Data Compression Conference 1992

DCC '92
DATA COMPRESSION CONFERENCE

Edited by
James A. Storer
Martin Cohn

Sponsored by the **IEEE Computer Society**
Technical Committee on Computer Communications
in cooperation with **NASA/CESDIS**

IEEE Computer Society Press
Los Alamitos, California
Washington • Brussels • Tokyo

Published by the
IEEE Computer Society Press
10662 Los Vaqueros Circle
PO Box 3014
Los Alamitos, CA 90720-1264

IEEE Computer Society Press Order Number 2717
Library of Congress Number 92-70381
IEEE Catalog Number 92TH0436-6
ISBN 0-8186-2716-6 (microfiche)
ISBN 0-8186-2717-4 (case)

Additional copies can be ordered from

IEEE Computer Society Press	IEEE Service Center	IEEE Computer Society	IEEE Computer Society
Customer Service Center	445 Hoes Lane	13, avenue de l'Aquilon	Ooshima Building
10662 Los Vaqueros Circle	PO Box 1331	B-1200 Brussels	2-19-1 Minami-Aoyama
PO Box 3014	Piscataway, NJ 08855-1331	BELGIUM	Minato-ku, Tokyo 107
Los Alamitos, CA 90720-1264			JAPAN

Cover design: Alex Torres
Editorial production: Catherine Harris
Printed in the United States of America by Edwards Brothers, Inc.

THE INSTITUTE OF ELECTRICAL AND ELECTRONICS ENGINEERS, INC.

DCC 1992

This book contains the presentations from the second Data Compression Conference held March 24–27, 1992 at Cliff Lodge, Snowbird, Utah. This conference was sponsored by the IEEE Computer Society Technical Committee on Computer Communications (TCCC) in cooperation with NASA/CESDIS.

General Chair: James A. Storer, *Brandeis U.*
Committee Chair: Martin Cohn, *Brandeis U.*
Publicity Chair: Raymond Miller, *NASA/CESDIS*

Program Committee

Ronald B. Arps, *IBM*
Richard L. Baker, *PictureTel Inc.*
Anselm Blumer, *Tufts U.*
Martin Cohn, *Brandeis U.*
Renato M. Capocelli, *U. Rome*
Robert G. Gallager, *MIT*
Robert M. Gray, *Stanford U.*
Daniel S. Hirschberg, *UC Irvine*
Didier LeGall, *C-Cube Inc.*
Abraham Lempel, *Technion*
Bradley J. Lucier, *Purdue U.*
John H. Reif, *Duke U.*
Dafna Sheinwald, *IBM*
James A. Storer, *Brandeis U.*
James C. Tilton, *NASA*
Vishu R. Viswanathan, *TI Inc.*
Jeffrey S. Vitter, *Brown U.*
Victor K. Wei, *Bellcore*
Ian H. Witten, *U. Calgary*

Acknowledgments
The Program Committee gratefully acknowledges the support of
NASA/CESDIS and the Computer Science Department of Brandeis University.
We thank Nancy Campbell and Tracy Chamberlain of NASA/CESDIS and
Myrna Fox and Cathy Rossi of Brandeis University for their hard
work on the conference administration.

Technical Sessions

Session 5

Session 6

Session 7

Session 8

Session 9

Session 10

Posters Session

Technical Sessions

Subband Vector Quantization of Images Using Hexagonal Filter Banks [1]

Osama S. Haddadin, V. John Mathews, and Thomas G. Stockham, Jr.

Department of Electrical Engineering
University of Utah
Salt Lake City, Utah 84112

Abstract

Results of psychophysical experiments on human vision conducted in the last three decades indicate that the eye performs a multichannel decomposition of the incident images. This paper presents a subband vector quantization algorithm that employs hexagonal filter banks. The hexagonal filter bank provides an image decomposition similar to what the eye is believed to do. Consequently, the image coder is able to make use of the properties of the human visual system and produce compressed images of high quality at low bit rates. We present a systematic approach for optimal allocation of available bits among the subbands and also for the selection of the size of the vectors in each of the subbands.

1. Introduction

Vector quantization (VQ) is a very powerful approach to data compression and has been successfully applied to a variety of signals [7] [17] [20]. In VQ a sequence of continuous or high rate discrete k-dimensional vectors is mapped into a sequence suitable for transmission over a digital channel or storage. The simplest form of vector quantizer operates as follows. First, a codebook of k-dimensional vectors is created using a training set representative of the waveforms. Once the codebook is designed and the representative vectors are stored, the process of encoding the incoming waveform can begin. k consecutive samples of the waveform are grouped together to form a k-dimensional vector at the input of the vector quantizer. The input vector is successively compared with each of the stored vectors and a metric or distance is computed in each case. The representative vector closest to the input vector is identified, and the index of the closest vector is available at the output for transmission or storage.

While direct VQ as described above will work reasonably well, much can be gained by combining vector quantizers with schemes such as predictive coding [10] [14] [21] [27] or subband coding [1] [2] [5] [6] [28] [30] [31]. This paper deals with

---

[1] This work was supported in part by the National Science Foundation under Grant MIP-9016331

a particular type of subband vector quantizers that makes use of hexagonal filter banks.

The block diagram of a typical subband image coder is shown in Figure 1. It consists of an analysis filter bank that decomposes the image into several subband components, decimators, and quantizers for the decimated signals. At the receiver, the synthesis section reconstructs the coded image from quantized subband images by upsampling and filtering each of the subband images and then additively combining the results. A block diagram of a multichannel Analysis/Synthesis filter bank (ASFB) is shown in Figure 2.

The algorithm presented in the paper performs a subband decomposition of hexagonally sampled (or resampled [22] [23]) images using filter banks with hexagonal planes of support. There are several factors that motivate this approach. First, hexagonal sampling of images provides very efficient discrete representation of two-dimensional signals. Secondly, it is believed, on the bases of psychophysical experiments [3] [8] [9] [11] [12] [24] [25] [29], that the human eye decomposes the incident images into several channels based on the magnitude and orientation of the frequency components of the images. Subband decomposition using hexagonal filter banks provides a similar decomposition of the images and consequently, we can take advantage of the properties of the eye and design a quantizer in such a way that the distortions are in areas that the eye can tolerate. This will result in a subjectively more pleasing quantization for coded images. Finally, the filter bank we employ provides a multiresolution decomposition of the images which would be very useful in progressive transmission, browsing and other similar applications.

The rest of the paper is organized as follows. The next section describes in detail the subband vector quantizer. In our work, we have used vector quantization of each subband separately. Our experience has shown that forming vectors using elements belonging to each subband separately is better than forming vectors using elements belonging to different subbands. However, this will necessitate the need for developing a scheme for allocating the available bits in some optimal manner among all the subbands. This section also presents a systematic scheme for bit allocation as well as for optimal selection of the size of the vector dimension in each subband. The concluding remarks are made in Section 3.

2. System Description

The subband vector quantizer with hexagonal filter banks comprises of the following components:

i) An ASFB that uses hexagonal sampling. The resulting subbands have hexagonal shapes as shown in Figure 3. Also, note that the bandwidths are different (the higher subbands have twice the bandwidth as lower subbands) for different subbands. It is necessary to use nonseparable filter banks to obtain such a decomposition. Use of hexagonal sampling has many advantages: They offer many

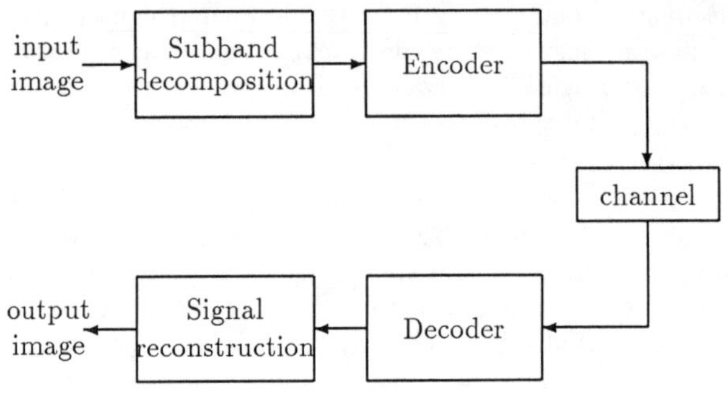

Figure 1: Subband coding of digital images.

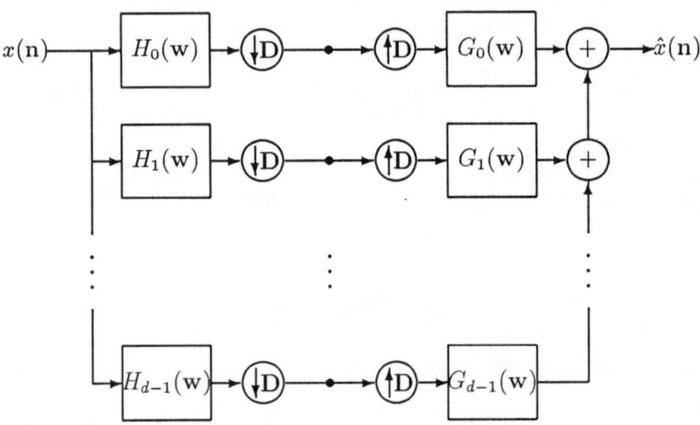

Figure 2: Multichannel analysis and synthesis filter bank

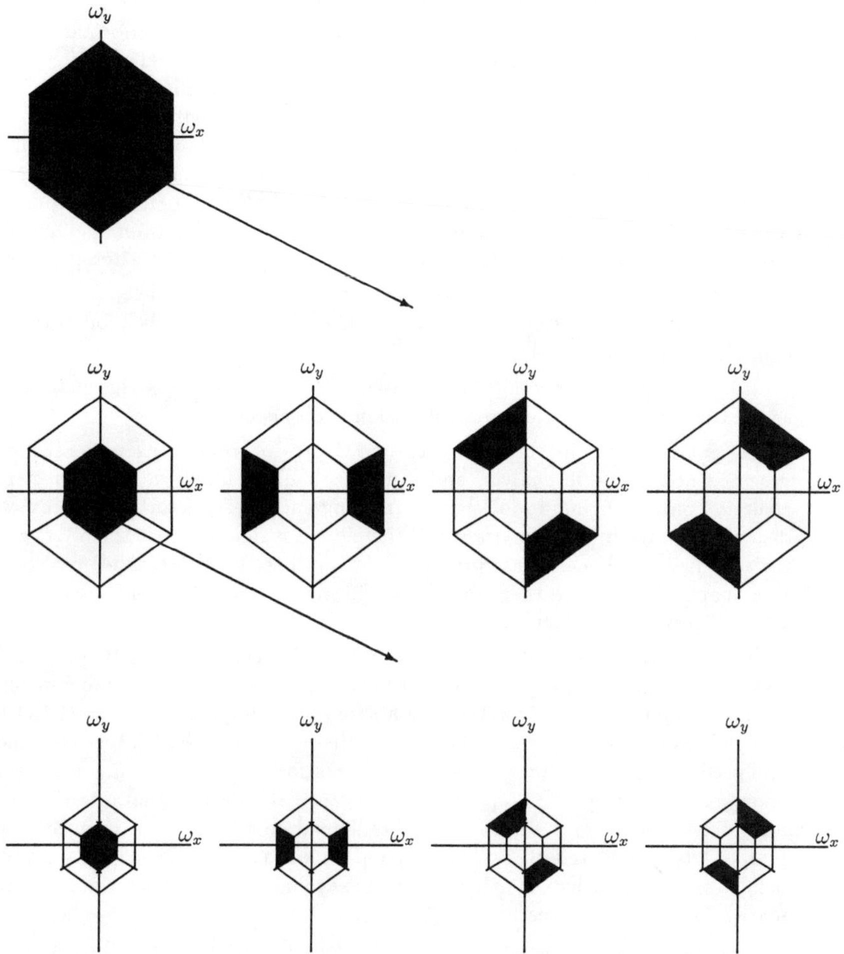

Figure 3: Idealistic frequency partitioning as indicated by the shaded regions in the middle level. The last level indicates further decomposition of lowest frequency subband into four more subbands. This process may be repeated a desired number of times.

advantages in computational simplicity. They provide the subbands with orientation properties that are not limited to vertical and horizontal directions.

Existing evidence in human vision suggest that the image information is processed by several frequency-selective channels (or bundles of cells) which combine to give the resulting human visual response. Each channel is a detector of a specific image feature. In particular experiments involving contrast threshold [8] [25] and electrical stimulation [9] imply the existence of elements which convey information about a region localized in space, frequency, and orientation. This discussion suggests that the basic structure of the hexagonal ASFB subband decomposition is similar to the processing that takes place in the human visual system [3] [32]. Therefore we believe that one can gain from designing the ASFB that attempts to mimic the behavior of the human visual system.

ii) Vector quantization of each subband separately. The bit allocation scheme is presented in this section.

iii) The synthesis section at the receiver that reconstructs the quantized images. Conditions for perfect reconstruction is discussed next.

Recent advances in the theory of ASFB provide conditions under which the designed nonseparable analysis and synthesis bank of filters satisfy perfect reconstruction of the original input signal. Aliasing and phase distortions are extremely disturbing to the human observer, and therefore it is required that the filters guarantee alias free and linear phase processing. Filter banks which provide a reconstruction that is alias free with negligible amplitude and phase distortions are referred to as Perfect Reconstruction Filter Banks (PRFB).

In this work, we restrict our study to maximally decimated ASFB systems. That is, the total number of samples in all the channels is equal to the number of samples in the original input signal. We also assume finite impulse response (FIR) filters of equal sizes for both the analysis and synthesis sections. FIR filters are generally preferred over infinite impulse response filters for image processing because they allow exact linear phase response, and because stability is guaranteed. Let the multidimensional input signal, $x(\mathbf{n})$, be defined on a hexagonal integer sampling grid, or lattice, denoted by Λ. The subband signals, $y_i(\mathbf{n})$ for $i = 0, ..., d-1$, are then defined on a sublattice Λ_D, that is also hexagonal provided that the subsampling matrix $\mathbf{D}$ is chosen correctly.

Using the convolution property and the definition of downsampling, we describe the Fourier transform of the output signal of the $i - th$ analysis channel as

$$Y_i(\omega) = \frac{1}{d} \sum_{j=0}^{d-1} H_i(\mathbf{D}^{-T}\omega + 2\pi\mathbf{D}^{-T}\mathbf{k}_j)X_i(\mathbf{D}^{-T}\omega + 2\pi\mathbf{D}^{-T}\mathbf{k}_j) \qquad (1)$$

where d represents the number of subbands in the decomposition, and $\mathbf{k}_i$ is a shift vector associated with the sublattice of the $i - th$ analysis channel. The output of the ASFB system (refer to Figure 2) is

$$\hat{X}(\omega) = \sum_{i=0}^{d-1} Y_i(\mathbf{D}^T\omega)G_i(\omega) \qquad (2)$$

The conditions for perfect reconstruction are given by [26]

$$\sum_{i=0}^{d-1} H_i(\omega)G_i(\omega) = d \tag{3}$$

$$\sum_{i=0}^{d-1} H_i(\omega + 2\pi\mathbf{D}^{-T}\mathbf{k}_j)G_i(\omega) = 0 \quad j = 1, \ldots, d-1. \tag{4}$$

A family of filters that do satisfy Equations 3 and 4 are the quadrature mirror filters [13] [15], defined for the hexagonal case [26] as

$$H_0(\omega) = G_0(-\omega) = F(\omega) = F(-\omega) \tag{5}$$

$$H_1(\omega) = G_1(-\omega) = e^{j\omega^T \mathbf{s}_1} F(\omega + 2\pi\mathbf{D}^{-T}\mathbf{k}_1) \tag{6}$$

$$H_2(\omega) = G_2(-\omega) = e^{j\omega^T \mathbf{s}_2} F(\omega + 2\pi\mathbf{D}^{-T}\mathbf{k}_2) \tag{7}$$

$$H_3(\omega) = G_3(-\omega) = e^{j\omega^T \mathbf{s}_3} F(\omega + 2\pi\mathbf{D}^{-T}\mathbf{k}_3) \tag{8}$$

where the $\mathbf{s}_i$ are known as the spatial shift vectors. $\mathbf{s}_i$ for $i = 1, 2, 3$ are chosen such that the system is alias free, and F is a function that is invariant under negation of it argument. Using Equations 5 through 8 in Equations 3 and 4, for $d = 4$, reduces the design problem to that of finding a filter with $F(\omega)$ satisfying the constraints

$$\sum_{i=0}^{3} \left| F(\omega + 2\pi\mathbf{D}^{-T}\mathbf{k}_i) \right|^2 = 4. \tag{9}$$

and

$$F(\omega + 2\pi\mathbf{D}^{-T}\mathbf{k}_j)F(-\omega) = 0 \tag{10}$$

where $\mathbf{k}_j$ can be any one of the non-zero shift vectors. Approaches to solving this optimization problem are discussed in [26] [31].

We will now very briefly discuss the vector quantizer. The codebook for each subband is created using a training set formed by the corresponding subband decomposition of a representative set of waveforms that the system will process. We have used the Linde, Buzo, Gray (LBG) algorithm [18] for codebook design. The size of the codebook and the vector dimension for each subband play an important role in the overall performance of the system. Techniques for selecting these parameters involve searching the bit-rate versus distortion plane for the optimal solution. However, most of such techniques ignore the dependency of the distortion on the vector dimension. In this paper, we will discuss, and employ, a new bit allocation technique which provides the complete solution (i.e. bit rate and vector dimension) to the problem. This technique is based on an adaptation of the scheme introduced by Bradley, Stockham and Mathews [6]. In the remainder of this section we provide a brief review of this scheme.

Our technique attempts to minimize a distortion function, $\mathbf{E}(\mathbf{r}, \mathbf{k})$, defined as

$$\mathbf{E}(\mathbf{r}, \mathbf{k}) = \sum_{i=0}^{d-1} e_i(r_i, k_i) \tag{11}$$

where e_i is the distortion introduced is quantizing the $i-th$ channel, and is a function of that channel's rate r_i and vector size k_i. The vectors $\mathbf{r}$ and $\mathbf{k}$ are d-dimensional and are defined as

$$\mathbf{r} = [\, r_0 \ldots r_{d-1} \,] \tag{12}$$

$$\mathbf{k} = [\, k_0 \ldots k_{d-1} \,] \tag{13}$$

Bradley, et. al. [6] demonstrated that e_i can be approximated as

$$e_i(r_i, k_i) = \beta(k_i)e^{-\gamma(k_i)r_i} \tag{14}$$

when the Euclidean distortion measure is employed. The parameters $\beta(k_i)$ and $\gamma(k_i)$ are estimated empirically. Thus we may write Equation 11 as

$$\mathbf{E}(\mathbf{r}, \mathbf{k}) = \sum_{i=0}^{d-1} \beta(k_i)e^{-\gamma(k_i)r_i} \tag{15}$$

Now, the optimization problem may be stated as that of minimizing Equation 15 subject to a bit rate constraint given by

$$\sum_{i=0}^{d-1} r_i \;=\; Total\ bit\ rate \tag{16}$$

where $r_i \geq 0$ for $i = 0,\ ...,\ d-1$, and a complexity constraint given by

$$\sum_{i=0}^{d-1} 2^{r_i k_i} \;\leq\; Maximum\ codebook\ size. \tag{17}$$

The constraint optimization problem is solved using a projected gradient algorithm [6] [16] [19].

3. Concluding Remarks

In this paper, we presented an algorithm for image coding that employs vector quantization of subband signals obtained using hexagonal filter banks and hexagonal sampling. The decomposition provided by the hexagonal filter bank shares several properties with the image decomposition that takes place in the visual cortex. Consequently, a compression scheme that makes use of such a decomposition can provide better subjective quality for the images. Experiments, the results of which are not reproduced here, have provided very good quality reproductions of coded monochrome still images at bit rates that are fractions of one bit per pixel.

References

[1] E. Adelson, E. Simoncelli and R. Hingorani, "Orthogonal pyramid transforms for image coding," *SPIE Visual Communication and Image Processing II*, vol. 845, pp. 50-58, 1987.

[2] R. Baseri, Vector Quantization of Monochrome Images using a Visual Masking Function, *M. S. Thesis*, University of Utah 1991.

[3] B. S. Baxter, Image Processing in the Human Visual System, *Ph. D. Dissertation*, University of Utah, 1973.

[4] C. Blakemore and F. W. Campbell, "On the Existence of Neurones in the Human Visual System Selectively Sensitive to the Orientation and Size of Retinal Images," *Journal of Physiology*, London, vol. 203, pp. 237-260, 1969.

[5] J. N. Bradley, Subband Image Coding with Vector Quantization, *Ph. D. Dissertation*, University of Utah 1989.

[6] J. N. Bradley, T. G. Stockham, Jr., and V. J. Mathews, "Subband Coding with Vector Quantization," submitted to *IEEE Transactions on Communications*

[7] A. Buzo, A. H. Gray, Jr., R. M. Gray, and J. D. Markel, "Speech coding based upon Vector Quantization," *IEEE Transactions on Information Theory*, vol. IT-28, no. 5, pp. 562-574, October 1980.

[8] F. W. Campbell and J. G. Robson, "Application of Fourier Analysis to the Visibility of Gratings," *Journal of Physiology*, London, vol. 197, pp. 551, 1968.

[9] F. W. Campbell, F. F. Cooper and C. Enroth-Cudgell, "The Spatial Cells of the Cat," *Journal of Physiology*, London, vol. 203, pp. 223, 1969.

[10] P. Chang and R. M. Gray, "Gradient Algorithms for Designing Predictive Vector Quantizers," *IEEE Transactions on Acoustics, Speech, and Signal Processing*, vol. ASSP-34, no. 4, August 1986.

[11] P. Colas-Baudelaire, Digital Picture Processing and Psychophysics: A Study of Brightness Perception, *Ph. D. Dissetation*, University of Utah, 1973.

[12] T. N. Cornsweet, *Visual Perception*, Prentice-Hall, 1970.

[13] A. Croiser, D. Esteban, and C. Galand, "Perfect channel splitting by use of interpolation/decimation/tree decomposition techniques," *International Conference on Information Sciences and Systems*, Patras, pp. 443-446, August 1976.

[14] V. Cuperman and A. Gersho, "Vector Predictive Coding of Speech at 16 kbits/s," *IEEE Transactions on Communications*, vol. COMM-33, no. 7, pp. 685-696, July 1985.

[15] D. Esteban and C. Galand, "Application of quadrature mirror filters to split band voice coding scheme," *Proceedings of IEEE International Conference on Acoustics, Speech, and Signal Processing*, pp. 191-195, 1977.

[16] P. E. Gill, W. Murray, and M. H. Wright, *Practical Optimization*, Academic Press, 1981.

[17] R. M. Gray, "Vector Quantization," *IEEE Acoustics, Speech, and Signal Processing magazine*, vol. 1, pp. 4-29, April 1984.

[18] Y. Linde, A. Buzo, and R. M. Gray, "An Algorithm for Vector Quantization Design," *IEEE Transactions on Communications*, vol. COM-28, pp. 84-95, January 1980.

[19] D. C. Luenberger, *Linear and Nonlinear Programming*, Reading, Addison Wesley Publishing Company, 1984.

[20] J. Makhoul, S. Roucos and H. Gish, "Vector Quantization in Speech Coding," *Proceedings of the IEEE*, vol. 73, no. 11, pp. 1551-1558, November 1985.

[21] V. J. Mathews, R. W. Waite, and T. D. Tran, "Image Compression Using Vector Quantization of Linear (one-step) Prediction Errors," *Proceedings of the IEEE International Conference on Acoustics, Speech, and Signal Processing*, pp. 733-736, Dallas, Texas, April 1987.

[22] R. M. Mersereau, "The Processing of Hexagonally Sampled Two-Dimensional Signals," *Proceedings of the IEEE*, vol. 67, no. 6, pp. 930-949, June 1979.

[23] R. M. Mersereau and T. C. Speake, " The processing of periodically sampled multidimensional signals," *IEEE Transactions on Acoustics, Speech, and Signal Processing*, vol. ASSP-31, no. 1, pp. 188-194, February 1983.

[24] D. A. Pollen and S. F. Ronner, "Phase relationship between adjacent simple cells in the visual cortex," *Science*, vol. 212, pp. 1409-1411, 1981.

[25] F. Ratliff, *Mach Bands: Quantitative Studies on Neural Networks in the Retina*, Holden-Day, 1965.

[26] E. P. Simoncelli and E. Adelson, "Non-separable Extensions of Quadrature Mirror Filters to Multiple Dimensions," *Proceedings of the IEEE*, vol. 78, no. 4, pp. 652-664, April 1990.

[27] B. Vasudev, "Predictive VQ Schemes for Gray Scale Image Compression," *Proceedings of GLOBECOM'87*, pp. 436-441, Tokyo, Japan, November 1987.

[28] M. Vetterli, J. Kovacevic and D. Legall, "Perfect Reconstruction Filter Bank for HDTV Representation and Coding," *Signal Processing: Image Communication*, vol. 2, pp.349-363, 1990.

[29] A. B. Watson and A. J. Ahumada, Jr., "A Hexagonal Orthogonal-Oriented Pyramid as a Model of Image Representation in Visual Cortex," *IEEE Transactions on Biomedical Engineering*, vol. 36, no. 1, January 1989.

[30] J. W. Woods and S. D. O'Neil, "Subband coding of images," *IEEE Transactions on Acoustics, Speech, and Signal Processing*, vol. ASSP-34, October 1986.

[31] J. W. Woods, ed., *Subband Image Coding*, Klumer Academic Publishers, 1991.

[32] Z. Xie, Previsualized Image Vector Quantization, *Ph. D. Dissertation*, University of Utah, 1989.

Complexity Optimized Vector Quantization:
A Neural Network Approach

Joachim Buhmann

Lawrence Livermore National Laboratory
Physics Division, P.O.Box 808, L-270
Livermore, CA 94550, USA
`jb@s1.gov`

Hans Kühnel

Technische Universität München
Physik Dep., T35, Boltzmannstraße
D–8046 Garching, Fed. Rep. Germany
`Hans.Kuehnel@physik.tu-muenchen.de`

Abstract

We discuss a vector quantization strategy which *jointly optimizes* distortion errors and complexity costs. A maximum entropy estimation of the vector quantization cost function yields an optimal codebook size, the reference vectors and the assignment frequencies. We compare different complexity measures for the design of image compression algorithms which quantize wavelet decomposed images. An online version of complexity optimized vector quantization is implemented by an artificial neural network with *winner-take-all* connectivity. Our approach establishes a unifying framework for different quantization methods like K-means clustering [1] and its fuzzy version [2, 3], entropy constrainted vector quantization [4] or self-organizing topological maps [5, 6] and competitive neural networks [7].

Costs for Complexity Optimized Vector Quantization

Vector quantization is a combinatorial optimization problem to represent a given data set $\{\mathbf{x}_i | i = 1, \ldots, N\}$ with large information content by a reduced set of reference vectors $\{\mathbf{y}_\alpha | \alpha = 1, \ldots, K\}$. These prototypical vectors correspond to feature detector cells or specialized neuronal groups in neural systems or to models in pattern recognition. To determine an appropriate number K of reference vectors and to find their positions $\mathbf{y}_\alpha$ and their occupation probabilities p_α is the primary objective in designing a codebook. The assignments $\{M_{i\alpha} | \alpha = 1, \ldots, K; i = 1, \ldots, N\}$, $M_{i\alpha} \in \{0, 1\}$ of data point $\mathbf{x}_i$ to cluster α are chosen such that the residual distortion error $\mathcal{D}_{i\alpha}(\mathbf{x}_i, \mathbf{y}_\alpha)$ between data point $\mathbf{x}_i$ and codebook vector $\mathbf{y}_\alpha$ is minimized and that the resulting complexity of the codebook is limited. $M_{i\alpha^*} = 1$ denotes that data point $\mathbf{x}_i$ is uniquely assigned to cluster α^* implying the uniqueness constraint $\sum_\alpha M_{i\alpha} = 1$. The most commonly used distortion measures are powers of the squared Euclidian distance $\mathcal{D}_{i\alpha}(\mathbf{x}_i, \mathbf{y}_\alpha) = \|\mathbf{x}_i - \mathbf{y}_\alpha\|^r$. According to rate distortion theory (see [8]) the optimal choice of $\mathbf{y}_\alpha$ has to be the centroid of cluster α, i.e., $\sum_i M_{i\alpha} \frac{\partial}{\partial \mathbf{y}_\alpha} \mathcal{D}_{i\alpha}(\mathbf{x}_i, \mathbf{y}_\alpha) = 0$. The complexity $\mathcal{C}_\alpha$ of cluster α depends on the specific information processing application at hand, in particular, we assume that $\mathcal{C}_\alpha$ is only a function of the occupation probability $p_\alpha \equiv \sum_{i=1}^N M_{i\alpha}/N$. The proposed cost function for vector quantization

$$\mathcal{E}(\{M_{i\alpha}\}) = \sum_{i=1}^{N} \sum_{\alpha=1}^{K} M_{i\alpha} \Big(\mathcal{D}_{i\alpha}(\mathbf{x}_i, \mathbf{y}_\alpha) + \lambda \mathcal{C}_\alpha(p_\alpha) \Big). \tag{1}$$

compromises between distortion costs and complexity costs, thereby determining an optimal size K of the codebook. $\mathcal{E}(\{M_{i\alpha}\})$ solely depends on the assignments $\{M_{i\alpha}\}$ since p_α, $\mathbf{y}_\alpha$ are fixed for a particular choice of $\{M_{i\alpha}\}$. This cost function has to be optimized in an iterative fashion: (i) vary the assignment variables $M_{i\alpha}$ for a fixed codebook size such that $\mathcal{E}(\{M_{i\alpha}\})$ decreases; (ii) increment the codebook size $K \rightarrow K + 1$ and optimize $\{M_{i\alpha}\}$ again. The optimized cluster parameters $\mathbf{y}_\alpha$, p_α and K are determined by the configuration with minimal costs.

An application dependent complexity could be the mass storage space of a storage medium, the processing hardware in electronics, the number of neurons in brains or the channel bandwidth in communication systems. Complexity costs which penalize small, rarely used reference vectors, i.e., $\mathcal{C}_\alpha = 1/p_\alpha^s, s = 1, 2, \ldots$, favor equal occupation probabilities, thereby emphasizing the hardware aspect of a vector quantization solution. The special case $s = 1$ with complexity costs strictly proportional to the number of clusters ($\mathcal{C}_\alpha = 1/p_\alpha \Rightarrow \sum_i \sum_\alpha M_{i\alpha}/p_\alpha = NK$) corresponds to an iterative version of the K-means clustering algorithm. An alternative complexity measure, which provides a lower bound on encoding costs in the context of data compression and bandwidth limited data transmission, is the Shannon entropy of a codebook $\langle \mathcal{C} \rangle = -\sum_\alpha p_\alpha \ln p_\alpha$ [4] with $\mathcal{C}_\alpha = -\ln p_\alpha$. We refer to this choice of $\mathcal{C}_\alpha$ as *entropy optimized vector quantization*.

Estimation of $\mathbf{y}_\alpha$ and p_α

To derive a robust, preferably parallel algorithm for vector quantization, we study the optimization problem (1) in a probabilistic framework [3]. This design philosophy for optimization algorithms is motivated by the success of simulating annealing [9] and of neural optimization algorithms [10]. The most likely distribution of assignment variables $M_{i\alpha}$ can be determined by the maximum entropy principle [11], and equals the Gibbs distribution $P(\{M_{i\alpha}\}) = \frac{1}{Z} \exp(-\beta \mathcal{E})$. The "computational temperature" $T = 1/\beta$, which plays the role of a Lagrange parameter for the average quantization costs, controls the randomness in the assignment process. The partition function Z normalizes the Gibbs distribution. We use the formalism of statistical mechanics (e.g. see [12, 13]) to maximize the entropy at a fixed temperature which is equivalent to minimizing the free energy

$$\mathcal{F} = -\sum_\alpha p_\alpha \hat{p}_\alpha - \frac{1}{\beta N} \sum_i \ln \left(\sum_\alpha \exp[-\beta(\mathcal{D}_{i\alpha} + \lambda \mathcal{C}_\alpha + \hat{p}_\alpha)] \right). \tag{2}$$

with respect to the variables $p_\alpha, \mathbf{y}_\alpha$. The term $\hat{p}_\alpha \equiv \lambda p_\alpha \dfrac{\partial \mathcal{C}_\alpha}{\partial p_\alpha}$ enforces the constraint $p_\alpha = \sum_{i=1}^{N} M_{i\alpha}/N$. The resulting re-estimation equations for the expected occupation probabilities and the expected centroid positions are

$$p_\alpha \;=\; \frac{1}{N}\sum_i \langle M_{i\alpha}\rangle, \tag{3}$$

$$0 \;=\; \frac{1}{N}\sum_i \langle M_{i\alpha}\rangle\frac{\partial}{\partial \mathbf{y}_\alpha}\mathcal{D}_{i\alpha}(\mathbf{x}_i,\mathbf{y}_\alpha), \tag{4}$$

$$\langle M_{i\alpha}\rangle \;=\; \frac{\exp\left[-\beta(\mathcal{D}_{i\alpha}+\lambda\mathcal{C}_\alpha+\hat{p}_\alpha)\right]}{\sum_{\nu=1}^{K}\exp[-\beta(\mathcal{D}_{i\nu}+\lambda\mathcal{C}_\nu+\hat{p}_\nu)]}. \tag{5}$$

We have identified $p_\alpha, \mathbf{y}_\alpha$ in Eqs. (2-5) with their expectation values which is justified in the large N limit. The probability $\langle M_{i\alpha}\rangle$ can be interpreted as a fuzzy membership of data point $\mathbf{x}_i$ in cluster α.

The global minimum of the free energy (2) with respect to $p_\alpha, \mathbf{y}_\alpha$ determines the maximum entropy solution of the cost function (1). Note that the K^N dimensional optimization problem (1) has been reduced to a $K(d+1)$ dimensional minimization of (2). To find the optimal parameters $p_\alpha, \mathbf{y}_\alpha$ and the optimal size of the codebook K we minimize the free energy using the following algorithm:

0.) `Initialization: Compute the centroid of the data set and place` `the first codebook vector there` $(K=1)$`.`

1.) `Determine a random order of codebook vectors` $\mathbf{y}_\alpha$`; list index` $\kappa \equiv 1$`.`

2.) `Split codebook vector` κ`, i.e.,` $\mathbf{y}_{K+1}^{\mathrm{new}} = \mathbf{y}_\kappa + \mathbf{z}$`,` $\mathbf{y}_\kappa^{\mathrm{new}} = \mathbf{y}_\kappa$`,` $p_{K+1}^{\mathrm{new}} = p_\kappa^{\mathrm{new}} =$ $p_\kappa/2$`, (`$\mathbf{z}$ `is a ''small'' random vector with` $\|\mathbf{z}\| \ll \|\mathbf{y}_\kappa\|$`).`

3.) `Reestimate` $p_\alpha, \mathbf{y}_\alpha$ `using Eqs. (3,4).`

4.) `If` $\mathcal{F}^{\mathrm{new}} < \mathcal{F}^{\mathrm{old}}$ `then accept new codebook with` $K+1$ `vectors,` `increment` $K \leftarrow K+1$ `and goto step 1.`

5.) `If` $\mathcal{F}^{\mathrm{new}} \geq \mathcal{F}^{\mathrm{old}}$ `then reject new codebook and increment` κ`. If` $\kappa > K$ `then quit, else goto 2.`

An iterative splitting strategy is required since we compare solutions with different codebook sizes. Furthermore, we found experimental evidence that this splitting and reestimation strategy tracks local minima with low quantization costs. This property of the algorithm is particularly valuable since the optimization problem is plagued with numerous local minima. The resulting configuration is stable under single cluster splitting, but we are not assured to find the global minimum.

Quantization results at zero temperature for the logarithmic complexity measure are shown in Fig. 1. At high complexity costs (b) the algorithm finds four clusters located at the centers of the Gaussians. In the limit of very small complexity costs (c) the best clustering solution densely covers the data distribution. The specific choice of $\mathcal{C}_\alpha = -\ln p_\alpha$ causes an almost homogeneous density of quantization levels, a phenomenon which is explained by the vanishing average complexity costs $\lim_{p_\alpha \to 0} p_\alpha \ln p_\alpha = 0$ of very sparsely occupied clusters (see [14, 15]). Analytical results of the asymptotic (K very large) level density for different complexity measures are discussed in [15].

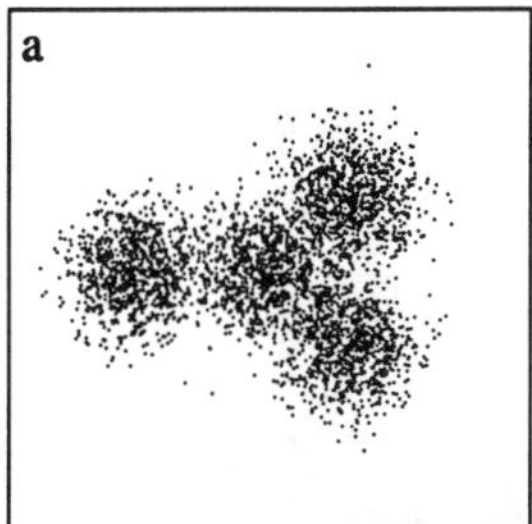 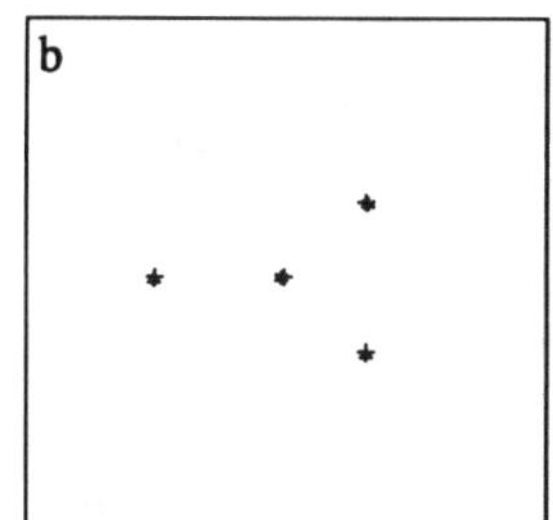 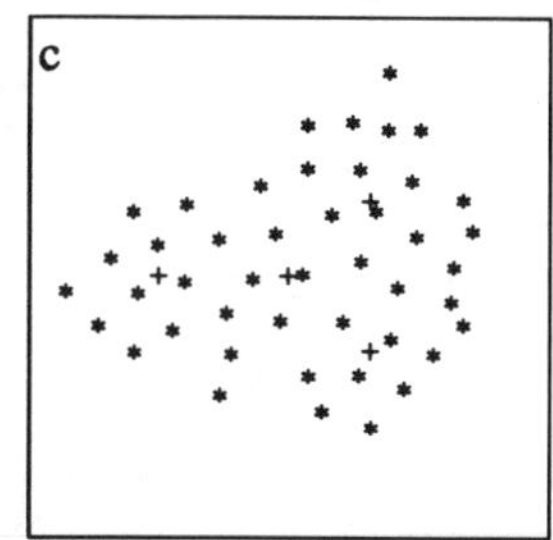

Figure 1: A data distribution (4000 data points) (a), generated by four normally distributed sources, is quantized with the complexity measure $\mathcal{C}_\alpha = -\ln p_\alpha$. Two zero temperature solutions for $\lambda = 2.5, 0.4$ are shown in (b,c) where plus signs (+) denote the positions of the Gaussians and stars ($\star$) denote codebook vectors.

Compression of Wavelet-decomposed Images

Lossy image compression is a *"real-world"* information processing problem which is well suited to study the influence of different complexity measure on the performance of vector quantization algorithms. In this section we use the image compression task to compare the efficiency of the K-means clustering scheme ($\mathcal{C}_\alpha = 1/p_\alpha$) with entropy optimized clustering ($\mathcal{C}_\alpha = -\ln p_\alpha$). The data set $\{x_i\}$ are three dimensional vectors composed of wavelet coefficients which are extracted from 8 Bit gray level images of human faces. These wavelet coefficients essentially are a combination of lowpass filtering in x-direction and bandpass filtering in y-direction (Ψ^1) or vice versa (Ψ^2) or bandpass filtering in both directions (Ψ^3). The frequency support of the filters Ψ^ν, $\nu = 1, 2, 3$ in Fourier space is shown in Fig. 2. The wavelet data format is supposedly optimal for natural images since the coefficients are statistically independent if we average over a large set of natural images [16, 17].

Using the subband decomposition algorithm [18] based on quadrature mirror filtering we generate an orthonormal multiresolution representation of our training images, called the wavelet representation. Starting with an image $\mathcal{I}$ of size 128×128 the wavelet algorithm calculates bandpass coefficients and lowpass coefficients for both image directions on a subgrid reduced by a factor of 2^{-1} in each direction (for details of the algorithm see [18]). We combine the three wavelet coefficients $(D^\nu_{2^{-\rho}}\mathcal{I})(i)$, $\nu = 1, 2, 3$ at position i (notation as in [18]) to a three-dimensional vector x_i (see Fig. 2). The index ρ denotes the reduction factor $2^{-\rho}$ of the bandpass filter. On the first frequency level ($\rho = 1$) this data set, refered to as $\mathcal{L}^1 = \left\{ x_i = \left((D^1_{2^{-1}}\mathcal{I})(i), (D^2_{2^{-1}}\mathcal{I})(i), (D^3_{2^{-1}}\mathcal{I})(i) \right) \right\}$, is of size 4096 vectors. The whole procedure is iterated once more on the lowpass filtered image of size 64×64, which generates the set $\mathcal{L}^2$ of size 1024 and a lowpass filtered image $A^2 = \left\{ x_i = \left(A_{2^{-2}}\mathcal{I} \right)(i) \right\}$ of size 32×32.

The training data for the K-means algorithm and the complexity optimized vector quantizer are the union of $\mathcal{L}^2$-sets, the union of $\mathcal{L}^1$-sets and the union of A^2 sets,

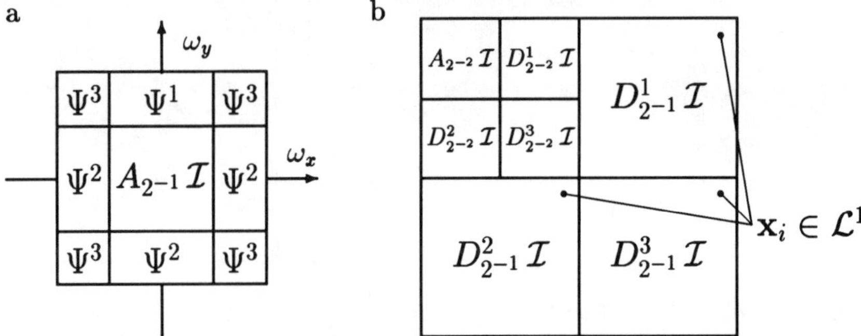

Figure 2: (after [18]) (a) Approximate frequency support of the wavelet filters Ψ^1, Ψ^2 and Ψ^3 in Fourier space. (b) Wavelet coefficients of image $\mathcal{I}$ arranged in matrix form: The upper index $\nu \in \{1,2,3\}$ of $D^\nu_{2-\rho}\mathcal{I}$ refers to the respective filter function Ψ^ν, the lower index ρ denotes the reduction factor. $A_{2^{-1}}\mathcal{I}$ and $A_{2^{-2}}\mathcal{I}$ are the lowpass filtered images after one or two reductions steps, respectively. Filter coefficients from a particular image position i are combined to a three-dimensional vector $\mathbf{x}_i$.

all taken from 10 different face images. During the training stage we solve Eqs. (3,4) for each of these training sets and for both complexity measures which are under comparison. This procedure yields three codebooks for entropy optimized quantization and three codebooks for K-means clustering. All distortions are measured as the squared Euclidian distance $\mathcal{D}_{i\alpha} = (\mathbf{x}_i - \mathbf{y}_\alpha)^2$. The complexity weights λ in the K-means clustering case are adjusted such that the compression ratio of both quantization schemes is the same, i.e., we require that K-means clustering and entropy optimized clustering compress the training data with the same resulting entropy. The error between an original test image and its reconstruction from the quantized wavelet representation allows us to quantify the efficiency of the complexity measures $\mathcal{C}_\alpha = 1/p_\alpha$ and $\mathcal{C}_\alpha = -\ln p_\alpha$ for image compression.

In the first series of compression experiments we set $\lambda = 5$ for entropy optimized vector quantization of $\mathcal{L}^1$ and $\mathcal{L}^2$ and $\lambda = 0.5$ for entropy optimized scalar quantization of A^2. The resulting codebooks for $\mathcal{L}^1$, $\mathcal{L}^2$, A^2 had size $K = 112, 123, 146$, respectively. The codebooks for K-means clustering were determined such that they quantized the training data generating the same entropy as the codebooks for entropy optimized quantization. (The resulting entropies of the test data might differ for both quantization schemes). The K-means clustering codebooks for $\mathcal{L}^1$, $\mathcal{L}^2$, A^2 had sizes $K = 12, 40, 104$. Note that the codebooks for K-means clustering are much smaller than the codebooks for entropy optimized quantization. This computational disadvantage of entropy optimized quantization is outweighted by the considerably smaller error rate of compressed images.

The following table summarizes four different compression experiments. The first three test images were taken from the same gallery as the training images, the fourth face image (terry) was generated under different lighting conditions with another camera setting. The entropy optimized quantizers produce a 10%-20% smaller error for comparable or superior compression ratios than K-means clustering. Furthermore, face images which have been compressed by optimizing the complexity $C_\alpha = -\ln p_\alpha$, look more natural than the results from K-means clustering. Psychophysically important image features like edges generate large wavelet amplitudes in the high frequency band which shows a fall off of the power spectrum as $1/\omega^2$ in natural images [16]. The corresponding outlier regions of $\mathcal{L}^1$ and $\mathcal{L}^2$ are more accurately sampled by entropy optimized quantization than by K-means clustering.

face images	pixel entropy	entropy of			average error	compr. ratio	efficiency
		$\mathcal{L}^1$	$\mathcal{L}^2$	A^2			
doro	5.9	1.57 1.77	1.01 1.05	1.47 1.44	2.83 3.14	10.9 9.9	14.8%
brix	4.6	1.88 1.81	1.05 1.05	1.31 1.28	2.46 3.01	7.4 7.6	22.4%
yildir	6.2	1.76 1.82	1.04 1.07	1.76 1.82	3.08 3.63	10.3 10.1	17.8%
terry	7.0	2.39 2.17	1.18 1.15	1.55 1.49	3.60 4.66	9.1 9.9	29.4%

Table 1: Summary of four compression trials: The upper numbers in the stacks refer to entropy optimized quantization, the lower numbers result from K-means clustering experiments. The average error is the average, absolute difference between the original pixel value $\mathcal{I}(i)$ and its reconstructed value $\mathcal{I}^c(i)$, i.e., $\frac{1}{N} \sum_{i=1}^{N} |\mathcal{I}(i) - \mathcal{I}^c(i)|$. The efficiency is defined as the relative difference in reconstruction error between the two quantization methods.

Online Vector Quantization

The vector quantization procedure as described so far requires in the style of *batch* processing that all data points $\mathbf{x}_i$ are available at once, a highly restrictive constraint for applications with a large data volume. *Adaptive* vector quantization algorithms process a data stream sequentially by updating $\mathbf{y}_\alpha$ and p_α iteratively after a new data point $\mathbf{x}_i$ has been processed. Such an algorithm is implemented by a competitive two-layer neural network with d neurons in the input layer and K neurons in the output or classification layer. The architecture is depicted in Fig. 3. Unit α in the classification layer receives activity from the input units weighted by the synaptic vector $\mathbf{y}_\alpha$. The units in the classification layer are connected by a *winner-take-all* network. Due to mutual competition each data point $\mathbf{x}_N$ is assigned to one unit α. The partial costs $\mathcal{D}_{N\alpha} + \lambda C_\alpha + \lambda p_\alpha \dfrac{\partial C_\alpha}{\partial p_\alpha}$ for assigning $\mathbf{x}_N$ to unit α determine the activation level m_α of the neuron α in the classification layer. A relaxation dynamics $dm_\alpha/dt = -m_\alpha + \langle M_{N\alpha} \rangle$ as found in many analog neural systems [12] returns the classification result for $\mathbf{x}_N$. The reference vector $\mathbf{y}_\alpha$ can be interpreted as the receptive field in data space of neuron α.

Learning after $N - 1$ data points have been processed results in the incremental

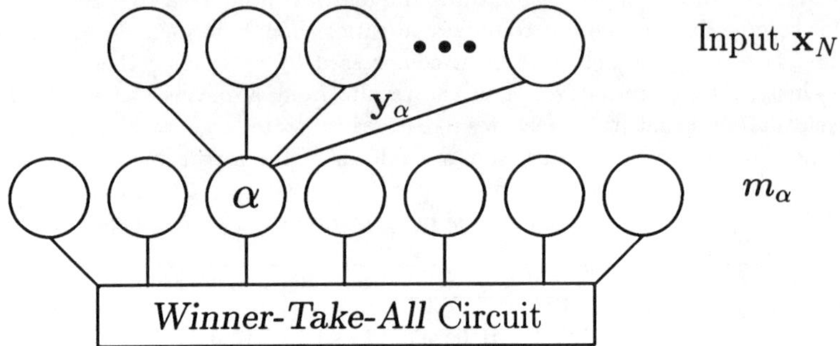

Figure 3: Architecture of a two layer competitive neural network for data clustering with d neurons in the input layer and K neurons in the output or classification layer.

changes

$$\Delta p_\alpha \equiv p_\alpha^{(N)} - p_\alpha^{(N-1)} = \frac{1}{N}\left(\langle M_{N,\alpha}\rangle - p_\alpha^{(N-1)}\right), \tag{6}$$

$$\Delta \mathbf{y}_\alpha \equiv \mathbf{y}_\alpha^{(N)} - \mathbf{y}_\alpha^{(N-1)} = -\frac{\langle M_{N,\alpha}\rangle \frac{\partial}{\partial \mathbf{y}_\alpha}\mathcal{D}_{N\alpha}(\mathbf{x}_N, \mathbf{y}_\alpha^{(N-1)})}{\sum_{i=1}^{N}\langle M_{i\alpha}\rangle \frac{\partial^2}{\partial \mathbf{y}_\alpha{}^2}\mathcal{D}_{i\alpha}(\mathbf{x}_i, \mathbf{y}_\alpha^{(N-1)})}. \tag{7}$$

To derive Eqs. (6,7) we have expanded Eqs. (3,4) up to linear terms in $\Delta p_\alpha, \Delta \mathbf{y}_\alpha$, keeping $\langle M_{N\alpha}\rangle$ fixed. All terms proportional to $\partial\langle M_{i\alpha}\rangle/\partial\Delta\mathbf{y}_\gamma$, $\partial\langle M_{i\alpha}\rangle/\partial\Delta p_\gamma$ vanish in the hard clustering limit ($T \to 0$).

In the case of Euclidean distortions Eq. (7) reduces to the form

$$\Delta \mathbf{y}_\alpha = \frac{1}{N p_\alpha^{(N)}}\langle M_{N,\alpha}\rangle(\mathbf{x}_N - \mathbf{y}_\alpha^{(N-1)}) \tag{8}$$

which is similar to learning in competitive neural networks. $\mathbf{y}_\alpha^{(N-1)}$ is moved towards the most recent data point $\mathbf{x}_N$ proportionally to the mismatch $\mathbf{x}_N - \mathbf{y}_\alpha^{(N-1)}$ and proportional to $\mathbf{x}_N$'s membership in cluster α. In addition to that, the update formula (8) weights any change in $\mathbf{y}_\alpha^{(N)}$ by the number of data points $N p_\alpha^{(N)}$ which are already assigned to cluster α. The learning parameter $1/(N p_\alpha^{(N)})$ treats different reference vectors according to their history and, thereby, avoids too quickly freezing in of clusters at suboptimal positions. The online optimization of the codebook size K can be achieved in the following way: we introduce a heuristics for the creation of codebook vectors. A data point $\mathbf{x}_i$ initializes a new reference vector $K+1$ with $\mathbf{y}_{K+1} = \mathbf{x}_i$ if the quantization costs by assigning $\mathbf{x}_i$ to an already existing reference vector exceeds the complexity costs of the new vector $K+1$, i.e., $\mathcal{C}_{K+1} < \min_\alpha\left(\mathcal{D}_{i\alpha}(\mathbf{x}_i, \mathbf{y}_\alpha) + \lambda\mathcal{C}_\alpha\right)$. We found in a series of vector quantization experiments that this strategy causes a slight overestimation of the codebook size but the resulting codebooks yield comparable quantization results (i.e. comparable costs) to codebooks designed with the respective batch algorithm. Deletion of codebook vectors has not been considered in the quantization experiments described in this paper, although a deletion heuristics is indispensible in cases of nonstationary data distributions.

Topology Preserving Vector Quantization

So far, we have dealt with quantization problems which are invariant under a permutation of the codebook vectors. In this section, we will establish the connection to quantization algorithms which favor a topological order like self-organizing feature maps [5, 6]. Luttrell [19] discovered in his studies of hierarchical vector quantizers that the topology of self-organizing feature maps can be related to the characteristics of a fictitious noise process in the communication channel between sender and receiver as depicted in the following block diagram:

$$\boxed{\text{noise } \mathrm{T}_{\alpha\gamma}}$$
$$\downarrow$$
$$\{\mathbf{x}_i\} \rightarrow \boxed{\text{Encoder } \mathbf{x}_i \rightarrow \mathbf{y}_\alpha} \rightarrow \alpha \rightarrow \boxed{\text{Channel}} \rightarrow \gamma \rightarrow \boxed{\text{Decoder}} \rightarrow \{\mathbf{y}_\gamma\}$$

The additional distortions due to the channel noise have to be taken into account when we estimate the most likely assignment variables and, thereby, the centroid positions and the occupation probabilities. A codebook, which is adapted to the distortions induced by the channel noise, implements a procedure for *soft-error correction coding*.

Let us denote the transition probability from index α to index γ by $\mathrm{T}_{\alpha\gamma}$. The average costs to quantize the data set $\{\mathbf{x}_i\}$ amount to $\mathcal{H} = \sum_i \sum_\alpha M_{i\alpha} (\langle\!\langle \mathcal{D}_{i\alpha} \rangle\!\rangle + \lambda \mathcal{C}(p_\alpha))$ with the averaged distortions $\langle\!\langle \mathcal{D}_{i\alpha} \rangle\!\rangle \equiv \sum_\gamma \mathrm{T}_{\alpha\gamma} \mathcal{D}_{i\gamma}(\mathbf{x}_i, \mathbf{y}_\gamma)$, the centroids $\mathbf{y}_\alpha$ being defined by $\sum_i \sum_\gamma M_{i\gamma} \mathrm{T}_{\gamma\alpha} \frac{\partial}{\partial \mathbf{y}_\alpha} \mathcal{D}_{i\alpha}(\mathbf{x}_i, \mathbf{y}_\alpha) = 0$. The transition matrix $\mathrm{T}_{\alpha\gamma}$ induces a topology onto the set of clusters, e.g. a tridiagonal matrix $\mathrm{T}_{\alpha\alpha} = 1 - \eta, \mathrm{T}_{\alpha+1,\alpha} = \mathrm{T}_{\alpha,\alpha+1} = \eta/2$ orders the clusters as a linear chain with nearest neighbor transitions. The maximum entropy estimation of the assignments $M_{i\alpha}$ is analogous to the non-topological case, i.e., we calculate the free energy and minimize it with respect to the cluster parameter $p_\alpha, \mathbf{y}_\alpha$. The expected occupation probabilities and the expected centroid position for topology preserving clustering are

$$p_\alpha = \frac{1}{N} \sum_i \langle M_{i\alpha} \rangle, \tag{9}$$

$$0 = \frac{1}{N} \sum_i \sum_\gamma \mathrm{T}_{\gamma\alpha} \langle M_{i\gamma} \rangle \frac{\partial}{\partial \mathbf{y}_\alpha} \mathcal{D}_{i\alpha}(\mathbf{x}_i, \mathbf{y}_\alpha), \tag{10}$$

$$\langle M_{i\alpha} \rangle = \frac{\exp\left[-\beta(\langle\!\langle \mathcal{D}_{i\alpha} \rangle\!\rangle + \lambda \mathcal{C}_\alpha + \hat{p}_\alpha)\right]}{\sum_{\nu=1}^K \exp[-\beta(\langle\!\langle \mathcal{D}_{i\nu} \rangle\!\rangle + \lambda \mathcal{C}_\nu + \hat{p}_\nu)]}, \quad \hat{p}_\alpha \equiv \lambda p_\alpha \frac{\partial \mathcal{C}_\alpha}{\partial p_\alpha}. \tag{11}$$

The iterative update equations for p_α and $\mathbf{y}_\alpha$ in the topological case are identical to Eqs. (6,7) if we replace the fuzzy membership variables $\langle M_{i\alpha} \rangle$ by the effective membership $\hat{M}_{i\alpha} \equiv \sum_\gamma \mathrm{T}_{\gamma\alpha} \langle M_{i\gamma} \rangle$. For Euclidean distortion costs we derive the following update rule:

$$\Delta\mathbf{y}_\alpha = \frac{1}{N\sum_\gamma T_{\gamma\alpha}p_\gamma^{(N)}}\ \tilde{M}_{N,\alpha}(\mathbf{x}_N - \mathbf{y}_\alpha^{(N-1)}). \qquad (12)$$

The learning rate $1/(N\sum_\gamma T_{\gamma\alpha}p_\gamma^{(N)})$ of a particular cluster α is adapted to its history as in Eq. (8). The update rule (12) exhibits a striking similarity to self-organizing feature maps [5, 6]. Note, however, two important differences between our clustering approach an feature maps: (i) complexity optimized clustering determines the optimal length of the chain or, for a more general noise distribution, an optimal size of the cluster set; (ii) the general update rule and its specific version for Euclidean distortions (12) introduces cluster specific learning rates which promises faster convergence [20].

Conclusion

Complexity optimized vector quantization is a maximum entropy approach to design the vector quantization algorithms which determine the optimal size of a codebook as a compromise between distortion error and complexity of a codebook. The complexity term turns out to be as important for the design of a codebook as the distortion measure is. Compression experiments on gray level images of human faces have demonstrated the superior performance (10%-20% less quantization error) of entropy optimized quantization over standard K-means clustering. We have derived a batch and an online version of the proposed quantization algorithm; the online algorithm maps onto a *winner-take-all* network which suggests hardware implementations analogous to Boltzmann machines. Topology preserving vector quantization establishes a connection to topological feature maps and suggests a cost function based approach to determine the size of such mappings. The proposed framework for vector quantization unifies traditional vector quantization techniques like K-means clustering, entropy constraint clustering or fuzzy clustering with neural network approaches as topological feature maps or competitive networks.

Acknowledgement: It is a pleasure to thank C. Anderson, H. Sompolinsky, P. Tavan and T. Tishby for stimulating discussions. HK is a recipient of a graduate fellowship, Technische Universität München. JB has been supported by the German Federal Ministry of Science and Technology (ITR-8800-H1) and by AFOSR (88-0274) while working at the Center for Neural Engineering of the University of Southern California, Los Angeles, Ca 90089. Part of this work has been performed under the auspices of the U.S. Department of Energy by the Lawrence Livermore National Laboratory under Contract W-7405-Eng-48.

[1] Y. Linde, A. Buzo, and R. M. Gray, "An algorithm for vector quantizer design," *IEEE Trans. on Communications COM*, vol. 28, pp. 84–95, 1980.

[2] J. C. Bezdek, "A convergence theorem for the fuzzy isodata clustering algorithms," *IEEE Transactions on Pattern Analysis and Machine Intelligence*, vol. 2, no. 1, pp. 1–8, 1980.

[3] K. Rose, E. Gurewitz, and G. Fox, "Statistical mechanics and phase transitions in clustering," *Physical Review Letters*, vol. 65, no. 8, pp. 945–948, 1990.

[4] P. A. Chou, T. Lookabaugh, and R. M. Gray, "Entropy-constrained vector quantization," *IEEE Trans. on Acoustics, Speech and Signal Processing ASSP*, vol. 37, pp. 31–42, 1989.

[5] T. Kohonen, *Self–organization and Associative Memory*. Berlin: Springer, 1984.

[6] H. Ritter, T. Martinetz, and K. Schulten, *Neural Computation and Self-organizing Maps*. New York: Addison Wesley, 1992.

[7] D. E. Rumelhart and D. Zipser, "Feature discovery by competitive learning," *Cognitive Science*, vol. 9, pp. 75–112, 1985.

[8] R. M. Gray, "Vector quantization," *IEEE Acoustics, Speech and Signal Processing Magazine*, pp. 4–29, April 1984.

[9] S. Kirkpatrick, C. Gelatt, and M. Vecchi, "Optimization by simulated annealing," *Science*, vol. 220, pp. 671–680, 1983.

[10] R. Durbin and D. Willshaw, "An analogue approach to the travelling salesman problem using an elastic net method," *Nature*, vol. 326, pp. 689–691, 1987.

[11] E. T. Jaynes, "Information theory and statistical mechanics," *Physical Review*, vol. 106, pp. 620–630, 1957.

[12] D. Amit, *Modelling Brain Function*. Cambridge: Cambridge University Press, 1989.

[13] J. Hertz, A. Krogh, and R. G. Palmer, *Introduction to the Theory of Neural Computation*. New York: Addison Wesley, 1991.

[14] H. Gish and J. N. Pierce, "Asymptotically efficient quantizing," *IEEE Trans. on Information Theory IT*, vol. 14, pp. 676–683, 1968.

[15] J. Buhmann and H. Kühnel, "Vector quantization with complexity costs." Preprint, 1991.

[16] D. Field, "Relations between the statistics of natural images and the response properties of cortical cells," *Journal of the Optical Society of America A*, vol. 4, no. 12, pp. 2379–2394, 1987.

[17] B. Wegmann and C. Zetsche, "Statistical dependence between orientation filter outputs used in an human vision based image code," in *SPIE Proceedings of the Visual Communications and Image Processing'90* (M. Kunt, ed.), vol. 1360, pp. 909–923, 1990.

[18] S. G. Mallat, "A theory for multiresolution signal decomposition: The wavelet representation," *IEEE Transactions on Pattern Analysis and Machine Intelligence*, vol. 11, pp. 674–693, 1989.

[19] S. P. Luttrell, "Hierarchical vector quantisation," *IEE Proceedings*, vol. 136, pp. 405–413, 1989.

[20] C. Darken and J. Moody, "Note on learning rate schedules for stochastic optimization," in *Neural Information Processing Systems 3*, (San Mateo, California), pp. 832–838, Morgan Kaufmann, 1991.

Nearly Optimal Vector Quantization
via Linear Programming *

Jyh-Han Lin and *Jeffrey Scott Vitter*

Department of Computer Science
Brown University
Providence, R. I. 02912–1910

Abstract

We present new vector quantization algorithms based on the theory developed in [LiV]. The new approach is to formulate a vector quantization problem as a 0-1 integer linear program. We first solve its relaxed linear program by linear programming techniques. Then we transform the linear program solution into a provably good solution for the vector quantization problem. These methods lead to the first known polynomial-time full-search vector quantization codebook design algorithm and tree pruning algorithm with provable worst-case performance guarantees. We also introduce the notion of *pseudo-random pruned tree-structured vector quantizers*. Initial experimental results on image compression are very encouraging.

1   Introduction

A full-search vector quantizer partitions a signal space into regions each of which is represented by a representative vector [Ger, GeG, Gra]. In full-search vector quantization, the distortion between an input vector and each representative vector (codeword) in an unstructured codebook is computed. The input vector is then represented by the index of the codeword with minimum distortion. On the other hand, a tree-structured vector quantizer partitions a signal space into a hierarchy of regions. An input vector is quantized by traversing a root-to-leaf path in the tree.

---

*Support was provided in part by an National Science Foundation Presidential Young Investigator Award CCR–9047466 with matching funds from IBM, by NSF research grant CCR–9007851, by Army Research Office grant DAAL03–91–G–0035, and by the Office of Naval Research and the Defense Advanced Research Projects Agency under contract N00014–91–J–4052, ARPA order 8225. The authors can be reached by electronic mail at jhl@cs.brown.edu and jsv@cs.brown.edu, respectively.

The goal of vector quantization is good data compression. The design of the codebook is a central issue in vector quantizer performance. The methods for codebook design usually involve the use of a training sequence. The training sequence is a collection of sample signal from the source to be coded. The most popular algorithm for full-search codebook design is the generalized Lloyd algorithm [GKL, LBG], an iterative clustering descent algorithm that produces a locally optimal codebook with respect to a training sequence. For tree-structured codebook, Chou, Lookabaugh, and Gray [CLG] propose a tree pruning heuristic based on the BFOS algorithm [BFO] in which a given initial tree is pruned back according to certain optimization criterion. Their heuristic traces the lower convex hull of the distortion-rate function and the final pruned subtrees are optimal for their rates. However, if there is no point (pruned subtree) on the lower convex hull at a desired rate, it requires time-sharing between two neighboring points (pruned subtrees). Lin, Storer, and Cohn [LSC] show that the tree pruning problem is $\mathcal{NP}$-hard in general.[1]

In this paper, we propose a new approach for codebook design based on linear programming. We demonstrate our methods by presenting the first known approximation algorithms with worst-case performance guarantees for a full-search codebook design problem and the tree pruning problem. An algorithm that may not lead to the optimal result is called an *approximation algorithm*. We are interested in approximation algorithms with guaranteed performance, in which we can prove that the solution they produce is not too far from the optimal solution. We remark that in practice, approximation algorithms may perform much better than their performance guarantees suggest.

Many $\mathcal{NP}$-hard optimization problems can be formulated as integer linear programs. One of the most important strategies for obtaining provably good approximation algorithms to an integer program is to drop the integrality constraints, solve the resulting linear programming problem,[2] and then round the solution to an integral solution. Much work along this line has been done, for example [Chv, Lov, Rag, RaT]. In [LiV], we build on previous work and propose new transformation methods for obtaining provably good solutions from linear program relaxation of a type of 0-1 optimization problems. These methods can be applied to codebook design problems.

In Section 2, we present a greedy full-search codebook formation algorithm. We discuss possible extensions of our algorithm for dealing with rates of codebooks and for designing *k-nearest-neighbor vector quantization* codebooks. Section 3 deals with the tree pruning problem and introduces the notion of *pseudo-random pruned tree-structured vector quantizers*. Initial experimental results on image compression are reported in Section 4. Section 5 concludes with further discussions.

---

[1] On the other hand, Lin, Storer, and Cohn also show that the tree pruning problem can be solved in polynomial time if the trees are binary and the cost constraint is the number of leaves. Our approximate tree pruning algorithm works for general trees and applies to other cost constraints, such as the average path length and the leaf entropy.

[2] The linear programming problem can be solved in polynomial time by the ellipsoid algorithm [Kha] or by the interior point method [Kar]. In practice, the simplex method [Dan] has been proven to be very efficient, although its worst case performance is not polynomial.

2 Full-Search Vector Quantization

In this section, we present an approximation algorithm for the *(discrete) full-search (vector quantization) codebook design problem.* We denote the signal space by (X, d_X), where d_X is a metric on X. Let $S = \{t_1, \ldots, t_n\}$ be a set of training signal data (training vectors) and let s be a given bound on the size of codebooks. The goal is to select a subset $\mathcal{U} \in S$ of s training vectors as codewords such that the mean squared error $\frac{1}{n} \sum_{i=1}^{n} \min_{t_j \in \mathcal{U}} d_X^2(t_i, t_j)$ is minimized. We remark that our algorithm also works for other distortion measures. The full-search codebook design problem can be formulated as an integer program of minimizing

$$\frac{1}{n} \sum_{i=1}^{n} \sum_{j=1}^{n} d_X^2(t_i, t_j) x_{ij} \tag{1}$$

subject to

$$\sum_{j=1}^{n} x_{ij} = 1, \qquad i = 1, \ldots, n, \tag{2}$$

$$\sum_{j=1}^{n} y_j \leq s, \tag{3}$$

$$x_{ij} \leq y_j, \qquad i, j = 1, \ldots, n, \tag{4}$$

$$x_{ij}, y_j \in \{0, 1\}, \qquad i, j = 1, \ldots, n, \tag{5}$$

where $y_j = 1$ if and only if t_j is chosen as a codeword, and $x_{ij} = 1$ if and only if $y_j = 1$ and t_i is quantized as codeword t_j.

The linear program relaxation of the above program is to allow y_j and x_{ij} to take rational values between 0 and 1. Clearly, the optimal fractional solution (linear program solution) is a lower bound on the solutions of the full-search codebook design problem.

The $\mathcal{NP}$-hardness result in [Pap] can be easily modified to show that the full-search codebook design problem is $\mathcal{NP}$-hard.

2.1 A Greedy Codebook Formation Algorithm

The following is the greedy codebook formation algorithm:

1. Solve the linear program relaxation of the full-search codebook design problem by linear programming techniques; denote the fractional solution by $\widehat{y}, \widehat{x}$.

2. For each i, compute $\widehat{D}_i = \sum_{j=1}^{n} d_X^2(t_i, t_j) \widehat{x}_{ij}$. Given $\epsilon > 0$, for each j such that $\widehat{y}_j > 0$, construct a set S_j. A vector t_i is in S_j if and only if $d_X^2(t_i, t_j) \leq (1+\epsilon)\widehat{D}_i$.

3. Apply the greedy set covering algorithm [Chv, Joh, Lov]: Choose the set which covers the most uncovered vectors. Repeat this process until all vectors are covered. Let U be the set of indices of sets chosen by the greedy heuristic. Output $\mathcal{U} = \{t_j\}_{j \in U}$ as the codebook.[3]

---

[3]The codebook can be further improved by the generalized Lloyd algorithm.

By the results in [LiV], we have the following application:

Corollary 1 *Given any $\epsilon > 0$, the greedy codebook formation algorithm outputs a codebook $\mathcal{U}$ of size at most $(1 + 1/\epsilon)s(\ln n + 1)$ such that $\frac{1}{n}\sum_{i=1}^{n} \min_{t_j \in \mathcal{U}} d_X^2(t_i, t_j) \leq (1+\epsilon)\widehat{D} \leq (1+\epsilon)D$, where $\widehat{D}$ is the mean squared error of the optimal fractional solution for the full-search codebook design problem and D is the optimal mean squared error of codebooks of size at most s.*

2.2 Extensions

2.2.1 Dealing with Rates

If the bound is on the rate of the codebook rather than on the codebook size, we may apply entropy-coding methods to the codebook produced by the greedy codebook formation algorithm. Alternatively, given a bound R on the rate of codebooks, we may formulate the codebook formation problem as a nonlinear program of minimizing

$$\frac{1}{n}\sum_{i=1}^{n}\sum_{j=1}^{n} d_X^2(t_i, t_j)x_{ij} \tag{6}$$

subject to

$$\sum_{j=1}^{n} x_{ij} = 1, \qquad i = 1, \ldots, n, \tag{7}$$

$$\frac{1}{n}\sum_{i=1}^{n} x_{ij} = p_j, \qquad j = 1, \ldots, n, \tag{8}$$

$$\sum_{j=1}^{n} p_j \log \frac{1}{p_j} \leq R, \tag{9}$$

$$x_{ij} \leq y_j, \qquad i, j = 1, \ldots, n, \tag{10}$$

$$x_{ij}, y_j \in \{0, 1\}, \qquad i, j = 1, \ldots, n, \tag{11}$$

where $y_j = 1$ if and only if t_j is chosen as a codeword, $x_{ij} = 1$ if and only if $y_j = 1$ and t_i is quantized as codeword t_j, and p_j is the relative frequency of training vectors quantized as t_j. In this case, heuristics may be needed to solve the nonlinear program.

2.2.2 k-Nearest-Neighbor Vector Quantization

In traditional vector quantization, an input vector is quantized as its nearest codeword in the codebook. In the *k-nearest-neighbor vector quantization*, an input vector is quantized as the weighted average of its k-nearest codewords in the codebook. In the context of image compression, this mapping may have the effect of smoothing images and preventing distracting blockiness.

Given a sequence of training vectors $t_1, t_2, \ldots, t_n$ and a bound s on the codebook size, the *k-nearest-neighbor (vector quantization) codebook design problem* is to select a subset $\mathcal{U}$ of s training vectors as codewords such that the mean squared error minimized. Our greedy codebook formation algorithm can be adapted for solving the k-nearest-neighbor codebook design problem with similar performance guarantees.

3   Tree-Structured Vector Quantization

The computational advantage of tree-structured vector quantizers (TSVQ) over full-search quantizers is that the mapping from a vector to a quantization bin can be done quickly by tree traversal. Tree-structured vector quantizers also have a distinguished "successive approximation" and "graceful degradation" character.

In this section we present an approximate tree pruning algorithm. Besides pruned tree-structured vector quantization (PTSVQ), the tree pruning problem has many other applications such as regression trees, decision trees, and computer graphics [BFO, CLG]. Our notations in this section follow that of [CLG].

A tree T is a finite set of nodes, $t_0, t_1, \ldots, t_n$, with a unique root node t_0. The set of leaves of a tree T is denoted by $\widetilde{T}$. A subtree S of tree T is a tree rooted at some node $root(S) \in T$ and the following condition holds: For each internal node t of T, if any of the children of t is in S, then all of children of t must be in S as well. The leaves $\widetilde{S}$ of a subtree S are not necessarily a subset of $\widetilde{T}$; the leaves of S may be the internal nodes of T. If $\widetilde{S} \subseteq \widetilde{T}$, then S is called a branch of T and is denoted by $T_{root(S)}$. For $t \neq t_0$, we denote the parent node of t as $parent(t)$. For $t \in T - \widetilde{T}$, let $children(t)$ be the set of children for node t. We define $path(t)$ as the set of nodes, including t, from t_0 leading to t. We call a subtree S of T a *pruned subtree* and write $S \preceq T$ if the root of S is t_0.

Definition 1 Let $u(t) \geq 0$ be an arbitrary function on the nodes of T. A *linear tree functional u* on subtrees is:
$$u(S) = \sum_{\widetilde{t} \in \widetilde{S}} u(\widetilde{t}).$$

Let $\Delta u(S) = u(S) - u(root(S))$. A tree functional u is monotonic nondecreasing if and only if for any subtree S of T, we have $\Delta u(S) \geq 0$. Similarly, u is monotonic nonincreasing if and only if $\Delta u(S) \leq 0$ for any subtree S of T.

Let $\mathcal{C}$ be a monotonic nondecreasing tree functional and $\mathcal{D}$ be a monotonic nonincreasing tree functional. We call $\mathcal{C}$ the *cost functional* and $\mathcal{D}$ the *distortion functional*. For example, in vector quantization, we have the following setting: Let P be a probability function such that $P(t_0) = 1$ and for all $t \in T - \widetilde{T}$, we have $P(t) = \sum_{t' \in children(t)} P(t')$. Let d be a distortion function on nodes satisfying $P(t)d(t) \geq \sum_{t' \in children(t)} P(t')d(t')$. Usually we let $\mathcal{D}(S)$ be the average distortion of subtrees. Possible definitions for $\mathcal{C}(S)$ include the average path length, the leaf entropy, or the number of leaves.

Given a tree T and a bound C on the cost, the *tree pruning problem* is to find a pruned subtree S of T such that $\mathcal{C}(S) \leq C$ and $\mathcal{D}(S)$ is minimized. We may formulate the tree pruning problem as an integer linear program as follows: For each node $t \in T$, let x_t be a decision variable such that $x_t = 1$ if and only if node t is a leaf in the final pruned subtree, $x_t = 0$ otherwise. The integer linear program for the optimal tree pruning problem is to minimize the cost

$$\sum_{t \in T} x_t \mathcal{D}(t) \tag{12}$$

subject to

$$\sum_{t \in path(\tilde{t})} x_t = 1, \qquad \tilde{t} \in \tilde{T}, \tag{13}$$

$$\sum_{t \in T} x_t \mathcal{C}(t) \leq C, \tag{14}$$

$$x_t \in \{0,1\}, \qquad t \in T. \tag{15}$$

Lin, Storer, and Cohn [LSC] show that, in general, the tree pruning problem is $\mathcal{NP}$-hard. Therefore, we have to use heuristics in practice [BFO, CLG].

3.1 Approximate Tree Pruning

The following is an outline of the approximate tree pruning algorithm:

1. Solve the linear program relaxation of the tree pruning problem by linear programming techniques; denote the fractional solution by $\hat{x}$.

2. Given $\epsilon > 0$, in a top-down and breadth-first fashion, we prune the tree at any node t where $\sum_{t' \in path(t)} \hat{x}_{t'} \geq 1/(1 + \epsilon)$.

The results in [LiV] imply the following:

Corollary 2 *Given any $\epsilon > 0$, the approximate tree pruning algorithm outputs a pruned subtree S satisfying $\mathcal{C}(S) \leq (1 + 1/\epsilon)C$ and $\mathcal{D}(S) \leq (1 + \epsilon)\widehat{D} \leq (1 + \epsilon)D$, where $\widehat{D}$ is the distortion of the optimal fractional solution for the tree pruning problem and D is the optimal distortion of pruned subtrees with cost at most C.*

3.2 Pseudo-Random PTSVQ

In this section we introduce a new kind of vector quantizers called *pseudo-random pruned tree-structured vector quantizers (pseudo-random PTSVQ)*. We first define a more general notion of *probability search trees*. Probability search trees are an interesting interpretation of the fractional solution of the integer linear program for the tree pruning problem.

Definition 2 A *probability search tree* $\widehat{T} = (T, q)$ is a tree T with augmented probability function q on tree nodes, which satisfies $\sum_{t \in path(\tilde{t})} q(t) = 1$, for all $\tilde{t} \in \tilde{T}$. Let us define $Q(t) = 1 - \sum_{t' \in path(t)} q(t')$. A search along a path through node t will continue at node t, assuming the search reaches node t, with probability $Q(t)/Q(parent(t))$. We may see $Q(t)$ as the probability that the search passes through node t and $q(t)$ as the probability that the search stops at node t.

We can extend tree functionals to probability search trees in the following way:

Definition 3 Let $\widehat{T} = (T, q)$ be a probability search tree. Given a linear tree functional u, we define the *probability tree functional u^** on subtrees as

$$u^*(S) = \sum_{t \in S - \widetilde{S}} q(t)u(t) + \sum_{\widetilde{t} \in \widetilde{S}} Q(parent(\widetilde{t}))u(\widetilde{t}),$$

and we define $\Delta u^*(S) = u^*(S) - u^*(root(S))$. A probability tree functional u^* is monotonic nondecreasing if and only if for any subtree S of T, we have $\Delta u(S) \geq 0$. Similarly, u^* is monotonic nonincreasing if and only if $\Delta u(S) \leq 0$ for any subtree S of T.

The results in [LiV] imply the following monotonic properties of probability tree functionals:

Corollary 3 *If a linear tree functional u is monotonic nondecreasing (nonincreasing), then the probability tree functional u^* is also monotonic nondecreasing (nonincreasing).*

We can interpret an optimal fractional solution $\widehat{x}$ as an augmented probability function q by setting $q(t) = \widehat{x}_t$. The resulting probability search tree can be used as a pseudo-random PTSVQ, which statistically has the potential of outperforming the optimal PTSVQ in terms of the average path length:

Corollary 4 *Let $\widehat{T} = (T, q)$ be a probability search tree with $q(t) = \widehat{x}_t$, where $\widehat{x}$ is an optimal fractional solution for the tree pruning problem, and let $C(S)$ be the average path length of subtrees. Then we have $C^*(\widehat{T}) \leq C$ and $\mathcal{D}^*(\widehat{T}) = \widehat{D} \leq D$, where $\widehat{D}$ is the distortion of the optimal fractional solution for the tree pruning problem and D is the optimal distortion of pruned subtrees with cost at most C.*

In pseudo-random PTSVQ, the encoder and decoder use the same pseudo-random number generator for making stopping decisions. For encoding, the encoder selects a random seed r for the pseudo-random number generator and then encodes each input vector as a path according to the search procedure for probability search trees. The random seed r is transmitted along with the binary sequence. For decoding, the decoder uses the same random seed r and traverses the tree according to the encoded binary sequence and the search procedure for probability search trees.

4 Experimental Results

4.1 Full-Search Vector Quantization

The solution of linear programs dominates the time and memory requirement of the greedy codebook formation algorithm. The number of variables in the linear program is $O(n^2)$ and the number of constraints is also $O(n^2)$. A straightforward implementation of the simplex method for linear programming requires $O(n^4)$ space. By the decomposition technique in [GNR], the space requirement can be reduced to $O(n^2)$. Unfortunately, for image compression, the number of training vectors can be in the order of 10^6. Therefore, it may require gigabytes of memory to solve the linear program. Currently we are studying ways for reducing the space requirement and for speeding up the linear programming.

Initial experimental results with hundreds of training vectors show that the greedy algorithm terminates with optimal solutions regularly. That is, with $\epsilon = 1$, often the codebook size is exactly s and the mean squared error is exactly $\widehat{D}$.

4.2 Tree-Structured Vector Quantization

The number of variables in the linear program for the tree pruning problem is $O(n)$ and the number of constraints is also $O(n)$. The space requirement is therefore $O(n^2)$. In fact, the number of nonzero entries in the constraint matrix is only $O(n \log n)$, and the space requirement can be greatly reduced by sparse-matrix techniques.

We used the USC database for our experiments. The test image was the well-known Lenna image. The code vectors were 4×4 pixel blocks. The average rate is the average path length of trees. A complete TSVQ of length 12 was designed using the training sequence. PTSVQs of average rate $0, 1, \ldots, 12$ were obtained by the approximate tree pruning algorithm. (We solved the linear programs by the Stanford MINOS package.) We also constructed a series of pseudo-random PTSVQs from the fractional solutions for the linear programs. The resulting peak signal-to-noise ratio (PSNR), which is defined as

$$10 \log_{10} \frac{(\text{peak input amplitude})^2}{\text{MSE}},$$

for each vector quantizer is plotted against its rate in Figure 1.

The results indicate that the performances of PTSVQs and pseudo-random PTSVQs are very similar. Compared with similar experiments by Riskin in [Ris], our approximate tree pruning algorithm performs at least as well as the generalized BFOS algorithm, although we use a different initial tree. We also note that the PSNRs can be further improved by predictive coding techniques as indicated in [Ris].

5 Conclusions

In this paper, we propose a new approach for vector quantization codebook design problems. Our method is to formulate a codebook design problem as a 0-1 integer linear program. We first solve its linear program relaxation and then transform the fractional solution to a provably good 0-1 solution. The codebook design problems we look into include a full-search codebook formation problem and the tree-structured vector quantizer pruning problem.

Initial experimental results indicate that our approximation algorithms perform much better in practice than their (worst-case) performance guarantees suggest. The

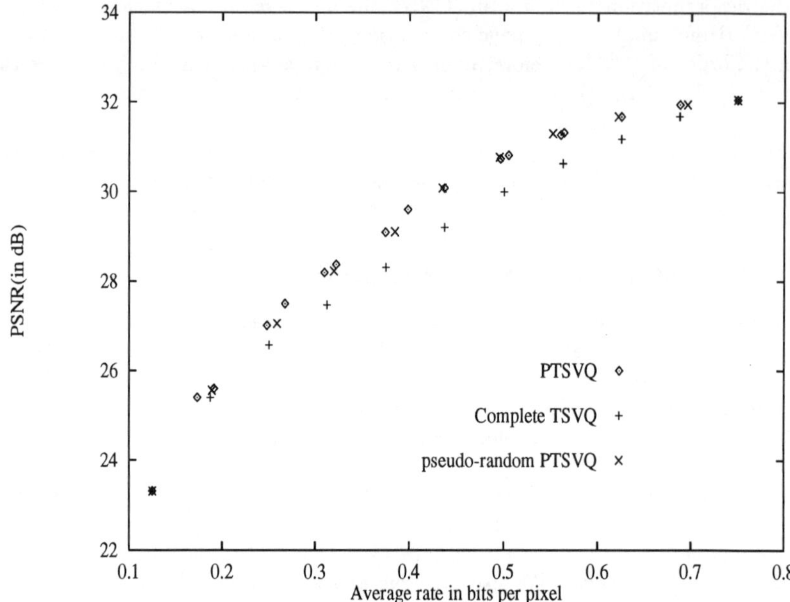

Figure 1: PSNR vs. Average Rate: USC database. The PTSVQs are obtained by the approximate tree pruning algorithm. The pseudo-random PTSVQs are constructed from the fractional solutions for the linear programs.

approximation algorithm for forming full-search codebook may not be practical at this moment due to the huge size of linear programs. On the other hand, the linear programs used by the approximate tree pruning algorithm are of moderate size and can be solved efficiently.

It is of interest to apply our approach to other problems related to vector quantization and data compression in general.

References

[BFO] L. Breiman, J. H. Friedman, R. A. Olshen, and C. J. Stone, *Classification Trees and Regression Trees*, Wadsworth, Belmont, CA, 1984.

[CLG] P. A. Chou, T. Lookabaugh, and R. M. Gray, "Optimal Pruning with Applications to Tree-Structured Source Coding and Modeling," *IEEE Transactions on Information Theory* (1989), 299–315.

[Chv] V. Chvátal, "A Greedy Heuristic for the Set-Covering Problem," *Mathematics of Operations Research* 4 (1979), 233–235.

[Dan] G. Dantzig, "Programming of Interdependent Activities, II, Mathematical Models," in *Activity Analysis of Production and Allocation*, John Wiley & Sons, Inc, New York, 1951, 19–32.

[GNR] R. S. Garfinkel, A. W. Neebe, and M. R. Rao, "An Algorithm for the M-Median Plant Location Problem," *Transportation Science* 8 (1974), 217–236.

[Ger] A. Gersho, "On the Structure of Vector Quantizers," *IEEE Transactions on Information Theory* 28 (March 1982), 157–166.

[GeG] A. Gersho and R. M. Gray, *Vector Quantization and Signal Compression*, Kluwer Academic Press, Massachusetts, 1991.

[Gra] R. M. Gray, "Vector Quantization," *IEEE ASSP Magazine* (April 1984), 4–29.

[GKL] R. M. Gray, J. C. Kieffer, and Y. Linde, "Locally Optimal Block Quantizer Design," *Information and Control* 45 (1980), 178–198.

[Joh] D. S. Johnson, "Approximation Algorithms for Combinatorial Problems," *Journal of Computer and System Sciences* 9 (1974), 256–278.

[Kar] N. Karmarkar, "A New Polynomial-Time Algorithm for Linear Programming," *Combinatorica* 4 (1984), 373–395.

[Kha] L. G. Khachiyan, "A Polynomial Algorithm in Linear Programming," *Soviet Math. Doklady* 20 (1979), 191–194.

[LSC] J. Lin, J. A. Storer, and M. Cohn, "On the Complexity of Optimal Tree Pruning for Source Coding," in *Proceedings of the Data Compression Conference*, J. A. Storer and J. H. Reif, eds., Snowbird, Utah, April 1991, 63–72.

[LiV] J.-H. Lin and J. S. Vitter, "ϵ-Approximations with Minimum Packing Constraint Violation," submitted for publication.

[LBG] Y. Linde, A. Buzo, and R. M. Gray, "An Algorithm for Vector Quantizer Design," *IEEE Transactions on Communications* COM-28 (January 1980), 84–95.

[Lov] L. Lovász, "On the Ratio of Optimal Integral and Fractional Covers," *Discrete Mathematics* 13 (1975), 383–390.

[Pap] C. H. Papadimitriou, "Worst-case and Probabilistic Analysis of a Geometric Location Problem," *SIAM Journal on Computing* 10 (1981), 542–557.

[Rag] P. Raghavan, "Probabilistic Construction of Deterministic Algorithms: Approximating Packing Integer Programs," *Journal of Computer and System Science* 37 (1988), 130–143.

[RaT] P. Raghavan and C. D. Thompson, "Randomized Rounding: A Technique for Provably Good Algorithms and Algorithmic Proofs," *Combinatorics* 7 (1987), 365–374.

[Ris] E. A. Riskin, *Variable Rate Vector Quantization of Images*, Ph. D. Dissertation, Stanford University, 1990.

Optical Techniques for Image Compression*

John H. Reif   Akitoshi Yoshida

Department of Computer Science
Duke University
Durham, NC 27706.
Email: reif@cs.duke.edu, ay@cs.duke.edu

ABSTRACT

Optical computing has recently become a very active research field. The advantage of optics is its capability of providing highly parallel operations in a three dimensional space. We propose optical architectures to execute various image compression techniques.

We optically implement the following compression techniques:

- transform coding
- vector quantization
- interframe coding

We show many generally used transform coding methods, for example, the cosine transform, can be implemented by a simple optical system. The transform coding can be carried out in constant time.

Most of this paper is concerned with a sophisticated optical system for vector quantization using holographic associative matching. Limitations of conventional vector quantization schemes are caused by a large number of sequential searches through a large vector space. Holographic associative matching provided by multiple exposure holograms can offer advantageous techniques for vector quantization based compression schemes. Photorefractive crystals, which provide high density recording in real time, are used as our holographic media. The reconstruction alphabet can be dynamically constructed through training or stored in the photorefractive crystal in advance. Encoding a new vector can be carried out by holographic associative matching in constant time.

An extension to interframe coding is also discussed.

1 Introduction

1.1 Image Compression

Image compression is crucial for many applications [1, 2]. The objective of image compression is to reduce the bit rate for signal transmission or storage while maintaining an acceptable image quality for various purposes. In video signal transmission, one can compress original images so that the high quality images which would require high bandwidth can be transmitted through a medium with relatively low bandwidth. In medical imaging, one can use image compression techniques to store a large number of x-ray pictures that are routinely produced at hospitals.

Compression techniques generally exploit the redundancy in the image. The transform coding such as the fourier transform coding or the cosine transform coding decomposes an

---

*Research supported in part by DARPA/ISTO Contracts N00014-88-K-0458, N00014-91-C-0114 and N00014-91-J-1985, NASA subcontract 550-63 of prime contract NAS5-30428, and US-Israel Binational NSF Grant 88-00282/2.

input image into its spectral components. One can achieve compression by appropriately coding the spectral components which are above a certain threshold value. Unfortunately, the difficulties of implementing the transform coding arise from the complexity of transforming algorithms, which require $O(n \log n)$ time for an n-point transformation.

A vector quantizer is a system that maps a set of continuous or discrete vectors into a finite set of discrete vectors that are suitable for transmission or storage. The vector quantization techniques for compressing image and speech signals have been extensively investigated by many researchers [3, 4, 5]. The basic algorithm using full search in the vector space requires an extremely large number of computations. Although the algorithm is guaranteed to find a locally optimal quantizer, its computational complexity can be prohibitive. A similar approach using tree search has less computational complexity but requires larger storage and needs still a quite large number of computations.

The problem is caused by sequential execution of the algorithm on conventional electronic computers. Although, some parallelism can be obtained by standard parallel processing hardware, electrically implemented interconnection may not provide enough bandwidth to handle a large number of computations.

1.2 Power of Optical Computing

Optical computing has recently become a very active research field [6, 7, 8, 9]. The obvious advantage of optics is its freedom in space. A set of light beams can establish communication links among optical logic gates in a three dimensional space, whereas the VLSI model must confine electrical wires on a two dimensional plane.

From a theoretical computational point of view, for a given problem, there is a lower bound on the circuit area and its computational time. One such lower bound on the planar VLSI model called "AT^2 bounds" states that $AT^2 = \Omega(I^2)$, where A is the circuit area, T is the time used by the circuit, and I is information content[1] of the problem (See Ullman [10]). In a three dimensional electro-optical model described by Barakat and Reif called VLSIO, the similar lower bound can be expressed as $VT^{3/2} = \Omega(I^{3/2})$ [11]. This implies that as the information content becomes larger, the VLSI circuit requires a larger and larger area to solve the problem in a fixed amount of time. Using three dimensional optical systems as in the VLSIO model, we can overcome this interconnection problem by utilizing space in a volume. As an example, a $n \times n$ two-dimensional fourier transform can be computed by a simple optical system of volume $O(n^{3/2})$ in constant time. A n-point fourier transform has $AT^2 = \Omega(n^2 \log^2 n)$ in the VLSI model, whereas in the VLSIO model it has $VT^{3/2} = \Omega(n^{3/2} \log^{3/2} n)$. In fact, there is an optical system which implements a n-point fourier transform in constant time using volume $n^{3/2}$ [12]. This is optimal within a polylog factor.

1.3 Optics for Image Compression

Although the advantages of optics are well known, the realization of a general purpose optical computer is yet to come. On the other hand, special purpose optical computers have been implemented for areas such as image and signal processing [13, 14], associative memory [15], and neural networks [16, 17]. These systems exploit the advantages of optics such as the ability to perform a matrix-vector multiplication and a two dimensional fourier transform in constant time or, to implement associative memory using holograms.

A lens can compute the fourier transform of an input image [18]. A transparency whose transmittance represents the input image is placed at the front focal plane of the lens. The amplitude of the light passing the transparency is modulated by the transmittance. The complex amplitude of the light at the back focal plane represents the fourier transform of the input image.

---

[1]Information content is the number of bits that must cross a boundary in order to solve the problem. The boundary separates the circuit into two sides, each of which holds approximately half the input bits.

Holograms have been used for associative matching [19, 20, 21, 22, 23]. One can record multiple images on a single holographic medium using distinct reference beams as their associative keys. Later, the stored image can be reconstructed by using its corresponding reference beam as a key associated to the image. Recently, dynamically modifiable holographic media such as photorefractive crystals (i.e., iron doped $LiNbO_3$) have been widely investigated. The refractive index of these media can be optically changed to store holograms. The thickness of the media allows the superposition of many holograms in a common volume in the crystal. A large number of holograms can be stored in a volume by using a recording reference beam that has a distinct angle for each hologram. Later, each hologram can be read out using its corresponding reference beam. Photorefractive crystals are particularly attractive as holographic media, since they provide high density recording in real time.

In this paper, we consider compression techniques using volume holograms in photorefractive crystals. We discuss their advantages and limitations. We also discuss an extension to interframe video compression.

Our results are:

- Cosine transform of a $n^{1/2} \times n^{1/2}$ image with n pixels can be carried out in constant time with the VLSIO model in volume $O(n^{3/2})$.
- Encoding a vector by an N-level k-dimensional vector quantizer can be carried out in constant time with the VLSIO model in volume $O(N^{3/2} + k^{3/2})$.
- Vector quantization of a $n^{1/2} \times n^{1/2}$ image with n pixels by an N-level k-dimensional quantizer can be carried out in constant time with the VLSIO model in volume $O((N^{1/2} + k^{1/2})n)$.

In the following, section 2 gives optical implementation of the cosine transform coding. Section 3 starts with a background in vector quantization and holographic associative matching, and describes our holographic vector quantizer. Section 4 discuss its extension to interframe coding. Section 5 concludes this paper.

2 Optical Implementation of Cosine Transform Coding

The cosine transform [24, 25] is a member of sinusoidal transforms. The fourier transform decomposes a spatially encoded input image into its spectral components. For an image with high inter-pixel correlation, high spatial frequency components are often small and negligible. Thus, appropriately encoding only significant components leads to compression of data.

An optical implementation of a two-dimensional cosine transform is quite simple, as depicted in Figure 1. The input image is copied and flipped three times to form a symmetric image. A two-dimensional fourier transform can be computed optically in constant time using a lens. The symmetry of the input image allows its cosine transform to be obtained at the focal plane. The amplitude of each spectral component represents its corresponding fourier coefficient.

Encoding
Our optical system is used to compute the two dimensional cosine transform of an input image in constant time. Threshold operations are applied to each spectral component to cut off some components. The resulting components are appropriately quantized and encoded by a computer.

Decoding
The same optical system used for encoding can be used to decode the spectral components.

Theorem 2.1 *Cosine transform of a $n^{1/2} \times n^{1/2}$ image with n pixels can be carried out in constant time with the VLSIO model in volume $O(n^{3/2})$.*

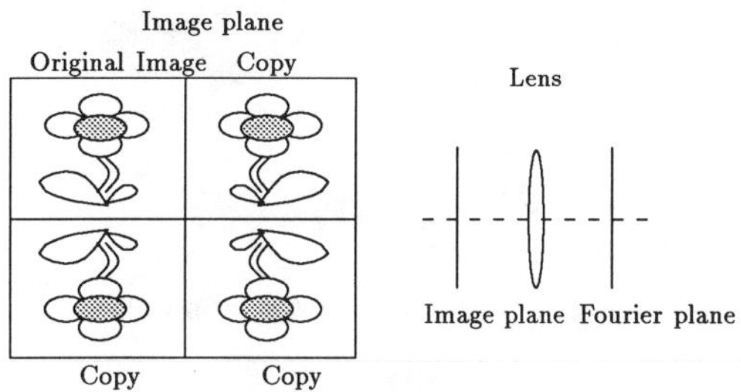

Figure 1: Optical cosine transform.

Proof: Let d_i and d_o represent the spacings between input pixels and detector pixels, respectively. The highest spatial frequency can be written as $1/d_i$. At the fourier plane, this spectral component is displayed at $\lambda f/d_i$, where λ is the wavelength, and f is the focal length of the lens. Since the detector array is of size $n^{1/2} \times n^{1/2}$, the spacing between detector pixels, d_o, becomes $2\lambda f/d_i n^{1/2}$. Assuming $d_i = d_o$, we obtain $f = O(n^{1/2})$. Thus, we can place the whole optical system in volume of size $O((n^{1/2})^3)$

3   Holographic Vector Quantization

3.1   Vector Quantizer

Extensive studies of vector quantizers have been made by many researchers [3, 4, 5].

An N-level k-dimensional vector quantizer can be defined as a mapping of a k-dimensional input vector $x = (x_1, \ldots, x_k)$ into a reproduction vector $\hat{x} = q(x)$, which is an element of a finite reproduction alphabet $\hat{A} = \{y_i | i = 1, \ldots, N\}$. The goal of quantization is to produce the best possible reproduction vectors for a set of input vectors under some given constrains. The performance of a quantizer is determined by using a distortion measure such as the squared error distortion measure defined by $d(x, \hat{x}) = ||x - \hat{x}||^2$

3.2   Holographic Associative Matching

Consider two mutually coherent beams interfering with each other on a photosensitive plate. After the plate is developed, the resultant intensity distribution is stored as a spatial modulation of the transmittance of the plate. When the plate is later illuminated by one of these beams, the incident beam will be diffracted by the modulation of the transmittance. Then, the resulting wavefront from the plate will be observed as if there are both beams incident on the plate. For detail, see the textbook by Collier, Burckhardt and Lin [26].

Holograms recorded in volume media are considered as a spatial modulation of the dielectric constant (phase gratings) or the absorption constant (absorption gratings). When two plane waves are used in recording, the interference of the two beams causes either the dielectric constant or the absorption constant to vary sinusoidally in the volume. A set of equally spaced planes that are loci of the constant dielectric or absorption constant are drawn in Figure 2 (a). Two waves represented by E_i and E_j enter the holographic medium. The wavelength in the medium is λ. Two vectors, $\vec{k}_i$ and $\vec{k}_j$, are called the wave vectors of E_i and E_j, respectively. The length of a wave vector is $2\pi/\lambda$, and its direction is parallel to the direction of the wave propagation in the medium. A vector, $\vec{K}_{i,j}$ is called the grating vector between wave E_i and wave E_j, and normal to the fringe planes. The length of the

36

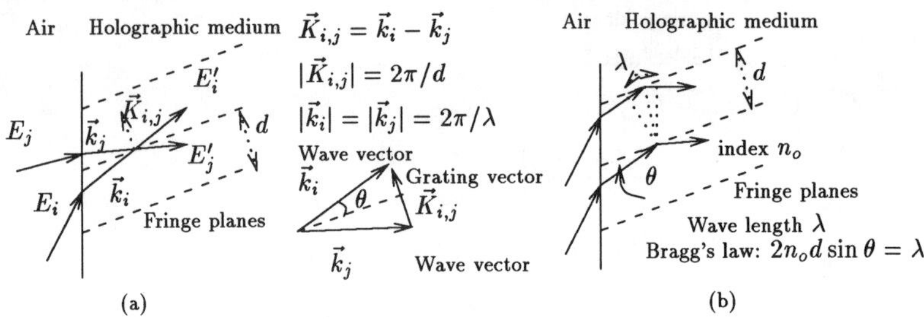

Figure 2: Formation of Holograms and the Bragg condition.

grating vector is defined as $2\pi/d$, where d is a distance between the fringe planes. Later, when the hologram is illuminated by a reconstruction beam, the incident beam is scattered by the set of planes. Only the reconstruction beam that satisfies the Bragg condition can constructively interfere with its scattered waves to maximize its diffraction efficiency, which is defined as the ratio of the incident intensity to the diffracted intensity. This is shown in Figure 2 (b). Thus, the Bragg condition gives volume holograms strong angular selectivity upon reconstruction.

Volume media are suited for multiple exposure holograms because of their strong angler selectivity. A large number of holograms have been recorded in a volume of dynamic media such as $LiNbO_3$ [27, 28, 29].

3.3   Design of Holographic Compression
3.3.1   General Configuration
For a given image, we partition the image into a set of blocks (vectors). Let the size of each block be $\sqrt{k} \times \sqrt{k}$. We use two arrays of liquid crystal light valve (LCLV) [30] spatial light modulators (SLM) at the input plane: one for the input image array, S_1, and the other for the label array, S_2. The first array, S_1, is of size $2\sqrt{k} \times \sqrt{k}$ and is used to represent each vector of the input image. Each pixel of the input vector is represented in S_1 by two pixels of complementary intensity values. A pixel with an intensity value c is encoded into two pixels: one with an intensity value c and the other with an intensity value $\bar{c}$, which is equal to the maximum intensity value minus value c. This encoding scheme keeps each encoded block at a constant intensity level, maintaining an equal energy incident on the holographic medium for every input vector. The other array, S_2, is of size $\sqrt{N} \times \sqrt{N}$, and provides one of N label beams to the holographic medium. We have two arrays of photodetectors at the output plane: one for the reconstruction vector array, D_1, and the other for the label array, D_2. The detector array, D_1, is of size $2\sqrt{k} \times \sqrt{k}$ and is used for reconstructing the decoded vector. The other array, D_2, is of size $\sqrt{N} \times \sqrt{N}$ and is used to detect the best matching label for the input vector.

Figure 3 (a) shows a configuration of the system. Two mutually coherent beams illuminate array S_1 and array S_2. Two fourier lenses are used to form fourier transform holograms in the photorefractive crystal placed between the lenses.

We consider each pixel in the input plane as a point source. Each point source produces a plane wave after passing the first lens. There are $2k$ pixels in S_1 and N pixels in S_2. At the output plane, there are $2k$ pixels in D_1 and N pixels in D_2. We give a global index number to each pixel of the vector arrays and the label arrays. The pixels of the vector arrays are indexed from 1 to $2k$, and those of the label arrays are indexed from $2k + 1$ to

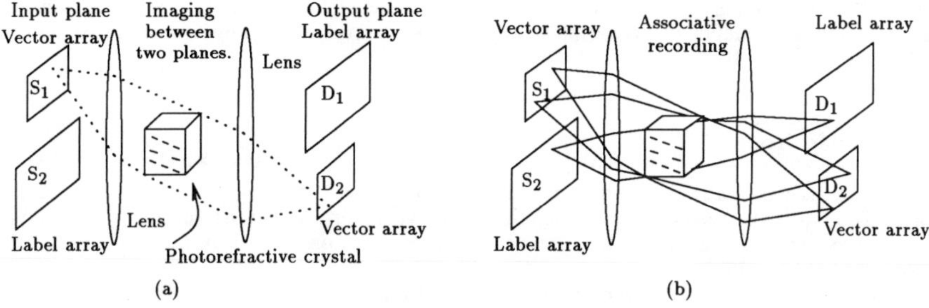

Figure 3: (a) Holographic Vector Quantizer and (b) Recording vector and its associated label.

$2k + N$. The image of the i-th pixel in the input plane is formed at the position of the i-th pixel in the output plane via two fourier lenses.

In photorefractive crystals, holograms are recorded via the modulation of the index of refraction by the space charge field induced by a spatially varying optical intensity distribution. Interaction between light waves and multiple gratings in the volume can be treated as linear if the diffraction efficiencies of the gratings are very small [31]. In this case, each incident plane wave interacts with every grating in the volume independently. The diffracted light for an arbitrary configuration of the input pixels is thus computed as a sum of each diffracted wave via each grating. Each grating formed by recording a pair of two plane waves is capable of connecting the pair of pixels.

Let η_{ij} be the diffraction efficiency of the grating connecting the i-th pixel and the j-th pixel. The intensity of light at the j-th pixel due to a light wave from the i-th pixel with intensity I_i is given by [32]

$$I_j = I_i\eta_{ij} + \sum_{p \neq i}\sum_{q \neq j} I_i\eta_{pq}\, \mathrm{sinc}^2(K_{pq}(i,j)L/2)$$

where $K_{pq}(i,j)$ denotes the phase mismatch of the wave from pixel i to pixel j due to the grating connecting the p-th pixel and the q-th pixel, and L is the thickness of the crystal.

The phase mismatched crosstalk term in the above summation can be eliminated under several conditions [31, 32]. One condition is satisfied when the phase mismatch term $K_{pq}(i,j)$ is larger than $2\pi/L$. Another condition requires that the diffracted light waves do not propagate to any one of the output pixels. Then, recording a hologram connecting a pair of pixels increases the connection between the pair without seriously affecting the connections between other pairs. If we assume the phase mismatched crosstalk term is negligible, we can consider the photorefractive crystal as a linear mapping from input plane vector P_{in} to output plane vector P_{out}. P_{in} is a vector of length $2k + N$ whose elements correspond to the intensity values of pixels at the input plane. Similarly, P_{out} is a vector of length $2k + N$ whose elements correspond to the intensity values of pixels at the output plane. Then, the mapping from the input plane to the output plane can be written as a matrix vector multiplication form.

$$P_{out} = H P_{in}$$

where H is a $(2k + N) \times (2k + N)$ matrix whose (i,j) entry is η_{ij}.

In this paper, we assume the above model to characterize photorefractive crystals. However, the nonlinear dynamics of multiple exposure holograms make it extremely difficult

38

to characterize analytically the recorded holograms. It is not possible to record multiple holograms independently. The exposure of each new hologram partially erases previously recorded holograms. For more complete analysis, one may have to rely on computer simulations or experiments.

3.3.2 Encoding
Static Code Book
First, we consider a case where the reconstruction alphabet of size N is already stored in the photorefractive crystal. The photorefractive crystal is initialized by a uniform plane light wave. To record the reconstruction alphabet, each vector in the reconstruction alphabet is loaded into array S_1 one at a time. Array S_2 can produce one of the N label beams as in Figure 3 (b).

The exposure of a pair of each vector wave and its associated label beam increases the connection strength by an amount proportional to the intensity of each pixel. The photorefractive crystal stores each η_{ij} as an element in matrix H [17]. A reproduction alphabet $\hat{A} = \{y_i | i = 1, \ldots, N\}$ is represented by a set of vectors $\{z_i = y_i \bar{y}_i | i = 1, \ldots, N\}$, where $\bar{y}_i$ denotes the complement of vector y_i. Each vector z_i is of length $2k$ and is represented with intensity. Each diffraction efficiency η_{ij} is proportional to the product of the intensity values of the i-th pixel and the j-th pixel. Thus, after recording each vector in this alphabet, we have

$$
H \propto \begin{pmatrix} H_{11} & z_1 & \cdots & z_N \\ z_1^t & & & \\ \cdots & & I & \\ z_N^t & & & \end{pmatrix}
$$

where z_i^t denotes the transposed vector of z_i, and H_{11} is the sum of outer products $z_i z_i^t$ for all i.

Consider encoding a new vector z. The input plane vector P_{in} and its corresponding output plane vector P_{out} can be written as

$$
P_{in} = (\underbrace{z^t}_{2k}, \underbrace{0, \ldots, 0}_{N})^t \qquad\qquad P_{out} \propto (\underbrace{(H_{11} z^t)^t}_{2k}, \underbrace{z_1^t z, z_2^t z, \ldots, z_N^t z}_{N})^t
$$

The first $2k$ elements of P_{out} correspond to the intensity values at D_1 and are not of our interest. The rest of N elements correspond to the intensity values at label array D_2. Each pixel receives intensity proportional to the inner product of the input vector and the recorded vectors. In the LBG algorithm, the distortion measure of two vectors x and y_i is written as

$$
d(x, y_i) = ||x - y_i||^2 = ||x||^2 + ||y_i||^2 - 2x y_i
$$

Our complementary encoding scheme keeps the first two terms constant. Thus, minimizing the distortion measure in vector quantization corresponds to maximizing the inner product in our holographic matching. We choose the label of the pixel which has the maximum intensity value as an encoded symbol.

Thus, once the reconstruction alphabet is recorded, encoding a new vector is simple and fast, as depicted in Figure 4 (a). There are no explicit computations or searches required to find the best vector in the reconstruction alphabet. Each new vector can be loaded into array S_1, which in turn illuminates the photorefractive crystal to retrieve its associated label. The retrieved light reaches some pixels at array D_2. Array D_2 selects the pixel with the largest intensity and transmits its label as an encoded symbol.

The speed of the system is only limited by the switching speed of the SLM.

Dynamic Code Book
Each vector from the training sequence is loaded into array S_1 one at a time. Array S_1 illuminates the photorefractive crystal. The diffracted waves from the crystal are detected

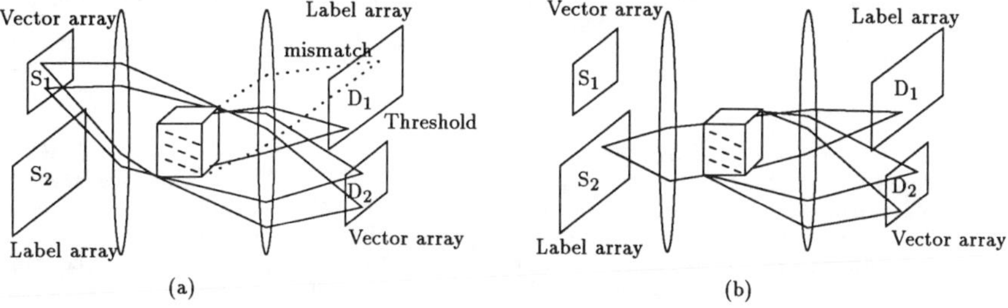

Figure 4: (a) Encoding a new vector and (b) Decoding a label.

by array D_2. If there is a pixel that has intensity greater than a threshold value t_r, we select the index of the pixel as a quantized label for the input vector. Otherwise, we arbitrarily select any unused label pixel that has intensity greater than a threshold value, t_u. The corresponding label is then loaded into array S_2 to create a new label beam for recording. Both S_1 and S_2 then illuminate the holographic medium, and the pair is recorded. After all the training vectors are presented to the system, the convergence of the system can be examined as follows. First, we illuminate the photorefractive crystal with a label beam. We then load its associated image vector that is obtained at array D_1 into array S_1. We then examine whether the illumination from array S_1 produces its associated label at array D_2. For each label beam, we repeat this process to see if there is any mismatch. If there is, we may repeat the recording phase.

Theorem 3.1 *Encoding a new vector by an N-level k-dimensional vector quantizer can be carried out in constant time with the VLSIO model in volume $O(N^{3/2} + k^{3/2})$.*

Proof: Using a similar argument as before, we have volume of size $O((N^{1/2} + k^{1/2})^3)$.

3.3.3 Decoding

For a given label, the reconstruction of its associated image vector is straight forward. The label is loaded into array S_2 that will illuminate the photorefractive crystal. By associative matching of the holograms, the image vector associated with the label will be obtained at array D_1 as shown in Figure 4 (b).

Consider decoding a label s, which is the i-th label vector. The input plane vector P_{in} and its corresponding output plane vector can be written as

$$P_{in} = (\underbrace{0,\dots,0,}_{2k} \underbrace{s}_{N})^t \qquad P_{out} \propto (\underbrace{z_i^t,}_{2k} \underbrace{\dots,0,1,0,\dots}_{N})^t$$

The first $2k$ elements of P_{out} correspond to a reconstruction vector of the i-th vector in the alphabet.

3.4 Increased Parallelism: Coding a Frame in Parallel

If the technology permits, one may construct an array of our holographic vector quantizers to encode and decode a whole image frame in parallel. As we showed in our theorem, each encoder of an N-level k-dimensional vector quantizer occupies a volume of $O(N^{3/2} + k^{3/2})$. In order to encode a $n^{1/2} \times n^{1/2}$ image with n pixels, we need a $(n/k)^{1/2} \times (n/k)^{1/2}$ array of the quantizers. Thus, for a fixed ratio N/k, the total volume becomes $O((N^{1/2} + k^{1/2})n)$.

Theorem 3.2 *Vector quantization of a $n^{1/2} \times n^{1/2}$ image with n pixels by an N-level k-dimensional quantizer can be carried out in constant time with the VLSIO model in volume $O((N^{1/2} + k^{1/2})n)$.*

Proof: From the above argument, the theorem follows.

3.5   Advantages and Limitations

Advantages of our holographic vector quantizer are its speed and size. Encoding a vector is carried out in constant time. The size of the encoder is optimal within a polylog factor.

Limitations are caused by a maximum degree of multiple-exposures in a photorefractive crystal. Although $LiNbO_3$ has large dynamic range to allow a number of multiple exposures, a large number of exposures may reduce the dynamic range of the image.

4   Interframe Compression, Motion Detection

In this paper, we consider only coding of the lateral movement of each block in the image frame. In our further research, we investigate coding methods for the movement of multiple objects and for zooming.

We use dynamic cross-correlation filters to track the movement of the image. Optical correlators are divided into two types, the matched filtering correlator [33] and the joint transform correlator [34, 35, 36]. The matched filtering correlator requires a preparation of a fourier hologram of the model in advance. The joint transform correlator is well suited for real-time applications such as interframe coding, since it provides real-time pattern recognition without requiring preprocessed holograms.

We describe our interframe coding method using the joint transform correlator and our holographic quantizer. Suppose the first frame is already decomposed into blocks and encoded by the previous algorithm. The encoded labels for each block are stored in memory. Each block of the second frame is encoded as follows. First, its previous label is used to reconstruct the previous block. The fourier transform of the reconstructed block is formed on an SLM array that implements a cross correlation filter. The fourier transform of the block from the second frame is formed on the SLM. The light passing the filter forms the cross-correlation of the previous block and the current block at a detector array via another fourier lens. If there is a correlation peak at the detector array, the value of its displacement is transmitted as a movement of the block. If there is no correlation peak, the holographic vector quantizer is used to assign the block a new label.

5   Conclusion and Further Research

We considered several compression techniques using optical systems. Optics can offer an alternative approach to overcome the limitations of current compression schemes. We gave a simple optical system for the cosine transform. We designed a new optical vector quantizer system using holographic associative matching and discussed the issues concerning the system. We also discussed an extension of this optical system to interframe coding.

Further research will include computer simulation and the construction of a small prototype system.

References

[1] A. K. Jain, "Image Data Compression: A Review," *Proceedings of the IEEE* **69**, 349-389 (1981).

[2] —, *DCC' 91 Data Compression Conference*, J. A. Storer and J. H. Reif, ed. (IEEE Computer Society Press, Los Alamitos, California, 1991).

[3] Y. Linde, A. Buzo, and R. M. Gray, "An Algorithm for Vector Quantizer Design," *IEEE Trans. Commun.* **COM-28**, 84-95 (1980).

[4] R. M. Gray, "Vector Quantization," *IEEE ASSP Mag.* April, 4-29 (1984).

[5] N. M. Nasrabadi and R. A. King, "Image Coding Using Vector Quantization: A Review," *IEEE Trans. Commun.* **COM-36,** 957-971 (1988).

[6] J. W. Goodman, F. J. Leonberger, S. Kung, and R. A. Athale, "Optical interconnections for VLSI systems," *Proceedings of the IEEE* **72,** 850-866 (1984).

[7] A. A. Sawchuk and T. C. Strand, "Digital optical computing," Proceedings of the IEEE **72,** 758-779 (1984).

[8] T. E. Bell, "Optical Computing: A field in flux," *IEEE Spectrum* **23(8),** 34-57 (1986).

[9] D. Feitelson, *Optical Computing, A Survey for Computer Scientists,* (MIT Press, Cambridge, Mass., 1988).

[10] J. D. Ullman, *Computational Aspects of VLSI,* (Computer Science Press, Rockwille, Md., 1984).

[11] R. Barakat and J. H. Reif, "Lower Bounds on the Computational Efficiency of Optical Computing Systems," *Appl. Opt.* **26,** 1015-1018 (1987).

[12] J. H. Reif and A. Tyagi, "Efficient Parallel Algorithms for Optical Computing with the DFT Primitive," *10th Conference on Foundations of Software Technology and Theoretical Computer Science, Lecture Notes in Computer Science,* (Springer-Verlag, Bangalor, India 1990).

[13] K. Preston, *Coherent optical computers,* (McGraw-Hill, New York, 1972).

[14] F. T. S. Yu, *Optical information processing,* (Wiley, New York, 1983).

[15] T. Kohonen, *Self-Organization and Associative Memory,* 2nd ed. (Springer-Verlag, New York, 1988).

[16] N. Farhat, D. Psaltis, A. Prata, and E. Paek, "Optical implementation of the Hopfield model," *Appl. Opt.* **24,** 1469-1475(1985).

[17] D. Psaltis, D. Brady, and K. Wagner, "Adaptive optical networks using photorefractive crystals," *Appl. Opt.* **27,** 1752-1759 (1988).

[18] J. W. Goodman, *Introduction to Fourier Optics,* (McGraw-Hill, New York 1968).

[19] H. J. Caulfield, "Associative mapping by optical holography," *Opt. Commun.* **55,** 80-82 (1985).

[20] A. Yariv, S. Kwong, and K. Kyuma, "Demonstration of an all-optical associative holographic memory," *Appl. Phy. Lett.* **48,** 1114-1116 (1986).

[21] B. H. Soffer, G. J. Dunning, Y. Owechko, and E. Marom, "Associative holographic memory with feedback using phase conjugate mirrors," *Opt. Lett.* **11,** 118-120 (1986).

[22] Y. Owechko, G. J. Dunning, E. Marom, and B. H. Soffer, "Holographic associative memory with nonlinearities in the correlation domain," *Appl. Opt.* **26,** 1900-1910 (1987).

[23] H. Kang, C. X. Yang, G. G. Mu, and Z. K. Wu, "Real-time holographic associative memory using doped LiNbO$_3$ in a phase-conjugating resonator," *Opt. Lett.* **15,** 637-639 (1990).

[24] N. Ahmed, T. Natarajan, and K. R. Rao, "Discrete cosine transform," *IEEE Trans. Comput.* **C-23,** 90-93 (1974).

[25] R. J. Clarke, *Transform Coding of Images,* (Academic Press, London, 1985).

[26] R. J. Collier, C. B. Burckhardt, and L. H. Lin, *Optical Holography,* (Academic Press, Orlando, Florida, 1971).

[27] D. L. Staebler, W. J. Burke, W. Phillips, and J. J. Amodei, "Multiple storage and erasure of fixed holograms in Fe-doped LiNbO$_3$," *Appl. Phys. Lett.* **26,** 182-184 (1975).

[28] W. J. Burke, D. L. Staebler, W. Phillips, and G. A. Alphonse, "Volume Phase Holographic Storage in Ferroelectric Crystals," *Opt. Eng.* **17,** 308 (1978).

[29] A. C. Strasser, E. S. Maniloff, K. M. Johnson, and S. D. D. Goggin, "Procedure for recording multiple-exposure holograms with equal diffraction efficiency in photorefractive media," *Opt. Lett.* **14,** 6-8 (1989).

[30] W. P. Bleha, L. T. Lipton, E. W. Wiener-Avner, J. Grinberg, P. G. Reif, D. Casasent, H. B. Brown, and B. V. Markevitch, "Application of the Liquid Crystal Light Valve to Real-Time Optical Data Processing," *Opt. Eng.* **17,** 371-384 (1978).

[31] H. Lee, "Volume holographic global and local interconnecting patterns with maximal capacity and minimal first-order crosstalk," *Appl. Opt.* **28,** 5312-5316 (1989).

[32] H. Lee, X. Gu and D. Psaltis, "Volume holographic interconnections with maximal capacity and minimal cross talk," *J. Appl. Phys.* **65,** 2191-2194 (1989).

[33] A. VanderLugt, "Coherent optical processing," *Proceedings of the IEEE* **62,** 1300-1319 (1974).

[34] D. Casasent, "Coherent optical pattern recognition," *Proceedings of the IEEE* **67,** 813-825 (1979).

[35] B. Javidi and J. L. Horner, "Single spatial light modulator joint transform correlator," *Appl. Opt.* **28,** 1027-1032 (1989).

[36] T. D. Hudson and D. A. Gregory, "Joint transform correlation using an optically addressed ferroelectric LC spatial light modulator," *Appl. Opt.* **29,** 1064-1066 (1990).

Textual Image Compression [1]

Ian H. Witten [2]
Timothy C. Bell [3]
Mary-Ellen Harrison [2]
Mark L. James [2]
Alistair Moffat [4]

We describe a method for lossless compression of images that contain predominantly typed or typeset text—we call these *textual images*. They are commonly found in facsimile documents, where a typed page is scanned and transmitted as an image. Another increasingly popular application is document archiving, where documents are scanned by a computer and stored electronically for later retrieval. Our project was motivated by such an application: Trinity College in Dublin, Ireland, are archiving their 1872 printed library catalogues onto disk, and in order to preserve the exact form of the original document, pages are being stored as scanned images rather than being converted to text. Our test images are taken from this catalogue (one is shown in Figure 1). These beautifully typeset documents have a rather old-fashioned look, and contain a wide variety of symbols from several different typefaces—the five test images we used contain text in English, Flemish, Latin and Greek, and include italics and small capitals as well as roman letters. The catalogue also contains Hebrew, Syriac, and Russian text.

The best lossless compression methods for both text and images base their coding on 'contexts'—a symbol is coded with regard to adjacent ones. However, the contexts used for coding text usually extend over significantly more characters than those used in images. In text compression, the best methods make predictions based on up to three or four characters [2, 7], while with black-white images, the most effective contexts tend to have a radius of just a few pixels [6, 8].

One possibility for textual image compression is to perform optical character recognition (OCR) on the text, and only transmit (or store) the ASCII (or equivalent) codes for the characters, along with some information about their position on the page. There are several problems with this. Considerable computing power is required to recognize characters accurately, and even then it is not completely reliable, particularly if unusual fonts, foreign languages or mathematical expressions are being scanned.[5] OCR systems can require 'training' to learn a new font, and an operator may have to adjust parameters such as the contrast of the scan to ensure that errors are corrected and small marks are removed from the page. Ironically, although the image may look better, it is actually *noisier*, because it does not faithfully represent the original image. Smudged or badly printed characters are replaced with what the OCR system has interpreted them as, rather than leaving human viewers to make their own interpretation. Dirt or ink-stains, which may have given valuable clues to a researcher, are lost. Even the typeface may not be reproduced accurately, affecting the look of the document. For typed business letters, this sort of 'noise' may be acceptable, even desirable, but for archives where the interests of future readers are unknown, there is a strong motivation to record the document as faithfully as possible.

The compression methods investigated here are noiseless, so the original document can be reproduced exactly from its compressed form. This is done by attempting to separate the text and noise in the document. The two components are then compressed independently using a method appropriate for each.

---

[1]Please direct all correspondence to *both* `ian@cpsc.UCalgary.CA` and `tim@cosc.canterbury.ac.NZ`.

[2]Department of Computer Science, University of Calgary, Calgary T2N 1N4, Canada. Telephone +1 403 220–6780.

[3]Department of Computer Science, University of Canterbury, Christchurch, New Zealand. Telephone +64 3 642–352.

[4]Department of Computer Science, University of Melbourne, Parkville, Victoria 3052, Australia.

[5]One of the authors has spent considerable time editing a scanned document where the letters 'r' and 'n' were run together and read as an 'm'. The scanned version was particularly entertaining where words like 'turn' and 'burn' occurred in the text.

Method of compression

Before proceeding with a detailed description, we briefly summarize the new compression method images with reference to a particular example. Figure 1 shows a test image. The actual library pages are formatted in two columns with a vertical separating line and a full-width header at the top. However, these structural elements are detected in a pre-processing stage and our system is presented with bitmap files representing single columns of text.

First, the image is segmented into individual groups of pixels, called 'symbols.' As each is identified it is checked against a growing library of symbols that have been seen so far. This involves testing the newly-segmented item against every member of the library. If no sufficiently close matches are found, the new symbol is added to the library. The library of symbols that is created from the test image is shown in Figure 3. Symbols occur in order of their appearance in the image.

The textual part of the image is the sequence of symbol numbers that have been encountered in it. Symbols are quite similar to characters; however, characters with disconnected parts like 'i' and 'j' are represented by pairs of library elements, one for the body and the other for the dot on top. The second column of Figure 2 shows the sequence of symbol numbers, and using the library in Figure 3 the symbols can be identified and read off the original picture. The first column gives an approximation to the corresponding library symbols, for easy reference.

It is also necessary to code the (x, y) coordinate offsets between one symbol and the next. These inter-symbol gaps are recorded in the last two columns of Figure 2, which show the x- and y-offsets from the right-hand bottom corner of one symbol to the left-hand bottom corner of the next. Occasionally the x-offset will be small and negative (for example, following the body of a 'i' when returning to the dot on top), or large and negative (when returning from the end of one line to the beginning of the next).

Using these symbol numbers, most of the original image can be reconstructed from the library. The result is an approximation to the original image that we call the 'reconstructed text'; it is shown in Figure 4. It differs from the original image in three ways. First, small groups of pixels are rejected by the segmentation process; these correspond to specks in the image and do not appear in the reconstructed text. Second, because matching is approximate, a halo of pixels often appears around the edge of symbols caused by a mismatch between the library element and the actual symbol in the image. Third, symbols that only occur once are not entered into the library and so do not appear in the reconstructed text.

To complete the original picture, it is exclusive-OR'd with the reconstructed text image to form a bitmap called the 'residue,' shown in Figure 5. This is coded using image compression techniques. As can be seen, much of the text can be made out from the residue, which indicates that the text itself should be of considerable help in compressing it. In fact, the reconstructed text is used as part of the context used to code the residue.

Details of the individual steps

Symbol extraction

The first stage in symbol extraction is to identify lines of text so that symbols can be detected in their natural order. This is done in an ad hoc manner—the problem has already been addressed by numerous optical character-recognition programs (though we were unable to locate detailed descriptions of the algorithms they use). The rectangle of pixels that the program identifies as a line of text is called a 'window.' To find the top of the first window we scan down the image seeking a connected group of pixels, in any horizontal position, whose height exceeds some prespecified minimum (currently 15 pixels). The bottom of the window is essentially assumed to be the first point at which a clear white line extends right across the image. However, this may be marred by a slight overlap (say, between subscripts on one line and superscripts on the next) or by a speck of dust. To cope with this, the scan continues until a full-width strip of a certain minimum height (again, 15 pixels) is encountered for which there is no connected black line that extends from top to bottom. This means that there must be a connected white line extending through this strip right across the image, and this is taken as the bottom of the window.

Next, the window is scanned in transposed raster order from bottom to top, moving one pixel rightward after each scanline. This visits the symbols in left to right order, and in general finds a symbol before any disconnected part that lies above it. For example, the body of an 'i' will be encountered before its dot; the accent on an 'é' will come after the letter itself. As soon as a symbol is found, it is removed from the window. Thus if 'ü' is encountered, the 'u' is found first and removed, then the first dot, and finally the second one. To cope with cases where a high superscript in the next line intrudes into the window, any connected region that extends below the window is left in the image and dealt with as part of the next window.

Symbols are segmented by boundary tracing (we use 8-connectivity), and the result is extracted from the window as a candidate for inclusion in the library. Symbols comprising less than 15 connected pixels are ignored. Other non-typographical symbols—specks of dust, annotations, coffee-stains, etc—are segmented as usual but will be removed from the library unless they occur again.

This method of symbol extraction is not robust and can easily be fooled. We recognize that a full system would have to address this issue but have not yet done so ourselves because, for us, these are not the most interesting research questions.

Template matching

As symbols are extracted, they are matched against those already in the library. With each library member a set is kept of all symbols that match it. If the current symbol matches an existing one, it is added to the set of matches for that library symbol; if not, it is entered into the library as a new symbol.

The template matching procedure is critical to the successful identification of symbols. A number of matching methods have been described in the literature. Holt [4] divides them into two categories depending on whether they use global or local criteria. The former measure the overall mismatch between the new symbol and a library template, while the latter seek local mismatches that comprise just a few pixels. Both work on an *error map* which is the bitwise exclusive-OR between the new symbol and a library member, and for this the two must be registered appropriately. On each symbol in the library, the new one is superimposed by aligning the lower left corners. Nine different registrations are used, corresponding to one-pixel displacements in the eight principal compass directions. In each registration the exclusive-OR between old and new symbols is calculated to yield the error map, and the tests below are repeated nine times. If the template is accepted in any of the registrations, the one with the best fit (i.e. minimum Hamming distance) is chosen.

Template-matching methods that use global criteria are intended to be size-independent. However, they must be trained on the fonts being used—if not, the results are unreliable. For example, the 'combined symbol matching' method [9] computes a weighted sum of pixels in the error map, where error pixels are weighted more highly if they occur in clusters. A match is rejected if this exceeds a threshold obtained from a training process, which varies depending on the size of the symbol. Holt and Xydeas [3] describe another global method that achieves slightly better performance.

Johnsen *et al.* [5] describe a template-matching method that uses local criteria, rejecting a match if any position in the error map is found to have four or more neighbors set to 1. In order to detect mismatches due to the presence of a thin stroke or gap in one image but not the other, another heuristic is used. Noticing that this method often produced false matches on small characters, Holt [4] used two different criteria to detect thin strokes or gaps—one for large characters and the other for small ones.

We began by simply rejecting the match if any square block of a certain size was found to be set in the error map. A crude normalization for symbol size was performed by rejecting if a 3×3 block was found, unless the height or width were less than 12 pixels in which case we rejected on the basis of a 2×2 block. However, this missed thin strokes—for example, c's were confused with e's. Consequently we implemented Holt's rule [4] to seek thin strokes in the error map. We had to modify this because our test images are digitized at 400 dpi, twice the resolution he used.

After some experimentation we settled on three categories of symbol: large ones (most uppercase letters, false ligatures, and g's) whose height and width both exceed 29 pixels; small ones (typically punctuation and thin lowercase letters such as 'i' and 'l') where height or width are less than 15 pixels; and the rest. For the first category a match is rejected outright if two or more 3×3 error blocks are found, while for the other categories a single 3×3 error suffices. In all cases, a thin line detector is implemented based on [4] but with slightly different criteria for the three categories of symbol. The reason why one 3×3 error is tolerated in the case of large symbols is that 'identical' letter g's often exhibit a difference of this size—and indeed the results show that the present algorithm still has a tendency to mismatch g's.

Of course, whereas in optical character recognition mismatches are serious errors, in our application they merely cause a small penalty in compression efficiency. The reproduced image will still be a faithful copy of the original.

Constructing the library

The result of template-matching is a provisional library which stores the first-encountered variant of each symbol, along with the set of all symbols that matched it. From this are discarded 'singletons,' that is, symbols that have occurred just once. This removes almost all the noise symbols (and also genuine characters that occur only once). Then each template in the library is replaced by an averaged version in which a pixel is set if it appears in more than half the symbols that matched. This removes the arbitrariness of storing the first-encountered variant, and minimizes the number of bits set in the residue.

Identifying white space

The symbol-extraction process does not recognize white space as a symbol in its own right—any space following a symbol will manifest itself merely as an unusually large x-offset. However, experiments with ordinary text files show that compression performance can deteriorate by up to 5% if space characters are removed. Therefore we experimented with inserting a special code, known in advance to encoder and decoder, into the text between words and at the end of lines. What distinguishes spaces from tabs from newlines is the size of the x (and y) offset associated with the symbol.

Coding the symbol numbers

The symbol numbers illustrated in the second column of Figure 2 are not conventional character codes. For one thing symbols are ordered in the sequence in which they happen to appear in the image, rather than alphabetically; for another, some characters (like 'i') generate more than one symbol. However, this does not affect text compression methods that begin with no preconceptions about the kind of information being coded, and any such 'adaptive' scheme is suitable. We use the well-known PPMC technique [1, 2, 7]. Its performance will depend on the success of the symbol extraction method. If, for example, two variants of a certain character find their way into in the library, (up to) one extra bit will be needed whenever the character occurs to distinguish them.

Coding the offsets

The x- and y-offsets are compressed by conditioning them on the symbol with which they are associated, and using adaptive coding. For every symbol, all offset values associated with it so far are stored, along with their frequency counts. If the present value has followed the symbol before, it is coded (using arithmetic coding) according to this frequency distribution. If not, an escape code is sent and the offset is coded according to the frequency distribution of all values that have occurred so far (regardless of what symbol they followed). If that particular offset value has never occurred

Component	Coding method	Single image	Average over five images	Fifth image using model from other 4
library of symbols	2-level coding	1435	2025	145
the symbol sequence	PPMC	752	1337	648
x- and y-offsets	order-1	1942	2539	1582
residue	see text	21710	27537	21264
Total:			25839	33438	23639
original image	2-level coding	34176	43556	33614
original 3900×1120 image	uncompressed	546000	546000	546000

Table 1: Size (in bytes) of each component of the representation for the test images

before, a further escape is sent and the value is coded according to a precomputed, fixed, probability distribution that corresponds to Elias's γ variable-length coding of the integers (see Appendix A of [1]).

Coding the library

The library of symbols is coded using normal image compression techniques. It is represented as an image from which members are extracted by the decoder using the same process that the encoder uses to extract symbols from text. Experiments show that the two-level coding scheme devised by Moffat [8], with the 22/10 bit context in his Figure 5, gives the best performance for sample library images.

Coding the residue

The residue is the bitwise exclusive-OR of the original image and the reconstructed text. Because of the success of the character extraction process, far fewer bits are set in it than in the original image. This would seem to indicate that the residue can easily be coded much more efficiently than the original. However, this is not so. When good compression methods are applied, there is little difference in their compressed size. In fact, with the best two-level coding scheme of [8], the compressed residue was slightly larger than the compressed form of the original image!

We found this result disappointing, although with hindsight it is perhaps not surprising. The original image is far more compressible than the residue precisely because most of the black pixels it contains form predictable parts of characters. When the symbols are extracted, what is left is the *noise*—the irregularities around the edges that are caused by deficiencies in the printing and scanning processes—and this is very difficult to compress.

Fortunately, the residue can be coded more efficiently. There is clearly considerable overlap in information content between it and the reconstructed text image—many of the characters can be discerned from the residue alone. Advantage can be taken of this by conditioning the coding of the residue on the reconstructed text image, as well as on that part of the residue coded so far. This is particularly effective because the entire reconstructed text is known before any of the residue is coded. Thus Moffat's 'clairvoyant' templates can be used [8], which assume that all pixel values surrounding the current one are known. We use as context *both* a regular template on the residue coded so far, *and* a clairvoyant template on the reconstructed text image.

Experimental results

Table 1 summarizes the overall result. The five test images from the Trinity College Library catalogue are each 3900×1120 pixels (they actually represent single columns from two-column pages). Using the best conventional compression method we could find, the two-level coding scheme [8] with a 22/10 bit context, the first image is reduced to only 6.2% (34,176 bytes). The new method reduces it to 4.7% (25,839 bytes). The average over the five test images is also shown: Moffat's method compresses them to 8.0% and the new method to 6.1%. The reason why better results are achieved on the first image is that it is a short column containing a large stretch of white space after the text.

These figures are for the situation where single images are coded in isolation. If several images are processed and then a further one is coded, significant economy is achieved because the overheads are reduced. The extra information needed to code the fifth image (chosen to be the one used for the single-image tests, and that of Figure 1) once the other four have been processed is shown in the final column of Table 1. The total is nearly 10% smaller than that for coding the image in isolation. If a conventional compression technique such as Moffat's is used, the gain from pre-adapting to the other four images is much smaller (1.6%).

We now review the success of the individual processes.

Coding the residue

The residue is by far the largest component of the compressed image. Different combinations of Moffat's regular (Figure 3 of [8]) and clairvoyant (Figure 6 of [8]) templates were evaluated (although in the latter we include the center pixel as well). The 4-bit regular template combined with a 13-bit clairvoyant one works best.

As can be seen from Figure 5, some unidentified symbols—singletons—appear in the residue. In order to determine whether these affect its compression significantly, we removed *all* symbols and re-coded it using the same technique. The size reduced to 20,931 bytes, down by only 4% from the figure in Table 1. It seems that most of the space occupied by the coded residue is inherent in the fact that it is a noisy image—it will be difficult to reduce its size much further.

Symbol extraction and library coding

For the five test images, 321 symbols were initially placed in the library, and this was reduced to 181 by the consolidation process (eliminating singletons). Of these, 124 were valid typographical symbols; 26 were duplicate copies of symbols; 6 were 'false ligatures,' which are double characters formed by two separate ones that have run together in the printing process (a 'true' ligature is a pair of letters such as 'ff' or 'fi' that are normally printed as a single symbol); 24 were fragments of characters where a printing imperfection has omitted part of a symbol or broken it in two; 1 was noise. Of course, all of these imperfections must have occurred twice in order to form part of the final library.

Of the 140 discarded singleton symbols, most were imperfectly formed variants of symbols that had already occurred. Although 26 of these appeared in the library, a further 52 occurred only once and hence were ignored. The next largest category is 44 fragments of characters that were broken up in the printing process; again, some of these appeared two or more times and hence made it into the library. Our connectivity criterion could easily be weakened in an attempt to rejoin such fragments; however, this would inevitably increase the false ligatures—of which there are a lot already.

The final library for the five images together is shown in Figure 6. The reconstructed text is more complete when the library is built from several images. Of the 40 symbols from the first image that were left in the residue (of which Figure 5 shows a part), and are therefore absent from the reconstructed text (of which Figure 4 shows a part), 19 occur again in the remaining four images and so find their way into the library (for example, the 'LOUIS' that can be seen prominently in Figure 5).

With regard to actually coding the library—the image of Figure 3—the best method found was two-level technique with a 22/10 bit context [8]. The average over all five images, coded individually, was 21.6 bytes per symbol in the library.

Coding the symbols and offsets

For the image of Figure 1 the symbol sequence itself, which contains 1806 symbols, is compressed by PPMC into 752 bytes, or 3.33 bit/symbol. Representing the 64-member alphabet directly would require just 6 bit/symbol, and so appreciable use is made of regularities present in the sequence—even for this rather short stretch of text. The average figure over the five images, coded individually, is 4.29 bit/symbol using PPMC as against 6.55 bit/symbol if the alphabet were represented directly. Extracting the characters in the correct sequence was difficult for some pages that were set with very little leading between the lines of type, and so the efficiency of the text coding might be improved if a better extraction method was used.

For the single test image, the x- and y-offsets are coded in 1942 bytes, or 4.30 bit/offset. The average value over the five images, coded individually, is 4.07 bit/offset.

Identifying white space

The idea behind the identification of white space was to improve the coding of both symbol sequence and character offsets: the former because representing spaces as symbols provides a word-boundary cue that is helpful for predicting character sequences; and the latter by making the set of offsets that follow a particular symbol more consistent, removing the exceptional condition that corresponds to word endings. In fact, this was only marginally successful.

Spaces are inserted fairly consistently, except of course in the above-mentioned case where symbols were extracted in the wrong order, which not surprisingly causes the space-insertion module considerable confusion. Some difficulty was encountered with punctuation, particularly the '.' symbol which serves double duty as a period and as the dot over 'i', 'j', ';', and ':'.

The final result was that the text, after compression, is about 7% to 10% larger after spaces have been inserted than it is without spaces. Considering that over 20% of the characters are spaces, this is not too bad. The offsets are about 2.5% smaller. These take more code space than the text, and the combined result just about breaks even—the space-insertion process causes the total compressed size to grow by about 0.5%. Probably if the characters had all been assigned to their correct lines of text (as they would be if the leading was greater), space-insertion would have proven just beneficial.

System considerations

Our research was motivated by the Trinity College Library catalogue problem, and it is instructive to consider the overall needs of that and similar applications. A typical catalogue will contain approximately 1,000 to 1,000,000 images. Users access it in various different ways: by browsing from page to page, giving a page number, or specifying other information such as a book title or author name (in which case all matching pages must be retrieved). We assume that all access is through bit-mapped display screens.

For most queries an approximate image is sufficient, and for this our proposed compression regime is particularly useful. To display a page in full, the symbol library must be decoded, then the list of symbols and (x, y) offsets, and finally the residue. The residue is an order of magnitude larger than the other components, and, although necessary to obtain a faithful reproduction, is not generally needed for an overview of the page. In the reconstructed image of Figure 4, the original text can be read without difficulty, certainly enough for a casual browser to decide whether it is of interest, and in most cases enough for a user to find the shelf location of a book being sought. Only by express command, or a request for a faithful printed copy, would the residual bitmap be retrieved and decompressed.

Although access will normally be to a single catalogue page, compression can be improved by building the symbol library for several pages and coding the symbols as a longer sequence. Decoding the residual image is the most intensive part of accessing the database, in terms of both bandwidth and processor time. Batching of the remainder of the information into blocks of pages has little impact upon retrieval performance, but improves the quality of the reconstructed text image (by gathering a more complete library) and yields a small compression saving (Table 1). The separation allows different media to be used for the different components. The symbol library and symbol list might be retained on fast magnetic disk, while the residual image could be held on a bulk storage device such as an optical disk or jukebox. This two-level structure caters particularly well to casual browsers, who tend to flick rapidly from one page to the next after a scan of just a few seconds.

We believe our compression techniques to be applicable to more general tasks of document archiving. Despite the phenomenal capacity of WORM optical disks, the huge space requirements of raw images make compression even more essential than for textual databases. Compared to decompression, the compression phase is relatively time consuming, which is unfortunate because this is the most frequent operation in a document archiving environment. We suggest that compression should be carried out as a background process, with new documents spooled to some temporary holding area until they can be added to the permanent collection.

Conclusion

We have described a mechanism for compressing textual images, based upon identifying any repeated symbols appearing in the image, encoding these symbols and their locations, and encoding a residual bitmap to allow faithful reproduction of the original image. Previous image compression algorithms were general purpose, in that they applied to any binary images; here, by exploiting knowledge of the contents, improved compression has been obtained. Experiments with pages of the Trinity College library catalogue show the technique to be effective, particularly when the two-stage progressive nature of the decompression process is taken into account.

The techniques we have described might also be applied to other families of source documents. For example, printed sheet music could be parsed into sequences of notes, which, together with the location of the staves, would give a crude representation of the image. Detailed information would be again coded as a residue image, so that an exact reproduction of any particular page would be obtainable.

Acknowledgements

We are most grateful to David Abrahamson of Trinity College, Dublin, for telling us about this problem and kindly supplying us with test images. This work is supported by the Natural Sciences and Engineering Council of Canada and the Australian Research Council.

References

[1] Bell, T.C., Cleary, J.G. and Witten, I.H. (1990) *Text compression*. Prentice Hall, Englewood Cliffs, NJ.

[2] Cleary, J.G. and Witten, I.H. (1984) 'Data compression using adaptive coding and partial string matching,' *IEEE Trans Communications* COM-32(4): 396–402; April.

[3] Holt, M.J.J. and Xydeas, C.S. (1986) 'Recent developments in image data compression for digital facsimile,' *ICL Technical Journal*: 123–146; May.

[4] Holt, M.J. (1988) 'A fast binary template matching algorithm for document image data compression,' in *Pattern Recognition*, J. Kittler (ed.) (Proc. Int. Conf., Cambridge). Springer Verlag, Berlin.

[5] Johnsen, O., Segen, J. and Cash, G.L. (1983) 'Coding of two-level pictures by pattern matching and substitution,' *Bell System Technical J* 62(8): 2513–2545; May.

[6] Langdon, G.G. and Rissanen, J. (1981) 'Compression of black-white images with arithmetic coding,' *IEEE Trans Communications* COM-29(6): 858–867; June.

[7] Moffat, A. (1990) 'Implementing the PPM data compression scheme,' *IEEE Trans Communications* COM-38(11): 1917–1921; November.

[8] Moffat, A. (1991) 'Two level context based compression of binary images,' in *Proc. DCC'91*, J.A. Storer and J.H. Reif (eds.), pp. 382–391. IEEE Computer Society Press, Los Alamitos, CA.

[9] Pratt, W.K., Capitant, P.J., Chen, W.H., Hamilton, E.R. and Wallis, R.H. (1980) 'Combined symbol matching facsimile data compression system,' *Proc IEEE* 68(7): 786–796; July.

— Resolutie van de staten generael der Vereenighde Nederlanden, dienende tot antwoort op de memorie by de ambassadeurs van sijne majesteyt van Vranckrijck.
's Graven-hage, 1678. 4°.   Fag. H. 2. 80. N°. 20.
    Fag. H. 2. 85. N°. 17.   Fag. H. 3. 42. N°. 4.

— Tractaet van vrede gemaeckt tot Nimwegen op den 10 Augusty, 1678, tusschen de ambassadeurs van [LOUIS XIV.] ende de ambassadeurs vande staten generael der Vereenighde Nederlanden.
    Fag. H. 2. 85. N°. 21.

— Nederlantsche absolutie op de Fransche belydenis.
Amsterdam, 1684. 4°.   Fag. H. 2. 50. N°. 22.

— Redenen dienende om aan te wijsen dat haar ho. mog. [niet] konnen verhindert werden een vredige afkomst te maken op de conditien by memorien van den grave d' Avaux van de 5 en 7 Juny, 1684, aangeboden.
[*s. l.*] 1684. 4°.   Fag. H. 2. 86. N°. 3.
    Fag. H. 2. 96. N°. 8.   Fag. H. 3. 44. N°. 52.

— Redenen om aan te wijsen dat de bewuste werving van 16000 man niet kan gesustineert werden te zullen hebben konnen strekken tot het bevorderen van een accommodement tusschen Vrankrijk en Spaigne.
[*s. l.*] 1684. 4°.   Fag. H. 2. 86. N°. 4.
    Fag. H. 2. 96. N°. 2.

— D' oude mode van den nieuwen staat van oorlogh.
[*s. l.* 1684]. 4°.   Fag. H. 2. 86. N°. 12.
    Fag. H. 2. 96. N°. 3.

— Aenmerkingen over de althans swevende verschillen onder de leden van den staat van ons vaderlant.
[*s. l.*] 1684. 4°.   Fag. H. 2. 92. N°. 1.
    Fag. H. 2. 98. N°. 16.   Fag. H. 3. 1. N°. 18.

— Missive van de staten generael der Vereenighde Nederlanden, ... 14 Maert, 1684.
's Graven-hage, 1684. 4°.   Fag. H. 2. 92. N°. 10.

— Missive van de staaten generael der Vereenigde Nederlanden, ... 11 July, 1684.
[*sin. tit.* 1684]. 4°.   Fag. H. 2. 96. N°. 13.
    Fag. H. 3. 44. N°. 69.

— Resolutie vande staten generael der Vereenighde Nederlanden, ... 2 Maart, 1684.
's Gravenhage, 1684. 4°.   Fag. H. 2. 92. N°. 11.
    Fag. H. 3. 44. N°. 9.

— Extract uyt de resolutien van de staten generael, ... 31 Maert, 1684.
[*s. l.*] 1684. 4°.   Fag. H. 2. 92. N°. 13.
    Fag. H. 2. 96. N°. 25.   Fag. H. 3. 44. N°. 11.
    . Fag. H. 3. 44. N°. 15.

— Antwoort van de staten generael der Vereenighde Nederlanden op de propositie van wegen sijne churf. doorl. van Ceulen, Maert 23, 1684, gedaen.
's Gravenhage, 1684. 4°.   Fag. H. 2. 92. N°. 12.

Figure 1   A test image

symbol	symbol number	x-offset	y-offset
start-of-page	0	19	62
—	1	24	7
R	2	2	-1
e	3	3	0
s	4	4	0
o	5	2	-1
l	6	3	0
u	7	3	0
t	8	3	0
l	9	-8	-25
.	10	7	25
e	3	15	0
v	11	3	-1
a	12	3	0
n	13	17	0
d	14	4	0
e	3	25	0
s	4	3	-1
t	8	3	0
a	12	3	0
t	8	3	0
e	3	3	-1
n	13	23	10
g	15	2	-10
e	3	3	-1
n	13	4	0
e	3	3	-1
r	16	3	-1
a	12	3	0
e	3	2	0
l	6	18	0
d	14	3	0
e	3	3	0
r	16	18	0
V	17	3	-1
e	3	1	0
r	16	3	0
e	3	3	-1
e	3	3	0
n	13	4	-1
l	9	-8	-24
.	10	6	35
g	15	0	-11
h	18	3	1
d	14	3	-1
e	3	-1012	53
N	19	4	0
e	3	2	0

· · · · ·

Figure 2   Symbols and x- and y-offsets created from the test image

‾Resoluti·vandgrVhN'wpm‾byJck's*Graven*ₕg16784°FH2
N53A[]*mttx*J*l*9Md¹*G*

Figure 3 Library of symbols created from the test image

— **Resolutie van de staten generael der Vereenighde
Nederlanden, dienende tot antwoort op de memo-
'e by de ambassadeurs van sijne majesteyt van
Vranckrijck.**
's Graven-hage, 1678.   4°.   Fag. H. 2. 80. N°. 20.
         Fa '. H. 2. 85. N°. 17.   Fag. H. 3. 42. N°. 4.

— **ractaet van vrede gemaeckt tot Nimwegen op
den 10 Augusty, 1678, tusschen de ambassadeurs
van [V.] ende de ambassadeurs vande
staten generael der Vereenighde Nederlanden.**

Figure 4 The 'reconstructed text' image, recreated from the information in Figures 2 and 3

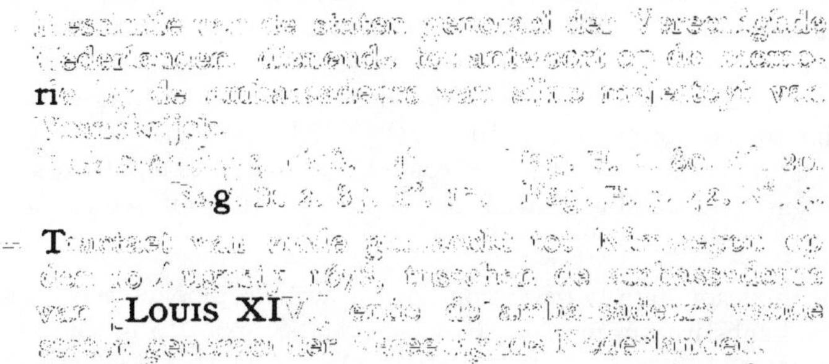

Figure 5 The 'residue' image, which is the difference between the original and reconstructed text

‾roJectvandₗuₗsgmtp7Jy"1684kh[*sl*]°FH29N3RVN*aven* ‾*h*
*g*5AVUbMWEG*r* q'rtD¹*t*S*L*ᵘ*d*Bf *A*ᵐTTTF‾ᵘGruryo&*DQ*
‾æ*B*GCEHˣP‾à()IWBOˣOoLPST·rvICMFUXLAГ¹tryvn
GɔIZ·ASˢˢD‾YffW"tsYR'R·fiAe·MITIf*O f*°ffi°ℇo入kⁱeg*tGr*d
*gg*l

Figure 6 Library of symbols created from the 5 test images together

Parallel Algorithms for Optimal Compression using Dictionaries with the Prefix Property

Sergio De Agostino and James A. Storer

Computer Science Department, Brandeis University, Waltham, MA 02254, USA

Abstract.   We study parallel algorithms for lossless data compression via textual substitution. Dynamic dictionary compression is known to be P - complete, however, if the dictionary is given in advance, we show that compression can be efficiently parallelized and a computational advantage is obtained when the dictionary has the prefix property. Our approach can be generalized to the sliding window method where the dictionary is a window that passes continuously from left to right over the input string.

1. Introduction

Textual substitution methods (often called "LZ" methods due to the work of Lempel and Ziv [1976]) replace substrings in the text with *pointers* to strings, called *targets* of the pointers, that are stored in a *dictionary*. The encoded string is a sequence of pointers (some of which may represent single characters). *Static* methods are when the dictionary is known in advance. By contrast, with *dynamic* or *adaptive* methods (often called "LZ2" methods due to the work of Ziv and Lempel [1978]) the dictionary may be constantly changing as the data is processed. A special way to change dynamically is the *sliding* dictionary method (often called "LZ1" method due to the work of Ziv and Lempel [1977]) where the dictionary is a window of the last n characters that passes continuously over the input from left to right. For references on serial algorithms for textual substitution, see the book of Storer [1988].

Parallel algorithms for data compression with a systolic pipeline have been provided for several substitution methods (Gonzalez and Storer [1985], Zito-Wolf [1990a], Zito-Wolf [1990b], Storer and Reif [1991]). These algorithms work on line with a linear number of processors and have linear processing time.

Here we consider parallel algorithms for data compression via textual substitution that can be implemented in polylogarithmic time with a polynomial number of processors with the PRAM CREW (concurrent read, exclusive write) model. We do not address the machine dependent issue of how data is input; we simply assume that a block of n input characters is available in processors 1 through n (and that a block of n output characters can be placed in processors 1 through n). Dynamic dictionary compression is shown to be P-complete in De Agostino [1991], and hence it is unlikely that polylogarithmic algorithms exist for such methods (see Gibbons and Rytter [1989] for an introduction to the class P and NC and the theory of P-completeness). By contrast, here we present polylogarithmic parallel algorithms to compress a string when the dictionary is given in advance; these algorithms can be generalized to the sliding window method. For most of this paper, we assume that the dictionary has the prefix property (if a string is in the dictionary, then so are all of its prefixes). Clearly, sliding windows have this property, and many of the practical textual substitution algorithms, including LZ2, produce dictionaries with this property. For the moment, We also make the following key assumption about the length of dictionary entries:

The maximum length of a string in a dictionary with n strings is $O(log(n))$.

The motivation for this assumption is that in practice the maximum length of a match is much smaller that the size of the dictionary. For example, when compressing english text with 16-bit pointers (a dictionary of 64,000 strings), the average match length will only be about 5 characters and there will be few or no matches of more than 100 characters; in fact, limiting the maximum match to 16 characters it is unlikely to have any significant effect on the total compression achieved (see Storer[1988] for a presentation of empirical results with English text).

Section 2 considers ineherent properties of optimal parsings. In Section 3 we present an algorithm requiring n^2 processors and $O(log(n))$ time to compute optimal compression with a dictionary given in advance having the above assumption. In section 4 we show that by increasing the time by only a logarithmic factor, optimal compression can be computed with a linear number of processors. In sections 5 and 6 we show how our results can be generalized to arbitrary dictionaries (ones without the prefix property and without arbitrary match length) and to the sliding window method.

2. Optimal Compression for the Static Dictionary Method

An *optimal parsing* of a string S with respect to a dictionary D is a shortest possible sequence of pointers to D such that the concatenation of the pointer targets is S. Since we assume that all strings of one character can be represented by a pointer, such a parsing always exists (but may not be unique). Wagner [1973] presents a dynamic programming algorithm for computing an optimal parsing that processes the string from right to left.

A *greedy parsing* is obtained by processing the string from left to right and finding at each step the longest match starting at the first character of the suffix yet to be parsed. Although the greedy parsing is not optimal, it works well in practice. Hartman and Rodeh [1985] show a way to compute on-line the optimal parsing with a dictionary with the prefix property by modifying the greedy parsing algorithm. Their on-line optimal algorithm is described in Figure 1 (this algorithm can be implemented in linear serial time with a modified suffix trie data structure). This algorithm looks not only at the position next to the last phrase but also at the ones of the largest proper suffix of the phrase and choose the one whose match

$j := 0;\ i := 0;$

repeat forever begin

    for $k = j + 1$ **to** $i + 1$ **do**

        begin

        let $h(k)$ be such that $x_k...x_{h(k)}$ is the longest match in the kth position

        end

    let k' be such that $h(k')$ is maximum

    $x_j...x_{k'-1}$ is a definitive phrase of the parsing

    $j := k';\ i := h(k')$

end

Figure 1: On-Line Optimal Algorithm

ends to the rightest. This operation is possible because of the prefix condition in the dictionary.

The parsing constructed by the algorithm of Figure 1 can be proved optimal as follows. Let p be a phrase of any parsing. We denote with $f(p)$ and $l(p)$ the position in the input string of the first and the last character of the phrase p. Let $P = p_1 \cdots p_h$ be any parsing and $Q = q_1 \cdots q_k$ be the parsing computed by the procedure above. After the ith step of the algorithm, we have computed a parsing $q_1 q_2 \cdots q_{i-1} q_i'$ of some prefix of the input string. The following lemma guarantees that $l(q_i') \geq l(p_i)$ so that $k \geq h$ and, hence, Q is an optimal parsing.

Lemma: Let $j(i)$ be such that $l(p_{j(i)}) \leq l(q_i') < l(p_{j(i)} + 1)$. Then $f(q_i') \leq l(p_{j(i)})$ and $j(i) \geq i$.

Proof. We prove the lemma by induction. The statement is true for $i = 1$. Let us see how to prove that the statement is true for $i + 1$, if we assume it is true for i.

At the $(i + 1)^{th}$ step the positions from $f(q_i') + 1$ to $l(q_i') + 1$ are considered.

Since $f(q_i') \leq l(p_{j(i)}) \leq l(q_i')$ then $f(q_i') + 1 \leq f(p_{j(i)+1}) \leq l(q_i') + 1$. It follows that $l(q_{i+1}') \geq l(p_{j(i)+1})$. So $j(i + 1) \geq j(i) + 1$ and since $j(i) \geq i$ then $j(i + 1) \geq i + 1$. Moreover, $f(q_{i+1}') \leq l(p_{j(i+1)})$ because $l(q_i') < l(p_{j(i)} + 1)$. ◇

Although the greedy parsing is often close to optimal in practice, in the worst case, it is not even a constant factor approximation of the optimal one. Consider the following example:

Example: $baba^k;\ k = f(n);$

dictionary: a, b, ba, bab, ba^i for $1 \le i \le k$

optimal parsing: ba, ba^k;

greedy parsing: $bab, a, a, ..., a, ...a$

Note that the greedy parsing is not a constant factor approximation of the optimal one, given any non-constant upper bound $f(n)$ to the maximum match length. Note also that in the example above, the dictionary has the prefix property.

The following theorem characterizes optimal parsings with respect to a dictionary with prefix property and provides insight as to why an on-line computation is possible.

Theorem. Let k be the number of phrases of an optimal parsing of a string X with dictionary D with the prefix property. Then for each i, $1 \le i \le k$, there exist an optimal parsing such that its ith phrase is a substring of the ith phrase of any other optimal parsing.

Proof. First of all, let us prove that the intersection of the ith phrases p_1^i and p_2^i of two optimal parsings $P_1 = p_1^1 \cdots p_1^k$ and $P_2 = p_2^1 \cdots p_2^k$ is nonnull.

Denote with $f(p)$ and $l(p)$ the first and the last position of a phrase p and suppose $l(p_2^i) < f(p_1^i)$. Let j be such that $f(p_1^j) \le l(p_2^i) \le l(p_1^j)$ and denote with $pref(p_1^j)$ the prefix of p_1^j such that $l(pref(p_1^j)) = l(p_2^i)$. Then the parsing $p_1^1 \cdots p_1^{j-1} pref(p_1^j) p_2^{i+1} \cdots p_2^k$ is composed by less than k phrases since $j < i$. It follows that p_1^i and p_2^i must have a nonnull intersection.

Suppose now that for any optimal parsing $P = p^1 \cdots p^k$, $f(p^i) \le f(p_1^i)$ and $l(p^i) \ge l(p_2^i)$. Then the parsing $p_1^1 \cdots p_1^{i-1} pref(p_1^i) p_2^{i+1} \cdots p_2^k$ is optimal and $pref(p_1^i)$ is a substring of the ith phrase of any other optimal parsing. $\diamond$

The presence of these *canonical* substrings identifying the set of ith phrases of all the possible optimal parsings is the reason why we don't need global information for the optimal parsing and we can compute it on line.

3. A $O(log(n))$ Time Algorithm Using $O(n^2)$ Processors

In this section we present an $O(log(n))$ time, $O(n^2)$ processors algorithm for optimal parsing with respect to a given dictionary that is a parallelization of the approach addressed in the previous section.

With a linear number of processors and logarithmic time we can find the longest match at each position of the input string by using a trie data structure for the dictionary. Let us define an $(n + 2)$ x n matrix M initialized to be the null matrix and let $M_{1,i} = M_{3,i} = i + m_i$, where m_i is the length of the longest match starting in position i; let $M_{2,i} = i$. Algorithm 1 can be used to fill in the other entries of M

in parallel for $1 \leq i \leq n$ **do**

    begin

    $f(i) := 3;$

    repeat

        let l_i be such that $M_{1,l_i}=\max(M_{1,k}: M_{f(i)-1,i}+1 \leq k \leq M_{f(i),i})$

        in parallel for $2 \leq j \leq n+2$ **do**

            if $j \leq f(l_i)$ **then** $M_{f(i)+j-2,i} := M_{j,l_i};$

        $f(i) := f(i) + f(l_i) - 2;$

    until $M_{f(i),i} = n+1;$

    end

Algorithm 1

in such a way that at its completion, the entries in the first column are the positions of the first characters of the phrases of an optimal parsing.

In each step the last two nonnull components of the ith column are in positions $f(i) - 1$ and $f(i)$. As depicted in Figure 2a, in parallel for each i we select a column l_i having the maximum value on the first row among the columns in position between $M_{f(i)-1,i} + 1$ and $M_{f(i),i}$. The search of the maximum value is made in constant time since we have to deal with a logarithmic number of components (due to the upper bound to the maximum match length) and n processors available. Then the nonnull components of column l_i, exclusive of the first one, are copied onto column i erasing its last nonnull component with the value l_i (Figure 2b). The iteration stops for a column when the value $n + 1$ is written on it.

The first column will provide us the optimal parsing, because its values are the positions of the first character of each phrase. This procedure requires n processors per column and at each step the number of components copied onto a column is doubled. Thus the algorithm requires $O(n^2)$ processors and $O(log(n))$ time.

4. A $O(log^2 n)$ Algorithm Using $O(n)$ Processors

In this section we show that by increasing the time by only a logarithmic factor, an optimal parsing with respect to a given dictionary can be computed with a linear number of processors by operating on a matrix initially defined as in the previous section. Unlike Algorithm 1, Algorithm 2 copies only the last two nonnull components of the selected column. Therefore, we have some sparse pairs of nonnull values on the first column that indicate $O(log(n))$ ranges of positions where matches of the parsing start. The first six values are generally nonnull and before the second

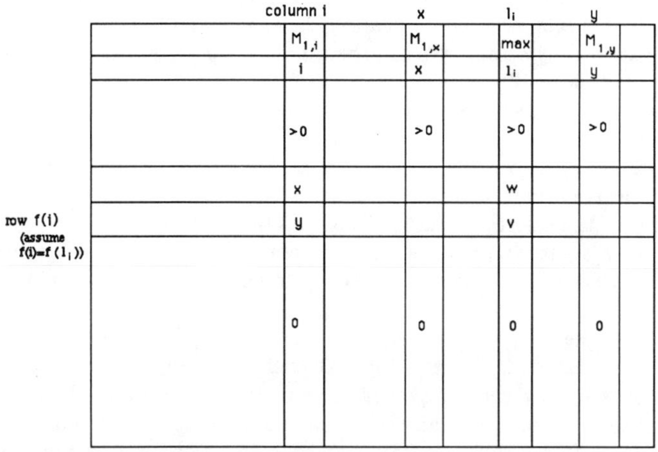

	column i		x		l_i		y	
	$M_{1,i}$		$M_{1,x}$		max		$M_{1,y}$	
	i		x		l_i		y	
	>0		>0		>0		>0	
	x				w			
row f(i) (assume $f(i)=f(l_i)$)	y				v			
	0		0		0		0	

figure 2a

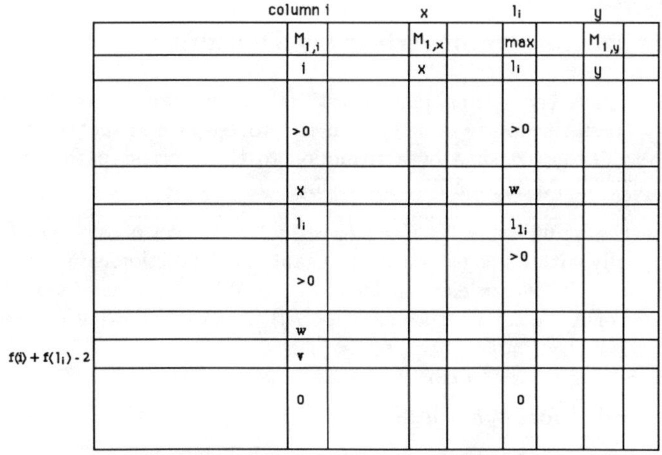

	column i		x		l_i		y	
	$M_{1,i}$		$M_{1,x}$		max		$M_{1,y}$	
	i		x		l_i		y	
	>0				>0			
	x				w			
	l_i				1_{l_i}			
	>0				>0			
	w							
$f(i) + f(l_i) - 2$	v							
	0				0			

figure 2b

loop of the procedure we fix the fourth component on the columns so that the only components that might need to be changed have a nonnull value next to the top and a zero next to the bottom. We call them *temporary* values. Let us consider the kth and $(k+1)^{th}$ nonnull components of the first column, say x and y, with x a temporary value. Then, we select the column maximizing the value on the first row in the range of positions determinated by x and its preceding nonnull component.

One processor copies on the first column all the nonnull values standing before y on the selected column (obviously exclusive of the first one). The value x is erased with the index of the selected column. This step takes $O(log(n))$ time because this is the order of magnitude of the number of nonnull values on each column and because the processor is able to access directly to the nonnul values and copy them in the right positions by keeping information of where the values are written in the first loop. This operation is executed in parallel for each temporary value. If we iterate this operation in $O(log(n))$ steps, at each step the only temporary values are still the ones having the component next to top nonnull and the next to the bottom equal to 0. In fact, we can verify that the number of consecutive zeros on the first column is always different from 4 and the first four components a processor copies from the selected column are not temporary. Thus, we get again the optimal parsing on the first column but the total time of the procedure is $O(log^2 n)$.

Unlike the matrix algorithm of the previous section, here we need only the first column of the matrix to be a vector of dimension n. The other columns need just $O(log(n))$ dimensions to hold their nonnull components. Thus, the algorithm can work using only $O(nlog(n))$ work space.

5. Generalization to an Arbitrary Dictionary

We can compute the optimal parsing with arbitrary match length and any type of dictionary (prefix property or not) with n^3 processors and $log^2(n)$ time or n^4 processors and $O(log(n))$ time by a reduction to the shortest paths problem on directed graphs. The reduction is the following:

let $x_1...x_n$ be the input string X, $V = (v_1...v_n, v_{n+1})$ the set of vertices of a graph $G(V, E)$ originally with no edges, k the cardinality of the dictionary D and $l(h)$ the length of the h-th dictionary element for $h = 1...k$. With k processors $p_{i,1}...p_{i,k}$ for each position i of X we can execute in $O(log(n))$ time the following procedure :

> **in parallel for** $1 \leq i \leq n$ **do**
>
> > **in parallel for** $1 \leq h \leq n$ **do**
> >
> > > **if** the h-th dictionary element matches X in position i
> > >
> > > **then** add a directed edge from v_i to $v_{i+l(h)}$ in G.

We obtain a directed acyclic with the vertices in topological order and we can see that the shortest path from v_1 to v_{n+1} provides the optimal parsing. In fact, each

in parallel for $1 \leq i \leq n$ **do**

    begin

    $k := 1$

    $r_{i,k} := 2$

    $f(i) := 3;$

    repeat

        let l_i be such that $M_{1,l_i}=\max(M_{1,k}\colon M_{f(i)-1,i}+1 \leq k \leq M_{f(i),i})$

        $M_{f(i)+f(l_i))-3,i} := M_{f(l_i)-1,l_i};$

        $M_{f(i)+f(l_i)-2,i} := M_{f(l_i),l_i};$

        $f(i) := f(i) + f(l_i) - 2;$

        $k := k + 1;$

        $r_{i,k} := f(i) - 1;$

        until $M_{f(i),i} = n + 1;$

    let l_i be such that $M_{1,l_i}=\max(M_{1,k}\colon M_{3,i}+1 \leq k \leq M_{4,i})$

    $M_{4,i} := l_i$

    for $j = 1$ **to** $\lceil logn \rceil$ **do**

        begin

        if $M_{i,1} \notin \{0, n+1\}$ **and** $M_{i-1,1} \neq 0$ **and** $M_{i+1,1} = 0$ **then begin**

            let l be such that $M_{1,l}=\max(M_{1,k}\colon M_{i-1,1}+1 \leq k \leq M_{i,1})$

            $k := 1$

            while $M_{i+r_{l,k}-1,1} = 0$ **do**

                begin

                $M_{i+r_{l,k}-2,1} := M_{r_{l,k},l};$

                $M_{i+r_{l,k}-1,1} := M_{r_{l,k}+1,l};$

                $k := k + 1$

                end

            end

        end

    end

Algorithm 2

path between two nodes v_i and v_j represents a parsing on the substring $x_i...x_{j-1}$ and the internal nodes of the path provide the position of the first character of each phrase.

Since with n^3 processors and logarithmic time we can compute the longest matches on each position of the string without assuming any bound to the match length, by assuming the prefix property in the dictionary we can apply the procedure in section 3 to obtain the optimal parsing with n^3 processors and $O(log(n))$ time.

Procedures to compute the greedy parsing are staightforward derivations from the algorithms presented above and have the same complexity without any need of the prefix property in the dictionary.

6. Sliding window method

The greedy parsing with a sliding window is optimal when the pointer size is fixed. With n^3 processors and logarithmic time we can compute the longest matches on each position of the string, with a sliding dictionary where the window is the whole prefix already read. A quadratic number of processors is sufficient if we assume a logarithmic upper bound to the match length. In (Naor [1991]), it is presented a probabilistic algorithm with a linear number of processors and expected logarithmic time on a CRCW PRAM (cuncurrent read, cuncurrent write) to compute the longest matches. It is also presented a parallelization of the decoding algorithm for the sliding dictionary method with $O(log(n))$ time and $O(n)$ processors. But it is errouneously claimed that it is possible with the same parallel complexity by means of a similar procedure to the one for decoding to find out the "breakpoints" defining the greedy parsing from the information about the matches on each position of the input string. The procedures for the greedy parsing with a static dictionary presented in this paper instead can be applied in this case.

7. Current Research

We have shown polylogarithmic algorithms for compression with a static dictionary that has the prefix property and for the sliding window method. Since dynamic dictionary compression is P - complete, we do not hope to find polylogarithmic algorithms for when the dictionary is dynamically changing. However, it is an interesting area of current research to find fast approximation algorithm for this problem. In addition, algorithms that handle dictionaries without the prefix property with less than n^3 are also of interest.

References

S. De Agostino[1991], P-Complete Problems in Data Compression, Technical Report

URLS - DM/NS - 90/001 (INFO), Dept. of Mathematics, University of Rome "La Sapienza", Italy.

M.E. Gonzalez and J.A. Storer [1985], Parallel Algorithm for Data Compression, *Journal of ACM* **32**, 344 - 373.

A. Gibbons and W. Rytter [1987], Efficient Parallel Algorithms, Cambridge University Press.

A. Hartman and M. Rodeh [1985], Optimal Parsing of Strings, *Combinatorial Algorithms on Words*, Springer - Verlag (A. Apostolico and Z. Galil, editors), 155 - 167.

A. Lempel and J. Ziv [1976], On the Complexity of Finite Sequences, *IEEE Transaction on Information Theory* **22**, 75 - 81.

A. Lempel and J. Ziv [1977], A Universal Algorithm for Sequential Data Compression, *IEEE Transaction on Information Theory* **23**, 337 - 343.

M. Naor [1991]. String Matching with Preprocessing of Text and Pattern, *Proceedings ICALP, LNCS*, 739 - 750

J.A. Storer [1988], *Data Compression: Methods and Theory* (Computer Science Press).

J.A. Storer and J.H. Reif [1991], A Parallel Architecture for High Speed Data Compression, *Journal of Parallel and Distributed Computing* **13**, 222 - 227.

R.A. Wagner [1973], Common Phrases and Minimum Text Storage, *Communications of the ACM* **16**, 148 - 152.

R.J. Zito-Wolf [1990a], A Systolic Architecture for Sliding Window Data Compression, *Proceedings IEEE VLSI Signal Processing Conference*, 339-351.

R.J. Zito-Wolf [1990b], Broadcast / Reduce Architecture for High Speed Data Compression, *Proceedings Second IEEE Symposium on Parallel and Distributed Processing*, 174-181

J. Ziv and A. Lempel [1978], Compression of Individual Sequences via Variable Rate Coding, *IEEE Transactions on Information Theory* **24**, 530 - 536.

Constructing Word-Based
Text Compression Algorithms

R. Nigel Horspool
Department of Computer Science
University of Victoria, P.O. Box 3055
Victoria, B.C., Canada V8W 3P6
`nigelh@csr.uvic.ca`

Gordon V. Cormack
Department of Computer Science
University of Waterloo
Waterloo, Ont., Canada N2L 3G1
`gvcormack@waterloo.edu`

Abstract

Text compression algorithms are normally defined in terms of a source alphabet Σ of 8-bit ASCII codes. We consider choosing Σ to be an alphabet whose symbols are the words of English or, in general, alternate maximal strings of alphanumeric characters and non-alphanumeric characters. The compression algorithm would be able to take advantage of longer-range correlations between words and thus achieve better compression. The large size of Σ leads to some implementation problems, but these are overcome to construct word-based LZW, word-based Adaptive Huffman, and word-based Context Modelling compression algorithms.

1 Introduction

Most text compression algorithms perform compression at the character level. If the algorithm is adaptive (as, for example, with any of the Ziv-Lempel methods), the algorithm slowly learns correlations between adjacent pairs of characters, then triples, quadruples and so on. The algorithm rarely has a chance to take advantage of longer range correlations before either the end of input is reached or the tables maintained by the algorithm are filled to capacity. If text compression algorithms were to use larger units than single characters as the basic storage element, they would be able to take advantage of the longer range correlations and, perhaps, achieve better compression performance. Faster compression may also be possible by working with larger units.

In this paper, we explore the use of *words* as the basic unit. When the source file is an English-language document, say, we have no difficulty in recognizing a word as consisting of a sequence of consecutive letters. Each word is separated from the next by space and/or punctuation characters. Following the same approach as Bentley et al. [2], we generalize slightly by considering a text file to consist of alternating alphanumeric-strings and punctuation-strings, where a word-string is a maximal sequence of alphanumeric characters and a punctuation-string is a maximal sequence of non-alphanumeric characters. We use the generic name *word* to refer to either an alphanumeric string or a punctuation string. The generalization permits us to decompose all kinds of text files — program source code, input to a word-processor, etc. — into sequences of words.

Existing compression algorithms that consider the input as a sequence of words are ad hoc in nature. The scheme described by Bentley et al. [2] maintains a list of words sorted into least-recently used order. A word is encoded by its position in this dynamically changing list. Words near the front of the list tend to have shorter codes than those near the end and, assuming words in frequent use stay near the front of the list, compression is achieved. The general approach is called Move-To-Front or MTF in [1]. Generalizations of the scheme that use other heuristics than MTF to manage the list appear in [5] and [6].

A less ad hoc approach would be to consider words as forming the symbols of an alphabet. Such an alphabet can, in principle, be used as the basis of any existing compression algorithm. For example, LZW (aka the UNIX *compress* command) [7] could work by encoding sequences of words instead of sequences of characters. If particular sequences tend to recur in the source text, compression would be achieved.

However, we need to overcome a major problem with word-based compression algorithms. The number of distinct words that the compression algorithm has to cope with is, for all practical purposes, unbounded. Thus it makes no sense to implement an algorithm that requires a pre-determined finite alphabet. To use LZW as an example again, we cannot initialize the LZW string table with all sequences of length one, as required in the usual implementations of LZW. Instead, we have to modify the algorithms so that they either pre-determine the set of words used in the source input (an inherently two-pass strategy) or they dynamically expand the source alphabet as each new word occurs. We, of course, advocate single-pass strategies as being more useful for practical applications.

The following sections of this paper will consider the problem of generalizing a compression algorithm to be word-based, then particular word-based algorithms will be described, and finally some experimental results will be reported.

2 Using Word-Based Alphabets

Following the scheme of [2], we can decompose textual input into a sequence of words, where alternate words are composed from alphanumeric characters and from non-alphanumeric characters. For example, a line of a Pascal source code file that reads

```
xCoord2 := xCoord2 + delta;
```

would be decomposed into the following elements, where spaces are made visible and the line-feed character at the end of line is shown as a C-style character constant '\n'.

"____"	"xCoord2"	"_:=_"	"xCoord2"	"_+_"	"delta"	";\n"
punct	*alpha*	*punct*	*alpha*	*punct*	*alpha*	*punct*

It is easy to transform an existing compression algorithm to operate on the alphabet of words if an extra pass over the source data is permitted. An initial pass enters the words (both alphanumeric and non-alphanumeric) into a dictionary. Once the pass is complete, we know all the symbols of the word alphabet and it should now be possible to construct a version of the compression algorithm that uses this new alphabet. Of course, the dictionary (or, more likely, a compressed form of the dictionary) must be transmitted with the output from the compression algorithm.

For the majority of applications, two passes over the source text are undesirable. An adaptive scheme that dynamically expands the dictionary as new words are encountered is preferable. A general mechanism for handling a new word involves the use of an escape code. When the compression algorithm hits a new word, it can output an escape code followed by some representation of the text of the new word. Then it can add the new word to the next available slot in the dictionary and continue as though the word had been present in the dictionary all the time.

This general escape mechanism, however, does not extract the maximum amount of redundancy from the compression algorithm. As the following examples show, it is possible to integrate the escape mechanism into the compression algorithm more tightly and do better. For one thing, we should be able to take advantage of the fact the the alphanumeric and non-alphanumeric words strictly alternate. Thus, we should use two word-based source alphabets Σ_A, the alphabet of alphanumeric words, and Σ_P, the alphabet of punctuation strings. If the symbols from the two alphabets are identified by symbol numbers, the numberings need not be disjoint, as the decoding algorithm should always know by context which source alphabet to expect. A second way in which the escape mechanism can be better integrated is by making either an occurrence of the escape code or the symbol that corresponds to a new word implicit. Such integration may increase the complexity of the implementation somewhat.

3 Some Word-Based Algorithms

3.1 Word-Based Adaptive Huffman Coding

Adaptive Huffman coding is the basis of the UNIX *compact* program. The compression program maintains a count of how many times each symbol has occurred so far in the source text. To encode the next symbol, the symbol counts are used as estimates of the relative probabilities of the symbols and a table of Huffman codes based on these frequencies is constructed. The Huffman code in the table is used to encode the next symbol. (A minor detail that needs to be taken into account is that symbols in the alphabet that have not yet occurred in the source text must be assigned a non-zero probability estimate.) The decoding algorithm can re-create the same set of symbol frequencies from its de-compressed text and use the table to re-construct the same table of Huffman codes. Thus it can uniquely decode one symbol, update the frequency count of that symbol, update its table of Huffman codes and then decode the next symbol, and so on.

Algorithms exist for efficiently updating the Huffman codes when small incremental changes to the probability estimates are made (as is the case here) [3], [4]. In spite of the widespread use of these algorithms in implementations, Adaptive Huffman coding is not renowned for its speed (nor for its compression performance).

The overall structure of a word-based Adaptive Huffman algorithm may take the form shown in Figure 1. The algorithm uses two tables of frequencies, `AFreq` and `PFreq`, and two tables of Huffman codes, `AHuffman` and `PHuffman`, for the two different alphabets Σ_A and Σ_P Details concerning the initialization and the proper termination of the algorithm at the end of input are omitted for brevity.

Figure 1 Word-Based Adaptive Huffman Algorithm

```
repeat
    read one alphanumeric word, AW;
    if AW ∉ Σ_A then
        output AHuffman[Escape];
        output text of AW;
        Σ_A := Σ_A ∪ {AW};
        AFreq[AW] := 1;
        AFreq[Escape] := AFreq[Escape] + 1;
    else
        output AHuffman[AW];
        AFreq[AW] := AFreq[AW] + 1;
    endif
    AHuffman := recomputed table of Huffman codes constructed
        from the frequency table, AFreq;
    read one non-alphanumeric word, PW;
    if PW ∉ Σ_P then
        . . .
        . . .    (* continuing similarly to the above *)
        . . .
until end of input is reached;
```

In what form should the text of new words be transmitted? New words occur in short input files with a relatively high frequency and efficient encoding of them is highly desirable. To be consistent with the top-level word-based compression strategy, we propose that adaptive Huffman coding be used for the individual characters of the words. Since an algorithm for updating the Huffman codes must already be available for the two source alphabets Σ_A and Σ_P, it would not impose a burden on the implementer to use it for four different source alphabets. (Four because the decoder knows whether a new word is going to be composed from alphanumeric characters or non-alphanumeric characters, and thus the two alphabets may be encoded separately.)

The compression performance of word-based Adaptive Huffman coding is excellent, as the experimental data at the end of this paper shows. The execution speed is not so good however. As the Σ_W and Σ_P alphabets grow in size, the time required to update the tables of Huffman codes slowly and inexorably increases. The average time complexity of the update algorithms appears to be $O(n)$, where n is the size of the alphabet; the worst-case time complexity is $O(n \log n)$. If word-based Adaptive Huffman coding were to become practical , some technique would be needed to prune infrequently used symbols from the Σ_W and Σ_P alphabets. (Certainly we should delete words whose Huffman codes become so long that fewer bits would be needed to re-transmit the word as a new word.) Several pruning strategies based on an analogy with page replacement algorithms in virtual memory systems are suggested in [6].

3.2 Word-Based LZW

The LZW (Lempel-Ziv-Welch) compression algorithm [7] is the basis of the UNIX *compress* program and of the compression strategies implemented in many commercial products, both hardware and software. Its main virtue is speed, while simultaneously achieving good, but not spectacular, compression performance.

LZW is easy to explain. The algorithm maintains a string table that associates a unique integer with each string. To encode the next segment of source text, the compression algorithm reads the longest possible sequence of characters that comprises a string in the table. It outputs the number associated with the string, using a simple binary numbering system. If the string that was read was ω and K is the following character in the source text, the new string ωK is added to the string table and the next unused number is associated with the string. The compression algorithm then continues, reading input characters starting with K looking for the longest string that is contained in the table.

The string table is initialized with all strings of length one. This guarantees that at least one character can be read from the input and matched against a string in the table. The strategy for adding new strings guarantees that if a string ω is in the table, then all prefixes of ω must also be present in the table. This property simplifies the task of matching a maximal length sequence of input characters against the strings in the table, and also permits the table to be implemented by an efficient data structure (such as a trie). As stated above, the encoding of string numbers is simple (and is another reason for the speed of LZW implementations). If, at some moment, the table holds N strings (and these will be numbered 0 through N-1), a binary number comprised of $\log(N+1)$ bits is used to encode the next string number to be output.[1]

A word-based LZW implementation cannot initialize the string table with all strings of length one. This is because the Σ_W and Σ_P alphabets may be very large and the symbols are not known in advance (unless a pre-pass over the text source is performed). Thus, we will again advocate the use of an escape mechanism.

The word-based LZW algorithm builds up two kinds of strings of symbols. All strings will consist of alternate symbols from Σ_W and Σ_P but we can segregate strings whose initial symbol is an element of Σ_W in a separate table from those strings whose initial symbol is an element of Σ_P Numbering of strings in the two tables need not be disjoint because the decoding algorithm can always deduce whether the next string it receives should begin with a Σ_W or a Σ_P symbol.

The structure of the main body of the algorithm has the form shown in Figure 2. We use λ to denote the empty string and $<<\alpha,b>>$ to denote a string constructed by appending the symbol b to the string α. The two tables of strings are named `ATable` and `PTable`. A string numbering scheme that reserves a code (presumably 0) for Escape must be used. The empty string λ may be implemented by the same number because an encoding of λ is never output.

Again, we must decide how the characters of a new word should be encoded. As before, the compression performance is compromised for small files unless a reasonably efficient coding scheme is used for the characters. Again, it is possible to apply the same

---

1. The original LZW algorithm, as described in [7], proposes a maximum table size of 4096 strings and that 12-bit numbers be used regardless of table occupancy.

Figure 2 Word-Based LZW Compression Algorithm

```
ω := λ;
repeat
    if currentIsAlph then read next alphanumeric word X;
    else read next non-alphanumeric word X; endif
    if X is a new word then
        if ω ≠ λ then output string number of ω endif
        output Escape;  output text of X;
        ω := λ;
        startIsAlph := not currentIsAlph;
    else
        if startIsAlph then search ATable for string <<ω,X>>;
        else search PTable for string <<ω,X>>; endif
        if <<ω,X>> was found then
            ω := <<ω,X>>;
        else
            output string number of ω;
            add <<ω,X>> to the appropriate table, ATable or PTable;
            startIsAlph := currentIsAlph;
            ω := <<λ,X>>;
        endif
    endif
    currentIsAlph := not currentIsAlph;
until end of input is reached;
```

basis algorithm for the lower-level encoding as at the higher word-based coding level.
There is a caveat however. LZW encodes sequences of characters. We must treat the end
of each new word as being equivalent to the end-of-file, otherwise the encoding of parts of
two consecutive new words would have to be combined. (We expect correlations between
characters at the end of one new word and characters at the beginning of the next new
word to be weak.)

Compression performance is again excellent. Speed degradation as the two word-
string tables fill up is hardly noticeable when they are implemented as very large hash
tables. However, a pruning strategy to prevent the tables from reaching too high an occupancy to permit fast look-ups (greater than 80% occupancy, say) is again desirable.

3.3 Word-Based First-Order Context Compression

The Adaptive Huffman coding algorithm, described above, uses a zero-order Markov
model to predict properties of the source text. Much better compression may be achieved
if a higher-order Markov model is used. Higher-order models form the basis of the PPM
(prediction by partial match) family of compression algorithms [1], for example.

When the symbols are English words, we can expect correlations between successive symbols. For example, the word 'the' would have a high probability of being followed by a word that is a noun or adjective but a low probability of being followed by
another article or a verb. An algorithm based on a first-order model could maintain statistics on the observed frequencies of word pairs in the text compressed so far. Then given

that the previous word to have been encoded is W_i, we can use the observed frequencies to estimate the conditional probabilities $P(W_j|W_i)$ for the next word. These probabilities may passed to an arithmetic coding subroutine for transmitting the next word.

If the compression algorithm is to be targeted to compression of natural language, we should treat the two alphabets differently. There should be strong correlations between successive alphanumeric words but, presumably, weak correlations between successive punctuation strings. Also, we can expect correlations between the punctuation and the alphanumeric words – for example, a punctuation string that contains a period would signify the end of a sentence and would therefore predict that the next alphanumeric word would begin with an upper-case letter (and would be quite likely to be an article). The algorithm structure shown in Figure 3 assumes only correlations between successive symbols from Σ_A. In the algorithm, the variable `PrevW` represents the previous alphanumeric word to have been transmitted. The arithmetic coding algorithm uses the frequency count `Freq[PrevW,X]` to estimate the relative probability for each word X in Σ_A.

The natural choice for encoding the text of punctuation strings and words is arithmetic coding applied to individual characters. The probability estimates needed as input to the algorithm can be based on the frequency of occurrence of each character. Compression performance is improved if probabilities obtained from the first-order model are blended with probabilities from the 0th-order model when the number of observations is too low to make reliable first-order predictions. Blending the two models is a scheme used in PPMC [1], for example. Blended probabilities are used to obtain the results reported in Table 1.

Another way to improve the significance of the statistics and also a way of reducing the volume of data that must be retained is to merge statistics for similar words. An obvious way to group words into a small number of classes is by their parts of speech in the English language. This gives rise to our final word-based algorithm. It is described in the following section.

Figure 3 Arithmetic Coding with Word-Based First-Order Context Model

```
PrevW := Escape;
repeat
    read next punctuation word AP and output text of AP;
    read next alphanumeric word, AW.
    if AW ∉ Σ_A then
        output Escape by arithmetic coding; output text of AW;
        Σ_A := Σ_A ∪ {AW};
        Freq[PrevW,AW] := 1;
        Freq[PrevW,Escape] := Freq[PrevW,Escape] + 1;
    else
        output AW by arithmetic coding;
        Freq[PrevW,AW] := Freq[PrevW,AW] + 1;
    endif
    PrevW := AW;
until end of input;
```

3.4 First-Order Context Modelling by Part-of-Speech

If we assume that the source text contains natural language, the sequence of words in the source should obey the rules of grammar for that language. For example, one possible form for an English language sentence is:

Subject   Verb   Object

where the *Subject* and the *Object* may be constructed as an *Article* followed by a *Noun*. The rules of grammar strongly influence the probabilities of certain words appearing in certain contexts. For example, after the word 'the' (an article), we would not expect to find another occurrence of an article or a verb, but we could find a noun or an adjective there. (However, the existence of a music group named 'The The' reminds us that we should not assume a zero probability for any combination of words, no matter how strange it seems.)

We therefore propose that a state-based model [1] be used for modelling the source text and be used for generating the prediction probabilities used by an arithmetic coding subroutine. For simplicity, we assume that there are just five parts of speech named *Article*, *Noun*, *Adjective*, *Verb* and *Other*. (We include pronouns such as 'she' and 'him' in the *Noun* category.) This yields a state diagram like the following:

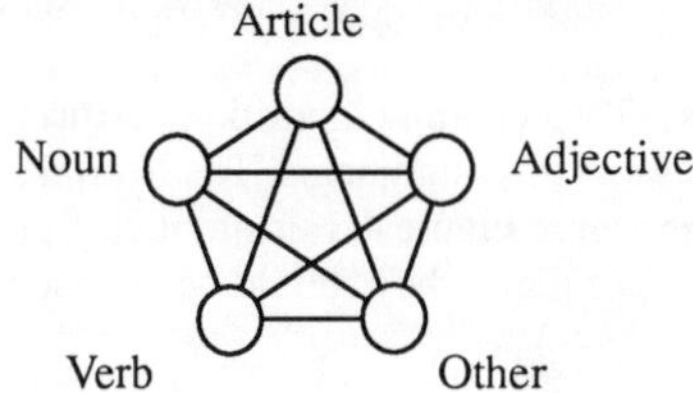

Each state provides a set of probability estimates for the symbols in Σ_A. If the current state is *Article* and the next symbol is the word 'funny', we would use the probability estimates associated with the *Article* state to encode the word 'funny'. Then we would make a transition to the *Adjective* state, since that is the part of speecf for the word 'funny'.

Implementation of this state-based model requires that we know or can determine the parts of speech for all the symbols in Σ_A. This requires that the compression algorithm be supplied with an initial vocabulary that specifies the appropriate part of speech for words in the vocabulary. (Presumably some heuristics, such as deciding that a word ending with the letters 'ly' is probably an adverb could also be useful.) But it is unreasonable to require every word that might appear in any document to be included in the initial vocabulary. Therefore, we need a mechanism for inferring an appropriate part of speech for a new word after an occurrence in the text.

The first time a word occurs, and the word is not contained in the vocabulary, we should assign that word the part of speech that is most likely to follow the part of speech for the preceding word. Subsequently, we keep statistics on how well that word fits into its assigned part of speech. For example, if the new word is W, we keep track of how efficiently those words that immediately follow subsequent occurrences of W would be encoded if W were assigned to the Noun class, to the Adjective class, and so on. If better compression would have been achieved with W in a different class, W is dynamically re-

Figure 4 Arithmetic Coding with State-Based Context Model

```
PW := any common symbol in Σ_A;   (* PW = Previous Word *)
State := PartOfSpeech[PW];
repeat
    read next word AW;
    if AW ∉ Σ_A then
        output code for Escape and output text of AW;
        Σ_A := Σ_A ∪ {AW};
        Freq[State,Escape] := Freq[State,Escape] + 1;
        Freq[State,AW] := 1;
        PartOfSpeech[AW] := most probable for a successor of State;
    else
        output code for AW;
        Freq[State,AW] := Freq[State,AW] + 1;
        for P := each possible state do
            Cost[PW,P] := Cost[PW,P] - logarithm of the probability
                predicted for word AW by state P;
        PartOfSpeech[PW] := P such that Cost[PW,P] is a minimum;
    endif
    PW := AW;  State := PartOfSpeech[AW];
until end of input;
```

assigned to that other class. The decoding algorithm performs the same calculations and can therefore perform the same re-assignments. The overall structure of the compression algorithm is therefore as shown in Figure 4. For simplicity, punctuation strings are ignored in the presentation of the algorithm – they should be encoded by some other means.

4 Experimental Results and Discussion

The four word-based algorithms described in this paper have been implemented and tested on several text files, using the UNIX *compress* program as a benchmark. The compression results are summarized in Table 1.The pair of numbers shown for the state-based context compression reflects the fact that the algorithm normally requires initialization with a vocabulary giving the parts of speech for words. In our experiments, the initial vocabulary contained all the words used in the first test document (the *csh* manual description). The upper number in each pair shows compression performance when that vocabulary is used; the lower number shows performance when *no* vocabulary at all is used. I.e., the algorithm simply assigns words to one of five classes as it seems to find appropriate.

The overall result is that performance is consistently better than our benchmark, the UNIX *compress* program, no matter which word-based method is used. Words apparently recur sufficiently often in the test files that any scheme for compressing repeated references to words will perform well. The compression scheme using a state model based on parts of speech in the English language has probably the most potential for improvement. The current crude scheme could be improved by monitoring the punctuation to check for a period (or other characters that terminate a sentence) and be used to reset the model state to the start of a new sentence. At present, two strings with different capitalization (e.g. 'the' and 'The') are treated as two different words, but they could be combined into a single entry and the end-of-sentence test could predict which form to use. The words 'A' and 'An' could be segregated into separate article classes and thus predict words that start with vowels or consonants. Word suffixes, such as 'ly', could be used to make better guesses as to a new word's part of speech, etc. Much further experimentation is required. For now, we recommend use of a simple and fast word-based algorithm for text file compression. And of the possibilities considered, word-based LZW would seem to be the closest fit.

Table 1   Comparative Compression Performance

	Original Size in bytes	Relative Size After Compression				
		UNIX compress	WB-Adpt Huffman	WB-LZW	State-Based	WB-First Order
On-line manual page for *csh*	66772	40.4%	29.8%	34.3	21.6% 29.3%	29.0%
On-line manual page for *make*	63761	42.7%	34.7%	35.8%	29.5% 33.6%	31.7%
LaTeX file	83106	44.7%	36.1%	32.0%	36.0% 35.2%	33.7%
C Source File	24706	39.2%	28.5%	26.4%	32.3% 27.0%	25.3%

Acknowledgements

We are grateful to Kenny Wong for programming the word-based Adaptive Huffman coding algorithm whose results are reported here. We also thank the Natural Science and Engineering Research Council of Canada for their financial support.

References

[1]   Bell, T.C., Cleary, J.G., and Witten, I.H. *Text Compression*. Prentice-Hall , 1990.

[2]   Bentley, J.L., Sleator, D.D., Tarjan, R.E., and Wei, V.K. "A Locally Adaptive Data Compression Scheme." CACM 29, 4 (April 1986), pp. 320-330.

[3]   Cormack, G.V., and Horspool, R.N. "Algorithms for Adaptive Huffman Codes." Inf. Processing Letters 18, 3 (March 1983), pp. 159-166.

[4]   Gallager, R.G. "Variations on a Theme by Huffman." IEEE Trans. on Inf. Theory, IT-24, 6 (Nov. 1978), pp. 668-674.

[5]   Horspool, R.N., and Cormack, G.V. "A General-Purpose Data Compression Technique with Practical Applications." Proc. of CIPS Session '84 (Calgary, Alberta), 1984, pp. 138-141.

[6]   Horspool, R.N., and Cormack, G.V. "Technical Correspondence on 'A Locally Adaptive Data Compression Scheme'." CACM 30, 9 (Sept. 1987), pp. 792-794.

[7]   Welch, T.A. "A Technique for High-Performance Data Compression." IEEE Computer 17, 6 (June 1984), pp. 8-19.

Coding for Compression in Full-Text Retrieval Systems

Alistair Moffat

Department of Computer Science,
The University of Melbourne, Parkville 3052, Australia.
`alistair@cs.mu.oz.au`

Justin Zobel

Department of Computer Science,
Royal Melbourne Institute of Technology,
GPO Box 2476V, Melbourne 3001, Australia.
`jz@kbs.citri.edu.au`

1   Introduction

Witten, Bell and Nevill [11] have described compression models for use in full-text
retrieval systems. They considered a sample text of 12 Mbyte, and showed that with
arithmetic coding and a variety of models this text could be stored in approximately
6 Mbyte, including sufficient indexing information to allow access by content. The
biggest drawback of their scheme is that the decoding process is slow, estimated to
be about 5 Kbyte per second.

Here we discuss other coding methods for use with the same models, and give
results that show our scheme yielding virtually identical compression, and decoding
more than forty times faster. One of the main features of our implementation is the
complete absence of arithmetic coding; this, in part, is the reason for the high speed.
Our implementation is also particularly suited to slow devices such as CD-ROM, in
that the answering of a query requires one disk access for each term in the query and
one disk access for each answer. All words and numbers are indexed, and there are
no stop words.

We have built two compressed databases. The first, to allow comparison with the
results of Witten *et al.*, is based upon a version of the Bible. Our second database
is built around the complete Commonwealth Acts of Australia, a large (132 Mbyte)
collection of legal documents. In this second example the compressed database, including all indexing structures and the text itself, requires less than 35% of the space
occupied by the uncompressed text. The corresponding figure for the Bible is 42%.

2   Full-Text Retrieval

A full-text retrieval (FTR) database stores a large number of *text fragments*, where
each fragment is some individually retrievable portion of text. For example, a fragment might be a sentence, a paragraph, a page, or an entire document.

Queries on the database specify a number of *terms*. To *answer* a query the FTR
mechanism must retrieve and display each fragment that contains all of the specified
terms. The FTR system must thus provide an indexing mechanism that is capable of

quickly identifying the fragments that contain any given term, as the alternative—a sequential scan through the full database—will normally be prohibitively expensive.

One method of providing the index is with an *inverted file*. In order of decreasing size the main components of an inverted file FTR database are the text of the records; the inverted file (sometimes known as the *concordance*); a *lexicon* (or *vocabulary*) of terms that appear; disk pointers to allow random access into the main text; and disk pointers to allow random access into the inverted file. In the sections that follow we discuss how each of these components might be efficiently coded.

We consider three sample databases. The first two are actual document collections, while the third is a hypothetical database that we use to indicate how the techniques we describe will scale. Various parameters of these collections are shown in Table 1.

	Collection Name		
	Bible	*Comact*	*Hypothetical*
Text Size (Mbyte)	4.36	132.11	1,000
Distinct Words	13,777	68,074	100,000
Distinct Non-Words	50	6,943	10,000
Word Occurrences	885,009	23,100,786	200,000,000
Fragments	31,102	261,829	1,000,000
Average Words per Fragment	28	88	200

Table 1: Sizes of Document Collections

Database *Bible* is stored as a collection of verses, with each fragment containing fields recording the book name, chapter number, verse number, and the text of the verse. Database *Comact* is a collection of records containing legal text, with fields in each fragment storing the act name, a section description, a unique page number, and one (short) page of text.

3 Coding the Main Text

We agree with Witten *et al.* [11] that a word-based model [8] is the most appropriate for use with full-text databases, and that the model should be constructed in a semi-static manner [1]. However we differ in our choice of coding method. Rather than arithmetic coding [12] we prefer to use Huffman coding [5, 6]. Although Huffman coding is non-optimal, when coding from a large alphabet in which no symbol dominates the inefficiency is small [2]. More importantly, it has a definite speed advantage in a semi-static environment, particularly when the alphabet is large.

A detailed description of the implementation is beyond the scope of this extended abstract, and can be found in [10]. Here we simply describe the observed performance characteristics. Table 2 summarises the resource requirements of the Huffman coded word-based model when applied to the whole of *Comact*, and compares it to the Unix utility *Compress*; *ZeroWord*, an adaptive word-based model [8]; and *PPMC*, a variable context character-based model [9]. None of these three allow decoding of individual fragments, and so they are not directly applicable to the problem we consider. Nevertheless, they provide reference points for speed and compression. All experiments were run on a Sun SPARCstation 2. Programs were written in C.

	Compress	*ZeroWord*	*PPMC*	Static Huffman
Pre-process text (cpu-sec)	—	—	—	1,133
Encode (cpu-sec)	598	3,265	2,366	848
Decode (cpu-sec)	372	2,262	3,051	314
Compressed Text (Mbyte)	40.59	45.74	24.44	34.32

Table 2: Times and effectiveness of compression of *Comact*

The Huffman coded word-based model requires 34.32 Mbyte to represent *Comact*, only slightly more than the 34.23 Mbyte needed when arithmetic coding is used with the same semi-static model. Moreover, the Huffman model decompresses at 400 Kbyte per second, faster than *Compress*, and approximately 40 times faster (even allowing for the difference in machines) than the 5 Kbyte per second estimated by Witten *et al.* During the *encoding* phase the semi-static Huffman coded variant is slower than *Compress*, but is still faster than arithmetic coding. More to the point, in the application we are considering, the resources required during encoding are of little concern, since the database is assumed to be static and re-created only relatively infrequently on a central computer.

The *PPMC* program gives significantly better compression, the result of the very good model formed on a long text. However when the same file is compressed with *PPMC* flushing the model at the start of each fragment, the compressed text grows to occupy 70 Mbyte—a clear illustration of the drawback of using an adaptive model.

4   Coding the Inverted File

The inverted file stores, for each unique word w in the database, the ordinal number d of every fragment that contains w, and is a relatively compact mechanism for storing a sparse bitmap. For example, allowing $\lceil \log_2 1,000,000 \rceil = 20$ bits for each value d stored, the space required by the inverted file of database *Hypothetical* would be about 4×10^9 bits ≈ 500 Mbyte, one twenty-fifth the size of the bitmap it represents. However this is still a great deal of space. In this section we describe a simple prefix code that allows the storage of all of the inverted file for *Hypothetical* in about 100 Mbyte. We first consider the representation of a single bitvector.

4.1   Representing a Bitvector

We suppose that V is a bitvector N bits long, and that there are p 1-bits in V. We seek a representation for V that is both compact and quickly decodable, and will compare the alternative representations by calculating the number of bits of storage required for each 1-bit in the vector. We call this the *efficiency ratio*.

For example, storing V in uncompressed bitvector form will result in an efficiency ratio of N/p. Although convenient, this is only efficient when $p \approx N/2$. Because most of the bitvectors will be sparse, we must consider other representations.

The coding method we prefer was suggested by the work of Golomb [4]; Gallager and Van Voorhis [3]; and McIlroy [7]. Those authors considered the representation of integers drawn from a geometric distribution, and described an easily computed prefix code to represent a stream of integers drawn independently and randomly from such a distribution. We will first describe the code, and then discuss the efficiency of the code for the problem of coding a bitvector with known parameters N and p.

Both encoding and decoding algorithms are controlled by a single parameter b, the *block size*, and we will refer to this coding method as a *b-block code*. The choice of b will be discussed below. To encode an integer $x \geq 1$, we first encode $(x-1)$ div b using a unary code, and then we encode $(x-1)$ mod b using a binary code of either $\lfloor \log_2 b \rfloor$ bits or $\lceil \log_2 b \rceil$ bits. Some example codes are shown in Table 3. To make the table a little easier to understand the boundary between the unary and binary section within each codeword has been indicated with a comma. This comma does not, of course, appear in the actual output code.

x	$b=1$	$b=2$	$b=3$	$b=5$	$b=10$
1	0,	0,0	0,0	0,00	0,000
2	10,	0,1	0,10	0,01	0,001
3	110,	10,0	0,11	0,10	0,010
4	1110,	10,1	10,0	0,110	0,011
5	11110,	110,0	10,10	0,111	0,100
6	111110,	110,1	10,11	10,00	0,101
7	1111110,	1110,0	110,0	10,01	0,1100

Table 3: Examples of b-block codes

To code a bitvector V, we first use the b-block code to encode the location of the first 1-bit in V, and then we encode the *differences* between successive 1-bits. This will result in p integers being coded—the run lengths of zeros in the initial vector.

4.2 Analysis

Coding for a Geometric Distribution

Gallager and Van Voorhis [3] proved that if θ is the probability of failure in a sequence of Bernoulli trials, and X is the random variable describing the number of trials until the first success, then the b-block code generates the infinite Huffman code corresponding to X, provided that b is chosen to satisfy

$$\theta^b + \theta^{b+1} \leq 1 < \theta^b + \theta^{b-1}.$$

Taking $\theta = (N-p)/N$ and solving for b gives

$$b = \left\lceil \log_\theta \frac{1}{1+\theta} \right\rceil. \tag{1}$$

Average Case for a Bitvector

To estimate the average number of bits required by the b-block code to represent V we suppose that each of the p inter-word gaps will require a binary component of average length $\log_2 b$ bits, plus a prefix unary code of at least one bit (the 0-bit that signals the end of the unary component). The 0-bit of itself does not cause any of the total length N of the bitvector to be consumed, but let us suppose that each of the binary codes following the 0-bit has expected value cb, where $c \geq 1/b$. That is, we assume that the binary codes average some fraction c of the block size, and so consume part of the total length N.

All leading 1-bits in the unary component of the code represent a distance of exactly b, and since there is now only a distance of $N - pcb$ unaccounted for, the total number of 1-bits in the unary prefixes is less than $(N - pcb)/b$. Thus the expected number of bits B_e required to represent the bitvector is

$$B_e \leq p \cdot (1 + \log_2 b) + \frac{N - pcb}{b} \tag{2}$$

We should choose b to minimise (2) and so take

$$b_e = \frac{1}{\log_2 e} \cdot \frac{N}{p} \approx 0.69 \frac{N}{p}. \tag{3}$$

With this value for b_e the expected length of the coded bitvector is given by

$$B_e \leq p \cdot \log_2 \frac{N}{p} + p \cdot (1 + \log_2 e - \log_2 \log_2 e - c) \approx p \cdot (\log_2 \frac{N}{p} + 1.91 - c) \tag{4}$$

A conservative value for c would be to suppose that on average each block is one third full, and so the expected efficiency ratio is about $\log_2(N/p) + 1.6$.

Note that in the limit $b = 1$ gives no compression, and so when $p > N/2$ it is more economical to code the complement of the bitvector.

Worst Case for a Bitvector

In the worst case each of the codes will be $\lceil \log_2 b \rceil$ bits long, and, to force this at minimal 'cost', each of the binary codes will correspond to a distance of exactly $2^{\lceil \log_2 b \rceil} - b + 1$. The total number of bits required then becomes

$$B_w = p \cdot (1 + \lceil \log_2 b \rceil) + \frac{N - p(2^{\lceil \log_2 b \rceil} - b + 1)}{b} \tag{5}$$

which, for $p \leq N/2$, is minimised at

$$b_w = 2^{\lfloor \log_2 \frac{N-p}{p} \rfloor} \tag{6}$$

with minimal value given by

$$B_w = p \cdot (1 + \log_2 b_w) + \frac{N - p}{b_w} \leq p \cdot (\log_2 \frac{N}{p} + 2). \tag{7}$$

Fortunately the question as to which of b_e or b_w should be preferred does not arise, as the worst case bound in (7) is also an upper bound for $b = b_e$. That is, the worst case error introduced by optimistically hoping for average case behaviour rather than pessimistically anticipating worst case behaviour is about 0.09 bits. For this reason we choose $b = b_e$.

A Lower Bound

The lower bound on the number of bits required, assuming that each p-bit combination of the N bits occurs with equal probability, is

$$\left\lceil \log_2 \binom{N}{p} \right\rceil \;\geq\; p \log_2 \frac{N}{p} + 1.44p - O\left(\frac{p^2}{N} + \log_2 N\right).$$

Hence when p is small relative to N the block based code is at most 0.56 bits inefficient in the worst case, with b chosen according to (6); and with b chosen according to (3) can be expected, on average, to be within about 0.2 bits.

Using Arithmetic Coding

By way of comparison, the exact arithmetic code used by Witten *et al.* [11] will require $-\log_2(1-\theta) - (x-1)\log_2 \theta$ to code integer x, where $\theta = (N-p)/N$, and so to code the entire sequence of p integers will require

$$-p\log_2(1-\theta) - \log_2 \theta \cdot \sum_{i=1}^{p}(x_i - 1) \;<\; p \log_2 \frac{N}{p} + 1.44p - O\left(\frac{p^2}{N^2}\right).$$

This is exactly equivalent to coding each of the bits in the bitvector individually using probabilities of θ for a 0-bit and $1 - \theta$ for a 1-bit.

Arithmetic coding results in compression close to the lower bound. However, the expected bound of Equation 4 is only slightly greater, and we anticipated that the two codes would give similar compression in practice.

4.3 Experimental Results

For the test database *Comact* we extracted a number of the bitvectors from the bitmap and coded them using the b-block code. The results of these experiments are shown in Table 4. In the table, 'b_w' is the greatest power of two less than or equal to $(N-p)/p$; 'b_e' is the value of b suggested by Equation 3; B_w is the worst case bound given by Equation 7; $B(b_w)$ and $B(b_e)$ are the measured number of bits per word pointer using b_w and b_e respectively; and 'Bound' is the value $\lceil \log_2 \binom{N}{p} \rceil / p$. Recall

word	p	b_w	b_e	B_w	$B(b_w)$	$B(b_e)$	Bound
'the'	208,965	1	1	1.25	1.25	1.25	0.91
'who'	20,836	8	9	5.45	5.18	5.12	5.03
'became'	2,089	64	87	8.94	8.70	8.40	8.40
'exports'	209	1024	868	12.22	12.00	11.48	11.71
'ambulance'	21	8192	8642	15.48	15.10	15.05	14.90
'aboriginals'	2	65536	90743	18.50	18.00	18.00	17.50
Comact	—	—	—	6.40	6.27	6.08	6.03

Table 4: Coding Inter-Word Gaps

that for *Comact* $N = 261,829$; the 23,100,786 words correspond to 14,219,078 actual inverted file pointers.

For a wide range of values of p the actual compression achieved is close to the lower bound, and well within the worst case upper bound. The last row of the table shows the cost of encoding the entire bitmap for *Comact* using the b-block code with b_w and b_e calculated individually for each of the bitvectors. Each of the word pointers is represented in an average of about 6 bits, and the storage for the entire bitmap (Table 5) requires 10.4 Mbyte—just 8% of the uncompressed text. Arithmetic coding the entire bitmap required an average of 6.02 bits per pointer, and again the difference between the arithmetic code and the prefix code is negligible.

5   Storing the Lexicon

In a large database the lexicon is small compared to the main text, and it is not necessary to use complex models to store it. In the full paper we describe a simple strategy that allows the lexicons for *Bible* and *Comact* to be stored on disk in 65 Kbyte and 341 Kbyte respectively (Table 5).

Of more importance is the need to reduce main memory usage during decoding. To obtain the fast decoding described in Section 3 the lexicon must be stored in a random access structure, requiring extra space for pointers—four bytes per token in a simple implementation. However if only one in four words is directly indexed as a *reference word*, the random access can be accomplished with only one overhead byte per word. The other three words are stored adjacent to the reference word, with the common prefix replaced by a 4-bit count indicating the number of common characters, thereby achieving further memory savings. Details of this structure, and of a mechanism for using an abridged lexicon when only a small amount of main memory is available, can be found in [10].

6   Coding the Disk Pointers

There are two places where disk pointers are required. An inverted file entry must be accessed for each term of a query, and then the compressed text of each fragment that is an answer to the query must be read. In both cases the retrieval should be directly from the disk, without going through any secondary indexing structure, so that the number of disk accesses can be restricted to 1 for each term in the query, plus 1 for each answer to the query.

In this section we consider how to represent these disk pointers economically so that they can be stored in main memory at run time. In the absence of compression and/or indexing each pointer will require 4 bytes, and even on a relatively small database might account for 1 Mbyte. In the sections that follow we show that in fact about 80 Kbyte of main memory is sufficient to provide 1-plus-1 access on *Comact*.

6.1   Coding Pointers to Variable Length Records

The problem we address is to provide economical random access into a file of variable length records. Fortunately, a solution is already at hand. If we consider the file to be a vector F of N bits, and imagine a second N-bitvector S in which bit i is 1 whenever bit i in F is the start of a record, we are again faced with the problem of storing a sparse bitvector. For S, p is the number of records in the file, and N is the total number of bits in the compressed file.

Each record of the file is prefixed with a b-block code indicating the length in bits of that record; and a number of records are grouped together to make a logical block. For convenience of transfer, the logical blocks should be padded with a small number of bits so that each block (but not each record within the block) starts on a byte (or perhaps word) boundary on the secondary storage device, where the aligned blocks are concatenated to make the file. Finally, one full 32-bit pointer giving the byte offset of the start of each logical block is kept in main memory, together with a 32-bit integer indicating the ordinal record number of the first record in the block.

To access a record we binary search the index to find the number of the block containing the record, and transfer the whole of that block into main memory. We then step through the prefix length fields of the records in the block, counting off records. The actual data in each record need not be decoded; we simply skip from one length field to the next, and only decode the contents of the actual record that is to be retrieved.

Each logical block should contain as many records as possible, subject to two constraints. First, the time taken decoding all of the length fields in one block must remain negligible compared with the disk access time; and second, the logical blocks should not become too large, so that buffer space is not excessive. With magnetic disk access times in the tens of milliseconds and CD-ROM access times in the hundreds of milliseconds we can certainly allocate 1–2 milliseconds to the decoding of length prefixes within a block, and transfers of 10–20 Kbyte will be only marginally slower than transfers of just a few hundred bytes. Experiments showed the b-block code to be decodable at in excess of 500 (compressed) Kbit/sec, and so we were prepared to allow as many as 1,000 bits of b-block codes in each logical block.

6.2 Pointers to the Main Text

The compressed text of *Comact* contains 261,829 records, and occupies 35,139 Kbyte. The average record is thus 1100 bits; the average b-block code required 11.6 bits; and the prefix lengths totalled 371 Kbyte, as shown in Table 5. Building logical blocks not exceeding 10 Kbyte and of at most 85 records meant that the in-memory index contained 3585 'record number, pointer' pairs, and that the total memory required, including the buffer, was 38 Kbyte.

6.3 Pointers to the Inverted File

The compressed inverted file is smaller than the main text, but there is much greater variability in record sizes. For *Comact* there are 68,074 entries, averaging 1280 bits, with the largest entries at 32,740 bytes. Each b-block length field consumed an average of 11.7 bits, and so bounding the block size at 32,740 bytes and 85 records implied that 859 blocks were required, and that the memory space needed to handle single term queries was 39 Kbyte.

6.4 Total Memory Requirements

In total, single term queries on *Comact* require 602 Kbyte—525 Kbyte for the partially compressed lexicon; 35 Kbyte for the two in-memory block indexes; 10 Kbyte for the main text buffer; and 32 Kbyte for a single inverted file buffer.

Multi-term queries require additional buffers for the inverted file, to allow two-into-one merging of inverted file entries, and storage of intermediate lists. Three buffers are sufficient to cope with all multi-term conjunctions. More complex queries, such as disjunctions of conjunctions, require correspondingly more space. Only one main text buffer is ever needed. Thus, for typical conjunctive queries involving several terms, about 700 Kbyte is sufficient for the in-memory structures.

7 Overall Performance

Table 5 summarises the secondary storage consumed by the various components of the FTR databases storing *Bible* and *Comact*. In calculating 'Raw' sizes it is assumed where appropriate that integers are coded in the minimal integral number of bits. If standard 32-bit integers are used the Raw values would be even larger. The column labelled '%' shows the percentage, relative to the original main text, occupied by each component of the compressed database. In terms of disk space only the main text and the inverted file are of any significance.

	Bible			Comact		
	Raw	Compressed	%	Raw	Compressed	%
Main Text						
— fragments	4,468	1,153	25.8	135,278	35,139	26.0
— record lengths	88	37	0.8	991	371	0.3
Inverted File						
— pointers	1,326	565	12.6	50,681	10,643	7.9
— record lengths	91	17	0.4	241	97	0.1
Lexicon	121	65	1.5	672	341	0.3
Disk Mappings						
— Main Text	2	2	0.0	24	24	0.0
— Inverted File	1	1	0.0	7	7	0.0
Total	6,097	1,840	41.2	187,894	46,622	34.5

Table 5: Summary of Compression (Kbyte)

Extrapolating these results to *Hypothetical*, it seems not unreasonable to conjecture that the main text would require approximately 25% of the initial data volume; that the compressed inverted file would require less than 10% of the original text; that decoding would require of the order of 1 to 1.5 Mbyte of main memory; and that all other resource requirements would be inconsequential.

Measured decompression rates on the main text show the Huffman coded models to operate roughly 40 times faster than the same models when represented with arithmetic coding. Access to the inverted file through the b-block code is just as fast. Because of these fast codes, query processing is limited almost entirely by the performance of the secondary storage device, and is relatively *in*sensitive to processor power, provided that the requisite main memory is available. We have even observed some queries for which a compressed database is *faster* than an uncompressed database, because of the reduced volume of information transferred from disk.

Acknowledgements

The authors are grateful to Tim Bell, who provided extensive information about the compression scheme described in [11]. This work was supported by the Australian Research Council.

References

[1] T.C. Bell, J.G. Cleary, and I.H. Witten. *Text Compression*. Prentice-Hall, January 1990.

[2] R.G. Gallager. Variations on a theme by Huffman. *IEEE Transactions on Information Theory*, IT-24:668–674, November 1978.

[3] R.G. Gallager and D.C. Van Voorhis. Optimal source codes for geometrically distributed alphabets. *IEEE Transactions on Information Theory*, IT–21(2):228–230, March 1975.

[4] S.W. Golomb. Run-length encodings. *IEEE Transactions on Information Theory*, IT–12(3):399–401, July 1966.

[5] D. Hirschberg and D. Lelewer. Efficient decoding of prefix codes. *Communications of the ACM*, 33(4):449–459, April 1990.

[6] D.A. Huffman. A method for the construction of minimum redundancy codes. *Proc. IRE*, 40(9):1098–1101, September 1952.

[7] M.D. McIlroy. Development of a spelling list. *IEEE Transactions on Communications*, COM–30(1):91–99, January 1982.

[8] A.M. Moffat. Word based text compression. *Software—Practice and Experience*, 19(2):185–198, February 1989.

[9] A.M. Moffat. Implementing the PPM data compression scheme. *IEEE Transactions on Communications*, 38(2):1917–1921, November 1990.

[10] A.M. Moffat and J. Zobel. Coding for compression in full-text retrieval systems. Technical Report 91/21, Department of Computer Science, The University of Melbourne, Parkville 3052, Australia, November 1991.

[11] I.H. Witten, T.C. Bell, and C. Nevill. Models for compression in full-text retrieval systems. In J.A. Storer and J.H. Reif, editors, *Proc. IEEE Data Compression Conference*, pages 23–32, Snowbird, Utah, April 1991.

[12] I.H. Witten, R. Neal, and J.G. Cleary. Arithmetic coding for data compression. *Communications of the ACM*, 30(6):520–541, June 1987.

Model Based Concordance Compression

Abraham Bookstein[1],   Shmuel T. Klein[2],   Timo Raita[3]

[1] Center for Information and Language Studies, University of Chicago, Chicago IL 60637, USA

[2] Depts. of Math. & CS and Economics & BA, Bar Ilan University, Ramat Gan 52900, Israel

[3] Department of Computer Science, University of Turku, SF–20520 Turku, Finland

1. Introduction

The development of optical disk technology has made it possible to widely distribute large, full text databases. But large as the capacity of CD-roms may be, it still doesn't match our ambitions for storing data [10]. In part, the desire to increase the amount of data that can be conveniently distributed via CD-rom has helped spur on interest in text compression. Today, text compression, which began as a set of unsystematic, though often ingenious, techniques [8], is quite well understood and rests on a firm theoretical base [12], [1].

It is often overlooked, however, that to be able to access and manipulate text, auxiliary data-structures must also be created and stored, and these often occupy as much space as the original text itself. Thus, to distribute a functional, full-text information retrieval system, consideration must be given how to compress these data structures. Though some work has been done on the compression of bit-maps [3], [2], [9], the concordance, one of the most important of these data structures, has been given relatively little attention. In this paper, we discuss concordance compression using the framework now customary in compression theory: we begin by creating a mathematical model of concordance generation, and then use optimal compression engines, such as Huffman or arithmetic coding, to do the actual compression.

It should be noted that in the context of a static information retrieval system, compression and decompression are not symmetrical tasks. Compression is done only once, while building the system, whereas decompression is needed during the processing of every query and directly affects the response time. One may thus use extensive and costly preprocessing for compression, provided reasonably fast decompression methods are possible. Moreover, compression is applied to the full files (text, concordance, etc.), but decompression is needed only for (possibly many) short pieces, which may be accessed at random by means of pointers to their exact locations. Therefore the use of adaptive methods based on tables that systematically change from the beginning to the end of the file is ruled out. However, our concern in this paper is less the speed of encoding or decoding than relating concordance compression conceptually to the modern approach of data compression, and testing the effectiveness of our models.

2. Background and Previous Work

Most large information retrieval systems are based on inverted files. In this approach, processing of queries does not involve directly the original text files (in which key words are located using some pattern matching technique), but rather the auxiliary *dictionary* and *concordance* files. The dictionary is the list of all the different words appearing in the text and is usually ordered alphabetically. Every occurrence of every word in the database can be uniquely characterized by a sequence of numbers that give its exact position in the text. Typically, such a sequence would consist of the document number d, the paragraph number p (in the document), the sentence number s (in the paragraph) and the word number w (in the sentence). The quadruple (d, p, s, w) is the *coordinate* of the occurrence, and the corresponding fields will be called for short the d-field, p-field, s-field and w-field. The concordance contains, for every word of the dictionary, the lexicographically ordered list of all its coordinates in the text; it is accessed via the dictionary that contains for every word a pointer to the corresponding list in the concordance.

The concordance is generally (depending on the omission or inclusion of the most frequent words, the so-called *stop-words*) of the order of magnitude of the text itself. There is therefore a real need to compress it, not only to save space, but also to save time by reducing the number of I/O operations needed to fetch parts of the concordance into main memory (see [10], [4], [13]). Since the list of coordinates of any given word is ordered, adjacent coordinates will often have the same d-field, or even the same d- and p-fields, and sometimes, especially for high frequency words, identical d-, p- and s-fields. In the *prefix-omission method* (POM) (see [5]), each coordinate is preceded by a header, giving the number of fields which can be copied from the preceding coordinate; these fields are then omitted. For instance in our model with coordinates (d, p, s, w), it would suffice to keep a header of 2 bits. The four possibilities are: don't copy any field from the previous coordinate; copy the d-field; copy the d- and p-field; and copy the d-, p- and s-field. Obviously, different coordinates cannot have all four fields identical.

For convenient computer manipulation, one generally chooses a fixed length for each field, which therefore has to be large enough to represent the maximal possible values. However, most stored values are small, thus there is usually much wasted space in each coordinate. The basic idea of the methods presented in [6] is to use a *variable length* representation of the integers stored in the fields of a coordinate. As in POM, each compressed coordinate will be prefixed by a header which will encode the information necessary to decompress the coordinate. The methods differ in their interpretation of the header. The choice of the length of every field is based on statistics gathered from the entire database on the distribution of the values in each field.

The codes in the header can have various interpretations: they can stand for a length ℓ, indicating that the corresponding field is encoded in ℓ bits; they can stand for a certain value v, indicating that the corresponding field contains that value; or they can be used as an index to a small static table which includes all the necessary information for the decoding.

These methods yield quite good results on the examples presented, but are not easily generalized to other systems, as the various parameters are being chosen *ad hoc*. Only recently has any attempt been made to relate concordance compression to the mainstream of compression methodology. Bookstein et al. [4] hinted at a more systematic approach in a paper describing a project to store a large, french language database on CD-rom. A similar approach was discussed in more detail by Witten et al. [13]. Our present work can be seen as a continuation of this effort.

3. Model based concordance compression

3.1 Concordance structure

For our model of a textual database, we assume that the text is divided into documents and the documents are made up of words. We thus use only a two level hierarchy to identify the location of a word, which makes the exposition here easier. The methods can, however, be readily adapted to more complex concordance structures, like the 4-level hierarchy mentioned above. In our present model, the conceptual concordance consists, for each word, of a series of (d, w) pairs, d standing for a document number, and w for the index, or offset, of a word within the given document:

$$
\begin{aligned}
\text{word}_1 : \quad & (d_1, w_1)\,(d_1, w_2)\,\cdots\,(d_1, w_{m_1}) \\
& (d_2, w_1)\,(d_2, w_2)\,\cdots\,(d_2, w_{m_2}) \\
& \cdots \\
& (d_N, w_1)\cdots(d_N, w_{m_N}) \\
\text{word}_2 : \quad & \cdots
\end{aligned}
\tag{1}
$$

For a discussion of the problems of relating this conceptual location to a physical location on the disc, see [4].

It is sometimes convenient to translate this model to an equivalent one, in which we indicate 1) the index of the next document containing the word, 2) the number of times the word occurs in the document, followed by 3) the list of word indices of the various occurrences:

$$
\begin{aligned}
\text{word}_1 : \quad & (d_1,\, m_1\,;\ \ w_1, w_2, \ldots, w_{m_1}) \\
& (d_2,\, m_2\,;\ \ w_1, \ldots, w_{m_2}) \\
& \cdots \\
& (d_N,\, m_N\,;\ \ w_1, \ldots, w_{m_N}) \\
\text{word}_2 : \quad & \cdots
\end{aligned}
\tag{2}
$$

Of course, we adopt this reorganization only if, on the average, it does not increase our storage requirements. For on the one hand, we store in (2) an additional number (m_i) for each document the word occurs in; on the other hand, the word occurrences themselves are then encoded by only $2 + m_i$ numbers instead of $2m_i$ for (1). Thus a simple rule of thumb, assuming that all these numbers are stored in the same way (say, in 2 bytes), would be to prefer representation (2) only if the average number of occurrences of a word in a document, $\bar{m}$, is larger than 2. A more precise rule would take into account the maximum number of bits needed to store any of these numbers. Therefore, if D denotes the number of documents, and M_W and M_m denote the maximal values of w_i (the length in words of the longest document) and of m_i (the maximal number of times a word occurs in the same document), then the condition for preferring (2) to (1) becomes $\lceil \log D \rceil + \lceil \log M_m \rceil + \lceil \log M_W \rceil \cdot \bar{m} < \bar{m}(\lceil \log D \rceil + \lceil \log M_W \rceil)$, i.e., $\bar{m} > (\lceil \log D \rceil + \lceil \log M_m \rceil)/\lceil \log D \rceil$. In the rest of our discussion, we assume the representation given in (2), but the methods to be described are easily adaptable to representation (1) as well.

Thus our task is to model each of the components of (2), and use standard compression methods to compress each entity. Below we assume that we know (from the dictionary) the total number of times a word occurs in the database, the number of different documents in which it occurs, and (from a separate table) the number of words in each document.

3.2 Choosing the encoding method

The compression algorithm below is based on predicting the probability distribution of the various values in the coordinates, devising a code based on the predicted distributions, and using the codeword corresponding to the actual value given.

We thus need to generate a large number of codes. If so, the Shannon-Fano method (as defined in [7]) seems the most appropriate if we are concerned with processing speed. Thus an element, which according to the model at hand appears with probability p, will be encoded by $\lceil -\log_2 p \rceil$ bits. Once the length of the codeword is determined, the actual codeword is easily generated. But Shannon-Fano codes are not optimal and might in fact be quite wasteful, especially for the very low probabilities.

While Shannon-Fano coding is fast, when high precision is required Huffman codes are a good alternative. Under the constraint that every codeword consists of an integral number of bits, they are optimal; however their computation is much more involved than that of Shannon-Fano codes, because here every codeword depends on the whole set of probabilities. Thus more processing time is needed, but compression is improved. On the other hand, Huffman codes are not effective in the presence of very high probabilities. Elements occurring with high probability have low information content, yet their Huffman codeword cannot be shorter than one bit. If this is a prominent feature, arithmetic coding must be considered.

Arithmetic coding [14] more directly uses the probabilities derived from the model, and overcomes the problem of high probability elements by encoding entire messages, not just codewords. Effectively, an element with probability p is encoded by exactly $-\log_2 p$ bits, which is the information theoretic minimum. While in many contexts arithmetic codes might not improve much on Huffman codes, their superiority here might be substantial, because the model may generate many high probabilities. There is of course a time/space tradeoff, as the computation of arithmetic codes is generally more expensive than that of Huffman codes.

In the sequel, we shall just refer to "codes"; the decision on which specific code to use will ultimately be based on the desired tradeoff between processing speed, programming convenience and compression savings.

3.3 Modeling document occurrence

3.3.1 Independence model

Initially we are at the beginning of the document list and are trying to determine the probability that the next (when we start, this is the first) document containing a term is d documents away from our current location. We know the number of documents that contain the term, say N, and the number of documents, say D, from which these are chosen. (More generally, after we have located a number of documents that contain the term, D and N will respectively represent the total number of remaining documents, and, of these, the number that contain the term. Our reasoning will then continue in parallel to that of the first occurrence.)

To compute these probabilities, we shall assume for this model that

1. Documents are approximately of the same size (this assumption could be relaxed at the cost of increased computational complexity).

2. There is little between-document clustering. That is, so far as term occurrence goes, there is little tie from document to document. Of course terms do cluster, but we assume this is just the tendency for words to occur within the same document.

3. Within a single document, words are independently distributed.

A breakdown of the independence assumptions, if serious, could be ameliorated either by increasing the number of levels in our hierarchy, or by using a more complex model.

Our first question, then, is: what is the probability distribution of the first/next document containing the term. Given our assumptions, this is equivalent to asking, if N different objects are selected at random from an ordered set of D objects, what is the probability that d is the index of the object with minimum index?

Because of the uniformity assumption, each of the $\binom{D}{N}$ ways of picking N out of D objects have same probability, viz, $1/\binom{D}{N}$. But of these, only $\binom{D-d}{N-1}$ satisfy the condition that d is the minimum index. That is, certainly one document must be the d-th one, so we only have freedom to choose $N - 1$ additional documents. Since all of these must have index greater than d, we have only $D - d$ options for these $N - 1$ selections. Thus the probability that the next document has (relative) position d is $\Pr(d) = \binom{D-d}{N-1} / \binom{D}{N}$.

We first note this is a true probability:

$$\sum_d \Pr(d) = \sum_{d=1}^{D-N+1} \frac{\binom{D-d}{N-1}}{\binom{D}{N}} = \sum_{k=N-1}^{D-1} \frac{\binom{k}{N-1}}{\binom{D}{N}} = \frac{\binom{D}{N}}{\binom{D}{N}} = 1,$$

where the last equality uses the well known combinatoric identity that permits summation over the upper value in the binomial coefficient [11]. Second, we note that we can rewrite the probability as

$$\left(\frac{N}{D-N+1}\right) \times \left(1 - \frac{d}{D}\right) \times \left(1 - \frac{d}{D-1}\right) \times \cdots \times \left(1 - \frac{d}{D-N+2}\right).$$

If $d \ll D$, this is approximately $(N/D) \times (1 - d/D)^{N-1}$, which is in turn approximately proportional to $e^{-d(N-1)/D}$ or γ^d, for $\gamma = e^{-(N-1)/D}$. This last form is that of the geometric distribution recommended by Witten et al. [13].

The encoding process is then as follows. We wish to encode the d-field of the next coordinates $(d, m; w_1, \ldots, w_m)$. Assuming that the probability distribution of d is given by $\Pr(d)$, we construct a code based on $\{\Pr(d)\}_{d=1}^{D-N+1}$. This assigns codewords to all the possible values of d, from which we use the codeword corresponding to the actual value d in our coordinate. If the estimate is good, the actual value d will be assigned a high probability by the model, and therefore be encoded with a small number of bits.

Next we encode the number of occurrences of the term in this document. Let us suppose that we have T occurrences of the term remaining (initially, this will be the total number of occurrences of the term in the database). The T occurrences are to be distributed into the N remaining documents the word occurs in. Thus we know that each document being considered must have at least a single term, that is, $m = 1 + x$, where $x \geq 0$. If $T = N$, then clearly $x = 0$ ($m = 1$), and we need output no code — m conveys no information in this case. If $T > N$, then we must distribute the $T - N$ terms not accounted for over the remaining N documents that contain the term. We assume, for simplicity, that the additional amount, x, going to the currently considered document is Poisson distributed, with mean $\lambda = (T - N)/N$. The Poisson distribution is given by $\Pr(x) = e^{-\lambda}\frac{\lambda^x}{x!}$. This allows us to compute the probability of x for all possible values ($x = 0, 1, \ldots, T - N$) and to then encode x using one of the encodings of Section 3.2.

We must finally encode all the m offsets. But this problem is formally identical to that of encoding the next document. The current document has W words, so the distribution of w, the first occurrence of the word, is given by the probabilities $\binom{W-w}{m-1}/\binom{W}{m}$. Once this is encoded, we have a problem identical to the initial one in form, except that we now have $m - 1$ positions left to encode and $W - w$ locations. This continues until the last term, which is uniformly distributed over the remaining word locations.

Then we encode the next document, but this is again a problem identical in form to the initial problem—only we now have one fewer document ($N - 1$) having the term, and d fewer target documents ($D - d$) to consider.

The formal encoding algorithm is given below. We begin with a conceptual concordance, represented for the purpose of this algorithm as a list of entries. Our concordance controls S different words. For each word, there is an entry for each document it occurs in, of the form $(d_i, m_i; w_1, \ldots, w_{m_i})$, where d_i, m_i and w_j are given similarly to the representation (2) defined above. Then the algorithm Compress is given as follows:

```
Compress (concordance)
{
        for s ⟵ 1 to S      /* for each word in concordance */
                D   ⟵     total number of documents
                T   ⟵     total number of occurrences of word s
                N   ⟵     total number of documents in which word s occurs
                d₀  ⟵     0

                for i ⟵ 1 to N      /* for each document containing word s */
                {
                        /* process document i */
                        output d_code(dᵢ − dᵢ₋₁, N − i, D)
                        if T > N
                                output m_code(mᵢ − 1,  (T − N)/N,  T − N)

                        /* process occurrences of word s in document i */
                        W   ⟵     total number of words in document i
                        w₀  ⟵     0
                        for j ⟵ 1 to mᵢ
                        {
                                output w_code(wⱼ − wⱼ₋₁, mᵢ − j, W)
                                W   ⟵     W − (wⱼ − wⱼ₋₁)
                        }

                        /* update parameters and continue */
                        D   ⟵     D − (dᵢ − dᵢ₋₁)
                        T   ⟵     T − mᵢ
                }
        }
}
```

d_code(d, N, D)
```
{
```
    construct a code $\mathcal{C}_1$ based on probabilities that $d = k$: $\left\{ \binom{D-k}{N} / \binom{D}{N+1} \right\}_{k=1}^{D-i+1}$

    return $\mathcal{C}_1(d)$
```
}
```

m_code(x, λ, max)
```
{
```
    $F \quad \longleftarrow \quad \sum_{k=0}^{max} e^{-\lambda} \frac{\lambda^k}{k!}$ /* correction factor for truncated Poisson distribution */

    construct a code $\mathcal{C}_2$ based on probabilities that $x = k$: $\left\{ \frac{1}{F} e^{-\lambda} \frac{\lambda^k}{k!} \right\}_{k=0}^{max}$

    return $\mathcal{C}_2(x)$
```
}
```

w_code(w, m, W)
```
{
```
    construct a code $\mathcal{C}_3$ based on probabilities that $w = k$: $\left\{ \binom{W-k}{m} / \binom{W}{m+1} \right\}_{k=1}^{W-i+1}$

    return $\mathcal{C}_3(w)$
```
}
```

Note that we do not encode the absolute values d_i and w_j, but the relative increases $d_i - d_{i-1}$ and $w_j - w_{j-1}$; this is necessary, because we redefine, in each iteration, the sizes D, W and T to be the *remaining* number of documents, number of words in the current document, and number of occurrences of the current word, respectively.

3.3.2   Cluster model

One should also deal with the possibility where the independence assumptions of the previous section are not necessarily true. In particular, we consider the case where terms cluster not only within a document, but even at the between document level. The details of this model will appear in the full paper.

4.   Discussion

One of the benefits of a theoretically based approach is that, if based on a good message generation model, it promises to provide near optimal performance. This assertion is justified by the theory itself. But methods exist that are not theory based and yet perform quite well. An additional important contribution of the theory is to explain the good performance of these other methods. That is, we would like to see the best *ad hoc* methods as incomplete or non-optimal expressions of the method suggested by the theory.

This is the case here. For example, the representation of the occurrences of a term in single document in the form (document index, number of occurrences; occurrence list) is a variant of run length encoding, with the "blanks" being members of the occurrence list, and their number being optimally encoded.

But the most common type of concordance compression, prefix omission, can also be understood in terms of this model. In prefix omission, the document number is encoded when it is first met, and all subsequent consecutive references to that document are represented by a smaller sized *ditto* code. For example: $(D_1, t_1), (ditto, t_2), \ldots,$ $(ditto, t_n), (D_2, t_1), \ldots$. But, seen in terms of the current model, this is equivalent to the representation: $(D_1, ditto, ditto, \ldots, ditto ; \ t_1, t_2, \ldots), (D_2, \ldots), \ldots$. In this form, it is clear that the portion $(D_1, ditto, \ldots)$ is simply an encoding of the document identifier and the number of occurrences of the term in the document.

Given the above interpretation, it is reasonable to ask why the direct encoding (document identifier, number of occurrences) is not often used. One explanation is that usually only one instance of a term will appear in any given document, and it is less costly to store a string of *ditto*'s only when necessary than to commit oneself to storing a number for every document. While this explanation may be valid for traditional encoding, it doesn't apply for us, since we don't use a fixed length integer to encode the number of occurrences. If usually only one token of a word appears in a document, that is, if the probability of one occurrence is near one, very little information is conveyed by a single occurrence. But using either arithmetic coding or Huffman coding with (D, number) encoded jointly, the number of occurrences consumes exactly the same amount of resources as it requires, and we don't have a loss by making it explicit. Given this interpretation, prefix omission can be seen as a non-optimal way of encoding the first two components of our representation.

5. Experiments

The database we chose for testing our method is the Hebrew Bible, consisting of 309631 words, which are partitioned into 929 chapters. The number of different words is 41197. We chose each chapter as a document, so $D = 929$. Other relevant statistics are: M_W (length of longest document) = 1153 words; M_m (maximum number of occurrences of a word in the same document) = 96; the number of coordinates of type $(d, m ; w_1, \ldots, w_m)$ is 192048, so that the average value of m is 1.612.

Table 1 summarizes the results. The rows correspond to the 3 fields of our coordinate: the d-, m- and w-fields. Each column corresponds to an encoding method and gives, in the appropriate row, the number of bits needed to encode that field. For the w-field, the value given is for a single value w_i. The **first** column is the straightforward encoding using fixed size (d, w) coordinates (representation (1)). The **second** column corresponds to POM, where one bit has been added to each coordinate, indicating whether to copy the d-field from the previous coordinate or not. The number of times the d-field could be copied is 117583. The **third** column corresponds to representation (2) with fixed sized fields (which, in our case, is worse than representation (1)). The **fourth** column is based on the full distributions of the possible values in each field, and gives the information theoretic minimum for a global encoding method; that is, if a certain value is always encoded in the same way when it appears, say, in the d-field, then averaged over all the possible values, we would need 7.0156 bits. The information theoretic bound can be approached very closely by arithmetic coding. The bound can, however, be beaten by adaptive methods, which take advantage of the increasing knowledge one gains during the scan of the concordance. This is the case with our method, the results of which, using arithmetic coding, are reported in the **last** column. As can be seen, the method reduces the average sizes for each field, and the total size to about 7.5% below the results of the preceding column.

	coordinate form (1)	POM	coordinate form (2)	arith. coding on full freqs.	new method
d-field	10	1 – 11	10	7.0156	6.5093
m-field	–	–	7	1.3298	1.2106
w-field	11	11	11	8.5007	7.8629
total size	812782	704507	833845	529349	489648
compression	2.5%	15.5%	–	36.5%	41.3%

Table 1: *Comparitive chart of compression results*

The last two rows of the table give the total size of the concordance (in bytes) for each method, and the compression savings in percent relative to the full concordance using representation (2).

As a final note we remark that the Bible was just used as an example, and is not a typical data base on which one would apply concordance compression. The Bible is too small (just about 1.5 MB), so that hardly any concordance is needed. On real life concordances, of the size of hundreds of MB, the compression savings are usually much more substantial (about 40% by POM on large data bases, versus 16% by POM here), so we expect there our method also to perform much better.

References

[1]   **Bell T., Witten I.H., Cleary J.G.,** Modeling for text compression, *ACM Computing Surveys* **21** (1989) 557–591.

[2]   **Bookstein A., Klein S.T.,** Optimal graphs for bit-vector compression, *Proc. 13-th ACM-SIGIR Conf.,* Brussels, Belgium (1990) 327–342.

[3]   **Bookstein A., Klein S.T.,** Flexible compression for bitmap sets, *Proc. Data Compression Conference,* Snowbird, Utah (1991) 402–410.

[4]   **Bookstein A., Klein S.T., Ziff, D.A.,** The ARTFL Data Compression Project, *Proc. RIAO–91 Conf.,* Barcelona, Spain (April 2–5, 1991) 967–985, an extended version will appear in *Information Processing & Management,* as "A systematic approach to compressing a full text retrieval system".

[5]   **Bratley P., Choueka Y.,** Processing truncated terms in document retrieval systems, *Inf. Processing & Management* **18** (1982) 257–266.

[6]   **Choueka Y., Fraenkel A.S., Klein S.T.,** Compression of Concordances in Full-Text Retrieval Systems, *Proc. 11-th ACM-SIGIR Conf.,* Grenoble (1988) 597–612.

[7]   **Hamming R.W.,** *Coding and Information Theory,* Prentice-Hall, Englewood Cliffs, NJ (1980).

[8]   **Held G.,** *Data Compression,* Wiley, NY (1983).

[9]   **Jakobsson M.,** Huffman coding in bit-vector compression, *Inf. Processing Letters* **7** (1978) 304–307.

[10]   **Klein S.T., Bookstein A., Deerwester S.,** Storing Text Retrieval Systems on CD-ROM: Compression and Encryption Considerations, *ACM Trans. on Information Systems* **7** (1989), 230–245.

[11]   **Knuth D.E.,** *The Art of Computer Programming, Vol I, Fundamental algorithms,* Addison-Wesley, Reading, Mass. (1973).

[12]   **Storer J.A.,** *Data Compression: Methods and Theory,* Computer Science Press, Rockville, Maryland (1988).

[13]   **Witten I.H., Bell T.C., Nevill C.G.,** Models for compression in full-text retrieval systems, *Proc. Data Compression Conference,* Snowbird, Utah (1991) 23–32.

[14]   **Witten I.H., Neal R.M., Cleary J.G.,** Arithmetic coding for data compression, *Communications of the ACM* **30** (1987) 520–540.

Arithmetic Coding for Memoryless Cost Channels

Serap A. Savari[1]   Robert G. Gallager[2]
Department of Electrical Engineering and Computer Science
Massachusetts Institute of Technology

Abstract: We analyze the expected delay for infinite precision arithmetic codes and suggest a practical implementation that concentrates on the issue of delay.

Arithmetic coding is a powerful and conceptually simple data compression technique (see Rissanen and Langdon (1979)). In the ideal situation where arithmetic calculations can be accomplished with infinite precision, arithmetic coding is unique in that it encodes exactly at the entropy rate with a delay whose expected value is bounded. In reality, arithmetic computations can be performed with only finite precision. The modifications that have been used to account for this problem and make arithmetic coding a more practical encoding scheme are complex and elusive to explain in an easy way; we refer the reader to Langdon (1984) for some historical perspective on these modifications. In this paper, we provide an alternate approach to arithmetic coding by concentrating on the issue of coding delay. We will analyze the expected delay for ideal arithmetic codes and suggest a practical implementation that focuses on delay. Our development closely follows Gallager (1991).

For notational simplicity, assume a source emitting independent identically distributed symbols from a finite set $\{0, 1, \ldots, K-1\}$. The letter probabilities $p_0, p_1, \ldots, p_{K-1}$ are strictly positive. We assume a noiseless channel with memoryless letter costs; i.e., the cost of transmitting any code letter depends only on that letter. Therefore, our channel is a device which accepts input from a specified set X of letters, say $\{0, 1, \ldots, N-1\}$ with (positive) letter costs $c_0, c_1, \ldots, c_{N-1}$, respectively.

Shannon (1948) demonstrated that under this assumption, the minimum expected cost per source symbol that can be achieved by any source coding technique is greater than or equal to $\frac{H(U)}{C}$ where $H(U) = -\sum_{i=0}^{K-1} p_i \log_2 p_i$ is the *entropy* of the source and C, the *capacity* of the channel, is the real root of the equation $\sum_{i=0}^{N-1} 2^{-Cc_i} = 1$.

We denote the random sequence produced by the source as $y = \{y_1, y_2, y_3, \ldots\}$ and let $y^{(m)} = \{y_1, y_2, \ldots, y_m\}$ for $m \geq 0$. Since the source is memoryless, $P[y^{(m)}] = \prod_{j=1}^{m} P[y_j]$ where $P[y_j = k] = p_k$, $0 \leq k \leq K-1$.

The idea in arithmetic coding is to map the initial source strings $y^{(m)}$ into subintervals of the unit interval that shrink to a point $x(y)$. The resulting subintervals are then represented by channel strings $z^{(n)} = \{z_1, z_2, \ldots, z_n\}$ that grow into the output channel sequence $z = \{z_1, z_2, \ldots\}$. First, we discuss the mapping of source strings into subintervals of the unit interval. Let $\mathcal{I}(y^{(m)})$ denote the subinterval correspond-

---

[1]Supported by an AT&T Bell Laboratories GRPW Fellowship and a Vinton Hayes Fellowship.
[2]Supported by NSF grant 8802991-NCR.

ing to source string $y^{(m)}$; $y^{(0)}$ denotes the null source string. As in earlier work on arithmetic coding, the mapping of source strings into (left half-closed) intervals has been selected to satisfy two requirements. The first is that for all source strings u, the width of interval $\mathcal{I}(u)$ is equal to the a priori probability that the string is a prefix of the source sequence. The other property is that for any source string u, we have that $\mathcal{I}(u0)\,,\ldots,\mathcal{I}(u(K-1))$ are disjoint intervals whose union is $\mathcal{I}(u)$. For the null string, $\mathcal{I}(\emptyset) = [0,1)$.

One way to implement these requirements is as follows. We define

$$f(i) \;=\; f_1(i) \;=\; \sum_{j=0}^{i-1} p_j \tag{1}$$

$$f(y^{(m)}) \;=\; f(y^{(m-1)}) + f_1(y_m) \cdot P(y^{(m-1)}), \; m > 1 \tag{2}$$

$$\text{and } \mathcal{I}(y^{(m)}) \;=\; [f(y^{(m)}), f(y^{(m)}) + P(y^{(m)})). \tag{3}$$

Figure 1 illustrates this procedure. We note that the mapping of source sequences

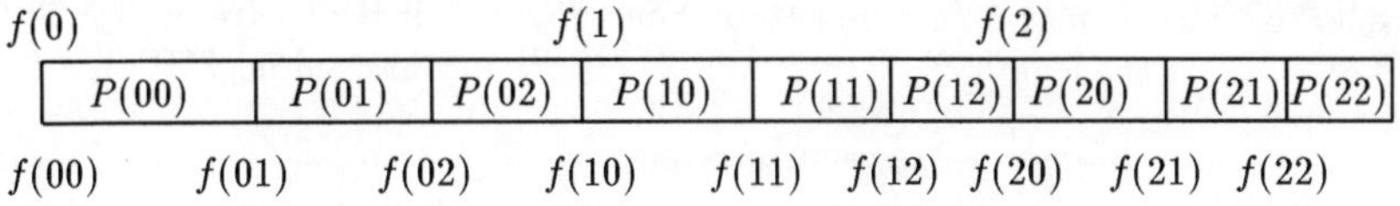

$f(0)$ $f(1)$ $f(2)$

$P(00)$	$P(01)$	$P(02)$	$P(10)$	$P(11)$	$P(12)$	$P(20)$	$P(21)$	$P(22)$

$f(00)$ $f(01)$ $f(02)$ $f(10)$ $f(11)$ $f(12)$ $f(20)$ $f(21)$ $f(22)$

Figure 1:

to points has the following monotonicity property: Given arbitrary distinct source sequences u and v, $x(u) > x(v)$ if and only if u is lexicographically larger than v.

Next consider mapping strings of channel letters into subintervals of the unit interval and vice versa. Let $z^{(n)}$ denote the initial string $z^{(n)} = \{z_1,\ldots,z_n\}$ and $\mathcal{J}(z^{(n)})$ denote the subinterval corresponding to this string; as before, $z^{(0)}$ represents the null channel string. Guazzo (1980) demonstrated that it is appropriate to associate a probability 2^{-Cc_i} with each channel letter i and then to map channel strings into subintervals in exactly the same way that source strings are mapped into subintervals. Therefore, if for any channel string σ, $c(\sigma)$ and $l(\sigma)$ denote the cost of transmitting σ and the length of $\mathcal{J}(\sigma)$, respectively, then we require that for all channel strings σ, $l(\sigma) = 2^{-C\cdot c(\sigma)}$ and $\mathcal{J}(\sigma0),\ldots,\mathcal{J}(\sigma(N-1))$ are disjoint intervals whose union is $\mathcal{J}(\sigma)$. The convention for the null symbol is that $\mathcal{J}(\emptyset) = [0,1)$.

To satisfy these requirements, we employ a mapping that is analogous to the mapping we used for source strings. We define

$$g(i) \;=\; g_1(i) \;=\; \sum_{j=0}^{i-1} l(j) \;=\; \sum_{j=0}^{i-1} 2^{-C\cdot c_j} \tag{4}$$

$$\begin{aligned} g(z^{(n)}) &\;=\; g(z^{(n-1)}) + g_1(z_n) \cdot l(z^{(n-1)}) \\ &\;=\; g(z^{(n-1)}) + g_1(z_n) \cdot 2^{-C\cdot c(z^{(n-1)})}, \; n > 1 \end{aligned} \tag{5}$$

$$\text{and } \mathcal{J}(z^{(n)}) \;=\; [g(z^{(n)}), \; g(z^{(n)}) + l(z^{(n)})) \;=\; [g(z^{(n)}), \; g(z^{(n)}) + 2^{-C \cdot c(z^{(n)})}). \tag{6}$$

Clearly, the mapping of channel sequences to points has the same lexicographic property as the mapping of source sequences to points.

For the inverse mapping, if we are given any subinterval $\mathcal{K}$ of the unit interval, the channel string associated with $\mathcal{K}$ is the longest string σ for which $\mathcal{J}(\sigma)$ contains $\mathcal{K}$.

We now have the tools to discuss the encoding of source sequence y. On observing $y^{(m)}$, the encoder knows that the limit point $x(y)$ lies in the interval $\mathcal{I}(y^{(m)})$. Thus, if $\mathcal{I}(y^{(m)})$ is contained in $\mathcal{J}(z^{(n)})$ for some channel string $z^{(n)}$, then the encoder can emit $z^{(n)}$ as the first n letters of z. Hence, as the source emits successive letters y_m, the interval $\mathcal{I}(y^{(m)})$ shrinks and more channel letters can be emitted.

To demonstrate the efficiency of the above procedure, we would like to show that when the source has emitted $y^{(m)}$, the encoder will have issued a channel string $z^{(n)}$ with cost of transmission close to $\frac{I(y^{(m)})}{C}$, where $I(y^{(m)}) = -\log_2 P[y^{(m)}]$, and that $z^{(n)}$ will be sufficient for the decoder to decode all but the last few letters of $y^{(m)}$. We first consider the number of letters $m(n)$ that the source must emit in order for the encoder to issue the first n channel letters. Since $P(y^{m(n)})$ is the length of $\mathcal{I}(y^{(m(n))})$, $2^{-C \cdot [\text{cost of } z^{(n)}]}$ is the length of $\mathcal{J}(z^{(n)})$, and $\mathcal{I}(y^{(m(n))})$ is contained in $\mathcal{J}(z^{(n)})$,

$$P(y^{m(n)}) \leq 2^{-C \cdot [\text{cost of } z^{(n)}]}. \tag{7}$$

Taking the logarithm of both sides of (7) and dividing the resulting inequality by $-C$ gives

$$\text{cost of } z^{(n)} \leq \frac{1}{C} I(y^{(m(n))}). \tag{8}$$

Since this inequality can be arbitrarily loose, we want to show that for each n, $E\left(\frac{I(y^{(m(n))})}{C} - [\text{cost of } z^{(n)}]\right)$ is bounded.

In order to accomplish this, let $z^{(n)}$ be fixed and let x be the final encoded point. The point x, conditional on $z^{(n)}$, is a uniformly distributed random variable in the interval $\mathcal{J}(z^{(n)})$, but we initially regard it as a fixed value. Define $D(x)$ as the distance between x and the nearest endpoint of $\mathcal{J}(z^{(n)})$ (see Figure 2). We note that

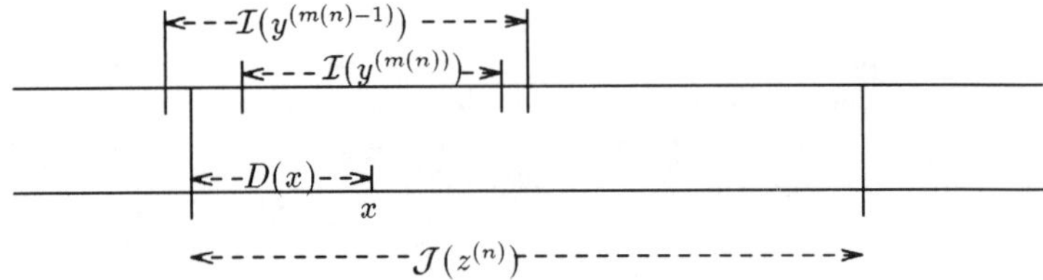

Figure 2:

the point x must be contained in $\mathcal{I}(y^{(m)})$ for all m. Also, since $m(n)$, by definition, is the smallest m for which $\mathcal{J}(z^{(n)})$ contains $\mathcal{I}(y^{(m)})$, we see that $\mathcal{I}(y^{(m(n)-1)})$ must contain one of the endpoints of $\mathcal{J}(z^{(n)})$ as well as x and thus must have width of at least $D(x)$. Hence $P(y^{(m(n)-1)} \mid x) \geq D(x)$, so

$$I(y^{(m(n)-1)} \mid x) \leq -\log_2(D(x)). \tag{9}$$

Now consider x as a random variable uniformly distributed over $\mathcal{J}(z^{(n)})$. $D(x)$ is then uniformly distributed between zero and half the length of $\mathcal{J}(z^{(n)})$. Using (9), we see that

$$E[I(y^{(m(n)-1)} \mid z^{(n)})] \leq -E[\log_2(D(x)) \mid z^{(n)}]. \tag{10}$$

Since $D(x)$ is uniformly distributed, we have that

$$\begin{aligned}
E[\log_2(D(x)) \mid z^{(n)}] &= \int_{D=0}^{\frac{1}{2} \cdot 2^{-C \cdot c(z^{(n)})}} 2 \cdot 2^{C \cdot [cost\ of\ z^{(n)}]}(\log_2 D)\, dD \\
&= -C \cdot [cost\ of\ z^{(n)}] - \log_2(2e).
\end{aligned} \tag{11}$$

Hence,

$$cost\ of\ z^{(n)} \geq \frac{1}{C} E[I(y^{(m(n)-1)} \mid z^{(n)})] - \frac{1}{C} \log_2(2e). \tag{12}$$

If p_{min} is the probability of the least likely source symbol, then for all $y^{(m)}$,

$$I(y^{(m)}) = I(y^{(m-1)}) + I(y_m) \leq I(y^{(m-1)}) + \log_2(\frac{1}{p_{min}}). \tag{13}$$

Therefore, (12) and (13) imply that

$$cost\ of\ z^{(n)} \geq \frac{1}{C} E[I(y^{(m(n))} \mid z^{(n)})] - \frac{1}{C} \log_2\left(\frac{2e}{p_{min}}\right). \tag{14}$$

We note that the above inequality is uniformly true for all $z^{(n)}$ and all n. (14) and (8) imply that the encoder generates cost, on the average, with the ideal of $\frac{H(U)}{C}$ per source symbol; however, there is a slight deficit in the cost of each code string that is produced since the encoder is storing the most recent information about the source sequence in order to correctly emit the next few channel letters. This deficiency in cost becomes increasingly insignificant as we average over longer and longer source strings.

We can use a very similar argument to bound the delay between the generation of channel letters at the decoder and the generation of decoded source symbols. For an arbitrary source string $y^{(m)}$, we let $n(m)$ denote the number of code letters that must be received at the decoder in order for the string $y^{(m)}$ to be decoded. Using a very similar derivation to that above, it is straightforward to show that

$$E[cost\ of\ z^{(n(m))} \mid y^{(m)}] \leq \frac{1}{C} I(y^{(m)}) + \frac{1}{C} \log_2\left(2^{Cc_{max}+1} e\right), \tag{15}$$

where c_{max} is the cost of the most costly channel letter.

We now combine (14) and (15). Consider a given string $y^{(m)}$ out of the decoder, and suppose that $z^{(n(m))}$ is the required code string to decode $y^{(m)}$. Figure 3 demonstrates the relationship between $\mathcal{I}(y^{(m)})$, $\mathcal{J}(z^{(n(m))})$ and $\mathcal{I}(y^{(m')})$ where $y^{(m')}$ is the extended source string required to produce $z^{(n(m))}$. Conditional on both $y^{(m)}$ and

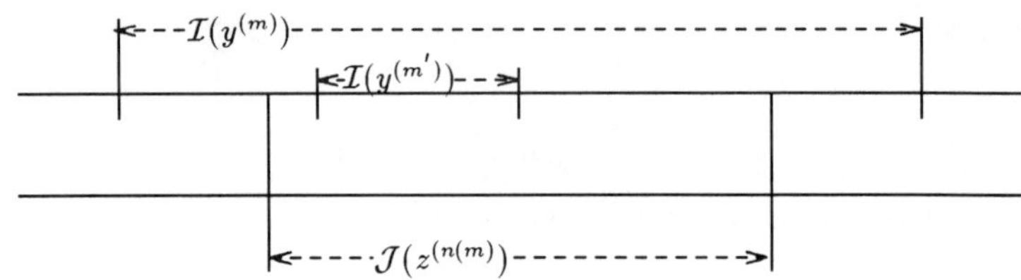

Figure 3:

$z^{(n(m))}$, we see that x is uniformly distributed over $\mathcal{J}(z^{(n(m))})$, and thus $y^{(m')}$ satisfies (from (14))

$$\text{cost of } z^{(n(m))} \geq \frac{1}{C} E[I(y^{(m')} \mid z^{(n(m))})] - \frac{1}{C} \log_2\left(\frac{2e}{p_{min}}\right). \qquad (16)$$

Using (15) to take the expected value of this over $z^{(n(m))}$, we see that for any given $y^{(m)}$, the expected self-information of the extended source string $y^{(m')}$ required from the source to produce the $n(m)$ channel letters needed to decode $y^{(m)}$ satisfies

$$E[I(y^{(m')} \mid y^{(m)})] - I(y^{(m)}) \leq \log_2\left(\frac{2^{Cc_{max}+2}e^2}{p_{min}}\right). \qquad (17)$$

The expectation here is over the source symbols y_{m+1}, y_{m+2}, $\ldots$ for the given string $y^{(m)}$. It is important to note that the bound does not depend on m or $y^{(m)}$. The upper bound in (17) states that on average there is very little delay from the encoder to the decoder. To convert this bound into a bound on the number of letters $m' - m$, let p_{max} be the maximum source letter probability. Then $\log_2\left(\frac{1}{p_{max}}\right)$ is the minimum possible self-information per source letter and

$$E[m' - m \mid y^{(m)}] \leq \frac{\log_2\left(\frac{2^{Cc_{max}+2}e^2}{p_{min}}\right)}{\log_2\left(\frac{1}{p_{max}}\right)}. \qquad (18)$$

The above analysis can be easily generalized to get an upper bound on the moment generating function for the delay distribution.

Implementation

In actual implementation, it is not possible to calculate the intervals used in encoding and decoding exactly. We view the arithmetic as being performed using binary fixed point arithmetic with M binary digits of accuracy. Assume that $2^{-M} <<$ $\min\{p_{min}, 2^{-Cc_{max}}\}$. There is some flexibility in how numbers are rounded to M bits, but it is vital that the encoder and decoder use exactly the same rule and the rounding is done at the appropriate time. In order to mitigate the effects of round-off, we will use a two-part arithmetic coder which is outlined in Figure 4. The outer arithmetic

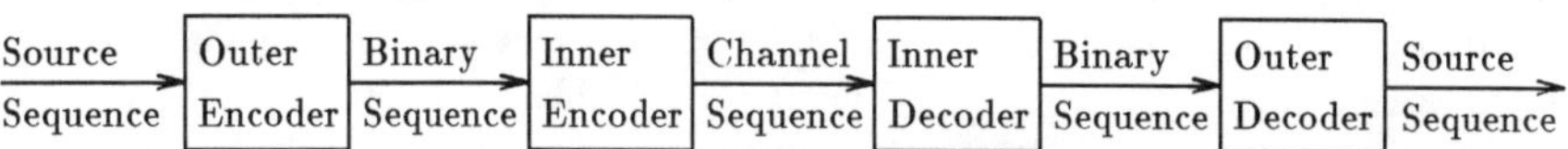

Figure 4:

coder will map source sequences into sequences from a binary channel with alphabet $\{0, 1\}$; this binary channel has memoryless digit costs and each digit is assumed to have a unit cost of transmission. We let x_b represent the point on the unit interval corresponding to the source sequence y and $b = \{b_1, b_2, \ldots\}$ be the corresponding binary sequence. The capacity of this binary channel is easily seen to be equal to one; therefore, our earlier results show that over the long term, the average number of binary digits per source symbol (for infinite precision arithmetic coding) is $H(U)$. Furthermore, since the mapping from source sequences to points on the unit interval is done so that the random variable b is uniformly distributed on the real line, each of the digits $b_1, b_2, \ldots$ in the binary expansion of b is independent and equiprobably equal to 0 or 1. The inner arithmetic coder will map the binary sequence b into a sequence of letters from the original channel alphabel. Since $b_1, b_2, \ldots$ are independent and equiprobably equal to 0 or 1, the entropy of the incoming binary sequence is 1. As before, the capacity of the channel is C. Hence, our earlier conclusions indicate that the second encoder generates cost, on the average, with the ideal of $\frac{1}{C}$ per binary digit. Combining these averages, we see that over a large source sequence, this double encoding procedure generates cost, on the average, with the ideal of $\frac{H(U)}{C}$ per source symbol. Therefore, in theory, we do not lose efficiency by splitting the coder into these two parts. However, it seems likely that there will be an increase in expected delay because coding is done in two steps. By using (18) twice, we see that the new upper bound on the delay between encoding and decoding is

$$E[m' - m \mid y^{(m)}] \le \frac{\log_2\left(\frac{8e^2}{p_{min}}\right)}{\log_2\left(\frac{1}{p_{max}}\right)} + \log_2(2^{Cc_{max}+3}e^2) \tag{19}$$

We will first discuss the behavior of the outer arithmetic coder. For the sake of simplicity, we begin with an algorithm that is not entirely correct. The outer encoder receives one source symbol at a time and calculates the corresponding interval with accuracy to M bits. Since $P(y^{(m)})$ is approaching 0 with increasing m, it is essential that the intervals be renormalized as binary digits are emitted. The encoder produces the longest binary string whose matching interval contains the current source string interval. If the length of this binary string is l, the encoder renormalizes by expanding the fraction of the unit interval which contains the source string interval by a factor of 2^l. This causes $p_{norm}(y^{(m)})$ to be multiplied by 2^l and $f_{norm}(y^{(m)})$ to be set to the fractional part of 2^l times the original value of $f_{norm}(y^{(m)})$.

More precisely, the outer encoder keeps in its memory a normalized interval starting at $f_{norm}(y^{(m)})$ and of width $p_{norm}(y^{(m)})$. We denote the right endpoint of this interval by $e_{norm}(y^{(m)})$. Initially, $m = 0$, $f_{norm}(\emptyset) = 0$, $p_{norm}(\emptyset) = 1$. In order to ensure that the intervals corresponding to different m tuples $y^{(m)}$ are disjoint and have $[0, 1)$ as their union, the interval end points are calculated directly and $p_{norm}(y^{(m)})$ is taken as the difference between the end points. The outer encoder employs the following algorithm.

1. Accept y_{m+1} into the encoder.

2. Calculate the new interval as follows:

$$
\begin{align}
f_{norm}(y^{(m+1)}) &= f_{norm}(y^{(m)}) + f_1(y_{m+1}) \cdot p_{norm}(y^{(m)}) \tag{20} \\
e_{norm}(y^{(m+1)}) &= f_{norm}(y^{(m)}) + f_1(y_{m+1} + 1) \cdot p_{norm}(y^{(m)}) \tag{21} \\
p_{norm}(y^{(m+1)}) &= e_{norm}(y^{(m+1)}) - f_{norm}(y^{(m+1)}) \tag{22} \\
\mathcal{I}_{norm}(y^{(m+1)}) &= [f_{norm}(y^{(m+1)}), \, f_{norm}(y^{(m+1)}) + p_{norm}(y^{(m+1)})) \tag{23}
\end{align}
$$

To use (21) when $y_{m+1} = K - 1$, we use the convention that $f_1(K) = 1$.

3. Find the longest binary string $B^{(l)} = \{b_1, \ldots, b_l\}$ for which $\mathcal{I}_{norm}(y^{(m+1)}) \subset [\sum_{i=1}^{l} b_i 2^{-i}, \sum_{i=1}^{l} b_i 2^{-i} + 2^{-l})$. Possibly, $B^{(l)} = \emptyset$, $l = 0$.

4. Emit the binary string $B^{(l)}$ as output.

5. Renormalize by

$$
\begin{align}
f_{norm}(y^{(m+1)}) &= 2^l f_{norm}(y^{(m+1)}) - \lfloor 2^l f_{norm}(y^{(m+1)}) \rfloor \\
p_{norm}(y^{(m+1)}) &= 2^l p_{norm}(y^{(m+1)})
\end{align}
$$

6. Increment m and goto step 1.

The purpose of step 5 is to eliminate the more significant binary digits that are no longer needed in the encoding and decoding and to add less significant digits that increase the precision as the intervals shrink. Note that renormalization is achieved with no additional round-off errors. We observe that if $b^{(n)} = b_1 b_2 \ldots b_n$ is the binary string emitted by the encoder before y_{m+1} enters the encoder, then the normalized interval $\mathcal{I}_{norm}(y^{(m+1)})$ corresponds to the actual interval, with round-off but no renormalization,

$$
\mathcal{I}(y^{(m+1)}) = [\tilde{b}^{(n)} + 2^{-n} f_{norm}(y^{(m+1)}), \, \tilde{b}^{(n)} + 2^{-n} e_{norm}(y^{(m+1)}))
$$

where $\tilde{b}^{(n)} = \sum_{i=1}^{n} b_i 2^{-i}$.

To obtain insights into the effect of the round-off errors, we consider the example of a ternary equiprobable source. First we examine the behavior of the encoder when the input consists of a long string of repetitions of the symbol 1. Without round-off errors, $\mathcal{I}_{norm}(y^{(1)}) = [\frac{1}{3}, \frac{2}{3})$, $\mathcal{I}_{norm}(y^{(2)}) = [\frac{4}{9}, \frac{5}{9})$, and in general, $\mathcal{I}_{norm}(y^{(m)}) = [\frac{1-3^{-m}}{2}, \frac{1+3^{m}}{2})$. Thus, for this string, $\mathcal{I}_{norm}(y^{(m)})$ continues to straddle the point $\frac{1}{2}$ and no binary digits are emitted by the encoder. Because arithmetic is performed with only M binary digits of accuracy, the left and right ends of these intervals must each be multiples of 2^{-M} and also must get close to $\frac{1}{2}$. For example, if the rounded off version of $\mathcal{I}(y^{(m)})$ is $[\frac{1}{2} - 2^{-M}, \frac{1}{2} + 2^{-M})$, then no binary digit can be emitted, and since the length of $\mathcal{I}(y^{(m)})$ is equal to $2 \cdot 2^{-M}$, it is impossible to split the interval into three distinct intervals to account for all possibilities of y_{m+1}. We will prevent this problem by changing the endpoints of certain intervals. The first revision is applicable for source intervals $\mathcal{I}_{norm}(y^{(m+1)})$ that straddle the point $\frac{1}{2}$ and have the property that the left endpoint is close to $\frac{1}{2}$. To facilitate renormalization, we move the left endpoint of this interval to $\frac{1}{2}$. This also allows a binary digit to be emitted. Let L be the largest integer for which $2^{-L} \geq \max\left(\frac{2^{-M}}{p_{min}}, \frac{2^{-M}}{2^{-C_{cmax}}}\right)$. We replace (20) with the following:

If $\frac{1}{2} - 2^{-L} \leq f_{norm}(y^{(m)}) + f_1(y_{m+1}) \cdot p_{norm}(y^{(m)}) < \frac{1}{2}$
and $f_{norm}(y^{(m)}) + f_1(y_{m+1} + 1) \cdot p_{norm}(y^{(m)}) > \frac{1}{2}$,

$$\text{then } f_{norm}(y^{(m+1)}) \;=\; \frac{1}{2} \tag{24}$$

$$\text{else } f_{norm}(y^{(m+1)}) \;=\; f_{norm}(y^{(m)}) + f_1(y_{m+1}) \cdot p_{norm}(y^{(m)}) \tag{25}$$

Since we are interested in producing a one-to-one onto mapping from the set of source sequences to the set of binary sequences, we must compensate for the truncation of any source string interval $\mathcal{I}_{norm}(\sigma)$. Here, we lengthen the interval of the string lexicographically preceding σ by relocating the right endpoint for that string's interval to $\frac{1}{2}$. We bring this about by changing (21) to:

If $\frac{1}{2} - 2^{-L} \leq f_{norm}(y^{(m)}) + f_1(y_{m+1} + 1) \cdot p_{norm}(y^{(m)}) < \frac{1}{2}$
and $f_{norm}(y^{(m)}) + f_1(y_{m+1} + 2) \cdot p_{norm}(y^{(m)}) > \frac{1}{2}$,

$$\text{then } e_{norm}(y^{(m+1)}) \;=\; \frac{1}{2} \tag{26}$$

$$\text{else } e_{norm}(y^{(m+1)}) \;=\; f_{norm}(y^{(m)}) + f_1(y_{m+1} + 1) \cdot p_{norm}(y^{(m)}) \tag{27}$$

Note that if the first condition above is satisfied, then $y_{m+1} + 2 \leq K$. Figure 5 illustrates the alterations. We selected L to ensure that the smallest interval that can straddle the point $\frac{1}{2}$ has length at least $\frac{2^{-M}}{p_{min}}$ to guarantee that the next source symbol to enter the encoder will receive a non-zero interval size without any unusual round-off rules. When we discuss the inner coder, it will become clear why we also insist on having $2^{-L} \geq \frac{2^{-M}}{2^{-C_{cmax}}}$. As a result of the modifications to (20) and (21), the

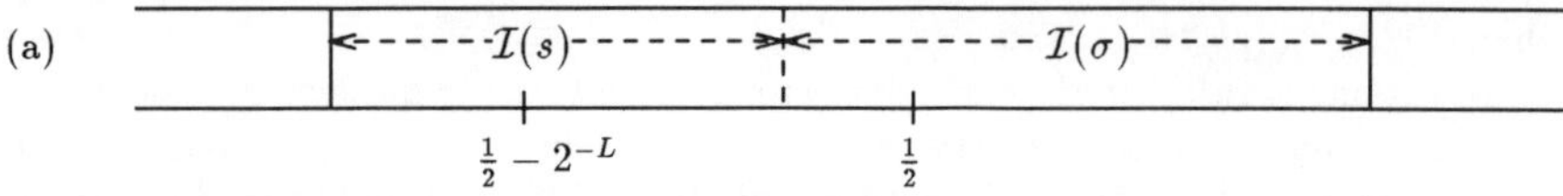

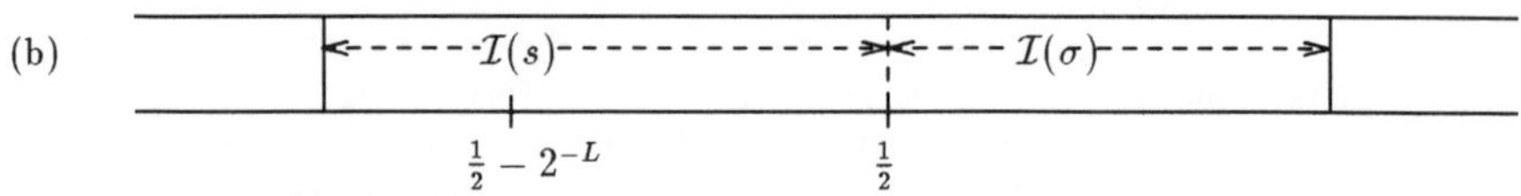

Figure 5:

Figure 5 illustrates the modification of adjoining intervals $\mathcal{I}(s)$ and $\mathcal{I}(\sigma)$ when $\mathcal{I}(\sigma)$ is an interval which straddles the point $\frac{1}{2}$ and has its left endpoint between $\frac{1}{2} - 2^{-L}$ and $\frac{1}{2}$. The left endpoint of $\mathcal{I}(s)$ is arbitrary.

binary output does not consist of digits that are equiprobably 0 or 1; however, for large M, it is fairly accurate to model the binary sequence in this way.

The above modifications are but one of many possible ways to handle the rarely occurring problem of normalized intervals that continue to straddle the point $\frac{1}{2}$. The only requirement in treating this issue is that the mapping from source sequences to binary sequences must be one-to-one onto.

We observe that when source string intervals are straddling the interval $[\frac{1}{2} - 2^{-L}, \frac{1}{2}]$, we experience some bounded delay in emitting binary digits and renormalizing. In all of the implementation schemes described in Langdon (1984), binary digits are emitted every time a source symbol is read in; however, it is often necessary to go back and correct the output.

We next consider the outer decoder. The decoder decodes one source symbol at a time and maintains both a queue of incoming binary digits and a replica of the encoder. Initially, $m = 1$ and the queue is empty. The decoder, in attempting to decode y_m, uses the same rules as the encoder to calculate $f_{norm}(y^{(m)})$ and $p_{norm}(y^{(m)})$ for all choices of y_m given $y^{(m-1)}$. As new binary digits enter the queue, we can consider the queued letters as a normalized binary fraction of j significant bits, where j is the queue length. When the interval corresponding to this fraction lies within one of the K normalized intervals calculated above, the decoder decodes y_m, renormalizes f_{norm} and p_{norm} by the encoder rules, and deletes the corresponding binary digits from the front of the queue. It then increments m and repeats the above procedure.

We note that when y_m enters the encoder, the interval end points are calculated to M binary digits of accuracy. Therefore, after the encoder emits M binary digits, the resulting interval must have size 2^{-M} and thus y_m is decodable at this point, if not before. Hence, decoding always occurs with at most M binary digits in the queue.

Therefore, by increasing M, we trade off smaller maximum delays between encoding and decoding for additional efficiency in terms of smaller round-off errors.

We now turn to the inner arithmetic coder which maps strings of binary digits into strings of channel letters. This coder functions independently of the outer coder. As we mentioned earlier, Guazzo associated a probability 2^{-Cc_i} with each channel letter i and then mapped channel strings into subintervals of the unit interval in exactly the same way that source strings are mapped into subintervals. We can again capitalize on that idea here. We saw that the outer coder created a one-to-one onto mapping of source sequences to binary sequences. We can use the identical technique to produce a one-to-one onto mapping of channel sequences to binary sequences by using the set of probabilities $\{2^{-Cc_{max}},\ldots,2^{-Cc_{N-1}}\}$ instead of $\{p_0,\ldots,p_{K-1}\}$. Since the inner encoder maps arbitrary binary strings into channel letters, its analogue in the outer coder is the outer decoder, which maps binary strings into strings of source symbols. The one-to-one onto nature of the encoding guarantees that the mapping of any binary string into a string of source symbols or channel letters is well-defined. Similarly, the counterpart of the inner decoder in the outer coder is the outer encoder. This duality between the inner and outer coders is the reason that we had selected L to satisfy $2^{-L} \geq \max\left(\frac{2^{-M}}{p_{min}}, \frac{2^{-M}}{2^{-Cc_{max}}}\right)$.

The previous analysis and implementation have been generalized to channels with finite-state letter costs. We refer the reader to Savari (1991) for the details. Finally, we note that there are no new complications in dealing with sources with memory or adaptive sources. In this case, the encoder and the replica of the encoder at the decoder use $P(y_m \mid y^{(m-1)})$ in place of p_m. We assume that none of these probabilities are smaller than some p_{min}.

Bibliography

Gallager, R. G. (1991) Class Notes for 6.441

Guazzo, M. (1980) "A general minimum-redundancy source-coding algorithm," *I.E.E.E. Trans. Inform. Theory* IT-26, 15-25

Langdon, G. G. (1984) "An introduction to arithmetic coding," *I.B.M. J. Res. Develop.* 28, 135-149

Rissanen, J. and G. G. Langdon, Jr. (1979) "Arithmetic coding," *I.B.M. J. Res. Develop.* 23, 149-162

Savari, S. A. (1991) "Source coding for channels with finite-state letter costs," M.S. thesis, Dept. of E.E.C.S., M.I.T., Cambridge, MA

Shannon, C. E. (1948) "A mathematical theory of communication," *Bell System Tech. J.* 27, 379-423, 623-656

ON THE CODING DELAY OF A GENERAL CODER

Marcelo J. Weinberger †, Abraham Lempel † † , and Jacob Ziv †

Technion - Israel Institute of Technology

Haifa 32000, Israel

Abstract. We propose a general model for a sequential coder, and investigate the associated coding delay. This model is employed to derive lower and upper bounds on the delay associated with commonly used encoders and decoders for noiseless data compression.

---

† Department of Electrical Engineering, Technion - Israel Institute of Technology.
† † Department of Computer Science, Technion - Israel Institute of Technology.

　　　　　　　　　　　　　　　

1. INTRODUCTION

This paper discusses the concept of coding delay of a general coder. The coding delay of a data compression system has been treated extensively [1,2] but, to the best of our knowledge, no general definitions are available. Instead, the notion of delay is adapted to the specific context of each application. The treatment of delay in [1] is in terms of a code, i.e., the combination of both encoder and decoder, rather than the delay of each coder as a separate entity. In addition, the codes treated in [1] are restricted to have a fixed, predetermined, set of input words, and coding delay is defined as the average length of the input words. This definition suggests a model where the encoder emits a codeword instantaneously after receiving a complete input word, and a decoder receives this codeword at the same time. Thus, the overall delay of the code can be interpreted as the (average) number of input symbols processed by the encoder, beginning with the first symbol of an input word and ending when that symbol is recovered by the decoder. In [2], there is no restriction on the set of codes (except for being finite-state and uniquely decipherable), but the definition of delay still involves the entire encoding/decoding process.

In this paper, we propose a general model for a sequential coder and its associated coding delay. We present lower and upper bounds on the delay associated with commonly used encoders and decoders for noiseless data compression. Roughly speaking, coding delay is defined as the maximum over all sequences up to a given length, of the elapsed time between the last input and the last output. It is shown that, with respect to the proposed model, this time is closely related to the length of the buffer that must be installed at the output of the coder in order to prevent any loss of information. Although the question of buffer length has been considered in the past [3,4], the approach proposed here is quite different.

In Section 2 we present the basic definitions (sequential coder, coding delay) of the model, obtain some preliminary results regarding the delay of a general coder, and show how this concept relates to buffer length. In Section 3, lower and upper bounds on the delay of the L-Z encoder [5] are presented, while in Section 4, the delay of a source encoder under a given compression ratio constraint is considered. In Section 5 we deal with the delay associated with noiseless data compression decoders.

2. DEFINITIONS AND PRELIMINARIES

Given discrete alphabets A and B of α and β letters, let A^* and B^* denote the sets of all finite sequences over the respective alphabets, including the null string λ. We denote by z_i^j the segment $z_i, z_{i+1}, \cdots, z_j$ of a sequence z in A^* or B^*, with $z_i^j \triangleq \lambda$ whenever $j < i$. Assume $\alpha = 2^k$ and $\beta = 2^l$, where k and l are positive integers. Let $

denote an end-of-sequence symbol appended to every sequence in A^* and define $\hat{A} \triangleq A \cup \{ \$ \}$. The convenience of using the additional symbol $\$$ will become clear below.

A function $C(\,\cdot\,,\,\cdot\,)$ from $A^* \times \hat{A}$ to B^* is called a sequential coder. For a sequence $x_1^n = x_1, x_2, \cdots , x_n$ in A^*, the coded image $C(x_1^n\$)$ of $x_1^n\$$ under C is defined as the sequence y_1^{n+1}, where $y_i \triangleq C(x_1^{i-1}, x_i)$, $1 \le i \le n$, and $y_{n+1} \triangleq C(x_1^n, \$)$. Note that $x_i \ne \$$ for $1 \le i \le n$ and that $C(x_1^n\$)$ is not necessarily a prefix of $C(x_1^{n+1}\$)$. The coder C is said to be uniquely decipherable (UD) if for every pair $x, z \in A^*, x \ne z$ implies $C(x\$) \ne C(z\$)$.

Let a prefix x_1^i of $x\$, x \in A^*$, be fed into a UD coder C, starting at time $t=1$ and ending at time $t(x,i)$. Let τ be the time at which the coder completes to output the last $y_j \ne \lambda$, $j \le i$, and let $T(y,i) = \max \{t(x,i), \tau\}$. The delay $d_C(x_1^i)$ introduced by the coder for the prefix x_1^i is defined as

$$d_C(x_1^i) \triangleq T(y,i) - t(x,i) \ .$$

The *maximal delay* $D_C(n)$ *of order* n introduced by the coder is defined as

$$D_C(n) \triangleq \max_{\substack{x_1^i \in A^i \\ 0 < i \le n}} d_C(x_1^i\$) \ .$$

Our model for the coder is a synchronous machine that can process one α-ary symbol, i.e., an input of k parallel bits, and output one β-ary symbol, consisting of l parallel bits, per unit of time. Now, the length of $y_i \in B^*$ can be more than one symbol, and we do not allow any loss of information. Consequently, the coder must include enough memory, in the form of a β-ary FIFO buffer so it can process any sequence up to a given length n, without overflow. The shortest feasible length of such a buffer will be denoted by $B(n)$. Notice that every coding scheme requires $B(n) \ge 1$.

We assume that the input symbols arrive sequentially, without interruptions. Thus, $t(x,i) = i$. We further assume that every computation is completed within one clock cycle. Hence, every $y_i \ne \lambda$, is fully in the buffer at time $i+1$. Let $z_i \in B \cup \{\lambda\}$ denote the buffer output at time i. Then, $z_i = \lambda$ if and only if the buffer is empty at time i. Moreover, with an initially empty buffer, $z_1 = \lambda$ while, for $i > 1$, $z_i = \lambda$ if and only if $T(y, i-1) = i-1$. Let $N(x,i)$ denote the number of null buffer outputs during the time interval $[1,i]$. We have

$$T(y,i) = L(y_1^i) + N(x,i) \ ,$$

where $L(y_1^i) \triangleq \sum_{j=1}^{i} length\,(y_j)$. It follows that

$$d_C(x_1^i) = L(y_1^i) + N(x,i) - i \ . \tag{1}$$

Now, let $B(x,i)$ denote the queue length of the buffer at time i (note that at this time z_i still resides in the buffer and, therefore, is part of the queue). The above assumptions imply

$$T(y,i) = i + B(x,i+1) \ , \ i \geq 1 \ ,$$

or, equivalently,

$$d_C(x_1^i) = B(x,i+1), \ i \geq 1 \ .$$

Lemma 1: $D_C(n) \leq B(n) \leq D_C(n) + 1.$

Lemma 1 implies the following recursive formula for the delay.

Lemma 2: The delay $d_C(x_1^i)$ for $x_1^i \in A^*\hat{A}$ satisfies the recursion

$$d_C(x_1^1) = length(y_1)$$
$$d_C(x_1^i) = length(y_i) + [d_C(x_1^{i-1}) \ominus 1] \ , \ i > 1 \ , \tag{2}$$

where $a \ominus b \triangleq \max(0, a-b)$.

Corollary: If $y_j = \lambda$ for $1 \leq m < j < i$, then

$$d_C(x_1^i) = length(y_i) + [d_C(x_1^m) \ominus (i-m)] \ . \tag{3}$$

Example: Block encoder

Let b denote the block length, and assume that $b \mid n$, and that we only consider input sequences where $ appears after an integer number of blocks. Let l_i denote the number of β-ary symbols in the i-th codeword (it is assumed that l divides the number of bits in every codeword). First, assume that the encoder cannot output any part of a codeword until the corresponding input block has been completely received. By the corollary to Lemma 2, the delay d_E introduced by the encoder satisfies

$$d_E(x_1^{bi}) = l_i + [d_E(x_1^{b(i-1)}) \ominus b] \ , \ 1 \leq i \leq \frac{n}{b} \ , \tag{4}$$

where $d_E(\lambda) \triangleq 0$. Let r denote the length of the longest codeword. By (4), the maximal delay $D_E(n)$ of order n introduced by the encoder is achieved when $l_i = r$ for all i, $1 \leq i \leq \frac{n}{b}$. Solving the recursion (4), and accounting for the $ symbol in the definition of $D_E(n)$, we obtain

$$D_E(n) = (\frac{n}{b} - 1)(r \ominus b) + r - 1 \ . \tag{5}$$

Note that unique decipherability implies $lr \geq bk$. Thus, $k \geq l$ guarantees $r \geq b$.

Now, if we consider an encoder that can begin the output of a codeword before receiving all the corresponding input block, it can be readily seen that, by (1), the economy is inconsequential.

3. THE MAXIMAL DELAY FOR THE L-Z ENCODER

In this section we present lower and upper bounds on the maximal delay $D_{LZ}(n)$ of order n introduced by the L-Z encoder (Theorem 1 below). To simplify the computations, we assume $\alpha=\beta=2$ (i.e., $k=l=1$), but the results can be easily extended to any value of k and l. Let u denote the infinite binary sequence formed by all distinct words of length one, followed by all distinct words of length two, and so forth, with words of the same length appearing, say, in lexicographic order. Let u_1^n denote the sequence formed by the first n symbols of u.

Theorem 1: For every $\varepsilon > 0$ and for sufficiently large n we have

$$\frac{2n}{\log n} \leq d_{LZ}(u_1^n \$) \leq D_{LZ}(n) \leq \frac{(3 + \varepsilon) \cdot n}{\log n} \ .$$

The sequence u used to lower-bound the maximal delay is not the worst case. For a given n, consider the sequence v_1^n obtained by reordering the phrases of u_1^n so that, for every point in the new order, the phrase appearing in that point is preceded by all its prefixes and is the longest phrase with the said property (in case of a tie, apply a lexicographic ordering). For example, with $p=3$ and $\Delta_p = 0$,

$$v_1^{34} = 0\,,\,00\,,\,000\,,\,001\,,\,01\,,\,010\,,\,011\,,\,1\,,\,10\,,\,100\,,\,101\,,\,11\,,\,110\,,\,111\ .$$

Clearly, the same code length $L(n)$ corresponds to v_1^n and to u_1^n. By the corollary to Lemma 2 and the structure of the sequence v, it can be shown that the number $N(v,n)$ of null buffer outputs satisfies

$$N(v,n) > \frac{n}{8 \log n} \tag{6}$$

which, by (1), implies

$$D_{LZ}(n) > \frac{(2+\frac{1}{8}) \cdot n}{\log n} \; ,$$

thus obtaining a lower bound tighter than that of Theorem 1. Moreover, there exist infinitely many values of n for which the multiplying constant in (6) is $\frac{4}{17}$, so the multiplying constant in the upper bound of Theorem 1 cannot be reduced below $2 + \frac{4}{17}$.

4. THE DELAY OF A SOURCE ENCODER UNDER A GIVEN COMPRESSION RATIO CONSTRAINT

In this section we restrict our discussion to source encoders. The definition of maximal delay stated in Section 2 implies a maximization over all possible input sequences up to a given length n. When we deal with source encoders, we are interested in "compressible" sequences, i.e., sequences x_1^n for which the normalized compression ratio $R(x_1^n)$ achieved by the encoder satisfies

$$R(x_1^n) \triangleq \frac{l \cdot L(y_1^{n+1})}{nk} \leq \rho \; ,$$

where ρ is a given constant satisfying $0 < \rho < 1$. (Note that, in this context, the concept of compressibility refers to the pair {sequence, encoder}, and not only to the sequence as in the original definition of [5]). Roughly speaking, the concept of coding delay under a compression ratio constraint is obtained as the result of maximizing the coding delay over the prefixes of sequences x_1^n for which $R(x_1^n)$ is approximately ρ. We present lower and upper bounds on this quantity for block and L-Z encoders. Note that this constraint is a function of both ρ and the specific encoder. In fact, a more interesting question in this context is one where the maximum delay of an individual sequence is a function of the sequence only, just as its compressibility. However, such formulation is outside the scope of this work.

Let ρ and $\Delta\rho$ denote given constants, with $0 \leq \rho - \Delta\rho < \rho$ (although typically $\rho < 1$, we do not require this condition), and define the range $\rho_- \triangleq [\rho - \Delta\rho, \rho]$. Let E denote a source encoder. The ρ-*maximal delay* $D_E(n, \rho_-)$ *of order* n introduced by E is defined as

$$D_E(n, \rho_-) \triangleq \max_{x_1^n \in S(n, \rho_-)} \max_{0 < i \leq n} d_E(x_1^i \$) \; ,$$

where $S(n, \rho_-) \triangleq \left\{ x_1^n \in A^n : \frac{(\rho - \Delta\rho)nk}{l} \leq L(y_1^{n+1}) \leq \rho\frac{nk}{l} \right\}$.

4.1. Block Encoder

As in Section 2, let b denote the block length, and assume $b \mid n$. We further assume that $D_E(n,\rho_-)$ is computed over values of i for which $b \mid i$. Let r and s denote the length (i.e., the number of β-ary symbols) of the longest and the shortest codewords, respectively. We can assume $\dfrac{lr}{kb} \geq \rho \geq \dfrac{ls}{kb}$, for if $\rho > \dfrac{lr}{kb}$ then either $S(n,\rho_-)$ is empty (in case $\rho - \Delta\rho > \dfrac{lr}{kb}$), or $D_E(n,\rho_-) = D_E(n)$, while if $\rho < \dfrac{ls}{kb}$ then $S(n,\rho_-)$ is empty. First, we consider encoders that cannot output any part of a codeword until the corresponding input block has been completely received. We can assume $s < b < r$, for otherwise the problem is trivial (in case $k \geq l$ and $s \neq r$, unique decipherability requires $b < r$).

Theorem 2: If $s < b < r$ then, for sufficiently large n, the ρ-maximal delay of order n introduced by a block encoder E satisfies

$$[(nF + b)\ominus r] + b - 1 \leq D_E(n,\rho_-) \leq nF + b - 1 \quad ,$$

where $F \triangleq \dfrac{(r-b)(\rho kb - ls)}{lb(r-s)} \geq 0.$

Notes:

1) If $bl(r-s)$ divides $lr - \rho kb$, then the upper bound holds with equality. If $F \neq 0$, we have $D_E(n,\rho_-) = n(F + O(n^{-1}))$.

2) If we consider an encoder E' that can begin the output of a codeword before receiving all of the corresponding input block, one can readily show, using an argument similar to that employed in Section 2, that $D_{E'}(n,\rho_-)$ and $D_E(n,\rho_-)$ differ by not more than a constant.

4.2. L-Z Encoder

As in Section 3, we assume $\alpha=\beta=2$ (i.e., $k=l=1$). Let

Theorem 3: For every $\varepsilon>0$, for sufficiently large n, and every $\rho>0$, the ρ-maximal delay $D_{LZ}(n,\rho_-)$ of order n introduced by the L-Z encoder satisfies

$$\frac{(2-\varepsilon)\cdot\rho n}{\log n} \leq D_{LZ}(n,\rho_-) \leq \frac{(3+\varepsilon)\cdot\rho n}{\log n} \quad .$$

The lower bound of Theorem 3 is obtained for a sequence formed by an all-zero segment, followed by a "counting" sequence from which the all-zero phrases have been deleted, with the length of each segment being such that the compression ratio is in the range ρ_- .

5. DECODING DELAY

5.1. The Maximal Delay

In this section we present bounds on the delay associated with the decoders for the data compression algorithms considered in the previous sections. The notation, definitions, and assumptions stated in Section 2 for a general coder remain in force. In particular, we assume that the decoder input symbols arrive sequentially, without interruptions. This is equivalent to the assumption that the beginning of decoding lags behind the beginning of encoding by at least the incurred encoding delay. Note that, with the definitions of Section 2, the delay of a decoder is determined with respect to the length n of the coded sequence, rather than that of the original sequence. Note also that adherence to the notation of Section 2 for alphabets and sequences, requires an obvious adjustment due to the interchange of encoder/decoder roles: for instance, now the input alphabet A denotes the alphabet of the compressed image, and the output alphabet B stands for the source alphabet. We assume that the end-of-sequence symbol $\$$ appears only at the end of the complete coded image of some β-ary sequence.

For the block decoder, it is easy to see that under the assumption $s \mid n$, the maximal delay $D_D(n)$ of order n is achieved when the encoded input is a concatenation of n/s codewords of length s. Proceeding as with the block encoder, we obtain

$$D_D(n) = (\frac{n}{s} - 1)(b \ominus s) + b - 1 .$$

If we require completeness for the α-ary tree defining the code, then $lb \geq ks$. Thus, $k \geq l$ guarantees $b \geq s$.

As for the L-Z decoder, we assume $\alpha = \beta = 2$ (i.e., $k=l=1$). The length n of the input (encoded) sequence must equal $Z(c) \overset{\Delta}{=} c + \sum_{j=1}^{c} \lceil \log j \rceil$, where c denotes the number of phrases in the incremental parsing of the decoded sequence. Let b_i denote the length of the i-th phrase in the decoded sequence. Again, by the corollary to Lemma 2, the delay d_{LZD} introduced by the decoder satisfies

$$d_{LZD}(x_1^{Z(i)}) = b_i + [d_{LZD}(x_1^{Z(i-1)}) \ominus (1 + \lceil \log i \rceil)] , \ 1 \leq i \leq c ,$$

where $d_{LZD}(\lambda) \overset{\Delta}{=} 0$. Since $b_i \leq i$, it can be readily seen that the maximal delay $D_{LZD}(n)$ is achieved when $b_i = i$ for all i, $1 \leq Z(i) \leq n$, namely, when the decoded sequence is the all-zero (or the all-one) sequence of length $\dfrac{c(c+1)}{2}$. Assuming $c \geq 3$ (i.e., $n \geq 6$) and solving the recursion, we obtain

$$d_{LZD}(x_1^n) = \sum_{i=4}^{c} i - \sum_{i=4}^{c} (1 + \lceil \log i \rceil) + d_{LZD}(x_1^{m(3)}) = \frac{c(c+1)}{2} - n + 3 \ ,$$

implying

$$D_{LZD}(n) = \frac{c(c+1)}{2} - n + 2 \ .$$

Theorem 4 below states tight lower and upper bounds on $D_{LZD}(n)$ as a function of n only.

Theorem 4: For every $\varepsilon > 0$ and for sufficiently large n, the maximal delay $D_{LZD}(n)$ of order n introduced by the L-Z decoder satisfies,

$$\frac{(1-\varepsilon) \cdot n^2}{2 \log^2 n} < D_{LZD}(n) < \frac{(1+\varepsilon) \cdot n^2}{2 \log^2 n} \ .$$

5.2 The Delay Under a Given Compression Ratio Constraint

By Section 5.1, we see that for both decoders the maximal delay is achieved for the coded images of the most compressible sequences. With the L-Z algorithm, the asymptotic compressibility of this sequence is zero. Such cases are of minor importance so, as in Section 4, we consider the concept of decoding delay under a compression ratio constraint. Let ρ and $\Delta\rho$ denote given positive constants, with $\rho < 1$, and define the range $\rho_+ \triangleq [\rho, \rho + \Delta\rho]$. Let D denote a source decoder. The ρ-*maximal delay* $D_D(n, \rho_+)$ *of order* n introduced by D is defined as

$$D_D(n, \rho_+) \triangleq \max_{\substack{x_1^n \in S'(n, \rho_+)}} \max_{\substack{0 < i \leq n \\ x_1^i \in C(x, i)}} d_D(x_1^i \$) \ ,$$

where $C(x, i)$ is the set containing all the prefixes of x_1^n that are the coded image of some β-ary sequence under C, and where

$$S'(n, \rho_+) \triangleq \left\{ x_1^n \in C(x, i) : \ \frac{nk}{(\rho + \Delta\rho)l} \leq L(y_1^{n+1}) \leq \frac{nk}{\rho l} \right\} \ . \text{ I.e., we consider only those}$$

input (coded) sequences of length n that are images of a β-ary (source) sequence whose compression ratio is in the range ρ_+, and all their prefixes that are the coded image of some source sequence.

For the block decoder, we can assume $s < b < r$ and $kr \geq \rho lb > ks$ for otherwise, as in Section 4, the problem is trivial. We further assume that there exists a codeword of length $s+1$: this assumption ensures that the sequence attaining the lower bound in Theorem 5 below exists for every value of n.

Theorem 5: If $s < b < r$ then, for sufficiently large n, the ρ-maximal delay of order n introduced by a block decoder D satisfies

$$[nF'\ominus(\frac{kb\,(r-s)}{\rho lb-ks}+r)]+b-1\le D_D\,(n,\rho_+)\le nF'+b-1 \quad,$$

where $F'\triangleq\dfrac{(b-s)\,(kr-\rho lb)}{\rho lb\,(r-s)}\ge 0.$

Note that if $F'\ne 0$, then Theorem 5 implies $D_D\,(n,\rho)=n\,[F'+O\,(n^{-1})]$.

As for the L-Z decoder we assume, again, $\alpha=\beta=2$ and $0<\rho<1$.

Theorem 6: For every $\varepsilon>0$ and for sufficiently large n, the ρ-maximal delay $D_{LZD}\,(n,\rho_+)$ of order n introduced by the L-Z decoder satisfies

$$(\frac{1}{\rho}-1)\cdot n\le D_{LZD}\,(n,\rho_+)<(\frac{1}{\rho}-1+\varepsilon)\cdot n \quad.$$

The lower bound of Theorem 6 is obtained for a sequence formed by two segments: first, the coded image of a "counting" sequence, and then the coded image of an all-zero segment, with the length of each segment being such that the compression ratio is in the range ρ_+ .

Note that while the upper bound applies to the delay of every sequence in $S'(n,\rho_+)$, the lower bound may apply only to a subset of sequences in this set. However, by (1), we have $d_{LZD}\,(x_1^n\$)\ge(\dfrac{1}{\rho+\Delta\rho}-1)\cdot n$ for *every* sequence x_1^n in the set.

References

[1] R.E. Krichevsky and V.K. Trofimov, "The performance of Universal Encoding", IEEE Trans. Infor. Theory, vol. IT-27, pp. 199-207, March 1981.

[2] S. Even, "On information Lossless Automata of Finite Order", IEEE Trans. Electronic Computers, vol. EC-14, pp. 561-569, August 1965.

[3] A.D. Wyner, "On the Probability of Buffer Overflow under an Arbitrary Bounded Input-Output Distribution", SIAM J. Appl. Math., vol. 27, pp. 544-570, December 1974.

[4] N. Merhav, "Universal Coding with Minimum Probability of Codeword Length Overflow", IEEE Trans. Infor. Theory, vol. IT-37, pp. 556-563, May 1991.

[5] A. Lempel and J. Ziv, "Compression of Individual Sequences via Variable Rate Coding", IEEE Trans. Infor. Theory, vol. IT-24, pp. 530-536, September 1978.

[6] F. Jelinek, Probabilistic Information Theory, New York: McGraw-Hill, 1968.

On Binary Alphabetical Codes

Dafna Sheinwald

IBM Scientific Center

Technion City, Haifa 32000, Israel

dafna@haifasc3.vnet.ibm.com

Abstract

Binary alphabetical codes, which are prefix free, fixed-to-variable binary codes for discrete memoryless sources, in which the lexicographic order of the codewords agrees with the alphabet order of the respective source letters, are studied. A necessary and sufficient condition on the sequence of codeword lengths of any such code is proved. A new upper bounds on the redundancy of alphabetical codes relative to the optimal prefix free, fixed-to-variable codes – the Huffman codes – is proved. An adaptation of the Ziv-Lempel algorithm making it lexicographic order preserving, without any additional redundancy, is presented.

1 Introduction

Large amounts of data are usually archived in a compressed form. A search in a huge archive for a particular key value k involves the decompression of every key to be compared with k. However, if a coding scheme is used which preserves the lexicographic order of its inputs then the compressed archive can undergo a search for the compressed form of k. No decoding is needed.

In the class of fixed-to-variable codes for discrete memoryless sources, the redundancy of the Huffman codes, relative to the source entropy, is minimal [2, 6]. It lies between zero and one, depending on the source statistics. New tight bounds on that redundancy were recently proved by Capocelli and De Santis [1]. Huffman codes are not necessarily alphabetical. Preservation of lexicographic order of inputs usually has its price in the form of additional redundancy. Gilbert and Moore [4] introduced in 1959 an algorithm, linear in the size s of the source alphabet, for producing alphabetical codes whose redundancy, relative to the source entropy, lies between one and two. To a letter a of probability p, they assign a codeword of length $m + 1$ bits, where m is the integer satisfying $2^{-m} \leq p < 2^{1-m}$. Shannon code, which is not alphabetical, assigns to a a codeword of length m.

Algorithms for generating optimal binary prefix free alphabetical codes are known. These are the algorithms for producing optimal binary search trees [8]. One of them is the dynamic programming algorithm of time complexity $O(s^3)$ which was also introduced by Gilbert and Moore in [4]. The algorithm by Hu and Tucker [5], of time complexity $O(s \log(s))$, is another example. The redundancy of optimal alphabetical codes relative to the source entropy has not been studied as extensively as that of Huffman codes. Gilbert and Moore [4] did not prove a better upper bound than 2, which is obtained by their linear algorithm, for the optimal codes produced by their dynamic programming algorithm.

Recently, Nakatsu [10] studied the redundancy of alphabetical codes relative to Huffman code performance for a given source. He defined the notion of "minimal point", which is a source letter whose Huffman codeword length is smaller than that of its neighbors in the alphabet order of the source letters, and claimed the sum of probabilities of the minimal points to be an upper bound on the redundancy of an optimal alphabetical code relative to the expected code length of the Huffman code. While Gilbert and Moore code lengthens all codewords by one bit, relative to Shannon code, Nakatsu code lengthens by one bit the codewords of minimal points only, relative to Huffman code. Nakatsu also designed a measure on integer sequences, and proved that an alphabetical binary code exists with a given sequence of codeword lengths if and only if the measure on that sequence is less than 1.

In this paper we study the redundancy of binary alphabetical codes in the spirit of [10]. We develop a new measure on integer sequences, and prove that an alphabetical binary code exists with a given sequence of codeword lengths if and only if our measure on that sequence does not exceed 1. Our measure allows us to identify an error in the claim of [10], and improve on it, assuming it is not dramatically changed if corrected. Additionally, we show that the Kawabata-Yamamoto [7] version of the Ziv-Lempel [11] compression algorithm preserves lexicographic order in no cost of additional redundancy.

2 Depth of Leaves of Binary Trees

Given a number x, "position i of x" refers in this paper to the i-th position right of the decimal point in the binary representation of x. For example, $x = 1/4$ has '0' in its first position and '1' in the second.

For a binary number x and a positive integer i, let $\tau(x, i)$ denote the number obtained from x by truncating the bits in positions $i + 1$ and further right. Formally, $\tau(x, i) = \lfloor x \cdot 2^i \rfloor / 2^i$. Define $t(x, i)$ to be x if $\tau(x, i) = x$, and $\tau(x, i) + 2^{-i}$ otherwise. Formally, $t(x, i) = \tau(x, i) + \lceil x - \tau(x, i) \rceil / 2^i$. The following property is readily verified.

Property 1 *If $a < b$ then $t(a, i) \le t(b, i)$ for any positive integer i.*

Given a sequence $N = n_1, n_2, \ldots, n_s$ of positive integers, define $\varphi(n_1) = 2^{-n_1}$, and for $1 < i \le s$, $\varphi(n_i) = t(\varphi(n_{i-1}), n_i) + 2^{-n_i}$. Also define $\varphi(N) = \varphi(n_s)$.

Property 2 *Given a sequence $N = n_1, n_2, \ldots, n_s$ of positive integers and an index $1 \le j < s$ satisfying both conditions:* **C1:** *$\varphi(n_{j-1})$ [1] does not include any '1' bits in the n_j-th position and further right, that is, $\tau(\varphi(n_{j-1}), n_j - 1) = \varphi(n_{j-1})$, and* **C2:** *$n_j > n_{j+1}$. Then, the sequence $N' = n_1', n_2', \ldots, n_s'$ obtained from N by decrementing n_j, i.e., $n_i' = n_i$ for $i \ne j$ and $n_j' = n_j - 1$, satisfies $\varphi(N') = \varphi(N)$.*

Proof: By conditions C1 and C2,

$$\varphi(n_{j+1}) = \tau(\varphi(n_{j-1}), n_{j+1}) + 2^{-n_{j+1}} + 2^{-n_{j+1}} \tag{1}$$

and $\varphi(n_j') = \varphi(n_{j-1}') + 2^{-n_j'}$. The binary representation of $\varphi(n_j')$ is thus obtained from the binary representation of $\varphi(n_{j-1}')$ by changing to '0' all (possibly none) consecutive '1' bits in positions n_j' and left, and changing to '1' the '0' bit occupying the position, r, next to these '1' bits in $\varphi(n_{j-1}')$ on their left. (Note that by C1, no '1' bits appear in $\varphi(n_{j-1}')$ right of position n_j'.) By the definition of r, it follows that $\tau(\varphi(n_j'), m) = \varphi(n_j') = \tau(\varphi(n_{j-1}'), m) + 2^{-m}$ for all integers m in the range $r, \ldots, n_j'$.
Hence, for $n_{j+1}' \ge r$, which by condition C2 also satisfies $n_{j+1}' \le n_j'$, we have

$$\begin{aligned}
\varphi(n_{j+1}') &= \tau(\varphi(n_j'), n_{j+1}') + 2^{-n_{j+1}'} \\
&= \tau(\varphi(n_{j-1}'), n_{j+1}') + 2^{-n_{j+1}'} + 2^{-n_{j+1}'}.
\end{aligned}$$

---

[1]Throughout this paper, for $j = 1$, we take $n_{j-1} = n_{j-1}' = \varphi(n_{j-1}) = \varphi(n_{j-1}') = 0$.

By (1) and the identities $n_i = n'_i$ for all $i \neq j$, we infer that $\varphi(n'_{j+1}) = \varphi(n_{j+1})$ and therefore $\varphi(N') = \varphi(N)$. For $n'_{j+1} < r$, we have by the definition of r and φ and by the '1' bit in position r of $\varphi(n'_j)$ that

$$\begin{aligned}
\varphi(n'_{j+1}) &= \tau(\varphi(n'_j), n'_{j+1}) + 2^{-n'_{j+1}} + 2^{-n'_{j+1}} \\
&= \tau(\varphi(n'_{j-1}), n'_{j+1}) + 2^{-n'_{j+1}} + 2^{-n'_{j+1}}.
\end{aligned}$$

As before, by (1) and the identities $n_i = n'_i$ for all $i \neq j$, we infer that $\varphi(n'_{j+1}) = \varphi(n_{j+1})$ and therefore $\varphi(N') = \varphi(N)$ also when $n'_{j+1} < r$. $\square$

Property 3 *Given a sequence $N = n_1, n_2, \ldots, n_s$ of positive integers and an index $1 \leq j < s$ satisfying both conditions:* **C1:** *$\varphi(n_{j-1})$ does not include any '1' bits in the n_j-th position and further right, and* **C2:** *$n_{j+1} = n_j$. Then, the sequence $N' = n'_1, n'_2, \ldots, n'_{s-1}$ obtained from N by decrementing n_j and deleting n_{j+1}, i.e., $n'_i = n_i$ for $i < j$, $n'_i = n_{i+1}$ for $i > j$, and $n'_j = n_j - 1$, satisfies $\varphi(N') = \varphi(N)$.*

Proof: Denote $m = n_j$. By C1, C2, and the definition of N', $\varphi(n'_{j-1}) = \varphi(n_{j-1})$ and $\varphi(n_{j+1}) = \varphi(n_{j-1}) + 2^{-n_j} + 2^{-n_{j+1}} = \varphi(n_{j-1}) + 2^{-(m-1)} = \varphi(n'_{j-1}) + 2^{-n'_j} = \varphi(n'_j)$. Since $n'_{j+1}, \ldots, n'_{s-1} = n_{j+2}, \ldots, n_s$, we conclude that $\varphi(n'_{s-1}) = \varphi(n_s)$. $\square$

Given a binary tree T with s leaves, $l_1, l_2, \ldots, l_s$, indexed from left to right, i.e., l_1 is the leftmost leaf of T, l_s is the rightmost, and in between, l_k is left of l_{k+1}, let the *depth*, n_k, of leaf l_k be the length in edges of the path in T leading from the root down to l_k. The *depth sequence* associated with T is $N(T) = n_1, n_2, \ldots, n_s$.

Lemma 1 (necessary condition) *The depth sequence $N(T)$ associated with a binary tree T satisfies $\varphi(N(T)) \leq 1$.*

Proof: The proof is by induction on $n(T)$, the maximal value in $N(T)$. When $n(T) = 1$, T consists of either a root and one leaf, in which case $N(T) = 1$, or a root and two leaves, in which case $N(T) = 1, 1$, and in both cases the lemma holds. Assuming that the lemma holds whenever $n(T) < m$, let T be a binary tree with $n(T) = m$. Let $N(T) = n_1, n_2, \ldots, n_s$, and let j be the minimal index k such that $n_k = m$. Let T' be the tree constructed as follows. If l_j has a sibling, which must be l_{j+1} with $n_{j+1} = m$, then T' is the binary tree obtained from T by deleting l_j and l_{j+1} and making their parent a leaf. If l_j does not have a sibling then T' is obtained by deleting l_j and making its parent a leaf. In the first case, by the definition of m and j, Property 3 applies, and we have $\varphi(N(T')) = \varphi(N(T))$.

In the second case, $\varphi(n'_{j-1}) = \varphi(n_{j-1})$ and since $n_j > n_1, n_2, \ldots, n_{j-1}$, no '1' bits appear in $\varphi(n_{j-1})$ right of the n'_j-th position. Thus, $\varphi(n_j) = \varphi(n_{j-1}) + 2^{-n_j} < \varphi(n'_{j-1}) + 2^{-n'_j} = \varphi(n'_j)$. Since $n_{j+1}, \ldots, n_s = n'_{j+1}, \ldots, n'_s$, we have $\varphi(n_s) \leq \varphi(n'_s)$ by repeated application of Property 1, and hence $\varphi(N(T)) \leq \varphi(N(T'))$.

The number of leaves of depth m in T' is smaller than their number in T, and yet $\varphi(N(T)) \leq \varphi(N(T'))$. We can repeat the above process, until a tree $\tilde{T}$ is obtained whose leaves are all of depth less than m, i.e., $n(\tilde{T}) < m$, and still $\varphi(N(T)) \leq \varphi(N(\tilde{T}))$. By the inductive hypothesis, $\varphi(N(\tilde{T})) \leq 1$, and thus $\varphi(N(T)) \leq 1$. $\square$

Lemma 2 (sufficient condition) *If a sequence N of positive integers satisfies $\varphi(N) \leq 1$ then there exists a binary tree T for which $N = N(T)$.*

Proof: When $N = n_1$, the binary tree made of a root from which a path emanates, formed of n_1 left branches and ends at the single leaf of the tree, satisfies the lemma for any positive integer n_1. When $N = n_1, n_2$ then for any positive integers n_1 and n_2, satisfying the lemma is the binary tree made of a root from which two paths emanate: one formed of n_1 left branches and ends at the leftmost leaf of the tree, and the other formed of n_2 right branches and ends at the rightmost and second leaf. Other cases are covered by induction on $n(N)$, the maximal value in N. When $n(N) = 1$, either $N = 1$ or $N = 1, 1$; otherwise $\varphi(N) > 1$. As shown before, in both cases the lemma holds. Assuming that the lemma holds for all sequences of positive integers not exceeding $m - 1$, let $N = n_1, n_2, \ldots, n_s$, with $s > 2$, be a sequence of positive integers one or more of which equal m. Construct a sequence N' as follows. Let j be the minimal index k such that $n_k = m$. For $j = s$, N' is obtained from N by decrementing n_s. In this case, by the definition of m and j, $\varphi(n_s) = \varphi(n_{s-1}) + 2^{-m}$, with a '1' bit in the m-th position of $\varphi(n_s) = \varphi(N)$ and none to the right thereof. Since $\varphi(N) < 1$, it follows that the sum of 2^{-m} and $\varphi(N)$ does not exceed 1. Thus, $1 \geq \varphi(n_{s-1}) + 2^{-m} + 2^{-m} = \varphi(n'_{s-1}) + 2^{-(m-1)} = \varphi(n'_s) = \varphi(N')$.

Assume, now, that $1 \leq j < s$. If $n_{j+1} = m$ then take $N' = n'_1, n'_2, \ldots, n'_{s-1} = n_1, n_2, \ldots, n_{j-1}, m - 1, n_{j+2}, \ldots, n_s$. By the definition of m and j, Property 3 applies and we have $\varphi(N') = \varphi(N) \leq 1$. Clearly, if there were a tree T' for which $N(T') = N'$, then making the j-th leaf of T' a parent and hanging two leaves on it would yield a tree T satisfying $T = N(T)$.

If $n_{j+1} < m$ then take $N' = n'_1, n'_2, \ldots, n'_s = n_1, n_2, \ldots, n_{j-1}, m - 1, n_{j+1}, \ldots, n_s$. By the definition of N', m, and j, Property 2 applies, and we have $\varphi(N') = \varphi(N)$. Clearly, if there were a tree T' for which $N(T') = N'$, then making the j-th leaf of T' a parent and hanging a leaf on it would yield a tree T satisfying $T = N(T)$.

The number of elements of size m in N' is smaller than their number in N', and yet

$\varphi(N') \le 1$. If N' has only one or two elements, then there exists a tree T' satisfying $N' = N(T')$; otherwise, if N' has elements of size m, we can repeat the above process, until a sequence $\tilde{N}$ is obtained which consists of no more than two elements, or whose elements are all of size less than m, and still $\varphi(\tilde{N}) \le 1$. By the inductive hypothesis, a tree $\tilde{T}$ exists satisfying $\tilde{N} = N(\tilde{T})$. Going back from $\tilde{N}$ to N through all the intermediate stages, we construct T from $\tilde{T}$ satisfying $N(T) = N$. $\square$

3   Codeword Lengths for Fixed to Variable Codes

Let $S = \{a_1, a_2, \ldots, a_s\}$ be a discrete memoryless source of s letters, $2 \le s < \infty$, with respective positive probabilities $\{p_1, p_2, \ldots, p_s\}$. The entropy $H(S)$ of S is $-\sum_{k=1}^{s} p_k \log_2(p_k)$. A fixed to vairable binary code $C(S)$ for S is a set $\{c_1, c_2, \ldots, c_s\}$ of s distinct binary words together with the mapping of letter a_k to codeword c_k. We denote by n_k the length in bits of codeword c_k, and by $c_k(i)$ – its i-th binary digit; that is, $c_k = c_k(1)c_k(2)\cdots c_k(n_k)$. The *expected code length* of $C(S)$ is defined as $E(C(S)) = \sum_{k=1}^{s} p_k n_k$.

A codeword c_k is called a prefix of a codeword c_j if $n_k \le n_j$ and $c_k(i) = c_j(i)$ for $1 \le i \le n_k$. A *prefix free code* is a code where no codeword is a prefix of any other codeword. Let $a_1, a_2, \ldots, a_s$ be the alphabet order of the source letters. A prefix free code $C(S)$ is *alphabetical* if c_k precedes c_{k+1}, $1 \le k < s$, in the lexicographic order. Note that since $C(S)$ is prefix free, for any two codewords c_k and c_j, $j \ne k$, there is an index $i \le n_k, n_j$ such that $c_k(l) = c_j(l)$ for $1 \le l < i$ and $c_k(i) \ne c_j(i)$. Thus, determining the lexicographic order between any two codewords in $C(S)$ never calls for a comparison of bits and blanks, and the lexicographic order of concatenations of source letters is preserved under encoding.

A prefix free code $C(S)$ can be conveniently represented as a binary tree $T(C(S))$ of s leaves, where the leaves are labeled with the different source letters, the path from the root down to the leaf labeled a_k is of n_k edges, and the sequence of branches taken on that path corresponds to c_k: the i-th branch is left if $c_k(i) = 0$, and right – if $c_k(i) = 1$. Let $l_1, l_2, \ldots, l_s$ be the leaves indexed from left to right. If $C(S)$ is alphabetical then letter a_k labels leaf l_k.

A prefix free [alphabetical] code $C(S)$ is *optimal* if its expected code length is minimal over the expected code lengths of all prefix free [alphabetical] codes. It is easy to see that the binary tree associated with an optimal prefix free [alphabetical] code is full, [2] and thus the lengths of the codewords satisfy $\sum_{k=1}^{s} 2^{-n_k} = 1$. We denote by L_α the expected code length of an optimal alphabetical code for S.

A sequence $N = n_1, n_2, \ldots, n_s$ is said to be *alphabetically legal* if $\varphi(N) \leq 1$. By Lemma 1 and Lemma 2, there is an alphabetical code for S with codeword lengths $= N$ if and only if N is alphabetically legal.

Let $C_H(S)$ be a code for S constructed by the Huffman algorithm [6], where letter a_k is mapped to a codeword of length h_k. Let $H = h_1, h_2, \ldots, h_s$ be the sequence of codeword lengths, and $L_H = E(C_H(S))$ denote the expected code length of $C_H(S)$. We will show now ways to construct alphabetically legal sequences from H.

First, notice that if $\varphi(H) \leq 1$ then $C_H(S)$ is an optimal alphabetical code. Second, observe that $\varphi(H) < 2$ since none of the h_j contributes $2 \cdot 2^{-h_j}$ or more to $\varphi(H)$. Hence, the sequence $H' = h'_1, h'_2, \ldots, h'_s = 2h_1, 2h_2, \ldots, 2h_s$ is alphabetically legal, and we thus have:

Corollary 1 (Gilbert and Moore [4]) $L_\alpha \leq L_H + 1$.

We now consider the case $\varphi(H) > 1$. For the minimal value h in H, a positive integer q, and $0 \leq r < 2^{-h}$, we can write $\varphi(H) = q \cdot 2^{-h} + r$. Now, by the definition of φ, there exists a subsequence of indices $k_1, k_2, \ldots, k_q$ such that $\varphi(h_{k_j+1}) - 2^{-h_{k_j}+1} = j \cdot 2^{-h}$ for $j = 1, 2, \ldots, q$ when $r > 0$, and $j = 1, 2, \ldots, q - 1$ when $r = 0$. Let $\Pi(H) = \{Q_1, Q_2, \ldots, Q_{q+1}\}$ be the partition of $\{1, 2, \ldots, s\}$ where $Q_j = \{k_{j-1} + 1, k_{j-1} + 2, \ldots, k_j\}$ for $j = 1, 2, \ldots, q$ (with i_0 taken to be 0) and for $r = 0$ $Q_{q+1} = \{\}$ and for $r > 0$ $Q_{q+1} = \{i_q + 1, i_q + 2, \ldots, s\}$. Using the definition of φ and $\Pi(H)$, the following three lemmas are readily verified.

Lemma 3 *For any suffix $f_j = \{j, j + 1, \ldots, q + 1\}$, the sequence $H' = h'_1, h'_2, \ldots, h'_s$ obtained from H by taking $h'_i = h_i$ for $i \notin Q$ and $h'_i = h_i + 1$ for $i \in Q$, where $Q = \bigcup_{i \in f_j} Q_i$, satisfies $\varphi(H') \leq \varphi(H) - \frac{1}{2}r - \frac{1}{2}(q - j + 1)2^{-h}$.*

Lemma 4 *If $r < 2^{-(h+1)}$ then for any $g_j = \{j, j + 1, \ldots, q\}$, $j \geq 1$, the sequence $H' = h'_1, h'_2, \ldots, h'_s$ obtained from H by taking $h'_i = h_i$ for $i \notin Q$ and $h'_i = h_i + 1$ for $i \in Q$, where $Q = \bigcup_{i \in g_j} Q_i$, satisfies $\varphi(H') \leq \varphi(H) - \frac{1}{2}(q - j + 1)2^{-h}$.*

Lemma 5 *For any set of $2m$ distinct indices g which form m pairs of adjacent indices in the range $1, \ldots, q$, the sequence $H' = h'_1, h'_2, \ldots, h'_s$ obtained from H by taking*

---

[2]A binary tree is said to be full if every node, but the root, has a sibling.

$h'_i = h_i$ for $i \notin Q$ and $h'_i = h_i + 1$ for $i \in Q$, where $Q = \bigcup_{i \in g} Q_i$, satisfies $\varphi(H') \leq \varphi(H) - m \cdot 2^{-h}$.

Hence, given $\varphi(H)$, we can find a subset of indices $g \subseteq \{1, 2, \ldots, q + 1\}$ satisfying the above three lemmas, whose probability $p(g) = \sum_{k \in Q} p_i$, where $Q = \bigcup_{i \in g} Q_i$, is minimal and such that the sequence $H' = h'_1, h'_2, \ldots, h'_s$ obtained from H by taking $h'_i = h_i$ for $i \notin Q$ and $h'_i = h_i + 1$ for $i \in Q$ is alphabetically legal.

In [10] the minimal points are defined as follows: "if $h_{i-1} > h_i$ and $h_i < h_{i+1}$, i is called a minimal point. In general, if $h_{i-1} > h_i = h_{i+1} = \cdots = h_{i+k} < h_{i+k+1}$, and p_j is the smallest among $\{p_j\}_{(i \leq j \leq i+k)}$ then j is a minimal point". Nakatsu claimed that the sequence H' obtained from H by incrementing all its minimal points is alphabetically legal.

The claim in [10] seems erroneous, at least in the "general" case. It allows the production of an h'_j satisfying $h'_{j-1} < h'_j > h'_{j+1}$. Now, if H' is obtained from H by incrementing h_j only, and $h'_{j-1} < h'_j > h'_{j+1}$ then by Property 2, $\varphi(H') = \varphi(H)$, and hence if H is not alphabetically legal then so is H'. Incrementing h_i (using the above quoted notations) will not do the job for $H = 5, 5, 5, 3, 3, 3, 3, 3, 3, 5, 5, 5, 5, 5$ as example, and incrementing h_{i+k} will not do for $H = 5, 5, 5, 5, 5, 3, 3, 3, 3, 3, 3, 5, 5, 5$.

Now, since our definition does allow us to choose a set of minimal probability, and we have a clear measure of the minimum amount of changes needed for making H alphabetical, our results are better than those claimed for in [10]. For example, taking $H = 5, 3, 5, 4, 5, 4, 3, 5, 4, 3, 5, 5, 4, 3, 5, 5$ associated with a source S of $s = 16$ letters where $p_k = 2^{-h_k}$, we have a set of minimal points $D = \{2, 4, 7, 10, 14\}$, and hence by [10] we have $L_\alpha \leq L_H + \frac{9}{16}$. By our results, $\varphi(H) = 1\frac{3}{16}$. $h = 3$, $q = 9$ and $r = \frac{1}{16}$. Also, the partition $\Pi(H) = \{$ $\{1\}$, $\{2\}$, $\{3, 4\}$, $\{5, 6\}$, $\{7\}$, $\{8, 9\}$, $\{10\}$, $\{11, 12, 13\}$, $\{14\}$, $\{15, 16\}$ $\}$. Now $g = \{3, 4, 9\}$, yielding $Q = \{3, 4, 5, 6, 14\}$, satisfies Lemma 4 and Lemma 5, and assures H' with $\varphi(H') \leq 1$. This implies the better upper bound $L_\alpha \leq L_H + \frac{5}{16}$.

4 Variable Rate Codes

The universal encoder by Ziv and Lempel [11] asymptotically outperforms any finite state encoder on any given infinite sequence. This encoding algorithm is widely used, and even has been accepted as a world standard for computer communication. On a sequence of length m symbols, emitted from a discrete memoryless source, the redundancy per symbol of this encoding scheme is upper bounded by $O(\log \log m / \log m)$.

The following flavor of the original algorithm was introduced by Ma [9]. Given a binary input string, start with $S_0 = \{0, 1\}$, and then iterate the following for $i = 1, 2, \ldots$ until x is exhausted. Let w be the unique maximal prefix of x which is in S_{i-1}. Output the index $S_{i-1}(w)$ of w in S_{i-1} using $\lceil \log_2(i + 1) \rceil$ bits; remove w from x's head; and replace w in S_{i-1} by $w0$ and $w1$, producing S_i. The set S_i is implemented as a full binary tree T_i of $i + 2$ leaves. Each leaf is associated with, and labeled by the index of, the word in S_i which corresponds to the path leading in T_i from the root to that leaf. In Step $i + 1$ of the algorithm, the prefix of x directs a walk on a path in T_i from its root down to its leaves. When a leaf is reached, the index labeling it is output using $\lceil \log_2(i + 2) \rceil$ bits, two new leaves are hanged on that leaf, making it a parent, and its label is moved to one of the new leaves, while the other leaf is labeled $i + 3$. T_{i+1} is thus produced.

Kawabata and Yamamoto [7] combined this flavor of the Ziv-Lempel algorithm with a data structure which maintains a different labeling of the leaves. Their labeling is from left to right. Namely, the leftmost leaf of T_i is labeled 0, the rightmost is labeled $i + 1$, and in between, the leaf labeled j is to the left of the leaf labeled $j + 1$. Their data structure is in the form of a counter maintained in each inner node n of the tree, whose value is the number of leaves the left subtree of n has.

T_0 consists of a root, whose counter $= 1$ and pointers to both leaves $=$ nil. Step $i \geq 1$ of the algorithm starts with variable $I = 0$ and variable p pointing at the root of T_{i-1}. Then: (1) The next bit b is extracted from x. (2) If $b = 0$ then the counter of the node pointed by p is incremented by 1, and q is set to point to its left child. (3) If $b = 1$ then $I \leftarrow I+$ the value of the counter at the node pointed by p, and q is set to point to its right child. (4) If $q \neq$ nil then $p \leftarrow q$ and (1) is resumed. (5) ($q =$ nil) The value of I is output using $\lceil \log_2(i + 1) \rceil$ bits; T_i is constructed from T_{i-1} by generating a new node with both pointers to its children $=$ nil and counter $= 1$, and making it p's left child, if $b = 0$, or right child, if $b = 1$; Step $i + 1$ of the algorithm now begins.

Kawabata and Yamamoto introduced this algorithm for allowing the decoder, using the same data structure, to produce the encoded word w, given its encoding $S_{i-1}(w)$, bit by bit from w's left to its right. Decoding algorithms introduced so far, either climb up the tree from the leaf labeled $S_{i-1}(w)$ to the root, decoding w bit by bit from its right to its left, or are of a non-linear complexity.

In the context of this paper, it is easy to verify, by induction on the number of steps of the coding algorithm, that the Kawabata-Yamamoto scheme is a variation of the Ziv-Lempel algorithm, which, without changing the coding efficiency, preserves the lexicographic order of its input sequences. That is, if x and y are of the same length, and x precedes y in the lexicographic order, then the bit string which is the encoding of x by the Kawabata-Yamamoto algorithm precedes the encoding of y.

References

[1] R.M. Capocelli and A. De Santis, "New Bounds on the Redundancy of Huffman Codes", *IEEE Trans. Inform. Theory*, vol IT-37, pp 1095-1104, 1991.

[2] R.G. Gallager, *Information Theory and Reliable Communication*, New York: Wiley, 1968.

[3] R.G. Gallager, "Variations on a Theme by Huffman", *IEEE Trans. Inform. Theory*, vol IT-24, pp 668-674, 1978.

[4] E.N. Gilbert and E.F. Moore, "Variable Length Binary Encodings" *Bell Systems Technical Journal*, vol 38, pp 933-967, 1959.

[5] T.V. Hu and A.C. Tucker, "Optimal Computer Search Trees and Variable-length Binary Encoding", *SIAM J. Applied Math.*, vol 21, pp 514-532, 1971.

[6] D.A. Huffman, "A Method for the Construction of Minimum Redundancy Codes", *Proceedings of the IRE*, vol 40, pp 1098-1101, 1952

[7] T. Kawabata and H. Yamamoto, "A New Implementation of the Ziv-Lempel Incremental Parsing Algorithm", *IEEE Trans. Inform. Theory*, vol IT-37, pp 1439-1440, 1991.

[8] D.E. Knuth, *The Art of Computer Programming, Volume 3: Sorting and Searching*, Addison-Wesley Publishing Co.

[9] J.S. Ma, *Data Compression*, Ph.D. Dissertation, Dept. of Elect. and Comput. Eng., Univ. of Mass., Amherst, 1978.

[10] N. Nakatsu, "Bounds on the Redundancy of Binary Alphabetical Codes", *IEEE Trans. Inform. Theory*, vol IT-37, pp 1225-1229, 1991.

[11] J. Ziv and A. Lempel, "Compression of Individual Sequences via Variable Rate Coding" *IEEE Trans. Inform. Theory*, vol IT-24, pp 530-536, 1978.

A comparison of codebook generation techniques for vector quantization

Robert F. Sproull[1]
Ivan E. Sutherland[1]
Sun Microsystems Laboratories, Inc.
Mountain View, CA 94043

Successful vector quantization of images depends on constructing suitable codebooks: the quality of the final image depends critically on the quality of the codebook, and codebook construction techniques can be very slow. This paper examines tradeoffs between speed and quality of codebook-generation algorithms and offers new ways to produce excellent codebooks with only modest computation cost.

This paper compares the performance of four algorithms for constructing codebooks. The LBG method [7] produces the best codebooks but requires the most computation. The method by Equitz [2,3] produces codebooks nearly as good and requires somewhat less computation. This paper describes a new method based on eigenvector subdivision that produces useable codebooks in a fraction of the computational effort of either of the other methods. A fourth hybrid method yields very good codebooks with modest computation by using the eigenvector subdivision method to obtain a first approximation that is refined with LBG optimization.

Our eigenvector subdivision method divides the training set vectors into successively smaller sets based on the direction of the principal eigenvector of each subset. After each subdivision, a new principal eigenvector is computed for each subset to select a direction for the next subdivision. Because the principal eigenvector points in the direction of greatest variance in the subset, subdivision normal to the principal eigenvector breaks the subset into more nearly hyper-spherical pieces. When enough subsets have been formed, the centroid of each subset is used as a codeword.

This paper also offers some insight into the content of codebooks. We show a method for visualizing an n-dimensional codebook by drawing n^2 two-dimensional projections. These projections show clearly how little variance there is in the codebook in some directions, reflecting the small size of several eigenvalues of the training set data. Ignoring the thickness of the training set data in directions with small eigenvalues and assuming a uniform distribution in other directions leads to a simple estimate of RMS encoding errors for a vector quantizer. This estimate agrees quite well with measured RMS encoding errors.

1   Codebook geometry

Before turning to the algorithms, we first offer a pictorial view a codebook by plotting all possible two-dimensional views. Figures 1 and 2 show plots of a 16-dimensional

---

[1]Performed this work as consultants to Apple Computer.

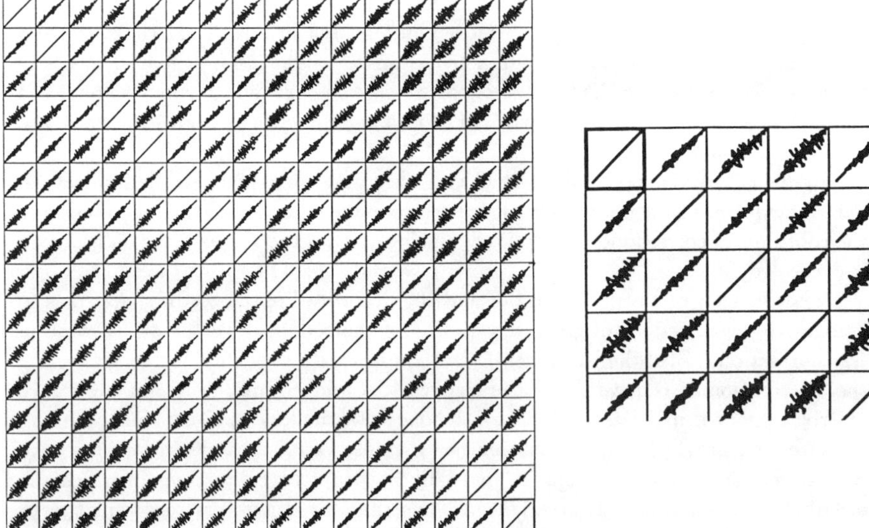

Figure 1: Visualization of a codebook for a 16-dimensional vector space. The plot in row i and column j plots values in the ith dimension against those in the jth dimension. The figure at the right is an enlarged view of the upper left corner of the figure at the left.

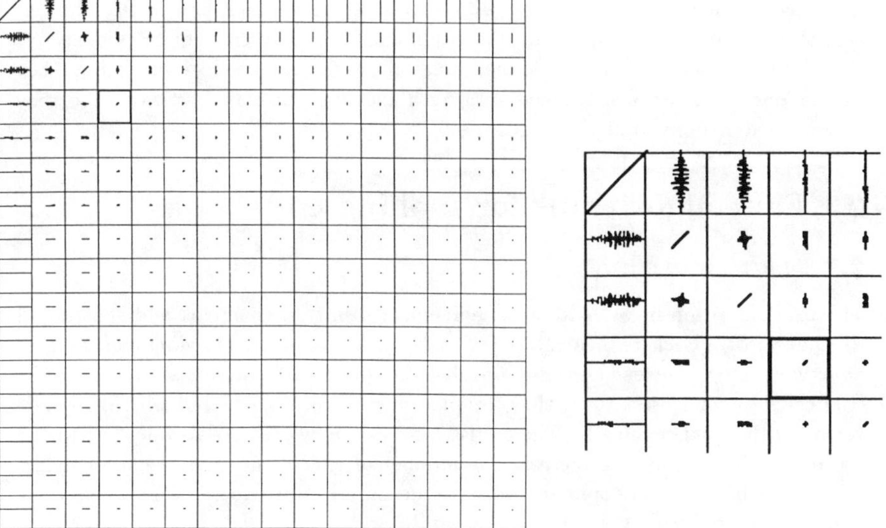

Figure 2: Visualization of a codebook for a 16-dimensional vector space after rotation by the Karhunen-Loève transformation.

vector quantizer codebook taken from a monochromatic image. Each 16-element vector contains the pixel values from a 4×4 square patch: the first four elements in the vector correspond to the top row of the patch, the next four to the next row, and so on. Since there are $16^2 = 256$ ways to choose two dimensions from 16 dimensions, there are 256 two-dimensional views.

Figure 1 shows a codebook plotted with axes that correspond to the intensity of particular pixels in the 4×4 patch. It is hard to make much out of this figure because the coordinates correspond to individual pixels and thus the shape of the distribution is concealed.

A better view of a codebook is obtained by first rotating the vector space so as to emphasize the directions of greatest variation of the codebook vectors. The rotation transformation, called the Karhunen-Loève transformation, is obtained by measuring the distribution of codewords by the eigenvectors and eigenvalues of its covariance matrix. The principal eigenvector, i.e., the one with the largest eigenvalue, points in the direction in which the distribution has greatest variance, and eigenvectors with successively smaller values point in mutually perpendicular directions in which the distribution has less and less variance. Thus the 16 eigenvectors represent the 16 orthogonal directions of a coordinate system that reveals the variance of the distribution. The Karhunen-Loève transformation rotates the original space so that these directions are aligned with coordinate axes.

The shape of a codebook rotated by the Karhunen-Loève transformation is clearly evident in Figure 2. The axes are shown in order of decreasing eigenvalue: the first dimension plotted is the direction of greatest variance in the data, the next dimension is a direction orthogonal to the first with next greatest variance, and so on. The fact that the distribution is long in one dimension and thin in others is quite evident. We think of such distributions as n-dimensional almonds, because like an almond they have a long axis, one or more medium length axes, and several short axes, and they are rounded or pointed at their ends.

2   Four algorithms for making codebooks

2.1   LBG algorithm

The LBG algorithm involves iterative refinement of a trial codebook and splitting of its codewords. Each refinement iteration has two steps, an *encoding* step and an *adjustment* step. The encoding step involves assigning each training set vector to the trial code vector closest to it, thus forming clusters, one associated with each code vector in the trial codebook. The adjustment step moves the trial codeword to the centroid of its cluster. To increase the number of codewords, one or more clusters with large distortion are split in two parts, usually by introducing a new codeword slightly displaced from the existing codeword.

A complete LBG algorithm applies the two-step refinement iteration and splitting a great many times. The algorithm must start with an initial trial codebook, and terminates when a refinement iteration fails to produce at least some minimal improvement in RMS encoding error of the training set. Many choices of initial codebook are possible. For example, purely random vectors or vectors chosen randomly from the training set may be used. Alternately, the output from another algorithm may be a good initial trial codebook [2].

The trouble with the LBG method is that it converges slowly. Because each refinement can only reduce the total distortion, the algorithm provably converges to a local optimum, but not necessarily the global optimum. Each refinement iteration produces a small improvement in the codebook but is slow because it must examine all of the training set vectors. Despite its large computational cost, our experiments indicate that the LBG algorithm routinely produces the best codebooks.

2.2 Equitz algorithm

Where the LBG algorithm builds up a codebook by adding codewords, the Equitz algorithm reduces the size of the training set gradually to produce the required codebook. The Equitz algorithm starts with the entire training set as a first approximation to the codebook, and reduces it by successive approximations. Each iteration finds the pair of vectors in the approximation that are closest together and combines them. The definition of close together weights previously combined clusters according to how many training-set vectors have been accumulated into them, so that "heavy" clusters will combine only if closer together than "light" ones. The effect is to perform the merge that will add the least distortion to the training set.

The algorithm hinges on a technique for finding the closest pair of vectors, which could be an expensive task. The obvious exhaustive search to find the closest pair of N vectors will require N^2 distance measurements. Equitz's method uses a faster approximation: he divides the training set into clusters of about 25 vectors each. Thereafter, the search for a vector's nearest neighbor is confined to the vectors in the same cluster as the vector, so that only slightly more than $25N$ distance measurements are required. The clusters are formed in a data structure called a k-d tree [1], which recursively splits the training set into clusters separated by cut planes aligned with a coordinate axis. We have developed a variant of Equitz's approach that uses a generalized k-d tree in which the cut planes are normal to the principal eigenvector of the distribution being cut [8].

2.3 Eigenvector subdivision algorithm

When we looked at pictures of codebooks such as Figure 2, we imagined finding clusters of training set data by recursively subdividing the data by cutting planes normal to the principal eigenvector. This notion led to devloping the generalized k-d tree [8] and a corresponding codebook-generation algorithm. A similar scheme, using cut planes aligned with axes, was used by Heckbert to build quantizers for color maps [6].

We think of the eigenvector subdivision method in geometric terms. The principal eigenvector of a distribution lies along its longest axis, so cutting the distribution near its center and normal to its principal eigenvector makes two more nearly hyper-spherical parts. If the principal eigenvalue is substantially larger than the next largest eigenvalue, the distribution is cigar-shaped, i.e., long in one direction, and we can expect more than one cut along nearly parallel planes, since cutting a long cigar in half leaves two pieces each of which is still cigar-shaped. In fact, the training set data we have examined using 4×4 squares of pixels as vectors is so highly correlated in the direction of average gray shade that the first eight or more cuts in the eigenvector method merely separate the data into groups of generally lighter and generally darker vectors, i.e., they cut normal to the "gray" axis.

If the two largest eigenvalues are substantially equal but larger than the third, the distribution is pancake-shaped. In this case it may be sensible to make two cuts at once, one normal to each of the two largest eigenvectors, but little harm is done by making them successively, as our programs do. The idea is always to cut in such a direction as to make the subdivided pieces more nearly hyper-spherical.

The eigenvector subdivision method places the training set data into a subdivision tree much like a k-d tree. Each subdivision, however, is made with a plane normal to the principal eigenvector of the data being split. Each node in the tree indicates the orientation and location of the cut plane and points to other tree nodes that further separate the data. The result is much like a k-d tree except that the orientation of the cut planes is data-dependent. In fact, our programs use the same code for eigenvector trees as for classical k-d trees, with a parameter to say how the orientation of the planes is to be selected. The algorithms for building and searching this kind of tree are given in detail in [8].

The algorithm builds the subdivision tree of the training-set vectors until there are as many leaf nodes as there are codewords in the required codebook. The centroid of the training set vectors in each leaf node of this tree then becomes the corresponding codeword.

The eigenvector method gives a rationale for selecting the orientation of each cut plane, but its location along the eigenvector can be chosen in many ways. We have experimented with two alternatives: pass the cut plane through the mean of the distribution being cut, or cut at the median value so as to place the same number of vectors on each side of the cut.

The eigenvector subdivision method for computing codebooks is very fast. It is fast because its only iterative processes operate on a very small amount of data, namely a covariance matrix. It is well adapted to run on vector processors because its major calculations are large inner products across the training set data. It makes only $O(logN)$ passes on the training set data to compute a codebook of size N. Finally, its output provides not only a codebook but also a set of subdivision planes suitable for use in a fast cut-plane encoding method.

2.4   Hybrid method

As we began to study the performance of the three algorithms described above, we looked for a compromise between the quality of the codebook produced by the slow LBG method and the speed of the eigenvector method. The obvious hybrid algorithm uses the fast eigenvector technique to build an initial codebook that is refined by the more accurate LBG algorithm. We ran several experiments in which the size of the initial codebook varies, i.e., changing how much subdivision is done by the eigenvector algorithm and how much splitting by the LBG algorithm. The hybrid technique is a good compromise between speed and quality.

3   Encoding

The job of encoding, or quantizing, an image is to find, for each vector in the image, the nearest codeword in the codebook. We have used two methods: a *full search* and a faster but less accurate *cut plane search*.

A full search of a codebook with N codewords would at first seem to require N distance measurements—an exhaustive linear search of the codebook. But if the codebook is loaded into a k-d tree data structure—either the classical form with axis-aligned cut planes or the form with cut planes normal to eigenvectors—the search is much faster. The speed of searches using the two kinds of trees is explored in [8].

When the codebook is produced using the eigenvector method, the cut planes of the subdivision tree that produced the codebook can be used to encode vectors. An image vector to be encoded is compared to the cut plane at the root node of the tree and the search proceeds to one of two child nodes depending on the relationship of the vector to the plane, and so on down the tree. When a leaf node is reached, the codeword associated with the leaf node is reported. Unlike full search, this technique does not always locate the codeword nearest to the data vector, so larger distortion results. In this respect, cut-plane searching is similar to *tree searching* of codebooks [5].

4   Experiments and results

To obtain credible performance measurements, we have coded all algorithms using one programming environment and one coding style. The three programs are written in C and use a common set of routines for accessing files, building and searching k-d trees, doing vector computations, computing averages, and so forth. The programs were written and debugged on a MicroVAX II and run against real data on a Cray YMP. No vectorization was used on the Cray.

The training set data consisted of five images supplied to us by Tom Stockham of the University of Utah. These images are called *park, parkcity, station, train,* and *tree;* they have appeared in other experiments. Each image is 512 pixels by 512 pixels in size carefully digitized from photographs. Each pixel is represented by a single 8-bit value representing log intensity. We used 4×4 square patches of pixels as vectors.

Table 1 summarizes experimental results. In each experiment we recorded the number of Cray seconds required and the RMS distortion for full search encoding the entire training set. For the eigenvector subdivision experiments we recorded also the RMS distortion for the faster cut-plane encoding. The table shows results only for codebooks with 1024 vectors; more complete results and discussion of algorithm variants can be found in a companion report [9].

The eight eigenvector subdivision experiments include all combinations of three binary variants. These are: (1) choice of which cluster to divide next, i.e., depth first *versus* worst distortion first; (2) orientation of cut planes in the k-d tree, i.e., cut planes running normal to eigenvectors *versus* cut planes normal to the coordinate axis with maximum data variance; and (3) location of the cut plane, i.e., cut plane positioned at the mean location of the cluster *versus* located at the median location. The best combination expands nodes with most distortion, uses eigenvector cut planes, and places the cut plane at the median of the cluster.

The seven Equitz algorithm experiments explore various ways of building the k-d tree used in its search: the size of buckets in terminal nodes of the tree, and the kind of cut planes used in the tree. Variants can build a tree of the entire training set ("infinite tiles") or can limit the number of tiles in memory before merge steps are performed. Not surprisingly, the least distortion is obtained when the entire training set participates in the merge, with large buckets, and cut planes that match the orientation of the data.

The LBG experiments differ in the settings of various parameters that control how new codewords are formed. The *split* parameter is the fraction of existing codewords that are candidates for splitting. The most interesting LBG experiment concerns splitting: how should the two new code vectors be related to the location of the code vector being split? In experiment 23 the codewords are aligned parallel to the principal eigenvector of the cluster being split rather than aligned randomly, as in all the other LBG tests. This not only reduces computing time by about 25% from the corresponding random vector experiment, number 17, but also gives the best codebook of any produced.

The final two experiments are hybrids. They both start with a codebook produced by the eigenvector method and then refine it using the LBG method. Experiment 24 uses an eigenvector codebook of the correct size, simply refining it by the LBG method, splitting codewords only when other codewords are deleted as too unpopular. It produces results in the same class as other LBG codebooks in about 1/4 the computing time. It is our best method in terms of its compromise between computing time and codebook quality. The final experiment primes the LBG method with a 256-word eigenvector codebook, but lets the LBG algorithm do further splitting. Again the RMS error is clearly like those of the other LBG algorithms, but so is the computing time. One should use the LBG algorithm to refine the location of codewords, not to split them.

Experiment	Description	Cray secs.	Distortion	Distortion (cut plane)
1	EV000: depth, eigenvector planes, median	189	7.52	8.10
2	EV001: depth, eigenvector planes, mean	150	7.09	7.47
3	EV010: depth, axis planes, median	150	7.81	9.34
4	EV011: depth, axis planes, mean	125	7.32	8.59
5	EV100: distortion, eigenvector planes, median	198	7.05	7.55
6	EV101: distortion, eigenvector planes, mean	156	<u>6.92</u>	7.31
7	EV110: distortion, axis planes, median	156	7.29	8.75
8	EV111: distortion, axis planes, mean	133	7.14	8.40
9	EQ000: infinite tiles, bucket (15,40), eigenvector planes	923	6.73	
10	EQ001: infinite tiles, bucket (15,40), axis planes	946	6.83	
11	EQ010: infinite tiles, bucket (30,80), eigenvector planes	2866	<u>6.68</u>	
12	EQ011: 8192 tiles, merge to 50%, bucket (15,40), eigenvector planes	718	6.80	
13	EQ100: 8192 tiles, merge to 90%, bucket (15,40), eigenvector planes	766	6.79	
14	EQ101: 4096 tiles, merge to 90%, bucket (15,40), eigenvector planes	762	6.79	
15	EQ110: 4096 tiles, merge to 50%, bucket (15,40), eigenvector planes	711	6.88	
16	LBG000: split 1.0, hit 0.1, delete 0.01	3304	6.56	
17	LBG001: split 0.5, hit 0.1, delete 0.01	3815	6.49	
18	LBG002: split 0.25, hit 0.1, delete 0.01	4755	6.50	
19	LBG003: split 0.125, hit 0.1, delete 0.01	5705	6.49	
20	LBG004: split 0.00625, hit 0.1, delete 0.01	43289	6.47	
21	LBG005: split 0.5, hit 0.0, delete 0.0	3794	6.49	
22	LBG006: split 0.5, hit 0.25, delete 0.125	3851	6.49	
23	LBG009: split 0.5, hit 0.1, delete 0.01, eigenvector	2961	<u>6.47</u>	
24	HY001: EV101+LBG001 refinement	1169	6.51	
25	HY002: EV101 256-word codebook+LBG001 split & refinement	2534	<u>6.50</u>	

Table 1: Experimental results for variants of four codebook-generation algorithms for 1024-vector codebooks: eigenvector (1–8), Equitz (9–15), LBG (16–23), and hybrid (24–25). The best results for each algorithm are underlined. The last column gives the distortion if the cut planes generated by the eigenvector algorithm are used for encoding rather than a "full search" of the codebook. Experiment 24 yields an excellent codebook with only modest computation.

Dim. n	Eigenvalue u	Square root $u^{1/2}$	Running product v	$(v/s)^{1/n}$ $s = 256$	$(v/s)^{1/n}$ $s = 1024$	$(v/s)^{1/n}$ $s = 4096$
1	31121.03	176.41	1.76×10^2	0.69	0.17	0.04
2	906.56	30.11	5.31×10^3	4.56	2.28	1.14
3	750.37	27.39	1.45×10^5	8.28	5.22	3.29
4	260.40	16.14	2.35×10^6	9.79	6.92	4.89
5	192.39	13.87	3.26×10^7	10.49	7.95	6.03
6	169.65	13.02	4.24×10^8	<u>10.88</u>	8.63	6.85
7	83.88	9.16	3.88×10^9	10.61	<u>8.71</u>	7.14
8	67.45	8.21	3.19×10^{10}	10.28	8.64	7.27
9	60.02	7.75	2.47×10^{11}	9.96	8.54	7.32
10	58.14	7.62	1.88×10^{12}	9.70	8.44	<u>7.35</u>
11	28.23	5.31	1.00×10^{13}	9.18	8.09	7.14
12	26.88	5.18	5.19×10^{13}	8.76	7.80	6.95
13	21.76	4.66	2.42×10^{14}	8.34	7.50	6.74
14	12.30	3.51	8.49×10^{14}	7.84	7.10	6.43
15	11.36	3.37	2.86×10^{15}	7.41	6.76	6.16
16	5.97	2.44	6.99×10^{15}	6.91	6.34	5.81

Table 2: Estimates of distortion for different codebook sizes. The inputs to the computation are the sixteen eigenvalues in the second column. Underlined in the last three columns are estimates of distortion for three different codebook sizes. Larger codebooks populate more of the "dimensions" of the distribution and thus have lower distortion.

5 A method for estimating codebook quality

The eigenvalues computed from a training set can be used to produce an estimate of the distortion that a good codebook of size s will introduce when encoding the training set. This estimate is based on a geometric argument and the fact that the eigenvalues computed from a distribution tell quite a lot about its geometry. In particular, if the distribution is a glob of data, perhaps extended in some directions more than in others, the eigenvalues give us a way to approximate the volume of the glob. The values in the second column of Table 2 are the eigenvalues of the covariance matrix of the training set vectors used in these experiments, sorted in order of decreasing value. The third column gives their square roots so as to measure RMS distortion. The product of square roots of the largest n eigenvalues, as shown in the next column, is approximately the n-dimensional volume, v, of the glob in the n-dimensional space of the corresponding eigenvalues.

A well-formed codebook of size s should fill the n-dimensional volume v. If we assume that image vectors are evenly distributed throughout this volume (which they are not), the codebook divides the volume v into s volumes of equal size, each occupying volume v/s. Moreover, those volumes will be roughly hyper-spherical, and so the average encoding error should be on the order of $(v/s)^{1/n}$, as shown in the fourth column in Table 2. Notice that the numbers in this column increase to a maximum and then decrease again.

The only question that remains is how many dimensions to consider for making an estimate of RMS error. In directions for which the square root of the eigenvalue is less than the expected encoding error, the volume associated with a codeword will stretch completely across the training set distribution. In other words, in such dimensions the distribution is so thin that its thickness will no longer contribute to encoding errors. We can thus ignore the effect of this and other dimensions with smaller eigenvalues. Thus the maximum value in the column of predicted RMS errors in Table 2 is the one to choose. These estimates compare quite well with distortions of actual codebooks.

6   Acknowledgements

We wish to thank Professor Thomas Stockham for his instruction in vector quantization techniques and for providing us with the image data we used. We thought of ourselves as his non-resident post-doctoral students. We also wish to thank Apple Computer for its support of this work and for providing the computing facilities required. Particular thanks to Al Alcorn and Larry Tesler of Apple whose encouragement and support made the project possible.

References

[1] J.L. Bentley. Multidimensional Binary Search Trees Used for Associative Searching. *Comm. ACM*, 18(9):509–517, September 1975.

[2] W. Equitz. Fast Algorithms for Vector Quantization Picture Coding. *ICASSP*, 18.1.1, 1987.

[3] W. Equitz. A New Vector Quanitization Clustering Algorithm. *IEEE Trans. ASSP*, 37(10):1568–1575, October 1989.

[4] J.H. Friedman, J.L. Bentley, and R.A. Finkel. An Algorithm for Finding Best Matches in Logarithmic Expected Time. *ACM Trans. Math. Software*, 3(3):209–226, September 1977.

[5] R.M. Gray. Vector Quantization. *ASSP Magazine*, p. 4–29, April 1984.

[6] P. Heckbert. Color image quantization for frame buffer display. *Computer Graphics*, 16(3):297–307, July 1982.

[7] Y. Linde, A. Buzo, and R.M. Gray. An algorithm for vector quantizer design. *IEEE Trans. Comm.*, COM-28(1):84–95, January 1980.

[8] R.F. Sproull. Refinements to nearest-neighbor searching in k-d trees. *Algorithmica*, 6:579–589, 1991.

[9] R.F. Sproull and I.E. Sutherland. A comparison of codebook generation techniques for vector quantization. Technical report, Advanced Technology Group, Apple Computer, 20525 Mariani Ave., Cupertino, CA, 95014, 1992.

Vector Quantizer Design by Constrained Global Optimization

Xiaolin Wu *

Department of Computer Science

University of Western Ontario

London, Ontario, Canada N6A 5B7

Abstract-Central to vector quantization is the design of optimal code book. The construction of a glabally optimal code book has been shown to be NP-complete. However, if the partition halfplanes are restricted to be orthogonal to the principal direction of the training vectors, then the globally optimal K-partition of a set of N D-dimensional data points can be computed in $O((N + KM^2)D)$ time by dynamic programming, where M is the intensity resolution. This constrained optimization strategy improves the performance of vector quantizer over the classic LBG algorithm and the popular methods of tree-structured recursive greedy bipartition of the training data set.

Key words: Vector quantization, optimization, dynamic programming, principal component analysis.

1 Introduction

For the last decade vector quantization has remained a very active research field. Its theoretical potential is being realized in signal compression practice thanks to intensive research efforts and ever-increasing computing powers. This paper only addresses the computational aspect of vector quantization. For a comprehensive introduction of the topic please refer to a new book by Gersho and Gray [7].

Central to the performance of a vector quantizer is the optimality of its code book. A VQ code book is designed on a large set S of training vectors that statistically represent the digital source signal to be compressed. A good VQ code book should contain K code words (vectors) that can well approximate individual training vectors. Thus VQ code book design is usually formulated as a clustering (classification) process as follows. The finite data set $S \subset \Re^D$ is partitioned into K subsets S_k, $1 \leq k \leq K$, $S_k \neq \phi$, $S_j \cap_{j \neq k} S_k = \phi$, $\cup_{1 \leq k \leq K} S_k = S$, and all vectors $\mathbf{x} \in S_k$ are

---

*Supported by grants from the Natural Science and Engineering Research Council of Canada.

mapped to a representative vector (code word) $\mathbf{z}_k \in S_k$. Given such a partition, the total quantization distortion is defined to be

$$E(S_1, S_2, \cdots, S_K) = \sum_{1 \leq k \leq K} \sum_{\mathbf{x} \in S_k} \|\mathbf{x}, \mathbf{z}_k\| \tag{1}$$

where $\|\mathbf{x}, \mathbf{z}_k\|$ is the quantization error in approximating $\mathbf{x}$ by $\mathbf{z}_k$. In this paper the ubiquitous mean square error is used to measure the quantization distortion. Ideally, one would like to minimize Eq(1) for given K and S over all possible K-partitions of S. The code book of the minimum total quantization distortion is called optimal code book. The fact that there are approaching K^{N^2} different partitions [1] makes the design of optimal code book a formidable combinatorial optimization problem. Many proofs for the NP-completeness of optimal K-clustering, for which optimal vector quantization is an instance, for variable K were given for various error functions [2, 6, 13]. When K is fixed, the problem is theoretically solvable in polynomial time [3, 5]. But the proposed algorithms run in $O(N^{cK})$ time, $c > 1$, even in 2-dimensional space $\Re^2$, having no practical significance.

The first practical optimal vector quantizer design algorithm was published in 1980 [9], known as the LBG algorithm. It is a generalization of Lloyd's method I for scalar quantizer design [10]. The LBG algorithm adopts a typical descent local optimization approach and thus converges to a local minimum of the distortion function.[1] In this paper, a new approach of constrained global optimization is proposed for optimal vector quantizer design. The chosen constraint facilitates an efficient global optimization scheme in clustering training vectors but does not adversely affect the Voronoi structure of an optimal code book.

To justify the new optimization approach, we will, in the next section, reexamine some heuristics currently used for vector quantizer design and reveal some inherent drawbacks of existing methods. In section 3, optimal K-partition of the training set in its principal axis is proposed for clustering training vectors. A dynamic programming algorithm is developed in section 4 to solve the proposed problem. Complexity analysis of the new algorithm is given in section 5 to demonstrate that the new optimization strategy can be made efficient enough to be practical. Section 6 shows how to combine optimal principal multicell quantization scheme with optimal recursive bipartition to complete the quantizer design process.

2   Previous Techniques and Their Limitations

Since the LBG algorithm tends to get trapped in a local minimum of the error function near the starting position of the algorithm, it is crucial to start the iterative clustering process at a set of good initial code words. A common technique is to bipartition the data set S recursively until K subsets S_j, $1 \leq j \leq K$, are formed, then the centroids of these subsets will serve as the initial code words. Conceptually,

---

[1] Unless the algorithm is accidentally initialized at a local maximum and gets stuck there.

the above recursive bipartition process can be described by a complete binary tree. The root of the tree is the entire training set S, each of its $K - 1$ internal nodes corresponds to a bipartition, and its K leaves are the final K subsets S_j, $1 \leq j \leq K$. Note that the K-partition of S embedded in the binary tree is a vector quantizer in its own right (tree-structured vector quantizer (TSVQ) [11]) if we use the centrods of S_j as final code words rather than as initial code words for the LBG algorithm.

In tree-structured vector quantizer design, each bipartition can be done by the LBG algorithm for $K = 2$, i.e., 2-means clustering. However, the optimality of a bipartition still heavily depends on the initial cutting halfplane. To minimize the quantization distortion the orientation of cutting halfplane should be made adaptive to data distributions. Wu and Zhang [16] proposed a bipartition technique that splits a data set with a cutting halfplane normal to the principal direction of data points, and the cutting position is optimized through a linear search.

The optimality of the tree-structured vector quantizer, and consequently the optimality of the initial code words it generates, also depends on the order in which the binary partition tree grows. The simplest order of successive bipartitions is blind recursion. Before growing to the next level, each internal node of the binary tree at the current level is split regardless of its statistic characteristic. Smaller quantization distortions may be achieved by more elaborated tree growing strategies. An obvious alternative is to always split the node with the largest variance; the other choice is to split the node whose bipartition yields the largest reduction in the total quantization distortion [14, 16]. Precisely let Ω_j, $1 \leq j \leq k < K$, be the k current subsets subject to further subdivisions, and $\Omega_{j,1}$ and $\Omega_{j,2}$ be the two subsets of Ω_j if it is split by the optimal cutting halfplane. Then the next subset to be split is Ω_t such that

$$t = \arg \max_{1 \leq j \leq k} \{ E(\Omega_j) - E(\Omega_{j,1}) - E(\Omega_{j,2}) \}. \tag{2}$$

A common drawback of all the above techniques is their extremely narrow optimization scope. The current subsets are treated one at a time with their interactions completely ignored. The quantizer optimality is further compromised by the greedy bipartition strategy. Namely, each bipartition aims at the immediate profit of minimizing $E(S_1) + E(S_2)$ regardless of its impact on further subdivisions of S deep down the binary partition tree. This greedy local criterion may contradict the global criterion of minimizing Eq(1). Even in 2-dimensional space it is not difficult to find such adverse cases. For instance, in Fig. 1, three successive greedy bipartitions clearly yield a bad 4-partition of the data set.

Recently Chou *et al.* [4] and Lin *et al.* [8] suggested to improve quantizer performance by growing a partition tree of more than K leaves, and then optimally pruning the tree back to a subtree of K leaves. But our experiments showed that the quantization distortion reduction by optimal tree pruning was minimal and hardly justified the additional computational cost. The main reason for the ineffectiveness of optimal tree pruning is that the decision is binary: a cut is either kept or removed but not adjustable. Furthermore, the top structure of the tree will remain immune from the optimal pruning.

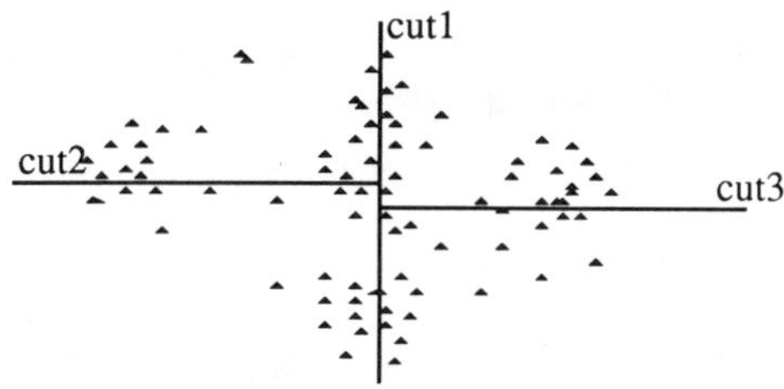

Figure 1: A bad 4-partition formed by greedy bipartitions.

To cure the above problems inherent to the greedy bipartition strategy, we need an approach which permits an optimization of multilevel partition in global sense.

3 Optimal Principal Multilevel Quantization

3.1 An observation

First we reveal an interesting observation of training vectors formed from image data which inspired our new optimization strategy. Suppose, as in our previous algorithm [16], that the data set S is split into S_1 and S_2 by the optimal cutting halfplane normal to the principal axis of S, and the binary partition tree grows in a look-ahead greedy fashion. Let $\{H_i : i = 1, 2, \cdots\}$ be the sequence of optimal cutting halfplanes generated by the above process. It was consistently observed that for some κ, the principal axes of the resulting subsets created by the first few cuts H_i, $1 \leq i \leq \kappa$, remained approximately the same as the principal axis of the original data set S. Consequently, the halfplanes H_i, $1 \leq i \leq i_0$, are almost parallel to each other and hence approximately normal to the principal axis of S. The critical value of κ varied around 30 depending on different images. An image model was found to explain our observation and will be presented in a forthcoming full-length paper but not in this extended abstract.

3.2 Problem formulation

For better quantizer performance we would like to optimize the cutting halfplanes H_i, $1 \leq i \leq \kappa$, together rather than choosing H_i one at a time. This accounts for the chain interactions between clusters which are ignored by the greedy approach, and minimizes the quantization distortion in a much broader scope. The question is how this global optimization approach can be made computationally feasible. Fortunately, the fact that halfplanes H_i, $1 \leq i \leq \kappa$, are almost parallel facilitates the following constrained global optimization scheme.

The basic idea is to optimize multiple cuts against the principal axis of the data set S. This axis can be determined by the classic principal component analysis technique [12], that is, by finding the largest eigenvalue λ_{max} and the corresponding principal eigenvector $\mathbf{v}$ of the covariance matrix $\mathbf{C}$ of S, i.e., $\mathbf{Cv} = \lambda_{max}\mathbf{v}$. Then all N training vectors $\mathbf{x} \in S$ will be sorted by their projections on the principal axis given by $\mathbf{v}$, i.e., establishing the order that $\mathbf{x}_i \leq \mathbf{x}_j$ if and only if $\mathbf{x}_i^T\mathbf{v} \leq \mathbf{x}_j^T\mathbf{v}$. In the computation, $\mathbf{v}$ needs to be normalized. The eigenvector transform and the sorting constitute a map $R : S \rightarrow \{1, 2, \cdots, N\}$, with $R(\mathbf{x}) = i$ meaning that the projection value $\mathbf{x}^T\mathbf{v}$ ranks i in the sorted list of N projections. Now we define a finite set

$$Q_n^k \equiv \{\mathbf{q} \mid 0 \equiv q_0 \leq q_1 < q_2 < \cdots < q_{k-1} < q_k \equiv n\} \subset \aleph^{k+1}, \tag{3}$$

where $\aleph$ is the set of all natural numbers. Then a $\mathbf{q} \in Q_n^k$ corresponds to a k-partition of the point set $S(0, n] = \{\mathbf{x} : 0 < R(\mathbf{x}) \leq n\}$ into subsets: $S(q_{i-1}, q_i] = \{\mathbf{x} : q_{i-1} < R(\mathbf{x}) \leq q_i\}$, $1 \leq i \leq k$. Notice that the intervals involved are open on the left but close on the right.

The vector $\mathbf{q} \in Q_n^k$ is called a $k : n$ principal quantizer for it quantizes n multivariate points into k parallel cells bounded by $k - 1$ cutting halfplanes normal to the principal axis of $S(0, n]$. The quantization distortion of the ith cell is

$$\mathcal{E}(q_{i-1}, q_i] = \sum_{\mathbf{x} \in S(q_{i-1}, q_i]} \|\mathbf{x}, \mathbf{z}_i\| \tag{4}$$

where $\mathbf{z}_i$ is the centroid of the point set $S(q_{i-1}, q_i]$. Given a critical parameter κ, the total distortion of a $\kappa : N$ principal quantizer $\mathbf{q} \in Q_N^\kappa$ is

$$E(\mathbf{q}) = \sum_{1 \leq i \leq \kappa} \sum_{\mathbf{x} \in S(q_{i-1}, q_i]} \|\mathbf{x}, \mathbf{z}_i\|. \tag{5}$$

Under the above formulation, minimizing $E(\mathbf{q})$ over all possible $\kappa : N$ quantizers $\mathbf{q} \in Q_N^\kappa$ means minimizing the total quantization distortion over all possible κ-partition of S generated by parallel halfplanes normal to the principal axis. We define the optimal $\kappa : N$ principal quantizer $\hat{\mathbf{q}}$ to be the one that minimizes Eq(5), i.e., $\hat{\mathbf{q}} = \arg\min_{\mathbf{q} \in Q_N^\kappa} E(\mathbf{q})$.

It is important to realize that $E(\mathbf{q})$ is still defined in $\Re^D$ not in $\Re$. Thus the $k : n$ principal quantizer $\mathbf{q} \in Q_n^k$ is a *vector* not scalar quantizer.

4 Dynamic Programming Algorithm

By restricting the cuts to be normal to the principal axis we reduce the problem domain from $O(K^{N^2})$ in minimizing Eq(1) to $|Q_N^\kappa| = \binom{N-1}{\kappa-1} = O(N^{\kappa-1})$ in minimizing Eq(5), which is already polynomial for fixed κ. But finding the optimum by enumeration is still intractable for modest N and κ, $\kappa \ll N$. More sophisticated algorithm is needed.

The first t cells of a $k : n$ principal quantizer $\mathbf{q} \in Q_n^k$, $1 < t < k$, $k < n$, give a t-partition of the point set $S(q_0, q_t]$, thus by definition, they form a $t : q_t$ principal quantizer. It can be proven by contradiction that the first t cells of the optimal $\kappa : N$

principal quantizer $\hat{q}$ must be the optimal $t : q_t$ principal quantizer on the subset $S(\hat{q}_0, \hat{q}_t]$. This property, called the principle of optimality in optimization literature, enables a dynamic programming algorithm to compute the optimal $\kappa : N$ principal quantizer $\hat{q}$, which is a generalization of the optimal scalar quantization process [15].

Denote by $\hat{q}_n^k$ the optimal principal $k : n$ quantizer, and let $L[k, n]$ be the $(k-1)^{th}$ parameter of $\hat{q}_n^k$, i.e., $L[k, n] \equiv (\hat{q}_n^k)_{k-1}$. Then the principle of optimality can be expressed as

$$L[k, n] = \arg \min_{k < i < n} \{ E(\hat{q}_i^{k-1}) + \mathcal{E}(i, n] \}, \quad 2 \leq k < n \leq N. \tag{6}$$

Hence $L[k, n]$ can be determined by a linear search provided that $E(\hat{q}_i^{k-1})$, $k \leq i < n$, are all known. Once $L[k, n]$ is determined $E(\hat{q}_n^k)$ also becomes known by

$$E(\hat{q}_n^k) = E(\hat{q}_{L[k,n]}^{k-1}) + \mathcal{E}(L[k, n], n], \quad 2 \leq k < n \leq N. \tag{7}$$

This suggests that $\hat{q}_N^\kappa$ can be constructed by bottom-up dynamic programming. First note that the distortions of one-level quantizers are trivially $E(\hat{q}_n^1) = \mathcal{E}(0, n]$, $1 \leq n \leq N$. Then by Eq(6) and Eq(7), $L[2, n]$ and $E(\hat{q}_n^2)$, $2 \leq n \leq N$, can be computed and stored as intermediate results for later use. In general, the dynamic programming process determines $L[k, n]$ and $E(\hat{q}_n^k)$, $k \leq n \leq N$, by referring to $E(\hat{q}_n^{k-1})$, $k - 1 \leq n \leq N$, and it remembers all the results just obtained to facilitate the computations of $L[k+1, n]$ and $E(\hat{q}_n^{k+1})$, $k+1 \leq n \leq N$. The process terminates when k has been incremented from 2 up to κ and $L[\kappa, N]$ is finally obtained. The parameters of optimal $\kappa : N$ quantizer $\hat{q}_N^\kappa$ can then be reconstructed backward from $\hat{q}_\kappa = N$ and the relation $(\hat{q}_N^\kappa)_i = L[i, (\hat{q}_N^\kappa)_{i+1}]$. The pseudo code of the algorithm is given below.

Algorithm. Optimal quantization by dynamic programming.
Input: N, κ, S, P.
Output: $\hat{q}_N^\kappa$.
Globals: $E[n] \equiv E(\hat{q}_n^{k-1})$, $L[k, n] \equiv (\hat{q}_n^k)_{k-1}$;
Initialization: $E[n] := \mathcal{E}(0, n]$, $1 \leq n \leq N$; $L[k, k] := k - 1$, $1 \leq k \leq \kappa$.
begin

```
        for k := 2 to κ do
            for n := k + 1 to N − κ + k do begin
                cut := n − 1; e := E[n − 1];
                for t := n − 2 downto k − 1 do
                if E[t] + ε(t, n] < e then begin
                    cut := t; e := E[t] + ε(t, n];
                end;
                L[k, n] := cut; E[n] := e;
            end;
            output Lchain(κ, N) as qN^κ;
```

end.

```
function Lchain(k, n) : q ∈ Q_n^k;
begin
        t := n;
        for j := k − 1 downto 1 do q_j := t := L[j + 1, t];
        return(q);
end
```

5 Complexity Analysis

In this section we will study the time and space complexities for computing optimal $\kappa : N$ principal quantizer $\hat{\mathbf{q}}_N^\kappa$. In general, all training vectors $\mathbf{x} \in S$ may have N distinct projection values $\mathbf{x}^T \mathbf{v}$, resulting a huge search domain for the dynamic programming algorithm. However, upon a second reflection, real arithmetic on the principal axis is unnecessary in practice since the intensity resolutions of frame buffer displays are discrete and have a small dynamic range, being typically integers from 0 to 255. Therefore, without loss of precision achievable by the digital devices, we put N projections into $M < N$ buckets, and approximated $\hat{\mathbf{q}}_N^\kappa$ by $\hat{\mathbf{q}}_M^\kappa$. This also allows a linear-time ordering of the N projections by bucket sort algorithm. In our experiments $M = 512$ was found sufficient.

The following analysis is based on M not on N, although the algorithm was first derived for N for conceptual clarity. In the kernel of the dynamic programming algorithm, the quantization distortions $\mathcal{E}(a, b]$, $0 \le l < r \le n$, are repeatedly evaluated. To gain efficiency, we can precompute $\mathcal{E}(a, b]$ for all possible pairs a and b and store them for future reference. Since there are $O(M^2)$ those pairs, such a preprocessing seemingly needed $O(M^3)$ time and $O(M^2)$ space. But the following manipulations lead to a linear-time scheme. Notice that

$$
\begin{aligned}
\mathcal{E}(a, b] &= \sum_{a < R(\mathbf{X}) \le b} (\mathbf{x} - \mathbf{z})^T (\mathbf{x} - \mathbf{z}) \\
&= \sum_{d=1}^{D} \left\{ \sum_{a < R(\mathbf{X}) \le b} x_d^2 - \frac{\left[\sum_{a < R(\mathbf{X}) \le b} x_d \right]^2}{\sum_{a < R(\mathbf{X}) \le b} 1} \right\}.
\end{aligned}
\tag{8}
$$

Now define the quantities:

$$
\begin{aligned}
W_2(n) &\equiv \sum_{0 < R(\mathbf{X}) \le n} \sum_{d=1}^{D} x_d^2, \\
W_1(d, n) &\equiv \sum_{0 < R(\mathbf{X}) \le n} x_d, \quad 1 \le d \le D, \\
W_0(n) &\equiv \sum_{0 < R(\mathbf{X}) \le n} 1,
\end{aligned}
\tag{9}
$$

where W_i are the ith cumulative moments, and use them to rewrite Eq(8) as

$$\mathcal{E}(a,b] = W_2(b) - W_2(a) - \frac{\sum_{d=1}^{D}[W_1(d,b) - W_1(d,a)]^2}{W_0(b) - W_0(a)}.$$ (10)

Therefore, if the 0th, 1st, and 2nd cumulative moments in Eq(9) are precomputed and stored for $1 \le n \le N$, $1 \le d \le D$, $\mathcal{E}(a,b]$ can be evaluated in $O(D)$ time. Consequently, the inner t loop of the dynamic programming algorithm can be executed in $O((n-k)D)$ time. Thus the total computational cost of the dynamic programming process is determined by the simple counting:

$$\sum_{k=2}^{\kappa} \sum_{n=k+1}^{M-\kappa+k} (n-k)D = \frac{\kappa-1}{2}[(M-\kappa)^2 + M - \kappa]D.$$ (11)

Clearly, $O(ND)$ time suffices to precompute and save the quantities $W_2(n)$, $W_1(d,n)$, $1 \le d \le D$, and $W_0(n)$, $1 \le n \le N$, and $O(\kappa)$ time is taken by the function Lchain(κ, M), being both insignificant at the presence of Eq(11). The cost of eigenvector transform prior to dynamic programming is dominated by the construction of covariance matrix $\mathbf{C}$, which takes $O(ND)$ time. Computing the N projections on the principal axis and ordering those projections by bucket sort each takes $O(ND)$ time. Adding all above costs up, we conclude that the optimal $\kappa : M$ principal quantizer can be computed in $O((\kappa M^2 + N)D)$ time considering that $\kappa \ll M$.

6 From Multicell Principal Quantization to Bipartition

As the bottom-up dynamic programming algorithm proceeds the distributions of training vectors in the quantization cells $S(\hat{q}_{i-1}, \hat{q}_i]$, $1 \le i \le k$, become less and less biased toward the principal axis of S for increasing k. The algorithm should terminate with the output $\hat{\mathbf{q}}_M^\kappa$ when for some $k = \kappa$ none of the data sets $S(\hat{q}_{i-1}, \hat{q}_i]$, $1 \le i \le \kappa$, has a strongly biased orientation in the principal direction of S. Otherwise, if the algorithm continues for $k > \kappa$, its output $\hat{\mathbf{q}}_M^k$ can differ significantly from the globally optimal k-cell quantizer. The critical parameter κ for the optimal principal quantizer $\hat{\mathbf{q}}_M^\kappa$ can be determined during the bottom-up dynamic programming process by examining the eigenvalues and eigenvectors of $S(\hat{q}_{i-1}, \hat{q}_i]$, $1 \le i \le k$, as k increases, to detect the shift of principal axes. The covariance matrix of $S(\hat{q}_{i-1}, \hat{q}_i]$

$$\mathbf{C} = E\{\mathbf{x}\mathbf{x}^T\} - E\{\mathbf{x}\}[E\{\mathbf{x}\}]^T$$ (12)

consists of D^2 covariances ($D^2/2 + D$ of them are distinct due to the symmetry of $\mathbf{C}$), namely,

$$x_{r,s} = \frac{\sum_{\mathbf{x} \in S(\hat{q}_{i-1}, \hat{q}_i]} x_r x_s}{\sum_{\mathbf{x} \in S(\hat{q}_{i-1}, \hat{q}_i]} 1} - \frac{\left[\sum_{\mathbf{x} \in S(\hat{q}_{i-1}, \hat{q}_i]} x_r\right]\left[\sum_{\mathbf{x} \in S(\hat{q}_{i-1}, \hat{q}_i]} x_s\right]}{\left[\sum_{\mathbf{x} \in S(\hat{q}_{i-1}, \hat{q}_i]} 1\right]^2} \quad 1 \le r, s \le D. \quad (13)$$

If the above matrix is to be evaluated straightforwardly for each subset $S(\hat{q}_{i-1}, \hat{q}_i]$, $1 \leq i \leq k$, at each level of dynamic programming, $O(\kappa N D)$ operations are needed just to correctly terminate the dynamic programming process. But a similar statistical preprocessing to Eq(9) can reduce this cost to $O((N + \kappa^2)D)$ thanks to the order already established on training vectors $\mathbf{x} \in S$ by their projections $\mathbf{x}^T \mathbf{v}$. Indeed, let

$$W_{r,s}(n) \equiv \sum_{0 < R(\mathbf{X}) \leq n} x_r x_s, \tag{14}$$

then precompute and store $W_{r,s}(n)$ for $1 \leq n \leq N$ and $1 \leq r \leq s \leq D$, we can simplify Eq(13) to

$$x_{r,s} = \frac{W_{r,s}(\hat{q}_i) - W_{r,s}(\hat{q}_{i-1})}{W_0(\hat{q}_i) - W_0(\hat{q}_{i-1})} - \frac{[W_1(r, \hat{q}_i) - W_1(r, \hat{q}_{i-1})]\,[W_1(s, \hat{q}_i) - W_1(s, \hat{q}_{i-1})]}{[W_0(\hat{q}_i) - W_0(\hat{q}_{i-1})]^2},$$

$$\tag{15}$$

where W_1 and W_0 are the cumulative comments introduced in the previous subsection. Therefore, a covariance $x_{r,s}$ can be evaluated in $O(1)$ time independent of the size of the subset $S(\hat{q}_{i-1}, \hat{q}_i]$. Clearly, precomputing $W_{r,s}(n)$, $1 \leq r, s \leq D$, requires $O(ND)$ time. It will not change the complexity order of the entire algorithm.

After the optimal principal quantizer $\hat{\mathbf{q}}_M^\kappa$ is computed and if $\kappa < K$ still, we need to further partition the subsets $S(\hat{q}_{i-1}, \hat{q}_i]$, $1 \leq i \leq \kappa$ until the required K clusters are formed. Unfortunately, we can no longer carry out a global optimization in the way the optimal principal quantizer is constructed because none of $S(\hat{q}_{i-1}, \hat{q}_i]$ now has a predominant enough principal axis to have two or more locally optimal cutting halfplanes parallel to each other. So we resort to local optimization approach and bipartition the current subsets $S(\hat{q}_{i-1}, \hat{q}_i]$ one at a time and under some optimization criteria as discussed in section 2.

A rather detailed description of an optimal bipartition algorithm based on principal analysis can be found in [16] and thus omitted here.

7 Performance and Remarks

The dynamic programming algorithm for vector quantizer design using the proposed constrained global optimization strategy was implemented and compared with all variants of tree-structured vector quantizer mentioned in section 2. The new algorithm consistently outperformed the previous methods, sometimes by a significant margin, with its mean square quantization error being 5 to 20 percent smaller than the others.

Finally, a word of warning for the sake of rigor, the optimal principal quantization defined by Eq(5), under the constraint of cutting orientation, is only a better heuristic method guided by a common statistical characteristic of image data to approximate the solution of the original NP-complete problem of optimal vector quantizer design. A nontrivial bound on the difference between the true global minimum quantization distortion and that of the new algorithm or any other heuristic algorithms still remains elusive.

References

[1] M. R. Anderberg, *Cluster Analysis for Applications*, Academic Press, New York, 1973.

[2] P. Brucker, "On the complexity of clustering problems" in *Optimization and Operations Research* (R. Henn, B. Korte, and W. Oettli, eds.), pp. 45-54, Springer-Verlag, 1977.

[3] V. Capoyleas, G. Rote and G. Woeginger, "Geometric clustering," *J. Algorithm*, vol. 12, pp. 341-356, 1991.

[4] P. A. Chou, T. Lookabaugh, and R. M. Gray, "Optimal pruning with applications to tree-structured source coding and modeling," *IEEE Trans. Inf. Theory.*, vol. IT-35, no. 2, pp. 299-315, 1989.

[5] Z. Drezner, "The p-center problem - heuristic and optimal algorithms," *J. Oper. Res. Soc.*, vol. 35, pp. 741-748, 1984.

[6] M. R. Garey, D. S. Johnson, H. S. Witsenhausen, "The complexity of the generalized lloyd-max problem," *IEEE Trans. Inf. Theory*, vol. IT-28, pp. 255-256, March 1982.

[7] A. Gersho and R. M. Gray, "Vector Quantization and Signal Compression," Kluwer Academic Publishers, Boston, 1991.

[8] J. Lin, J. Storer, and M. Cohn, "On the complexity of optimal tree pruning for source coding," *Proc. of Data Compression Conference*, IEEE Computer Society Press, pp. 63-72, 1991.

[9] Y. Linde, A. Buzo, R. M. Gray, "An algorithm for vector quantizer design," *IEEE Trans. Commun.*, vol. COM-28, pp. 84-95, Jan. 1980.

[10] S. P. Lloyd, "Least squares quantization in PCM," unpublished memo., Bell Lab., 1957; *IEEE Trans. Inform. Theory*," vol. IT-28, pp. 129-137, Mar. 1982.

[11] J. Makhoul, S. Roucos, and H. Gish, "Vector quantization in speech coding," *Proc. IEEE*, vol. 73, no. 11, pp. 1551-1587, Nov. 1985.

[12] B. F. J. Manly, *Multivariate Statistical Methods*, Chapman and Hall, London, 1986.

[13] N. Megiddo and K. J. Supowit, "On the complexity of some common geometric location problems," *SIAM J. Comput.* vol. 13, pp. 182-196, 1984.

[14] E. A. Riskin and R. M. Gray, "A greedy tree growing algorithm for the design of variable rate vector quantizers," *IEEE Trans. Signal Proc.*, Nov. 1991.

[15] X. Wu, "Optimal quantization by matrix-searching," *Journal of Algorithms*, vol. 12, no. 4, p. 663-673, Dec. 1991.

[16] X. Wu and K. Zhang, "A better tree-structured vector quantizer," *Proc. of IEEE Data Compression Conference*, IEEE Computer Society Press, pp. 392-401, 1991.

PERCEPTUALLY BASED CODING OF MONOCHROME AND COLOR STILL IMAGES

T. R. Reed, V. R. Algazi, G. E. Ford, and I. Hussain

CIPIC, The Center for Image Processing and Integrated Computing,
UNIVERSITY OF CALIFORNIA, DAVIS

1. INTRODUCTION

Most image coding techniques are directed to the efficient digital representation of original images of moderate quality. The quality of the original image serves as an implicit measure of the additional tolerable distortion that the coder may introduce. For very high quality images, a more suitable approach is to attempt to achieve an imperceptible quality degradation in coding. The effective design of such coders has to start with the properties of human visual perception. In this paper we describe an approach and report some results for this problem. The approach is based on the differential quantization of images, in which smooth approximations are subtracted from the image prior to quantization. We consider two such approximations. The first one is an approximation by splines obtained from a sparse and fixed subsampled array of the image. The second one segments the image into piecewise constant regions on the basis of the local activity of the image. Both these approximations result in remainders or residual images where large errors are localized in portions of the image of high activity. Because of visual masking the remainder image can now be coarsely quantized without visual impairment to the reconstructed image. The coarsely quantized remainder is now encoded in an error free manner. In such a perceptually based encoding method the mean square error is now dependent on the activity of the image. This method provides results substantially superior to the standard JPEG technique for the same high quality. In addition, because no structured artifacts are present in the reconstructed image, it is now possible to perform additional operations, such as interpolation or enhancement, without the intolerable artifacts that would result in the post processing of JPEG encoded images.

2. DIFFERENTIAL QUANTIZATION

There are three properties of human visual perception which can be used to achieve high image quality while reducing the information content, or bit rate. These are the nonlinear perception of luminance according to Weber's law, the very substantial decrease of the contrast sensitivity for spatial-frequencies above 8 cycles/degree, and the visual masking of perturbation or errors, by the activity of the image. Most common visual artifacts encountered in images encoded by current techniques occur in the vicinity of high contrast edges, or near the transition between image regions, and are caused by inadequate control of the spatial distribution of errors. Artifacts with a spatial structure, such as the block effect in transform coders, are quite perceptible and highly objectionable. Differential quantization circumvents this problem by providing an excellent approximation in flat portions of the image. The approximation is not as good near edges or in active portions of the images. But in these portions of the image, visual masking, which extends over several minutes of solid angle, allows for substantial errors to occur before they reach the visual threshold of perception. A diagram of the differential quantization approach which exploits these visual properties is shown in Figure 1.

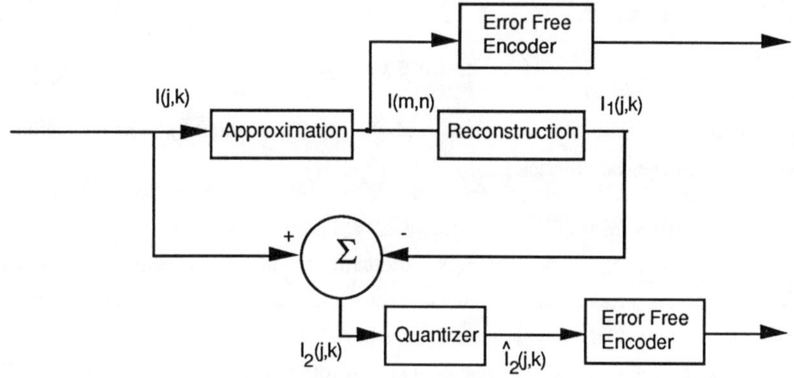

Figure 1: Differential Quantization

For an 8 bit image $I(j,k)$, the images obtained $I_1(j,k)$ after approximation and reconstruction also has 8 bits. We consider $\{I_1, \hat{I}_2\}$, with $\hat{I}_1 = I_1 + \hat{I}_2$ as an alternate representation of $I(j,k)$.

3.   APPROXIMATION TECHNIQUES

We have considered two approximation techniques to achieve the objectives of efficient differential quantization. In the first one, we subsample the original image in a 8×8 sub-array. The second method performs an image segmentation into a piecewise constant approximation.

A.   Subsampling and Spline Approximation

We consider now that the image is a surface in 3 dimensional space. The approximation by splines is obtained by subsampling a pre-processed version of the original full resolution image. After subsampling, we obtain a set of values u(p,q), p=0,...n; q=0,...m, on a rectangular grid. By the use of bicubic spline patches, we determine, from the $\{u(p,q)\}$ set, a smooth surface $I_1(x,y)$, that interpolates the sampled values. We obtain, in fact, a set of bicubic spline patches, which are given by :

$$I_{pq}(x,y) = \sum_{k,l=0}^{3} \gamma_{pqkl}(x-p)^k(y-q)^l \tag{1}$$

for each rectangular region

$$R_{pq} = \{(x,y): p \leq x \leq p+1, q \leq y \leq q+1\}$$

The whole image can thus be interpolated with the requirement that $I_{pq}(x,y)$ be continuous at each of the patches boundaries.

We have used subsampling by a factor of 8, based on consideration of the visual masking of errors in active image regions. Alternatives to the use of bicubic splines would be linear splines on a rectangular or quincunx sampling grid. We have found them slightly inferior for our purpose. Note that linear splines have been used in combination with VQ in a fairly low bit rate encoding scheme [1]. Another alternative is to use an FIR approximation to an ideal low pass both prior to sampling and for interpolation. We have found that approach unsatisfactory because of the serious visual artifacts caused by ideal low pass filtering or interpolation of images [2]. The subsampled array $\{u(p,q)\}$ which results from the sampling of the image is represented with an 8 bit accuracy and not encoded. For an 8×8 subsampling grid, this array requires 0.125 bit per original sample. From the spline interpolation, an approximation to the original image is obtained, and this approximation is subtracted from the original to obtained a remainder image encoded by methods discussed in section 4 of the paper.

B.   Image Segmentation Using Gibbs-Markov Random Fields

The interesting information in an image relates to the characteristics and relationships between the object or homogeneous segments which compose that image. The advantages in taking a region or object-based, rather than pixel-based, approach to coding have been well documented [3]. The method described below combines texture and contour models in order to find regions with smooth boundaries. A detailed explanation of the segmentation method used, in the context of coding, can be found in [4,5].

The first step in the segmentation algorithm is preprocessing. This step models Weber's law by taking the logarithmic response of the visual system into account [6]. This allows us to find a more natural partitioning of images, closer to the segmentation that perceived visually. After this step, the region growing algorithm is applied. This algorithm consists of three different phases, using a more sophisticated image model in each one. The first uses only the mean of the luminance of the regions in order to merge them. With this phase, we merge all regions with difference of means smaller than a given threshold. In the second, the variance of the region is also included in the model.

As typical in region growing methods, over merging of regions often occurs, resulting in a loss of detail. To regain the lost detail, a larger number of regions could be retained. This is undesirable from the standpoint of image compression, however, since each region must be coded. In order to obtain a better partition without increasing the number of regions, a third model is introduced. In this model, region contour and texture information are used jointly. The contour information is introduced by using a Gibbs-Markov random field (GMRF) to model the set of possible image partitions, penalizing irregular contours [7].

A labelled image partition Q can be modeled as a sample from a two dimensional GMRF, so that

$$P(Q) = \frac{1}{Z} e^{-U} \tag{2}$$

where

$$U = \sum_{c_i \subset Q} V(c_i) \tag{3}$$

is a potential function and $Z = \Sigma e^{-U}$ is a normalizing constant. For a GMRF of order 2, the c_i (cliques) consist of each possible pair of adjacent pixels. $V(c_i)$ is defined as

$$V(c_i) = \begin{cases} \alpha & \text{for inhomogeneous nearest neighbor pairs} \\ \beta & \text{for inhomogenous diagonal neighbor pairs} \\ 0 & \text{otherwise} \end{cases}$$

By filling the regions found in the above segmentation with their mean values, we obtain a base representation (approximation).

4. NON-UNIFORM QUANTIZATION AND TRANSPARENT CODING

The approximation of an image by splines or by piecewise constant image segments, and the subsequent digital representation of the remainder, is a form of information source decomposition of the original image or information source into multiple subsources. However the principal gain that can be achieved by the differential quantization scheme is to use more effectively the properties of the human visual system, by non-uniform coarse quantization.

A. Luminance and Chrominance

The use of 8 bits for grey scale images is due to the fact that at low luminance level, the just noticeable difference (JND) <u>in luminance</u> is approximately 1/256. In our scheme, the number of grey scale levels actually available is always more than 256 because of the additive contributions of both the approximation and the remainder. Further, the approximations are best in the low frequency subareas of the images. Therefore, coarser quantization of the remainder now becomes feasible. The flat areas of images are also critical when considering the quality of color representation, so that similar considerations hold for the chrominance components.

B. Visual Masking

It is known that errors in images are substantially less visible in active portions of the image [8]. This phenomenon of visual masking by image activity is generally difficult to exploit in image coding since it requires some analysis of the image. Here, since the remainder is the difference between a smooth approximation and the original, large values in the remainder correspond to the most active portions of the image, for which visual masking will be significant. It has been determined that visual masking, at a viewing distance of 6 time picture height, will occur a distance of up to six to seven pixels from a sharp transition. This is the reason for the use of a 8×8 subsampling grid, in the approximation by splines so that the maximum distance from the two dimensional grid of subsamples is less than six pixels. For the approximation by segmentation, large values of the remainder are also tightly localized in active image regions, in general.

C.   Non Uniform Quantization

Based on the above consideration, we devised a non-uniform quantization scheme for the remainder. Such a scheme provides a global fine quantization for the low frequency subareas, where the remainder is small, and allow for coarse quantization for the active portions of the images. We designed a minimum mean square error quantizer which provides the desired non uniform characteristic based on the first order probability density function of the remainder. The number of quantization levels was progressively decreased until we reached the threshold of perception for the quantization error. We find that, for all images, quantization of the remainder at approximately 5 bits or 32 levels, is sufficient to insure perceptual transparency. Further work, based on this statistically based quantizer, results in a "universal" non uniform quantizer which assures perceptual transparency for all images.

D.   Error Free Encoding of the Quantized Remainder

In the proposed scheme, the non uniform quantization is as coarse as possible while still maintaining high quality. Therefore, all subsequent encoding of the quantized remainder has to be error free so as to avoid additional and generally uncontrolled image quality degradations. We considered several schemes for this error free encoding. The first encoding method is error free DPCM, also used for error free encoding of the original image in the JPEG standard. Note that the prediction error is no longer guaranteed to fall on one of the allowed quantization levels. However the prediction error may be quantized so as to allow only the few values present in the remainder and thus lead to an error free reconstruction. The quantized values of the remainder can be indexed, and differences of indices can be performed, so as to concentrate the probability distribution of these indices and decrease entropy. Although derived for the spline approximation, we will use the same predictor for the segmentation case. The formulation of a predictor more closely tuned to the segmentation residual is expected to yield improved results.

5. RESULTS

A. Spline Approximation

The two approximation methods were applied to three representative 512×512 pixel, 8 bit/pixel images; buildings (Figure 2), wonder woman (wwoman) and mandrill.

The coding performance of this method, as compared to JPEG error free, is summarized in Table 1. Also shown are the remainder entropy and the bits required for the error free DPCM encoded remainders. All values are in bits per pixel. In each case, a significant improvement in performance (as compared to JPEG) is demonstrated, with no loss in image quality.

Image	buildings	wwoman	mandrill
Entropy	7.45	7.23	7.47
JPEG Error Free	4.11	3.46	6.40
Remainder entropy	4.06	3.12	4.40
DPCM encoded remainder	2.55	1.71	4.13
Total bits/pixel	2.68	1.84	4.25

Table 1. Error-free DPCM encoding of the quantized remainder for the spline approximation based method.

B. Segmentation

The result of applying the segmentation-based encoding method to the images lead to the relative performance of the segmentation method, compared to error-free JPEG, as shown in Table 2. The results for "buildings' are shown in Figure 3. The total bits per pixel for this method includes the Q-coded contour information (the boundaries of the segments), the list of mean values which fill the regions (8 bits/value) and the error-free DPCM encoded quantized difference image (remainder).

Figure 2.   The "buildings" image, encoded using spline approximation. From upper left to lower right: a) The original image. b) The reconstructed image. c) The spline approximation. d) The scaled remainder.

Figure 3.   The "buildings" image, encoded using the segmentation-based method. From upper left to lower right: a) The original image. b) The reconstructed image. c) The segmentaiton approximation. d) The scaled remainder.

Image	buildings	wwoman	mandrill
Entropy	7.45	7.23	7.47
JPEG Error Free	4.11	3.46	6.40
Remainder entropy	3.52	2.62	4.26
DPCM encoded remainder	2.96	2.47	4.31
Total bits/pixel	3.48	3.14	4.99
(With DPCM encoded remainder Q-coded contours and uncoded mean list.)			

Table 2. Error-free DPCM encoding of the quantized remainder for the segmentation-based method.

The remainder entropy and number of bits in the error free DPCM encoded remainder are also shown. While a reasonable degree of improvement is shown as compared to JPEG, it should be noted that the quantization and prediction (DPCM) strategies which were utilized are the same as for the spline approximation. However, particularly in the facial portrait, there are significant errors in some of the smoothly varying regions. This accounts to some extent for the somewhat lower compression obtained in this case, as shown above. It is expected that these results can be improved substantially by reexamining the design of the quantization and prediction schemes, to match them more closely to the characteristics of the segmentation - derived remainder. Therefore, although the segmentation based approach leads to higher bit rates as currently implemented, it has substantial promise with further refinements.

The same approach has been used on color images. Preliminary results indicate that the encoding of color for very high image quality requires only a modest increase in the number of bits used for the luminance component of the color image. Because the representation is very good in flat portions of a image, accurate reproduction of solid colors is achieved.

6. DISCUSSION AND CONCLUSIONS

In this paper, we have reported some preliminary results on the perceptually based coding of high quality images. In our approach, we account for the properties of human perception directly in the choice of the image representation and of the quantization parameters. It is clear that in cases where a coders has some adjustable quality parameters, it is possible to select such parameters to achieve high quality. However, schemes such as the DCT based coding of the JPEG standard, are not very effective at high image quality.

Further, since they introduce errors with a spatial structure, they are not robust to further processing and editing. For instance, we have applied techniques for the anisotropic enhancement of images based on properties of human vision to encoded images [9,10]. Images encoded by the methods described in this paper benefit from such postprocessing, while for DCT encoded images, the block structured artifacts are enhanced and make the results unacceptable.

REFERENCES

1.   H. M. Hang and B.J. Haskell, "Interpolative Vector Quantization of Color Images," *Transaction Communications,* 36(4):465-470. April 1988.

2.   T. A. Hentea and V. R. Algazi, "Perceptual Models and the Filtering of High-Contrast Achromatic Images," *IEEE Trans. on Systems, Man, and Cybernetics,* SMC-14(2):230-245. 1984.

3.   M. Kunt, A. Ikonomopoulos, and M. Kocher, "Second generation image coding techniques," Proceedings of the *IEEE*, 73(4)1549-575. April 1985.

4.   T. R. Reed, T. Ebrahimi, G. Giunta, T. Ebrahimi, F. Marqués, T. G. Campbell, and M. Kunt, "Image sequence coding using concepts in visual perception," In Proceedings of the *SPIE/SPSE Symposium on Electronic Imaging Science and Technology,* p. 272-283, Santa Clara, California, February 11-16, 1990.

5.   F. Marqués, A. Gasull, T. R. Reed, and M. Kunt, "Coding-oriented segmentation based on Gibbs-Markov random fields and human visual system kowledge," In Proceedings of the *IEEE 1991 International Conference on Acoustics, Speech and Signal Processing*, p. 2749-2752, Toronto, Ontario, Canada, May 14-17, 1991.

6.   Z. Xie and T. G. Stockham, "Toward the unification of three visual laws and two visual models in brightness perception," *IEEE Trans. on Systems, Man and Cybernetics,* 19(2):379-387, March/April 1989.

7.   V. Franke and R. Mesler, "Region based image representation with variable reconstruction quality," in T. R. Hsing, editor, *Visual Communications and Image Processing '88*, p. 178-186, Cambridge, Massachusetts, November 9-11, 1988.

8.   A. Netravali, B. Haskell, **Digital Images**, Chapter 4, Plenum Press, 1988.

9.   V. R. Algazi, "Fir Anisotropic Filters for Image Enhancement," *Proc. ICASSP*, vol. 3. 1986.

10. V. R. Algazi, G. E. Ford, and E. Hildum, "Digital Representation and Storage of High Quality Color Images by Anisotropic Enhancement and Subsampling," *Proc. ICASSP-89*, pp. 1846-1849. 1989.

Real Time Implementation of Pruned Tree Search Vector Quantization

Avanindra Madisetti, Rajeev Jain

Integrated Circuits and Systems Laboratory
Department of Electrical Engineering
University of California, Los Angeles
Los Angeles, CA 90024

Richard L. Baker

PictureTel Corporation
One Corporation Way
Peabody, MA 01960-7988

Abstract

This paper discusses the design of a CMOS integrated circuit for real time vector quantization (VQ) of images at MPEG rates. It has been designed as a slave processor which can implement binary, non-binary, and pruned tree search VQ algorithms. Inputs include the image source vectors, the VQ codevectors and external control signals that direct the search. The chip outputs the index of the codevector that best approximates the input in a mean square error sense. The layout has been generated using a 1.2μ CMOS library and measures $5.76\times6.6mm^2$. Critical path simulation with SPICE indicates a maximum clock rate of 40 MHz.

I. INTRODUCTION

Image and video compression are becoming increasingly common in business today for video conferencing and multimedia applications. Recent Investigations have been aimed at using Vector Quantization (VQ) as an alternative to scalar quantization in hybrid (DCT + VQ) transform coders. Many researchers have also proposed spatial coding schemes which replace the DCT with a vector quantizer, and several have been marketed successfully (e.g., Mitsubishi's Invite-64 and PictureTel's HVQ and SG3 video conferencing algorithms).

For a VQ based image coding system, the encoder compares each source vector X with N candidate approximations or *codevectors* Y^i , $i = \{1, \cdots, N\}$ prestored in a *codebook* and picks the closest codevector Y^n using the Euclidean norm. Data compression occurs as a result of transmitting the index n of the best match instead of the input vector itself. The decoder uses n to access Y^n from its copy of an identical codebook and places it in the corresponding block location. This can be implemented with a simple look up table. Thus a VQ based codec has a very simple decoder. This is particularly attractive in broadcast (point to multipoint) applications.

While vector quantization algorithms have attained a sufficient degree of maturity over the last decade, their translation to hardware is still relatively primitive. Implementation of the VQ algorithm requires the computation of the Euclidean distance and a running comparison of the distance measures to determine the index n of the best match. To perform this in real time, different architectural strategies have been reported. The computational complexity grows linearly with N and typically large N is required for acceptable performance. Most implementations [4] resort to multi-chip solutions to satisfy the complexity requirements. Other techniques [5] resort to sub-optimal VQ algorithms.

As discussed in *section II*, pruned tree search algorithms (BFOS, ROPA) [7-8] perform quite close to the rate-distortion bound and actually outperform the generalized Lloyd algorithm full search VQ. Pruning the tree results in an irregular tree structure in terms of tree depth and the number of children at any node. While this complicates the control flow of the algorithm, the computational complexity is significantly reduced by the tree. Thus a trade-off between computational complexity and control complexity can be made to achieve real time capability on a single chip.

To exploit this tradeoff, the approach presented in *section III* partitions the tree search VQ implementation into a slave-processor chip that computes the distances and an off-chip controller that directs the search. The architectural design of the slave processor described in *section IV* is suitable for searching irregular pruned tree-structured codebooks. Codebook size, codevector dimension, tree depth and number of children at any node are arbitrary. The design of a simple controller is given in *section V*. The IC design of the slave processor has been carried out in detail to verify the feasibility of a single chip implementation.

II. TREE SEARCH VQ

A. <u>*Tree Search*</u> :   Full search VQ can be performed by comparing the input source vector with *all* the codevectors in the codebook and is necessarily of order O(N). The computational complexity can be reduced to O(logN) by arranging the codevectors to lie on the nodes of a tree and traversing the tree in the following fashion: Let $C = \{Y^i\}$ be the set of all children of the current node. The tree search algorithm can be written as

descend to node labeled Y^n iff

$$\| Y^n - X \| \leq \| Y^i - X \| \, \forall \, i \, \neq \, n \, and \, \forall \, Y^i \, \& \, Y^n \, \epsilon \, C \tag{1}$$

At each step, moving to a child node Y^n eliminates the sub trees of all other children, significantly reducing computational complexity at the cost of a more complex control flow.

B. *Performance* :   The quality of a tree search VQ depends on the structure and design of the tree, The simplest is a binary tree where each node has only two children. Since only a portion of a tree structured codebook is searched, its performance can never be better (and typically is slightly worse) than a full search VQ having codebook size equal to the number of terminal nodes. Recently, a new class of tree structured VQ design algorithms have been developed (BFOS, ROPA) [7-8] which retain the desirable fast search, low complexity tree structure and which actually outperform traditional generalized Lloyd algorithm full search VQ designs.

The paths to the leaf codevectors are used to index the codevectors. Since path lengths differ, so does instantaneous codevector rate, so the improved performance comes at the cost of a variable depth structure. Figure 1 compares the mean square error performance of full search (FVQ), binary tree search (TSVQ), and pruned tree search VQ (BFOS and ROPA) at different rates. BFOS and ROPA can result in a performance quite close to the rate-distortion bound and outperform binary tree search and full search VQ.

C. *Complexity* : For a black and white video source with input pixel rate f_s and for k-dimensional vectors, the input vector rate is simply f_s/k. With a given processor, let T_c be the time in seconds to compute a single subtract and square operation and let N_d be the number of distance computations needed to find the minimum. For N_p processors operating in parallel, a minimum is found after kN_dT_c/N_p seconds. A simple upper bound on the number of distance calculations that be performed in real time is given by:

$$\frac{N_p}{kN_dT_c} \geq f_s/k \Rightarrow N_d \leq \frac{N_p}{T_cf_s} \tag{2}$$

Since N_d is exponentially smaller for tree searches, the number of processors required (N_p) is likewise reduced and a single chip implementation is feasible. Therefore, for a given hardware implementation, tree search schemes permit the search of exponentially larger codebooks and for practical purposes will not limit codebook sizes. It was decided to target the proposed implementation at pruned tree search. because of the reduced complexity with no degradation of SNR),

III. ARCHITECTURE FOR PRUNED TREE SEARCH VQ

Pruned tree search algorithms result in irregular trees, that is, trees with varying depths and possibly a variable number of children at any node. An implementation for pruned tree search can be partitioned into

(a) Distance computation : $\| Y^i - X \|_2^2$

(b) Minimization of distances.

(c) A branching decision.

Both the distance computation and minimization operations are iterative and indepen-dent of the exact tree structure. The branching decision depends on the particular tree structure.

Based on these considerations, we have partitioned the implementation of the VQ algorithm into the following subsystems (Figure 2).

(a) VQ Slave Processor : implements the distance computation and minimization

(b) Controller : implements the branching decision and provides slave processor timing.

(c) Codevector memory and offset memory.

Figure 2 depicts the overall VQ system and the interfaces. The VQ slave processor is responsible for distance computation and minimisation. The controller monitors the outcome of the minimisation and is responsible for fetching the next set of codevectors. The controller also reads information about the tree structure from the codebook memory. The controller provides all the control and timing information needed by the slave processor. The codebook memory has been partitioned into a codevector memory and an offset memory.

Codebook storage for a tree search based on the euclidean distance measure is larger (about twice) than that for full search VQ. However, reformulation of the distance measure to an inner product reduces both the storage and the number of multiplies. The distance calculation and minimization for VQ encoding can be reformulated as:

$$= min^{-1} \left\{ 0, \sum_{j=0}^{k-1} z_j{}^i x_j + d^i \right\} \tag{3}$$

where $\quad z_j{}^i = y_j{}^0 - y_j{}^i \quad$ and $\quad d^i = c^i - c^0$ and $c^i \equiv \sum_{j=0}^{k-1} \left(y_j{}^i \right)^2 / 2$ and
$i \in \{ \; children \; at \; the \; given \; node \}$

For a binary tree ($N_c = 2$), this halves the number of multiplications and results in a single distance computation per node. Thus, the inner product results in a 50 % saving for binary trees ($N_c = 2$), 33 % for three way ($N_c = 3$) etc.

The codevector memory in Figure 2. stores the codevector $\{Z^i\} = \{z_1^i, z_2^i, \cdots, z_k^i\}$ and the offset term d^i along with some information about the tree structure, such as the number of children at a node (N_c).

IV. THE VQ SLAVE PROCESSOR

The architecture of the slave processor is shown in Figure 3. The distance computation requires the computation of a k-dimensional inner product. The inner product $Z^i.X$ is calculated using the multiplier bank, the CSA tree, the barrel shifter and the accumulator. The inner product is added to the offset vector (d^i) to compute the distance value. The distance value is input to the minimizer which sets a flag *newout* whenever the current distance value is less than the previous minimum.

A. *Multiply and Accumulate* :   The computational core of the chip consists of a bank of eight $2 - bit \times 8 - bit$ serial-parallel multipliers. Inputs to each multiplier are eight bits of a dimension x_j of the source vector X stored on chip and two bits of the the jth dimension $z_j{}^i$ of the ith codevector Z^i.

The codevectors Z^i are input serially at each clock cycle, 2 bits at a time via a 16 bit wide data bus. The advantage of the serial-parallel configuration is that it permits the use of a slower on-chip memory for the source vector trading off speed for memory bandwidth. Even with the extra clock cycles required, the serial-parallel configuration is adequate for meeting the low throughput requirements of the tree search algorithm if a clock rate of 20 MHz can be achieved.

The accumulator adds the shifted partial sums and produces an eight-dimensional inner product once every four clock cycles. For the evaluation of a k-dimensional inner product, the control signal *accreset* must be exerted once every k/2 clock cycles. This permits a variable codevector dimension. This reset signal also latches out the 24 bit inner product which is in a carry-save format. The offset term d^i is then added to the carry save product to complete the distance evaluation. The distance value calculated at the output of the carry propagate adder is input to a multiplexer and a minimizer. The internal wordlength of 24 bits in the accumulator provides sufficient accuracy for a 256-dimensional inner product. The current distance is also multiplexed over 6 pins.

B. _Minimizer_ : For binary trees, the minimizer (Figure 4) needs only to compare the distance value against zero, which can be done by examining the MSB of the result. For non-binary trees, a Minimum Value Register (MVR) is needed to keep track of the local minimum during a node search.

The current distance value is latched into a New Value Register (NVR). The comparator compares the contents of the MVR and the NVR. Whenever a new value is less than the content of the MVR, the MVR latches the new value and flags the controller by setting *newout HIGH*. The controller then makes a decision and generates the address for the next node of the tree and the corresponding codevectors. A new distance value is computed and input to the NVR. At the end of the node search, the controller initializes the MVR to the maximum 24 bit value possible and the process begins for a new source vector.

C. _Source Vector Buffer_ : To reduce off-chip memory I/O, since the codevectors are already stored externally, it is advantageous to store the source vectors on chip on a dual port RAM. For pruned tree search, the codevector to be compared in a given cycle is not known until the comparison in the previous cycle is completed. This can result in idle processor cycles while the next codevector is being fetched. To avoid this, several source vectors are buffered on-chip and are interleaved in the processor as described in the next section.

V. CONTROLLER

The main task of the controller is to direct the execution of the tree search by the slave processor. The controller monitors the outcome of the minimization and generates the addresses of the codevectors for the next node to be searched as described in *section V.A.* For pruned tree search, the controller has to additionally take into account the pipeline latency to prevent degradation in the throughput. This is achieved by interleaving source vectors as described in *section V.B.*

A. _Codebook Address Generation_ : For very regular codebooks address generation can be performed by a simple finite state machine. For irregular codebooks, it is convenient to embed the tree structure into the codebook itself. Variable parameters in a tree can be

(1) dimension of codevector (k).

(2) number of children at any node (N_c).

(3) depth of tree (N_l).

Example : *Pruned Tree Search (N_c, N_l and k are variable)*
The codebook structure for a pruned tree search is shown in Figure 5. If a decison to branch to node i is made, the children of node i must be accessed for the next minimization. The addresses of all the children of node i can be stored along with the codevector Z^i. Thus, whenever Z^i is accessed from the codebook memory, the addresses of all its children also become available. If all the children of a node are constrained to occupy contiguous locations in the codebook memory, then it is sufficient to specify only the address of the first child. The number of bits allocated for the address of a child depends on the codebook size.

For a node i with N_c^i children, all the associated codevector slices occupy $\frac{kN_c^i}{2}$ contiguous locations in the codebook memory. A binary flag ($LC=$ last child) can be set $HIGH$ to mark the location of the last codevector slice of the last child. This allows a node to have an arbitrary number of children. $LC = HIGH$ marks the end of a node search. Another binary flag EOS is used to identify a leaf node. This signals an end of search for the given source vector. Two address bits (AB) store the address of the first child. Given this memory structure, an example for searching a pruned tree with 16-dimensional codevectors is described below.

For a 16-dimensional codebook, each codevector occupies eight contiguous locations of the codebook memory. Two address bits AB (shaded in Figure 5) spanning eight contiguous locations store the 16 bit address of the first child. The 16 bit address is sufficient to address upto 2^{16} nodes in a tree. For smaller trees with fewer nodes, all 16 address bits are not used.

Address generation using the circuit in Figure 6 occurs as follows : The address bits (AB) of the first child are serially input, two bits at a time, to the serial to parallel converter $(SERPAR)$ over eight clock cycles (a 16-d vector is accessed over eight clock cycles). The *newout* signal from the VQ slave processor always goes $HIGH$ after the first comparison. This latches the contents of the new address register (NAR) into the old address register (OAR). Thus, OAR stores the result of a running node comparison. When LC is $HIGH$, OAR contains the address of the child node which is the best match. This is latched into the Best Address Register BAR. BAR then provides the address of the child node to descend. This is used to generate the actual codebook memory address. The end of search flag (EOS) latches the contents of BAR into the $INDEX$ register which can then be transmitted.

B. *Source Vector Interleaving* :   For an implementation with dimensionality k, N_c children at any given node and capable of P scalar multiplies per clock cycle (T_c), each node search requires $k(N_c-1)$ multiplications and can be performed in $\frac{k(N_c-1)T_c}{P}$ seconds. For an address generation time of T_{addr} and codevector access time T_v, one can show that the number of source vectors that have to be interleaved to avoid idle time is given by

$$\text{Number of interleaved vectors} = (\text{idle time}) \,/\, (\text{time for one node search}) = \frac{(LT_c + T_{addr} + T_v)P}{(N_c - 1)kT_c}.$$

Interleaving complicates control since the controller must keep track of the branching addresses of all the interleaved vectors. Each source vector operates on a different set of codevectors which must be input to the slave processor (the codevectors cannot be shared between source vectors as permitted in a full search scheme). Also, a variable tree depth results in a variable search time for different source vectors. Both BAR and $INDEX$ registers must now replaced by FIFO's (First In First Out implemented as a shift register chain). The depth of the FIFO equals the number of source vectors being interleaved. Both EOS and LC are asynchronous signals and depend on the tree depth and number of children at any node respectively.

The controller can be implemented in a host processor which does other codec functions or in an FPGA for a stand-alone VQ board.

VII. CONCLUSION

Pruned trees are ideal candidates for the real time implementation of vector quantization for images. They significantly reduce computational complexity without degradation in SNR. Because of their low computational complexity (about 30 MOPS at MPEG rates), tree structured implementations are not severely constrained by I/O (finite pinout) and codevector access time limitations. The partitioning of the encoding problem into a programmable slave processor configured by an off-chip controller allows maximal flexibility in codebook structure. Tree depth, dimensionality and number of children at any node are variable parameters. A VQ slave processor, designed for distance computation and minimization, has been generated using a 1.2μ CMOS library (Figure 7) and measures $5.76 \times 6.6\ mm^2$. Clocking at a modest 40 MHz, the chip is capable of performing 80 MOPS which is quite adequate for searching tree codebooks. The design of a controller for address synthesis and node traversal has also been presented. The chip will permit the design of a single board VQ based encoder, and allow the implementation in real time, of pruned tree structured vector quantization algorithms.

References

[1] R. M. Gray, "Vector Quantization", IEEE ASSP Magazine, April 1984, pp. 4-29.

[2] Abut Huseyin, Tao B. and Smith Jack L., " Vector Quantizer Architectures for Speech and Image Coding", Proc. ICASSP, pp 756-59, 1987.

[3] G. Davidson and A. Gersho, "Application of a VLSI Vector Quantization Processor to Real-Time Speech Coding", IEEE JSAC., Vol. SAC-4, No. 1, Jan 1986, pp. 112-124.

[4] P.A. Ramamoorthy , B.Potu and T.Tran , Bit serial VLSI implementation of vector quantizer for real time image coding., IEEE CAS, Oct 89, Vol 36, pp 1281-1290.

[5] W.C.Fang, C.Y.Chang and B.J.Sheu, "Systolic Tree Searched Vector Quantizer for Real Time Image Compression" , VLSI Signal Processing IV, IEEE Press 1990, Edited by H.S.Moscovitz, Kung Yao and Rajeev Jain.

[6] R. Dianysian and R. L. Baker, "A VLSI Chip Set for Real Time Vector Quantization of Image Sequences", Proc. ISCAS, May, 1987.

[7] P. A. Chou, T. Lookabaugh, and R. M. Gray, "Optimal Pruning with Applications to Tree-Structured Source Coding and Modeling", Trans. Info Theory, 1988.

[8] S.Z. Kiang, G.J. Sullivan, C.Y. Chiu and R.L. Baker, "Recursive Optimal Pruning with application to tree-structured Vector Quantizers", ICASSP, May 1991, pp 2285-2288.

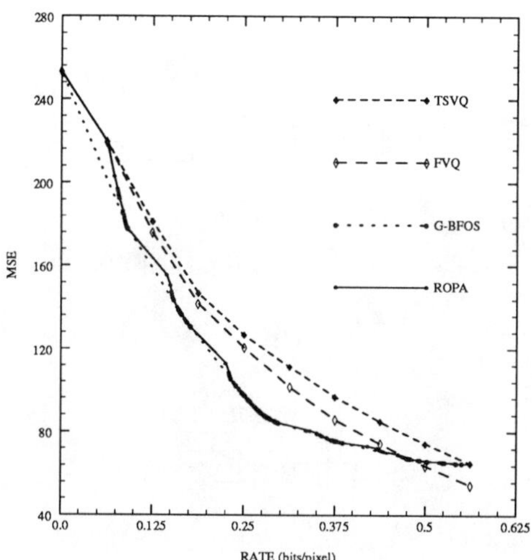

Figure 1: Performance Comparison of Full search, Binary Tree and Pruned Tree search, [8]

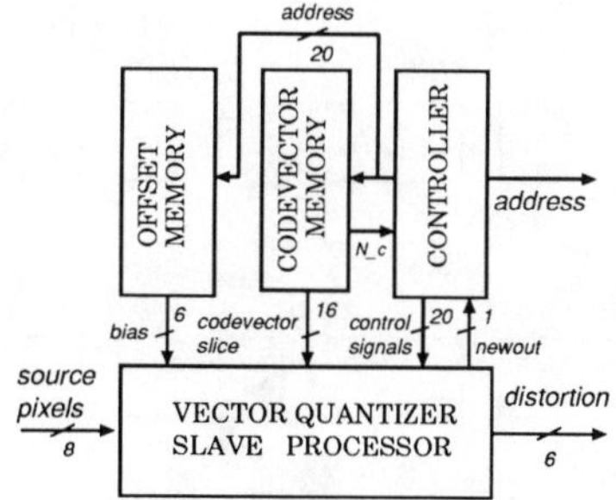

Figure 2: VQ Chip Interface

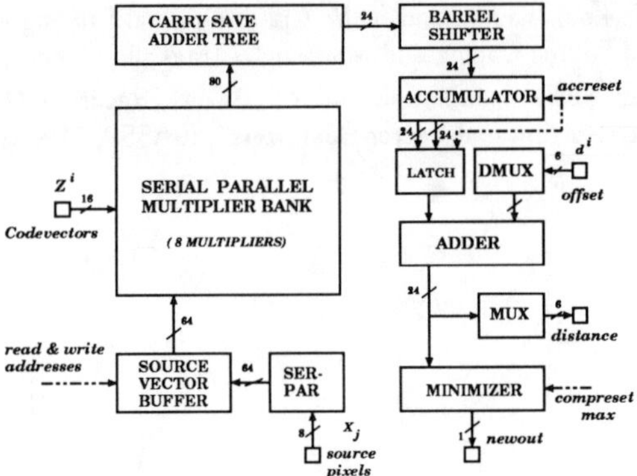

Figure 3: Chip Architecture and Floorplan

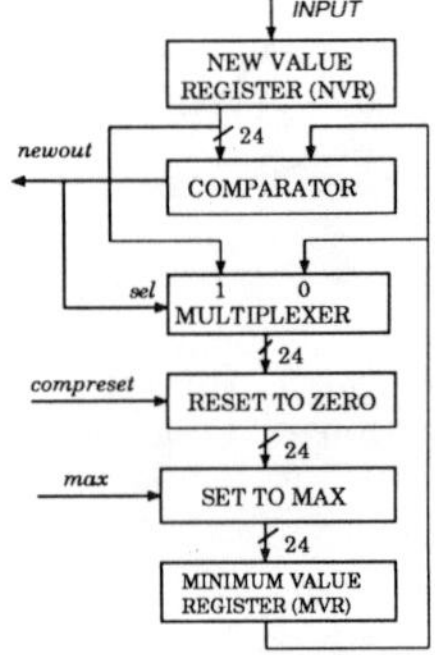

Figure 4: Block diagram of the Minimizer

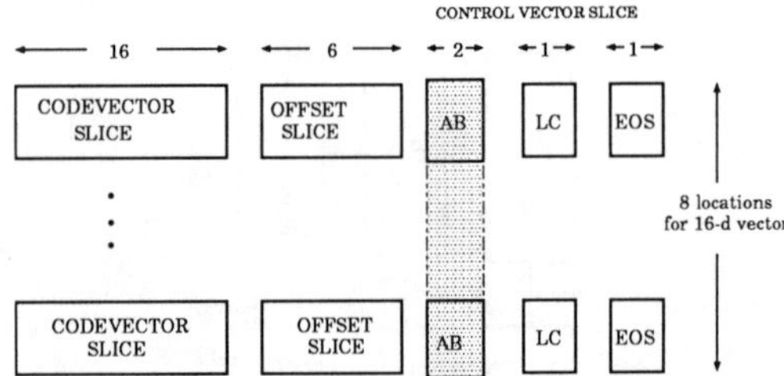

Figure 5: Codebook memory structure (Example)

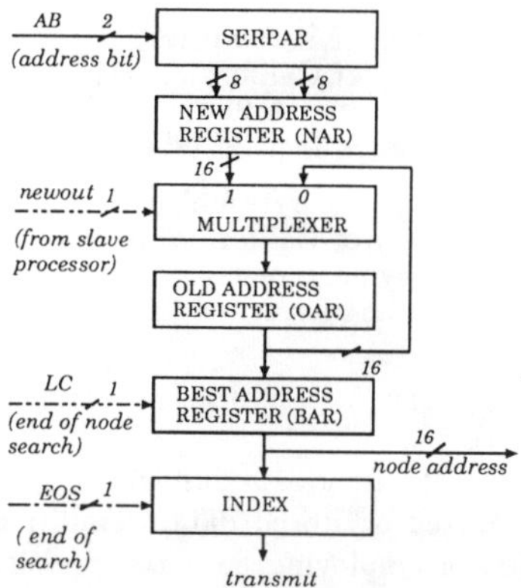

Figure 6: Address generation for pruned trees

- Scalable 1.2μ CMOS technology.

- 40 MHz input clock frequency.

- 31,000 transistors.

- 5.76×6.6 mm^2 die area.

- Two's complement data format.

- 24 bit carry save accumulation (max. dimension 256)

- Can search Binary, Non Binary and Pruned Tree codebooks

- 9 clock cycle Latency.

- 4K internal RAM for source vector interleaving and buffering.

- Cascadable

- Scan test design for registers

Features

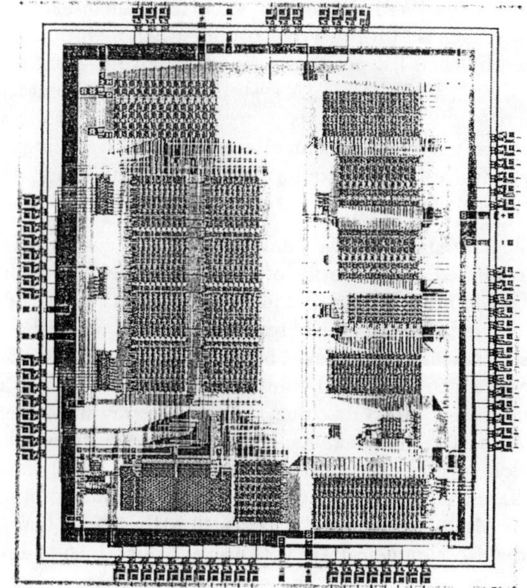

Figure 7: Chip Layout as generated by LagerIV

Transpose Coding on the Systolic Array

Lynn M. Stauffer
University of California, Irvine
Irvine, CA 92717
stauffer@ics.uci.edu

Daniel S. Hirschberg
University of California, Irvine
Irvine, CA 92717
dan@ics.uci.edu

1. Introduction

Data compression attempts to remove redundancy from data and thereby increases the density of transmitted or stored data. Traditionally, there has been a tradeoff between the benefits of employing data compression versus the computational costs related to encoding and decoding. Parallelism represents a means for speeding up data compression performance. The problem of compressing data as effectively as possible is a challenging one that has been extensively researched in the sequential setting [W91, BCW90, S88, LH87]. Included in this vast collection of sequential methods is Move-to-Front coding which maintains a dynamic list of words (to be encoded by their list position) using the move-to-front self-organizing list strategy [BSTW86, E87, R87, HC87]. A systolic array implementation of Move-to-Front has been described [TW89]. In this paper, we present systolic array implementations of Transpose coding, which uses an alternative self-organizing list strategy but otherwise is similar to Move-to-Front coding. We present implementations for fixed-length word lists which provide improved system bandwidth by accelerating Transpose coding.

The benchmark in software data compression systems is the UNIX[1] *compress* utility which is based on a variation of Ziv and Lempel coding due to Welch [W84, ZL78]. The UNIX *compress* system provides compression savings of up to 80% at a relatively high input bandwidth of 30 Kbytes per second on a 1 MIPS machine [TW89]. Higher compression savings are achieved by high-order Markov models and improved versions of *compress* which operate at limited input bandwidths of approximately 10 Kbytes per second on a 1 MIPS machine. A systolic array implementation of Move-to-Front running on a 40 MHz clock operates at a bandwidth of 40 Mbytes per second with compression savings ranging from 20% to 70% [TW89]. Several parallel compression systems based on dictionary coding achieve similar compression at input rates exceeding 25 Mbytes per second using a 40 MHz clock. Our implementations operate at a bandwidth commensurate with the systolic Move-to-Front system.

Our algorithms are implemented on a systolic array. Systolic arrays consist of a linearly-connected collection of synchronized rudimentary processing elements. Each processor has its own local memory and is assigned a unique identification number.

Section 2 describes the basic list compression method and several of its variants. Related work on systolic implementations of Move-to-Front coding is presented in

---

[1] UNIX is a trademark of AT&T Bell Laboratories

　　　　　　　　

Section 3. Our systolic designs for Transpose coding are given in Sections 4 and 5. Conclusions and areas for further investigation are the focus of Section 6.

2. List Compression

Data compression schemes can be categorized according to the method used to parse the input stream into individual encodable messages. In *defined-word* schemes, the context determines a set of source messages or words[2] (sequences of input symbols) that are candidates for encoding. There are a number of suitable definitions for the composition of a word. For instance, in text file compression, a word may be defined to consist of an individual character or a sequence of characters delineated by a space.

This paper considers a class of compression algorithms which maintain a sequential list of words using a self-organizing heuristic so that frequently accessed words appear near the front of the list. To distinguish the collection of compression techniques which utilize a self-organizing list from dynamic dictionary or Ziv and Lempel compression schemes, we will refer to this collection as *list compression* methods under a particular update heuristic.

A list compression method uses a self-organizing data structure to maintain a list of source messages and an encoding of the integers to compress list indices. A variable-length encoding of the integers, such as Elias codes, Fibonacci codes and start-step-stop codes, or a non-codeword based coding such as arithmetic coding can be used to compress list positions [BCW90]. To compress a word, it is located in the dynamic word list and encoded by its list position. After a word has been referenced, the list is reorganized appropriately. In Move-to-Front coding, the encoded word is removed from its current position and placed in the first list position. In Transpose coding, the encoded word is exchanged with the contents of the preceding list entry. By directing the encoded list position to a fixed-to-variable coder (located in a special-purpose processor at the tail of the array), the output is further compressed by assigning short codewords to positions near the front of the list. Arithmetic coding assigns shorter encodings to more frequently occurring list indices.

The move-to-front and transpose list organizing strategies are two update heuristics among a collection of many others (see [HH85] for a survey of self-organizing linear search). After reaching a steady state, where many further search requests are not expected to significantly impact the expected search time, the expected access cost will be less for transpose than for move-to-front. But the convergence time or number of accesses required to reach a steady state is greater for transpose than for move-to-front [HH85]. There are applications for which move-to-front and transpose outperform each other. Moreover, Horspool and Cormack report that the transpose heuristic performs as well as the move-to-front and is easier to implement since updates involve only local rearrangement [HC87]. For any particular application, simulations are necessary to determine the superior heuristic. This paper, by furnishing a systolic array implementation of transpose, provides the option of choosing between transpose and move-to-front for other applications.

---

[2] Bentley et al. refer to these source sequences as "words" [BSTW86].

3. Related Work in Move-to-Front Coding

Dictionary coding algorithms (which include list compression algorithms) function by replacing blocks of input with references to earlier occurrences of identical data. Systolic implementations have been developed for several variants of the general dictionary scheme. Parallel dictionary methods are surveyed in [SH91a]. Previous findings in parallel list compression are described below.

Thomborson and Wei investigate parallel implementations of Move-to-Front coding [TW89]. They distinguish two major algorithmic variants of Move-to-Front compression. The simpler procedure permutes a byte-level fixed-length list of symbols and the other approach divides the input stream into "words" and transmits words by a move-to-front code. VLSI implementation issues are the root of this distinction. That is, a general defined-word scheme requires words of arbitrary length to be present in the word list. In a systolic array, arbitrary word lengths place unreasonable demands on the number of input/output pins that must be placed on each processing element. Thomborson and Wei examine various alternatives, such as placing a limit on the length of words, and find that even permitting short words can be prohibitive.

For the simpler byte-level fixed-length Move-to-Front coding, Thomborson and Wei describe an array of 256 processing elements each of which stores an 8-bit number corresponding to an ASCII code [TW89]. The input stream enters the pipe and is encoded by detecting matches between the input characters and the bytes stored in the processing elements. When a match is detected, the input character is replaced by the identification number of the matching processor. By depositing the input character in the first processor as it enters the pipe and then cascading previous processing element contents down the array, the move-to-front behavior is realized. The output of the array, consisting of a sequence of 8-bit list indices, is fed into a fixed-to-variable length coding system. This byte-level design achieves compression savings of 19% to 38% and operates at a bandwidth of 40 Mbytes/second running on a 40 MHz byte clock.

Thomborson and Wei describe a systolic design for approximating general defined-word schemes [TW89]. The idea is to map variable-length words to an 8-bit hashcode using a hardwired hash table. These 8-bit codes are entered into the Move-to-Front list of target strings and manipulated as in the byte-level systolic encoder and decoder arrays. A closed hashing scheme with no collision resolution is used to obtain a high-speed, high-bandwidth design. These performance improvements, however, come at the expense of poorer compression performance. Unlike the sequential Move-to-Front codes in which the least-recently-used target word "falls" off the end of the list, the hashing approach randomly eliminates list words. This random behavior of the systolic design yields compression savings ranging from 25% to 65% and an input bandwidth of 40 Mbytes running on a 40 MHz clock.

4. Parallel Transpose Coding with Fixed-Length Words

Parallel transpose list compression is described by the following general paradigm. Encoder and decoder maintain identical word lists using the transpose heuristic.

Namely, after a word is used it is exchanged with the word stored in the position immediately preceding its original position. In general, to transmit word w on the systolic array, w is compared to the list entries of successive processors. If w matches the list entry in processor i, it is encoded as i. The encoder then updates the list by transposing the list entry (w) of processor i with the list entry in processor $i - 1$. When the decoder array receives list index i, it decodes it as the list word stored in processor i (which will be w) and then updates the list by exchanging w with the previous list entry stored in processor $i - 1$. Since several matches can be detected in parallel the list update procedure needs additional consideration.

In the sequential setting, a sequence of words that match the list structure in successive entries are handled in the same way as other matches. However, in the systolic environment, matches corresponding to successive entries in the array impose additional constraints when the list of words is being manipulated in parallel. That is, simultaneous matches occurring in different locations in the array may force global communication among the processors to determine the contents of the updated list. To illustrate this difficulty, consider the input string "abcdefgh" and the word list " h, g, f, e, d, c, b, a". Sequential transpose list compression outputs the sequence of positions 8, 8, 6, 6, 4, 4, 2, 2 and the final word list is identical to the original. In a sense, each pair of matches "cancels" the effect of their updates. On the systolic array, the input string pipes into the array and all eight matches are detected simultaneously. Handling the subsequent update may require global communication.

A systolic implementation may have difficulty allowing non-fixed-length words because of the unreasonable pin requirements [TW89]. Our initial designs are for defined-word methods which permute a list of fixed-length source messages. Section 5 describes systolic implementations which approximate the more general dynamic list compression method.

4.1 Systolic Implementations ENC1 and DEC1

This section gives systolic implementations (which we call ENC1 and DEC1) for encoding and decoding using the transpose fixed-length list compression model. For a list of length N, ENC1 consists of N processing elements (PE's) linearly connected by a two-way communication channel. PE i stores the list entry which is currently in position i in the list and a copy of the input word PE i considered on the previous clock cycle. The list entry will be referred to as $entry_i$ and the prior input word as $oldw_i$. The input stream enters the pipe from the right (PE 1) and the encoded message exits at the left (PE N). A schematic of the architecture is shown in Figure 1.

In order to prevent a contiguous sequence of matches from occurring concurrently, our design allows input packets to enter the array only on every other clock cycle. The word list is updated at the start of each encoding cycle. Later in the cycle, word matches are detected and encoded.

At the beginning of the ENC1 clock cycle, PE i receives 3-tuple (w, e, p) from PE $i - 1$ and bit m_{i+1} from PE $i + 1$. w is a word to be matched, e is the current

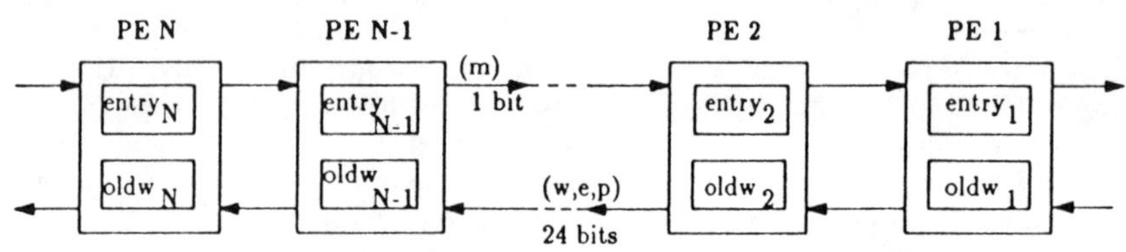

Figure 1
Systolic array for ENC1

contents of $entry_{i-1}$ that may be needed for a transpose update, p is the list position of w (0 is no match found yet) and m_{i+1} is a bit flag which is set if PE $i+1$ detected a match in the previous clock cycle. If m_{i+1} is set then PE i overwrites $entry_i$ with $oldw_i$. If w matches $entry_i$ then PE i carries out three tasks. Namely, PE i sets $p = i$, flags $m_i = 1$, and (if $i > 1$) overwrites $entry_i$ with input e (equivalently $entry_{i-1}$ obtained from PE $i - 1$).

At the close of the clock cycle, PE i overwrites $oldw_i$ with w and transmits (w, $entry_i$, p) to PE $i + 1$ and (m_i) to PE $i - 1$. Contention is avoided as a result of restricting input to every other cycle.

For $N = 256$, the ENC1 communication channel is 25 bits wide and each processing element has three 8-bit registers, an 8-bit identity comparator, two 8-bit multiplexers, and additional control logic. The critical path in PE i passes through three hardware components. First, $entry_i$ and $oldw_i$ pass through a multiplexer triggered by flag m_i. Second, $entry_i$ and the input word w enter the identity comparator. Finally, the output of the comparator determines if the input word should be encoded as i by triggering a second multiplexer. The critical path compares to the move-to-front systolic array [TW89].

Our first decoding algorithm DEC1a resembles ENC1. As in ENC1, input enters the pipe on every other clock cycle. At the outset of the cycle, the word list is updated. Unlike ENC1, where only a single bit is passed from PE i back to PE $i - 1$ to facilitate updating, DEC1a requires $entry_i$ be transmitted along with the single match bit. Following the list updating, list indices are replaced by word list entries. Details of DEC1a appear in [SH91b].

Our second decoding algorithm, DEC1b, processes packets on every system cycle and therefore operates at twice the rate of ENC1 and DEC1a. However, DEC1b restricts the input to a fixed predefined alphabet of size S. The symbols in this alphabet are arbitrarily given indices 1 through S. The output of ENC1 is a sequence of list positions which DEC1b receives as input and decodes in two stages. The first stage decodes list positions into indices and the second stage translates indices into symbols. PE i stores pos_i which is the list position of the alphabet symbol with index representation i. See [SH91b] for a detailed description of DEC1b.

For a fixed-length list, such as the 256 different 8-bit ASCII characters, each processor is initialized to contain one of the 8-bit bytes. Alternatively, new words can be added to the list until the list becomes full. Moreover, if an input word w is not in the current list of size K $(1 \leq K \leq N)$ the word is encoded by the index $K + 1$ followed by the word w and the list is updated by transposing w with the list entry K. If $K = N$ (i.e., the list is full), word w replaces the last list entry. The decoder "learns" the word list in a similar fashion. In the systolic array, an additional flag bit in each processor is used to delimit the current list. The processor holding the flag is designated as the first empty list entry. Initially, the flag bit in PE 1 is set.

4.1.1 Empirical Evaluation

Compression findings for fixed-length word implementations of Move-to-Front and Transpose coding are reported in Table 1. A systolic array consisting of 128 processing elements, each initialized to contain a 7-bit ASCII character, was simulated. The test files used are part of the Calgary/Canterbury text compression corpus [BCW90]. Transpose coding provides superior compression performance for large text files but, for small files (under 40 Kbytes), Move-to-Front gives better compression. These findings support the theoretical expectation that Transpose coding takes longer to reach a steady state but, after reaching a steady state, has a smaller expected access cost.

Input File	Size (Bytes)	Compression Savings – MTF	Compression Savings – Transpose
bib	111261	29.44	32.24
book1	768771	37.91	41.90
book2	610856	36.98	39.54
paper1	53161	34.19	34.33
paper2	82199	37.49	39.07
paper3	46526	36.63	36.81
paper4	13286	35.20	29.75
paper5	11954	33.71	26.64
paper6	38105	35.45	33.79
news	377109	31.48	34.43
progc	39611	30.72	30.70
progl	71646	38.72	38.61
progp	49379	35.26	34.99

Table 1

Compression savings delivered by Transpose and Move-to-Front Coding

4.2. Systolic Implementations ENC2 and DEC2 with Reduced Delay

The linear delay of the previous designs is determined by the piping of the input from PE 1 through to PE N. In this section we describe an architecture which combines a systolic array with trees, resulting in a logarithmic delay. The trees broadcast the input to the systolic array and reduce the simultaneous outputs of the processors. A similar architecture for dictionary coding is described in [Z90]. In addition to decreased delay, the restriction allowing data to enter the pipe only on every other system cycle is eliminated in systolic implementation ENC2 for Transpose coding.

For a list of size N, the ENC2 architecture consists of $3N - 2$ processors. The first N processors are arranged in a systolic pipe and the remaining processors are configured as two binary trees (each containing $N - 1$ processors) synchronized with the systolic array (see Figure 2). One of the binary trees (the *broadcast tree*) is placed on top of the systolic array. Input enters at the root of the broadcast tree and is propagated down the tree to each array processor. The other binary tree (the *reduction tree*) is placed below the systolic array. Results of the processors are reduced to a single non-null output via the propagation toward the root of the reduction tree. The tree interconnect provides total delay of $2 \log_2 N$.

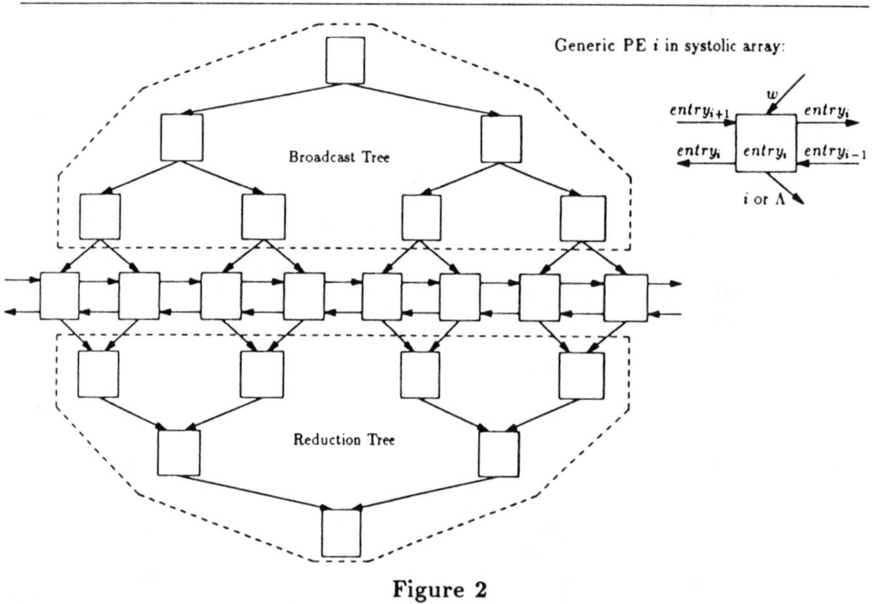

Figure 2
Broadcast/reduce architecture for ENC2 and DEC2

Processor PE i in the systolic array stores the list entry which is currently in position i in the list. As in ENC1, this entry is referred to as $entry_i$. PE i receives input from the broadcast tree and from PE $i - 1$ and PE $i + 1$. PE i transmits $entry_i$ to PE $i - 1$ and PE $i + 1$ and outputs match information to the reduction tree.

Processors in the broadcast tree simply pass their input to their outputs. Reduction processors receive two inputs which are either both zero or one is non-zero. In the first case, the reduction tree outputs zero. In the second case, the reduction processor transmits the non-zero input.

After the input has propagated down the broadcast tree to the array processors, encoding proceeds as follows. At the beginning of the clock cycle, PE i receives (w) from the broadcast tree, $(entry_{i-1})$ from PE $i-1$, and $(entry_{i+1})$ from PE $i+1$. w is the word to be encoded. If w matches $entry_i$ then w is set to i and $entry_{i-1}$ is written into $entry_i$. If w matches $entry_{i+1}$ (received from PE $i+1$ at the start of the cycle) then PE i overwrites $entry_i$ with $entry_{i+1}$ and sets w to 0. Otherwise, PE i sets w to 0. At the close of the clock cycle, PE i transmits $entry_i$ to PE $i+1$ and PE $i-1$ and sends w to its neighboring processor in the reduction tree. Thus, at the end of each clock cycle, exactly one processor (the one which matched the input symbol) outputs a non-zero value into the base of the broadcast tree. This non-zero value is propagated to the root of the reduction tree and finally output. Decompression (DEC2) mirrors ENC2 and is carefully described in [SH91b].

5. Parallel Transpose Coding with Arbitrary Words

The designs of Section 4 included only fixed-length words in the list. The more general word list compression scheme permits words of arbitrary lengths to be present. A straightforward extension of our previous designs allows arbitrary words. However, the 3-tuples that travel through the array, consisting of two words and a pointer, may lead to unreasonable VLSI implementation requirements. For example, the fixed-length implementations consisting of 256 processing elements require 24 bits per tuple or 48 input/output pins per systolic element. For words of length 8 or less on a systolic array of similar size, the pin requirement jumps to 272 input/output pins per chip. One simple solution to the problem of unbounded pin requirements is to place a bound on the maximum allowable word length. This bound enforces a limit on the pin requirements. The appropriate maximum word length is dependent on the application.

In order to avoid the potential VLSI issues, Thomborson and Wei approximate Move-to-Front coding by using a hardwired hash table to map arbitrary words onto an 8-bit byte [TW89]. This single byte is piped into the array and encoded as a fixed-length word. The increased throughput provided by the systolic design comes at the expense of lower compression savings. Their design provides compression savings ranging from 25% to 65% and an input bandwidth of 40 Mbytes running on a 40 MHz clock. This is considerably lower than the compression savings of 30% to 75% obtained by the sequential Move-to-Front codes. Implementing this hashing approach on our systolic transpose coders is straightforward. We suspect that the random behavior of the hashing scheme would result in compression savings similar to those of the Move-to-Front systolic implementation [TW89].

6. Topics for Future Investigation

Although we have outlined the design and compression performance of several systolic compressors for high-bandwidth applications, extensive empirical evaluations of our methods are needed to fully describe their behavior.

As supported by the empirical findings in Section 4.1.1, Move-to-Front coding performs well on small files and Transpose coding is superior for large files. This suggests the examination of a hybrid scheme which combines Move-to-Front and Transpose coding. Initially, Move-to-Front coding is utilized and at some point control is switched to a Transpose coding method.

The systolic designs for arbitrary word lengths are limited by the imperfect approximation behavior of the hashing scheme. Alternative methods are necessary to better emulate general sequential list compression.

As suggested by Thomborson and Wei, a high-bandwidth architecture for adaptive Huffman coding, other fixed-to-variable length coders or arithmetic coding which is capable of operating at a rate that is commensurate to the systolic list compression systems is also of great interest. Potentially, this high-bandwidth coder, when coupled with a systolic list compressor, will lead to improved compression performance.

References

[BCW90]   Bell, T. C., Cleary, J. G., and Witten, I. H. *Text Compression,* Prentice-Hall, Englewood Cliffs, New Jersey, 1990.

[BSTW86]   Bentley, J. L., Sleator, D. D., Tarjan, R. E., and Wei, V. K. A locally adaptive data compression scheme. *Commun. ACM 29,* 4 (April, 1986), 320–330.

[E87]   Elias, P. Interval and recency rank source coding: two on-line adaptive variable-length schemes. *IEEE Trans. Inform. Theory IT-33,* 1 (Jan., 1987), 3–10.

[HH85]   Hester, J. H. and Hirschberg, D. S. Self-organizing linear search. *ACM Comp. Sur. 17,* 3 (Sep., 1985), 295–311.

[HC87]   Horspool, R. N., and Cormack, G. V. A locally adaptive data compression scheme. Technical Correspondence. *Commun. ACM 30,* 9 (Sep., 1987), 792–794.

[LH87]   Lelewer, D. A. and Hirschberg, D. S. Data compression. *ACM Comp. Sur. 19,* 3 (Sep., 1987), 261–296.

[R87]   Ryabko, B. Y. A locally adaptive data compression scheme. Technical Correspondence. *Commun. ACM 30,* 9 (Sep., 1987), 792.

[SH91a]   Stauffer, L. M. and Hirschberg, D. S. Parallel data compression. Report 91-44. Info. and Comp. Sci. Dept., U. of California, Irvine, 1991.

[SH91b]   Stauffer, L. M. and Hirschberg, D. S. Systolic Implementations for Transpose Coding. Report 91-69. Info. and Comp. Sci. Dept., U. of California, Irvine, 1991.

[S88]   Storer, J. A. *Data Compression Methods and Theory,* Computer Science Press, Rockville, Maryland, 1988.

[TW89]   Thomborson, C. D. and Wei, Belle W.-Y. Systolic implementations of a move-to-front text compressor. In *Proceedings 1989 ACM Symposium on Parallel Algorithms and Architectures,* Sante Fe, New Mex., ACM, New York, 1989, pp. 283–290.

[W84]   Welch, T. A. A technique for high-performance data compression. *Computer 17,* 6 (June, 1984), 8–19.

[W91]   Williams, R. N. *Adaptive Data Compression,* Kluwer Academic Publishers, Norwell, MA, 1991.

[Z90]   Zito-Wolf, R. J. A broadcast/reduce architecture for high-speed data compression. In *Proceedings of the Second IEEE Symposium on Parallel and Distributed Processing,* Dallas, Texas, 1990.

[ZL78]   Ziv, J. and Lempel, A. Compression of individual sequences via variable-rate coding. *IEEE Trans. Inf. Theory 24,* 5 (1978), 530–536.

On the JPEG Model for Lossless Image Compression

Glen Langdon[†] *   Amit Gulati[† †]   Ed Seiler[‡]

langdon@cse.ucsc.edu   amitg@cse.ucsc.edu   seiler@amarna.gsfc.nasa.gov

[†]Department of Computer Engineering   [‡]NASA
University of California at Santa Cruz   Goddard Space Flight Center
Santa Cruz, CA 95064   Greenbelt, MD

ABSTRACT

The *JPEG lossless* arithmetic coding algorithm and a predecessor algorithm called *Sunset* both employ adaptive arithmetic coding with the *context model* and *parameter reduction* approach of Todd et al. We compare the Sunset and JPEG context models for the lossless compression of gray-scale images, and derive new algorithms based on the strengths of each. The context model and binarization tree variations are compared in terms of their speed (the number of binary encodings required per test image) and their compression gain. In this study, the Bostelmann technique is studied for use at all resolutions, whereas in the arithmetic coded JPEG lossless, the technique is applied only at the 16-bit per pixel resolution.

1 Introduction

A *context model* (model structure) [1, 2] operates recursively on the selected data items of the data sequence, and employs conditioning states x based on the past history of the data seen. In classical information theory, conditioning states x are in 1:1 correspondence with probability distributions. In [1], context function $G(x)$ selects the probability distribution for the next event by partitioning conditioning states x. Now each context (partition) z is in 1:1 correspondence with its probability distribution z.

In lossless predictive coding algorithms using a multiple-context model, *parameter reduction* [3] is one purpose for quantizing the error to form *error buckets*. In contrast, lossy algorithms quantize the error to reduce the amount of information, such that only the error bucket index is encoded. For encoding the *exact error* within the bucket (a necessary step in *lossless* algorithms) a large number of contexts are not needed since most of the benefit of conditioning falls to the bucket index (quantization range) statistics. In [3], the exact error within each bucket (the extrabits) was not conditioned, but had its own 0-order distribution.

A technique first described in [4], and published in [3], *selects* neighboring error-buckets (known to the decoder) as *contexts* for conditioning the prediction error. For *context selection* in [4], the buckets for prediction errors need not be the same buckets used to decompose the prediction error distributions. Conditioning with quantized prediction errors improves the compression over the zero-order

---

*This author partially supported by NASA Goddard Space Flight Center as a NASA Summer Faculty Fellow.

[†]This author partially supported by the UCSC Foundation through a gift of Glen and Marian Langdon.

lossless DPCM schemes by about 12% to 25%, see [3]. statistically Subsequent investigators (including the JPEG results) confirm this advantage for error-bucket contexts over the unconditioned error distribution.

2 Sunset: a hardware-oriented implementation

Sunset is a hardware-oriented approach [5, 6, 7] for [3], and was prototyped on a PC/AT card. Error buckets are based on the "power of two" exponent number of the *bit position* of the leading (most significant) bit of the absolute value of the prediction error. The mantissa (*extrabits* in [5]) and the exponent together determine the prediction error. The position of the leading prediction error bit, for statistical coding with a Huffman codeword appears due to [8], where the position within the bucket (extrabits) and sign bit are concatenated after the Huffman codeword. Another prediction error approach based on [8] appears in [9]. In Sunset, a "leading-one" circuit commonly used in floating-point arithmetic for normalization quickly identifies the bucket number.

Sunset uses adaptive binary arithmetic coding, and decomposes (binarizes) the prediction error with a binary tree. Sunset binarization has four steps; the first step determines if the error is zero. If not zero, the second step determines the sign of the nonzero error. This second step, unlike [3], lumps (blends) positive error buckets with the negative error bucket of the same exponent. The third step encodes the bucket number as a sequence of binary events in the form of a binary search. In the fourth step, the exact error (extrabits) are coded, otherwise the encoding would be lossy.

Sunset employed 8 nonzero absolute error buckets, the first nonzero bucket being an error of 1, the second such having errors of 2 or 3, the third having errors of 4 through 7, and so forth with the eighth bucket having errors of 128 through 255. If there are more than 256 gray levels, i.e., more than 8 bits per pixel, then nonzero bucket 8 can become a *catch-all bucket*. Instead of an extrabit part, bucket 8 may be followed by the desired pixel value itself. A catch-all bucket allows any number of bits per pixel to be conveniently handled by a hardware implementation as long as the encoder and decoder both know the number of bits per pixel in the original image.

Empirically, the distribution of the prediction error appears Laplacian (double-sided exponential). Therefore, use of the exponent of 2 for bucketing the prediction error suggests the bucket numbers may be approximately uniformly distributed. If so, then using a binary search tree for coding the bucket number is a means to reduce the number of coding operations. A Huffman tree for the relative frequency of each error bucket would optimally reduce the number of binary encodings.

The neighborhood context includes the *V-pixel* (vertically above the current pixel), the *H-pixel* (the pixel horizontally to the left), and the *D-pixel* (for diagonal) above the H-pixel. Between scanlines (at the image border) the context pixels "wrap around" as was done in [2]. A 4-bit context number identifies each context. Fifteen of these sixteen values represent buckets -7, through 0, to bucket +7. The sixteenth context bucket jointly represents buckets -8 and +8. For the D-pixel, the three most significant pixel magnitude bits were employed. The context index is 11 bits, and this version is called *Sunset-11*. For simplicity the prototype card also used the D-pixel context number, and this version is called *Sunset-12*. The first three steps of the binarization employ binary adaptation to the statistics of each context. The fourth step, the extrabits, does not adapt; each bit value is simply encoded under probability $\frac{1}{2}$. In another version, *Sunset-8*, only the 4-bit H- and V-pixel contexts are used. *Sunset-8x* statistically encodes the extrabits according to the approach suggested in [3].

3   JPEG lossless image compression

The JPEG (Joint Photographic Experts Group) working group is developing a still color image compression standard [10, 11]. In [12] a proposal called EXACT is made for an independent lossless gray-scale image compression algorithm. The JPEG baseline algorithm is a lossy algorithm for still color images based on the discrete cosine transform (DCT). It was not convenient to use the DCT version to exactly reproduce the original image. The independent JPEG lossless algorithm uses predictive coding. One version has Huffman coding as in [8]. The second JPEG lossless version, considered here, uses prediction with error bucketing for parameter reduction, does context selection based on bucketed prediction errors, encodes with an adaptive binary arithmetic coder called the QM-Coder, and uses a binarization of the prediction error. The QM-Coder is MPS-renorm driven as in [13]. See also [14] for a background and description of the adapter portion of Q-Coder type algorithms.

We explain this arithmetic coding version in terms of Sunset. JPEG lossless repeats the same four binarization steps, but the binarization of the error bucket of step 3 is determined by the same leading-one method *except* value 1 is first subtracted from the nonzero absolute error value. The bucket-coding of step 3 also differs: Sunset's *binary* search is replaced by a *sequential* search.

Following the subtraction of 1 from the nonzero absolute prediction error, the result is called Sz. The sequential search begins with event $Sz = 0$, followed by events called X1, X2, etc., through event X15. Events $Sz = 0$ and X1 have no extrabits. Bucket X2 corresponds to Sz values 2 and 3 (or absolute error value 3 and 4), and has one extrabit. The extrabits for buckets X2, X3, etc., are encoded under events respectively called B2, B3, etc.

The conditional distributions for the lossless JPEG algorithm are based on three context models as a function of the binary events in question. To encode the zero-error and the sign events, the first context model has 25 independent contexts, derived from the cross-product of 5-element subsets of the V-pixel and H-pixel error buckets. The five elements are denoted: $-L$ (large negative error), $-S$ (small negative error), 0 (zero error), $+S$ and $+L$. These context buckets are formed by grouping the prediction error buckets, where 0 is zero error. In the default, the Small errors are errors that lie in prediction error buckets X1 and

X2. As in Sunset, there is a separate context for each separate binary event. For example there are 25 distributions for the zero-error event, and another 25 for the sign event.

Binary event $Sz = 0$ is encoded under the second context model. This model has 50 contexts, formed from the set product of the 25-element first context model and the two-valued sign.

The third JPEG lossless context model has two probability distributions for each binary event using it. The third context model is the 2-element subset *Large* and *Not-Large*. Element *Large* consists of the set $\{-L, +L\}$ and element *Not Large* of set $\{-S, 0, +S\}$ of the V-pixel error bucket. Each of the remaining binary events X1,...,X15 (the bit-position number) and B2,...,B15 (corresponding to bit-positions with a nonzero number of extrabits) have their own distributions conditioned on the value of boolean variable *Large*.

There can be up to 16 bits per pixel for the lossless JPEG algorithm. With more than 8 bits per pixel, the error buckets continue to X9 for 9 bits per pixel, etc. For 16-bit pixels, ordinarily 17 bits of arithmetic is required; however for this pixel resolution, the technique of Bostelmann [15] is employed. We briefly describe the idea. For convenience, call the mod 2^{16} prediction error result the *Bostelmann number*. The most significant bit of the 16-bit Bostelmann number is treated as the sign bit. Each unique Bostelmann number represents two possible (or twin) error values. Since the range of the error for any unique predicted value has exactly $2^{16} - 1$ possible values in the 16 bit per pixel case, when one error value of the corresponding Bostelmann number is possible, the twin value is impossible. The *original error value* is exactly reconstructed as the modulo 2^{16} sum of the predicted value and the 16-bit Bostelmann number. In this work, we employ the Bostelmann technique for the 8-bit per pixel test files using modulo 2^8 arithmetic because we suggest using the Bostelmann technique at all pixel resolutions.

4   Context Model Performance and the Sparse Context Problem

In [1], the *ideal codelength* performance measure, also nicknamed *NlogN*, was introduced as a means to compare competing context models. The NlogN measure was used in [3]. Unfortunately, the NlogN measure is subject to the *sparse context problem*. When the number of contexts is increased, the symbol counts are dispersed among a larger number of contexts so each context receives fewer counts. Some sparse contexts have so little activity that only one of the symbols has a nonzero count and the ideal length summand is 0, giving a false indication of achievable compression. One way to study the problem is to define a measure N+logN+ that replaces a count of zero in an *active* context with a count of 1.

Another way to assess the sparse context problem is to use a one-pass measure. A closed form using factorials for enumerative counting appears in [16]. Here, the Ideal Code Length in [1] is augmented by the Enumerative Length (EL), or the *LogFac* measure [17]. The enumerative length employs the causal *Laplacian estimator* (based on Laplace's Rule of Succession) that estimates the relative

LENA	Context	NlogN	†N+logN+	LogFac
256x256	8-bit	136849.72	137389.72	140750.25
	9-bit	136114.27	138005.27	141346.17
	12-bit	123995.11	145292.12	146180.88
512x512	8-bit	508015.59	508758.59	512413.59
	9-bit	507028.06	509049.06	513307.69
	12-bit	491381.34	511966.41	518926.56

Table 4.1: Sunset's Sparse Context Problem for lena at multiple resolutions. Distribution of the same skew over several bins results in weaker performance. †The N+logN+ construction compensates for skews where one of the symbols did not occur. On the larger resolution lena, the problem isn't as pronounced.

frequencies for each next symbol based on the symbol counts so far, and is thus a realizable *one-pass* technique. See Table 4.1.

For the general case, the one-pass codelength for the stationarity assumption for a single context is the LogFac formula for EL given below. Letting alphabet A contain $|A|$ symbols: $A = \{a_1, \ldots a_i \ldots a_{|A|}\}$, then $EL(s) = \log(N + (|A| - 1))! - \sum_{a \in A} \log(c(a)!)$, where $c(a)$ is the number of times symbol a was seen. The above formula should have a term $(-\log(|A| - 1)!)$, which should subtract very little from the length estimate. Stirling's formula may be used to simplify the calculation for cases where the counts are large.

Table 4.1 makes the point that the use of the H-, V-, and D-pixels as contexts may encounter the sparse context problem on the size of images tested. In contrast, JPEG lossless uses fewer buckets per pixel, and only for the H- and V-pixels, and avoids sparse contexts. Context model Sunset-12 has 4096 members in the context set which appears too many. Context model Sunset-8 employs only the H- and V-pixels for an 8-bit context identifier and 256 members in the context set The EL measure LogFac penalizes the adapter "learning phase" required before the context becomes economical. Notice that as the number of contexts for the subsampled Lena image increases, that the LogFac metric also increases, as does N+logN+. In contrast, NlogN decreases with increasing contexts, as more and more binary contexts experience one count of value 0. The sparse context effect is less pronounced on the 512x512 images because each context experiences more count activity due to the quadrupling of the number of pixels. The sparse context problem of Sunset-12 appears to be solved with Sunset-8 due to the reduction in the number of contexts by a factor of 16.

Strategies against the sparse context problem include escaping out of them to a more highly populated context [18], or increasing the speed of adapting to the probability distribution when highly skewed (the "fast attack" aspect of the JPEG adaptive binary arithmetic coder called the QM-coder).

5 Speed considerations

The JPEG error buckets are not quite the same as the Sunset buckets, due to the JPEG subtraction of one, so the extrabit comparisons are comparable only between

Image	Number of Pels (8bits/pel)	Number of Encodings	
		JPEG	Sun8xb
lena	65536	300392	283936
lenna	262144	1090429	1047697
ba	65536	291729	281013
hh	262144	1103867	1107075
liver	262144	1039713	1016610
sjband1[§]	262144	687674	877627
tpd	65535	279836	273573

Table 5.1: Performance in terms of SPEED: Number of binary encodings per image for both JPEG and Sunset. [§]sjband1 was collected from an infrared camera and thus produces very small prediction errors.

the Sunset versions. JPEG uses more binary encodings for the error buckets and less extrabit encodings relative to Sunset. If the bucketing is sequentially ordered for binary encoding as in JPEG, then JPEG lossless averages a net loss in speed relative to the Sunset and [8] bucketing methods that do not subtract one from nonzero errors before bucketing. For example the fourth nonzero JPEG bucket (X3) corresponds to absolute error values of 5 through 8 (two errorbits). In Sunset, the two error-bit case is the third error bucket containing absolute values 4 through 7. Notice that subtracting 1 from the nonzero errors to form value Sz before bucketing has the overall detrimental effect of increasing the average number of binary events to be encoded by JPEG. In the example, errors 5, 6, and 7 require one more binary encoding for the JPEG bucketing. For error 6, the lossless JPEG approach encodes 8 events: (1) nonzero, (2) sign, (3) not Sz=0, (4) not X1, (5) not X2, (6) X3, (7) B3: first extrabit, and (8) B3: second extrabit. The corresponding error requires 7 sequential encodings if the error is not reduced in value by 1: (1) nonzero, (2) sign, (3) not 1, (4) not 2-3, (5) 4-6, (6) first extrabit, (7) second extrabit.

From a compression standpoint, the ideal code length is the same no matter how the binarization takes place (other considerations being equal). However, a factor affecting speed is the distribution governing the error buckets. For example, if the error buckets are equally likely, then a binary search offers fewer encodings to identify the error bucket. In fact, if the distribution is known, then a Huffman code tree offers the optimal speed for binarizing the error bucket. Table 5.1 indicates the number of binary encodings required for each of the test images by lossless JPEG and Sun8xb.

The Sunset method of decomposing the prediction error usually offers an advantage when the error bucket distribution is nearly equally likely, as would be expected with a Laplacian distribution for the prediction error. The speed advantage goes to JPEG for extrabit encodings, since subtracting 1 to form Sz means an error of 2 requires no extrabits (Sunset needs 1 extrabit), an error of 3 requires 1 extrabit (Sunset needs 2), etc. However, JPEG requires fewer error bucket encodings for error buckets with fewer error values, due to the sequential encoding. The Sunset speed advantage occurs with all but two of the test images shwon in the figure. Most images (with sjband1 being an exception) tend to have near-uniformly

Image	Algorithm	Buckets	Extrabits	Total
lena	sunset-12	233389.10	127255.15	360644.25
(256x256)	jpeg	248367.25	111400.88	359768.12
	sunset-8x	222984.33	126964.81	349949.16
	sun8xb	222765.04	126205.00	348970.03
lenna	sunset-12	857645.70	410299.62	1267945.38
(512x512)	jpeg	953825.80	339363.75	1293189.50
	sunset-8x	849441.41	409033.22	1258474.62
	sun8xb	849418.57	406056.62	1255475.25
liver	sunset-12	772561.41	409911.34	1182472.75
(512x512)	jpeg	839478.16	364745.22	1204223.38
	sunset-8x	765428.15	409467.12	1174895.25
	sun8xb	765361.34	406591.75	1171953.12
tpd	sunset-12	231928.43	112610.52	344538.94
(256x256)	jpeg	248450.32	97123.38	345573.69
	sunset-8x	223205.89	112431.02	335636.91
	sun8xb	221035.40	110294.45	331329.84
hh	sunset-12	882925.23	437538.53	1320463.75
(512x512)	jpeg	951136.77	384170.53	1335307.25
	sunset-8x	870214.70	436839.28	1307054.00
	sun8xb	869245.59	434930.69	1304176.25
ba	sunset-12	240509.01	120726.20	361235.22
(256x256)	jpeg	249189.75	105490.86	354680.62
	sunset-8x	227978.95	120569.77	348548.72
	sun8xb	249189.75	119909.95	347640.25
sjband	sunset-12	640210.05	92508.65	732718.69
(512x512)	jpeg	698458.16	30316.11	731475.44
	sunset-8x	641592.41	92502.31	734094.75
	sun8xb	641592.41	91508.38	733100.81

Table 6.1: Compression performance is reported for one-pass (LogFac) entropy on several images: lena , lenna, liver, tpd (tripod), hh (hurseley house), ba (boat), sjband1 (infrared). The Total is the sum of the Bucket length, extrabit lenght as well as the zero error and sign bucket lengths. Gains from 8-bit contexts, sunset decomposition, more sophisticated extrabit conditioning and bostelmann's error range reduction technique can be extracted from this table.

distributed bucket numbers (at least for buckets 1 to 6 and the test files used), which gives a speed advantage to Sunset's binary search over JPEG's sequential search.

Table 5.1 does not take into account the subraction that generates Sz. In software implementations the JPEG lossless approach requires an extra subraction operation, and in hardware implementations an extra subtractor unit is required.

6   Extrabit coding and use of Bostelmann approach

The study also addressed the context for the extrabits. Sunset-12 without statistical coding of the extrabits is inferior to JPEG lossless. An experiment was tried using the suggested 0-order method in [3]. The experiment showed a good compression gain per testfile.

A second experiment simplified the approach. Given a Laplacian (exponential) distribution, and (for example) for error bucket 4 with 3 extrabits, the 000 mantissa value is expected to be the most popular and 111 the least popular. Between these extremes, the smaller the mantissa value, the higher its probability in the Laplacian distribution. The first mantissa bit, by this reasoning, should have value

Image	LogFac	Q-coder [13]	QM-coder [19]
lenna (512x512x8)	1.67 (1255475.25)	1.60:1 (1311209)	1.62:1 (1293571)
liver (512x512x8)	1.79 (1171946.12)	1.73:1 (1208777)	1.76:1 (1194484)
sjband (512x512x8)	2.86 (733100.81)	2.75:1 (762120)	2.77:1 (756392)
jhotel (576x720x8)	1.63 (2040226.25)	1.56:1 (2121879)	1.58:1 (2096752)
jgirl (576x720x8)	1.71 (1942343.00)	1.64:1 (2020754)	1.66:1 (1996676)
jballoon (576x720x8)	2.30 (1444167.38)	2.22:1 (1496042)	2.24:1 (1481577)
jgold (576x720)	1.63 (2032307.38)	1.58:1 (2105044)	1.60:1 (2078417)

Table 6.2: Q-coder and QM-coder compression gains (derived as α/β where α is the size of the uncompressed data and β is the size of the compressed data [20]). Values in parenthesis are actual lengths in bits.

0 as the most popular bit. For the second bit, for either 0 or 1 as the first bit, the same reasoning suggests that again 0 should be the most popular extrabit value in the second bit position. This experiment simply compressed each extrabit under its position number. Thus for error bucket 4, the bucket-dependent *bit-position context*, is the set 0, 1, or 2 defined by the bit position number. The use of these 3 coding parameters performed nearly as well as the 7 coding parameter 0-order case. The use of the extrabit position, independent of which bucket, should show a slight loss in compression gain relative to the bucket-dependent use of bit-position as context.

The JPEG lossless algorithm lumps all extrabits for a given bucket size into the same binary event context so the lesser significant positions, whose skewness is fairly flat, dilutes the more significant positions that have more skew and offer better compression. Results obtained are summarized for several test images in Table 6.1. Sunset-8x uses the H-pixel and V-pixel context components and encodes the extrabits under bit-position contexts.

The current best, named *Sun8xb*, is Sunset-8x with the addition of the Bostelmann technique to reduce the number of bits in the resulting prediction error. Since both the encoder and decoder know there are K bits per pixel, then application of the Bostelmann technique at any such resolution would employ modulo 2^K arithmetic in determining the prediction error. For test images of 8 bits per pixel, the prediction error arithmetic is done modulo-256.

References

[1] J. Rissanen and G. Langdon. Universal modeling and coding. *IEEE Trans. Info Theory*, IT-27(1):12–23, January 1981.

[2] G. Langdon and J. Rissanen. Compression of black-white images with arithmetic coding. *IEEE Trans. Commun.*, COM–29(6):858–867, June 1981.

[3] S. Todd, G. Langdon, and J. Rissanen. Parameter reduction and context selection for compression of the gray-scale images. *IBM Jl. Res. & Develop.*, 29(2):188–193, March 1985.

[4] G. Langdon, J. Rissanen, and S. Todd. On lossless compression of gray scale images. In *IBM Internal Conference on Data Compression*, Yorktown Heights, NY, March 18–20 1980. IBM Research Division. (Available from IBM Research Division as RJ-8026, March 18, 1991. Refereed version is [3]).

[5] G. Langdon. Further developments in lossless gray-scale image compression. In *IBM Internal Conference on Pattern Recognition and Image Processing*, Yorktown Heights, NY, November 1984. IBM Research Division. Declassified as IBM Research Report RJ6426, 9/8/88.

[6] G. Langdon. Compression of Multilevel Signals, U. S. Patent 4,749,983, June 7, 1988. (Filed April 29, 1986).

[7] G. Langdon. Sunset: a hardware-oriented algorithm for lossless compression of gray scale images. *Proc. SPIE, (Medical Imaging V: Image Capture, Formatting, and Display)*, 1444:272–282, March 1991.

[8] O. Pahlm, P. O. Borjesson, and O. Werner. Compact digital storage of ECGs. *Computer Programs in Biomedicine*, 9:293–300, 1979.

[9] G. Einarsson. An improved implementation of predictive coding compression. *IEEE Trans. Commun.*, COM-39:169–171, February 1991.

[10] W. B. Pennebaker and J. L. Mitchell. Standardization of color image compression. I. Sequential coding. In *Electronic Imaging '89 East*, Boston MA, October 1989.

[11] G. Wallace. Overview of the JPEG (ISO/CCITT) still image compression standard. *Proc. SPIE (Image Processing Algorithms and Techniques)*, 1244:220–233, 1990.

[12] W. B. Pennebaker and J. L. Mitchell. EXACT - an algorithm for lossless coding of continuous tone images. Working group document JPEG-186, ISO/IEC/ JTC1/SC2/WG8, September 1988.

[13] W. B. Pennebaker, J. M. Mitchell, G. G. Langdon, and R. B. Arps. An overview of the basic principles of the Q-Coder adaptive binary arithmetic coder. *IBM Jl. Res. Develop.*, 32(6):717–726, November 1988.

[14] G. Langdon. Probabilistic and Q-Coder algorithms for binary source adaptation. In *Data Compression Conference 91*, pages 12–22. IEEE Computer Society, April 1991.

[15] G. Bostelmann. A simple high quality DPCM-Codec for video telephony using 8 Mbit per second. *Nachrichtentechn. Z.*, 27:115–117, 1974.

[16] J. G. Cleary and I. H. Witten. A comparison of enumerative and adaptive codes. *IEEE Trans Inf. Theory.*, IT-30(2):306–315, March 1984.

[17] Glen Langdon. On adaptation to multiple-context binary sources. Research Report RJ 7845, IBM Research Division, Almaden Research Center, San Jose CA 95120-6099, November 1990.

[18] J. G. Cleary and I. H. Witten. Data compression using adaptive coding and partial string matching. *IEEE Trans Commun.*, COM-32(4):396–402, April 1984.

[19] W.B. Pennebaker. JPEG technical specification, revision 8, August 1990. Informal Working Paper JPEG-8-R8, Aug. 1990.

[20] Ross Williams. *Adaptive Data Compression.* Kluwer Academic, 1991.

PROGRESSIVE VECTOR QUANTIZATION OF MULTISPECTRAL IMAGE DATA USING A MASSIVELY PARALLEL SIMD MACHINE

M. Manohar
USRA, Code 936,
GSFC, Greenbelt, MD 20771

James C. Tilton
Code 936, NASA/GSFC,
Greenbelt, MD 20771

Abstract: Progressive Transmission (PT) using Vector Quantization (VQ) is called Progressive Vector Quantization (PVQ) and is used for efficient telebrowsing and dissemination of multispectral image data via computer networks. The initial data renditions are obtained by applying VQ to a compression ratio of at least 20-30. The quantization residuals thus obtained are low entropy data which can be further vector quantized. Thus the residuals from previous quantization are iteratively quantized until the image is decomposed into required number of levels. The last residue however is compressed using a lossless compression to ensure exact or lossless reconstruction at the receiving end. This data can be retrieved from the database and transferred to remote sites across the computer networks keeping the transmission costs in check. Theoretically any compression technique can be used in PT mode. Here VQ is selected as the baseline compression technique because the VQ encoded images can be decoded by simple table lookup process so that the users are not burdened with computational problems for using compressed data. Codebook generation or training phase is the most critical part of VQ. Two different algorithms have been used for this purpose. The first of these is based on well-known Linde-Buzo-Gray (LBG) algorithm. The other one is based on Self Organizing Feature Maps (SOFM). Since both training and encoding are computationally intensive tasks, we have used MasPar, a SIMD machine for this purpose. The multispectral imagery obtained from Advanced Very High Resolution Radiometer (AVHRR) instrument images form the testbed. The results from these two VQ techniques have been compared in compression ratios for a given Mean Squared Error (MSE). The number of bytes required to transmit the image data without loss using this progressive compression technique is usually less than the number of bytes required by standard *unix compress* algorithm.

Introduction

The high spatial and spectral resolution instruments onboard EOS will send huge amounts of data to the ground. The data that will be collected from EOS platforms over its 15-year mission will be tens of Petabytes(Peta is 10^{15}). Some of the challenges faced by information engineers are archival, browsing, dissemination and prompt generation of data products for different scientific applications. Storage of this data offline in optical disks seems to be technically feasible. But browsing through the data to find interesting features in data seems to be almost impossible task. So it is highly desirable to have at least browse quality data online for this purpose being supported by residual data files at one or more precision levels offline. This philosophy of image database has the following advantages: (i) For a given online storage, larger number of images can be stored. (ii) The time required to browse the data is much less because much fewer bytes have to read from the disk. (iii) The transmission costs of the data are reduced significantly. The savings in transmission costs are especially significant when the user decides to terminate the data after examining the browse quality. On the other hand if the data is found to be useful from its browse level images, one or more residuals can be sent to the user depending on the application. When all successive residuals are added to the browse quality, the data is reconstructed without any loss of bits.

The the main considerations in the design of our data compression approach are: (i) the browse quality should be visually lossless at compression ratios of as much as 20-30 so that most users can make decisions on the usefulness of the data for their applications by looking at them (ii) encoding should be fast enough to handle data rates (50 kbits/sec) in real time (iii) decoding algorithm should be as simple as possible so that the data users are not burdened with unnecessary computations (in other words the saving in transmission and storage should not be annulled by the decoding computational costs) (iv) the compression algorithm should naturally exploit the higher dimensional (spatial and spectral) correlation in multispectral image data.

Vector Quantization (or quantizer) (VQ) is an extension of scalar quantizer to reduce the bit rate over communication channel or to reduce storage. VQ optimally builds up a dictionary of fewer representative vectors such that when the input vectors drawn from the image are mapped on them using minimum Euclidian distance criterion results in minimum mean squared error. The vectors are derived by extracting a block in the case of 2-D data or cube in the case of multispectral data in order to fully exploit both spatial and spectral correlations present in the data. In the encoding the address of the code word in the dictionary that most closely matches the input vector are transferred. At the receiving end the vector corresponding to the address bits is extracted as a table lookup process and the image is reconstructed.

VQ turns out to be the most suitable candidate for multispectral images by taking the aforementioned considerations into account. The main consideration in favor of VQ is the simple decoding. For VQ encoded images decoding is a just a table lookup process which can be done very fast on sequential computers. Most transform based compression techniques including the Joint Photographic Experts Group's (JPEG) Discrete Cosine Transforms (DCT) [1], have nearly same computational complexities both in encoding and decoding. The encoding using VQ however is not as efficient as the decoding because it involves searching codebook for matching code vector. This problem is overcome by employing massively parallel SIMD computer, MasPar. One extra step that is unique to VQ is training or optimal codebook generation. This is also computationally involved, but this can be done offline for given class of images just once. The training part of VQ is again performed on MasPar. The reason for using VQ based compression is its ability to exploit naturally the spatial and spectral correlations in the multispectral data.

The key issue in the VQ based approaches is generating an optimal codebook for a class of images. We have used two different approaches to generate codebooks, namely Linde-Buzo-Gray (LBG) [2] algorithm and a Self Organizing Feature Map (SOFM) due to Kohonen [3]. The first level approximation of the data or browse quality data are generated from these algorithms serve as the browse quality . The quantization residuals obtained from the browse quality data are further compressed using the same compression techniques generating second level of residuals. This can be continued to generate required number of levels of residual images. The residuals are low entropy images and so higher order residuals require less number of bits to represent. But larger number of residuals means more computational burdens. We generally provide two levels of residuals. The main objective of this research is to demonstrate the use of Progressive Vector Quantization (PVQ, not to be confused with Predictive Vector Quantization) methodology using VQ on data sets belonging to AVHRR instrument and to show that initial data renditions obtained from VQ algorithms are adequate for making a positive decision about the data quality.

Progressive Vector Quantization

Progressive Vector Quantization (PVQ) is nothing but VQ used in Progressive Transmission (PT) mode. PT is becoming increasingly popular due to increase in remote accessing of image data bases across computer networks. Browsing image data locally or across computer networks (telebrowsing) involves reading the data from the files, transmitting and displaying on the screen. Browsing the data in the database enables data users to decide whether the data are useful or not for the intended application. In the absence of any data hierarchy, this decision is as expensive as acquiring all the data sets. Progressive compression is intended to make this very decision most economical. In this scheme we decompose the original image file into a hierarchy, in which the highest level is the initial data rendition and typically requires 3 - 5% storage. The lower levels of the hierarchy comprise details that are missing in the upper levels. The data rendition at highest level of hierarchy, called browse data, should be good enough for making a decision whether the data is useful or not for the specific application. If the decision is negative the transmission costs are within 3-5% of getting the entire image. If the users need better precision, the successive images from the hierarchy can be transmitted. The transmission can be terminated as soon as the user decides the data are not useful or the required precision is obtained by adding details to the browse data. If the user intends to get the data without any loss, the entire hierarchy will be transmitted.

Any compression method such as naive subsampling to sophisticated VQ can be used in generating image compression hierarchy. The different approaches generally fall into one of pyramidal coding, transform coding and VQ encoding. Burt and Adelson [4] have smoothed images by using fixed size Gaussian like filter and subsampled the soothed images by 1/2 along row and column. By recursively performing various images can be generated as a pyramid structure. The progressive transmission then involves sending the top of the pyramid first and successive differences between the current image and the next in the pyramid. The main disadvantage with this technique is the requirement that the entire pyramid must be computed before the transmission is ready to begin. Hoffman and Troxel [5] have solved this problem by low-pass filtering by a separable Gaussian filter and then subsampled. The sigma of the Gaussian filter and subsampling rate are selected such that at least 60% information preserved. This image further compressed by DPCM and sent as the first approximation. The subsequent images correspond to error images which are coded using tapered quantizers. The disadvantages of pyramidal encoding are: (i) the image resolution from the from the first approximation is so small that it is hard to make positive decisions about the data. (ii) Using these techniques it is not easy to use spectral correlations in multispectral data. (iii) The reconstruction of the images from the transmitted information involves interpolation and is computationally expensive. A popular transform based PT is the the JPEG's DCT based PT [1] . In this scheme the transform coefficients are transmitted successively to the receiving end until the reconstruction quality is satisfactory. The disadvantage of this technique is that lossless reconstruction is not guaranteed, and the points (ii) and (iii) of Pyramidal progressive transform apply to DCT based PT. Wang and Goldberg [7] have used VQ in progressive transmission mode like one described here. The techniques described here however differ in implementation, and they are specifically designed for multispectral data.

Figure 1 shows a block schematic of PVQ scheme. The codebooks are assumed to be available. The input to VQ code block is multispectral data which can be visualized as data cube. The data is decomposed into subcubes of appropriate size depending on the targeted compression ratios. Every subcube extracted from the data cube is regarded as a vector. The coder accepts these vectors one by one and searches for closest match in the codebook and outputs the address bits of the closest match. This data is further compressed by any standard lossless compression technique (here we have used *unix compress*) and made available as browse data. The next step in PVQ involves locally decoding the browse code and taking the difference between the original image and the browse approximation. This image corresponds to quantization error residue. The error images thus generated are characterized by stationarity and low entropy. The property of low entropy makes this decomposition and compression more efficient than most single lossless compression techniques. The stationarity property enables us to use one codebook for all error images. The error image is further vector quantized by using a different codebook. The coded error image locally decoded and the difference between the original error and the quantized error forms second level residual. This can be repeated until required number of levels are obtained. Thus PVQ consists of encoding, decoding, and subtraction for each level. The PVQ decoding is exactly the reverse process as shown in Figure 2. The codebooks are assumed to be available at the receiving end. The first level browse quality is obtained by decoding the first data received from PVQ encoding scheme. Subsequent refinements can be obtained by decoding error data and adding to the previous renditions. When all the levels in the PVQ are used the images are reconstructed without any loss of bits.

Implementation of VQ on SIMD Machines

VQ consists of training and coding phases both of which are computationally involved. The basic computation involved in both these phases is to compute the closest match to the input vector from the codebook, called *winner*. In the case of training winner is updated using one of the two algorithms (LBG, SOFM) such that the error between the input vector and the winner is further reduced. The LBG, and SOFM algorithms are well known in VQ literature and are described in detail in our earlier work [8] and in [2,3]. In the case of coding the address of the winner is saved as the code for the given vector. Unless the codebook is organized ingeniously using tree [6] structures, the winner computation could be very expensive on sequential machine. The tree structured codebooks have other problems of increased codebook size which directly affects the decoding process which we are trying to keep as simple and straight forward as possible. An SIMD multiprocess is considered as solution to this problem. The motivation for SIMD implementation stems from the fact that in future special multiprocessor hardware can be designed to carry out compression onboard spacecraft.

MasPar is a SIMD machine with 8192, 4 bit Processing Elements (PEs), each PE having a local memory of 16 Kbytes (recently upgraded to 64 Kbytes). VQ is implemented on MasPar using a small fraction of the available memory. As shown in Figure 3, the input image data (multispectral image data) is vectorized such that spatially adjacent pixels in contiguous spectral channel form the elements of a vector. In this paper 4x4x2 data cube is extracted as vector in which first 16 elements of the vector belong 4x4 window of the first spectral band and next 16 elements are 4x4 window of the other spectral band.

Initially the codebook (Cv_1, Cv_2... Cvn) is assumed to be present in the local memory of the PE array as shown in the Figure 3. In the case of LBG algorithm, the initial codebook is generated by randomly selecting m out of n vectors in the input image where m is the size of the code book and n is number of vectors contained in input image set. While in the case of SOFM the initial codebook is generated by a random number generator producing floating point numbers between 0.0 and 1.0. For optimal performance it is necessary to have codebook size equal the size of the PE array. However codebooks smaller or larger than PE array size can be easily handled. Now, the given image is vectorized and each vector is broadcast to all PE local memory as shown in the Figure 3 (Vk's) . The Eucleadian distance between in the input vector and the code vectors is computed independently by all the processors simultaneously and the result is stored in the local memory (Dk's). This forms a parallel array of distance. The time taken for computation of this is proportional to the size of the vector (number of pixels per vector). The winner can be found by finding the least value in the distance parallel array. Its minimum value can be found out in a time proportional to the number of bits per one element of distance array (number of bits for real number, 32). The vector in the codebook corresponding to the location of this minimum distance value is the winner. In the case of training, this vector (or its neighboring vectors in SOFM) is updated. In the case of coding the address of the winner is considered as the code and saved in the output file. When this process is repeated for all the vectors from the input image data, it forms one iteration in the case of training and completes coding of the input image in the case of coding.

PVQ Performance and Tradeoffs

PVQ has been implemented on the MasPar with a VAX Station as host computer. The package has a user friendly point and click interface. We have used AVHRR data for demonstration of this package. The AVHRR data is 5-band 409x512, 16bits/pixel images. Using PVQ the first two bands have been decomposed into 4 levels of data. The five band data is split two parts so that spectral and spatial correlations can be optimally utilized. The results are however shown only for first two bands. The first two bands are shown in Figure 4 (a) . A spatial window of 4x4 along with two spectral bands (4x4x2) constitutes a vector. For remaining three bands a spatial window of 2x4 is selected (vector size in this case is 2x4x3). The results of PVQ using LBG algorithm generated codebooks on first two bands are shown in Figure 4 (b-h). The data shown in Figure 4 (b,c,e,g) correspond to the 4 level PVQ data packets. In Figure 4 (b) a browse quality data is shown with a compression ratio of more than 35 which looks visually lossless and may be good for some initial analysis. The data shown in Figure 4 (c) is first VQ coded residual which is added to initial browse quality to improve the quality. The improved data is shown in Figure 4 (d) which is visually indistinguishable from the browse data but is better by a factor of 4 in terms of MSE. The second VQ coded residual and the improved reconstructed data are shown in Figure 4 (e-f). Finally the bulk of the data is sent as final residue (VQ is not used in this data) as shown in Figure 4 (g). This is added to the data in Figure 4 (f) to reconstruct in the input data exactly (MSE = 0). As shown in Figure 4 (b-h) as the additional data are transmitted the effective compression ratio decreases and quality improves (MSE decreases). When all the data is transmitted the compression ratio is comparable to what one can obtain by using other efficient lossless encoding technique and the MSE becomes Zero. The compression ratio and MSE plots as a function of four data packets are shown in Figure 6 (a). The compression results on the same data using SOFM are shown in Figure 5(a-f). In this Figure the original image is same as shown in Figure 4(a) and reconstructed images after four level transmission is same as input image and so not shown in the figure. Figure 5(a) is browse data, (b) is VQ coded residue, (d) is VQ coded second residue, (f) is final residue. Figure 5 (c) and (d) correspond to the improvements over initial data renditions.

Another important aspect of PVQ is that the given data can be decomposed into a given number of data packets (levels) such that when all of them are added reconstructs the original data without any loss. In our experiments we have seen that 3 to four levels of decomposition is optimal. Decomposition to one level does not involve any VQ. The image set is compressed using unix compress and transmitted. In two level case the image is VQ coded and both coded data as well as residuals are compressed using unix compress and transmitted. As can be seen from plot of Figure 6 (b) as the number of levels increase fewer number of bytes need to be transmitted or higher the lossless compression ratio. From the plot it can be seen that after 3 levels the compression ratio does not improve significantly. The CR of 1.86 corresponding to level 1 is due to unix compress and as levels increase the CR increases up to 2.92 which is nearly an improvement of 57% over unix compress. The SOFM algorithm performs not quite as good as LBG. The CR, MSE plots with respect to number of levels are shown in Figure 7 (a) and the lossless CR plot is shown in Figure 7 (b).

Normally 3 to 4 level decomposition is adequate for many data sets. As number of levels increases the compression performance improves also, but the computational costs also go up. After certain number of decomposition levels the compression savings outweigh the computational burdens. Thus an optimal tradeoffs between transmission savings and computational costs have to be taken into account in using PVQ.

Conclusions

The scientific data volumes that are expected to be available from EOS platforms will be overwhelming. Data archival and dissemination are some of the challenges the data management engineers are facing. Data compression is very useful in reducing data volume. But users are concerned about the loss of information because of compression. The lossless data compression schemes unfortunately can reduce the data by no more than a factor of 2 on most NASA images. Progressive Vector Quantization will be satisfactory for users since the data can be reconstructed without loss if required. If the data is not found to be useful by examining first level transmission (that provides browse data) then the transmission can be terminated saving transmission costs.

This paper described VQ based progressive transmission which is implemented on a massively parallel machine. The decoding or reconstruction from the coded data is done on a sequential machine and is computationally very efficient. The performances of the two training techniques namely, LBG and SOFM, differ marginally with LBG performing slightly better most of the time. The advantages of progressive transmission combined with improvement in compression over other lossless techniques such as unix compress outweigh the marginal computational problems associated with reconstructing the data from PVQ.

REFERENCES

1. Pennebaker, "JPEG Technical Specification, Revision 8," Working Document No. JTC1/SC2/WG10/JPEG-8-R8 (Aug. 1990).
2. Gray, R. M., "Vector Quantization", IEEE ASSP Magazine, pp. 4-28, April 1984.
3. Kohonen, T., "The Self-Organizing Map," Proceedings of the IEEE, Vol. 78, No. 9, pp. 1464-1480, 1990.
4. P. J. Burt and E. H. Adelson, "The Laplacian Pyramid as a Compact Image Code", IEEE Trans on Comm., Vol. Comm-31, No. 4, April 1983, pp. 532-540.
5. W. D. Hoffman and D. E. Troxel, "Making Progressive Transmission Adaptive", IEEE Trans on Comm., Vol. Comm-34, No. 8, August 1986, pp. 806-813.
6. Chou, P. A., Lookagaugh, T. and Gray, R. M., "Optimal Pruning with Application to Tree-structured Source Coding and Modeling," IEEE Trans on Infor Theory, Vol. 35, No. 2, March 1989, pp. 299-315.
7. L. Wang and M. Goldberg, "Lossless progressive image transmission by residual error vector quantization", IEE Proceedings, Vol. 135, Part F, No.5, October, 1988, pp. 421-430.
8. J. Tilton, D. Han, and M. Manohar, "Compression Experiments with AVHRR data", Proceedings Data Compression Conference, Snowbird, Utah, April 8-11, 1991, pp. 411-420.

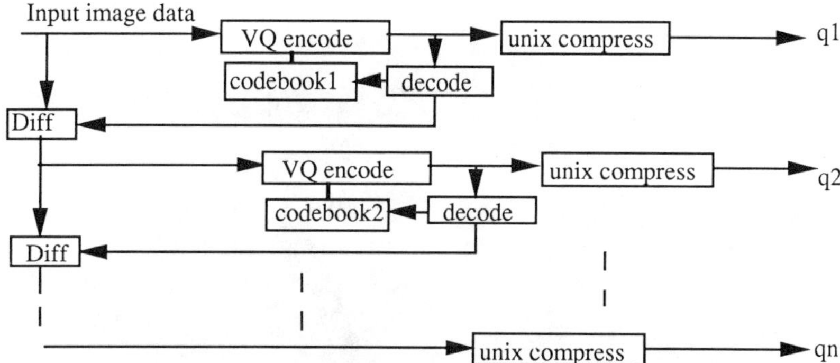

Figure 1. Image encoding using Progressive Vector Quantization; same codebook is used for all residual images: q1 is browse level approximation, q2 .. qn are quantization residuals.

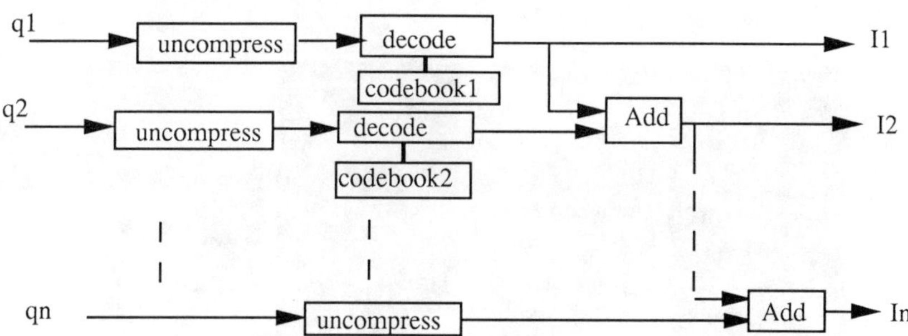

Figure 2. Progressive reconstruction from PVQ coded data I1, I2 .. In are reconstructed images.

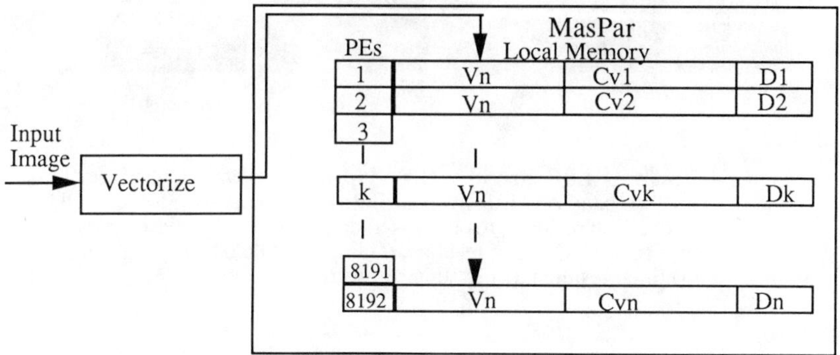

Figure 3. Vector Quantization on MasPar

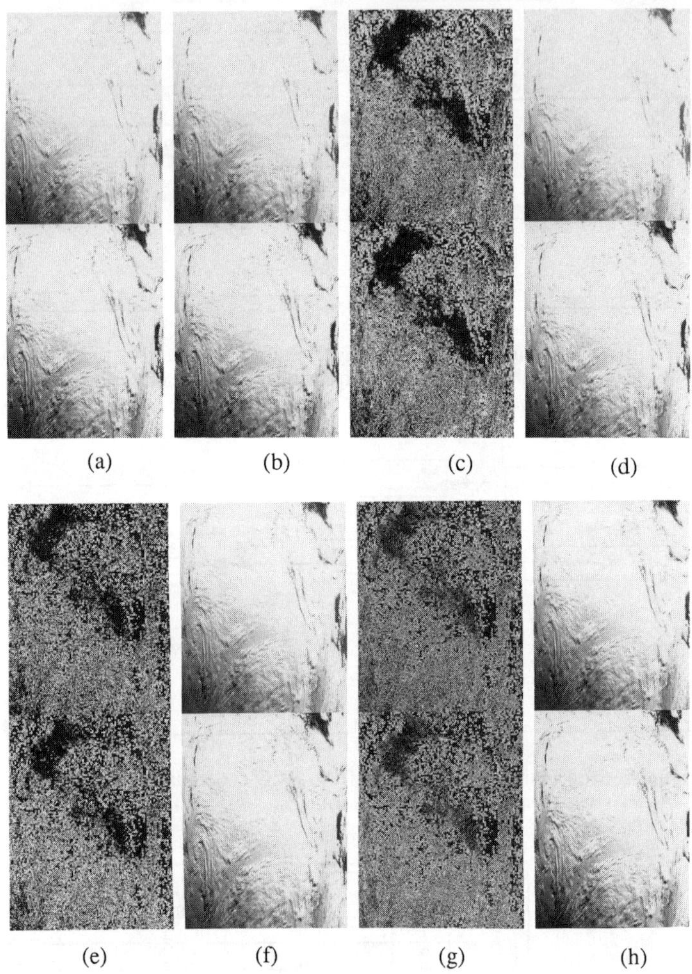

Figure 4. Results of LBG algorithm based Progressive Vector Quantizer.
(a) Two band AVHRR image, (b) Browse data (CR= 35), (c) VQ
coded first residual, (d) Improved data rendition by adding b and c,
(e) Second VQ coded residual, (f) Improved data by adding d and e,
(g) Final residual, (h) Exactly reconstructed image.

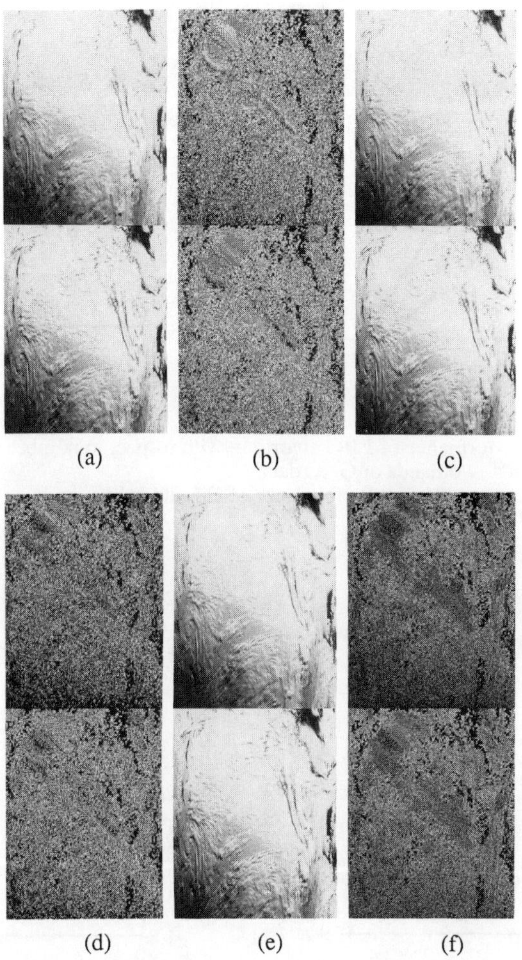

Figure 5. Results of SOFM algorithm based Progressive Vector Quantizer. (a) Browse data (CR= 39), (b) VQcoded first residual, (c) Improved data rendition by adding a and b, (d) Second VQ coded residual, (e) Improved data by adding c and d, (f) Final residual.

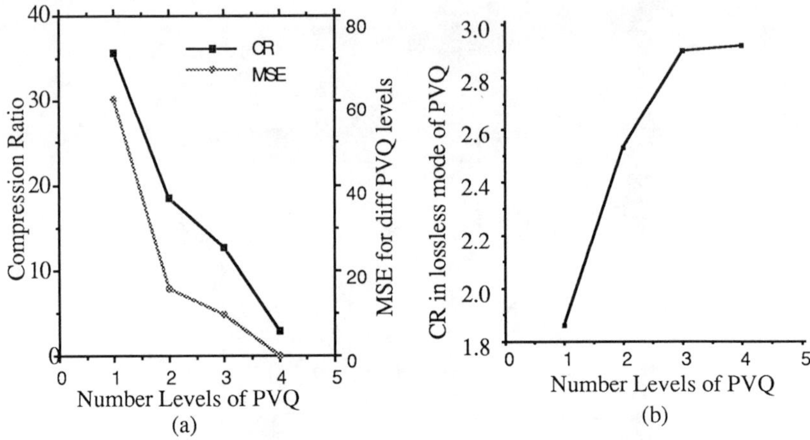

Figure 6. Performance of LBG algorithm with respect to number of PVQ levels
on first two bands of GAC data.
(a) lossy to lossless Performance of CR and MSE
(b) Lossless performance of CR

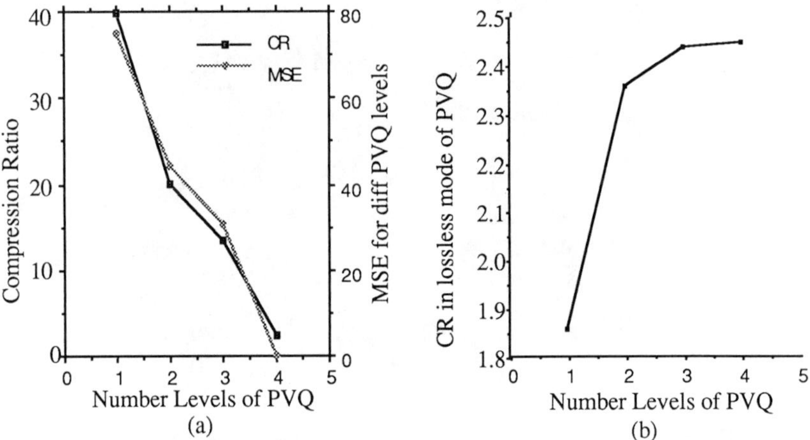

Figure 7. Performance of SOFM algorithm with respect to number of PVQ levels
on first two bands of GAC data
(a) Lossy to lossless Performance of CR and MSE
(b) Lossless performance of CR

POSSIBLE HARMONIC-WAVELET HYBRIDS
IN IMAGE COMPRESSION
Michael Rollins
Frank Carden
Center for Space Telemetering and Telecommunication Systems
Box 30001, Dept. 3-0 NMSU, Las Cruces, New Mexico 88003-0001

This Research Was Funded by Sandia National Laboratories
Contract Number 63-9092

This paper describes some image compression research at New Mexico State University. It explores the possibility of combining multi-resolution and harmonic analysis in signal decomposition. This is in recognition of the fact that both local and global characteristics are found in most images and that the ideal compression system should be able to contend with both types of features. A hybrid will be proposed and discussed.

Harmonic Features in Images

For Markov-1 signals with high correlation, it has been shown [1] that the Discrete Cosine Transform is asymptotically equivalent to the Karhunen-Loueve Transform which is optimal for decorrelation of information and therefore, compaction. This high correlation in terms of real images describes features with gradual changes in brightness over a wide (global) support of pixels (eg. clouds). For such images, it is possible to discard nearly all of the transform coefficients and reconstruct very good approximations. This is equivalent to a low-pass filtering of the image, which is fine if the important details of the image are of low spatial frequencies. Secondly, the DCT works well in compression of images with periodic features such as textures. This involves use of any of the transform coefficients as long as the coding scheme can take advantage of the sparse transform image.

The DCT, however, has trouble compressing wide-band features in images with edges. One can observe the long line-like distribution of non-zero coefficients in the DCT of an edge image. If one is not careful in quantizing the coefficients during the compression process, the reconstructed image will have fringes parallel to the edge and annoying to the observer. In fact, it is really not possible to avoid such fringes at high compression using the DCT. High frequency fringes can cause uncertainty in edge location, and low-frequency fringes cause discontinuities at the boundaries of the blocks into which the image has been partitioned.

Local Features in Images

Most images have important features which are local in nature. That is, they contain compact objects at specific locations in the support. The boundaries of these objects are generally fairly sharp edges which give the DCT poor performance. Intuitively, one would expect difficulty in correlating such local objects with the sinusoidal basis images of the DCT (See Fig. 1). Thus, one would look for a set of basis images with local features. This motivates the discussion of wavelets, which are functions with chiefly local support. Their name implies small (local) waves and they offer solutions to some of the problems discussed above for the DCT.

Wavelet Analysis

For some time, researchers in digital signal processing have been developing practical ways to split a signal into low and high pass "sub-signals" which are orthongonal to each other. This seems straight forward in the normalized frequency domain. Why not just split the spectrum of the signal cleanly at some frequency and allocate each half to their respective sub-signal outputs at half the original sample rate. The reason is that this cannot be done in hardware without an unreasonable delay in the output since this involves use of an arbitrarily large number of previous samples. To avoid this, mirror filters have been designed which decompose the signal spectrum into two mirror image spectrums with some overlap. These mirror filters output signals at half the sample rate but aliasing in the two data streams is canceled at reconstruction. The filter taps of some mirror filters have a special quality. They represent discrete coefficients of scaling functions which can be used to generate discrete and continuous wavelets [2]. The discrete wavelets along with their scaling functions can be used to form a set of orthonormal vectors for a basis. Decomposition of signals in terms of such bases can give sparse transformation matrices ideal for compression of local features. The Haar system is one such wavelet basis.

Reconciling Multi-Resolution and Harmonic Decomposition.

The preceding discussion has characterized images in terms of local or global features. A perfect definition of "local" and "global" which would allow us to separate features into these categories is elusive. If one considers the Haar Transformation matrix, for instance, none of its rows (save that corresponding to DC) could replace any rows in the DCT matrix to form an orthonormal complete set. However, taking

$$[DCT \ (NxN)] \otimes [HrT \ (MxM)] = [Hybrid \ X\text{-}Form \ (\{MxN\}x\{MxN\}) \ ]$$

where $\otimes$ is the kronecker product operator between the two transformation matrices, one gets a hybrid transformation matrix which is unitary   The basis vectors in this larger dimensional space are of the form $[a,b,0,0,...,0,0,c,d,0,0,...0,0,e,f,0,0,...]^T$ which is essentially a pulse train of wavelets with expanses of zeroes between. In images, this would be like tree branches with uniform sky between. A good compression scheme using such a transform is beyond the scope of this article (See [3]). Lacking a suitable, single transformation matrix for the desired hybrid we continue.

A Wavelet-DCT Hybrid

In the initial design, the Haar transform, due to ease of calculation, has been chosen to accompany the DCT. The Haar Transform itself is notoriously poor for image compression of natural images. Textures and most other global features with continuous transition require functions with much greater smoothness and regularity for concise approximation. The Haar wavelet is very blocky (eg. [0,0,0,1,-1,0,0,0]) and its continuous form has only zero-order continuity. For decomposition of natural images, smoother wavelets with wider support (eg. [0,0,.683,-1.183, .317,.183,0,0] derived by Daubechies [4] and called D4 in [2]) give better compaction.

The hybrid is implemented as follows (See Figure 2): Perform the Haar transform of the image first.

$$[H] = [HrT][Im][HrT]^T$$

194

Truncate all but most significant coefficients,

$$[H] \rightarrow [H']$$

where

$$H'_{ij} = \{ H_{ij} \backslash H_{ij} \ni \{\text{greatest N coeff}\}\}$$
$$= \{0 \text{ e.w.}\}$$

and reconstruct and subtract from the original image.

$$[Diff] = [Im] - [HrT]^T [H'][HrT]$$

Then, perform the DCT on this "difference" image and truncate:

$$[D] = [DCT][Diff][DCT]^T$$

$$[D] \rightarrow [D']$$

where

$$D'_{ij} = \{ D_{ij} \backslash D_{ij} \ni \{\text{greatest M coeff}\}\}$$
$$= \{0 \text{ e.w. }\}$$

Send this "difference DCT" as well as the retained Haar coefficients and reconstruct at the receiver.

$$[Im'] = [DCT]^T [D'][DCT] + [HrT]^T [H'][HrT]$$

If the difference DCT [D'] has fewer significant coefficients than a DCT of the original image, then one has successfully separated some of the local features from the textures (harmonic features). The challenge is to be sure that the sum of transmitted Haar and difference DCT coefficients is less than the number of transmitted DCT coefficients for the original image at the same mean-square error. Regardless of how coarsely the Haar or other wavelet transform image is quantized, the process is lossless until the quantization following the DCT. This is because the difference image plus the crude image exactly equals the original and how the difference image is treated determines the loss.

Figure 3 shows (from upper-left to lower right, left to right) the original image of an object (toy tank), its Haar Transform (16x16), the original again and its Cosine Transform, reconstructed using the most intense 32 out of 256 transform coefficients. Note the fuzzy boundaries, especially at the front of the tank. The mean square error is 61.5. Note also, the shadow above the tank. Now compare with Figure 4 where the hybrid has been implemented.

Figure 4 shows (from upper-left to lower-right) the original image of the object, its reconstructed Haar Transform image (16x16 blocks), the difference image and finally, the sum of the reconstructed DCT and Haar images. Of the 256 coefficients in the transform domains, the 16 most intense were retained and the rest set equal to zero for both the DCT and the Haar Transform. Thus, the total number of transform coefficients used was 32 as in Figure 3. In Figure 4 (lower right), the vehicle boundaries are more sharply defined as are other roof-edge type features (MSE=66.7). Yet this uses the same number of bytes of information as in Figure 3. Certainly, choosing the N most intense coefficients (rather than by proper normalization and quantization) is not the best way to compress an image, but the result suggests the merit of employing both local and global basis functions in image decomposition/compression.

In this study, we were careful to show an object aligned horizontally and vertically to avoid the stair-step artifacts which occur when the Haar decomposition encounters a diagonal edge. The choice of the Haar wavelet is not necessarily the best. Smoother wavelets with wider support would have a diminished stair-step effect. Using the 4 coefficient Daubechies' wavelet given above, the combination of 24 DCT and 8 wavelet coefficients yields a sharpened image with a lower MSE - 57.4 (Fig. 5). Thus for this image, the hybrid has given greater clarity and a lower MSE than just using the DCT alone.

It is clear that in such a hybrid which involves wavelet as well as DCT coding, we no longer have the convenient "zig-zag" scanning of coefficients as in pure DCT coding. However, if motion pictures are involved, interframe coding can take advantage of the fact that the significant wavelet coefficients retain fairly rigid spatial relationships with each other for rigid objects, allowing one to use predictive coding.

In comparing compaction between the DCT and any wavelet or hybrid transform, we have used a performance measure

$$\text{relative compaction} = \sum_{(i,j)} |avg^2 - V^2(i,j)|$$

where $V(i,j)$ is the transform image coefficient at i,j and avg is the original image's average intensity for the given block. Since orthonormal transformations conserve energy, this measure essentially finds the sum of differences in energy between the average of the original image and each element of the transformed image. If compaction has occurred, the difference within the absolute value will generally be large since more energy will be lumped among few coefficients causing a highly negative difference there and a highly positive difference where $V^2(i,j)$ is close to zero. We have found that this compaction measure often agrees to the third decimal place between the DCT and the wavelet transform being used. For the 2 compactly supported wavelets discussed in this paper, the DCT nearly always shows greater compaction over the 256 coefficients in a block, but not necessarily over the top 20 or 30 most significant ones. Other wavelets will probably perform better.

Finally, we point out that use of wavelets to decompose some features in an image is simply a short-hand method of using a much larger number of DCT basis images. In essence, each wavelet basis image can be seen as a linear combination of DCT basis images.

REFERENCES

[1] K. R. Rao, P. Yip, *Discrete Cosine Transform; Algorithms, Advantages and Applications* , Academic Press, New York 1990.

[2] G. Strang, *Wavelet and Dilation Equations: A Brief Introduction,* SIAM Review, Vol **31**, No. 4, pp 614-627, December 1989.

[3] K. R. Rao, M. A. Narasimhan, K. Revuluri, *Image Data Compression by Hadamard-Haar Transform,* Proc. Natl. Electron. Conf., Chicago, Illinois, **29**, 336-341 (1974).

[4] I. Daubechies, *Orthonormal Bases of Compactly Supported Wavelets,* Comm. Pure Appl. Mathematics, **41**, 909-996.

IMAGES WELL-SUITED FOR DCT COMPRESSION:

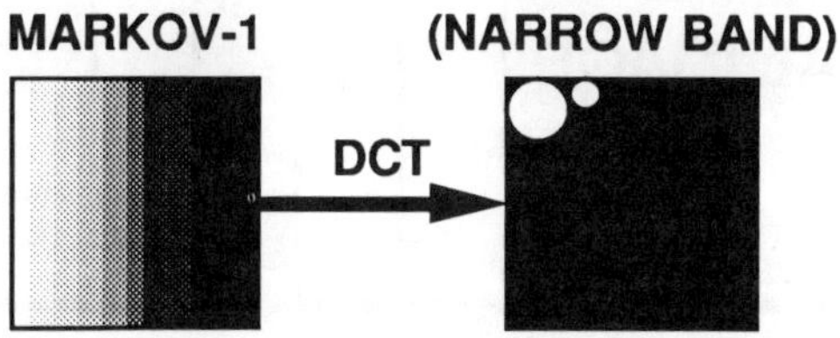

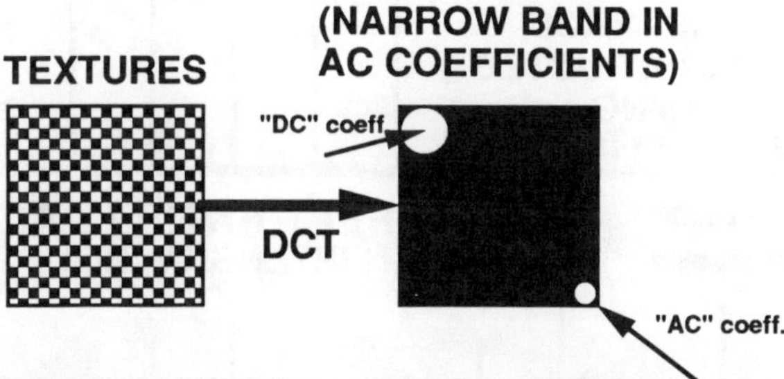

IMAGES ILL-SUITED FOR DCT COMPRESSION :

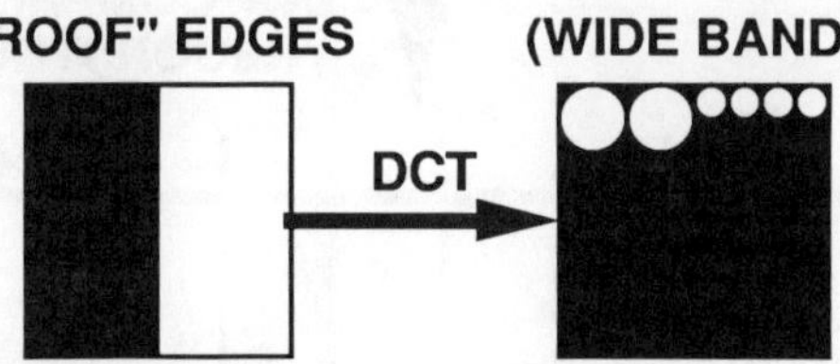

VERY LOCAL DISCONTINUITIES
(eg.. STAR IN SPACE)

(VERY WIDE BAND)

Figure 1:

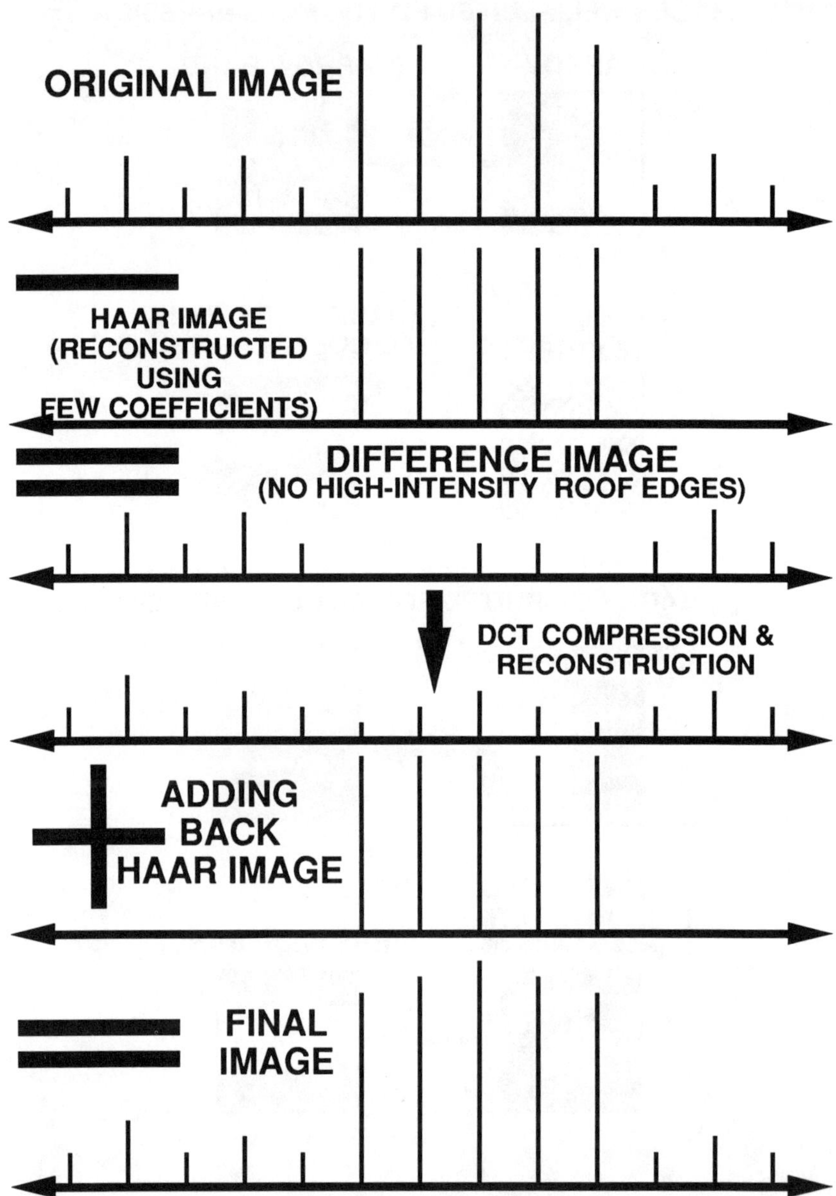

Figure 2: 1-Dimensional Compression Sequence

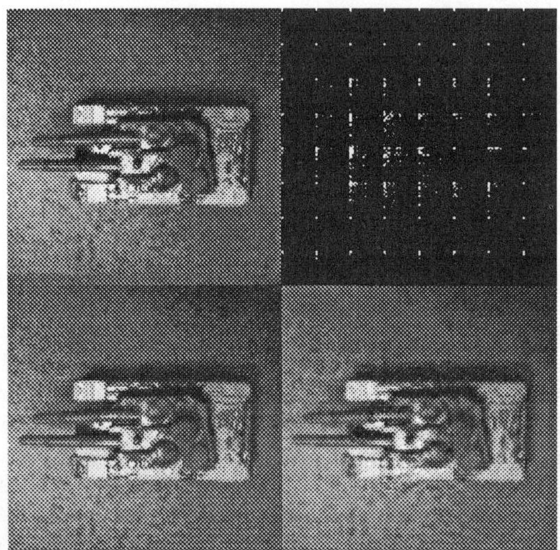

Figure 3: DCT - 32 coefficients

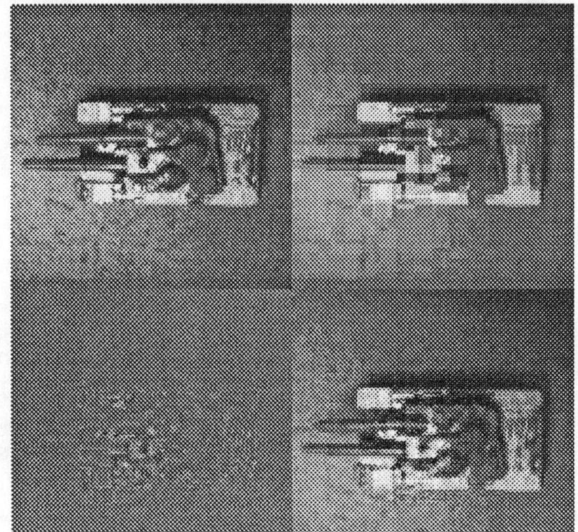

Figure 4: DCT-Haar Hybrid

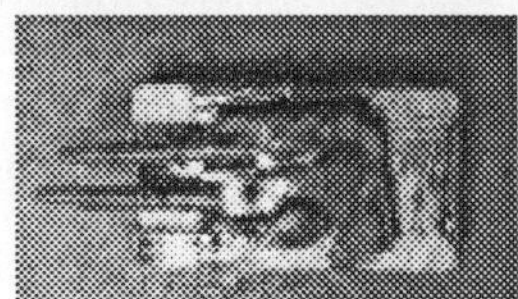

Figure 5: DCT-D4 Hybrid

Multispectral KLT-Wavelet Data Compression for Landsat Thematic Mapper Images

Benjamin R. Epstein, Rajesh Hingorani,
Jerome M. Shapiro, and Martin Czigler

David Sarnoff Research Center
CN5300, Princeton, N.J. 08543-5300

Abstract

We report a methodology that enhances the compression of Landsat Thematic Mapper (TM) multispectral imagery, while reducing image information loss. The method first removes interband correlation of the image data by use of the Karhunen-Loeve transform (KLT) to produce the image principal components. Each principal component is spatially decorrelated using a discrete wavelet transform. The resulting coefficients are then quantized and losslessly encoded. Image compressions of typically 80:1 demonstrate that the method should be quite suitable for rapid browsing applications where small amounts of image loss are tolerable.

1. Introduction

The wide and growing use of multispectral satellite imagery calls for more efficient methods of viewing, distributing, and storing such image data. This need for efficiency becomes even more apparent when multispectral images must be analyzed over many spectral bands and over time. The anticipated data flows of the Earth Observation System (EOS) present a further challenge in image data handling, where terabytes/day of image information is anticipated. Data compression plays an important role in achieving rapid delivery and analysis of multispectral imagery while easing data transmission and storage requirements.

Recent work[1] related to multispectral and hyperspectral data compression has been reported by Baker and Tse [2], where predictive coding, block truncation coding, discrete cosine transformation (DCT), and various forms of vector quantization (VQ) were applied to hyperspectral image data. The effectiveness of these methods was evaluated in the context of a spectral signature matching and mixture component analysis application for remote sensing. Mean-residual and gain-shape VQ yielded the most favorable results in these applications at 20:1 compression ratios. VQ was also applied to Landsat TM data by Giusto [6], who also investigated a hybrid VQ method with polynomial prediction. "Straight" VQ was found to yield preferable results, with a compression of typically 35:1. Presumably, the Landsat Thematic Mapper (TM) bands were treated separately during the encoding. Tilton *et. al.* [13] further investigated the use of VQ as applied to multispectral Advanced Very High Resolution Radiometer (AVHRR) image data. Their results yielded visually favorable restored images at about 24:1 compression.

In a non-VQ study, Tilton [12] described "hierarchical data compression," which pro-

---

[1]The results quoted from the mentioned studies serve only to show past work performed in multispectral data compression and are not intended to serve as a comparison of the compression methods discussed.

vided an integrated approach to data compression with high loss (for browsing), moderate loss, and no loss. Techniques used included block averaging, quadtrees, and iterative parallel region growing. Results for compression ratios up to 27:1 were reported. All Landsat TM bands were treated separately. An earlier study by Chen *et. al.* [4] showed that considerable spatial correlation exists in Landsat TM imagery. Entropy computations by these investigators show that exploitation of this correlation can result in 3:1 lossless compression. The authors also show that spatial correlation yields better data compression than the use of the weaker spectral correlation. Slightly improved lossless compression of Landsat images was demonstrated by Howard and Vitter, who used spatial predictive coding techniques combined with arithmetic encoding [7].

The VQ approaches discussed above depend on carefully constructed codebooks. In the event that the image characteristics change, the codebooks have to be updated to avoid the risk of excessive image distortion. Of course, compared to transform-based compression methods, VQ offers the strong advantage of simple image decoding hardware and software. Regarding hierarchical data compression, more sophisticated techniques can yield higher compression ratios for browsing and other applications where some information loss is tolerable. One such technique, which is described herein, draws from past work in quadrature-mirror filter (QMF) pyramid image compression [1]. In this earlier work, multiresolution image pyramid structures were constructed that effectively created subband filtered versions of the image. The filtered representations were then scalar quantized, runlength encoded, and Huffman encoded to form compressed bit streams of the original image. In the present work, we carry out the procedure of the earlier work not directly on the original image bands of a multispectral image, but on the principal components of the original images. The principal components are derived by applying the Karhunen-Loeve transform (KLT) to the original image bands. This transform effectively creates a representation of the original multispectral image where much of the interband correlation is removed. Removal of the correlated data from the set of images results in reduced data redundancy and thereby contributes to the enhanced data compression.

2. Interband Karhunen-Loeve Transform

There often is a large amount of correlation present in landsat TM images since the sensors are co-located and the spectral weighting functions have some overlap. An effective way of exploiting this correlation is to compute the image-dependent KLT. This involves performing an eigenvalue decomposition on the interband correlation matrix, and projecting the images, pixel-by-pixel, onto the orthonormal basis functions defined by the eigenvectors. The resulting principal component images each correspond to a different eigenvector. The amount of compression attainable depends on the eigenvalue spread, where a larger spread implies a higher coding gain[2].

Note that there is some overhead associated with the KLT that must be transmitted. In the results discussed below, the seven means for each original band and the 49 elements of the eigenvector matrix are represented as 32-bit floating point numbers for a fixed overhead of 1792 (56 x 32) bits. This precision is probably unnecessary for large images, and

---

[2]The coding gain is defined as the ratio of the arithmetic mean to the geometric mean of the eigenvalues [8], and represents the signal-to-noise ratio (SNR) improvement attainable for a given bit rate and memoryless scalar quantizer-coder pair in coding the principal component images over the original images.

amounts to an overhead of only 0.007 bits/pixel in a 512x512 7-band image. A larger drawback of the KLT approach is the computational burden in computing the KLT at the encoder. A fixed sub-optimal transformation, perhaps based on physical considerations of the sensors, may be more practical at the cost of reduced coding gain.

3. Wavelets and Data Compression

Once the interband correlation has been removed via the KLT, the spatial correlation within each principal component image is then removed. In contrast to the spectral decorrelation, where the number of elements in each basis function is fixed by the number of bands, it is not practical to apply a full KLT decorrelation spatially.

One common approach for spatial decorrelation is to apply the DCT, because it is nearly optimal for a stationary first-order Markov process as the correlation coefficient approaches unity [8]. A key assumption that is often overlooked is the notion of stationarity. Large block sizes are not generally used in image coding because qualitative aspects of pictures, or what we loosely call "picture statistics," change over large block size, thereby reducing the energy compaction. In other words, the block size is chosen such that the picture statistics are well modeled by a stationary process. However, the optimal block size depends on the persistence of periodicities within a local region. Therefore, a fixed block size may be too small for low frequency coarse features and too large for high frequency non-periodic features such as edges.

Wavelets have recently been introduced to signal processing as a methodology for signal representation that is localized in both time and frequency [5,9,10,11]. Wavelets are attractive for spatial decorrelation because for a wavelet basis, low frequency basis functions have a long spatial extent, whereas high frequency basis functions have a short spatial extent. However, there are many more high frequency basis functions than low frequency basis functions since all the basis functions for a given subband (except DC) are shifted versions of each other, with only a finite number of non-zero samples. It makes sense that low frequency non-stationary data can be modeled as stationary over larger spatial regions than high frequency data, whereas, high frequency data statistically changes over a much smaller area. Thus wavelets are an ideal tool for describing non-stationary processes because they relieve the user from having to determine *a priori* the area over which the data can be treated as stationary; i.e., the block size. Wornell [14] has recently shown that wavelets can also be used in Karhunen-Loeve-like expansions for $1/f$ processes, which are non-stationary processes often applied to image and texture modeling. Although not a direct consequence of this result, the implication is that wavelet transforms can also be used to spatially decorrelate images.

The wavelets used in this paper are based on 7-tap QMF filter banks [1] that have linear-phase analysis and synthesis filters, but are not perfect reconstruction. They have been appropriately scaled so that the discrete wavelet transform constructed using these filters is nearly orthogonal. These filters were chosen because, empirically, they lead to good compression without objectionable artifacts under moderate quantization.

4. Application of Method

Landsat 5 TM images of Kuwait were obtained, as part of a cooperative effort, from the

USGS EROS Data Center (Sioux Falls, SD) to serve as sample images in our study. Landsat TM data are produced by 7 sensors, where each sensor corresponds to a band of imagery data. Bands 1 to 3 correspond to visible spectra, Band 4 corresponds to near IR spectra, Bands 5 and 7 mid IR spectra, and Band 6 thermal spectra. The instantaneous filed of view (IFOV) for all sensors is about 30 x 30 m, except Band 6, which has an IFOV of 120 x 120 m. Images were of size 512 x 512 pixels at 8 bits/pixel.

To visualize the impact of the compression methodology described above, the following steps were used to compress, expand, and display the images:

1. Mean values were subtracted from each of the seven original image bands.

2. Seven principal components were generated by computing and applying the KLT to the seven mean-subtracted bands.

3. The resulting seven principal components were each spatially decorrelated using the wavelet transform.

4. The decorrelated samples were then quantized and coded using run-length encoding of the occurrences of zeros and non-zero values.

5. Huffman encoding followed for each of a) the run-lengths of zeros, b) the run-lengths of non-zeros, and c) non-zero values.

6. The resulting bit stream therefore contained a reduced representation of the original seven bands. Mean values and eigenvectors were included in the bit stream for later decoding and image restoration.

7. The run-length and Huffman encoding of the bit stream were decoded, with the results fed into a wavelet expansion process. This restored the original principal components, but with loss.

8. Original images were restored from the lossy principal component images.

9. Mean values were added to the restored images.

Figure 1 summarizes the procedure. On a SUN 4/260 workstation, encoding and decoding times for a 512 x 512 image were about 10 sec/band, whereas the computation of the principal components, which is only required for the encoder, required about 2 min.

In our process, the degree of compression and the amount of numerical precision preserved in the subband samples were regulated by varying the quantizer bin sizes of the band-passed images during wavelet compression. Since the KLT is an orthonormal transform and the wavelet transform is nearly orthonormal, the amplitude units of the resulting subband samples can be treated as gray scale units. For the images examined, quantizer bin sizes ranged from 1 gray scale unit (resulting in no perceptible image distortion) to 32 units. Figure 2 and Table 1 compare all seven bands before and after compression/expansion. Even with a bin size of 32 gray scale units, which corresponds to about 0.1 bit/pixel for each band (or almost an 80:1 compression rate), the image quality remains quite acceptable for many browsing applications. Similar results were obtained for other Landsat TM images.

To show the impact of compressing principal components rather than the original bands, the original seven bands were compressed separately using equivalent quantizer bin sizes. As implied by Table 1, compression of the principal components resulted in typically a 40% improvement in data compression, with a similar reduction in mean-square error.

Table 1

bin size	bits/pixel^2	MSE^2	bin size	bits/pixel^2	MSE^2
1	19.52	0.51	1	22.83	0.83
16	1.55	25.11	16	2.51	40.02
16,32[1]	0.76	46.83	16,32[1]	1.06	73.82
32	0.73	47.96	32	1.06	76.66

(A) Compression rate and error over 7 bands by compressing principal components.

(B) Compression rate and error over 7 bands by summing compression rates and errors of separately compressed bands.

[1]Bin size of 16 assigned to lowest frequency (Gaussian) image; all other subbands assigned bin size of 32.

[2]Values stated are over all seven bands collectively. Average value per band is obtained by dividing stated values by 7.

5. Discussion

The large amount of compression achieved in the above results suggests that the method described herein may be suitable for Landsat TM browsing and target search applications, as well as similar uses from other multispectral imaging platforms (e.g., AVHRR and future EOS platforms). We emphasize that by condensing the bulk of the image variability into the first few principal components, extra amounts of data compression can be obtained with no visual impact.

The results discussed above represented a "blind" approach to treating Landsat TM images in that strong correlations within the band sets 1,2,3 and 5,7 were ignored for the purposes of generality [3]. By transmitting compressed versions of principal components formed by grouping correlated images (i.e., band groups 1,2,3 and 5,7 and 4 and 6), further compression could be achieved with minimal impact on image quality. As mentioned earlier, the computational overhead associated with computing the principal components may be eliminated by using a generalized set of principal component eigenvectors tuned to the Landsat TM sensors. This technique requires further investigation.

Adjustments in wavelet kernel sizes were also investigated. It was found that tap sizes ranging from 7 to 9 generally yielded similar results. Larger tap sizes did not provide any additional compression or improved image quality, and only increased the computational requirements of the wavelet encoding and decoding. On the other hand, tap sizes too small (4 and below) yielded excessive image distortion upon restoration. Note that the quantization in the results presented herein was uniform across and within all subbands. Attempts to selectively increase bin sizes for higher frequency subband image components, which results in a coarser quantization of the high frequencies, resulted in minimal effect (see Table 1).

Acknowledgments

This work was funded by the National Information Display Laboratory (NIDL). We wish to thank the staff at the USGS EROS Data Center (Sioux Falls, SD) for cooperating in this study.

References

[1] E.H. Adelson, E. Simoncelli, and R. Hingorani, "Orthogonal pyramid transforms for image coding," *Proc. SPIE*, Oct. 1987.

[2] R.L. Baker and Y.T. Tse, "Compression of high spectral resolution imagery," *Proc. SPIE: Applications of Digital Image Processing*, August, 1988, San Diego, CA, pp. 255-264.

[3] P.S. Chavez Jr., and A.Y. Kwarteng, "Extracting spectral contrast in Landsat thematic Mapper image data using selective principal component analysis," *Photogrammetric Engineering and Remote Sensing*, vol. 55, no. 3, March 1989, pp. 339-348.

[4] T.M. Chen, D.H. Staelin, and R.B. Arps, "Information content analysis of Landsat image data for compression," *IEEE Trans. on Geoscience and Remote Sensing*, vol. GE-25, no. 4, July 1987, pp. 499-501.

[5] I. Daubechies, "the wavelet transform, time-frequency localization and signal analysis," *IEEE Trans. Information Theory*, vol. 36, pp. 961-1005, Sept. 1990.

[6] D.D. Giusto, "On the compression of multispectral images," *Proc. International Geoscience and Remote Sensing Symposium*, 1990, pp. 1651-1654.

[7] P.G. Howard and J.S. Vitter, "New methods for lossless image compression using arithmetic coding," *Proc. Data Compression Conf.*, April 1991, pp. 257-266.

[8] N.S. Jayant and P. Noll, *Digital coding of Waveforms*, Prentice-Hall, Englewood Cliffs, NJ, 1984.

[9] S. Mallat, "A theory for multiresolution signal decomposition: The wavelet representation," *IEEE Trans. Acoustics, Speech and Signal Processing*, vol. 37, Dec. 1990, pp. 2091-2110.

[10] G. Strang, "Wavelets and dilation equations: A brief introduction," *SIAM Review*, vol. 4, Dec. 1989, pp. 614-627.

[11] J.C. Tilton, "Hierarchical data compression: Integrated browse, moderate loss, and lossless levels of data compression," *Proc. of the international Geoscience and Remote Sensing Symp.*, 1990, pp. 1651-1654.

[12] J.C. Tilton, D. Han, and M. Manohar, "Compression experiments with AVHRR data," *Proc. Data Compression Conf.*, April 1991, pp. 411-420.

[13] G.W. Wornell, "A Karhunen-Loeve expansion for $1/f$ processes via wavelets," *IEEE Trans. Information Theory*, vol. 36, July 1990, pp. 859-861.

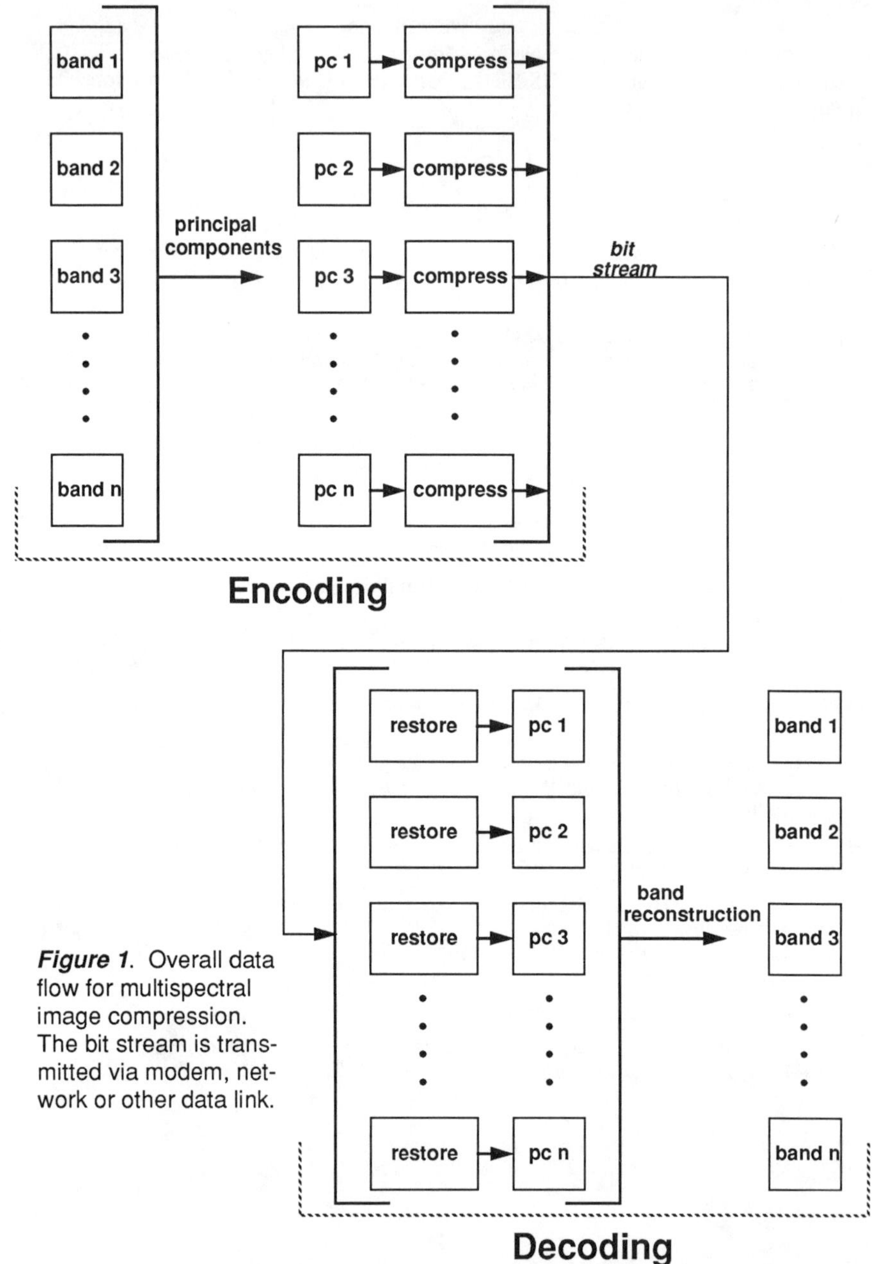

Figure 1. Overall data flow for multispectral image compression. The bit stream is transmitted via modem, network or other data link.

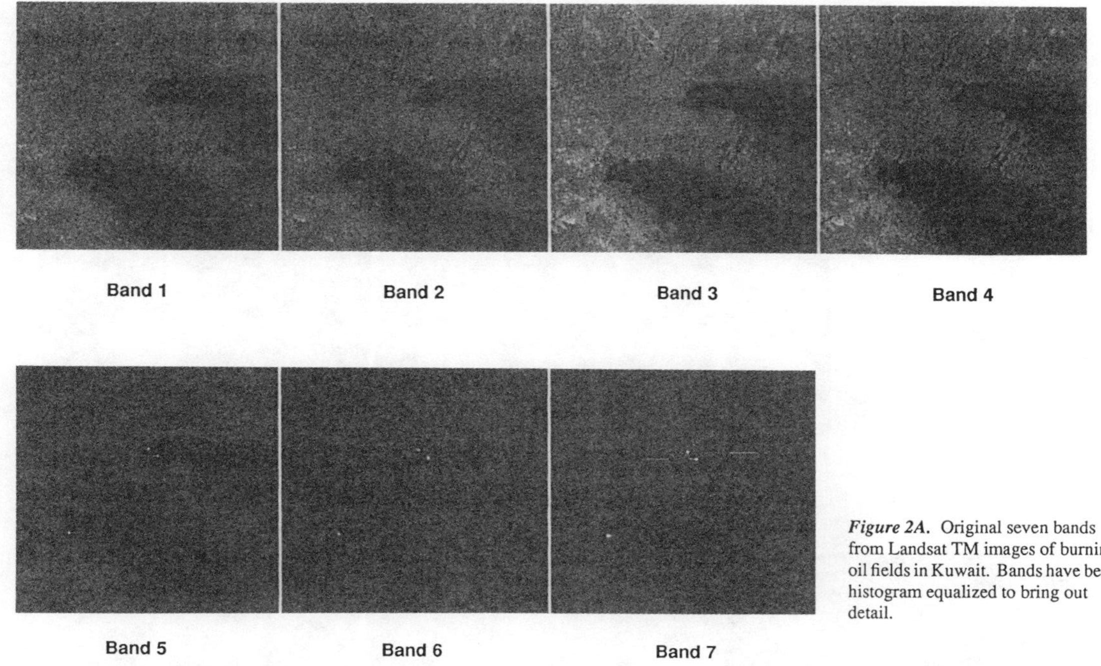

Figure 2A. Original seven bands from Landsat TM images of burning oil fields in Kuwait. Bands have been histogram equalized to bring out detail.

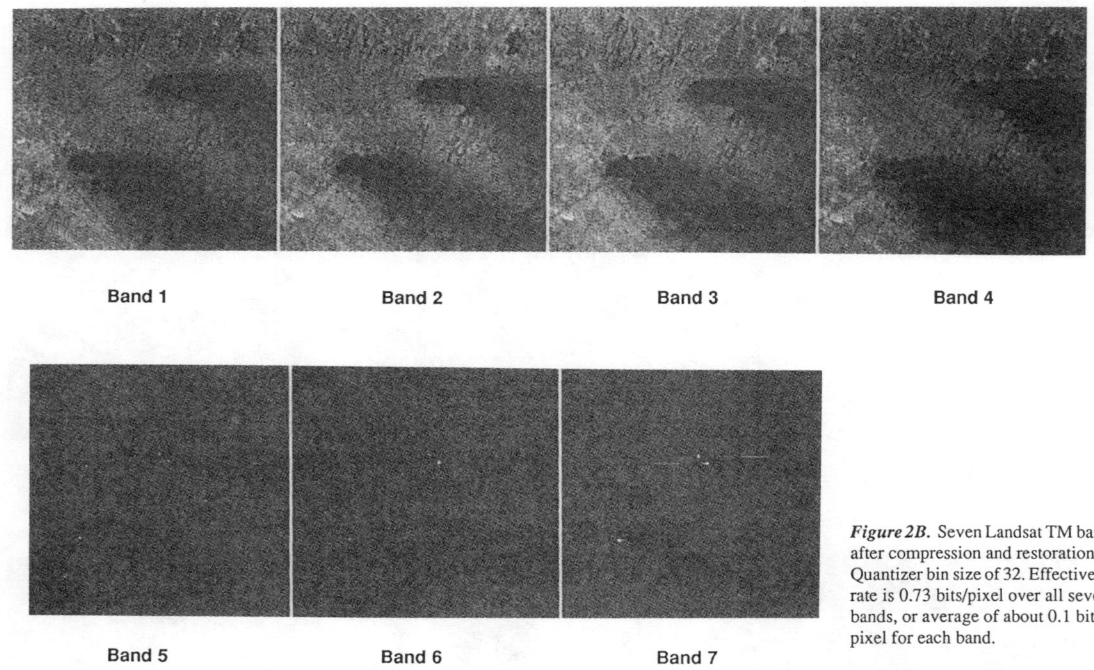

Figure 2B. Seven Landsat TM bands after compression and restoration. Quantizer bin size of 32. Effective bit rate is 0.73 bits/pixel over all seven bands, or average of about 0.1 bit/pixel for each band.

Convolutional Interpolative Coding Algorithms

Masoud R. K. Khansari, Indra Widjaja
A. Leon-Garcia
Department of Electrical Engineering
University of Toronto
Toronto, Ontario, Canada

1   Introduction

Traditionally, real time digital communication takes place as shown in Figure 1. The transmitter takes the source sequence $x(n)$ and tries to reduce the redundancy of the sequence as much as possible so that the amount of channel bandwidth required to transmit $x(n)$ is minimized. This reversible redundancy-reducing procedure results in a *residual* sequence which is then quantized and sent through the channel.

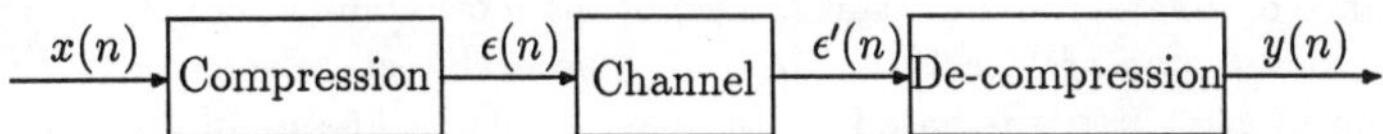

Figure 1 : Block diagram of general point-to-point communication.

In this paper, we will first assume noiseless coding so that the residual sequence $\epsilon(n)$ is sent through the channel. At the receiver, the sequence $\epsilon'(n)$ is received through the channel and de-compressed to produce $y(n)$, which is the replica of $x(n)$. Assuming the channel is noise free, then $\epsilon'(n) = \epsilon(n)$ and $y(n) = x(n)$ for all n.

One of the common compression schemes is the class of *convolutional coding* methods. In the convolutional coding methods such as *Differential Pulse Coded Modulation(DPCM)*, the redundancy of each input sample is reduced by estimating it based on the other samples available at the transmitter. The difference $\epsilon(n)$ between the sample $x(n)$ and its estimate $\hat{x}(n)$ is then transmitted through the channel.

Let I_n be the information transmitted to the receiver up to time index n, then

$$I_n \triangleq \{\cdots, \epsilon(-1), \epsilon(0), \epsilon(1), \cdots, \epsilon(n)\}.$$

In predictive coding the estimate of the $x(n)$ depends only on its *past*[1] and the source sequence up to time n can be recovered from I_n. In this paper, we are interested in *non-causal prediction* or *interpolation* or *smoothing* [1] [3] [5], where the estimate depends both on the past and the future of $x(n)$. This type of coding is of interest in data storage applications where the real-time constraint is absent.

Interpolation achieves smaller mean square estimation error than prediction. However, the decoding procedure is not as straightforward as in the case of prediction.

---

[1]By the past of $x(n)$, we mean $\{\cdots, x(-1), x(0), x(1), \cdots, x(n-1)\}$ and by its future we mean $\{x(n+1), x(n+2), \cdots\}$

"

Since each estimate not only depends on the past but also on the future, the decoder needs to have residual information of future samples which are not available at time n. In this paper we will present a method for recovering $x(n)$.

An interesting property of interpolation is its symmetry with respect to time. It is possible to decode an interpolatively coded data in any direction and from any arbitrary starting point. This feature makes interpolation an attractive candidate for applications such as storage where *play-back* and *random access* are required.

In section 2, we review some of the properties of interpolation for the general class of *auto-regressive* processes and find the minimum mean square error interpolator for these processes. In section 3, we outline a decoding procedure for interpolative coding schemes and demonstrate that it is possible to reconstruct the sequence x from sequence ϵ. We also investigate different trade-offs among decoding delay, estimation gain and interpolator parameters.

In practice, most compression systems contain some sort of quantization. The addition of the quantizer raises new issues such as its placement in the encoder and the performance of different architectures. Two of the most commonly used methods are open and closed loop architectures. In open loop architecture such as D^*PCM, the estimation of $x(n)$, $\hat{x}(n)$, is based on the past of $x(n)$. The main disadvantage of these encoding schemes is that the quantization error of each sample propagates and affects the reconstruction of the future samples, which results in a reduced end-to-end SNR. To counter this problem, in closed-loop architecture such as $DPCM$, the estimation of $x(n)$ is based on $\{\cdots, \hat{x}(n-2), \hat{x}(n-1)\}$. This means that the encoder emulates the decoder. In the case of the interpolation, where the estimation is non-causal, the realization of the closed loop architecture is not easily achieved. In section 4, we demonstrate the performance of the open-loop interpolative encoder in the presence of the quantizer. In section 5, we show how the close-loop circuit can be realized and compare its performance with the open-loop case. For simplicity, we are only considering the case where the input process, $\{x\}$, is an $AR(1)$ process but add that the algorithm can be extended, without any difficulty, to a general $ARMA(N, M)$ processes.

2   Interpolation

We assume the underlying process of the random sequence x is pth order autoregressive. In other words,

$$x(n) = \sum_{i=1}^{p} a_i x(n-i) + \omega(n),$$

where ω is a zero mean white-noise random sequence independent of the past inputs. Then, using orthogonality principle, the optimal interpolator which minimizes the mean square error of the interpolation error is: [1],

$$\hat{x}(n) = \sum_{i=1}^{p} h_i \left\{ x(n-i) + x(n+i) \right\},$$

where h_i is given by,

$$h_i = -\frac{\sum_{k=0}^{p-i} a_k a_{i+k}}{\sum_{k=0}^{p} a_k^2}, \qquad a_0 \triangleq -1$$

In contrast to the optimal prediction error, the interpolation error is not white. In fact for an $AR(p)$ source, the interpolation error is pth order moving average process [1] [4]. The correlation coefficients of the interpolation error are given by,

$$r_\epsilon(k) = \beta_\epsilon^2 \left[\delta_{k,0} - \sum_{i=1}^{p} h_i \left(\delta_{k,i} + \delta_{k,-i} \right) \right],$$

where $\delta_{k,i}$ is Kronecker's delta function and,

$$\beta_\epsilon^2 = \frac{\mathbf{E}[\epsilon^2]}{\sum_{i=1}^{p} a_i^2}.$$

For example, for an $AR(1)$ process, $x(n) = \rho x(n-1) + \omega(n)$, the optimal interpolator is given by,

$$\hat{x}(n) = \frac{\rho}{1+\rho^2} \left\{ x(n-1) + x(n+1) \right\},$$

and, the interpolation error process is given by,

$$\epsilon(n) = \frac{-\rho}{1+\rho^2}\omega(n+1) + \frac{1}{1+\rho^2}\omega(n).$$

Note that $\epsilon(n)$ is the time *reversed* first order moving average process, $MA(1)$. We define the **estimation gain G**, as

$$G = \frac{\mathbf{E}[x^2]}{\mathbf{E}[\epsilon^2]}.$$

Thus, in the case of the interpolation for $AR(1)$, $G_{inter} = \frac{1+\rho^2}{1-\rho^2}$ and for prediction, $G_{pred} = \frac{1}{1-\rho^2}$. This demonstrates the fact that using interpolation the dynamic range of the error signal is smaller than in prediction. For example, for $\rho = 0.9$, $G_{pred} = 7.21\ dB$ and $G_{inter} = 9.79\ dB$. It should be noted that the above estimation gain may or may not translate into an actual *end-to-end SNR* gain.

3 Algorithms

In the noiseless case where there is no quantizer, a transmitter using a two-tap interpolator sends $\epsilon(n)$ at time n which is

$$\epsilon(n) = x(n) - a\{x(n-1) + x(n+1)\},$$

where a is the interpolator parameter. We will now propose an algorithm for recovering $x(n)$ from the sequence of residuals $\epsilon(n)$. The receiver has a buffer to store the

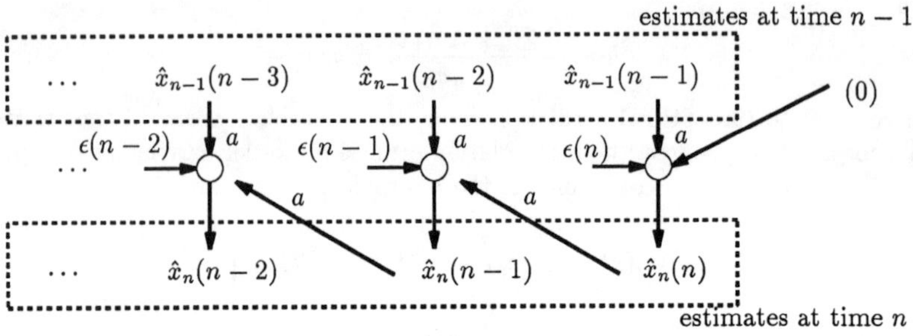

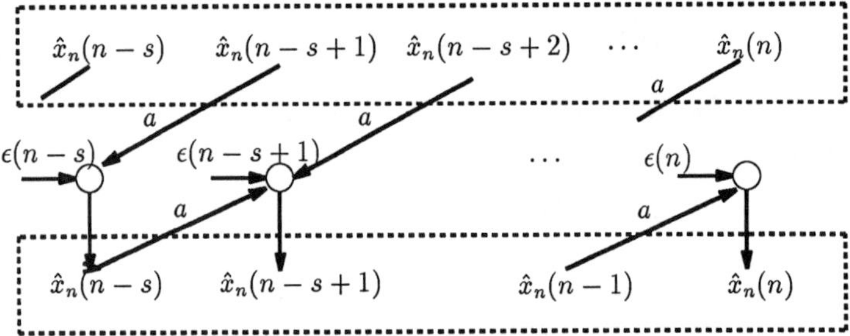

Figure 2: Backward and forward refinements at the decoder.

previous estimates of the sequence x. Let $\hat{x}_k(n)$ be the estimate of $x(n)$ at time k. After receiving $\epsilon(n)$ at time n, the receiver updates the estimates as follows. First, the present estimate of $x(n)$, $\hat{x}_n(n)$, is updated according to

$$\hat{x}_n(n) = \epsilon(n) + a(\hat{x}_{n-1}(n-1) + \hat{x}_n(n+1)),$$

which is obtained by solving the interpolator equation for $x(n)$. Since no estimate of $x(n+1)$ is available at time n, its mean (which is assumed zero) is used for $\hat{x}_n(n+1)$. Now, that the estimate of $x(n)$ has changed, the receiver modifies the estimate of $x(n-1)$ as

$$\hat{x}_n(n-1) = \epsilon(n-1) + a(\hat{x}_{n-1}(n-2) + \hat{x}_n(n)).$$

Similarly, the same procedure is applied to the estimates of $x(n-2), x(n-3), \cdots$. Figure 2, demonstrates the above procedure which we call *backward* refinement. How far the algorithm goes back into the past to update the samples is an issue that needs to be addressed. The simplest method is to terminate updating the estimates after the decoder reaches a specific number of samples into the past, namely s, from the current sample. At this point the decoder outputs $\hat{x}_n(n-s)$ as an estimate for $x(n-s)$. In this case, the operation of the decoder is *synchronous*. It is clear that when the decoder terminates too soon (i.e s is small), the estimate is not very accurate. On the other hand, a desired estimate can be obtained by increasing s at the expense of long decoding delay. A more elaborate decoding procedure implements the termination point dynamically(i.e. s can vary). In this case the number of the output samples of the decoder at each time index varies and the operation of the decoder is *asynchronous*.

Backward refinement is terminated after it reaches $(n-s)$th sample at time n. Clearly, the $(n-s+1)$th sample can be improved using the new estimate of $(n-s)$th sample. Similarly, the other estimates $\hat{x}_n(n-s+2), \hat{x}_n(n-s+3), \cdots, \hat{x}_n(n)$ can also be improved. We call this procedure *forward* refinement, as shown in Figure 2. More passes can be added, but it was found that two passes are sufficient. To show that the encoded sequence is uniquely decoded, it is sufficient to show that $\lim_{k\to\infty} \hat{x}_k(n) = x(n)$ pointwise. In other words, after a finite number of iterations the estimate of $x(n)$, $\hat{x}(n)$, can be made arbitrarily close to $x(n)$. The decoding algorithm when operating asynchronously is summarized as follows,

input: receive $\epsilon(n)$
step1: update current estimate of $\hat{x}_n(n)$
$\hat{x}_n(n) \leftarrow \epsilon(n) + a\hat{x}_{n-1}(n-1)$
$k \leftarrow n$; counter $\leftarrow C$
step2: update past estimate $\hat{x}_k^n$ (backward refinement)
$k \leftarrow k - 1$
$\hat{x}_n(k) \leftarrow \epsilon(k) + a\left(\hat{x}_n(k+1) + \hat{x}_{n-1}(k-1)\right)$
if $\hat{x}_n(k)$ does not change significantly from its previous value
counter $\leftarrow$ counter -1
else counter $= C$
step3: **if** counter $\neq 0$ **and** $k > j$ **goto** step2
else if counter $= 0$
output: $\hat{x}(i) = \hat{x}_n(i), \quad$ for $j \leq i \leq k$
$j \leftarrow k$
goto step4
step4: update past estimate $\hat{x}_n(k)$ (forward refinement)
$k \leftarrow k + 1$
$\hat{x}_n(k) \leftarrow \epsilon(k) + a\left(\hat{x}_n(k+1) + \hat{x}_n(k-1)\right)$
step5: **if** $k \neq n$ **goto** step4
else stop

For the encoder to be stable, that is for the ϵ sequence to be bounded, it is necessary and sufficient to have the poles of the interpolation filter inside the unit circle of the complex plane. Therefore, it is necessary to have the interpolator parameter $a < \frac{1}{2}$. We will demonstrate that the convergence rate depends mainly on the interpolator parameter and not on the underlying random process x.

We define the *mean-delay* as the average number of required refinements for each sample. Figure 3 and 4 show the mean-delay and estimation gain versus a. Notice that when a is small, the compression gain and the delay are also low. As we increase a, both the compression gain and delay increase, but in a different way. The compression gain initially increases quickly and then slowly saturates near $a_{opt} = \frac{\rho}{1+\rho^2}$, whereas the delay increases slowly for a small a and then goes up rapidly near a_{opt}.

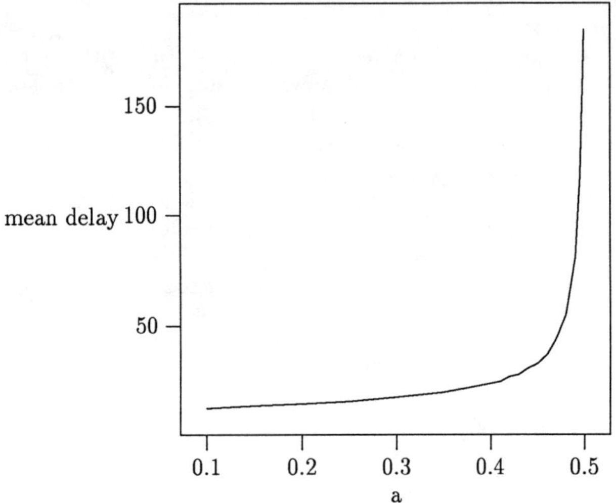

Figure 3: Mean-delay vs. interpolation parameter a.

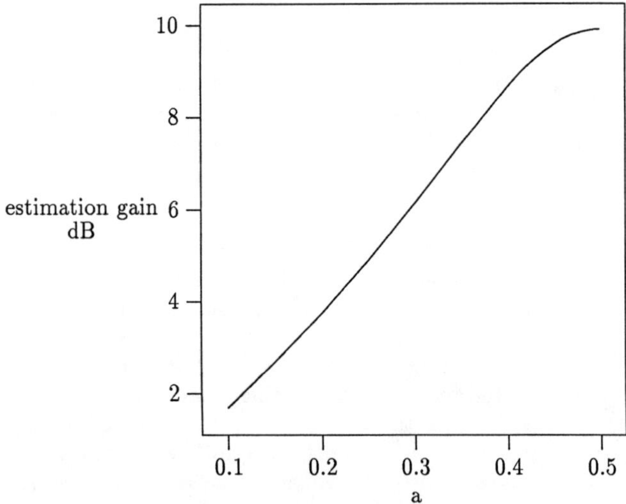

Figure 4: Estimation gain vs. interpolation parameter a.

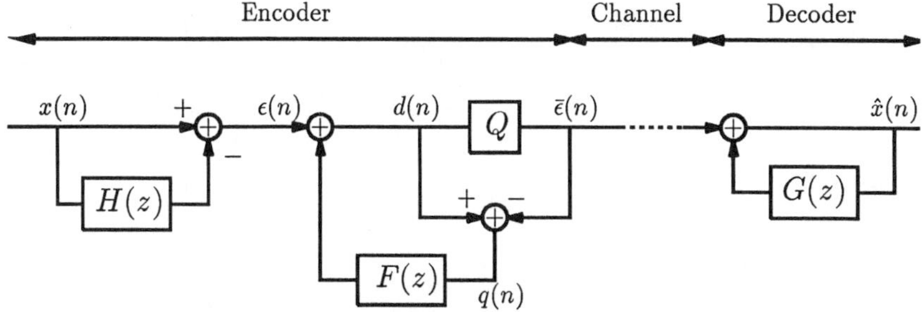

Figure 5: Block diagram of the encoder-decoder circuits.

Thus, there is a trade-off between maximizing compression gain and minimizing decoding delay. For $\rho = 0.9$, $a_{opt} \simeq 0.497$ which is close to 0.5, and results in a slow convergence of the decoder. Hence, we decided to use a sub-optimal encoder, such as $a_{sub} = \frac{\rho}{2}$. Estimation gain in this case is 9.57 dB which is 0.33 dB less than the optimal case. And the mean delay is 33 steps in comparison to 151 steps for the optimal case. Although the estimation gain is slightly lower than the optimal case, considerable improvement in the convergence rate is achieved. For the processes with lower correlation coefficient(ρ), a_{opt} is not close to $\frac{1}{2}$ and mean-delay of the optimal interpolator decreases considerably.

4   Open-loop Performance

Figure 5 shows the encoder and the decoder circuits in the most general set-up. $H(z)$ and $G(z)$ are estimation filters used in the encoder and the decoder, respectively [2]. These two filters are not necessarily the same. The input to $F(z)$ is the quantization error and the output is fed back and added to the estimation error. For open loop structures such as D^*PCM, $F(z) = 0$. In this case, the optimal $G(z)$ is not necessarily the same as $H(z)$. If $F(z)$ is taken to be the same as $H(z)$, the structure is equivalent to $DPCM$. In this case, the quantization error does not propagate and it can be shown that the optimal[2] $G(z)$ is $H(z)$. In the general case of *noise feedback coding*, $H(z) = G(z)$ but $F(z)$ can be different from $H(z)$.

Using open-loop architecture, $F(z) = 0$ and the quantizer is outside of the encoder loop. Therefore, there is no extra complexity in the implementation with respect to the noiseless encoder. After including the quantizer at the encoder, one has to consider other parameters in the design of the codec. One of these parameters is the signal-to-noise ratio, SNR, which is an indication of the end-to-end reconstruction error. Let $e(n) = x(n) - \hat{x}(n)$, then the SNR is defined as

$$SNR \triangleq 10 \log \frac{\sigma_x^2}{\sigma_e^2},$$

---

[2]Optimal in the sense of minimizing end-to-end reconstruction error.

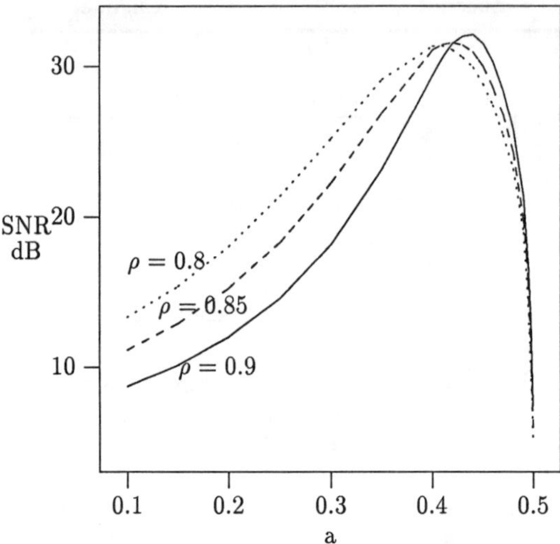

Figure 6: SNR vs. a (open-loop).

where $\sigma_e^2 = \mathbf{E}[e(n)^2]$ and $\sigma_x^2 = \mathbf{E}[x(n)^2]$ and x and e sequence are zero mean processes. Figure 6 shows the SNR vs. interpolator parameter a for $AR(1)$ processes with different correlation coefficient ρ. It is clear from this figure that for low values of a, the SNR increases as ρ decreases. However, the maximum achievable SNR increases as ρ increases. This means that processes with high correlation are more sensitive than processes with lower correlation to the variation in the interpolator parameters. Also, for the values of a close to $\frac{1}{2}$, the SNR drops sharply as a approaches 0.5. This is another indication that operating at optimal a is not necessarily suitable. For example for $\rho = 0.9$, the maximum SNR occurs at $a = 0.44$ and is 32 dB. For $a_{opt} = \frac{\rho}{1+\rho^2}$, the SNR achieved is 13 dB which is clearly not suitable.

5 Closed-Loop Implementation and Performance

In predictive coding, the estimate is based on the past and as a result, the filters $H(z), F(z)$ and $G(z)$ are all causal. Consequently, both feed-forward and feedback circuits can be implemented without any difficulty. If interpolation is used, the filters are non-causal. In this case, the feed-forward circuits can be easily implemented using delay elements. However, the implementation of the feedback circuits with a non-casual filter, such as decoding the interpolatively encoded data, is not straightforward.

In the closed-loop circuits such as $DPCM$, the quantization is done in a feedback loop. The quantization error is first filtered and then added to the estimation error. This is necessary to avoid quantization error propagation. If interpolation is used, the filter is non-causal and depends on the future which is not available. In principle, this problem is exactly the same as the implementation of the decoder investigated

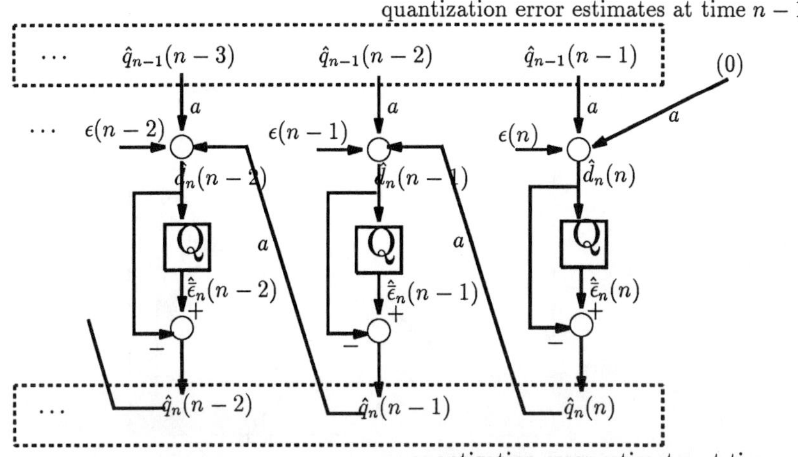

Figure 7: Quantization feedback loop circuit.

in section 3. Therefore, we propose to use the same approach to implement the noise feedback circuit. Figure 7 shows the implementation of the quantization feedback loop, where q is the quantization error sequence and $\bar{\epsilon}$ is the signal transmitted to the decoder. $\hat{q}_n(k)$ and $\hat{\bar{\epsilon}}_n(k)$ are the estimates of $q(k)$ and $\bar{\epsilon}(k)$ at time n, respectively. After the sequence q converges, the sequence $\bar{\epsilon}$ is calculated and transmitted through the channel to the decoder. The algorithm can be generalized to more than one-pass in a similar fashion as section 3.

Figure 8 compares the performance of the codec with open and closed loop circuits. The input process is as before, an $AR(1)$ with correlation coefficient $\rho = 0.9$. The codec behavior has similar pattern in both cases with closed-loop outperforming the open-loop architecture. Around the region $0.4 < a < 0.45$, the SNR is about $4dB$ greater in the case of the closed-loop circuit. This is achieved at the expense of delay at the encoder. Also as a approaches 0.5, SNR decreases as in the open-loop circuit.

6   Conclusion

We proposed a method for decoding interpolatively encoded data. This class of coding scheme achieves higher estimation gain and are symmetric with respect to time which makes them a good candidate for storage application. We showed that different trade-off parameters are involved and investigated their relationships. These parameters are estimation gain, delay experienced by the encoder and the decoder and end-to-end signal-to-noise ratio. We also showed the implementation and the effect of incorporating quantizers in the circuits. Specifically, we investigated two extreme open and closed loop architectures and compared their performances. Generalization of the above algorithm to noise feedback coding can be achieved easily.

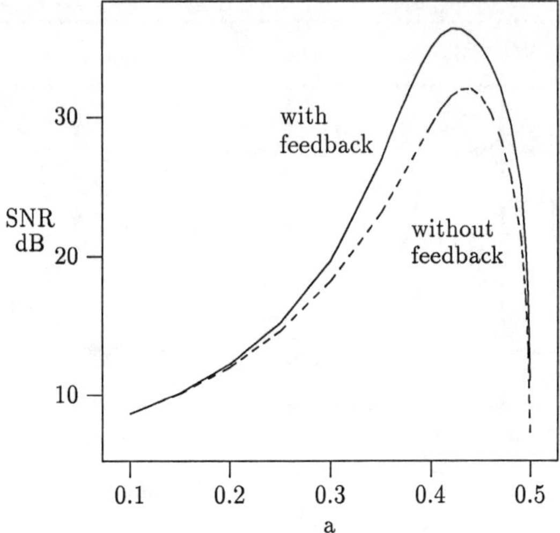

Figure 8: SNR vs. interpolation parameter a.

References

[1] A. K. Jain, "Advances in mathematical models for image processing," *Proceeding of IEEE*, vol. 69, 502-528, May 1981.

[2] N.S. Jayant and P. Noll, *Digital coding of waveforms*, Prentice-Hall, New Jersey, 1984.

[3] A.N. Kolmogorov, "interpolation and extrapolation of stationary random sequences," Izv. Akad. Nauk SSSR, Ser. Mat., 5, 3, 1941.

[4] B. Picinbono and J. Kerilis, "Some properties of Prediction and Interpolation Errors," IEEE Trans. on ASSP, Vol. 36, 525-531, April 1988.

[5] B. Friedlander, M. Morf, "Least Square Algorithms for Adaptive Linear-Phase Filtering", IEEE Trans. on ASSP, Vol. 30, 381-390, June 1982.

A Forward-Mapping Realization of
the Inverse Discrete Cosine Transform

Leonard McMillan

Lee Westover

Sun Microsystems, Inc.
Research Triangle Park, NC 27709

Abstract

This paper presents a new realization of the Inverse Discrete Cosine Transform
(IDCT). It exploits both the decorrelation properties of the Discrete Cosine
Transform (DCT) and the quantization process that is frequently applied to
the DCT's resultant coefficients. This formulation has several advantages
over previous approaches, including the elimination of multiplies from the
central loop of the algorithm and its adaptability to incremental evaluation.
The technique provides a significant reduction in computational requirements
of the IDCT, enabling a software-based implementation to perform at rates
which were previously achievable only through dedicated hardware.

1. Introduction

Since its introduction, the DCT [Ahmed74] has found widespread use in the field
of image processing. [Jain79] has demonstrated that for data exhibiting high
correlation, the DCT performs close to the ideal Karhunen-Loeve Transform. The
DCT representation of a data sequence tends to concentrate the most variance
(energy) into the fewest transform coefficients. This results in a transform domain
description which is sparse compared to the original input sequence.

The application of the DCT to many interesting classes of data, particularly continuous tone images, has motivated the search for fast and efficient algorithms. The
earliest fast algorithms were based on approaches originally developed for the Fast
Fourier Transform, in which the periodicity and recursive nature of the underlying
basis functions were exploited [Narasimha78][Tseng78][Vetterli84]. Later, other fast
algorithms were developed by considering various factorizations of the DCT's basis
matrix [Chen77][Lee84][Ligtenberg87].

The structural similarities of the DCT to its inverse, the IDCT, has enabled each
of the fast DCT algorithms to be easily adapted to their dual IDCT formulation.
As a consequence, there has been little concentration on specific formulations of the
IDCT and the unique statistical properties of this transform domain description.

Both IDCT and the DCT are easily expressed as a constant-coefficient linear
system in which each output element is expressed as a finite weighted sum of
input elements. Systems where each output value is directly evaluated in this
fashion are called *inverse-mapping* systems [Wolberg90]. An alternate evaluation
approach is to express each input element's contribution to the entire set of output

220

elements independently. This formulation is referred to as a *forward-mapping system* [Wolberg90]. A system can calculate a weighted average by either gathering energy from each contributing input to calculate each output, or by spreading the energy from each input to all affected outputs. The final result is independent of the evaluation order of these energy contributions.

We will introduce a forward-mapping derivation of a fast IDCT algorithm (FMIDCT) which exploits the statistical properties of its input sequence. Although the discussion will concentrate on the 2-D IDCT algorithm, the techniques described are easily adapted to other dimensions and other orthogonal transforms with similar statistical properties. We also discuss a further optimization to the FMIDCT which takes advantage of the quantization of the transform domain coefficients. Finally, we will demonstrate the unique capability of the FMIDCT to trade-off reconstruction quality in exchange for reductions in computation.

2. FMIDCT Evaluation

A type II, $N \times N$, 2-D IDCT, which is commonly used in image compression, is expressed as

$$o(x, y) = \sum_{v=0}^{N-1} \sum_{u=0}^{N-1} f(u)f(v)i(u, v) \times \cos\left(\frac{\pi(2x + 1)u}{2N}\right) \cos\left(\frac{\pi(2y + 1)v}{2N}\right), \tag{1}$$

$$x, y: \to [0, N - 1] \quad \text{and} \quad f(i) = \begin{cases} \frac{\sqrt{2}}{2}, & \text{for } i = 0; \\ 1, & \text{otherwise.} \end{cases}$$

This equation expressed as a linear system is $\bar{O} = C\bar{I}$, where $\bar{I}$ and $\bar{O}$ are N^2-dimensional vectors constructed from the row-ordered enumeration of the $N \times N$ transform domain input sequence, $i(u, v)$, and the reconstructed output sequence, $o(x, y)$, respectively. The $N^2 \times N^2$ system matrix, C, is composed of the input weighting terms and is defined as follows:

$$c(yN + x, vN + u) = f(u)f(v)\cos\left(\frac{\pi(2x + 1)u}{2N}\right) \cos\left(\frac{\pi(2y + 1)v}{2N}\right).$$

Equation (1) may be evaluated using either matrix decompositions, inverse-mapping procedures, or forward-mapping procedures. Previously, fast algorithms [Chen77][Lee84][Ligtenberg87][Kamangar82] have concentrated almost exclusively on matrix decomposition evaluation procedures, where the system matrix, C, is factored into a set of sparse matrices.

Inverse-mapping procedures are equivalent to calculating each element of the output vector, $\bar{O}$, by taking the inner-product of a corresponding row in the system matrix, C and the input vector, $\bar{I}$. Let $L = N - 1$ and $M = N^2 - 1$, then

$$\bar{O} = \bar{R}\bar{I} \quad \text{or} \quad O_{xy} = R^{xy}\bar{I}, \quad \text{where} \quad R^{xy} = [r_0^{xy} r_1^{xy} \ldots r_M^{xy}]$$

with

$$r_k^{xy} = f(k \bmod N)f(k \operatorname{div} N)\cos\left(\frac{\pi(2x + 1)(k \bmod N)}{2N}\right) \cos\left(\frac{\pi(2y + 1)(k \operatorname{div} N)}{2N}\right).$$

As a matrix equation, this is written as:

$$
\begin{bmatrix} o_{00} \\ o_{01} \\ \vdots \\ o_{xy} \\ \vdots \\ o_{LL} \end{bmatrix}
=
\begin{bmatrix} r_0^{xy} & r_1^{xy} & r_2^{xy} & \cdots & r_M^{xy} \end{bmatrix}
\begin{bmatrix} i_{00} \\ i_{01} \\ \vdots \\ i_{uv} \\ \vdots \\ i_{LL} \end{bmatrix} .
$$

When using the forward-mapping approach, the output vector is formed by the successive accumulation of each system matrix column scaled by the corresponding input value.

$$
\bar{O} = \sum_{uv} i_{uv} C^{uv} \qquad \text{where} \qquad C^{uv} = \begin{bmatrix} c_0^{uv} \\ c_1^{uv} \\ \vdots \\ c_M^{uv} \end{bmatrix}
$$

with

$$
c_k^{uv} = f(u)f(v) \times \cos\left(\frac{\pi(2(k \ mod \ N)k + 1)u}{2N} \right) \cos\left(\frac{\pi(2(k \ div \ N) + 1)v}{2N} \right).
$$

As a matrix equation, this is written as:

$$
\begin{bmatrix} o_{00} \\ o_{01} \\ \vdots \\ o_{LL} \end{bmatrix}
= i_{00} \begin{bmatrix} c_0^{00} \\ c_1^{00} \\ \vdots \\ c_M^{00} \end{bmatrix}
+ i_{01} \begin{bmatrix} c_0^{01} \\ c_1^{01} \\ \vdots \\ c_M^{01} \end{bmatrix}
+ \ldots + i_{LL} \begin{bmatrix} c_0^{LL} \\ c_1^{LL} \\ \vdots \\ c_M^{LL} \end{bmatrix}
$$

[Westover90] [Westover91] has demonstrated the efficiency of the forward-mapping approach for volumetric reconstruction. The advantages are pronounced when the input vector is sparse. The forward-mapping process incrementally accumulates the energy contributed from each input element into the output vector. Each transform domain coefficient scales the corresponding matrix column. We call this matrix column vector the *reconstruction kernel* of the input coefficient. The scaled reconstruction kernel is then accumulated with the output vector, $\bar{O}$.

3. Properties of FMIDCT

Previous algorithms have been formulated to be computed in some minimal, yet constant, number of operations. This leads to constant time evaluation, which is independent of the input sequence applied. However, the FMIDCT is input sequence dependent, since the amount of computation required is proportional to the number of non-zero coefficients. This situation is similar to that of the well known quicksort algorithm [Knuth73], in which its worst case behavior varies significantly from its average case behavior. In such cases it is useful to not only discuss the average behavior, but also the likelihood of the worse case scenario.

There are three ways in which the FMIDCT reduces computation. First, the reconstruction kernels exhibit considerable symmetry thereby reducing the number of unique multiplies required in the scaling process. Furthermore, since the transform domain coefficients are frequently quantized to a small number of reconstruction levels, this multiply can be replaced by a table-look-up. Second, zero-valued coefficients will make no contribution to the output vector, thereby eliminating the scaling and accumulation steps. Since there is a high incidence of these zero-valued coefficients, due to the decorrelation properties of the DCT and the subsequent quantization, this results in a significant reduction in computation. Finally, the FMIDCT provides a continuous quality versus computation time trade-off.

3.1 Table Driven Multiplication

Although the unit-valued reconstruction kernels are composed of N^2 values, the magnitude of at most $\frac{N^2+2N}{8}$ of these values is unique. This repetition allows the scaling multiply to be calculated only once and accumulated into the output vector at each repeated position. This is demonstrated by the following example 8×8 IDCT kernels. Let

$$C_{xy} = f(x)f(y)\cos\left(\frac{x\pi}{16}\right)\cos\left(\frac{y\pi}{16}\right),$$

$$k(0,1) = \begin{bmatrix} C_{01} & C_{03} & C_{05} & C_{07} & -C_{07} & -C_{05} & -C_{03} & -C_{01} \\ C_{01} & C_{03} & C_{05} & C_{07} & -C_{07} & -C_{05} & -C_{03} & -C_{01} \\ C_{01} & C_{03} & C_{05} & C_{07} & -C_{07} & -C_{05} & -C_{03} & -C_{01} \\ C_{01} & C_{03} & C_{05} & C_{07} & -C_{07} & -C_{05} & -C_{03} & -C_{01} \\ C_{01} & C_{03} & C_{05} & C_{07} & -C_{07} & -C_{05} & -C_{03} & -C_{01} \\ C_{01} & C_{03} & C_{05} & C_{07} & -C_{07} & -C_{05} & -C_{03} & -C_{01} \\ C_{01} & C_{03} & C_{05} & C_{07} & -C_{07} & -C_{05} & -C_{03} & -C_{01} \\ C_{01} & C_{03} & C_{05} & C_{07} & -C_{07} & -C_{05} & -C_{03} & -C_{01} \end{bmatrix},$$

$$k(1,1) = \begin{bmatrix} C_{11} & C_{13} & C_{15} & C_{17} & -C_{17} & -C_{15} & -C_{13} & -C_{11} \\ C_{13} & C_{33} & C_{35} & C_{37} & -C_{37} & -C_{35} & -C_{33} & -C_{13} \\ C_{15} & C_{35} & C_{55} & C_{57} & -C_{57} & -C_{55} & -C_{35} & -C_{15} \\ C_{17} & C_{37} & C_{57} & C_{77} & -C_{77} & -C_{57} & -C_{37} & -C_{17} \\ -C_{17} & -C_{37} & -C_{57} & -C_{77} & C_{77} & C_{57} & C_{37} & C_{17} \\ -C_{15} & -C_{35} & -C_{55} & -C_{57} & C_{57} & C_{55} & C_{35} & C_{15} \\ -C_{13} & -C_{33} & -C_{35} & -C_{37} & C_{37} & C_{35} & C_{33} & C_{13} \\ -C_{11} & -C_{13} & -C_{15} & -C_{17} & C_{17} & C_{15} & C_{13} & C_{11} \end{bmatrix} \quad \text{and}$$

$$k(4,4) = \begin{bmatrix} C_{44} & -C_{44} & -C_{44} & C_{44} & C_{44} & -C_{44} & -C_{44} & C_{44} \\ -C_{44} & C_{44} & C_{44} & -C_{44} & -C_{44} & C_{44} & C_{44} & -C_{44} \\ -C_{44} & C_{44} & C_{44} & -C_{44} & -C_{44} & C_{44} & C_{44} & -C_{44} \\ C_{44} & -C_{44} & -C_{44} & C_{44} & C_{44} & -C_{44} & -C_{44} & C_{44} \\ C_{44} & -C_{44} & -C_{44} & C_{44} & C_{44} & -C_{44} & -C_{44} & C_{44} \\ -C_{44} & C_{44} & C_{44} & -C_{44} & -C_{44} & C_{44} & C_{44} & -C_{44} \\ -C_{44} & C_{44} & C_{44} & -C_{44} & -C_{44} & C_{44} & C_{44} & -C_{44} \\ C_{44} & -C_{44} & -C_{44} & C_{44} & C_{44} & -C_{44} & -C_{44} & C_{44} \end{bmatrix}.$$

Notice that only 4 unique multiples are necessary for the accumulation of the $k(0,1)$ kernel, 10 for the $k(1,1)$ kernel, and only 1 for $k(4,4)$. Table 1 depicts the number of unique coefficients of the unit-valued reconstruction kernels in each of the 8×8 cases.

$$\begin{array}{c|cccccccc}
v/u & 0 & 1 & 2 & 3 & 4 & 5 & 6 & 7 \\
\hline
0 & 1 & 4 & 2 & 4 & 1 & 4 & 2 & 4 \\
1 & 4 & 10 & 8 & 10 & 4 & 10 & 8 & 10 \\
2 & 2 & 8 & 3 & 8 & 2 & 8 & 3 & 8 \\
3 & 4 & 10 & 8 & 10 & 4 & 10 & 8 & 10 \\
4 & 1 & 4 & 2 & 4 & 1 & 4 & 2 & 4 \\
5 & 4 & 10 & 8 & 10 & 4 & 10 & 8 & 10 \\
6 & 2 & 8 & 3 & 8 & 2 & 8 & 3 & 8 \\
7 & 4 & 10 & 8 & 10 & 4 & 10 & 8 & 10
\end{array}$$

Table 1:Unique entries for each DCT coefficient

This suggests that an 8×8 IDCT can be accomplished with just 384 multiplies instead of the 4096 implied by the matrix equation. This reduction is less impressive than the 128 required multiplies achievable through other fast 2-D algorithms [Kamangar82], however, the computation requirements of the FMIDCT can be further reduced using techniques which are not amenable to other fast algorithms.

In most applications the IDCT is preceded by a dequantization process. This leads to a finite limit on the actual number of reconstruction levels. Generally, dequantization is performed prior to the IDCT. In the FMIDCT, the dequantization and the scaling may be combined into a single step. Since there are a finite number of reconstruction levels for each coefficient and each coefficient is treated independently, this step may be realized as a table look-up, as described in the Software Implementation Detail section.

The fact that existing fast implementations of the IDCT do not treat each input value independently limits the usefulness of performing multiplications by table-look-ups. In these algorithms, linear combinations of several input values, generated by the matrix products of the previously applied matrix decompositions, are multiplied by scalar constants. While these linear combinations are also constrained to take on a finite number of unique values, this number quickly becomes impractical for implementation by table look-up, since it is proportional to the product of the number of reconstruction levels for each of its constituent inputs.

3.2 Special Case of Zero Coefficients

Well known fast IDCT algorithms [Kamangar82] require as few as 400 adds and 128 multiplies per 8×8 block. If we assume each multiply is equivalent to 5 adds, (allowing 12-bits per scalar constant and assuming the use of Booth's algorithm), this results in more than 1024 adds per block or approximately 16 adds per result. More commonly used approaches, where the 2-D IDCT is separated into 2N 1-D IDCTs, require on the order of 128 additional multiplies resulting in 26 adds per output. While, in the worst case, a FMIDCT that utilizes table-driven multiplies, would require 63 adds per result, typically the algorithm requires less than 20% of that number, and in the best case, where the DC coefficient is the only non-zero coefficient, requires no adds. The highly uncorrelated data sequences which are necessary to generate a large number of adds are rare in practice and furthermore, they are generally ill-suited for DCT coding.

One of the most important properties of the DCT that is often exploited in compression algorithms is the high probability, after appropriate quantization, of zero valued coefficients [Wallace91][LeGall91][Liou91]. These coefficients imply no work for the FMIDCT. Table 2 gives the average number of non-zero AC coefficients occurring in a variety of images out of a possible 63. Since each non-zero coefficient implies the accumulation of a scaled reconstruction kernel, this number indicates the average number of additions required for each pixel. This data suggests that the FMIDCT required only 6% to 17% of the additions implied by the worst case. Futhermore, based on the multiplier equivalence arguments presented earlier, this algorithm is between 2 to 6 times faster than other well known approachs.

3.3 Quality versus Speed Trade-off

This formulation of the IDCT is unique in providing a quality versus computation-time trade-off. Since each input is handled independently, we can accumulate the various spatial frequency inputs in a priority order. Such an ordering can be approximated by zig-zag ordering. The accumulation of reconstruction kernels can be stopped at any point in order to achieve a given performance level. We call this approach *incremental evaluation*. This notion is similar to that of progressive transmission of images [Wang88][Tzou87], where an approximate reconstruction of an image is gradually built up with increasing fidelity while a viewer controls how long the process should continue. The motivation for progressive transmission is to make effective use of channel bandwidth at the cost of requiring many invocations of the IDCT. In contrast, the incremental evaluation approach places a upper limit on the computational cost for the IDCT, trading off image quality for decoding speed. These two techniques may be combined, where each successive component in the progressive scheme implies one additional accumulation in the FMIDCT.

4. Results

We have implemented a baseline JPEG decoder in software that utilizes the FMIDCT which can perform in excess of 50,000 8 × 8 transforms per second on a 40 Mhz Sun SparcStation 2. This implementation is capable of decoding and displaying 320 × 240 image sequences at rates in excess of 10 frames per second. In our implementation, each 16 × 16 pixel macroblock is represented by 4 8 × 8 blocks of luminance values and 2 8 × 8 blocks of subsampled chrominance values. These frames have 280 macroblocks, so each image requires 1680 8 × 8 IDCTs. Less than one third of a sequence's playback time is spent in the IDCT and related routines. Another third of a sequence's playback time is spent in the conversion of the luminance/chrominance representation to red, green, blue and dithering routines. About one fifth of a sequence's playback time is spent in the bit-stream parsing and Huffman decoding routines, while the remaining time is spent in various bookkeeping routines.

Table 2 gives some statistics on a few sample image sequences. The "target" sequence is the 30 second Sun Microsystems, Inc. client-server computing commercial. The "mifkin" sequence is a 60 second sequence with 19 scene changes. The f16, Lenna, mandrill, and Zelda images are commonly studied in the image processing field.

image	Resolution	Frames	IDCTs	non-zero Coeffs	Mults	$\frac{Mults}{IDCT}$
f16	512×496	1	5952	4.90	4183	0.703
Lenna	512×496	1	5952	4.67	3726	0.626
mandrill	512×496	1	5952	11.28	5328	0.895
Zelda	512×496	1	5952	4.33	3336	0.560
target	320×224	300	504000	5.08	5425	0.011
mifkin	320×224	600	1008000	3.80	5167	0.006

Table 2:Result Table

4.1 Software Implementation Details

The FMIDCT uses table look-ups for most of its multiplications. The current implementation has a separate table or cache for each DCT coefficient. The lower bits of the quantized input value act as the index into the cache. If the last key-value stored in the cache is the same as the current input value, the system simply uses the results that are stored in the cache. If the values disagree, the system dequantizes the value, performs the required multiplies needed for this DCT coefficient and loads these results in the cache. Choosing the least significant bits of the quantized value guarantees that the most probable values, (1, -1, 2, and -2) do not map to the same cache location, and increases the likelihood that these values may stay in the cache once they are calculated.

The values in Table 2 illustrate the effectiveness of this approach. For the sample images, each DCT block has between 4 and 12 non-zero AC coefficients on average. Each of these coefficients require between 1 and 10 multiplies to scale their respective reconstruction kernels. Yet, the average number of multiplies per block is below 1 for all cases, and is approaching 0 for the long sequence.

The current cache implementation uses approximately 112 kilobytes of storage. Since we use the least significant 7 bits as an index to the cache, there are 128 different cache locations for each of the 64 different caches. The size of the cache can be reduced by using fewer bits as the index. Since the number of quantization levels and the variance of the coefficient's distribution varies for each coefficient, the system could size each cache accordingly.

4.2 Hardware Realization Potential

Another advantage of the FMIDCT is its suitability for VLSI implementation. The FMIDCT can be accomplished using a simple accumulator block repeated $N \times N$ times as shown in Figure 1.

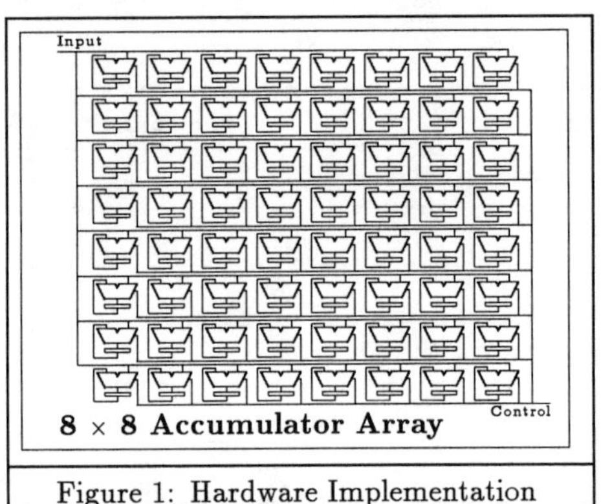

Figure 1: Hardware Implementation

It is possible to precede the data-path described with a single multiplier to perform both dequantization and scaling by the unit-reconstruction kernel. However, it is probably more efficient for a supporting controller to perform this operation using the caching techniques described earlier, given the infrequency of multiplies. Every accumulator in the array could be made to share a common data input I, with distributed control for each accumulator. Each accumulator is only required to perform four distinct operations. $A_{xy} \leftarrow I, A_{xy} \leftarrow A_{xy}, A_{xy} \leftarrow A_{xy} + I, A_{xy} \leftarrow A_{xy} - I$. The IDCT applys the scaled unique values of the reconstruction kernel to the array along with an appropriate control word, for each non-zero coefficient.

The amount of control circuitry can be reduced by recognizing that each reconstruction kernel can be categorized into one of four possible forms.

$$\begin{bmatrix} [Q] & [H] \\ [V] & [D] \end{bmatrix}, \qquad \begin{bmatrix} [Q] & -[H] \\ [V] & -[D] \end{bmatrix}, \qquad \begin{bmatrix} [Q] & [H] \\ -[V] & -[D] \end{bmatrix}, \qquad \begin{bmatrix} [Q] & -[H] \\ -[V] & [D] \end{bmatrix}$$

where:

$$H = QR, \quad V = RQ, \quad D = RQR \quad \text{and } \mathbf{R} \text{ is defined as} \quad R = \begin{bmatrix} 0 & 0 & 0 & 1 \\ 0 & 0 & 1 & 0 \\ 0 & 1 & 0 & 0 \\ 1 & 0 & 0 & 0 \end{bmatrix}$$

Therefore, independent control is only required for the accumulators within a single quadrant of the array, with an addition two-bits to select the appropriate symmetry.

One could also further reduce the control circuitry required by recognizing that there are fewer than 384 actual configurations of a given quadrant, as implied by Table 1.

Thus, with a highly regular structure requiring a single input of approximately 16-bits and 10-12 controls bits, a low cost and high-speed implementation of a 2-D 8×8 IDCT can be realized. Futher enhancements might include combining the look-up tables and the accumulator array on the same chip along with a suitable state-machine which would automatically step through each of the kernel values corresponding to a given quantized coefficient value.

5. Conclusions

We have presented an algorithm for the efficient evaluation of the IDCT which uses a forward-mapping approach. It typically requires 2 to 6 times less computation than other fast algorithms. Our approach takes unique advantage of the decorrelation properties of the DCT, in that it requires no work for zero valued coefficients. Multiplies are essentially eliminated through the use of table look-ups and caching. The FMIDCT also provides a unique tradeoff that exchanges quality for further reductions in computation. Thus, in addition to being amenable to a simple and regular hardware realization, this technique allows for an efficient software-only realization that provides performance previously only achievable via hardware assisted approaches, yielding a low-cost playback-only solution for DCT based compression standards.

6. References

Ahmed, N., T. Natarajan, and K. R. Rao, [1974] "Discrete Cosine Transform," *IEEE Trans. on Computers, vol. 23*, pp. 90-93, Jan 1974.

Chen, W. H., C. H. Smith, and S. C. Fralick, [1977] "A Fast Computational Algorithm for the Discrete Cosine Transform," *IEEE Trans. on Communication, vol. 25*, pp. 1004-1009, Sept 1977.

Jain, A. K., [1979] "A Sinusoidal Family of Unitary Transforms," *IEEE Trans. on Pattern Analysis and Machine Intelligence, vol 1*, **no. 4**, pp. 356-365, Oct 1979.

Kamangar, F. A. and K. R. Rao, [1982] "Fast Algorithms for the 2-D Discrete Cosine Transform," *IEEE Trans. on Computers, vol. C-31*, **no. 9**, pp. 899-806, Sept 1982.

Knuth, D. E., [1973] *Art of Computer Programming, Volume 3: Sorting and Searching* Addison-Wesley, Reading, Mass., 1973.

LeGall, D., [1991] "MPEG: A Video Compression Standard for Multimedia Applications", *Com. of the ACM, vol. 34*, **no. 4**, pp. 46-58, April 1991.

Lee, B. G., [1984] "A New Algorithm for the Discrete Cosine Transform," *IEEE Trans. on Acoustics, Speech, and Signal Processing, vol 32*, pp. 1243-1245, Dec 1984.

Ligtenberg, A. and J. H. O'Neil, [1987] "A Single Chip Solution for an 8 by 8 Two Dimensional DCT," *International Symposium on Circuits and Systems*, **ISCAS 87**, pp. 1128-1131, Philadelphia, Pa, May, 5-7, 1987.

Liou, M. [1991] "Overview of the px64 kbit/s Video Coding Standard", *Com. of the ACM, vol. 34*, **no. 4**, pp. 59-63, April 1991.

Narasimha, M. J., and A. M. Peterson, [1978] "On the Computation of the Discrete Cosine Transform," *IEEE Trans. on Com., vol. 26*, pp. 934-946, June 1978.

Tseng, B. D. and W. C. Miller, [1978] "On Computing the Discrete Cosine Transform," *IEEE Trans. on Computing, vol. 27*, pp. 966-968, Oct 1978.

Tzou, K. H., [1987] "Progressive image transmission: a Review and Comparison," *Optical Engineering, vol. 26*, pp. 581-580, July 1987.

Vetterli, M. and H. Nussbaumer, [1984] "Simple FFT and DCT Algorithms with Reduced Number of Operations," *Signal Processing, vol. 6*, pp. 267-278, Aug 1984.

Wang, L. and M. Goldberg, [1988] "Progressive Image Transmission by Transform Coefficient Residual Error Quantization," *IEEE Trans. on Communication, vol. 36*, pp. 75-87, Jan 1988.

Wallace, G. K., [1991] "The JPEG Still Picture Compression Standard", *Com. of the ACM, vol. 34*, **no. 4**, pp. 30-44, April 1991.

Westover, L. A., [1990] "Footprint Evaluation for Volume Rendering," *Computer Graphics, vol. 24*, **no. 4**, pp. 367-376, Aug 1990.

Westover, L. A., [1991] *SPLATTING: A Parallel, Feed-Forward Volume Rendering Algorithm.* Ph.D. Dissertation, Technical Report TR91-029, University of North Carolina, Chapel Hill, NC, 1991.

Wolberg, G., [1990] *Digital Image Warping*, IEEE Computer Society Press, Los Alamitos, CA, 1990.

Appendix

The follow C code fragment demonstrates the forward-mapping evaluation of the $k(4,2)$ reconstruction kernel:

```c
short key[4][128];
short table[4][128][2];

splat42(tile, value, qindex)

short tile[8][8];
short value;
short qindex;
{
    register short hash = value & 127;
    register short *tptr = table[qindex][hash];
    register short c0, c1, c2, c3;
    register int coeff;

    if (key[qindex][hash] != value) {
        /* dequantization step */
        coeff = value * quantizer[qindex][32];
        key[qindex][hash] = value;
        tptr[ 0] = c0 = (coeff * COS_03 + 128) / 256;
        tptr[ 1] = c1 = (coeff * COS_07 + 128) / 256;
        tptr[ 2] = c2 = (coeff * COS_01 + 128) / 256;
        tptr[ 3] = c3 = (coeff * COS_05 + 128) / 256;
    } else {
        c0 = tptr[ 0];
        c1 = tptr[ 1];
        c2 = tptr[ 2];
        c3 = tptr[ 3];
    }
    tile[0][0] += c0; tile[0][1] -= c1; tile[0][2] -= c2; tile[0][3] -= c3;
    tile[0][4] += c3; tile[0][5] += c2; tile[0][6] += c1; tile[0][7] -= c0;
    tile[1][0] -= c0; tile[1][1] += c1; tile[1][2] += c2; tile[1][3] += c3;
    tile[1][4] -= c3; tile[1][5] -= c2; tile[1][6] -= c1; tile[1][7] += c0;
    tile[2][0] -= c0; tile[2][1] += c1; tile[2][2] += c2; tile[2][3] += c3;
    tile[2][4] -= c3; tile[2][5] -= c2; tile[2][6] -= c1; tile[2][7] += c0;
    tile[3][0] += c0; tile[3][1] -= c1; tile[3][2] -= c2; tile[3][3] -= c3;
    tile[3][4] += c3; tile[3][5] += c2; tile[3][6] += c1; tile[3][7] -= c0;
    tile[4][0] += c0; tile[4][1] -= c1; tile[4][2] -= c2; tile[4][3] -= c3;
    tile[4][4] += c3; tile[4][5] += c2; tile[4][6] += c1; tile[4][7] -= c0;
    tile[5][0] -= c0; tile[5][1] += c1; tile[5][2] += c2; tile[5][3] += c3;
    tile[5][4] -= c3; tile[5][5] -= c2; tile[5][6] -= c1; tile[5][7] += c0;
    tile[6][0] -= c0; tile[6][1] += c1; tile[6][2] += c2; tile[6][3] += c3;
    tile[6][4] -= c3; tile[6][5] -= c2; tile[6][6] -= c1; tile[6][7] += c0;
    tile[7][0] += c0; tile[7][1] -= c1; tile[7][2] -= c2; tile[7][3] -= c3;
    tile[7][4] += c3; tile[7][5] += c2; tile[7][6] += c1; tile[7][7] -= c0;
}
```

Image Reconstruction for Hybrid Video Coding Systems[*]

Qin-Fan Zhu, Yao Wang and Leonard Shaw
Department of Electrical Engineering
Polytechnic University, Brooklyn, NY 11201

Abstract

This paper presents a new technique for image reconstruction from partially received information for hybrid video coding systems using DCT and motion compensated prediction and interpolation. The technique makes use of the smoothness property of typical video signals by requiring the reconstructed samples be smoothly connected with their adjacent samples, both spatially and temporally. This is fulfilled by minimizing the differences between neighboring pixels in the current as well as adjacent frames. The optimal solution is obtained through three linear transformations. This approach can yield more satisfactory results than the existing algorithms, especially for images with large motions or scene changes.

1 Introduction

With the fast advances of fiber optical and VLSI techniques, video services will become ubiquitous in the near future. Because of the extremely high data rate of video signals, various coding methods have been developed to reduce the bitrate to a level affordable by practical applications. One still open problem is how to handle signal loss inevitable in physical channels. Losing any part (even a single bit) of a highly compressed bit-stream can lead to objectionable degradations in the reconstructed video signals.

Two approaches have been proposed to solve this problem. One is to use error control coding[1]. Problems with this approach are three fold. First, it adds additional redundancy which may cause more traffic congestion, hence an even higher loss probability [2]. Secondly, due to the burstiness of compressed video data, error control coding may introduce extra delays that are not acceptable in some applications. And last, but not least, is the fact that conventional error control coding techniques do not make use of the properties of video signals and the human visual system. While the fact that human eyes can tolerate some degree of distortion in image signals has been partially employed in the encoding stage, this visual redundancy can be used to

---

[*]This work was supported by the New York State Science and Technology Foundation as part of its Center for Advanced Technology program.

further advantage.

The other approach is to perform error concealment, which intends to conceal the signal loss effect at the receiver side by exploiting the redundancies of video signals and the human visual systems without adding additional information at the coder. Two methods have been proposed for implementing this approach. The first one is *layered coding* [3, 4] which separates compressed video data into two categories with different priorities. The high priority signal is delivered through a very high performance channel. The low priority signal is transmitted through a lossy channel and can be thrown away in case of channel congestion. When some of the low priority signal is lost, the lost part can be replaced by zeros without producing noticeable distortion. However, this requires a very costly error-free channel. In the case that the high priority signal is damaged due to adverse conditions, the reconstruction becomes extremely difficult if not impossible. Another concealment technique makes use of temporal and/or spatial correlations in image signals and interpolates the damaged region of an image from its adjacent frames or regions [5, 6]. A simple and yet quite effective temporal interpolation method is to replace the damaged region with its corresponding part in the previous frame. This method will be referred to below as the *copying algorithm.* Although it generally works well, it cannot produce satisfactory results when the video sequence contains fast moving objects or encounters lighting changes. Another difficult situation is when loss occurs during a scene change and the two adjacent frames are uncorrelated. The copying algorithm will completely fail in this case.

In [7], a maximally smooth reconstruction technique has been presented for still image codecs using DCT coding. It exploits the spatial correlations in image signals more thoroughly than other interpolation methods do. In this paper, we present a reconstruction scheme for video codecs using DCT and motion compensated prediction and interpolation. It employs both spatial and temporal correlations in an "optimal" fashion by minimizing a certain smoothness measure. It is an extension of the reconstruction algorithm for still images presented in [7] and includes the copying algorithm as a special case. Our simulation results have shown that this method can yield significant improvement over the existing algorithms.

2   Smoothness Criterion and Optimal Reconstruction

The reconstruction algorithm in this paper is developed for hybrid video codecs using motion compensated DPCM and DCT which have been adopted in several international standards for video coding[8, 9]. In such a coder, an image is divided into non-overlapping contiguous square blocks which are then processed independently. There are three coding modes: intraframe mode, interframe prediction mode, and interframe interpolation mode. The prediction and interpolation modes are different only in the way the prediction is performed. The reconstruction scheme to be described is valid for both modes. To be concise, we will call both the prediction mode from now on. In the intraframe mode, a frame is coded as an independent still image using DCT coding. This is performed periodically to eliminate error propagation introduced by interframe prediction. In the prediction mode, temporal redundancy is first removed by motion compensated prediction. Then the prediction error signals undergo the DCT transform. The DCT coefficients are then quantized, entropy coded and transmitted. If all the information is correctly received, the receiver can perform the corresponding inverse operations and arrive at the original sequence with added quantization error. But if some of the coded bits are lost or corrupted during transmission, an appropriate recovery scheme is needed to obtain acceptable images.

Image reconstruction from partial information is generally an ill-posed problem. By imposing additional constraints, the problem can be regularized. It is well known that the spectra of most common images have low pass characteristics. In the spatial domain, this is reflected by the existence of large areas with constant brightness or little variation. Even in edge areas, the transition is often slow. In the temporal domain, this corresponds to the fact that the difference between adjacent frames is in general very small. Such spatial and temporal redundancy is utilized in the proposed reconstruction algorithm. In this paper we only consider the reconstruction for interframe coded images. The technique presented in [7] can be applied directly to the reconstruction of intraframe coded images.

In the following, we derive the proposed reconstruction technique. Let $\mathbf{f}$ be the vector consisting of the samples in an image block in the current frame to be coded, and $\mathbf{f}_p$ the (uni- or bi-directionally) predicted block. Then the error vector is

$$\mathbf{e} = \mathbf{f} - \mathbf{f}_p. \tag{1}$$

This signal is DCT transformed and transmitted. Let the DCT transform pair be defined by

$$\mathbf{a} = \mathbf{T}^T \mathbf{e}, \tag{2}$$

where $\mathbf{T}$ consists of the basis vectors of the two-dimensional DCT defined in [8]. Let $\tilde{\mathbf{a}}$ be the coefficient vector after quantization. Then in absence of transmission error, the prediction error and the original image block can be reconstructed by:

$$\tilde{\mathbf{e}} = \mathbf{T}\,\tilde{\mathbf{a}} \quad \text{and} \quad \tilde{\mathbf{f}} = \tilde{\mathbf{e}} + \mathbf{f}_p \tag{3}$$

Suppose that some of the DCT coefficients are lost during transmission. Let $\tilde{\mathbf{a}}_r$ represent the subvector containing the correctly received coefficients and $\hat{\mathbf{a}}_l$ the subvector including the estimates of the lost coefficients. Further, let $\mathbf{T}_r$ and $\mathbf{T}_l$ be the submatrices composed of the basis vectors in $\mathbf{T}$ corresponding to the entries of $\tilde{\mathbf{a}}_r$ and $\hat{\mathbf{a}}_l$, respectively. Then the reconstructed error and the original vector can be described by

$$\hat{\mathbf{e}} = \mathbf{T}_r \tilde{\mathbf{a}}_r + \mathbf{T}_l \hat{\mathbf{a}}_l \quad \text{and} \quad \hat{\mathbf{f}} = \hat{\mathbf{e}} + \mathbf{f}_p \tag{4}$$

As mentioned before, for a common image, the decoded block should be smoothly connected to its adjacent blocks in the same frame, and to its predicted block, due to spatial and temporal correlations. We would like to find a good estimate of $\hat{\mathbf{a}}_l$ in the sense that it minimizes the smoothness measure defined as follows:

$$
\begin{aligned}
\Psi(\hat{\mathbf{a}}_l) &= \frac{1}{2}\{w(\|\mathbf{S}_w\hat{\mathbf{f}} - \mathbf{b}_w\|^2 + \|\mathbf{S}_e\hat{\mathbf{f}} - \mathbf{b}_e\|^2 + \|\mathbf{S}_n\hat{\mathbf{f}} - \mathbf{b}_n\|^2 + \|\mathbf{S}_s\hat{\mathbf{f}} - \mathbf{b}_s\|^2) + (1-w)\mathbf{e}^T\mathbf{e}\} \\
&= \frac{1}{2}\{w(\hat{\mathbf{f}}^T\mathbf{S}\hat{\mathbf{f}} - 2\mathbf{t}^T\hat{\mathbf{f}} + c) + (1-w)(\mathbf{T}_r\tilde{\mathbf{a}}_r + \mathbf{T}_l\hat{\mathbf{a}}_l)^T(\mathbf{T}_r\tilde{\mathbf{a}}_r + \mathbf{T}_l\hat{\mathbf{a}}_l)\},
\end{aligned}
\tag{5}
$$

where

$$
\begin{aligned}
\mathbf{S} &= (\mathbf{S}_w^T\mathbf{S}_w) + (\mathbf{S}_e^T\mathbf{S}_e) + (\mathbf{S}_n^T\mathbf{S}_n) + (\mathbf{S}_s^T\mathbf{S}_s), \\
\mathbf{t} &= \mathbf{S}_w^T\mathbf{b}_w + \mathbf{S}_e^T\mathbf{b}_e + \mathbf{S}_n^T\mathbf{b}_n + \mathbf{S}_s^T\mathbf{b}_s, \\
c &= \mathbf{b}_w^T\mathbf{b}_w + \mathbf{b}_e^T\mathbf{b}_e + \mathbf{b}_n^T\mathbf{b}_n + \mathbf{b}_s^T\mathbf{b}_s, \\
0 &\leq w \leq 1.
\end{aligned}
\tag{6}
$$

The matrices $\mathbf{S}_w, \mathbf{S}_e, \mathbf{S}_n$ and $\mathbf{S}_s$ depend on the smoothing constraints in four different directions and $\mathbf{b}_w, \mathbf{b}_e, \mathbf{b}_n$ and $\mathbf{b}_s$ are the vectors containing the sample values in the four one pixel wide boundaries outside the damaged block. More detailed definitions can be found in [7]. In equation (5), the first term is the measure of spatial smoothness and the second term the temporal smoothness. The spatial term is essentially a weighted sum of squares of pixel-wise differences, which forces the pixels to be connected smoothly with each other within the block and with the boundary pixels outside the block. The temporal term requires the error vector to be as small as possible to enforce a smooth transition between adjacent frames. Choice of the weighting factor w is dependent on the relative importance of the spatial and temporal smoothing constraints. Ideally it should vary according to the motion content of the block. In the presence of large motion, the spatial smoothness constraint should be emphasized more and hence a large value of w should be used. On the other hand, if there is little motion, the spatial constraint should be relaxed by using a smaller w. A special case is when all the coefficients are lost (i.e. $\tilde{\mathbf{a}}_r = \mathbf{0}$) and the weighting is chosen to be $w = 0$. Then the optimal solution is

$$\hat{\mathbf{a}}_l = \mathbf{0} \quad \text{and} \quad \hat{\mathbf{f}} = \mathbf{f}_p. \tag{7}$$

which corresponds to the copying algorithm.

Notice that equation (5) is a quadratic function of $\hat{\mathbf{a}}_l$, since $\hat{\mathbf{f}}$ is linearly related to $\hat{\mathbf{a}}_l$ according to (4). Hence it has only one minimum and reaches its minimal point $\hat{\mathbf{a}}_{opt}$ when the gradient vanishes, i.e,

$$\frac{\partial \Psi}{\partial \hat{\mathbf{a}}_{opt}} = \mathbf{T}_l^T\{w[\mathbf{S}(\mathbf{f}_p + \mathbf{T}_r\tilde{\mathbf{a}}_r + \mathbf{T}_l\hat{\mathbf{a}}_{opt}) - \mathbf{t}] + (1-w)(\mathbf{T}_r\tilde{\mathbf{a}}_r + \mathbf{T}_l\hat{\mathbf{a}}_{opt})\} = \mathbf{0}. \tag{8}$$

The optimal solution $\hat{\mathbf{a}}_{opt}$ is given by

$$\hat{\mathbf{a}}_{opt} = (\frac{1-w}{w}\mathbf{I} + \mathbf{T}_l^T\mathbf{S}\mathbf{T}_l)^{-1}\mathbf{T}_l^T[\mathbf{t} - \mathbf{S}\mathbf{f}_p - (\mathbf{S} + \frac{1-w}{w}\mathbf{I})\mathbf{T}_r\tilde{\mathbf{a}}_r] \qquad (9)$$

$$= \mathbf{A}\mathbf{t} - \mathbf{B}\tilde{\mathbf{a}}_r - \mathbf{C}\mathbf{f}_p, \qquad (10)$$

where

$$\mathbf{A} = (\frac{1-w}{w}\mathbf{I} + \mathbf{T}_l^T\mathbf{S}\mathbf{T}_l)^{-1}\mathbf{T}_l^T, \quad \mathbf{B} = \mathbf{A}(\mathbf{S} + \frac{1-w}{w}\mathbf{I})\mathbf{T}_r, \quad \mathbf{C} = \mathbf{A}\mathbf{S}. \qquad (11)$$

The solution defined in (10) can be implemented in two ways. The direct approach is to compute the matrices $\mathbf{A}, \mathbf{B}$ and $\mathbf{C}$ in real time according to actual coefficient loss pattern (different $\mathbf{T}_r$ and $\mathbf{T}_l$) and the weighting factor w. An alternative is to store the matrices for different combinations of coefficient loss patterns and weighting factors beforehand. Such a mechanism is simpler but is only partially adaptive to the loss pattern and the weighting factor.

Up till now, we have assumed that each damaged block is surrounded by undamaged blocks. When several adjacent blocks are lost, each block can be first reconstructed using an inverse DCT transform directly with the missing coefficients set equal to zero. The optimal solution defined in (10) can then be applied to the damaged blocks repeatedly, using the values reconstructed from a previous iteration as the boundary information for the next iteration. It has been found from our simulations that on an average twenty iterations can yield satisfactory results.

3 Simulation Results

The proposed algorithm has been applied to the luminance components of two video sequences: *Football* and *Susie*. They are first coded by the *MPEG* algorithm [8]. A uniform random generator is used to generate the random bit error locations. Due to the use of run-length and entropy coding in *MPEG*, once a bit error occurs in a scan of 16 lines, all the subsequent blocks in the same scan will also be damaged. For each damaged block, we estimate the lost coefficients with the algorithm presented in the previous section. Since the reconstruction is based on a smoothness criterion, it can only effectively recover the low frequency coefficients. The optimally reconstructed high frequency coefficients are in most cases zeros. After both subjective (visual evaluation) and objective (PSNR) testing, we choose to estimate only the first 15 coefficients in the zigzag order. The rest of the lost coefficients are simply replaced by zeros.

Four cases of transmission loss are tested in our simulation. Case 0 simulates the situation when all the information of the damaged blocks is lost, which includes the coding modes (*Intra/Non-intra, MC/No-MC*, etc) [8], motion vectors and DCT coefficients. Since no mode information is available , we treat each damaged block as an intra-coded block and perform reconstruction using a weighting factor of $w = 1$. In this way only spatial smoothing constraint is imposed. Case 1 simulates the situation when the coding mode is available but all the other information is lost. For *Intra-coded* blocks, the reconstruction is fulfilled in the same way as in Case 0. The blocks coded with mode "No MC, Non 8-ESC, and Not coded" [8] is simply reconstructed by copying from spatially corresponding blocks in the previous frame (As is done in the copying algorithm). The rest of the coding modes are clustered into three groups according to the relative significance of the spatial against the temporal correlation in these modes. (More clusters will produce a better result but will also increase the complexity.) Each group is assigned a different weighting factor $(0 < w < 1)$ which is proportional to the amount of spatial correlation in that group. The lost motion vectors of a damaged block are estimated from its upper and lower neighboring blocks by a linear interpolation since its two horizontally neighboring blocks are often also damaged as well. In Case 2, we assume all the side information (Coding modes and motion vectors) is present but the DCT coefficients are completely lost. Since the motion vectors are available, the temporal smoothing constraint can be imposed more reliably. Therefore, a smaller weight is used for blocks coded in prediction modes with nonzero motion vectors. For ease of implementation (i.e., only four groups of $\mathbf{A}, \mathbf{B}$ and $\mathbf{C}$ need to be computed and stored beforhand), we still use the previous three weighting factor values but recluster the coding modes. In Case 3, only part of the low frequency coefficients (the DC plus the first five low frequency) in the zigzag order are lost while the rest of the high frequency coefficients are available. The reconstruction process is the same as in Case 2 except that we only need to estimate the six low frequency coefficients instead of fifteen in the previous three cases.

Figure 1 shows the peak signal-to-noise ratio (PSNR) values versus the frame numbers for the *Football* and the *Susie* sequences using different methods. The simulated bit error rate is 0.002 for *Football* and 0.005 for *Susie*, which lead approximately to a block loss rate of 0.022 for *Football* and 0.055 for *Susie* due to error propagation effect in run-length and entropy coding. The top dashed lines represent the PSNRs for the original coded sequences. The curves labeled with *Zero* are the PSNRs for case 0 when lost information is replaced by zeros. Curves labeled with *Copying* show the PSNRs of the images with the damaged blocks simply repaced by their correspondent blocks (motion vectors are used if available) in the previous frame. The rest are the reconstruction results for four different loss cases using the proposed algorithm. For both sequences, the proposed algorithm outperforms the zero-replacing and copying algorithms. Even in the worst case (Case 0), an average of 2dB gain can still be achieved over the method of zero-replacing or copying. Figure 2 compares the images reconstructed using different methods for frame 5 of the *Football* sequence. For this particular frame, 21 blocks out of 330 are damaged, which corresponds to a block loss rate of 0.064. Part (a) is the original image and part (b) is the image coded by *MPEG*. Parts (c) and (d) are the images obtained from the zero-replacing and copying algorithms. Images after reconstruction with the proposed algorithm for case 0 to 3 are shown in parts (e) to (h). We see that the visual image quality agrees well with the PSNR shown in Figure 1, with case 3 affording the best reconstruction. Some artifacts are still observable, especially for Case 0. But when the images are displayed in real time at thirty frames per second, these defects are much less annoying.

To evaluate the convergence behavior of the proposed algorithm, Figure 3 shows the PSNRs of three reconstructed frames of *Football* at successive iterations. It is seen that 20 iterations are sufficient. Subjective observation yields a similar conclusion. Figure 4 gives the reconstructed images of frame 5 of the *Football* sequence after iteration times 1, 5, 20 and 50, respectively. There is no substantial improvement from iteration time 20 to 50 visually.

4 Conclusion

We have considered the problem of image reconstruction for hybrid video communication systems. By employing temporal and spatial correlations, the proposed algorithm can reconstruct an image block satisfactorily even when many low frequency DCT coefficients are lost. Both objective measures (PSNR) and pictures of reconstructed images have been provided for evaluation of the proposed algorithm. It has been shown that the proposed technique yields better reconstruction image quality than other error concealment methods. In particular when signal loss occurs in regions with large motion or during a scene change, this technique can still produce quite satisfactory results while many other concealment techniques would fail. The algorithm is expected to function more effectively for HDTV signals since the smoothness criterion employed in the proposed reconstruction algorithm is more valid due to the stronger spatial and temporal correlations in such signals.

5 Acknowledgment

The authors would like to thank Dr. S. Singhal of Bellcore at Morristown for providing the video sequences used in the simulations.

6 References

[1] S. H. Lee, P. J. Lee and R. Ansari, "Cell loss detection and recovery in variable rate video", *Proc. of Third Int. Workshop on Packet Video*, Morristown, March 1990.

[2] G. Karlsson, and M. Vetterli, "Sub-band coding of video signals for packet-switched networks," *Proc. of SPIE Conf. on Visual Communications and Image Processing*, pp 446–456, Oct. 1987.

[3] M. Nomura, T. Fujii and N. Ohta, "Layered packet-loss protection for variable rate video coding using DCT", *Int. Workshop on Packet Video*, Torino, Italy, September 1988.

[4] M. Ghanbari, "Two-layer Coding of video signals for VBR networks", *IEEE J. on Select. Areas in Commun*, Vol.7, pp771-781, June 1989.

[5] V. Thomas, "Influence of cell losses on the performance of a TV coding algorithm," *Proc. of Third Int. Workshop on Packet Video*, Morristown, March 1990.

[6] G. Aarsten *et al.*, "Error resilience of a video codec for low bit rates,", in *Proc. ICASSP '88*, New York, pp. 1312–1315, April 1988.

[7] Y. Wang and Q. F. Zhu, "Signal loss recovery in DCT-based image and video codecs", *SPIE Conf. Visual Communication and Image Processing*, Boston, Nov. 1991, pp. 667–678.

[8] ISO-IEC/JTC1/SC2/WG11, "MPEG Video Simulation Model Three (SM3)," July 1990.

[9] CCITT Draft Revision of Recommendation H.261, "Video Codec for Audiovisual Services at px64 kbits/s," CCITT SG XV, "Description of Ref. Model 8 (RM8)," Doc 525, June 1989.

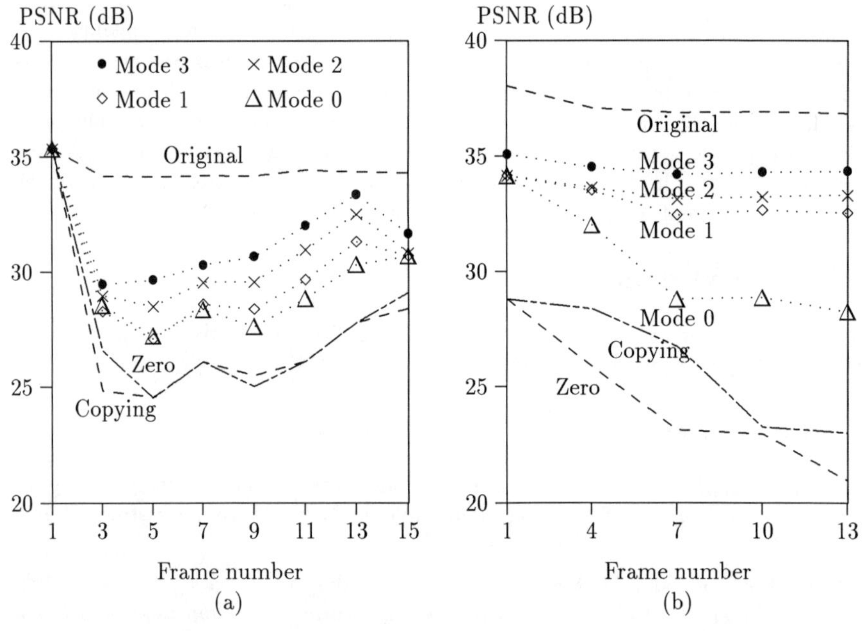

Figure 1   PSNRs vs. Frame Number: (a) *Football*, (b) *Susie*

Figure 2   Reconstructed images of frame 5 of *Football* using different methods. From left to right, top to bottom: (a) original, (b) coded, (c) zero-replacing, (d) copying, and (e) to (h) reconstructed images with the proposed algorithm for cases 0 to 3.

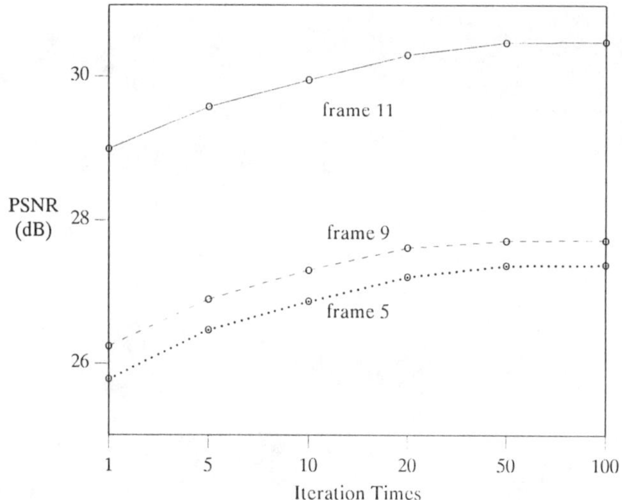

Figure 3 Convergence rate for *Football* sequence in Mode 0

Figure 4   Reconstructed images of frame 3 of *Football* after, from left to right and top to bottom, 1, 5, 20 and 50 iterations.

A Split-Merge Parallel Block-Matching Algorithm for Video Displacement Estimation

Bruno Carpentieri
Dipartimento di Informatica ed Applicazioni
Università di Salerno
84081 Baronissi (SA), Italy
and
Computer Science Dept.
Brandeis University
Waltham, MA 02254

James A. Storer
Computer Science Dept.
Brandeis University
Waltham, MA 02254

Abstract

Motion Compensation is one of the most effective techniques used in interframe data compression. In this paper we present a parallel block-matching algorithm for estimating interframe displacement of small blocks with minimum error. The algorithm is designed for a grid architecture to process video in real time. The blocks may have variable size depending on a split-and-merge technique. The algorithm performs a segmentation of the image into regions (objects) moving in the same direction and uses this knowledge to improve the transmission of the displacement vectors.

1   Introduction

Data Compression is essential for the storage and transmission of digital video, where large amounts of data must be handled by devices with a limited bandwidth. For example, digital High Definition Television (HDTV) requires more than 1 billion bits per second in uncompressed form. Knowledge of motion or displacement of groups pixels in successive frames can be the basis of video compression algorithms and can be used in addition to other classical single-image compression techniques, such as transform, interpolation and quantization algorithms to greatly reduce the amount of data transmitted.

Here we will restrict our attention to the translational component of the motion and we will refer to the algorithms that compute the trajectory information of a pixel or a block of pixels as *displacement estimation algorithms.*

[MPG85] divides the recent displacement estimation algorithms into three classes:

- Recursive Displacement-Estimation Algorithms: in which the prediction of the displacement for each pixel is computed recursively from its neighboring pixels that have already been coded; [NR79] [CR83]

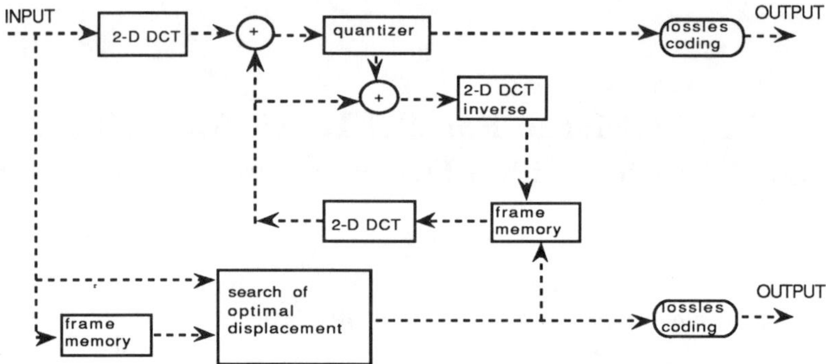

Figure 1: **Displacement Estimated Image Coding**

- Block-Matching Displacement Estimation Algorithms: in which the image is divided into a number of rectangular blocks and the displacement vector is computed for each block by correlating the block with a search area in the previous frame; [JJ81] [KIH*81] [SR84]

- Feature-Based Displacement Estimation Algorithms, in which the edges delimiting the objects in the picture are extracted and then one recursive or block-matching algorithm is used to estimate the displacement of each edge; [MW82] [Kre83]

In this paper we present a real-time parallel algorithm for displacement estimation using a two dimensional grid architecture. The algorithm is based on a block-matching approach to the problem and uses a split and merge technique: the blocks (*superblocks*) have a variable size that is determined at each step of the algorithm from the previous step and the input data. In fact the algorithm performs a segmentation of the image into objects moving in the same direction and uses this knowledge to improve the transmission of the displacement vectors of the elementary blocks.

In the next section we outline a general displacement-estimated motion-compensation encoding method for video sequences and the displacement estimation sequential algorithm presented in [JJ81]. In Section 3 we present our parallel algorithm for displacement estimation. Section 4 is devoted to the analysis of the algorithm, and Section 5 discusses future work.

2   Image Coding and Displacement Estimation

In this section we outline first the general displacement estimated motion compensation encoding method and review the sequential displacement measurement algorithm proposed by Jain and Jain [JJ81]. This algorithm and its assumptions have been a guideline for more recent work in the field, a similar approach is taken by [PHS87].

Figure 1, proposed by [JJ81], describes the encoder part of a typical algorithm for displacement estimated image coding: the frame is segmented into blocks and for each block a displacement vector is computed and sent to the decoder, moreover the encoder computes the difference between the 2-D DCT transform of the original frame and the 2-D DCT transform of the frame that the decoder could reconstruct from the displacement vectors, and sends this difference image to the decoder. All data sent from the encoder to the decoder may eventually go through an additional entropy coding phase.

2.1   Jain and Jain's Algorithm

The algorithm proposed in [JJ81] is based on a block-matching approach. An image is segmented into fixed-size small rectangular blocks, each block assumed to be undergoing independent translation. If these areas are small enough, rotation, zooming, etc. of larger objects can be closely approximated by piecewise translation of these smaller areas. The goal is to approximate interframe motion by piecewise translation of one or more areas of a frame relative to a reference frame. Let U be an $M \times N$ size block of an image and U_r be an $(M + 2p) \times (N + 2p)$ size area of a reference (neighboring) image, centered at the same spatial location as U, where p is the maximum displacement allowed in either direction in integer number of pixels. The algorithm requires for each block a search of the *direction of minimum distortion (DMD)*, i.e. of the displacement vector that minimizes a given distortion function. In their paper, Jain and Jain consider a mean distortion function between U and U_r defined as:

$$D(i,j) = \frac{1}{MN} \sum_{m=1}^{M} \sum_{n=1}^{N} g(u(m, n - u_r(m + i, n + j)), \qquad -p \leq i, j \leq p$$

where $g(x)$ is a given positive and increasing distortion function of x. The direction of minimum distortion is given by (i, j), such that $D(i, j)$ is minimum.

One problem of this approach is that finding the direction of minimum distortion requires the evaluation of $D(i, j)$ for $(2p + 1) \times (2p + 1)$ directions per block. For example even for motions up to 5 pixels along either side of the axes a search of 121 directions is required. The solution proposed in [JJ81] is to assume as hypothesis that the data is such that the distortion function monotonically increases as we move away from the DMD along any direction in each of the four quadrants. This assumption makes possible a search procedure for the DMD that is an extention in two dimensions of the standard logarithmic search in one dimension [Knu83].

In the next section we present a parallel algorithm that eliminates the need for this hypothesis and which can be implemented to run on-line on a practical two-dimensional grid architecture.

3   A Split-and-Merge Parallel Block-Matching Algorithm

In this section we present a new parallel block-matching algorithm for displacement estimation based on a split-and-merge technique taking advantage of the fact that tipically blocks move in the same direction if they are part of the same object. The encoding algorithm computes the displacement vectors (in parallel) and sends them in compact form to the decoder. The decoder receives the data and constructs an approximate version of the image, which will be corrected in the next step of the general encoding algorithm.

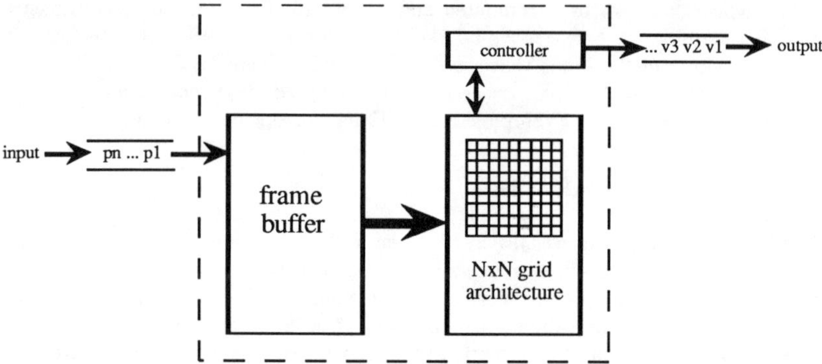

Figure 2: **Displacement Estimation Encoder**

3.1   The Model of Computation

The encoding algorithm is designed to run on a $N \times N$ grid of processors, numbered by row from processor 1 to processor $N \times N$. For all of what follows we let n denote the number of pixels per frame and $N^2 = N \times N$. We assume that each of the N^2 processors has $O(n/N^2)$ local memory, therefore if the number of processor grows linearly with n, each processor shall have a constant amount of local memory. In what follows we will assume that $N^2 = kn$ for $0 < k \leq 1$. Each frame is divided into N^2 rectangular blocks numbered in the same way as the processors; we assume that at time t processor i receives as input block i from the t-th frame. Since each processor corresponds to a block, and vice versa, from now on we will use the terms processor and block interchangeably.

The encoding algorithm implies the use of a sequential "Controller" to monitor the execution of the algorithm. The Controller will need $O(N^2)$ dynamic memory and will perform communication operations only with processor 1. We will identify this "Controller" with processor 1 itself by allocating to this processor an additional $O(N^2)$ local dynamic memory. The encoder computes the displacement vectors and transmits them in a compact form to the decoder on a serial line. The decoder is a serial machine with $O(n)$ memory.

Figure 2 depicts our model of computation. The input frames come to the frame buffer on a serial line, in time proportional to n. The data flows from the frame buffer to the grid architecture that performs the search of the DMD for each block. The communication between the frame buffer and the grid architecture has to be performed fast enough to allow the grid time to perform the necessary computation on the actual frame before receiving the next frame. In fact the bold arrow implies that this commuinication should be performed either in parallel or on a serial line kn/N^2 time faste, where k is a system dependent constant

3.2   The Encoder Algorithm

Each processor at time t computes in parallel the displacement of the block that it represents (in frame t) with respect to a search area in frame $t - 1$. We will assume for simplicity that for each block the search area is limited to its adjacent blocks. Processor i

at time t keeps the description of the block it was representing at time $t-1$ in the variable $block_{pf}(i)$ (the subscrit pf is short for "previous frame". If at time $t-1$ a number of adjacent blocks have the same displacement vector, then at time t they are considered to be a well-defined *superblock*: *superblock*(i) where i is the leader of the *superblock* (the processor with minimum ID). If they continue to move together in the same directon, just a single displacement vector for the whole superblock has to be sent from the encoder to the decoder. Each processor is not aware of the shape of the *superblock* to which it belongs, but is aware of the adjacent processors that move in its same direction (*coblock*). The union of *coblock*s for adjacent processors that move in the same direction will define a *superblock*.

At each time t the algorithm can be divided into three steps. In Phase 1 (*the compute phase*) the displacement vector for each single block is computed and each processor compares its displacement with the displacement of the adjacent processors. Each processor i keeps a list of the adjacent processors that move in its own direction *coblock(i)*. In Phase 3 these lists will be merged together into *superblocks* whenever possible. At time $t+1$ a unique displacement vector will be sent from the encoder to the decoder for all the processors in a *superblock* that still move in the same direction.

In Phase 2 (*the split and send phase*) processor 1 becomes the Controller and communicates with the others processors, gathering information on their displacement vectors, deciding their belonging to a *superblock* or the occurrence of a *split*, i.e. whereby processors leave a *superblock* because their motion differs from that of the majority. We address the complexity of this operation in the next section. Being aware of all the displacement vectors for the $N \times N$ processors, the Controller, for each *superblock*, tests if *split*s have occurred and contructs the *list-of-splits*, i.e. the list that specifies which processors that were assumed to be part of a *superblock* are no longer part of it because they are now moving in a different direction respect to the rest of the *superblock*. If the length of *list-of-splits* is less than a threshold T, monitoring when it is convenient in terms of amount of data sent to the decoder to send both *list-of-splits* and the *superblock*s displacement vectors instead of the displacement vectors for each single block, then the Controller sends the *list-of-splits* and the displacement vectors for the *superblock*s, otherwise it sends the displacement vectors for each single block.

In Phase 3 the *superblock*s at time $t+1$ are built from the *coblock* of each processor. The encoder and the decoder maintain dynamically a list of the *superblocks*, telling which block belongs to which *superblock*. No information needs to be sent from the encoder to the decoder when two or more *coblock*s *merge* in a *superblock*, whatever the shape of the superblock: the decoder can in fact decide by itself which blocks will belong to a *superblock* at time $t+1$, being aware of all the displacement vectors at time t. Instead, as we have seen, at every time t a list of the positions in which a *split* has occurred needs to be sent from the encoder to the decoder so as to make the decoder able to interpret the displacement vectors for the *superblock*s that are sent from the encoder.

3.3 How To Build *list-of-splits*

One of the critical points of the algorithm is the communication from the encoder to the decoder of the *list-of splits*, i.e. of the list of the processors that at time t, belonged to a *superblock* but no longer do, and of their displacement vectors. There are two requirements that the *list-of-splits* must satisfy: it must be computationally easy to build, and the list

Phase 1: (COMPUTE)

for each processor i in parallel do:
    begin
    1)   for every adjacent processor *neighbor* do get $block_{pf}(neighbor)$
    2)   COMPUTE (brute force) its own displacement vector $\vec{v}_t(i)$
    3)   for every adjacent processor *neighbor* do get $\vec{v}_t(neighbor)$
    4)   set $coblock(i)$ = set of adjacent processors *neighbor* such that $\vec{v}_t(neighbor) = \vec{v}_t(i)$
    end

Phase 2: (SPLIT and SEND)

Controller do
    begin
    1)   for $i = 1$ to N^2 do
           get $\vec{v}_t(i)$ and store it into the record representing i in the *superblock* to which i belongs
    2)   for each *superblock* do
           begin
    2.1)   SPLIT the *superblock* into *group*s of processors j having the same displacement vector $\vec{v}_t(j)$
    2.2)   let *pmin* be the processor with minimum ID in the larger *group*
    2.3)   if *pmin* is not the *leader* of the current *superblock* then make a new *superblock* with
           leader *pmin* and displacement vector $\vec{v}_t(superblock(i))$
    2.4)   add the other *group*s to *list-of-splits*
    2.5)   if *pmin* is not the *leader* of the current *superblock* then delete the current *superblock*
           end
    3)   if length(*list-of-splits*) $\geq T$
           then for $i = 1$ to N^2 do SEND $\vec{v}_t(i)$
           else   begin
                    SEND *list-of-splts*
                    for each $superblock(i)$, in ascending i order SEND $\vec{v}_t(superblock(i))$
                    end
    end

Phase 3: (MERGE)

Controller do
    begin
    1)   for $i = 1$ to N^2 do get $coblock(i)$
    2)   from the *coblock*s at time t construct the new *superblock*s at time $t + 1$
    end

Table 1: **The Algorithm at time** t

itself must have a concise encoding, otherwise the saving obtained by sending only one displacement vector for each *superblock* could be negated from the necessity of sending also *list-of-splits*.

The *list-of-splits* is dynamically built: In line 2.4 of Phase 2 *group*s of processors are added to the list. A unique displacement vector corresponds to each group. We can therefore keep a hash table of the possible displacement vectors. Each time a group is added to the list we compute the hash value of its displacement vector. Then we associate to the corresponding entry in the table the displacement vector of the *group* and we add the list of its processors. The list begins with the ID of the smaller processor, then follow IDs of the other processors follow each coded in terms of the displacement with respect to the previous one. Given that the processors were part of the same *superblock* and that they are still moving in the same direction (even if this is no longer the direction in which the *superblock* is now moving) we can expect their ID numbers to be very close, thereby getting good compression with this simple heuristics. When the encoder has to send the *list-of-splits*, it sends for each non-zero entry in the table the displacement vector associated with that entry and the the *group*s in the *list-of-splits* that move in the direction of the vector.

3.4   When There Is More Than One Displacement Vector Per Block

There might be more than one solution to the computation in Line 2 of Phase 1. The block examined could match optimally more than one block in the search area, or else we may want to consider in the next Phase more than one direction in which the block can move, in such a way to have more options when it is time to consider the belonging of the block to a *superblock*. A way to do this is to save for each block all the displacement vectors that allow an error less than a threshold T when the block is matched in the search area. In this case, in line 1 of Phase 2, the processor sends to the Controller not only a single vector but a list of possible vectors.

To determine the eventuality of a *split*, in line 2.1 of Phase 2, the Controller will have to compute which of the possible directions is in the majority of the processors moves. The number of possible directions is finite and can be limited in advance by limiting the length of each list of possible vectors to an appropriately chosen constant L. Phase 3 is not affected by considering more than one displacement value per vector in Phase 2 because a single displacement vector per block has been sent from the encoder to the decoder in Phase 2, and now only that vector has to be considered in Phase 3 for the information available to the decoder to be consistent.

3.5   The Decoder Algorithm

The decoder receives at time t the information sent from the encoder during Phase 2. It is aware of the shape of the *superblock*s at time t so it can compute for each block the correspondent displacement vector. Finally, at this point it has enough information to compute which blocks will be in which *superblock*s at time $t+1$. The decoder is not necessarily a parallel machine; one single processor suffices to perform the necessary operations. The decoder will need $O(n)$ memory and will decode each frame in $O(n)$ time.

4 Analysis of the Algorithm

In this section we analyze the encoder algorithm in terms of time complexity, space complexity, fidelity and compression.

4.1 Time Complexity

Let N^2 be the number of processors in the grid. In Phase 1 lines 1 and 3 involve direct neighbor communication on a grid and take constant time. The computation involved in line 2 is the most expensive part of Phase 1, but it still takes constant time, where the constant depends on the size of the search area.

The for loop in line 1 of Phase 2 at a first look seems to involve $O(N^2)$ communication on a grid architecture, because processor 1 has to interact with all the other processors. But consider the blocks in the image numbered as in a matrix, by row and column. The for loop in line 1 can now be easily pipelined. For instance when processor 1 receives the required data from processor 2, at the same time processor i, $3 \le i \le n$, is passing the data for processor 1 to its upper, left or right neighbor in order to form a snakelike pipeline. Therefore processor 1 will always interact at each iteration of the loop with an adjacent processor: processor 2 and the loop will take $O(N^2)$ time. In line 2 (2.1-2.5) each processor in a *superblock* is touched a constant number of times. The *superblock*s are pairwise disjoint sets therefore line 2 has a time complexity of $O(N^2)$. The same is true for line 3 and line 4.

As in line 1 of Phase 2, so the for loop of line 1 of Phase 3 can easily be pipelined on a grid and takes $O(N^2)$. The *coblock*s have for each vector a constant size (each processor has at most eight neighbors) therefore line 2 will take $O(N^2)$.

Therefore the algorithm as a whole has at each time t a time complexity $O(N^2)$, i.e. linear in the size of the input, and is an on-line algorithm.

4.2 Space Complexity

Each processor, with the exception of the Controller, needs a constant amount of memory. The Controller needs $O(N^2)$ dynamic memory to represent the *superblock*s and to store the *coblock*s and the displacement vectors via linked lists.

4.3 Fidelity

The displacement vectors computed by our algorithm are certainly at least as accurate and generally more then the ones computed by Jain and Jain's algorithm. In fact we do not assume any a priori hypothesis to simplify the search for the direction of minimum distortion for each block; rather we search all the possible directions.

4.4 Compression

From the point of view of amount of data sent from the encoder to the decoder, our algorithm in the worst case performs as Jain and Jain's algorithm and may transmit much less data.

The size of the blocks is chosen in such a way to approximate different movements of an object by piecewise translation of the blocks themselves. This implies that an object is generally composed of a large number of blocks, all of which move in the same direction. Therefore the *superblocks* will generally consist of many processors and the length of the *list-of-splits* will be negligible respect to the cardinality of the *superblocks* and at each time t a sensible reduction in size of the data sent from the encoder to the decoder is expected.

However when the length of the *list-of-splits* becomes significant and bigger than an opportunely chosen threshold T, the Controller sends to the decoder the displacement vectors block by block, starting from $\vec{v}_t(1)$ to $\vec{v}_t(n)$ and not *list-of-splits* and the *superblocks* displacement vectors, therefore sending to the decoder the same amount of data that the algorithm in [JJ81] would have sent. The decoder can infer that the displacement vectors received refers to the blocks and not to the *superblocks* from the number of vectors received.

5 Conclusion and Future work

We have presented a new on-line parallel algorithm for displacement estimation based on the block-matching approach. Our algorithm compares successfully both in terms of accuracy of optimality of the displacement vectors found and in terms of minimizing the amount of data transmitted with the previous sequential algorithms.

At each time t both the decoder and the encoder have available the description of the *superblocks* computed at time $t-1$. Each *superblock* is a set of contiguous blocks that move in the same direction. Therefore there is a strict correspondence between *superblocks* and objects in the image. The partition of the image in *superblocks* corresponds to an approximate segmentation of the image into areas (objects) that move in the same direction. The quality of the approximation depends on the granularity chosen (i.e. the size of the blocks).

Our algorithm uses this knowledge of the segmentation of the image to optimize the transmission of the displacement vectors. This knowledge is retained at each step t and can therefore be used for for other purposes. Other uses for this knowledge is an interesting area for future research.

References

[CR83] C. Cafforio and F. Rocca. The differential model for motion estimation. In T. S. Huang, editor, *Image Sequence Processing and Dynamic Scene Analysis*, Springer-Verlag, Berlin, Germany, 1983.

[JJ81]   Jaswant R. Jain and Anil K. Jain. Displacement measurement and its applications in interframe image coding. *IEEE Transactions on Communications*,
COM-29(12):1799–1808, December 1981.

[KIH*81] T. Koga, K. Inuma, A. Hirano, Y. Iijima, and T Ishiguro. Motion-compensated
interframe coding for video conferencing. In *NTC 81, Proc.*, New Orleans, LA,
December 1981.

[Knu83]   D. E. Knuth. *Searching and Sorting, Vol. 3 The Art of Computer Programming*.
Addison-Welsey, 1983.

[Kre83]   F. Kretz. Edges in visual scenes and sequences: application to filtering, sampling
and adaptive dpcm coding. In T. S. Huang, editor, *Image Sequence Processing
and Dynamic Scene Analysis*, Springer-Verlag, Berlin, Germany, 1983.

[MPG85]   Hans George Musmann, Peter Pirsch, and Hans-Joachim Grallert. Advances in
picture coding. *Proceedings of the IEEE*, 73(4):523–548, April 1985.

[MW82]   F. May and W. Wolf. Picture coding with motion analysis for low bit rate transmission. In *ICC Proceedings*, June 1982.

[NR79]   A. N. Netravali and J. D. Robbins. Motion compensated television coding - part
1. *Bell Syst. Tech. J.*, 58:631–670, March 1979.

[PHS87]   A. Puri, H. M. Hang, and D. L. Shilling. An efficient block matching algorithm
for motion compensated coding. In *Proceedings of ICASSP*, pages 25.4.1–25.4.4,
1987.

[SR84]   R. Srinivasan and K. R. Rao. Predictive coding based on efficient motion estimation. In *ICC Proceedings*, May 1984.

Lossless Interframe Compression of Medical Images

Xiaolin Wu *
Department of Computer Science
University of Western Ontario
London, Ontario N6A 5B7

Yonggang Fang [†]
Department of Electrical Engineering
Tsinghua University
Beijing, P. R. China

Abstract-A sequence of medical images is converted to a 4-dimensional volumn of bits using gray code. Then an interframe sequential and intraframe interlacing prediction scheme is used for reversible image sequence compression. Higher compression ratios than the current intraframe compression methods are achieved due to interframe decorrelation.

Key Words: Lossless image compression, gray code, arithmetic coding.

1 Introduction

The amount of acquired digital image data in medical communities is so rapidly growing that image archiving and transmission are putting prohibitively heavy burdens on communication bandwidth and computer storage. Without effective image compression some physical limits have been or will soon be reached in utilizing the ever-increasing wealth of digital medical images. To make the matter worse, unlike in commercial and entertainment fields, most medical applications have no or very little error tolerance, demanding either lossless image compression or image reconstruction of ultra high fidelity.

*Supported by grants from the Natural Science and Engineering Research Council of Canada.
[†]Currently visiting the first author's department.

Except for some simple images like binary synthesized graphics, lossless image compression has had very limited success. The compression ratios achieved by the current lossless compression methods [3, 1, 2, 7] on natural gray scale images seem not to exceed 3:1.

Due to the nature of CT and MRI imaging technologies medical images are often organized as a sequence of two-dimensional cross-sections of a 3-dimensional object. This sequence is commonly represented as a 3-dimensional array of voxels $g(x, y, z)$, $0 \leq x < N_x$, $0 \leq y < N_y$, and $0 \leq z < N_z$, where N_x, N_y, N_z define the image resolution, and $0 \leq g(x, y, z) < 2^m$ is an integer encoded by m bits. The key to the compression of the above data source will be the removal of correlations among $g(x, y, z)$ values. To the best of our knowledge the current medical image compression algorithms [4, 5] only remove intraframe redundancy. They employed existing two-dimensional image coding techniques to compress the medical images frame by frame. However, interframe correlation, although significantly weaker than the intraframe correlation, does exist. Indeed, it is the dependency between adjacent frames that provides the rationale for interpolation-based 3-dimensional reconstruction and visualization. Needless to say, for the highest compression ratio possible one should take advantage of both interframe and intraframe correlations.

2   Four-dimensional Bit Volumns in Gray Code

According to studies by Roos *et al.* [5] and Lo *et al.* [4] on intraframe medical image compression, the best performed compression technique for intraframe medical image coding is a two step process: decorrelation by two-dimensional polynomial interpolation of pixel values and entropy coding of prediction errors. This scheme can be generalized from two-dimensions to 3-dimensions for compressing a sequence of medical images. That is, take every other voxel in each of x, y, and z directions, and then predict the voxel values in between by 3-dimensional polynomial interpolation of the known voxels. But due to the uneven sampling rates in different directions in medical imaging practice (the interframe distance is usually much larger than the distance between adjacent samples in xy plane, typically around 5 mm versus around 0.7 mm.), 3-dimensional interpolation of voxel values does not work well. Facing this failure, we develop the following new technique.

First, as in [2], gray level values of voxels are encoded by gray codes. The reason for this is that gray code guarantees that the binary representation of the codes of adjacent integer gray levels differ by only one bit. Let $g_{m-1} \cdots g_1 g_0$ be the intensity value encoded by gray code. Then for a fixed j, $0 \leq j < m$, the bits g_j of all voxels of an image sequence constitute a 3-dimensional $N_x \times N_y \times N_z$ array of 0's and 1's. We call this array the jth significant bit volumn V_j of the image sequence. Consequently the whole image sequence consists of a 4-dimensional volumn of bits in which V_j, $0 \leq j < m$, are the layers of subvolumes. In the sequel, we denote by $b(x, y, z, j)$ the jth significant bit of the integer voxel value $g(x, y, z)$.

Due to the adjacency property of gray code, for larger j's (higher significant bits of gray code), V_j will have large connected components of uniform bits, or large chunks of 0's and 1's, if the 3-dimensional intensity function $g(x, y, z)$ is reasonably smooth. This is the case for typical medical images because organs usually consist of approximately uniform substance and their spatial occupancy is continuous.

The bit volumn V_j can be of course encoded by octree-like methods. But we lose code efficiency because the uniform connected components have too arbitrary shapes, orientations and locations to be exactly described by a small number of artificial octree cells. For higher compression ratios we will develop a 4-dimensional prediction scheme in the next section.

3   Prediction Hierarchy

To predict the bit $b(x, y, z, j)$ we use its neighboring bits in the 4-dimensional bit volumn: $b(r, c, d, s)$, $x - 1 \leq r \leq x + 1$, $y - 1 \leq c \leq y + 1$, $z - 1 \leq d \leq z + 1$, and $j - 1 \leq s \leq j + 1$. Just as a constant j specifies a 3-dimensional bit volumn V_j, constant index pair j and z specify a bit plane $H_{j,z}$. For algorithmic reasons to be clarified later, bit contexts in three bit planes $H_{j,z}$, $H_{j,z-1}$, and $H_{j-1,z}$ are used to predict the unknown bit $b(x, y, z, j)$. Precisely, define the set

$$A(x, y, z, j) \equiv \{b(r, c, z, j) : x - 1 \leq r \leq x + 1, y - 1 \leq c \leq y + 1\} \subset H_{j,z} \qquad (1)$$

then the bit contexts involved in our prediction scheme are $A(\cdot, \cdot, z, j)$, $A(\cdot, \cdot, z - 1, j)$ and $A(\cdot, \cdot, z, j - 1)$.

The bit volumns V_j will be encoded sequentially for increasing j, i.e., from lower to higher significant bits. This order means that the previous bit volumn V_{j-1} is known when encoding V_j if we ignore the initialization of the algorithm for now. Thus the bit context $A(\cdot, \cdot, z, j - 1)$ is available for prediction. Within a given bit volumn V_j the bit planes $H_{j,z}$ will be encoded sequentially for increasing z. Such an order allows the bit context $A(\cdot, \cdot, z - 1, j)$ to be used, too.

Since the strongest correlation exists inside a frame, the intraframe decorrelation should be done as thoroughly as possible. To this end, an interlacing prediction scheme is used within a bit plane $H_{j,z}$. The bit plane is sampled in a step of two in both row and column, i.e., bits $b(2r, 2c, z, j)$, $0 \leq r < N_x/2$, $0 \leq c < N_y/2$, are encoded. At this moment nothing about the current bit plane is known, we can only

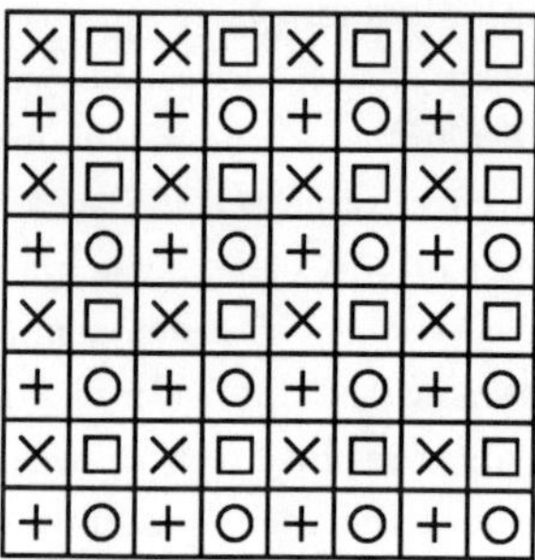

Figure 1: Intraframe interlacing prediction scheme.

use the bit contexts $A(2r, 2c, z - 1, j)$ and $A(2r, 2c, z, j - 1)$. This first quartile of bits in $H_{j,z}$ to be encoded are labeled by o in Figure 1. The second quartile of bits to be encoded will be those marked as $\times$ in the figure, i.e., $b(2r + 1, 2c + 1, z, j)$, $0 \leq r < N_x/2$, $0 \leq c < N_y/2$. Now define the corner context to be

$$
\begin{aligned}
C_\times(x, y, j, z) &= \{b(x - 1, y - 1, z, j), b(x + 1, y - 1, z, j), \\
&\quad b(x - 1, y + 1, z, j), b(x + 1, y + 1, z, j)\}
\end{aligned}
\tag{2}
$$

which contains the bits to the northwest, northeast, southwest, and southeast corners of the bit $b(x, y, j, z)$. Note that in Figure 1 the bits $\times$ have their corner contexts $C_\times(2r + 1, 2c + 1, z, j)$ to be the known bits o. Thus bits $\times$ can be better predicted than bits o using their conner contexts in the same bit plane $H_{j,z}$ in addition to $A(2r + 1, 2c + 1, z - 1, j)$ and $A(2r + 1, 2c + 1, z, j)$.

Likewise, we can define the so-called cross context C_+ and square context $C_\square$ to be

$$
\begin{aligned}
C_+(x, y, j, z) &= \{b(x, y - 1, z, j), b(x - 1, y, z, j), b(x + 1, y, z, j), b(x, y - 1, z, j)\} \\
C_\square(x, y, j, z) &= C_+(x, y, j, z) \cup C_\times(x, y, j, z).
\end{aligned}
\tag{3}
$$

In digital geometry, the cross context consists of 4-connected bit neighbors and the square context consists of 8-connected bit neighbors in the bit plane $H_{j,z}$. The dependency of a bit on its cross context is stronger than on its corner context for most images because the corner bits have distance $\sqrt{2}$ from the center bit while the cross bits have distance 1 from the center. The square context is the union of the corner and cross contexts, hence the dependency of a bit on its square context is the strongest among the three. But in order to utilize the cross context the bits o and $\times$ must have been known first as clearly indicated in Figure 1. Thus the bits marked by $+$ in the figure, Namely, $b(2r + 1, 2c, z, j)$, $0 \leq r < N_x/2$, $0 \leq c < N_y/2$, are encoded after bits o and $\times$ using $C_+(2r + 1, 2c, z, j)$, $A(2r + 1, 2c, z - 1, j)$ and $A(2r+1, 2c, z, j-1)$. The remaining quartile of bits (those marked by $\square$ in Figure 1) in the bit plane $H_{j,z}$: $b(2r, 2c+1, z, j)$, $0 \leq r < N_x/2$, $0 \leq c < N_y/2$, have their square contexts available, and hence can be predicted most accurately by $C_\square(2r, 2c+1, z, j)$, $A(2r, 2c + 1, z - 1, j)$ and $A(2r, 2c + 1, z, j - 1)$.

In summary the proposed interplane-Sequential and intraplane-Interlacing Prediction Hierarchy (SIPH) is described by the following pseudocode.

```
for j = 1 to m − 1 do
    for z = 1 to N_z − 1 do
        begin
            predict bits o with A(·, ·, z, j − 1) and A(·, ·, z − 1, j);
            predict bits × with C_×(·, ·, z, j), A(·, ·, z, j − 1) and A(·, ·, z − 1, j);
            predict bits + with C_+(·, ·, z, j), A(·, ·, z, j − 1) and A(·, ·, z − 1, j);
            predict bits □ with C_□(·, ·, z, j), A(·, ·, z, j − 1) and A(·, ·, z − 1, j);
        end
```

4   A Simple Predictive Coding Algorithm

Different from all current prediction models for image compression, our prediction model is discrete and binary. In the SIPH scheme the 4-dimensional bit contexts for prediction are bit patterns and the random variable $U = b(x, y, z, j)$ being predicted is binary. We can encode instances of a prediction bit context as binary numbers, and treat these values as outcomes of a random variable V. If the prediction bit context consists of w bits, then the random variable V is drawn from a discrete probability space of size 2^w. Correlations between adjacent voxels in the image sequence are reflected by the conditional probability $P(U|V)$. The discrete density of $P(U|V)$, namely, $P(0|v_i)$ and $P(1|v_i) = 1 - P(0|v_i)$, $0 \leq i < 2^w$, where v_i is a particular bit context, can be approximated by sample frequencies in practice. To get a good approximation of $P(U|V)$ a sufficiently large number of sequences of 3-dimensional gray level images should be converted to the 4-dimensional bit volumns in gray code. Then these bit volumns are swept by each of the 4-dimensional windows defined by the chosen bit contexts to set

$$P(0|v_i) = \frac{\text{the number of 0 bits associated with } v_i}{\text{the number of } v_i \text{ occurrences}}. \tag{4}$$

Since gray code tends to generate clusters of uniform bits in bit volumns, the bit contexts y of greater uniformity or clear structure have either high $P(0|v)$ or high

$P(1|v)$, whereas noisy bit contexts y can hardly predict the center bits with $P(0|v)$ or $P(1|v)$ being close to 0.5. A simple predictive coding method is to classify all bit contexts into two classes: those of either high $P(0|v)$ or high $P(1|v)$ values so that they can predict the center bits with high probability and the remaining ones. Both the encoder and decoder keep an identical table Γ that records those bit contexts v_i in the first class and their predictions $\phi(v_i) \in \{0, 1\}$.

The table Γ serves as a code book. It should be constructed by analyzing a large enough training data set for a given class of images, and used for that class. With the code book available, encoding a sequence of medical images becomes straightforward. We convert the image sequence into a 4-dimensional bit volumn in gray code and then scan the bit volumn by SIPH method. The SIPH scanning of a bit volumn generates a sequence of bit contexts $v_0 v_1 \cdots$ and the corresponding bit string $u_0 u_1 \cdots$ to be predicted, with v_i being observations of V and u_i being observations of U. If $v_i \in \Gamma$ then the exclusive OR of its prediction $\phi(v_i)$ and u_i is performed and the result $\phi(v_i) \oplus u_i$ is concatenated to a bit string $S_\oplus$; if $v_i \notin \Gamma$, then u_i is concatenated to another bit string S_o. After the SIPH scan is finished, the encoder employs a lossless compression method, say, arithmetic coding [6], to compress strings $S_\oplus$ and S_o separately. Very high compression was obtained on $S_\oplus$ using arithmetic coding since $S_\oplus$ consists of predominantly 0's thus highly predictable. The structure of S_o, on the other hand, is weak if exists at all. Not much compaction can be achieved on S_o. Fortunately, the adjacency property of gray code means that $S_\oplus$ is much longer.

With the same code book Γ available, the decoding process is simple and fast. The bit strings $S_\oplus$ and S_o can first be reconstructed since they are encoded by a reversible code. Then the decoder will reconstruct the bit volumn in gray code from $S_\oplus$ and S_o by the same SIPH traversal as at the encoder side and by interpreting $S_\oplus$ using Γ. Finally the sequence of images can be reconstructed error free by converting the 4-dimensional bit volumn in gray code to a 3-dimensional $N_x \times N_y \times N_z$ array of voxels whose values are encoded by conventional binary code.

5   Optimization Issues

There is much room for improvement on the above basic lossless image sequence coding algorithm. In this extended abstract we will only sketch two optimization processes that can increase the compression ratio.

5.1 Code Book Optimization

In designing the code book Γ for the proposed image sequence coding algorithm we have to decide whether a bit context v_i can successfully predict the unkown center bit. Thus a threshold q must be set. Bit context $v_i \in \Gamma$ if and only if it satisfies

$$|P(0|v_i) - 0.5| \geq q. \tag{5}$$

Let $S_\oplus(q)$ and $S_o(q)$ be the bit strings generated from the training data for the threshold q. Then the optimal threshold q_{opt} is the one that minimizes the total code length of $S_\oplus(q)$ and $S_o(q)$ after they are compressed by an entropy coding method. To compute q_{opt} we can discretize the interval $[0, 0.5]$ to an M-point grid, and carry out a linear search on the grid. In the search for q_{opt} we do not have to actually encode $S_\oplus(q)$ and $S_o(q)$ to get the total code length. Instead we may form blocks of bits in $S_\oplus(q)$ and $S_o(q)$, and use the entropy of the blocks in $S_\oplus(q)$ and the entropy of the blocks in $S_o(q)$ to estimate the total code length. Of course, the block size should be consistent with whatever block size adopted by the chosen entropy coding method. Once q_{opt} is obtained the code book Γ_{opt} associated with q_{opt} will be the optimal one for the the class of images represented by the training sequences.

In the previous development we classify the bit contexts into two classes, and consequently generate two bit strings $S_\oplus$ and S_o. But this design is soly for the sake of simplicity. The bit contexts can be classified into more than two classes. In general, one can set multiple thresholds $0 \equiv q_0 < q_1 < \cdots < q_{K-1} < q_K \equiv 0.5$, such that bit context $v_i \in \Gamma_k$ if and only if

$$q_{k-1} \leq |P(0|v_i) - 0.5| < q_k, \quad 0 < k \leq K. \tag{6}$$

We may treat Γ_k, $0 < k \leq K$, as a set of K code books. Given the source bit string $u_0 u_1 \cdots$ with the corresponding context string $v_0 v_1 \cdots$, the result of $\phi(v_i) \oplus u_i$ is concatenated to a string S_k if $v_i \in \Gamma_k$. By the conditions in Eq(6) different Γ_k's contain bit contexts of different prediction accuracies. Thus different strings S_k will have different densities of 1's that indicate prediction errors. Specifically, the lower the k value, the higher the density. Assume that prediction errors are independent of each other. Then by splitting the previous string $S_\oplus$ into S_k, $0 < k \leq K$, according to the ratios between 0's and 1's, we obtain individual strings S_k of different levels of uniformity. Thus entropy coding methods will perform better on strings S_k separately than on the long compounded string $S_\oplus$ whose statistics may change considerably from substrings to substrings.

The thresholds q_k, $0 < k < K$, can be optimized using dynamic programming technique. Although the optimization is computationally expensive, it is one time

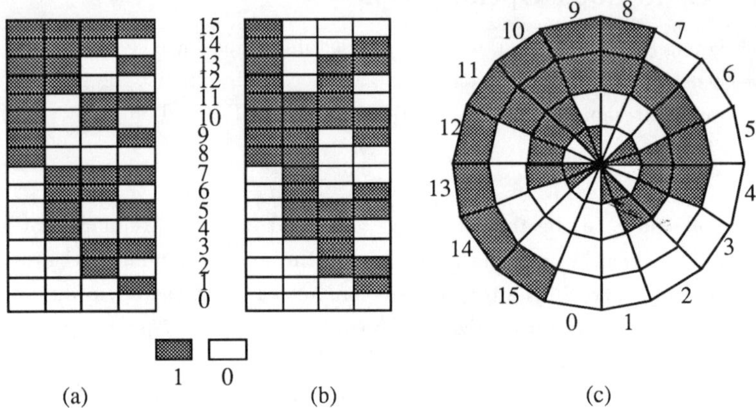

Figure 2: (a) Binary code. (b) Gray code. (c) Gray code cycle.

investment required only for designing a set of optimal code books Γ_k on training data. The details of this optimization will be provided in the full-length version of this extended abstract.

5.2 Optimal Gray Code Assignment

The reason that we use gray code rather than binary code in our coding algorithm is that the gray code has better bit adjacency (few jumps between 0's and 1's in the same significant bit) as clearly illustrated by Figure 2. The conversion between gray code and binary code can be found in [2] and hence omitted here. It is interesting to note that the bit adjacency of gray code is cyclic (see Figure 2(c) which is obtained by connecting the head and the tail of gray code sequence in Figure (b)). In the cycle of Figure 2(c) any two adjacent gray codes differ from each other only in one bit. Therefore, if the intensity values $g(x, y, z)$ are originally encoded by w bits then we can have as many as 2^w one-to-one maps between the binary code and a gray code by aligning binary code $00 \cdots 0$ to a position in the gray code cycle. We define the optimal binary-gray map to be the one under which the highest compression ratio is achieved by the proposed lossless image sequence coding algorithm.

If computational cost is not a concern then the optimal map can be found by encoding an image sequence for every possible map between the two codes and selecting the best. However, an efficient heuristic code optimization approach was proven to be quite effective. The fact that the higher significant bits of gray code form contiguous uniform bit regions suggests that $g(x, y, z)$ values in a relatively large dynamic range will cause no or very little changes at these bits. This is the very property that we want to preserve in order to create large clusters of uniform bits in the bit volumn being encoded. To this end we should place as many $g(x, y, z)$ values as possible in a large uniform bit region. Before encoding the input image sequence we can first obtain the intensity histogram of the entire sequence. Then we can shift the histogram in the gray code cycle and search for the best position at which the least number of gray values straddle the borders between the 0 and 1 bit segments in gray code. It should be pointed out that if we treat all significant bits equally, then the above optimization is meaningless, because every position in the gray code cycle has a transition between 0 and 1 at some bit. But since the lower significant bits are more likely to represent noise, we should lower their weighting in the optimization accordingly.

6   Performance and Discussions

The new lossless image sequence compression algorithm was implemented and extensively tested on MRI medical images. The test images were 256×256 in xy plane and had 10 bits gray scale. Both long and short image sequences were used with the number of slices ranging from 16 to 48. Due to much higher intraframe correlation than interframe correlation, the compression ratio largely depends on the image type rather than on the image sequence length. Nevertheless, the interframe decorrelation did increase the compression ratios. On a set of 20 MRI brain images our algorithm obtained an average compression ratio of 2.31 versus 1.78 by the polynomial interpolation method [4], the best previously reported. On a set of 40 MRI knee images the corresponding comparison is 1.94 versus 1.63.

It should be pointed out that the high level of noise usually existing in MRI images greatly deteriorates the effectiveness of our 4-dimensional prediction model. In fact, more than 95 percent of compression was gained on the first 6 significant bits. In other words, 40 percent of source data are almost incompressible. For the first 6 significant bits in gray code, the new algorithm obtained average compression ratios of 8.04 for brain images and 4.95 for knee images, while the polynomial interpolation intraframe compression method reached average compression ratios of 4.49 and 4.45. This means that if the true information range in the MRI images does not include few least significant bits, as suggested by the studies in [4], thus a controled lossy compression is acceptable, then much more significant improvement is achieved by the new image sequence coding algorithm over the intraframe coding methods.

The proposed lossless interframe image coding technique can be readily applied to other image sequences as well, for instance, satellite images of different bands.

If there is some correlation between the bands then higher compression ratios than intraframe coding should be expected.

7   Conclusion

A promising lossless image sequence coding technique is proposed. The technique exploits both interframe and intraframe correlations. The correlations are captured through a four-dimensional bit space formed by a sequence of two-dimensional images whose intensity values are encoded by gray code.

References

[1] E. Kawaguchi and T. Endo, "On a method of binary-picture representation and its application to data compression," *IEEE Trans. Machine Intel. Patt. Anal.*, vol. PAMI-2, no. 1, pp. 27-35, Jan. 1980.

[2] E. Kawaguchi, T. Endo, and J. Matsunaga, "Depth-first expression viewed from digital picture processing", *IEEE Trans. Machine Intel. Patt. Anal.*, vol. PAMI-5, no. 4, pp. 373-384, July 1983.

[3] G. G. Langdon and J. J. Rissanen, "Compression of black-white images with arithmetic coding," *IEEE Trans. Comm.*, vol. COM-29, no. 6, pp. 858-867, June 1981.

[4] S. B. Lo, B. Krasner, and S. K. Mun, "Noise impact on error-free image compression," *IEEE Trans. Medical Imaging*, vol. 9, no. 2, pp. 202-206, June 1990.

[5] P. Roos, M. A. Viergever, M. C. A. Van Dijke, and J. H. Peters, "Reversible intraframe compression of medical images," *IEEE Trans. Medical Imaging*, vol. 7, no. 4, pp. 328-336, Dec. 1988.

[6] I. H. Witten, R. M. Neal, and J. G. Cleary, "Arithmetic coding for data compression," *Com. of ACM*, vol. 30, pp. 520-540, 1987.

[7] J. Ziv, and A. Lempel, "A universal algorithm for sequential data compression," *IEEE Trans. Inf. Theory*, vol. IT-23, no. 3, pp. 337-343, May.

$$W(x) = \begin{pmatrix} a & b \end{pmatrix}\begin{pmatrix} x \end{pmatrix} + \begin{pmatrix} e \end{pmatrix} = (ax + by + e)$$
$$(y) \quad (c \quad d)(y) \quad (f) \quad (cx + dy + f)$$

If the translations, rotations, and scalings that make up W are known in advance, then the coefficients may be calculated by:

	$a = r \cos q,$	$b = - s \sin f,$	$c = r \sin q,$	$d = s \cos f,$
where:	r = scaling factor on x,		s = scaling factor on y	
	q = angle of rotation on x,		f = angle of rotation on y	
	e = translation on x,		f = translation on y	

The affine transformations can be implemented by the hardware that we have developed using the IRS (TMC2301). This chip performs image transformations according to the equations, [2]:

The Geometric   { $x(u,v) = Au^2 + Bu + Cuv + Dv^2 + Ev + F$

Transformation Equations   { $y(u,v) = Gu^2 + Hu + Kuv + Lv^2 + Mv + N$

where: the coefficients A to N define the transformation,

      x,y = source image coordinates, u,v = destination image coordinates.

The 2nd order terms are ignored since affine transformations are only first order transformations, thus the geometric equations simplify to:

$$x = a(x') + b(y') + e \qquad\qquad y = c(x') + d(y') + f$$

where: $B = a, \ E = b, \ F = e, H = c, \ M = d, N = f.$

Calculation of Transformation Coefficients

There are six unknown coefficients to be solved for the Geometric Transformation equations. Therefore, by selecting six points in the destination image (x', y'), the 'Control Points', and finding their corresponding coordinates in the source image (x, y), two systems of linear simultaneous equations can be set up with six equations in each system and six unknowns. These two systems may be solved by Gaussian Elimination to obtain the required coefficients values.

The selection of the six control points for calculating the coefficients is critical because, they must be:

uniquely identifiable - they must be traceable in the source image,

evenly spread in the cell - they must reflect changes all over the cell's area.

If the points are chosen to be on a cell's boundaries, then the advantages are:

each point can be used for calculating the coefficients of two adjacent cells,

reduction by ½ the number of points traceable from the destination to source image,

smooth transition transformations from one cell to the next may be obtained.

Figure 2a shows an example of nine adjacent cells in the new (Destination) frame with the six control points for each cell, **Figure 2b** shows how these points may map into the previous (Source) frame. For each cell three points are selected, one on the right hand border and two on the bottom border. In order to calculate the coefficients of cell ''E'', for example, control points ''E1,E2,E3,B1,B2,D3'' would be utilised.

To enable the edges of objects in the image whose points are most likely to be uniquely identifiable to be found - edge detection operation is performed using convolution with sobel operators, in order to select the control points. Using this technique, the intercept points in each cell where the edges in the image intercept the right hand border which is nearest to the border's centre, and the two points nearest to the border's ''one third intervals'' for the bottom border of the cell, are found and selected.

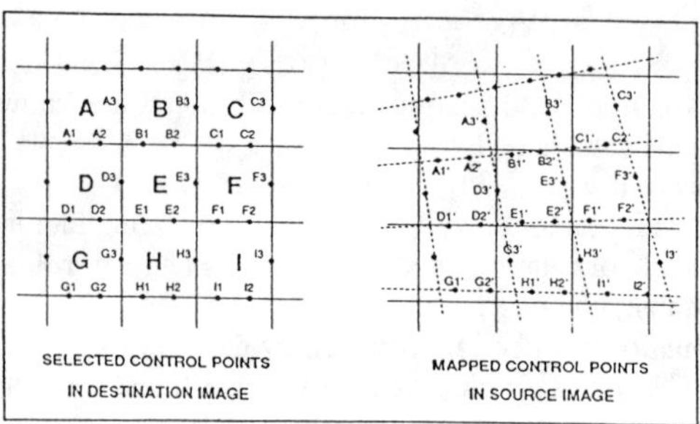

Figure 2. Control Points

A motion detection algorithm is then applied to establish where those points were in the source frame, by Search Block Matching using a Mean Absolute Error algorithm.

II) Hardware Implementation

To perform the image processing operations a Modular Image Processing System [3] is being developed, whose architecture will offer both high speed processing and hardware flexibility. The system consists of a central processing module responsible for the overall system management, and a number of parallel dedicated hardware modules for performing specific image processing operations. **Figure 3** shows a block diagram of the overall architecture of the system. One of the parallel modules is the IRS used to implement the affine transformations.

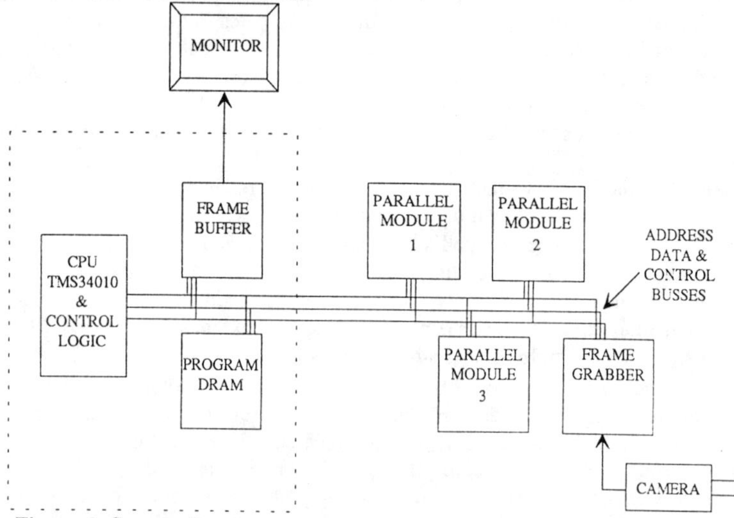

Figure 3. System Outline of a Modular Parallel Digital Image Processor

The system central controller is a TMS34010 Graphics System Processor(GSP) [4] - a graphics orientated microprocessor that offers a rich general purpose and graphics instruction set. The GSP's Address, Data and Control busses expand out of the central processing module to provide an interface for the parallel modules. The Frame Buffer is capable of storing and displaying up to 512x512 pixel images with 8 bits per pixel depth (256 gray levels). **IMAGE Resampling Module** performs 1st and 2nd order geometric transformations, bilinear interpolation or convolution filtering using two TMC2301 IRSs as local processors. **Convolver Module** performs convolution in real-time with kernels of up to 8x8 size using the PDSP16488 convolver (Plessey) as the local processor. **IMAGE Compression Module** - The Fractal Compression Module to perform encoding is under development. A Discrete Cosine Transform (DCT) module to compress image data: can perform both Forward and Inverse DCT and also low pass filtering has already been built. It uses the IMS A121 DCT chip as the local processor. A number of **Motion Estimation Modules** performs search block matching using mean absolute error. These modules use STI3220 Motion Estimation Processors as the local processors: used for finding in the source image, the coordinates of the control points, which were selected in the destination image. **IMAGE Difference Module** - calculates mean absolute error between corresponding cells, in the new and previous frames, and also in the new and reconstructed frames. At the transmitter the data compression system will require all the above modules in order to perform all the operations necessary for encoding the sequence. At the receiver, however, much less processing is required for decoding. The receiver will only need to have the Image Resampling Module for performing the geometric transformations according to the parameters that it receives, decoding of IFS code can be achieved in software alone at the receiver, this can be stored as ROM.

III) How to find and decode IFS codes

The complex representation of an IFS code is required to calculate its moment and match it with the moment of the image segment it is to represent. The points (x, y) in the real 2-d space may be thought of as points z in the complex plane C, then the affine transformation w_i can be expressed in the complex form $w_i(z)$ where:

$$z = x + i\, y,$$
$$w_i(z) = c_i\, z + (d_i\, z)^* + b_i, \quad i = 1,...N. \text{ where: } z^* = x - i\, y.$$

Comparing this with the polar form of the affine transformation (the probabilities stay the same in either case) the complex variables of the affine transform are found to be:

$$c_i^r = \tfrac{1}{2} (r \cos q + s \cos f) \qquad r^2 = (c_i^r + d_i^r)^2 + (c_i^c + d_i^c)^2$$

$$c_i^c = \tfrac{1}{2} (r \sin q + s \sin f) \qquad \tan q = (c_i^c - d_i^c)/(c_i^r + d_i^r)$$

$$d_i^r = \tfrac{1}{2} (r \cos q - s \cos f) \qquad s^2 = (c_i^r - d_i^r)^2 + (c_i^c + d_i^c)^2 \qquad b_i^r = e$$

$$d_i^c = \tfrac{1}{2} (-r \sin q + s \sin f) \qquad \tan q = (c_i^c + d_i^c)/(c_i^r - d_i^r) \qquad b_i^c = f$$

Relationship between Complex Moment and Complex form of IFS

The moment of an IFS is defined[5] by:

$$M_n = \int_k z^n\, d\mu\,(z) : n = 0,1,2,...$$

where z = points generated by affine transformation w_i.

Consider our fractal image to be made up of m points z_k, then moment M_n is:

$$M_n = \sum_{k=1}^{m} z_k \frac{n}{m}$$

For an IFS with $r = s$ and $q = f$ (e.g. of the form $w_i(z) = a_i z + b_i$, $i = 1,...N$) then:

$$M_n = \sum_{i=1}^{N} p_i \int_k (a_i z + b_i)^n d\mu(z)$$

M_n can be simplified to:

$$M_n = \left(1 - \sum_{i=1}^{n} p_i a_i^{\ n}\right)^{-1} \sum_{i=1}^{N} p_i \sum_{j=0}^{n-1} (^nC_j)\, a_i^{\ j}\, b_i^{\ n-j} M_j$$

The equation for M_n is obtained given in terms of the previous moments M_j, $j = 0,..., n-1$ and the form of the affine transformation a_i, b_i, and p_i, $i = 1,...,N$. Since $M_0 = 1.0$, the rest of the moments may be calculated, without the need for points z_k generation. Thus saving valuable computation time where 10,000 or more points may need to be generated to obtain accurate moments. Thus an IFS that describes an image may be found by attempting to make the moments of the IFS as close to the moments of the image. This only holds for the case $r = s$ and $q = f$. For the more general case, the general moment definition has to be used:

$$M_{jk} = \int_k z^j z^{*k} d\mu(z) \quad : j,k = 0,1,2,...$$

In this case a matrix equation for the moments M_{jk} with $j+k = n$ has to be solved [6], this is in the form of: $- C = (A - I)\, M_{array}$

where: M_{array} = vector $(M_{0n}, M_{1(n-1)}, M_{2(n-2)},...,M_{n0})^T$,

A = matrix, size = $(n+1) \times (n+1)$, elements are IFS parameter dependant,

I = Identity matrix, I_{ii} 1.0, $I_{ij} = 0.0$ if i is not equal to j,

C = IFS parameters and moments M_{jk} (where $j+k < n$) dependant vector.

Thus using $M_{00} = 1.0$ and the IFS code, the moment M_{jk} can be solved.

1) The moment library search method

The moments have to be normalised so that fractal images that are the same except for a global scaling may be compared. By having a large database of IFS codes and its associated normalised moments, this library may be used to search for an IFS code whose moment is closest to the normalised moment of an image to be encoded. This IFS code may then be retained and passed as the fractal transform of that image segment to use directly to compress that segment or instead the IFS code obtained may be used as a starting point to some non-linear solution method to find a closer IFS code.

2) Newton's Method to find an IFS code close to an image

Newton's method can be used to solve an equation of the form: $f(x) = 0$. The problem is essentially: $\underline{f}(\underline{x}) = f_1(\underline{x}) - f_1(\underline{x}_{image\ segment})$

where: $\underline{f}_1(\underline{x})$ = normalised moments function of an IFS code

$\underline{f}_1(\underline{x}_{\text{image segment}})$ = normalised moments of an image

calculated explicitly from the points of the image.

When $\underline{f}(\underline{x}) = 0$, then the vector form of the IFS code $\underline{x}$ has been found.

3) Simulated Annealing method to find an IFS code close to an image [6] [7] [8]

This is a better method of minimising functions of many variables as it will not go immediately to the local minima of a function - a problem inherent with Newton's Method. The problem concerns the thermodynamics of metal cooling and annealing given by the equation:

$$\text{Prob (E)} \approx \exp\left(\frac{-E}{kT}\right)$$

where: E = energy of system, T = temperature (Kelvin), B = Boltzmann's constant.

The method requires parameters that are analogues of T whose value is lowered as the method gets closer to the minima, and energy E, where energy is the value of the system to be minimised. At initial higher T's, changes to higher energy states are much more likely to be accepted and it is this feature of the method that allows the algorithm to find the global minima of a function rather than one of many local minima. The method may be used to find an IFS whose moments are close to a given set of moments. The following are required:

1) Description of system - use vector $\underline{x}$, size N_{ofx} = # of points in image segment:

$$\underline{x} = (c_1^r,\ c_1^c,\ d_1^r,\ d_1^c,\ b_1^r,\ b_1^c,\ ...,\ d_{N_{\text{Affines}}}^r,\ d_{N_{\text{affines}}}^c,\ b_{N_{\text{affines}}}^r,\ b_{N_{\text{affines}}}^c)^T$$

2) A random system change generator. Accomplished by random vector $\underline{dx}$ variable of length randomly chosen between 0 and given length dl. dl and T was lowered simultaneously creating a new vector $\underline{x}_{\text{new}}$:

$$\underline{x}_{\text{new}} = \underline{x}_{\text{old}} + \underline{dx}$$

Check vector for valid IFS code production, if invalid then a new $\underline{dx}$ was generated.

3) The energy of the system, E, whose minimisation was required, was substituted by:

$$E = |\underline{f}(\underline{x})|^2 = \sqrt{\sum_{i=1}^{N_{\text{off}}} f_i(\underline{x})^2}$$

where $\underline{f}(\underline{x}) = \underline{f}_1(\underline{x})$ - $\underline{f}_1(\text{image})$. Use unnormalised moments for $\underline{f}_1(\underline{x})$ and $\underline{f}_1(\text{image})$.

4) The parameter T and a method of lowering T. T governs the changes in the function E. Consider E value carefully as affects the energy change, ΔE, that can be acceptable.

How to decode an IFS code - the Random Iteration Algorithm -a summary[6] [7]

1) Initialization: x = 0, y = 0.

2) For n = 1 to Number_of_points_ in_image, do steps (3) and (4).

3) Choose k to be one of the numbers 1,2,...,m, with probability P_k.

4) Apply the transformation W_k to the point (x,y) to obtain (x', y').

5) Set (x,y) equal to the new point: x=x', y=y'.

6) If n > number_points_required_to_obtain_attractor, then plot (x',y').   7) Loop.

More points are added to an image by increasing the variable Number_of_points_in_image. This may be required to obtain an image with a greater resolution, e.g. for HDTV. Zooming may also be achieved by using an increased scale factor. The variable of (6) is around 100, but may be minimised by empirical methods. The ability of the random iteration algorithm to produce the same image time and time again independent of the random sequence of events chosen has been proven:

1) by carrying out computer-graphical math experiments;

2) by rigorous theoretical foundation of the mathematician John Elton of Georgia Institute of Technology, Georgia, USA.

IV) Motion Video Compression Using Geometric Transformations

The hardware may also be used to compress motion video. The initial frame of the sequence will be sent in its IFS encoded form. The preceding frames may be constructed using geometric transformations to describe inter-frame image changes, whilst simultaneously IFS encoding of a new frame sequence may be occuring. If a frame cannot be sent using geometric transformations then it will be sent as IFS codes. Loss of channel link will not mean loss of image as the image will be stored in a framestore. Infact the framestore may temporarily freeze the last frame whilst the new frame is being encoded as IFS codes.

i) The 1st frame of the sequence is sent in its IFS encoded form, which is regenerated using the Random Iteration Algorithm at the decoder, this can be performed in real-time and entirely in software if necessary.

ii) The new frame to be sent is split-up into rectangular domain blocks, as shown in **Figure 4**. Comparison between the domain block of the new frame and the previous frame is made to determine which cells have altered using an Image Difference operation on the cells and forming the Mean Absolute Error. If the error is below a preset threshold then assume no change in the corresponding cell, otherwise, assume that it has changed.

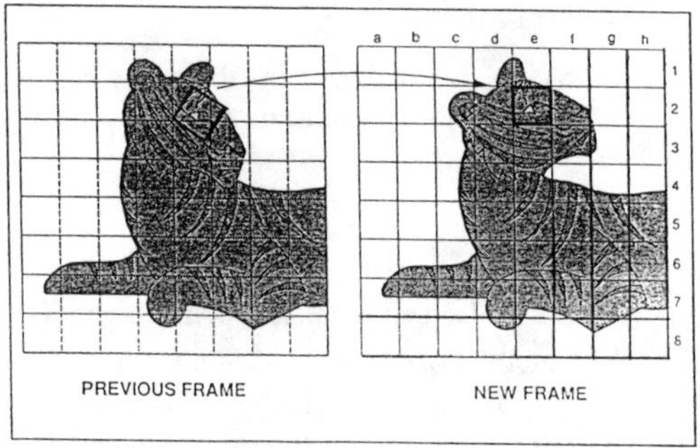

Figure 4 Example of Consecutive Frames in a Sequence

iii) No new information is transmitted for unaltered cells. Altered cell are constructed by geometrically transforming parts of the previous frame. For example, cell "e2" in the new frame of **Figure 4** can be reconstructed by rotating and translating the highlighted part in the previous frame.

iv) After the reconstruction of each cell, it is compared with the actual cell in the new frame to determine whether the reconstruction was successful or not. The comparison is again performed as in (ii) with an Image Difference operation on the cells, finding Mean Absolute Error. If this reconstruction is successful, then only the transformation coefficients need to be transmitted.

v) Otherwise, the cell is sent in its IFS encoded form.

Reasons for Cell Reconstruction Failure

Completely new information may have come into the image such as:

- hidden views of objects which are revealed by 3-dimensional rotations,

- movement of another object which was obscuring the camera's field of view,

- higher than 2nd order terms being necessary to accurately describe intra-cell changes.

V) Compression Ratios

The overall CR will depend on the nature of the frame sequence. In general there will be three categories of cells, the average CR will depend on the percentage of cells that fall into these, cells that have:

i)　remained unaltered since the last frame,

ii)　altered and can be described by 2nd order geometric transformations,

iii) altered and cannot be described by 2nd order geometric transformations.

Assuming an image of size of 512x512 pixels with 8 bits per pixel depth, and being divided into 64 domain blocks, then the bitmap size of each cell will be 4096 bytes. If this cell falls into the 2nd category above, then it can be described with a set of 16 programmable parameters, which can be used by a pair of IRS devices (TMC2301) to reconstruct the cell. These parameters require 42 bytes of data giving a CR of 97.5:1. The programmable parameters which need to be stored or transmitted are directly related to the Geometric Transformation Equation coefficients. From the Table below, the worst case IFS CR is ~76:1, which is 3.8 times higher than that obtained by using conventional DCT. The Fractal CR is variable and depends on the image and image quality required. Large compression factors of 10,000:1 may be obtained for some images.

Cell Category	Compression Ratios
Unchanged Cells	Infinite
Cells That Can Be Geometrically Reconstructed	97:1
Cells That Cannot Be Reconstructed - Compressed Using IFS codes	~76:1 to 10,000:1
Cells That Cannot Be Reconstructed - Compressed Using DCT	20:1

VI) Conclusions

An Image Data Compression technique for frame sequences of digital images has been described, which promises CRs well above those offered by conventional Data Compression Methods.

The major advantage of using fractal techniques is that it offers very large image CRs from 76:1 to 10,000:1. The work being conducted using just the geometric transformation module has given CRs of 97.5:1. Using IFS codes - a type of fractal equation - to compress image segments has been explained. The difficult inverse problem of finding a suitable IFS code whose fractal image is to represent the real image and hence achieve compression is being investigated through the use of: a library of IFS codes and complex moment and the method of simulated annealing, for solving non-linear equations of many parameters. The implementation of the fractal encoder is still under development. The application of simulated annealing is being investigated. IFS codes are robust - thus they are ideal for transmission through noisy distortion inducing communication channels - since small deviation of the IFS codes will still produce recognizable images with minimal distortion. The resolution independence of the decoded image from the IFS code makes fractal coding the compression technique for implementing HDTV and ensuring compatibility with non-HDTV equipments.

A Modular Image Processing System has also been presented which can be used to perform the operations required to implement the coding and decoding for this technique. The hardware complexity of the system is concentrated in the coding end of the system which means that it is well suited for applications where a single encoder is used to provide coded information to many decoders, i.e. in broadcasting.

VII) References

1. HO.Peitgen, D.Saupe, The Science of Fractal Images. Springer Verlag, 1988. Fig1.4, p.29.

2. J.Eldon R.Wegner, Using the TMC2301 Image Resampling Sequencer, TRW Application Note TP-37.

3. C.Papadopoulos, T.Clarkson "Parallel Processing of Digital Images Using a Modular Architecture". IEE Proc 6th Int. Conf. on DSP in Communications, Sept 1991.

4. TMS34010 User's Guide, Texas Instruments (1988).

5. MF.Barnsley, V.Ervin, D.Hardin, J.Lancaster, "Solution of an inverse problem for fractals and other sets", Proc. Natl. Acad. Sci., USA, Vol.83, pp1975-77, April 1986.

6. D.Wilson, "Fractal Image Compression", computer science MSc project report, Sept 1988, Imperial College of Science, Technology & Medicine, University of London.

7. MF.Barnsley, AD.Sloan, "A better way to compress images", BYTE, Jan 1988, pp 215-223.

8. S.Kirkpatrick, CD.Gelatt Jr, MP.Vecchi, "Optimisation by simulated annealing", Science, Vol.220, No.4598, pp671-679, 13 May 1983.

ERROR MODELING FOR HIERARCHICAL LOSSLESS IMAGE COMPRESSION

Paul G. Howard[1] *and Jeffrey Scott Vitter*[2]

Department of Computer Science
Brown University
Providence, R. I. 02912–1910

Abstract

We present a new method for error modeling applicable to the MLP algorithm for hierarchical lossless image compression. This method, based on a concept called the *variability index*, provides accurate models for pixel prediction errors without requiring explicit transmission of the models. We also use the variability index to show that prediction errors do not always follow the Laplace distribution, as is commonly assumed; replacing the Laplace distribution with a more general distribution further improves compression. We describe a new compression measurement called *compression gain*, and we give experimental results showing that the using the variability index gives significantly better compression than other methods in the literature.

1   Introduction

In [2] we introduced a paradigm for lossless image compression including four components: pixel sequence, prediction error modeling, and coding. We also introduced an algorithm for progressive coding based on a hierarchical pixel sequence. This *multi-level progressive* algorithm is called MLP. In this paper we focus on the error modeling component of MLP, and present a practical method of modeling prediction errors that leads substantial improvements in compression efficiency.

In the MLP algorithm, the pixels in an image are divided into levels, each level having twice as many pixels as the preceding one. The pixels in a level are arranged in a (possibly rotated) checkerboard pattern. Within a level we apply three operations to each pixel:

1. We predict the pixel's intensity based on the intensities of other nearby pixels known from earlier levels, and compute the prediction error (the difference between the actual and predicted values).

[1] Support was provided in part by NASA Graduate Student Researchers Program grant NGT–50420 and by a National Science Foundation Presidential Young Investigator Award grant with matching funds from IBM. Additional support was provided by a Universities Space Research Association/CESDIS associate membership.

[2] Support was provided in part by a National Science Foundation Presidential Young Investigator Award grant with matching funds from IBM, by NSF grant CCR–9007851, by Army Research Office grant DAAL03–91–G–0035, and by the Office of Naval Research and the Defense Advanced Research Projects Agency under contract N00014–83–J–4052, ARPA order 8225. Additional support was provided by a Universities Space Research Association/CESDIS associate membership.

2. We find an appropriate model for the prediction error, consisting of a probability distribution and an estimated variance.

3. We encode the prediction error using the estimated model in conjunction with a statistical coder, such as arithmetic coding.

The best predictions come from linear combinations of the nearest 4 or 16 pixels, the coefficients being chosen to perform polynomial interpolation. Arithmetic coding can encode the prediction errors optimally with respect to any given error model.

Finding a good error model is at least as important for compression efficiency as making good predictions. Using too flat a distribution gives too low a probability (and hence an excessively long code) to small error values, which occur frequently. On the other hand, using too peaked a distribution allocates too little probability to large errors.

To keep the code length short, we prefer that the error modeling be done implicitly, with no need to transmit side information about the models used. Of course, any computations used in modeling the error for encoding must be computable by the decoder as well.

In this paper we introduce the notion of error modeling by *variability index*. In Section 2 we present and motivate the algorithm. In Section 3 we use the variability index as an experimental tool to show that prediction errors are not always Laplace distributed, as is widely assumed. We also indicate a family of distributions that can provide more accurate error models. In Section 4 we describe experiments showing that application of the variability index algorithm to Laplace distributions leads to an improvement in compression efficiency of about 4 percent compared with implementations with explicit transmission of variances; further refinement by allowing a wider family of error distributions gives another 1 percent improvement. In Section 5 we discuss the direction of our current work.

2 Modeling by Variability Index

In this section we assume that prediction errors are random variates from a Laplace (or symmetric exponential) distribution with zero mean. This assumption is based on considerable experimental evidence beginning with O'Neal [3].

Our goal is to estimate the local variance of the pixel prediction errors in a given level of the MLP encoding. This will allow us to select the appropriate Laplace distribution (the one with the estimated variance) to use in encoding each prediction error by arithmetic coding. Using a single variance for the entire level (as in [2]) disregards local variations in the image; estimating and explicitly encoding variances for small sections of the image (also done in [2]) incurs considerable overhead. It would seem that previously encountered prediction errors of nearby pixels would be related to a given pixel's error, but there is no obvious way to use them directly.

We estimate the variance by an indirect method: for each pixel we compute a *variability index*, a quantity with strong correlation to the local variance. On the supposition that pixels with similar variability index will have similar error models, we adaptively estimate the local variance based on the variability index. The algorithm is as follows:

1. We initialize the variance estimate V.

2. For each pixel, we compute the variability index.

3. We sort the pixels in variability index order.

4. For each pixel (in order of decreasing variability index):

    (a) We code the prediction error d, using V as the variance.

    (b) We use the prediction error d to update V. The variance is just the mean squared error; our variance estimate is an exponentially weighted mean squared error, computed by exponential smoothing:

$$V := f \cdot V + (1 - f) \cdot d^2.$$

Note that the variability index is used only for sorting the pixels, then discarded. We use decreasing variability index order because compression efficiency is less dependent on accurate variance estimates for large variances; hence we encode pixels with large variances first in each level, before our variance estimate has stabilized. The sorting step removes any natural ordering of the pixels, so both the encoder and the decoder must maintain the pixel coordinates.

We have tried several different quantities for the variability index, including both intensity values and prediction errors of pixel neighborhoods of various sizes. Empirically, the most effective is simply the variance of the four nearest pixels. The smoothing parameter f must also be selected. Experiments show that the best results come from a large value like 0.992; smaller values make the estimated variance too sensitive to random fluctuations in the variability index.

3   Distribution Selection

When we code the pixels of a level in variability index order, we can plot histograms of the error distributions for different values of the variability index. A typical set of plots is shown in Figure 1. Two facts are apparent. First, the error distributions are not always Laplacian; in fact, for large variability index they appear closer to normal. Second, the distributions become closer to the Laplace distribution for smaller values of variability index.

This leads us to consider a family of generalized symmetric exponential distribution functions which includes both the Laplace distribution and the normal distribution. Distributions in this family have the form

$$f_{n,\sigma}(x) = \frac{\alpha_n}{\sigma} \exp\left(-\beta_n \left|\frac{x}{\sigma}\right|^n\right). \tag{1}$$

From the constraints on a probability distribution with variance σ^2, we can find α_n and β_n:

$$\alpha_n = \frac{n}{2}\left(\frac{\Gamma(3/n)}{\Gamma(1/n)^3}\right)^{1/2}, \qquad \beta_n = \left(\frac{\Gamma(3/n)}{\Gamma(1/n)}\right)^{n/2}.$$

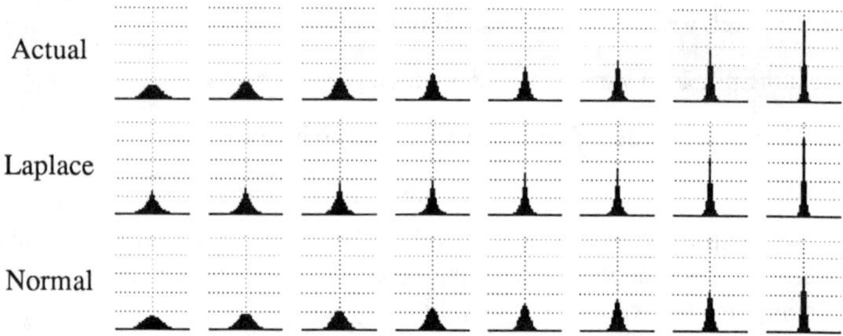

Figure 1: Histograms showing distributions of prediction errors. The top row shows the actual distributions of prediction errors for eight batches of 16,384 points each taken from the last level of the coding of Band 4 of the Donaldsonville data set. The variability index decreases from left to right. The second and third rows show the discretized Laplace distributions and normal distributions with the same variances as the actual data in the corresponding column. The horizontal lines are at intervals of 10 percent probability; prediction errors from -20 to $+20$ are plotted.

For the Laplace distribution ($n = 1$), we have $\alpha_1 = 1/\sqrt{2}$ and $\beta_1 = \sqrt{2}$; for the normal distribution ($n = 2$), we have $\alpha_2 = 1/\sqrt{2\pi}$ and $\beta_2 = 1/2$.

We can use these distributions to optimize the exponent n in Equation (1), either image by image or for a class of images. Optimal values of n for our individual test images range from 1.15 to 2.0; a reasonable value for the set of images is $n = 1.35$. It is possible to vary the exponent within each level, but doing so gives no improvement.

It appears that the distributions we see are actually mixtures of normal or near-normal distributions. High variability indices arise only from regions with high local variance, so the mixture distribution contains contributions only from a small range of distributions. Low variability indices, on the other hand, can come either from regions with low local variance or from the (not unusual) occurrence of small deviates from regions with high local variance. The resulting mixture has contributions from many different distributions, and tends to be more peaked near zero; this gives the characteristic Laplace distribution shape.

4 Comparative Results

Our experiments involved compressing 21 Landsat Thematic Mapper images. We report our results both in terms of compression ratio (original size divided by compressed size) and in terms of a new measure called *compression gain*, described in Section 4.1. In Section 4.2 we briefly describe the test images and the compression methods compared, and present the results in narrative, tabular and graphical form. We conclude that error modeling by variability index gives better compression than other methods in the literature.

Washington, D.C.

Donaldsonville, Louisiana

Ridgely, Maryland

Figure 2: A 256×256 section of Band 4 of each data set.

4.1 Compression gain

A robust measure of compression performance, called *compression gain*, is introduced in [2]. It is measured in decibels (dB) with respect to the zero-order entropy of the image, and is defined to be

$$10 \log_{10} \frac{H_0/8}{L/t}, \tag{2}$$

where t is the size of the input image in bytes, L is the total code length of the compressed file in bytes, and H_0 is the zero-order entropy of the original image in bits per input symbol. As an example, a gain of 3.01 dB means that the image is compressed to half the size of the output of a theoretical zero-order entropy compressor. For completeness we also give the *reference gain* of the zero-order entropy with respect to the original image length, namely $10 \log_{10}(8/H_0)$. The zero-order entropy of the image is a natural choice for the reference value since it is an easily computed property of all images, independent of the word size of the data representation, and it indicates the inherent compressibility of the file.

The logarithms give us additivity, so we can simply add the compression gain and reference gain to obtain the total gain, $10 \log_{10}(t/L)$, if desired. Coding effects, often expressed as percentages of code length, can be given as losses that can simply be subtracted from the compression gain of the modeling method. In this form we can clearly separate coding and modeling, and we can see how tiny the coding effects are. The *gain/loss* terminology is natural: larger numbers mean better compression. A further benefit is that the difference in compression gain between two compression methods is roughly constant; this can be seen clearly in Figure 3.

4.2 Experimental results

Our test data consists of three seven-band Landsat Thematic Mapper data sets consisting of 8-bit grayscale images, over Washington, D.C., Donaldsonville, Louisiana (90 kilometers west of New Orleans), and Ridgely, Maryland (70 kilometers southeast of Baltimore). The Washington and Donaldsonville images are 512×512 pixels; the Ridgely images are 368×468 pixels. Portions of three of the images, contrast enhanced, are shown in

Figure 2. Each data set contains one highly compressible image (compressible to better than 8 : 1) and six "normal" images.

We compare our results with the newly available JPEG lossless mode. The CCITT/ISO Joint Photographic Experts Group (JPEG) has recently developed a proposed standard for image compression [1] that addresses both lossless and lossy compression. The JPEG lossless mode is based on prediction by one, two, or three points, followed by Huffman coding or arithmetic coding; encoding proceeds in raster scan order. The standard gives some latitude to implementors; we report results from an implementation based on two-point prediction with arithmetic coding. For all except the three highly compressible images, two-point prediction provides 0.2 to 0.4 dB more compression gain than three-point prediction. We also include results for the Minimax coder, AT&T's original lossless compression submission to the JPEG, and for the UNIX *compress* program.

We report results from the original MLP algorithm, with limited error modeling: a single variance is computed and transmitted for each level. We give results for the method described in Section 2, using $f = 0.992$, and the version obtained by using the variability index technique in conjunction with a non-Laplace distribution; we use $n = 1.35$ as the exponent in Equation (1).

In Tables 1 and 2 and Figure 3, we denote the various compression methods by the following abbreviations:

Abbreviation	Compression Method
H_0	Reference gain (zero-order entropy compared to original)
comp	UNIX *compress*
JPEG	JPEG lossless mode (two-point prediction)
MM	AT&T Minimax coder (two-point prediction)
MLP	Our MLP method, using a single variance for each level
MLP-VI	Our MLP method with variance estimation by variability index
MLP-VI-EXP	Our MLP method with variability index, exponent=1.35

5 Conclusions

In our experiments we find that using MLP with the variability index technique gives the best compression for all files. We conclude that using the variability index for the error modeling component of the MLP algorithm is extremely effective. It gives good estimates of local pixel variances without requiring any overhead (side information) to describe the models. We obtain compression gain of about 0.16 dB (3.6 percent) with respect to the original version of MLP. In addition, the use of the variability index to classify pixels according to their local variability allows us to see that prediction errors are best modeled by a Laplace distribution only for groups of pixels with low variability; this leads us in turn to the use of a different distribution which provides another 0.03 dB (0.7 percent) of compression gain. Since the original MLP algorithm gives results better than the JPEG

Washington, D.C.

Band	comp	JPEG	MM	MLP	MLP-VI	MLP-VI-EXP
1	1.70	2.07	2.15	2.16	2.20	2.21
2	2.21	2.67	2.76	2.74	2.82	2.83
3	1.92	2.28	2.36	2.37	2.43	2.44
4	1.46	1.81	1.88	1.90	1.92	1.93
5	1.34	1.68	1.74	1.76	1.78	1.79
6	5.36	7.92	8.08	8.66	9.65	9.77
7	1.70	2.10	2.17	2.20	2.22	2.24
All	1.86	2.30	2.38	2.40	2.45	2.46

Donaldsonville, Louisiana

Band	comp	JPEG	MM	MLP	MLP-VI	MLP-VI-EXP
1	1.79	2.26	2.34	2.27	2.40	2.41
2	2.36	3.07	3.16	2.92	3.23	3.24
3	1.99	2.58	2.65	2.45	2.72	2.72
4	1.34	1.85	1.91	1.89	1.97	1.98
5	1.34	1.82	1.87	1.83	1.94	1.94
6	6.14	9.25	9.35	9.61	11.14	11.27
7	1.65	2.17	2.23	2.21	2.30	2.31
All	1.87	2.49	2.56	2.48	2.65	2.66

Ridgely, Maryland

Band	comp	JPEG	MM	MLP	MLP-VI	MLP-VI-EXP
1	1.79	2.28	2.38	2.40	2.44	2.46
2	2.26	2.94	3.07	3.04	3.14	3.18
3	1.86	2.45	2.56	2.55	2.64	2.66
4	1.76	2.24	2.33	2.32	2.41	2.42
5	1.34	1.78	1.85	1.85	1.92	1.94
6	1.58	2.08	2.15	2.17	2.23	2.25
7	5.50	7.43	7.85	8.06	8.70	8.78
All	1.91	2.49	2.60	2.60	2.69	2.71

Table 1: Compression ratios (original file size divided by compressed file size) for three data sets. Each data set consists of seven spectral bands (images); each band is encoded independently of the other bands.

Washington, D.C.

Band	H_0	comp	JPEG	MM	MLP	MLP-VI	MLP-VI-EXP
1	2.32	−0.03	0.84	1.00	1.01	1.09	1.11
2	3.18	0.27	1.09	1.23	1.19	1.32	1.34
3	2.69	0.15	0.89	1.05	1.05	1.16	1.18
4	1.68	−0.04	0.89	1.07	1.10	1.15	1.18
5	1.49	−0.21	0.77	0.92	0.98	1.03	1.05
6	3.66	3.63	5.32	5.41	5.71	6.18	6.23
7	2.26	0.04	0.96	1.11	1.16	1.21	1.24
All	2.41	0.28	1.20	1.36	1.39	1.48	1.50

Donaldsonville, Louisiana

Band	H_0	comp	JPEG	MM	MLP	MLP-VI	MLP-VI-EXP
1	2.19	0.33	1.35	1.49	1.36	1.61	1.63
2	2.83	0.89	2.05	2.17	1.83	2.26	2.27
3	2.23	0.75	1.88	2.00	1.65	2.11	2.11
4	1.02	0.24	1.64	1.78	1.74	1.92	1.94
5	1.13	0.14	1.46	1.58	1.48	1.74	1.75
6	3.80	4.08	5.86	5.91	6.03	6.67	6.72
7	1.79	0.39	1.57	1.69	1.65	1.83	1.85
All	2.05	0.66	1.90	2.02	1.89	2.18	2.19

Ridgely, Maryland

Band	H_0	comp	JPEG	MM	MLP	MLP-VI	MLP-VI-EXP
1	2.18	0.34	1.40	1.59	1.62	1.69	1.74
2	2.69	0.85	1.98	2.17	2.14	2.28	2.33
3	2.10	0.60	1.80	1.98	1.97	2.11	2.15
4	2.23	0.23	1.26	1.44	1.42	1.58	1.60
5	1.14	0.15	1.38	1.54	1.54	1.71	1.74
6	1.66	0.33	1.52	1.68	1.71	1.82	1.87
7	4.33	3.07	4.38	4.62	4.73	5.06	5.11
All	2.24	0.57	1.72	1.90	1.91	2.05	2.09

Table 2: Compression gains (in dB) for three data sets. Each data set consists of seven spectral bands (images); each band is encoded independently of the other bands.

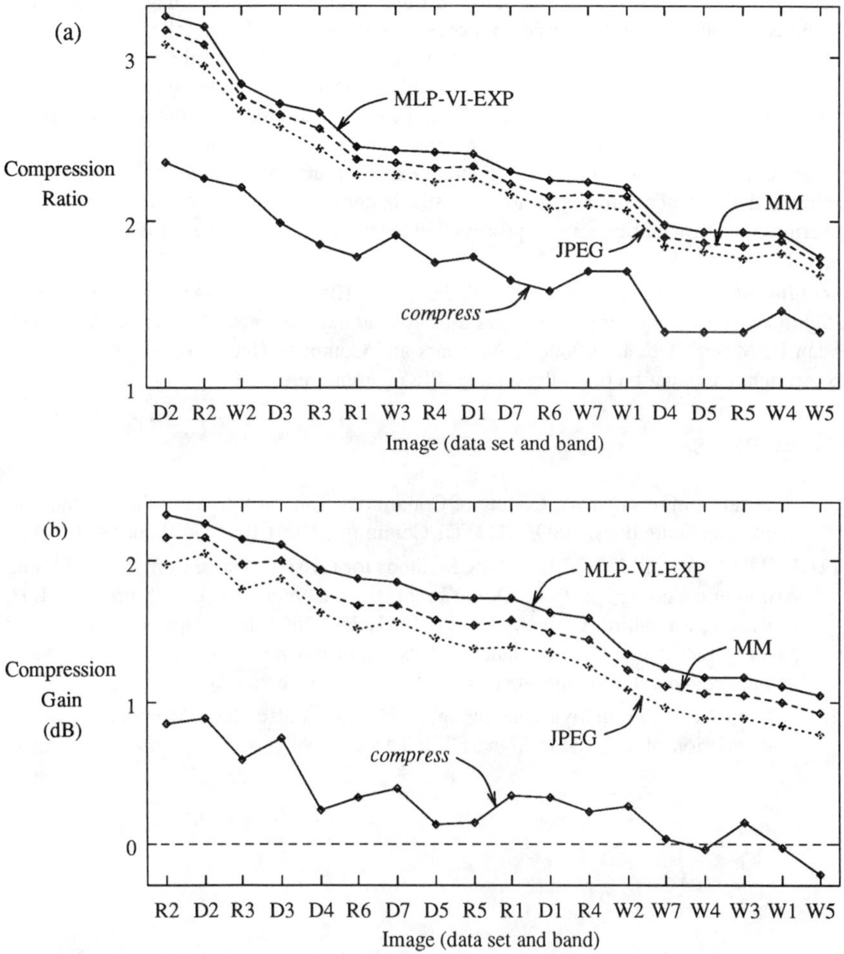

Figure 3: (a) Compression ratios from Table 1, arranged in order of decreasing compressibility, measured by the compression ratio using MLP-VI-EXP. (b) Compression gains from Table 2, arranged in order of decreasing compressibility, measured by the compression gain using MLP-VI-EXP. Images are identified by data set (Washington (**W**), Donaldsonville (**D**), or Ridgely (**R**)) and band number. Images **D6**, **W6**, and **R7** are not included: they are all highly compressible, and would appear off the scale. Results from methods MLP and MLP-VI are omitted to avoid cluttering the graphs.

lossless mode and comparable to the AT&T Minimax coder, we see that the variability index technique improves substantially on other available lossless image compression methods. We also retain MLP's advantages of progressivity and parallelizability.

We are currently investigating several questions. We wish to find a theoretical basis for the variability index; we expect that this will enable us to estimate the variance directly from the variability index, without the sorting step and the indirect adaptive estimation. We are also investigating the choice of exponent in Equation (1); an understanding of the factors that combine to produce the optimal exponent at a given pixel will enable us to estimate the exponent directly, leading to still better compression. A related issue is to determine the distribution mixing process that leads to the observed error distributions.

Acknowledgments. We wish to thank James C. Tilton of the NASA Goddard Space Flight Center for supplying the images used for our experiments. We also wish to thank Allan R. Moser of E. I. duPont de Nemours and Company (Inc.) for assisting us with experimental evaluation of lossless mode JPEG compression.

References

[1] "Digital Compression and Coding of Continuous-Tone Still Images, Part 1, Requirements and Guidelines," ISO/IEC JTC1 Committee Draft 10918–1, Feb. 1991.

[2] P. G. Howard and J. S. Vitter, "New Methods for Lossless Image Compression Using Arithmetic Coding," in *Proc. Data Compression Conference*, J. A. Storer and J. H. Reif, eds., Snowbird, Utah, Apr. 8–11, 1991, 257–266, also to appear as an invited paper in the special issue on data compression in *Journal of Information Processing and Management*, also appears as Brown University Technical Report CS–91–47 .

[3] J. B. O'Neal, "Predictive Quantizing Differential Pulse Code Modulation for the Transmission of Television Signals," *Bell Syst. Tech. J.* 45 (May–June 1966), 689–721.

Efficient Two-Dimensional Compressed Matching

Amihood Amir[*]
College of Computing
Georgia Institute of Technology

Gary Benson[†]
Department of Computer Science
University of Maryland

Abstract

Digitized images are known to be extremely space consuming. However, regularities in the images can often be exploited to reduce the necessary storage area. Thus we find that many systems store images in a compressed form. We propose that compression be used as a time saving tool, in addition to its traditional role of space saving.

We introduce a new pattern matching paradigm - *Compressed Matching*. A text array T and pattern array P are given in compressed forms $c(T)$ and $c(P)$. We seek all appearances of P in T, *without decompressing T*. This achieves a search time that is sublinear in the size of the uncompressed text $|T|$.

We show that for the two-dimensional run-length compression there is a $O(|c(T)|\log|P| + |P|)$, or *almost optimal* algorithm. The algorithm uses a novel multi-dimensional pattern matching technique - *two-dimensional periodicity analysis*.

1   Introduction

Pattern matching is a fundamental and well studied problem in computer science. It is interesting from both theoretical and practical points of view. Another well-studied area is data compression. The main thrust in the study of data compression has been in achieving compression that is efficient in packing while also being practical in time and space. We are interested in a new paradigm for this problem. We would like the compression to have the additional property of allowing **pattern matching** in the **compressed data**.

The *compressed pattern matching problem* is the following: Let c be a given compression algorithm, let $c(D)$ be the result of c compressing data D.

INPUT: Compressed text $c(T)$ and compressed pattern $c(P)$.

OUTPUT: All locations in T where pattern P occurs.

A compressed matching algorithm is *optimal* if its time complexity is $O(|c(T)|)$. It is *efficient* if for T such that $|c(T)| << |T|$ its time complexity is $o(|T|)$. This definition of *efficient* may seem somewhat strange. It is motivated by the following observation. The size of the compressed data will vary depending on the internal structure of the data. In the

---

[*]Partially supported by NSF grant IRI-9013055.

[†]Partially supported by NSF grant IRI-9013055.

worst case it may be $O(|T|)$. Any algorithm that is not optimal would then be worse than decompression and then matching. However, there is an implicit assumption that compression is beneficial, *i.e.* $|c(T)| << |T|$. This leads to our definition of efficient compressed matching. In particular, efficient algorithms with complexity $O(|c(T)|\text{polylog}(|c(T)|))$ we call *almost optimal.*

In one dimension (strings), an optimal compressed matching algorithm is readily apparent for the run-length compression [ALV-90]. The run-length compression is defined as follows:

Let $S = \sigma_1\sigma_2\cdots\sigma_n$ be a string over some alphabet Σ. The *run-length compression* of string S is the string $S' = \sigma_1'^{r_1}\sigma_2'^{r_2}\cdots\sigma_{\hat{n}}'^{r_{\hat{n}}}$ such that: (1) $\sigma_i' \neq \sigma_{i+1}'$ for $1 \leq i < \hat{n}$; and (2) S can be described as the concatenation of $\hat{n}$ *segments*, the symbol σ_1' repeated r_1 times, the symbol σ_2' repeated r_2 times, ..., and the symbol $\sigma_{\hat{n}}'$ repeated $r_{\hat{n}}$ times. For example, the run length compression of string $S = aaabbcccc$ is $S' = a^3b^2c^4$.

Again in [ALV-90], a simple two-dimensional generalization of the run-length representation was considered, namely, the concatenation of the run-length compression of all the matrix rows (or columns). For simplicity's sake we will refer to this compression as the *two-dimensional run-length compression.* In [ALV-90], an efficient compressed matching algorithm was presented for the two-dimensional run-length compression. However, the time complexity of that algorithm is $\Omega(|T|/\sqrt{|P|})$. For a large but very compressible T, and a small P, this result, while efficient, is not very attractive.

The **main contributions** of this paper are the formal introduction of the **compressed matching paradigm** and the presentation of a $O(|c(T)|\log|P| + |P|)$ time algorithm for the two-dimensional run-length compression. We believe that the run-length compression problem is interesting for the following two reasons: 1) It is the first **almost optimal** multidimensional compressed search algorithm. 2) It is the first algorithm that makes use of the concept of **two-dimensional periodicity**. We thus feel that both the problem and the solution techniques are novel.

The paper is organized as follows. In Section 2, we give a formal definition of the two-dimensional run-length compressed matching problem that we solve. In Section 3, we review two-dimensional periodicity as presented in [AB-92] and outline its application by describing an overview of our algorithm. In Section 4, we discuss the pattern preprocessing step of the algorithm. In Section 5 we solve the two-dimensional compressed matching problem for non-periodic patterns.

2   Two-Dimensional Run-Length Compressed Matching

The problem of *two-dimensional run-length compressed matching* is defined as follows:

Input: Two-dimensional run-length compressed text matrix T in both row compressed and column compressed forms; Compressed two-dimensional pattern matrix P.

Output: All locations in T where P occurs.

We want the running time of our algorithm to be insensitive to the size of the output, therefore we do not allow trivial patterns. A *trivial matrix* is one in which every element contains the same character. If the text and the pattern are both trivial with the same character, then the output size is $O(T)$ which is not efficient for any compression scheme. All other patterns contain a *seam*, that is, an occurence of two different, adjacent characters. Since the number of seams in the text is $O(|c(T)|)$ for run length compression, the output size is optimal.

3 Periodic Matrices and Matching

In [AB-92], periodicity in two-dimensional arrays is defined. They show that there are four classes of periodicity for rectangular arrays based on the ability of A to overlap itself without a mismatch in the overlapping elements. We give here a simplified summary of the periodicity classes which we illustrate with square arrays (figure 1). The concept generalizes to all rectangular arrays. Let $A[0..m-1, 0..m-1]$ be an $m \times m$ square *pattern* array. Consider any $\frac{m}{2} \times \frac{m}{2}$ block B of *text*. The periodicity class of A is determined by the number and arrangement of copies of A that could originate in B:

1. *Non-Periodic.* Only one copy of A can originate in B.

2. *Lattice Periodic.* Multiple copies of A can originate in B, but identical elements in the copies must lie on the *nodes of a lattice* determined by A.

3. *Line Periodic.* Multiple copies of A can originate in B, but identical elements in the copies must lie on a *single line* determined by A.

4. *Radiant Periodic.* Similar to line periodic, except that identical elements are monotonic. Identical elements are *monotic* if they can be ordered so that both the row index and the column index are non-decreasing. Intuitively, monotonic sources can form a jagged line in B.

We present below an overview of our algorithm. In the discussion that follows, the term *candidate source* or merely *source* refers to a location in the *text* that *may* correspond to the element $P[0,0]$ of an actual occurence of the pattern. A set of sources is *compatible* if for any two sources in the set, the two copies of the pattern originating at the sources overlap without any mismatches. Our use of two-dimensional periodicity will be apparent from the overview.

Algorithm Overview:

As in many pattern matching algorithms (e.g. [KMP-77, Bi-77, B-78, V-85]) our algorithm consists of a *pattern preprocessing* part and a *text scanning* part.

Pattern Preprocessing: The pattern is analyzed for periodicity as described in [AB-92]. From this analysis we obtain the period class of the pattern and a witness table which indicates compatibility of two candidate sources or the location of a mismatch in their overlap.

Text Scanning: Performed in three phases:

1) The **restriction phase** is a crude text scan in which preliminary *candidate* sources are selected.

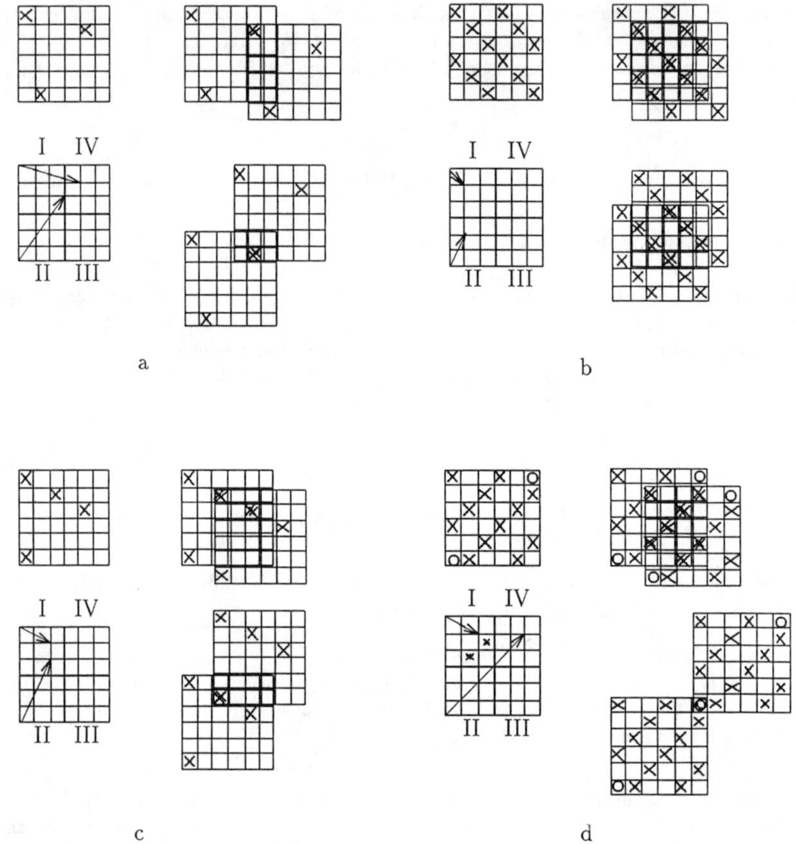

Figure 1:
Examples of the four classes of periodicity. The arrows indicate the nearest location of a
second copy of the array. a) non-periodic   b) lattice periodic   c) line periodic
d) radiant periodic – the locations of two possible non-monotonic copies
of the array are marked. Both can not appear in the text

2) The **compatibility phase**, partitions the portion of the text having candidate sources into blocks of size $\frac{m}{2} \times \frac{m}{2}$. Within each block, only compatible sources remain.

3) The **unmasking phase** is a triple scan of the text to verify which of the remaining candidates are actual occurrences of the pattern.

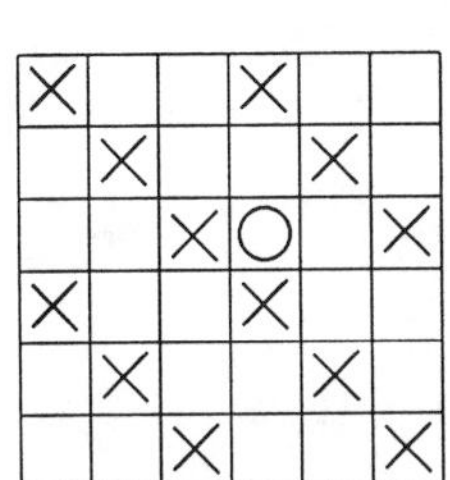 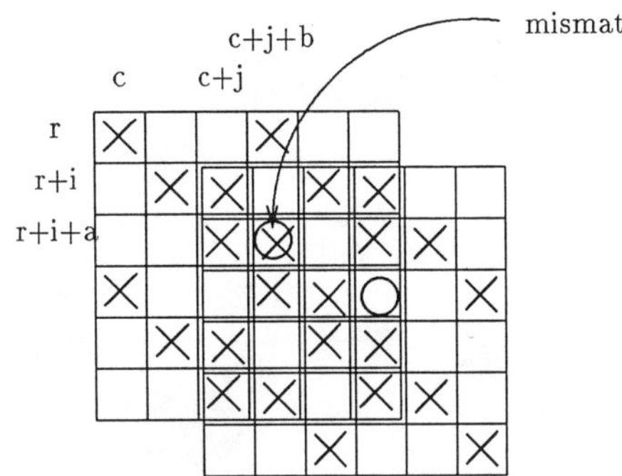

Figure 2:
The witness table gives the location of a mismatch (if one exists) for two overlapping patterns: $WITNESS[i,j] = (a,b)$

4 Pattern Preprocessing

The input to this part of our algorithm is the $m \times m$ pattern P. (For the remainder of this paper, we assume the pattern is a square array to simplify the explanation although, *our algorithm applies to any rectangular array.*)

P. Pattern Preprocessing

Step P1: Analyse pattern for periodicity

This analysis is described in detail in [AB-92]. The output of this step is 1) the pattern's periodicity class and 2) a table $WITNESS[-\frac{m}{2}\ldots\frac{m}{2}, 0\ldots\frac{m}{2}]$. $WITNESS$ indicates whether two potential sources are compatible or if not, gives a location that witnesses a mismatch in the overlap of the patterns. Specifically (figure 2), given a source S_1 at text location $T[r,c]$ and a source S_2 at text location $T[r+i,c+j]$, if $WITNESS[i,j] = (m,m)$ then the sources are compatible. Otherwise, if $WITNESS[i,j] = (a,b)$, then text location $T[r+i+a,c+j+b]$ matches at most one of pattern locations $P[a,b]$ (the pattern for S_2) or $P[i+a,j+b]$ (the pattern for S_1).

Step P2: Select a pattern characteristic seam. If no seam exists then rotate pattern and text and select a pattern characteristic seam. For every pattern row, note the closest non-stripe row below and above it

Recall that a *seam* is a row location where two adjacent characters are different. The importance of seams is that they appear explicitly in the run-length compression. A *stripe* is a row (or column) without a seam. If a pattern consists entirely of row stripes then it does not have a seam. However, then we rotate the pattern and text by 90°. Now a seam is guaranteed, otherwise all rows and all columns are stripes and the pattern is trivial. The closest stripe information is used in the unmasking phase.

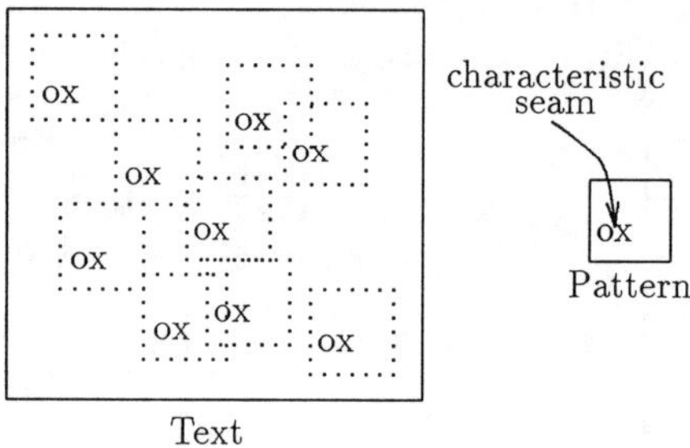

Figure 3:
Text and candidate patterns at the end of the restriction phase.

5 Text Analysis for the Non-Periodic Pattern

Our general text analysis algorithm is presented in [B-92]. For didactic reasons, we present Algorithm A, below, which finds exact occurrences of *non-periodic* patterns in the text. It is constructed in the same way as the general algorithm but does not need to handle the details of the different periodicity classes. Thus, the essentials of the algorithm are clearer to the reader. Algorithm A and the general algorithm both run in time $O(|c(T)| \log |P|)$. The input to Algorithm A is 1) The compressed representations of the text and the pattern oriented, so that the pattern has a characteristic seam, and 2) the output from the pattern preprocessing stage.

A1 The Restriction Phase

> Step A1: Scan each compressed row of the text for characteristic seams. If such a seam is found, compute the indices $T[r, c]$ of the potential source, create a candidate source with these indices and put on column list C_c.

Because there can be no more seams in the text than $|c(T)|$, this phase provides an important initial limit on the number of candidates considered in the remaining phases of the algorithm (figure 3). Each candidate is stored on a column list C_i used in the compatibility and unmasking phases, where i corresponds to the column of the text in which the candidate source occurs. The text is scanned row-by-row from left to right and top down, so that at the end of the scan, the column lists are ordered by increasing row index.

A2 The Compatibility Phase

> Step A2: For $j := 1$ to $\log m - 1$ do steps A2.1, A2.2 and A2.3.

Here we partition the text into disjoint, occupied blocks of size $\frac{m}{2} \times \frac{m}{2}$. An *occupied* block contains a candidate source. As a result of the restriction phase, the text is partitioned into occupied blocks of size 1×1 each containing one candidate source. Step A2 initially combines

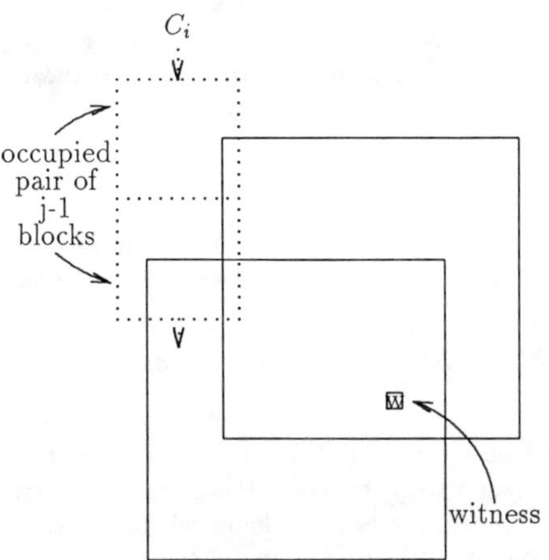

Figure 4:
Non-periodic candidates must be incompatible and thus have a witness.

vertical pairs of these blocks into blocks of size 2×1 and then combines horizontal pairs of these blocks into blocks of size 2×2. Repeating in a similar fashion for $\log m - 1$ stages, we obtain blocks of size $\frac{m}{2} \times \frac{m}{2}$. Blocks are combined vertically by scanning down one list (steps A2.1 and A2.2) and horizontally by scanning down two adjacent lists simultaneously (step A2.3). After each stage, the number of lists is reduced by half, until there are $\frac{2n}{m}$ lists at the end of this phase.

> Step A2.1: For each column list C_i, $i = 0 \ldots \frac{n}{2^{j-1}} - 1$ scan the list from the top down. If the list contains a pair of occupied blocks, look up the witness for the candidates in the WITNESS table from the pattern preprocessing step and put onto the witness list.

The two candidates are incompatible and thus have a witness since two compatible sources for non-periodic patterns can not co-exist within a block of size $\frac{m}{2} \times \frac{m}{2}$ or smaller (figure 4).

> Step A2.2: Bucket sort the witness list. Scan the text to determine the character in each witness. Rescan each list C_i and for each pair of candidates with a witness, determine which one or both of the candidates mismatches the text character and eliminate the appropriate candidate(s) from list C_i.

As the blocks are combined, we use witness locations from the pattern analysis and refer to the text to eliminate incompatible candidates. Since the text is stored in row lists due to its compressed representation, it is not possible to directly access a witness location in $O(1)$ time. So, for each stage, we first determine all the witness locations, sort them (bucket sort) and then do a complete scan of the text to determine which character is in each witness.

Step A2.3: For each pair of lists C_{2i}, C_{2i+1}, $i = 0\ldots\frac{n}{2^j} - 1$, scan down both lists simultaneously. If the lists contain two horizontally adjacent occupied blocks, find the witness for the candidates and put on a witness list. Repeat step A2.2 except the remaining candidates are linked onto a new list C_i.

A3 The Unmasking Phase

For the final phase of the algorithm, we present only an outline. Details can be found in [B-92]. In testing the candidates against the text, we employ the following main ideas:

- For each segment of the text, at most nine candidates contain the first character of the segment.

- Long segments (with length $> m$) in the text, may represent a stripe in several candidates. We will note that a stripe occurs in these candidates without actually marking each one, therefore, we will not actually know whether the stripe character matches the pattern stripe, only that a stripe occurs in the correct row of the candidate.

- Testing one candidate column against the text determines if the stripes match the expected pattern stripes.

A3.1 The Nine Blocks

For each segment S of the text, if a candidate contains the first character of S, then we test if S matches the expected segment of the candidate. If a mismatch occurs, we eliminate the candidate. Consider the first character of a text segment at location $T[r, c]$. Any candidate that overlaps this character must have its source in one of nine contiguous blocks (figure 5). Let

$$k \cdot \frac{m}{2} \leq r < (k+1) \cdot \frac{m}{2}$$

$$l \cdot \frac{m}{2} \leq c < (l+1) \cdot \frac{m}{2} \quad k, l = 0\ldots\frac{2n}{m} - 1$$

Then, the sources for candidates that can contain $T[r, c]$ are in the $\frac{m}{2} \times \frac{m}{2}$ size blocks encompassing text locations

$$T[(k-i) \cdot \frac{m}{2}\ldots(k-i+1) \cdot \frac{m}{2}, (l-j) \cdot \frac{m}{2}\ldots(l-j+1) \cdot \frac{m}{2}] \quad i, j = 0\ldots2$$

These blocks are on lists C_{l-j}. Number the blocks consecutively row-by-row from upper left. Then $T[r, c]$ occurs in block B_9. Candidates with sources in blocks $B_4 - B_6$ always overlap row r. Candidates with sources in blocks $B_1 - B_3$ and $B_7 - B_9$ may be, respectively, completely above row r or completely below row r. We move down each column list C_i as we move down the rows of the text, so there is no time penalty for finding the (possibly) nine candidates to test for each segment.

A3.2 Long Text Segments

For a long segment, if we had to mark each candidate that it passes through, the algorithm's time complexity would become $O(|c(T)|m)$ because we could mark each candidate $O(m)$ times. Instead, for each candidate, we maintain information on the next non-stripe row

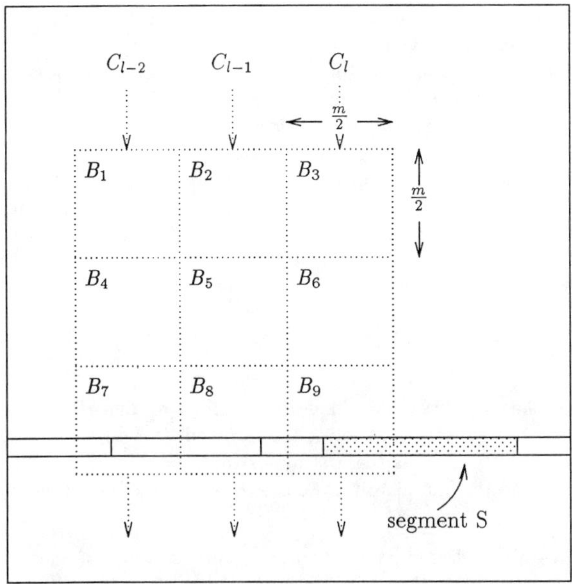

Figure 5:

The nine blocks which can contain a candidate that overlaps the first character of segment
S.

expected to be tested. If, when we actually test the next row of the candidate, we find
that the next expected non-stripe row has been skipped over, we eliminate the candidate.
We may not test the last rows of a candidate if they are covered by long segments in the
text, so, we do a final test of all the candidates to confirm that the last non-stripe row was
tested.

A3.3 Verifying the Stripes

At this point, the remaining candidates match the pattern except for the possible occurrence
of mismatched stripes. *If the pattern contains no row stripes, we are done.* Otherwise, we
do a final test using the column compressed form of the text. We scan down compressed
text column $i \cdot \frac{m}{2}$ and candidate list C_{i-1}, $i = 1 \ldots \frac{2n}{m}$ simultaneously, matching segments
as in the description of the nine blocks. For a long text column segment, we now test that
candidates it covers contain a stripe of the same character in the appropriate column. At
this point, the remaining candidates must be occurrences of the pattern. All non-stripe
rows have been tested and every stripe row is matched by a long segment of the correct
character.

Complexity of Algorithm

The pattern preprocessing requires time $O(|P| \log |\Sigma|)$ where Σ is the alphabet [AB-92].
If the alphabet size is finite, then this is just $O(|P|)$. The restriction phase requires time

$O(|c(T)|)$ since both the number of candidates and the number of lists is $O(|c(T)|)$. For the compatibility phase, each stage requires one pass through the text (size $|c(T)|$) and two passes through the lists C_i (size $O(|c(T)|)$. Sorting the witnesses is done by bucket sort in time $O(|c(T)|)$. Each stage thus requires time $O(|c(T)|)$ and the entire compatibility phase requires time $O(|c(T)| \log m) = O(|c(T)| \log |P|)$. For the unmasking phase, the time is $O(|c(T)|)$. There are $|c(T)|$ text segments and $O(|c(T)|)$ candidates. In the scan of the text rows, each segment is tested against at most 9 candidates. In the scan of the text columns, each short segment is tested against at most 3 candidates and each candidate is tested against at most one long segment. The total time for the run-length compressed matching algorithm is therefore $O(|c(T)| \log |P| + |P|)$.

6   Summary

We have described the compressed matching problem for two-dimensional run-length compression and given an algorithm that solves this problem (for all but trivial patterns) in time $O(|c(T)| \log |P| + P)$. This is the first almost optimal multidimensional compressed matching algorithm and the first algorithm to use the concept of two-dimensional periodicity.

It is our hope that this modest start will encourage further study of one and multidimensional compressed search algorithms. Such a study should find efficient search techniques for known compressions as well as stimulate the definition of interesting new compressions that enable efficient compressed search.

7   References

[AB-92] A. Amir and G. Benson, "Two-Dimensional Periodicity and its Application", *Proc. 3rd ACM-SIAM Symposium on Discrete Algorithms*, 1992.

[ALV-90] A. Amir, G.M. Landau and U. Vishkin, "Efficient Pattern Matching with Scaling", *Proc. 1st ACM-SIAM Symposium on Discrete Algorithms*, 1990, pp. 344-357.

[B-92] G. Benson, Doctoral dissertation, University of Maryland, College Park, Md., 1992.

[B-78] T.P. Baker, "A Technique For Extending Rapid Exact-Match String Matching to Arrays of More Than One Dimension", *SIAM J. Comput.*, Vol. 7, No. 4, 1978, pp. 533-541.

[Bi-77] R.S. Bird, "Two Dimensional Pattern Matching", *Information Processing Letters*, Vol. 6, No. 5, 1977, pp. 168-170.

[KMP-77] D.E. Knuth, J.H. Morris and V.R. Pratt, "Fast Pattern Matching in Strings", *SIAM J. Comp.*, Vol. 6, 1977, pp. 323-350.

[V-85] U. Vishkin, "Optimal Parallel Pattern Matching in Strings", *Information and Control*, Vol. 67, 1985, pp. 91-113.

Vector Run-length Coding of Bi-level Images

Yao Wang
Dept. of Electrical Engineering
Polytechnic University
Brooklyn, NY 11201

Jen-Ming Wu*
Dept. of Electrical Engineering
Univ. of Southern California
Los Angeles, CA 90089

Abstract —— *Run-length Coding (RC) is a simple and yet quite effective technique for bi-level image coding. A problem with the conventional RC which describes an image by alternating runs of white and black pixels is that it only exploits the redundancy within the same scan line. The Modified Relative Address Run-Length Coding (MRC) used in Group III facsimile transmission is more efficient by making use of the correlation between adjacent lines. This paper presents a vector run-length coding (VRC) technique which exploits the spatial redundancy more thoroughly by representing images with vector or block patterns and vector run-lengths. Depending on the coding method for the block patterns, various algorithms have been developed, including single run-length VRC (SVRC), double run-length VRC (DVRC), and block VRC (BVRC). The conventional RC is a special case of BVRC with block size of 1×1. The proposed methods have been applied to the CCITT standard test documents and the best result has been obtained with the BVRC method. With a block dimension of 4×4, it has yielded compression gains higher than the MRC with $k = 4$ by 15.5% and 22.7%, when using a single and multiple run-length codebooks, respectively.*

1   Introduction

Most of the current approaches for bi-level image coding employ *Run Length Coding* (RC) [1], in which the numbers of adjacent samples with the same intensity, black or white, are determined and coded, line by line. This is a simple and yet very effective technique for exploiting the one-dimensional redundancy in common bi-level images. The *Modified Relative Address Run-Length Code* (MRC) used in Group 3 facsimile

---

*The major part of the work was performed when the authors were together with Polytechnic University. All the correspondence should be addressed to the first author. This work was supported by the New York State Science and Technology Foundation as part of its Center for Advanced Technology program.

transmission [2, 3, 4] further makes use of the two dimensional correlation by specifying the *relative* run-length between two adjacent lines. The algorithms proposed here exploit the two dimensional redundancy in a more general way by coding vector or block patterns and run-lengths of column vectors, and hence the name *vector run-length coding* or VRC. In the most general version, it segments an image into separate regions, each starting with a varying block containing a set of contiguously changing columns and followed by a constant block containing vectors with the same pattern as the last one in the varying block. The varying block can contain a fixed or variable number of column vectors. The constant block is represented by its length, while the varying block can be represented in various ways. Depending on the coding method for the latter, various versions of VRC have been developed, including single run-length VRC (SVRC), double run-length VRC (DVRC), and block VRC (BVRC). These methods have different trade-offs between compression gain and complexity. The conventional RC can be considered as a special case of BVRC with block size of 1×1.

In the following, we first describe different versions of the VRC technique. We then present simulation results and compare them with the conventional RC and MRC methods. Finally, we conclude the paper by suggesting future investigations.

2 Single Run-Length VRC (SVRC)

The basic idea of VRC is to code the run-length of a vector instead of just one pixel, where a vector is composed of n samples in the same column. The SVRC algorithm segments every n scan lines of an image into separate regions, each consisting of column vectors with the same pattern. Every region is coded by a product code, a pattern codeword specifying the first vector pattern followed by a run-length codeword specifying the number of vectors having this pattern. A vector appearing only once has a run-length of zero. Note that the run-length defined here is one less than the definition in the conventional RC method in that a vector appearing only once has a run-length zero instead of one. Since only one run-length is used to describe each region, this method is called single run-length VRC (SVRC).

Usually the first few pixels of each scan line are white. We assume that this is true and start the coding of each group of n scan lines by the run-length of the all white vector. If the first vector pattern is not all white, the encoder inserts a codeword for the run-length of zero. The coder then codes the next new vector and its run-length repeatedly until the end of the scan is reached. The run-length of the last vector in the scan is replaced with an "EOL" (End of Line) symbol. This process is illustrated in Fig. 1.

To specify the vector pattern and run-length, two classes of codebooks are re-

R	V	R	V	R	⋯	⋯	⋯	⋯	⋯	⋯	R	V	R	V	E

Figure 1: Coding format of SVRC: **R**, **V** and **E** represent the codewords for run-length, vector pattern, and "EOL", respectively.

quired. Since the statistics of the run-lengths for different vectors differ, ideally, separate codebooks should be designed for the run-lengths of different vectors. To reduce implementation complexity, we can also cluster vector patterns into a few groups according to their run-length statistics and design a codebook for each group based on the joint statistics of the run-lengths within the group. Although using more codebooks can lead to a lower bit rate, a single codebook may be preferred for simplicity. Another alternative is to use two codebooks: one for the all-white pattern, and the other for the non-white patterns. This is to take advantage of the fact that various vector patterns have similar run-length characteristics, except the all white pattern, which usually has much longer run-lengths.

Let s_{ik} be the probability of the run-length k in the i-th group, $k = 0, 1, \cdots, L-1$, where L is the maximum length of a scan. Then the per pixel entropy and mean values of the run-length for the i-th group are respectively:

$$H_{r_i} = -\frac{1}{n} \sum_{k=0}^{L-1} s_{ik} \log s_{ik} \quad \text{and} \quad E_{r_i} = \sum_{k=0}^{L-1} k s_{ik} \, .$$

According to Shannon's information theory, H_{r_i} is the lower bound on the average bit rate for the run-length of the i-th group. Let p_i be the probability that a region starts with a pattern in the i-th group and I the total number of groups. Then the average bit rate for the run-length and the average run-length are:

$$H_r^I = \sum_{i=1}^{I} p_i H_{r_i} \quad \text{and} \quad E_r = \sum_{i=1}^{I} p_i E_{r_i} \, .$$

For the vector patterns, a codebook with $N_v = 2^n$ codewords is required. Let v_j be the probability of a vector run starting with the j-th pattern, the lower bound on the bit rate for the vector pattern is

$$H_v = -\frac{1}{n} \sum_{j=1}^{N_v} v_j \log v_j.$$

Since each pair of the run-length and pattern codewords describes, on an average, $n(E_r + 1)$ pixels with $n(H_r^I + H_v)$ bits, the final average bit rate (bits per pixel or bpp) of SVRC using I codebooks for the run-length is bounded by

$$R_{\text{SVRC}}^I = \frac{H_r^I + H_v}{E_r + 1} \, . \tag{1}$$

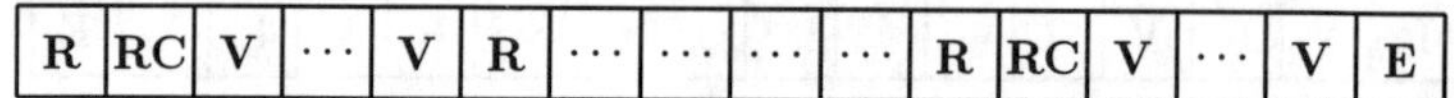

Figure 2: Coding format of DVRC: **RC** represents the changing run-length codeword.

Note that although a larger vector dimension n facilitates the exploitation of the vertical redundancy and hence the reduction of H_v, the average bit rate for the vector pattern, it also reduces the efficiency of run-length coding since E_r, the average run-length of a vector is smaller for larger vector dimensions. In addition, a larger vector dimension requires a bigger codebook and hence more memory space. Hence the dimension of the vector should be chosen appropriately to achieve a good compromise between compression gain and implementation complexity.

3   Double Run-Length VRC (DVRC)

A problem with SVRC is that it cannot represent a rapidly changing region efficiently, where the run-length of each vector is very short. In the extreme case when every new column is different from the previous one, the zero run-length codeword is repeated after each vector, which is actually redundant. Hence, it may be more appropriate to specify the changing vectors contiguously. With the double run-length VRC (DVRC) algorithm, an image is segmented into separate regions, each containing a set of contiguously changing vectors followed by non-changing vectors with the same pattern as the last one in the preceding changing region. Every such a region is specified by a codeword specifying the number of changing vectors, or the *changing run-length*, and then the codewords for all the intermediate vectors, and finally the codeword for the number of non-changing vectors, or the *non-changing run-length*. If a new vector does not change immediately, such as during the transition between two constant regions, the changing run-length is considered to be one. Again, the algorithm assumes that each scan starts with an all white vector and codes the run-length of the all white vector first. It then specifies the run-length of the following changing vectors and each intermediate vector. The run-length of the last vector in the previous changing pattern is next coded. The repeated process for each scan is illustrated in Fig. 2.

The non-changing run-length and the vector pattern can be coded as described in the last section. Either multiple codebooks or a single codebook can be used for the non-changing run-length. For the changing run-length, multiple codebooks can also be designed, each for the changing run starting from a different previous vector. Since the dependency of the changing run-length on the beginning vector pattern is not as strong as with the non-changing run-length, the gain from using multiple codebooks

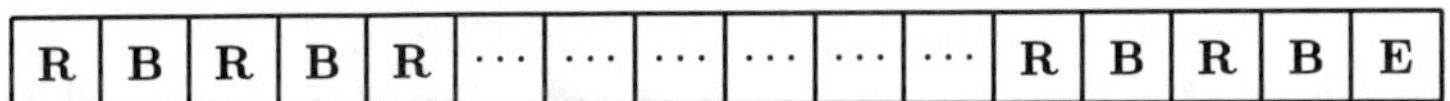

Figure 3: Coding format of BVRC: **B** represents the block pattern codeword

may not be as significant. Therefore, only the single codebook case is studied. Let t_l be the probability of the changing run-length l. Then the entropy , H_{rc}, and average length E_{rc} of the changing run-length can be determined as

$$H_{rc} = -\frac{1}{n}\sum_{l=1}^{L} t_l \log t_l \quad \text{and} \quad E_{rc} = \sum_{l=1}^{L} l\, t_l \,.$$

The entropy H_{rc} represents the lower bound on the bit rate for specifying the non-changing run-length. The final average bit rate for DVRC using I codebooks for the non-changing run-length is bounded by

$$R^I_{\text{DVRC}} = \frac{H^I_r + H_{rc} + E_{rc}H_v}{E_r + E_{rc}} \,. \tag{2}$$

Compared to SVRC, DVRC requires more memory space for storing the codebooks. In practice, for further simplification, a single codebook can be designed for the non-changing and changing run-lengths based on their joint satistics. But since the statistics of these two are very different, this simplification may reduce the compression gain substantially.

4 Block/Vector Run-Length Coding (BVRC)

With DVRC, a changing region is specified by successive vector patterns. The entropy coding of the vector patterns only makes use of the redundancies in the vertical direction. The correlation in the horizontal direction is ignored. The BVRC algorithm is a hybrid method which combines the VRC with block coding. It represents each image region by a fixed size block pattern consisting of m vectors, or a block of $n \times m$ samples, and the non-changing run-length of the last vector in the preceding block pattern. When the $(m+1)$-th vector is still different from the m-th, the run-length of the m-th vector is considered to be zero. The value of m should be close to the average length of a changing pattern in order to reduce the appearance of the zero run-length codeword. A special case of BRVC is when $m = 1$, which reduces to the previous SVRC. The coding format is shown in Fig. 3.

Similar to previous methods, either multiple codebooks or a single codebook can be used for the vector run-length. For the block patterns, a single codebook for all the

$N_b = 2^{nm}$ possible patterns is needed. Let the probability of the i-th block pattern be b_j, $j = 1, 2, \ldots, N_b$. Then the average entropy per pixel of the block patterns is

$$H_b = -\frac{1}{nm} \sum_{j=1}^{N_b} b_j \log b_j.$$

When I codebooks are used for the run-length, the average bit rate for BVRC is bounded by

$$R_{\text{BVRC}}^I = \frac{H_r^I + m\, H_b}{E_r + m}. \tag{3}$$

Compared to SVRC and DVRC, BVRC is more efficient. But it also requires more memory space for storing the codewords for block patterns.

5 Simulation Results

We have applied the VRC algorithms described in the previous sections to the eight CCITT recommended standard test documents for bi-level image coding [1]. For SVRC and DVRC, vector sizes of 4×1 and 8×1 have been simulated. For BVRC, block sizes of 4×4 and 8×4 have been considered. For SVRC and DVRC, both cases using a single and multiple codebooks for the non-changing run-length have been tested. For DVRC, separate codeboks are used for the non-changing and changing run-lengths and a single codebook is used for each. In the case of BVRC with 8×4 blocks, to limit the codebook size for the pattern, each block pattern is divided into two 4×4 blocks and these sub-blocks are coded separately using a single codebook for the 4×4 pattern. The compression ratios (compared to 1 bpp) obtained with different methods and vector/block dimensions are given in Table 1. The results are determined from the entropy estimates according to (1), (2), and (3). It can be seen that for SVRC and DVRC, vector size of 8×1 is in general better than 4×1. For BVRC, using 8×4 is slightly better than 4×4, even though the 8×4 pattern is coded as two 4×4 patterns. Note that the optimal vector/block sizes vary from images: simple images containing line drawings (such as Documents 2 and 6) ask for a larger vector or block, while complicated images full of small letters (such as Document 4) prefer a smaller size.

When using a single codebook for the non-changing run-length, DVRC gives slightly better results than SVRC. With multiple (two or N_v) codebooks, SVRC outperforms the single codebook DVRC. But it is still not as good as the BVRC using a single codebook. BVRC with N_v codebooks gives the highest compression gain. Of course, it is also most expensive in terms of memory space. Note that when the maximum run-length $L \geq 2^8$, the total codebook size for the BVRC using a 4×4

block pattern codebook and a single run-length codebook is smaller than that for the SVRC with vector dimension 8×1 and using N_v run-length codebooks. Therefore, the BVRC with block sizes 4×4 or 8×4 is overall a better scheme. For further compression gain, multiple codebooks can be used for the run-lengths in the BVRC method at expense of additional memory space.

For ease of comparison with the conventional RC and MRC, the compression ratios of these methods for the same test images are also presented in Table 1. For the RC (equivalent to BVRC with block size 1×1, the pattern need not be coded), the results obtained from using a single or two separate codebooks for the black and white runs are both given. With MRC, one dimensional RC is executed every k lines to limit transmission error propagation [2]. The error propagation effect in MRC and VRC will be similar if $k = n$. Hence for a fair comparison, we have simulated MRC with $k = 4$ and $k = 8$. For $k = 4$, the first set of results is obtained using the modified Huffman code (MHC) recommended in [2] and the result given here is copied from [5]. The second one and that using $k = 8$ are determined with actual Huffman codes (HC) designed based on the run-length statistics of individual images. In the following, the MRC method using MHC is referred to as MRC-MHC, while that using HC is called MRC-HC. The MRC-MHC requires a smaller codebook size, but is sub-optimal and requires a higher bit rate than the MRC-HC. Since our results are determined based on entropy calculation, it is more appropriate to compare with the MRC-HC algorithm. From the simulation results, we see that SVRC and DVRC methods with a single codebook is much better than RC, but not as good as MRC when $n = k$. However, the SVRC with multiple codebooks and the BVRC with a single or multiple codebooks outperform MRC by noticeable margins. A comprehensive comparison is given in Table 2. Note that the results for our methods are estimated from entropy values and the actual bit rates after Huffman coding may be slightly reduced.

6 Conclusion

A new lossless coding technique for bi-level images has been presented. It exploits the redundancy in common image signals more thoroughly than the conventional RC and MRC methods by combining vector or block coding with vector run-length coding. The potential compression gains of various versions of the VRC technique have been explored. From our simulation results, the highest compression can be obtained with the BVRC method using multiple run-length codebooks. The BVRC using a single codebook and the SVRC using multiple codebooks are inferior to the BVRC with multiple codebooks, but still outperform the RC and MRC methods. For the eight CCITT test documents, the average compression ratios obtained by the multiple codebook and single codebook BVRC with block dimension 4×4 and multiple codebook SVRC with vector dimension 4×1 are 21.4, 20.1, and 19.1, higher than the MRC-HC method with $k = 4$ by 22.7, 15.5, and 9.9 %, respectively. Although these algorithms require more memory space to store the codebooks, they can be implemented with the current VLSI technologies at a modest cost increase.

The proposed algorithms allow lossless rendition of the original images. In applications where certain degrees of distortion are accepted, the vector/block pattern can be coded by a codebook containing only typical patterns. The generalized Lloyd algorithm, also known as the LBG algorithm, for vector quantization [6] can be employed to design pattern codebooks that can minimize a given distortion criterion.

The extension of the VRC technique to dithered images will also be of great practical as well as theoretical interests. One possible approach is to make use of the run-length of a block instead of a vector. This requires further studies.

7 References

[1] A. N. Netravali and B. G. Haskell, *Digital Pictures*. Plenum Press, 1988.

[2] CCITT Recommendation, "Standardization of Facsimile Apparatus for Document Transmission," 1980. Amended 1984.

[3] H. Musmann and D. Preuss, "Comparison of Redundancy Reducing Codes for Facsimile Transmission of Documents," *IEEE Trans. Commun.*, vol. COM-25, pp. 1425–1433, Nov 1977.

[4] Y. Yasuda *et al.*, "Advances in FAX," *Proc. IEEE*, vol. 73, pp. 706–730, Nov 1985.

[5] A. K. Jain, *Fundamentals of Digital Image Processing*. Prentice Hall, 1989.

[6] R. M. Gray, "Vector Quantization," *IEEE ASSP Magazine*, vol. 1, pp. 4–29, Apr. 1984.

Acknowledgement

The authors are grateful to Dr. D. Duttweiler of AT&T Bell Laboratories, Holmdel, for providing the CCITT test images used in the simulations.

Table 1: Compression Ratios for CCITT Standard Test Documents

Methods	Doc.1	Doc.2	Doc.3	Doc.4	Doc.5	Doc.6	Doc.7	Doc.8	Ave.
RC									
One codebook	18.79	22.92	10.31	5.65	9.28	14.33	5.26	11.93	12.30
Two codebook	20.63	25.87	11.46	5.99	10.28	16.47	5.81	13.32	13.73
MRC									
k=4 (MHC)	19.77	26.12	12.58	6.27	11.63	18.18	6.30	15.55	14.55
k=4 (HC)	23.35	33.70	14.49	6.71	12.92	22.17	6.56	19.34	17.40
k=8 (HC)	24.97	38.17	15.81	6.99	14.09	24.95	6.91	21.90	19.22
BVRC ($I = N_v$)									
4x4	28.23	41.49	17.83	7.83	15.66	28.31	8.11	23.34	21.35
8x4	27.64	43.47	18.00	7.42	15.69	30.10	8.04	25.29	21.96
BVRC ($I = 1$)									
4x4	26.67	39.12	16.83	7.36	14.67	26.46	7.61	21.99	20.09
8x4	26.45	41.16	17.18	7.10	14.97	28.47	7.68	23.94	20.87
SVRC ($I = N_v$)									
4x1	24.57	39.33	15.70	6.49	13.60	25.33	6.92	21.03	19.12
8x1	24.48	41.79	16.70	6.34	14.17	28.23	6.93	22.94	20.20
SVRC ($I = 2$)									
4x1	22.86	35.15	14.70	6.22	12.76	23.08	6.59	19.63	17.62
8x1	23.39	38.82	15.97	6.17	13.59	26.43	6.75	21.88	19.12
SVRC ($I = 1$)									
4x1	22.19	33.77	14.02	5.94	12.21	21.89	6.34	18.13	16.81
8x1	22.96	37.62	15.52	6.01	13.25	25.45	6.52	20.75	18.51
DVRC ($I = 1$)									
4x1	22.73	34.83	14.27	6.02	12.40	22.40	6.40	18.62	17.21
8x1	23.23	38.27	15.67	6.04	13.35	25.80	6.56	21.04	18.75

Table 2: Compression Gain of VRC over RC and MRC †

	1-D Runlength Coding (RC)		Modified READ Code (MRC)		
	One Codebook	Two Codebook	k=4(MHC)	k=4 (HC)	k=8 (HC)
BVRC ($I = N_v$)					
4x4	73.57%	55.26%	46.73%	22.69%	–
8x4	78.51%	59.91%	–	–	14.24%
BVRC ($I = 1$)					
4x4	63.33%	46.32%	38.08%	15.46%	–
8x4	69.67%	52.00%	–	–	8.58%
SVRC($I = N_v$)					
4x1	55.44%	39.25%	31.41%	9.89%	–
8x1	64.23%	47.12%	–	–	5.10%
SVRC($I = 2$)					
4x1	43.25%	28.33%	21.10%	1.26%	–
8x1	55.45%	39.26%	–	–	-0.52%
SVRC ($I = 1$)					
4x1	36.67%	22.43%	15.53%	-3.39%	–
8x1	50.49%	34.81%	–	–	-3.69%
DVRC ($I = 1$)					
4x1	39.92%	25.35%	18.28%	-1.09%	–
8x1	52.43%	36.56%	–	–	-2.45%

† The gain value in each entry is determined according to $(Y - X)/X * 100\%$, where Y and X represent the average compression gains of the methods in the corresponding row and column, respectively.

is at most $nL/2$, so the number of phases in the first superphase is at most L.

The same reasoning holds for all superphases. The number of superphases needed to reduce the number of remaining pixels from n to p is $\lg(n/p)$, so the number of phases needed is just $L\lg(n/p)$. Once p or fewer pixels remain, we fall back to bit-transpose coding, which may require L late phases, so the total number of phases needed is at most $L\lg(2n/p)$.

We defer the probabilistic analysis of the expected number of reallocations required to the full version of the paper. In various scenarios we can show that the number of early phases is small with high probability.

2.5 Parallel Huffman coding in practice

We have simulated parallel Huffman compression for a set of 21 Landsat Thematic Mapper 8-bit grayscale images; the images are described in [5]. We simulate only the last level of coding ($n = 131{,}072$ pixels) for each image, using $p = 4{,}096$ processors. For our test images, the number of early phases is at most 7, the average being 5.6. It usually happens, however, that the remaining code lengths take on many of the possible possible values, so the number of late phases is large. The average value of L in the simulations is 23.7, and the average number of late phases is 13.7.

To improve compression time, we must reduce the number of phases. Using the variability index technique described in Section 4.2, we can more evenly balance the output bits among the processors. The result is a reduction in the number of early phases for most of the images; a few stayed the same. The average falls to 4.6. The number of late phases is essentially unaffected.

By reducing L, the length of the longest code, we can reduce the number of late phases. We can do this by substituting a special IGNORE code for the codes of pixels longer than a certain threshold θ. These *long pixels* must then be transmitted separately. There are not very many of them and their code lengths are long, so we lose very little compression efficiency by sending them unencoded at the end of the level; this is easy to do in parallel after a prefix operation to assign long pixels to processors. The IGNORE code itself can be of length θ. In simulations with $\theta = 10$ using the variability index technique, the average number of late phases falls to 9.1. The average loss in compression is only 196 bytes.

We can further reduce the number of early phases by performing local reallocations. Instead of using time $2\lceil \lg p_t \rceil$ to reallocate all untouched pixels when one processor completes its pixels, we can arrange local exchanges between neighboring processors, thus lengthening the time between full reallocations.

3 Parallel Quasi-Arithmetic Coding

Huffman coding is nearly optimal in that it produces an average code length close to the entropy of the source model used for coding. Its suboptimality can be appreciable, however, whenever one input event has a probability near 1. In image compression, this happens when the variance of the Laplace distribution describing model is small, in which case the zero-error event has high probability. For example, when the variance of a Laplace distribution is less than 1.04, the probability of a zero error is more than 0.5; when the variance is less than 0.26, the probability of a zero error is more than 0.75.

When Huffman coding is inadequate, we can turn to arithmetic coding. Arithmetic coding can theoretically achieve exactly optimal compression for a given source model when it is implemented using exact (slow) arithmetic. Practical implementations of arithmetic coding use fixed precision arithmetic [4,9], but they still run slowly because of the multiplications (and sometimes divisions) required. Recent research has focused on approximations to the arithmetic that reduce the time required without sacrificing much coding efficiency. Work by Rissanen and Mohiuddin [8] and Chevion *et al.* [1] has involved approximate multiplication. In [6] we present complete details of an alternative practical approach using table lookups, which we call *quasi-arithmetic coding*. We review quasi-arithmetic coding in Section 3.1. Quasi-arithmetic coding can be viewed as a generalization of Huffman coding, so the extension of the algorithm in Section 2.3 is natural.

3.1 Quasi-arithmetic coding

In arithmetic coding we code a sequence of input events by identifying each possible sequence with a subinterval of the real line, then selecting the interval corresponding to the actual input. Quasi-arithmetic coding is based on the observation that the intermediate intervals computed by the coder can be thought of as states of the coder. A full precision arithmetic coder has an infinite number of possible states; practical coders use a large finite number of states. By limiting the number of possible states, we can obtain a coder small enough that it can be represented in lookup tables; the only arithmetic involved is in precomputing the tables. A one-state coder corresponds to Huffman coding. As we increase the number of states, we increase the precision of the coder and hence its efficiency. Using just a few states often provides efficiency considerably greater than that of Huffman coding. Quasi-arithmetic codes, like arithmetic codes, are not instantaneous codes; nevertheless, they are uniquely decodable with bounded coding delay.

Constructing a quasi-arithmetic code for a multi-symbol alphabet is a three-step process.

1. We design a multi-state code table for a two-symbol alphabet with various possible symbol probabilities.

2. We decompose the multi-symbol alphabet into a binary tree with the alphabet symbols at the leaves, such that the product of the edge probabilities from the root to each leaf approximately equals the corresponding symbol probability.

3. We follow all paths through the tree of Step 2, using the table from Step 1 to compute an output codeword and next state for each alphabet symbol from each possible starting state.

Example 1: We construct a two-state code for the three-symbol alphabet $\{A, B, C\}$, with $p_A = 0.7$, $p_B = 0.2$, and $p_C = 0.1$. First we construct a two-state binary code. In this example we use a very simple binary code, in which we merely distinguish the input symbols as more or less probable; a more complete two-state code would also allow the two probabilities to be approximately equal. We indicate the more probable symbol by MPS and the less probable symbol by LPS; the probability of MPS can be taken to be about 0.71.

	From state S_0		From state S_1	
Input	Output	Next state	Output	Next state
MPS	-	S_1	1	S_0
LPS	00	S_0	01	S_0

Next we construct a binary tree with each branch labeled either MPS or LPS, the probability of MPS being 0.71.

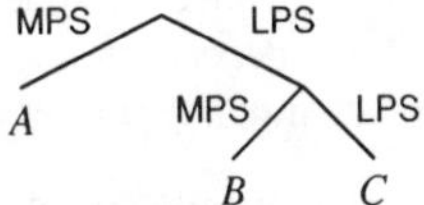

We then use the tree and the table to derive the following code.

	From state S_0		From state S_1	
Input	Output	Next state	Output	Next state
A	-	S_1	1	S_0
B	00	S_1	01	S_1
C	0000	S_0	0100	S_0

Note that this code is uniquely decodable even though it does not have the prefix property. For example, from state S_0, the code for B (**00**) is a prefix of the code for C (**0000**); but a B input leads to state S_1, and the first two bits output from state S_1 are never **00**; hence from state S_0, a B will not be decoded as a C.

The asymptotic average code length for this code is 1.171 bits per symbol. The entropy of the source is 1.157 bits per symbol, so we obtain 98.8 percent efficiency[4], or a compression loss[5] of about 0.05 dB. The Huffman code for this source has an average code length of 1.3 bits per symbol; its efficiency is only 89.0 percent, and the compression loss is 0.51 dB, almost 10 times as large. In this example we used a two-state code; using more states usually gives even more efficiency. □

Note that the two-symbol code is used only for constructing the multi-symbol code. The multi-symbol code tables and coding algorithm are similar to the Huffman tables and algorithm, but with added state information. In MLP we would precompute the set of Laplace distributions, then precompute a quasi-arithmetic code for each of them.

---

[4]*Compression efficiency* as defined in [8] equals optimal average code length (i.e., entropy) divided by actual average code length.

[5]*Compression loss* is introduced in [3]; it equals $-10\log_{10}$(efficiency) and is expressed in decibels (dB). For small losses the compression loss is about $4.3 \times (1 - \text{efficiency})$.

3.2   Parallel algorithm

We can apply the reallocation coding protocol of Section 2.3 directly to quasi-arithmetic coding. The only complication arises when the last pixel of a processor's allocation leaves the processor in a state other than the starting state. We deal with this by providing each processor with one additional "event," to be encoded after the last allocated pixel has been encoded. This event is designed to force the processor back to the starting state by the output of a small number of bits. (Often just one bit is required.)

Example 2: If we were using the three-symbol code in Example 1, and if the last symbol to be output by a processor (starting in state S_0) were B, we would output **00**; then we would have to force the processor back to state S_0. This can be done by outputting **1** or **01**; of course we would choose the shorter string. Without the extra bit, the decoder would not know whether the last symbol was B or C, since the codes for both of them begin with **00**. After reading the **1** and decoding B, the decoder would know that the processor had no more data to encode, so it would not attempt any further decoding.   □

In effect, we have a number of arithmetically coded output streams; we have to solve the end-of-file problem for each of them. It is not difficult, merely a nuisance.[6]

The algorithm for parallel quasi-arithmetic coding is as follows:

1. We assign each pixel to a processor, assigning the same number of pixels to each processor. The pixels may be assigned randomly or, even better, we may attempt to give each processor approximately the same number of bits to output, as discussed in Section 4.2.

2. Each processor proceeds sequentially through its assigned pixels, writing one bit to a preassigned location at each time step. If a pixel completes all its assigned pixels, and it is in the starting state, it writes **1** to the completion register. If a completing processor is not in the starting state, it begins the finishing-up procedure described above. After finishing up, it writes **1** to the completion register (unless a reallocation has taken place, giving the processor more pixels to work on).

3. When the completion register becomes **1**, processing is interrupted for pixel reallocation. Pixels currently being processed remain with their current processor. The untouched pixels are divided among all the processors. Processors that have begun but not completed the finishing-up procedure must complete the procedure.

4. If a reallocation leaves any processors with no pixels and no finishing up to do, those processors are deactivated. We perform a prefix operation on the remaining pixels to determine the location of each processor's next output bit.

After reallocation, we return to Step 2, and repeat until no pixels of the current level remain.

---

[6]A simpler solution, reverting to a Huffman code for the last pixel of a processor's allocation, does not work: toward the end of processing, a pixel with a long code may *become* a processor's last pixel through reallocation, even though it was not the last when the processor began working on it. This happened to pixel 10 in the example of Figure 1.

4 Parallel Prediction and Error Modeling

In order to code images using the MLP algorithm, we must predict the value of each pixel and model the error of our prediction. Both of these steps can be parallelized.

4.1 Prediction

The prediction step for a pixel involves computing a linear combination of the values of a fixed constellation of nearby pixels whose values are already known. Clearly the encoder, having access to all pixel intensities at the beginning of the computation, can predict all values simultaneously; the decoder can make the same predictions, but only level-by-level, since the predictions depend on values from preceding levels.

4.2 Modeling

Error modeling is most effective when done implicitly. In [5] we give an implicit method for estimating local image variances that leads to better compression than any other published lossless image compression method. Our method involves computing an index number, called the *variability index*, for each pixel, sorting the pixels by variability index, then using the same error model (i.e., Laplace distribution variance) to encode all pixels with similar variability index. Like the intensity prediction, the variability index computation depends only on the values of a few nearby pixels, known from a previous level, so it can be done in parallel by both encoder and decoder with no loss of efficiency. The assignment of variances to values of the variability index can be done implicitly in a sequential environment, adaptively estimating the variance while working through the pixels in order of variability index. For parallel coding the use of side information is more appropriate: we can group the pixels after sorting (sorting can be done efficiently in parallel), then compute the variance of each group and transmit it in coded form. Each variance requires only a few bits to transmit, typically four or fewer; if we divide each level of n pixels into $\sqrt{n}$ groups, only about $(\sqrt{2}+1)m$ variances must be transmitted for an $m \times m$ image. For a 512×512 image this amounts to 1236 variances, or only 618 bytes of side information.

The variability index technique has the effect of classifying pixels by local variance. This translates roughly into a classification by code length, since distributions with larger variances usually have larger average code length. Using this classification we can assign pixels to processors in a way that divides the *code length* (not just the number of pixels) approximately evenly among the processors, thus reducing the number of pixel reallocations needed. The simulation results described in Section 2.5 confirm the usefulness of this technique.

5 Conclusions

We have shown that efficient parallel lossless encoding and decoding of images is feasible, using either Huffman coding or, more surprisingly, a version of arithmetic coding; we have presented algorithms and analysis. Current work involves a more detailed analysis, including the time needed to route pixels to processors during reallocation and the time needed to look up code words. Our algorithm uses randomization to limit the number of reallocations, but the variability index technique provides sufficient balancing of output bits to obviate randomization. Our current plans are to implement the algorithm on a Connection Machine (CM–2) and report experimental timings in the final version of the paper.

We note that although we have presented our algorithms in terms of image compression, the ideas extend to any compression problem in which the model needed to encode each event is fixed ahead of time.

References

[1] D. Chevion, E. D. Karnin, and E. Walach, "High Efficiency, Multiplication Free Approximation of Arithmetic Coding," in *Proc. Data Compression Conference*, J. A. Storer and J. H. Reif, eds., Snowbird, Utah, Apr. 8–11, 1991, 43–52.

[2] R. W. Hamming, *Coding and Information Theory*, Prentice-Hall, Englewood Cliffs, NJ, 1980.

[3] P. G. Howard and J. S. Vitter, "New Methods for Lossless Image Compression Using Arithmetic Coding," in *Proc. Data Compression Conference*, J. A. Storer and J. H. Reif, eds., Snowbird, Utah, Apr. 8–11, 1991, 257–266, also to appear as an invited paper in the special issue on data compression in *Journal of Information Processing and Management*, also appears as Brown University Technical Report CS–91–47 .

[4] P. G. Howard and J. S. Vitter, "Analysis of Arithmetic Coding for Data Compression," in *Proc. Data Compression Conference*, J. A. Storer and J. H. Reif, eds., Snowbird, Utah, Apr. 8–11, 1991, 3–12, invited paper, also appears as Brown University Technical Report CS–91–03.

[5] P. G. Howard and J. S. Vitter, "Error Modeling for Hierarchical Lossless Image Compression," IEEE Data Compression Conference, Snowbird, Utah, Mar. 1992.

[6] P. G. Howard and J. S. Vitter, "Practical Implementations of Arithmetic Coding," Proc. International Conference on Advances in Communication and Control (COMCON 3), Victoria, British Columbia, Canada, Oct. 16–18, 1991, also to appear in *Data Compresion*, J. A. Storer, ed., also appears as Brown University Technical Report CS–91–45.

[7] D. A. Huffman, "A Method for the Construction of Minimum Redundancy Codes," *Proceedings of the Institute of Radio Engineers* 40 (1952), 1098–1101.

[8] J. J. Rissanen and K. M. Mohiuddin, "A Multiplication-Free Multialphabet Arithmetic Code," *IEEE Trans. Comm.* 37 (Feb. 1989), 93–98.

[9] I. H. Witten, R. M. Neal, and J. G. Cleary, "Arithmetic Coding for Data Compression," *Comm. ACM* 30 (June 1987), 520–540.

COMPRESSION OF GREY-SCALE FINGERPRINT IMAGES

Tom Hopper
Federal Bureau of
Investigation
10th & Pennsylvania Ave NW
Washington DC 20537

Fred Preston
United Kingdom Home Office
Science and Technology Group
Horseferry House
Dean Ryle Street
London SW1P 2AW England

I   Background

The FBI is pursuing a strategic plan to improve the
essential identification services provided to the law
enforcement community. In essence the plan focuses on the
development and implementation of an integrated automated
system which will incorporate an Automated Fingerprint
Identification System (AFIS). An essential part of this
plan involves the conversion of the data base of
fingerprints, held largely as inked impressions on card, to
electronic images.

Currently the FBI maintains about 25 million criminal
records with fingerprints. The image capture will follow a
standard being established in cooperation with vendor and
user communities and the National Institute of Standards
and Technology (NIST). Fingerprint images will be captured
at 500 pixels per inch at 256 levels of grey (8 bits). The
area containing finger impressions to be captured is a
little over 39 square inches. This amounts to about 9.8 M
bytes of image data per fingerprint card. The total for 25
million cards is 245 T bytes of data, uncompressed.

Ridges are not necessarily continuous across the impression
but suffer interruptions - ridge endings or bifurcations
(also referred to as forks). Collectively these
interruptions are known as minutiae. The definitive
information used to determine that one fingerprint matches
another is in the fine detail of the ridges - the minutiae
and their relationships. For the fingerprint application
it is essential that the fidelity of the ridge detail is
retained in compression and subsequent decompression.

Once captured the images will be required by two "types of
user". They will be used as source images for the
automatic process where they will be submitted to pattern
recognition algorithms and they are required by fingerprint
experts for verification. A compression technique must
therefore support both of these uses.

Early in the research work the discrete cosine transform
based compression technique defined by the Joint
Photographic Experts Group (JPEG) was investigated. It

soon became apparent that advantages could be gained by
using other techniques. A program was therefore
established to research appropriate techniques and
investigate their validity to the fingerprint application.

II. Evaluation Algorithms

Test implementations include:

- ISO/CCITT JPEG (baseline) - Cosine transform
  based developed by the Joint Photographic Experts
  Group.

- Local Cosine Transform (LCT) - Cosine transform
  based with adjustments to minimize tiling
  artifacts. Developed at Yale University.

- Best Basis (BBW) - Adaptive wavelet transform
  plus uniform quantization. Developed at Yale
  University.

- Wavelet Vector Quantization (WVQ) - Wavelet
  transform plus vector quantization. Developed at
  Los Alamos National Laboratory.

- Wavelet Scaler Quantization (WSQ) - Wavelet
  transform plus scaler quantization. Developed at
  the FBI as the simplest possible wavelet
  algorithm. Originally intended as a baseline for
  comparison to the more complex algorithms.

III. Components of a compression algorithm

In this section each of the algorithms are viewed from a
multifrequency or subband decomposition perspective. This
approach is particularly effective in identifying
similarities between the algorithms. The general strategy
with subband decomposition is to divide the input image
into two or more frequency bands and then quantize and code
the bands separately.

The three wavelet algorithms use lowpass and highpass
filters, based on the Discrete Wavelet Transform (DWT), to
split the original image into subbands. The subbands are
then subsampled by 2 which doubles the scale while the
filter halves the resolution. Thus the decomposition is
often referred to as multiscale rather then multifrequency
[RIO91].

<u>Wavelet Selection</u> Wavelets are a large class of functions
and the success of the compression algorithm depends, in
part, on selecting the right one. Grey-scale fingerprint
images have soft edges and are best modeled with a smooth
wavelet. The length of the wavelet is also a consideration

since, among other things, it affects the speed of the compression software and image quality.

An indication of the relative importance of wavelet selection is shown in Figure 2. The two algorithms labeled Fixed Basis Wavelet only differed in the wavelet used. The difference is small but it is uniform across all compression levels. Note that the root mean square error (RMSE) of the reconstructed image does not track with visual measures of image quality, but it can provide insight into the relative merits of various approaches.

<u>Number of Subbands</u> The three wavelet algorithms have totally different strategies in subband decomposition. The BBW uses an optimization approach that continues to split and re-split the subbands until it concentrates the maximum energy/information into the fewest coefficients [WIC89]. The subband decomposition is different for each image and usually exceeds 2,000 subbands. The result is the 'best' decomposition in terms of energy concentration for each image.

The WVQ algorithm uses a 13 subband decomposition which blends well with vector quantization [BRA90]. The focus here is on efficient quantization rather then energy concentration.

The decomposition used in the final wavelet approach, WSQ, is in between the other two. It uses 67 bands (Fig. 3) selected to give good energy concentration and perceptually optimized for fingerprints. This level of decomposition is efficiently implemented and de-correlates the coefficients enough to use scaler quantization.

<u>Quantization</u> Quantization usually involves removing detail from the image. The exact quantization procedure is normally dictated by the design decisions that are made in the above areas. A common approach is to concentrate losses in certain frequency bands. For example, one could try to preserve the frequencies corresponding to ridges and pores while quantizing the other bands more aggressively. WSQ, LCT and JPEG all use this approach, sometimes called error shaping.

The WVQ algorithm uses vector quantization, a procedure which treats coefficients in small groups or cells rather than one at a time [BRA90]. This approach produces efficient quantization but has additional CPU costs.

<u>Entropy Coding</u> All the test implementations use LZW [WIL91] type compression except JPEG and WVQ which use Huffman Coding. It is envisioned that the algorithm chosen for operational use will be converted to Huffman coding if required.

IV. Preliminary Findings

Candidate algorithms are undergoing formal evaluation to determine their performance in all phases of fingerprint identification. In preparation for this evaluation several ad hoc tests were conducted. The following observations are based on this preliminary experience and summarized in the table below.

<u>Feature Detection</u> Traditionally, minutiae detection and related processing have taken place before compression and storage in an image data base. In the new environment being developed compression will normally come first and must support current and future feature detection methodologies. A small study was conducted to get a preliminary assessment of how the various algorithms affected minutiae detection. Images from JPEG, BBW and WSQ, at two levels of compression, were run through the encoder stage of the Home Office matcher [MIL83]. Within the study, JPEG compression always decreased the number of correctly detected minutiae while WSQ always increased the same total. Study results are contained in Fig. 4. Further AFIS performance evaluation is planned.

An additional requirement in this area is support for emerging technology in pattern recognition. Advances in pattern recognition techniques may soon have application in automated classification and identification. Since this area is still developing it is difficult to specify the requirements precisely. However, recent reviews [CRA91] and [RIO91] indicate that multiscale approaches, such as the wavelet transform, seem promising.

<u>Image Quality</u> The JPEG algorithm produces significant tiling at both 15:1 and 20:1 compression. The LCT algorithm avoids the sharp edges with its localization technique but still demonstrates some distortion at 20:1.

The three wavelet algorithms all produce a good quality image at 20:1, however they each have their own character. The WSQ algorithm accurately preserves ridge structure and excels in its ability to retain pores and islands (Figures 5 and 6). This is consistent with results reported by Rompelman [WOO91] where scalar quantization of the subband elements produced results comparable to more complex approaches.

Algorithm Characteristics

	JPEG	LCT	BBW	WVQ	WSQ
Transform	cosine	cosine center weighted	D6 wavelet	BO wavelet	BO wavelet
Subbands	64 per tile	256 per tile	adaptive > 1,000	13	67
Quantization	by frequency within tiles	by frequency within tiles	uniform	vector quantization by frequency subband	by frequency subbands
Image quality at 20:1 compression	low	medium	high	high	high
CPU requirements Compress - Decompress -	1:06 1:04	0:41 0:41	3:27 0:43	0:41 0:56	0:50 0:39
Feature detection compatibility	low	medium	high multi-scale	high multi-scale linear phase	high multi-scale linear phase
Support for progressive transmission	complex	-	direct	direct	direct

REFERENCES

[ANT90] M. Antonini, M. Barlaud, P. Mathieu and I. Daubechies, "Image Coding Using Vector Quantization in the Wavelet Transform Domain", in Proc. 1990 IEEE Int. Conf. Acoust., Speech, Signal Proc., Albuquerque, NM. Apr. 3-6, 1990.

[BRA90] J.N. Bradley, C.M. Brislawn, "Image Compression by Vector Quantization of Wavelet Coefficients", preprint Los Alamos National Laboratory, 1991.

[COI90] R.R. Coifman, Y. Meyer, S. Quake, M.V. Wickerhauser, "Signal Processing and Compression With Wavelrt Packets", 5 April 1990, preprint Yale University.

[CRA91] C. Crawford, E. Mjolsness, "Automated Fingerprint Identification", September 1991, report from Yale University and U.S. Naval Academy

[DAU88] I. Daubechies, "Orthonormal Bases of Compactly Supported Wavelets", Comm. Pure Appl. Math. 41 (1988) 909-996.

[MIL83] K. Millard, "Developments on Automatic Fingerprint Recognition", 1983 International Carnahan Conference on Security Technology, pp.173-178, 4 October 1983.

[RAB91] M. Rabbani, P.W. Jones, "Digital Image Compression Techniques", SPIE Press, 1991

[RIO91] O. Rioul and M. Vetterli, "Wavelets and Signal Processing", IEEE SP Mag. (Oct 1991) pp. 14-38.

[WIC89] M.V. Wickerhauser, "Acoustic Signal Compression with Wavelet Packets", preprint Yale University, 1989.

[WIL91] R.N. Williams, "Adaptive Data Compression", Kluwer Academic Publishers, 1991.

[WOO91] J.W. Woods, "Subband Image Coding", Kluwer Academic Publishers, 1991.

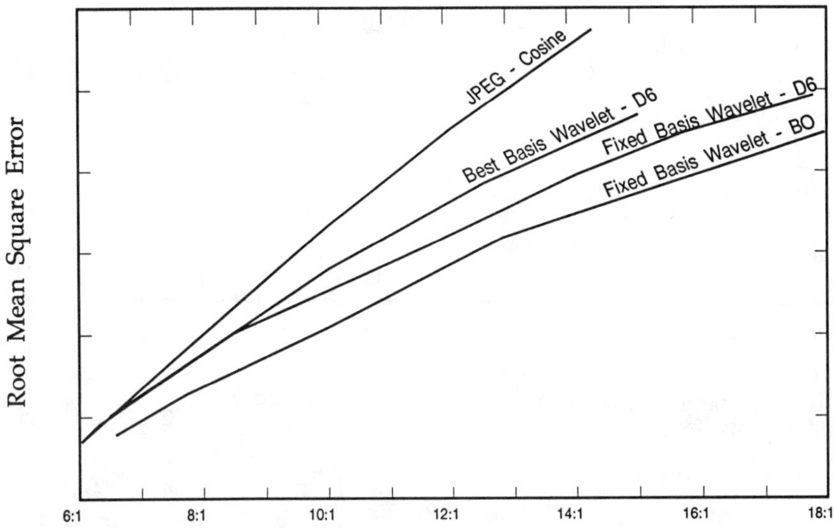

Fig. 2. Comparative RMSE Curves

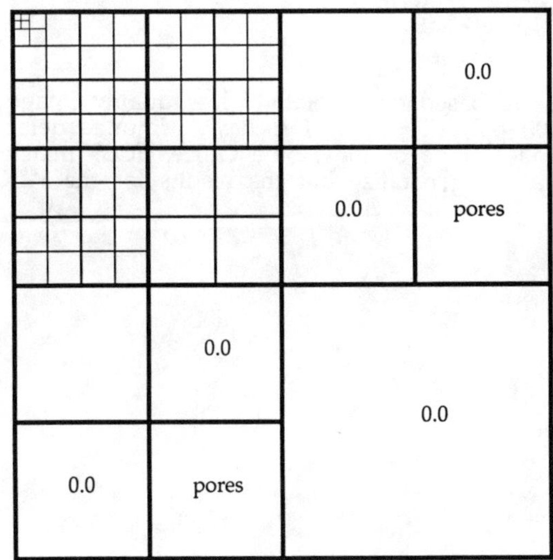

Fig 3. Subband Decomposition

Numbers of minutiae	15:1			20:1		
	JPEG	WSQ	BBW	JPEG	WSQ	BBW
Correctly detected in original and compressed	72	72	69	67	73	68
Correctly detected only in original	8	8	11	13	7	12
Correctly detected only in compressed	6	10	9	10	11	11
Change with compression	-2	+2	-2	-3	+4	-1
Missed in both original and compressed	25	21	22	21	20	20
Total false detected in original	41	41	41	41	41	41
Total false detected in compressed	34	16	30	30	29	22
Change with compression	-7	-25	-11	-11	-12	-19

These results are based on a relativly low quality image (Fig. 17) scanned at 500 ppi, 1.54 by 1.54 inches. Minutiae detection counts are from the encoder stage of the Home Office HO39 matcher. The sample size is to small to generalize but the results for the WSQ algorithm are encouraging.

Fig. 4.   Minutiae Detection

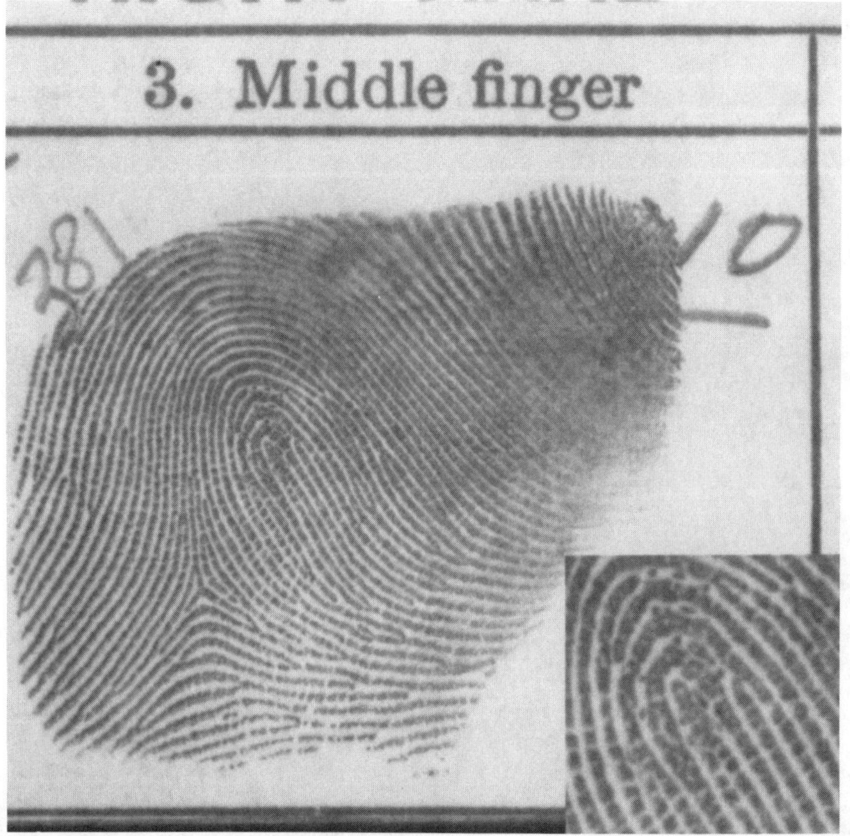

Fig. 5. Original image

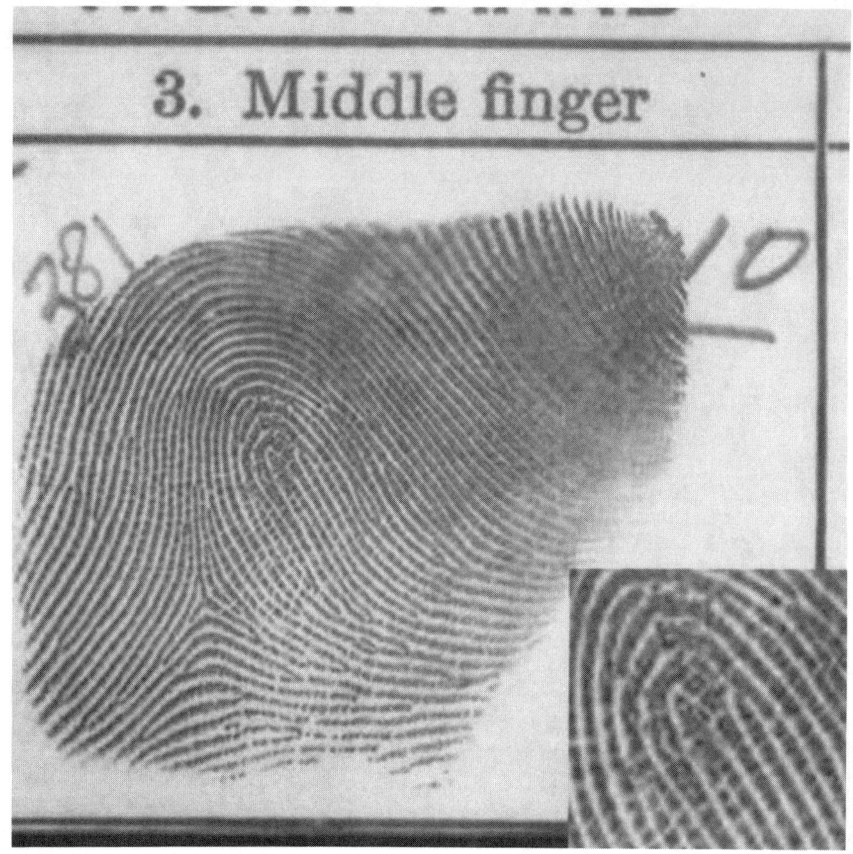

Fig. 6. WSQ compression at 20:1

Variable Precision Representation
for Efficient VQ Codebook Storage

Raffi Dionysian and Miloš D. Ercegovac

Computer Science Department

University of California, Los Angeles

Los Angeles, CA 90024

Abstract

In Vector Quantization (VQ) with fast search techniques, the storage available limits the number of codevectors used in VQ. Variable Precision Representation (VPR) is a simple codebook compression scheme. VPR for each vector $\mathbf{y}$ stores the number $e(\mathbf{y})$, the number of leading bits which are zero in all elements, and avoids storing those leading bits.

When storing the difference of codevectors in a binary tree structured VQ codebook, VPR can save from 24% to 44% in storage. Storing the codevector difference removes the redundancy between similar codevectors. Also as the mean square error of the VQ encoder is lowered, on the average, the difference becomes smaller and yields to better compression.

To process vectors in VPR format, the operator uses a bit-serial, element-parallel scheme to evaluate the inner product. The operator's throughput can be increased by replicating its core.

1   Introduction

In this paper we present a scheme for reducing the storage required for implementation of Vector Quantization (VQ). VQ is a promising method for data compression. For example, it is used in compressing video: the images are broken into blocks of K pixels (*source vectors*), $\mathbf{x}$; the encoder compares each with C potential replacements (*codevectors*) $\hat{\mathbf{x}}^c$, $c = 1, \cdots, C$, prestored in a *codebook*; it transmits the index c of the best matching (least distorting) codevector to the receiver. In decompression, the index is the mean to approximate $\mathbf{x}$ using $\hat{\mathbf{x}}^c$ from an identical codebook. Survey papers by Nasrabadi *et. al.* [NK88], and Makhoul *et. al.* [MRG85] discuss a variety of VQ codebook building techniques.

In real-time VQ of video and speech with large codebooks, typically exhaustive search of the replacement vector $\hat{\mathbf{x}}^c$ is computationally prohibitive. A variety of codebook structures [NK88], [MRG85] have been devised to reduce the search time at some nominal increase in additional storage. An example is Tree Structured VQ (TSVQ) which uses a tree structure to search C codevectors in $O(\log(C))$ time. TSVQ, however, typically stores up to twice as many codevectors. It needs to store the codevectors on the tree branches, in addition to storing the leaves $\mathbf{x}^c$, $c = 1, \cdots, C$. If the leaf codevectors are used only in encoding, binary TSVQ can avoid the increase in the number of vectors stored. In binary TSVQ, in every tree branch, the two mean square error evaluations can be replaced with an inner product with the vector normal to the plane separating the two leaves [DH73]. This reduces the storage and computation.

Storage of codevectors in vector quantization is large and costly. This is more significant with schemes such as Pruned TSVQ (PTSVQ) [CLG88], where the search time is computationally feasible. Larger codebooks are known to decrease the distortion in VQ. With better codebook storage, larger codebooks can fit in a given amount of memory.

Source coding schemes [JN84] themselves can be used for compressing codebook. In speech coding, μ-law coding [JN84] has been used for speech samples which compresses 12-bit samples to 8-bit μ-law coded numbers. We, however, focus on lossless coding which can apply to both speech and video, and does not increase the distortion in VQ.

We note the inherent property of codevectors: *the difference between two neighboring codevectors is small.* By encoding the difference between codevectors, the redundancy between codevectors is removed, lowering the entropy. Even a simple scheme of coding the difference can provide significant compression.

For storing codevector difference, Variable Precision Representation (VPR) is an effective vector compression scheme. As a source coding scheme, VPR chooses from one of several codes based on the max(.) or $L_\infty(.)$ of the vector. For each vector, VPR chooses the precision based on number of bits the largest element in magnitude requires. For many vectors, all the vector elements are small enough not to need one or more of the leading bits in their representation. On average, this decreases the number of bits stored. By comparing the number of bits against the entropy coded vector elements, VPR efficiency can be measured.

Direct entropy coding such as Huffman coding, however, would have drawbacks. The decoding is serial: Huffman code is a variable length code whose length cannot be determined prior to decoding. The decoding is also complex: It requires a PLA to convert the code into a representation more permissive to computation. It also needs barrel shifters for unpacking of vector elements. In VQ source decoders where the codevector elements are accessed serially, we expect the marginal gain offered by this method to become attractive, when transistors per chip increase and chip design becomes simpler. VPR, on the other hand, does not impede higher throughput in codevector access, and does not require decoding.

The next section describes variable precision representation (VPR) and discusses storing the codebook as difference of codevectors. Section 3 shows the reduction in storage possible with VPR, the gains as the number of codevectors increases, and the gains from storing the codevector difference. Section 4 looks at the memory organization for VPR, and design of associated variable precision arithmetic.

2 Variable Precision Representation (VPR)

Variable precision representation is similar to Block Floating Point (BFP) [Opp70]. BFP is a floating point system with a single exponent for all the elements of a vector $\mathbf{y}$. Originally used in digital filters [Opp70], BFP represents a vector $\mathbf{y}$ of n-bit 2's complement integers as a vector of fractions and a single exponent.

$$\begin{aligned} \mathbf{y} &= (y_1 2^{n-1}, y_2 2^{n-1}, \cdots, y_K 2^{n-1}) \\ &= (y_1, y_2, \cdots, y_K)\, 2^{n-1}, |y_i| \le 1 \ \forall i \end{aligned}$$

BFP has the advantages of floating point numbers, while by having a common exponent for all the vector elements, it needs less storage.

In BFP, leading bits which are zero in all the elements are eliminated. When there are zero leading bits, we shift left all the elements by e bits,

$$(y_1', y_2', ..., y_K') = (y_1 2^e, y_2 2^e, \cdots, y_K 2^e)\, 2^{n-1-e} \ \exists\, |y_i'| \ge 1/2$$

where $\mathbf{y}$ is before and $\mathbf{y}'$ is after block normalization; both $\mathbf{y}$ and $\mathbf{y}'$ are in fractional 2's complement form. The floating point radix is two to maximize the bit reduction offered by VPR. Normalization chooses the smallest e such that:

$$|y_i| < 2^{-e} \ \forall i$$

In words, e designates the smallest interval which contains all the vector elements. Equivalently,

$$e(\mathbf{y}) = -\lfloor \log_2(\max_{\forall i} |y_i|) \rfloor$$

BFP, through normalization, avoids overflow (or underflow) [Opp70].

VPR, on the other hand, views normalization as compression. VPR, through normalization, reduces vector precision. This eliminates e bits per element. Let's show an example.

Figure 1 shows the two different ways to store $\mathbf{y} = ($ -1/32, 13/128, 5/128, -1/32 $)2^7$ ($n=8$). Fixed precision 2's complement representation needs $4 \times 8 = 32$ bits. VPR eliminates three leading bits ($e = 3$), it needs $4 \times (8 - 3) + 3 = 23$ bits. Note that when a negative number is converted to 2's complement, the leftmost bits which were zero become extension of the sign.

As shown in the previous example, VPR uses fewer bits than conventional representation to represent a vector. The n-bit fixed precision requires nK bits for the K element vector $\mathbf{y}$. In comparison, VPR requires $(n - e(\mathbf{y}))K$ bits for vector elements and $\lceil \log_2(n) \rceil$ bits for vector range e. When $e(\mathbf{y})$ is one or greater, VPR uses fewer bits.

Reducing Storage

Instead of storing C codevectors independently, we save more bits by storing their differences. VPR compresses most when representing the difference of similar vectors. That is, when $\hat{\mathbf{x}}^i$ and $\hat{\mathbf{x}}^h$ are similar, $e(\hat{\mathbf{x}}^i - \hat{\mathbf{x}}^h)$ is large. To maximize the sum of the exponent $e(\hat{\mathbf{x}}^i - \hat{\mathbf{x}}^h)$ of the codevector difference, we try different enumerations of C codevectors such that:

$$\max_{\forall enumerations} \sum_{i=2}^{C} e(\hat{\mathbf{x}}^i - \hat{\mathbf{x}}^{i-1})$$

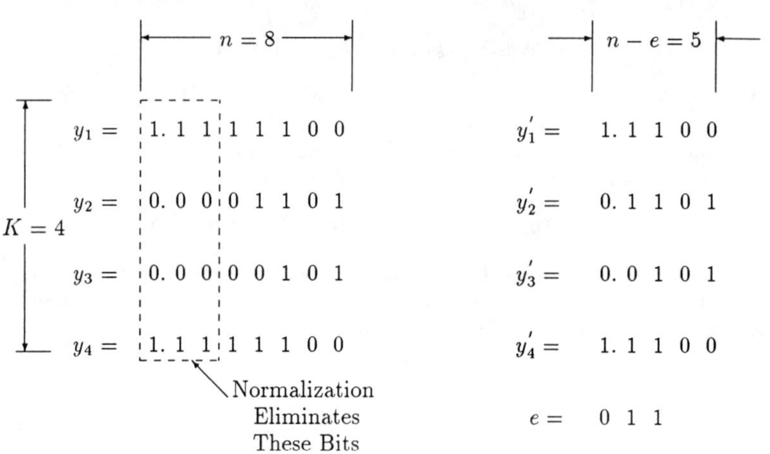

Figure 1: As Shown for $\mathbf{y} = (-1/32, 13/128, 5/128, -1/32)2^7$, Variable Precision Representation (VPR) Reduces Required Storage.

This is akin to the traveling salesman problem, and can be solved with similar heuristics. To access a codevector $\hat{\mathbf{x}}^j$, we would have to access all the previous codevectors in the tour:

$$\hat{\mathbf{x}}^j = \hat{\mathbf{x}}^1 + \sum_{i=2}^{j}(\hat{\mathbf{x}}^i - \hat{\mathbf{x}}^{i-1})$$

Where we store: $\hat{\mathbf{x}}^1, \hat{\mathbf{x}}^2 - \hat{\mathbf{x}}^1, \hat{\mathbf{x}}^3 - \hat{\mathbf{x}}^2, \cdots, \hat{\mathbf{x}}^C - \hat{\mathbf{x}}^{C-1}$.

3 Performance

Experiment

The computation in selecting one of the two branches in the binary TSVQ, referred to as a hyperplane test [DH73], is:

$$sign(\mathbf{x}\mathbf{y}^t + b)$$

where $\mathbf{y} = (\hat{\mathbf{x}}^i - \hat{\mathbf{x}}^h)$ is the hyperplane and $b = (\|\hat{\mathbf{x}}^h\| - \|\hat{\mathbf{x}}^i\|)/2$ is the bias term. To avoid overflow, an element of $\mathbf{x}$, x_i, is 9-bits – it is the difference of an 8-bit pixel from the pixel prediction. An element of $\mathbf{y}$, y_i is 10-bits – it is the difference of two 9-bit elements. In VPR, we evaluate

$$sign(\sum_{\forall i} x_i y_i' + b')$$

where y_i' is $(10 - e(\mathbf{y}))$ bits, and $b' = b/2^{2e}$.

We generated the codebooks with k-means clustering [LBG80] and two different sets of images. The first training data set was 32 pixel blocks ($K = 32$) from 10 256x256 pixel images, the second data set was 32 pixel blocks from 15 512x512 pixel images. The two mean/residual product codebooks [Bak84] had 2^{10} and a 2^{12} codevectors. The third training data set encoded 10 256x256 images with Interpolative VQ [HH88] using 2^{10} codevectors. All codebooks used binary TSVQ, which was then pruned [KBSC92] to different depths.

Table 1: Reduction in Storage for Two Pruned Codebooks

Code book	Training Data Set	Number of codevectors	Root Mean Square Error	$\mathcal{E}[e]$ (bits)	Storage Reduced
1	Set 1	292	$14.1/2^8$	2.65	26%
2	"	511	$13.4/2^8$	2.82	28%
3	"	718	$10.7/2^8$	3.00	30%
4	"	913	$9.4/2^8$	3.30	33%
5	Set 2	1292	$14.1/2^8$	2.38	24%
6	"	3467	$11.0/2^8$	2.76	28%
7	"	4538	$10.1/2^8$	2.97	30%
8	"	5526	$8.4/2^8$	3.22	32%
9	Set 3	875	$10.9/2^8$	3.36	34%
10	"	896	$10.6/2^8$	3.37	34%
11	"	922	$10.4/2^8$	3.40	34%

Table 2: Analysis of Bits Required in Storage

			For Added Vectors			
Code book	Added vectors	Root Mean Square Error	$\mathcal{E}[e]$ (bits)	$n - H(Y)$ (bits)	$n - H(\hat{X})$ (bits)	Efficiency $\mathcal{E}[e]/(n-H(Y))$
1	292	$14.1/2^8$	2.65	3.35	2.32	79%
2	219	$13.4/2^8$	3.05	3.70	2.44	82%
3	207	$10.7/2^8$	3.44	3.82	2.55	90%
4	195	$9.4/2^8$	4.40	4.48	2.93	98%
5	1292	$14.1/2^8$	2.38	3.06	2.15	78%
6	2175	$11.0/2^8$	2.99	3.47	2.45	86%
7	1071	$10.1/2^8$	3.65	3.96	2.68	92%
8	988	$8.4/2^8$	4.37	4.31	2.81	100%
9	875	$10.9/2^8$	3.36	3.68	2.06	91%
10	21	$10.6/^8$	3.95	4.33	2.20	91%
11	26	$10.4/2^8$	4.42	4.44	3.12	100%

Table 2 uses the entropy [JN84] of the codevectors to give an upper bound in compressing the codevectors $\hat{\mathbf{x}}$, and their difference the codevectors $\mathbf{y}$. The entropy

H of a random variable Y is defined as,

$$H(Y) \;=\; \sum_{\forall i} -p_i(Y) \log_2(p_i(Y))$$

where the random variable Y is the elements of all the $\mathbf{y}$ vectors and $p_i \equiv P(Y = i)$. Entropy measures the information, in bits, required for representing elements of the vector independent of each other. Since the correlation between elements is mostly removed with subtraction of the similar vectors, entropy $H(Y)$ is an approximate bound on the possible reduction in storage of vector elements.

Discussion

As shown in Table 1, the compression ranges from 24% to 34 %. For a given training set, as the number of the codevectors increases VPR saves more storage. We have the following explanation: As the number of codevectors increases, the K-dimensional space they are placed in becomes crowded. The smaller distance of codevectors from each other results in higher $\mathcal{E}[e(\mathbf{y})]$. The increase in the exponent e is correlated more closely with the root mean square error in encoding images from the training set.

As shown in Table 2, the compression for branches added to the tree structure is even better. It is more than 40%, or average of 4 bits per element. In other words, on the average, all the vector elements are 1/16 of the maximum. The efficiency with respect to Huffman coding also increases from 78% to 100%. In a way, VPR groups vectors based on exponents and codes each group differently. This notes the variety in vector type. On the other hand, Huffman codes elements of all vectors with a single coder. Moreover, the probability mass function, being result of centroid averaging, is smooth which lowers the yield of entropy coding the elements.

Table 2 also shows that the processing prior to VQ accounts for part of the increase in $\mathcal{E}[e]$, and subtracting the codevectors always improves the performance. We analyze the effect of preprocessing on codevectors by noting that a codevector is the centroid of source vector clusters. Since codevectors, through training on the source vectors, share the characteristics of the source vectors, any preprocessing affects source vectors and codevectors similarly. Preprocessing reduces the energy of the signal to be VQ'd, which reduces the max($\mathbf{y}$) or L_∞ of the vector $\mathbf{y}$. For example, subtracting the mean reduces vector energy and on average increases e of codevector. The entropy of the difference of two similar codevector decreases by at least one bit, even though storing the difference of two numbers needs an additional bit of dynamic range.

4 Architecture

Memory Organization

Let's look at arranging one vector in the storage. As the precision varies one bit, the number of bits required for representation varies by increments of K-bits. For best

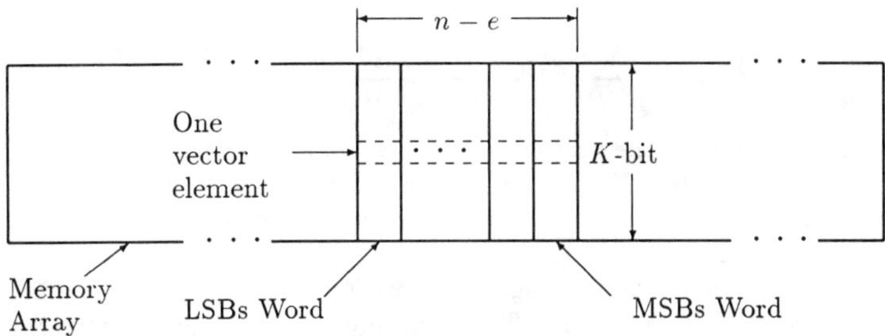

Figure 2: Bit-Serial Memory Organization of Vector Elements in Variable Precision Representation (VPR)

saving from VPR, a vector is stored with K-bit words. The vector $\mathbf{y}$ then requires $(n - e(\mathbf{y}))$ words. A bit-parallel access would require a barrel shifter to unpack the words. We show the alternative scheme which avoids unpacking. It accesses the bits of the same weight together which then can be fed to K bit-serial multipliers.

As shown in Figure 2, a vector of K elements is stored as K-bit words. Each word groups bits of the same weight of all the vector elements. For example with $K = 32$ and $n = 10$, each vector $\mathbf{y}$ needs $(10 - e(\mathbf{y}))$ 32-bit words per vector. Alternatively, this memory organization spreads bits of an element across $(n - e(\mathbf{y}))$ words. In Figure 2, the dashed line demarcates one of the vector elements. In the next section, we describe an inner product operator which evaluates $\mathbf{y}$ in the same order as it is stored in Figure 2.

Bit-Serial Inner Product

An approach to evaluation would be to read the numbers in VPR format, convert them to fixed point, and use parallel multiplier and adders. To have a simple interface to storage, we perform bit-serial evaluation as the codevector is read in VPR format. This results in sequential processing of the codevector in $n - e(\mathbf{y})$ iteration. Since the processor is designed to evaluate an inner product in n cycles, when $e(\mathbf{y}) > 0$ the processor idles for $e(\mathbf{y})$ cycles.

In a conventional bit-serial implementation, K conventional sequential multipliers [RPT89] would be used. The sequential multiplier consists of a partial product generator and an accumulator which collects the sums of partial products. At the end of multiplication, it transfers the result to an auxiliary latch. A new set of multiplications begins while the results are summed with auxiliary adders.

We chose the inner product operator used in Variable Precision Classification (VPC) [DE90]. As shown in Figure 3, it decomposes the inner product's multiplications to the addition of partial products – the multiplication of x_i with j-th bit of y_i.

$$\mathbf{x}\mathbf{y}^t = \sum_{\forall i} x_i y_i$$

$$\mathbf{xy}^t \;=\; -\sum_{\forall i} x_i y_{i,0}' + \sum_{j=1}^{n-1} 2^{-j} \sum_{\forall i} x_i y_{i,j}'$$

and then in each cycle sums all the partial products which have the same weight. A parallel adder and a latch replace K bit-serial adders and K parallel auxiliary latches which would sum the multipliers' output. Moreover, if it is not bit-level pipelined, there is no equivalent of an accumulation latch.

The inner product result is read by a sign detector. For fast cycle time, the inner product accumulates in carry-save form. The sign detector adds the accumulated saved carries to the sum and outputs the sign. The sign detector is based on a fast carry propagation adder. For example, it could be a carry look ahead adder, stripped to the circuitry needed to calculate the output's sign.

VPR conforms to the VPC [DE90] architecture; VPC architecture speeds the computation by skipping the superfluous LSBs. It proceeds in bit-serial evaluation from MSB to LSB as shown in Figure 3. It, however, keeps track of the error of the inner product $(\mathbf{xy}^t + b')$. When the error is less than the estimate of the inner product, the sign of the output cannot change with succeeding evaluation. At this point it terminates the evaluation. VPC can be easily modified to accept vector elements in VPR format, further reducing the execution time.

VPR can also accommodate higher throughput, by packing m K-bit words into a mK-bit word, and replicating the partial product generators m times. Alternatively, we can merge the m partial product generators of an element together in to K $m \times n$ sub-multipliers. When vectors are accessed randomly, as is in binary TSVQ, one of the words is shared by two vectors. The inner product operator needs to mask out the portion of the word belonging to other vector causing less efficient use of memory bandwidth.

5   Conclusion

Variable precision representation (VPR) is simple to implement. VPR determines the vector elements' leading bits which are sign extension. VPR for each vector stores the number $e(\mathbf{y})$, and avoids storing $e(\mathbf{y})$ leading bits of each vector element. The accompanying variable precision arithmetic uses a bit-serial, element-parallel inner product operator. It requires fewer latches than conventional serial-parallel multiplier based design. The throughput also can be increased by replicating the core of the inner product operator.

VPR is effective in reducing storage, especially when storing the difference of the codevectors. The compression of the codevector difference is better than the original codevectors. For storing a binary tree structured VQ codebook, VPR can save from 24% to 44% in storage. The compression improves as the mean square error of VQ encoder decreases.

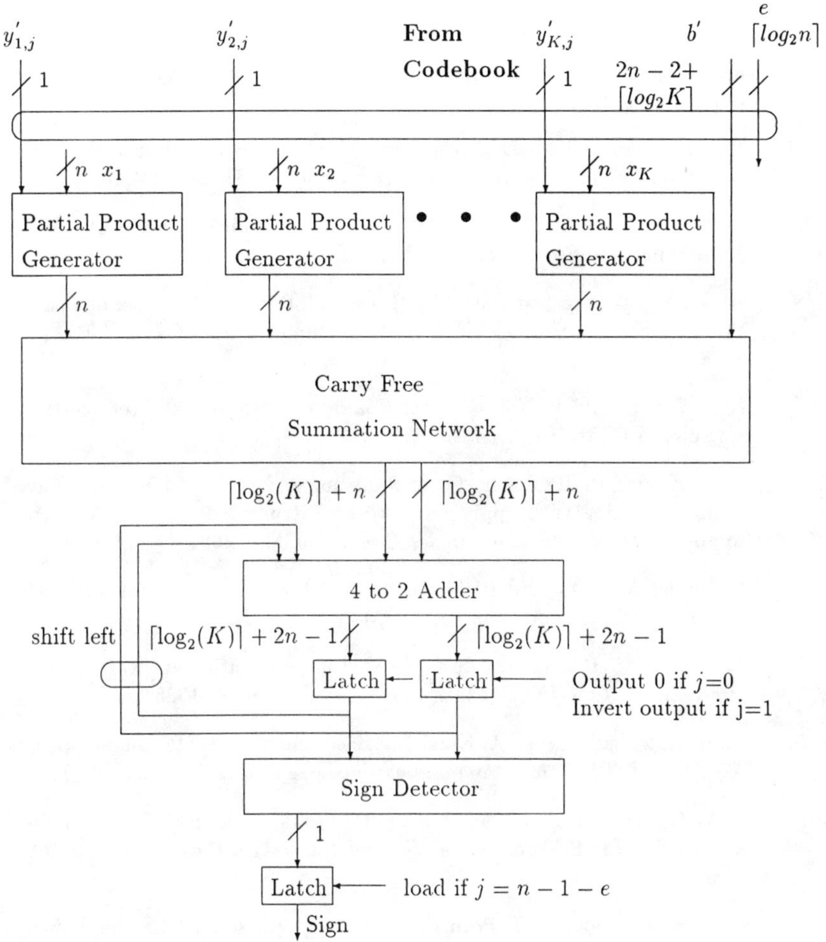

Figure 3: Inner Product Data-Path in j-th Cycle Evaluates $\mathbf{x}y'_j$: the Inner Product of $\mathbf{x}$ with Bit Vector of $\mathbf{y}$ Elements' j-th Significant Bit.

References

[Bak84] R. L. Baker. *Vector Quantization of Digital Images*. Stanford University, Electronics Laboratory, Stanford University, Stanford, CA 94305, 1984.

[CLG88] P. A. Chou, T. Lookabaugh, and R. M. Gray. Optimal pruning with applications to tree-structured source coding and modeling. *IEEE Trans. Info Theory*, 1988.

[DE90] R. Dionysian and M. D. Ercegovac. Variable-precision linear classifier. *IEEE Workshop on VLSI Signal Processing*, Vol. IV:285–294, 1990.

[DH73] R. O. Duda and P. E. Hart. *Pattern Classification and Scene Analysis*. John Wiley and Sons, Inc., New York, 1973.

[HH88] Hsueh-Ming Hang and Barry G. Haskell. Interpolative vector quantization of color images. *IEEE Trans. Commun.*, COM-36:465–470, April 1988.

[JN84] N. S. Jayant and P. Noll. *Digital Coding of Waveforms*. Prentice-Hall, Englewood Cliffs, NJ, 1984.

[KBSC92] S. Z. Kiang, R. L. Baker, G. J. Sullivan, and C. Y. Chiu. Recursive optimal pruning with applications to tree-structured vector quantizers. to appear *IEEE Trans. on Signal Processing*, May 1992.

[LBG80] Y. Linde, A. Buzo, and R. M. Gray. An algorithm for vector quantizer design. *IEEE Trans. Commun.*, COM-28:84–95, January 1980.

[MRG85] J. Makhoul, S. Roucos, and H. Gish. Vector quantization in speech coding. *Proceedings of the IEEE*, pages 1551–1588, November 1985.

[NK88] N. M. Nasrabadi and R. A. King. Image coding using vector quantization: A review. *IEEE Trans. Communications*, pages 957–971, August 1988.

[Opp70] A. V. Oppenheim. Realization of digital filters using block floating point arithmetic. *IEEE Trans. on Audio and Electroacoustics*, pages 130–136, June 1970.

[RPT89] P. A. Ramamoorthy, B. Potu, and T. Tran. Bit-serial VLSI implementation of vector quantizer for real-time image coding. *IEEE Trans. on Circuits and Systems*, pages 1281–1290, October 1989.

Universal Coding of Band-Limited Sources by Sampling and Dithered Quantization

Ram Zamir and Meir Feder
Dept. of Electrical Engineering - Systems,
Tel-Aviv University,
Tel-Aviv, 69978, ISRAEL

I. Introduction

Nyquist's well known sampling theorem states that a band-limited signal can be faithfully represented via its samples taken at a rate twice its bandwidth. The samples may have continuously many values. In practice, the samples are quantized leading to a distorted representation of the original signal. The rate-distortion characteristics of of this digitization scheme can be analyzed via classical quantization theory. Furthermore, the optimal performance in compressing the continuous time band-limited source is given by the rate-distortion function of the discrete time process, sampled at Nyquist's rate.

In theory, then, there is no need to sample the process at a rate higher than Nyquist's rate. However, when practical quantization is examined instead of the theoretically optimal rate-distortion function, increasing the sampling rate over Nyquist's rate may be advantageous. Furthermore, by increasing the sampling rate we reduce the required quantization resolution and still achieve comparable rate-distortion characteristics in compressing the original signal. Using a smaller number of quantization levels may be practically preferable; the recently popular sigma-delta techniques provide such an example.

In this paper we analyze a scheme for encoding continuous time band-limited signals in which the input is sampled at Nyquist's rate or faster, the samples undergo dithered uniform or lattice quantization and the quantizer output is entropy coded. This analysis leads to explicit expressions for the trade-off between sampling rate and quantization accuracy. Also, we provide expression for the scheme's redundancy (i.e. its excess rate over the rate distortion function) in terms of the both the sampling rate and quantization resolution parameters. This work uses extensively the results of [1] where the rate-distortion performance of dithered quantization for vector sources have been analyzed.

II.   Scheme Description

Let $x(t)$ be a sample function of a band-limited source. It is assumed that the source is stationary and its power spectrum function is limited to the frequency band $-B \leq f \leq B$, i.e.

$$S_x(f) = 0, \quad \text{for all } |f| > B. \tag{1}$$

In the proposed scheme for coding $x(t)$ the signal is sampled at a rate $F_s \geq 2B$ samples per second where $2B$ is the Nyquist's rate. The discrete sampled signal is denoted $x[n]$. The samples undergo dithered uniform (or lattice) quantization where the mean square error of the quantizer is denoted ϵ (i.e. $\epsilon = \Delta^2/12$ for scalar uniform quantizer where Δ is the quantizer step, or $\epsilon = G_K \cdot V^{2/K}$ for the general lattice quantizer case where V is the volume of the K dimensional lattice Voronoi region and G_K is its normalized second moment, see [2]). The output of the quantizer is losslessly encoded ("entropy encoded"). The decoder, then, decodes the lossless code and reconstruct the quantized samples, assuming that the dither realization is available and may be subtracted. The reconstructed discrete signal is denoted $\hat{x}[n]$ which is a concatenation of reconstructed source vectors

$$\hat{\underline{x}}_K = Q_K(\underline{x}_K + \underline{z}_K) - \underline{z}_K \ , \quad \hat{\underline{x}}_K \in \mathcal{R}^K \tag{2}$$

where $\underline{z}_K$, the dither vector, is drawn independently for every new K block. Finally, a continuous-time distorted signal, denoted $\hat{x}(t)$, is reconstructed via digital-to-analog conversion and low-pass filtering. This digital coding scheme is illustrated in Figure 1.

III. General Expressions for Rate-Distortion Performance

The rate of the coding scheme is determined by the conditional entropy of the quantizer output. To find this rate we consider first the discrete part of the system. Let the dither signal be denoted $z[n]$ and define $N[n] = \hat{x}[n] - x[n]$, i.e., $N[n]$ is the quantization error signal. We first recall the following theorem:

Theorem 1 $N[n]$ *is independent of* $x[n]$ *and distributed as* $-z[n]$. *(i.e. when the lattice is symmetric, $N[n]$ is distributed as the dither.)*

This theorem is well known at least for scalar dithered quantization (see e.g. [3] pp.170). For completeness it is proved in [4] for the general lattice case. The theorem shows that as far as the input/output relations are considered dithered quantization is equivalent to a discrete *additive* noise channel, whose input is $x[n]$ and its output is $\hat{x}[n] = x[n] + N[n]$, and the entire coding scheme is equivalent to the continuous *additive* noise channel depicted in Figure 2, whose input is $x(t)$ and its output $\hat{x}(t)$ is obtained by a low pass filtering of $\tilde{x}(t) = x(t) + N(t)$, where $N(t)$ is the continuous-time representation of the discrete quantization error signal,

$$N(t) = \sum_n N[n] \frac{\sin \pi(t - nT)/T}{\pi(t - nT)/T}. \tag{3}$$

In Theorem 2 below it is further shown that the rate, or the entropy, of the quantizer output equals to the mutual information between input and output of this channel.

Specifically, let $\underline{x}, \underline{\hat{x}}, \underline{z}$ and $\underline{N}$ denote blocks of length n composed of n/K blocks of length K (assuming K divides n) of the corresponding discrete signals. Denote by $H\left(Q_K(\underline{x} + \underline{z})|\underline{z}\right)$ the rate (in bits) of the randomized K-dimensional quantizer in encoding $\underline{x}$, where the conditional entropy is considered since it is assumed that the decoder has access to $\underline{z}$. We claim:

Theorem 2

$$H\left(Q_K(\underline{x} + \underline{z})|\underline{z}\right) = I(\underline{x}; \underline{\hat{x}}) = I(\underline{x}; \underline{x} + \underline{N}). \tag{4}$$

Proof: Observe that

$$H\left(Q_K(\underline{x}+\underline{z})|\underline{z}\right) = H\left(Q_K(\underline{x}+\underline{z})\underline{z}|\underline{z}\right) = H(\hat{\underline{x}}|\underline{z}). \tag{5}$$

Since $\underline{x}$ and $\underline{z}$ determine $\hat{\underline{x}}$, $H(\hat{\underline{x}}|\underline{x},\underline{z}) = 0$ and we have

$$H(\hat{\underline{x}}|\underline{z}) = H(\hat{\underline{x}}|\underline{z}) - H(\hat{\underline{x}}|\underline{x},\underline{z}) = I(\underline{x};\hat{\underline{x}}|\underline{z}). \tag{6}$$

However, $\underline{z}$ is deterministically given by $\hat{\underline{x}}$ (it is $\underline{l}(\hat{\underline{x}}) - \hat{\underline{x}}$ where $\underline{l}(\hat{\underline{x}})$ is the nearest lattice point to $\hat{\underline{x}}$) and so $H_0(\underline{x}|\hat{\underline{x}}) = H_0(\underline{x}|\hat{\underline{x}},\underline{z})$, where $H_0(\cdot)$ denotes differential entropy. Also, since $\underline{z}$ is independent of $\underline{x}$, $H_0(\underline{x}) = H_0(\underline{x}|\underline{z})$. Thus,

$$I(\underline{x};\hat{\underline{x}}|\underline{z}) = H_0(\underline{x}|\underline{z}) - H_0(\underline{x}|\hat{\underline{x}},\underline{z}) = H_0(\underline{x}) - H_0(\underline{x}|\hat{\underline{x}}) = I(\underline{x};\hat{\underline{x}}). \tag{7}$$

Combining (5), (6) and (7) leads to the desired relation (4). $\blacksquare$

The result (4) originally appeared in [1] and it has re-derived here using different (simpler) technique. In light of the theorems above, the channel of Figure 2 is equivalent to our coding system in both rate and distortion performances. The asymptotic rate of encoding the continuous-time source, after normalization to bits per second, is given by

$$R_Q = \lim_{n\to\infty} \frac{1}{nT} I(\underline{x};\underline{x}+\underline{N}) = I\left(x(t); x(t)+N(t)\right). \tag{8}$$

As for the distortion in encoding the continuous-time source, let $N_B(t)$ be the signal achieved by further low-passing $N(t)$ to the frequencies $-B \leq f \leq B$. This is also the error signal, i.e., $N_B(t) = \hat{x}(t) - x(t)$. Explicit calculation of the distortion using this signal is straight-forward. Consider, for example, the uniform scalar quantizer, where $N[n]$ is white, and each sample is uniformly distributed over $[-\Delta/2, \Delta/2]$, i.e. it has zero mean and variance $\epsilon = \Delta^2/12$. The variance of $N(t)$ is also ϵ and since it has a flat spectrum over the band $-1/2T \leq f \leq 1/2T$ its spectral level is $\epsilon \cdot T$. As a result, passing $N(t)$ through an ideal low-pass filter whose band is $-B \leq f \leq B$, we get that the power spectrum of $N_B(t)$ is also flat at a level $\epsilon \cdot T$. Since in this case $N_B(t)$ is wide sense stationary, the quantizer MSE is constant, equal to its variance,

$$D = \int_f S_{N_B}(f)df = \epsilon \cdot T \int_{-B}^{B} df = \epsilon \cdot T \cdot 2B. \tag{9}$$

As the sampling rate is increased (T is decreased) the distortion is linearly reduced. A similar simple calculation can be made for general symmetric lattice quantizer. A spectral picture, showing a typical source and the additive quantization noise, is illustrated in Figure 4.

IV. Limit Case: Equivalent Additive Gaussian Noise Channel

For any source and any quantizer one can use (8) to examine how the rate changes with the sampling rate and the trade-off between sampling and quantization resolution; however, an explicit trade-off formula for the rate may be complicated. Simpler expression for this trade-off are provided in this section in the asymptotic case as the (optimal) lattice dimension becomes large (at any sampling rate). In this case the rate-distortion expressions approaches the mutual information and the distortion associated with the input and output of an additive *Gaussian* noise channel, with a noise, $G(t)$, having a flat spectrum of level $\epsilon \cdot T$. Clearly, in this case the MSE distortion is the variance of $G_B(t)$ i.e. $\epsilon \cdot T \cdot 2B$. As for the rate, it is given by the mutual information between $x(t)$ and $\hat{x}(t) = x(t) + G_B(t)$, and so as long as $\epsilon \cdot T$ is kept constant we get the same rate (notice that for the the case of additive Gaussian noise, only the in-band noise contributes to the mutual information in the channel).

Let us consider the optimal lattice for quantization under the MSE criterion ([2]). It follows from a conjecture made in [5] that the normalized second moment of the optimal lattice satisfies,

$$\lim_{K \to \infty} G_K^* = \frac{1}{2\pi e} \approx 0.058823, \tag{10}$$

where G_K^* is the minimal value of G_K over all lattices of dimension K. Note that it is well known, e.g. [2], that $1/2\pi e$ is the limit of the minimal second moment of any structure, lattice or not. The asymptotic Gaussian behavior of the equivalent channel follows from the claim:

Theorem 3 *Assuming conjecture (10) holds. Then, using the optimal lattice, almost all finite blocks of noise samples $\{N[n]\}$ of the equivalent discrete channel have a limit distribution of an i.i.d. Gaussian vector with zero mean and a variance (of each component) $\epsilon = G_K \cdot V^{2/K}$.*

One may point out, of course, that the quantizer noise samples, distributed as the dither, are such that each K-block of them is uniformly distributed over the lattice cell. Nevertheless, our claim follows from an argument used in the central limit theorem leading to convergence in distribution. This convergence is sufficient for our purposes since we are only interested in the rate-distortion performance which is defined by moments and information function that only depend on the distribution. The detailed proof is omitted for lack of space.

V.   The Redundancy of the Scheme

The rate-distortion function of a continuous time source, measured in bits per second, is defined for the square error distortion measure (see [6]) as,

$$R(D) = \min_{\{u(t):E\{(x(t)-u(t))^2\}\leq D\}} I\left(x(t); u(t)\right) = \lim_{n\to\infty} \frac{1}{nT} I(\underline{x}; \underline{u}) \tag{11}$$

where $\underline{x}$ and $\underline{u}$ are n-vectors containing samples of the band limited signals $x(t)$ and $u(t)$, sampled faster than Nyquist's rate, i.e. at $F_s = 1/T \geq 2B$.

The redundancy of the coding scheme, which in general depends on the distortion, is denoted $\rho(D)$ and defined

$$\rho(D) = R_Q(D) - R(D), \tag{12}$$

where for square error distortion measure, as shown above, $D = \epsilon \cdot T \cdot 2B$.

Consider again the equivalent channel, depicted in Figure 2, and recall that the independent additive noise in this channel is $N(t)$ given by (3). Define by C the capacity of this channel when the input is constrained to be band-limited to $-B \leq f \leq B$ (i.e. as the signal to be coded), and to have a limited power $E\{x^2(t)\} \leq D$. This capacity, measured in bits per sample, is,

$$C = \lim_{n\to\infty} \frac{1}{nT} \max_{\underline{x}\in\mathcal{X}} I(\underline{x}; \underline{x} + \underline{N}) \tag{13}$$

where $\underline{x}$ was defined above, $\underline{N}$ is an n-vector representing a block of length n of $N[n]$, the samples of $N(t)$, and $\mathcal{X}$ is the set of random vectors such that the second moment of each component is bounded by D and the auto-covariance can be interpolated to yield the band-limited spectrum. The Following theorem provides an upper bound for the redundancy:

Theorem 4

$$\rho(D) \leq C \tag{14}$$

The proof follows the same steps as in the proof of Theorem 2 of [1] and is given in [4].

Comments:

1. This theorem extends Theorem 2 of [1]. Indeed, when operating at Nyquist's rate, the noise band equals the signal band and the band-limitedness constraint is not effective. In this case, the capacity bound is the same as the bound calculated in [1], i.e. for scalar quantizer it is approx. $1/2 \log 4\pi e/12 \approx 0.754$ bits per Nyquist sample, or $B \log 4\pi e/12 \approx 0.754B$ bits per second. For a general lattice quantizer the capacity bound is $B \log 4\pi e G_K$ bits per second, which approaches B bits per second (or 0.5 bits per Nyquist rate) as the lattice dimension $K \to \infty$ since in this case, by the conjecture in [5], $G_K \to 1/2\pi e$.

2. As the sampling rate increases the band-limitedness constraint becomes effective. Since the channel is not necessarily Gaussian (except from the case described in section 4), the high spectral components of the noise depend on the in-band noise components, which in turn increases the capacity, i.e., the upper bound in (14). On the other hand, from the central limit theorem, as the sampling rate increases and the noise bandwidth becomes wider, the in-band noise becomes Gaussian, which in turn decreases the capacity bound in (14). The total effect of increasing the sampling rate is not fully understood yet.

3. The capacity bound is tight for the high distortion case. The redundancy of the source that maximizes the mutual information in (13) is exactly the capacity bound. This source is band-limited and its power is $\epsilon T \cdot 2B$, i.e. as the allowed distortion D. The rate distortion function of this source at distortion D is of course <u>zero</u> and so the redundancy is the quantizer rate which is the mutual information or, for this source, the capacity (13) of the channel.

4. In general, following the results of the previous sections and the derivation in [1], a composite bound on the redundancy can be obtained. This bound has a simple behavior for the asymptotic Gaussian case (at any sampling rate): It will tend to zero (i.e. it will be tighter by at least B bits per second or 0.5 bits per Nyquist rate) at the low distortion (high resolution) case. This behavior is demonstrated in the next section via examples.

VI.   Examples

The performance of the proposed coding scheme will be demonstrated more specifically via examples. For simplicity we consider the limit case where the noise in the equivalent channel becomes Gaussian. In this case we have to calculate the mutual information between our source $x(t)$ and $x(t) + G_B(t)$. Suppose our source has a power spectrum $S_x(f)$. Then, for square error distortion measure the rate of the coding scheme satisfies (8),

$$R_Q(D) \leq \frac{1}{2} \int_{-B}^{B} \log \left(1 + \frac{S_x(f)}{\epsilon T} \right) df = \frac{1}{2} \int_{-B}^{B} \log \left(1 + \frac{S_x(f)}{D \cdot T_{Nq}} \right) df \tag{15}$$

where $D = \epsilon \cdot T \cdot 2B$ is the square error distortion, $1/T_{Nq} = 2B$ is the Nyquist rate and the rate is measured in bits per seconds. The upper bound in (18) is achieved by a Gaussian source. We can get a simple expression when the Gaussian source has a flat spectrum S_x. The rate-distortion function in this case is $R(D) = B \cdot \log \frac{S_x}{D/2B} = B \cdot \log \frac{\sigma_x^2}{D}$ where $\sigma_x^2 = 2B S_x$ is the source's variance. From (18), the rate of our scheme for a Gaussian source with flat spectrum is $B \cdot \log \left(1 + \frac{\sigma_x^2}{D} \right)$. Thus the redundancy becomes, $\rho(D) = B \cdot \log \left(1 + \frac{D}{\sigma_x^2} \right)$. This redundancy expression holds for all distortion levels. At high distortion, $D/\sigma_x^2 \approx 1$ and we get $\rho = B$, i.e., 0.5 bits per Nyquist sample. This is also the capacity of an additive Gaussian noise channel when the input variance equals to the noise variance. At low distortion levels, where $D/\sigma_x^2 \to 0$, we find, as expected, that the redundancy approaches zero.

Figure 3 shows the rate-distortion performance of our scheme for the following two sources. The first is a white Gaussian source for which we have plotted the rate of our scheme (R_Q), and the rate-distortion function ($R(D)$) as given above. The second source is a Gauss-Markov source, with a $-3dB$ bandwidth $B_0 = 0.1B$. For this source we have plotted the rate of our scheme $R_Q(D) = \frac{1}{2}\log(1 + 0.067\frac{\sigma_x^2}{D}) + \sqrt{0.14\frac{\sigma_x^2}{D} + 0.02} \cdot \arctan\left(1/\sqrt{0.068\sigma_x^2/D + 0.01}\right) - 0.212$, and instead of its rate-distortion function, which is hard to calculate, we have plotted Shannon's lower bound $R_L(D) = \frac{1}{2}\log(0.067\frac{\sigma_x^2}{D}) + 1.23$. All plots are presented as a function of $SQNR = \frac{\sigma_x^2}{D}$, and normalized to bits per Nyquist sample.

References

[1] R. Zamir and M. Feder. On Universal Quantization by Randomized Uniform Lattice Quantizer. *IEEE Trans. Information Theory*, to appear, March 1992.

[2] J. H. Conway and N. J. A. Sloane. *Sphere Packings, Lattices and Groups.* Springer-Verlag, New York, N.Y., 1988.

[3] N. S. Jayant and P. Noll. *Digital Coding of Waveforms: Principles and Applications to Speech and Video.* Prentice-Hall, Englewood Cliffs, NJ, 1984.

[4] R. Zamir and M. Feder. Universal Coding of Band Limited Sources by Sampling and Dithered Quantization. in preparetion.

[5] A. Gersho. Asymptotically optimal block quantization. *IEEE Trans. Information Theory*, IT-25:373–380, July 1979.

[6] T. Berger. *Rate Distortion Theory: A Mathematical Basis fot Data Compression.* Prentice-Hall, Englewood Cliffs, NJ, 1971.

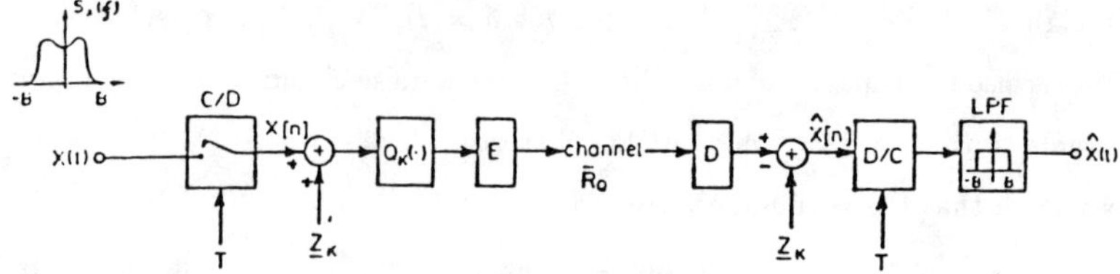

Figure 1: The Digital Coding Scheme

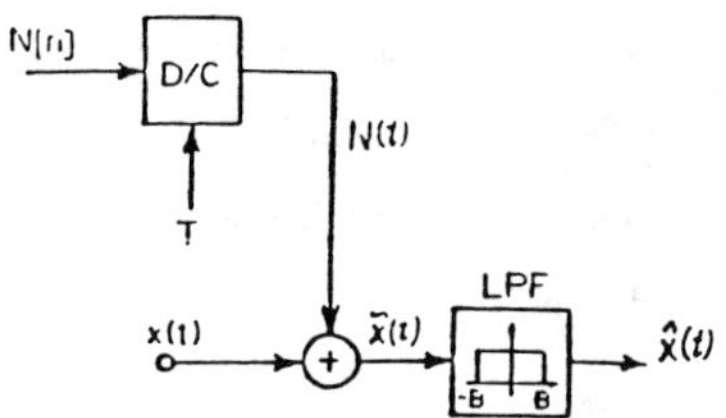

Figure 2: Equivalent Continuous Channel
for Rate and Distortion

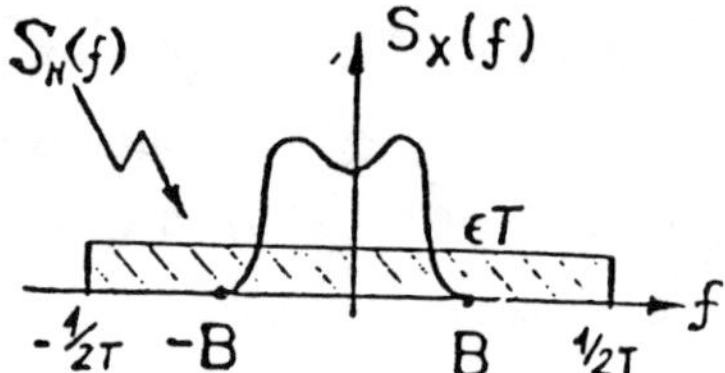

Figure 3: Spectrum of Source and Noise

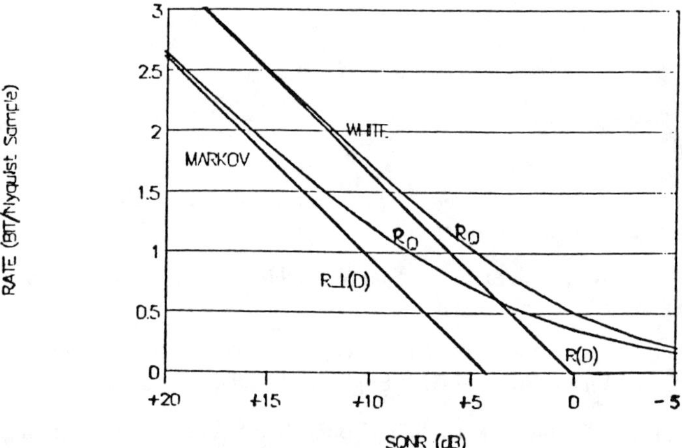

Figure 3: Rate-Distortion of the Coding Scheme for Flat spectrum and Gauss-Markov Sources, Compared with Optimal Performance

Improving Search for Tree-Structured Vector Quantization

Jianhua Lin
Department of Computer Science
Eastern Connecticut State University
Willimantic, CT 06226
and
Department of Computer Science
Brandeis University, Waltham, MA 02254

James A. Storer
Department of Computer Science
Brandeis University
Waltham, MA 02254

Extended Abstract

1 Introduction

Tree-structured vector quantization (TSVQ) is used to simplify the design and speed up the codebook search for vector quantizers. The efficiency is usually achieved at some cost of the quantization performance compared with full vector quantizers where no structural requirement is imposed on the codebook. Various algorithms have been proposed to improve the design of tree-structured vector quantizers to achieve performance close to that of full vector quantizers (Chou, Lookabaugh, and Gray [1989], Lin and Storer [1991], and Lin [1992]).

We view tree-structured vector quantization as an approximation to optimal vector quantization. This approximation can be divided into two levels, the approximation of the code vectors and the approximation of the partitioning regions on the input space. The code vectors are obtained through a design algorithm while the partitioning regions are determined by a search algorithm. Most of the effort in the past has been devoted to improving the design of tree-structured vector quantizers. Little is known, however, about the performance of approximate tree search in TSVQ.

In this paper, we analyze the approximate performance of tree search and provide tight upper bounds on the amount of error resulting from tree search for a single input vector. These bounds are not encouraging but fortunately, the performance of tree-structured VQ in practice does not seem to be as bad. However, our experimental results show that if we use a design algorithm such as the one presented in Lin, Storer, and Cohn [1992] for tree-structured VQ, the performance loss of TSVQ is almost entirely due to approximate tree search. It is thus evident that better performance of tree-structured VQ can be obtained by improving the search performance.

From our analysis, we derive a simple heuristic to improve the approximation of tree search. The strategy is to identify for each code vector some of its closest neighboring code vectors determined by the partition. After a code vector is found for an input vector by tree search, the closest neighboring code vectors are then searched for the best match. Unfortunately, the average number of neighboring code vectors of a given code vector can be as many as the total number of code vectors. Thus, the performance improvement of the strategy depends on the number of code vectors that are searched. Experimental results show that a number logarithmic in the size of the codebook provides significant performance gain while preserving the asymptotic search time complexity.

2 Optimal VQ and Tree-Structured VQ

For an input space, a vector quantizer partitions the space into a finite number of regions, each of which is assigned a *code vector*. An input vector is then quantized to the code vector representing the region to which the input vector belongs. Figure 1 shows an example of such a partition for a two-dimensional space. Each partitioning region A_i has a code vector $\vec{y}_i$. The collection of all the code vectors is called a *codebook*.

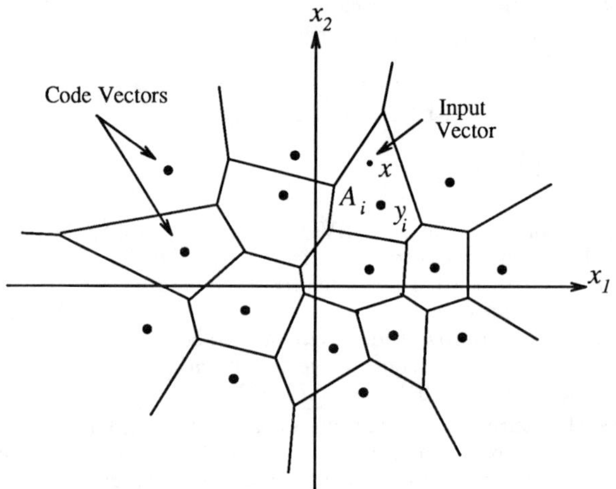

Figure 1: Partition of a two-dimensional space

When an input vector $\vec{x}$ is quantized to a code vector $\vec{y}$, a quantization error generally results and can be measured by a distortion $d(\vec{x}, \vec{y})$. If $f(\vec{x})$ is the probability density function of the random vector $\vec{x}$ of the input space, then the overall distortion of a vector quantizer of k code vectors is the expected value

$$D = E(d(\vec{x}, q(\vec{x}))) = \sum_{i=1}^{k} \int_{\vec{x} \in A_i} d(\vec{x}, \vec{y}_i) f(\vec{x}) d\vec{x}.$$

A vector quantizer is said to be an *optimal (minimum-distortion) quantizer* if the distortion is minimized over all vector quantizers of codebook size k. There are two necessary conditions for optimality. The first condition is that the optimal quantizer always quantizes an input vector to the *closest* code vector. The second condition is that each code vector is the *centroid* of its corresponding partitioning region.

These are, however, not sufficient conditions for a vector quantizer to be optimal. Finding an optimal vector quantizer is most likely difficult (Lin [1992], Capoyleas, Rote, and Woeginger [1991]), and heuristic design algorithm based on the necessary conditions such as the generalized Lloyd algorithm (Lloyd [1957], and Linde, Buzo, and Gray [1980]) has been widely used.

One of the other important techniques used to simplify vector quantizer design is to impose a structural requirement on the quantizer such as *tree-structured vector quantization* (Buzo, Gray Jr., Gray, and Markel [1980], Makhoul, Roucos, and Gish [1985]). A tree-structured VQ partitions an input space into a hierarchy of regions which can be represented in a tree structure. Figure 2 shows an example of a tree-partition for a two-dimensional space. The tree structure of the quantizer also

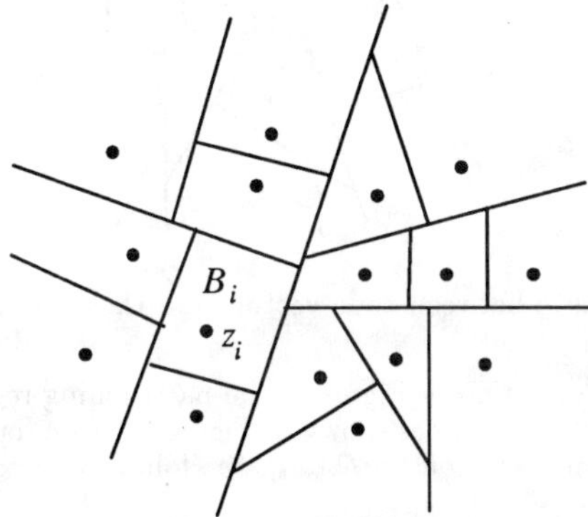

Figure 2: Tree-partition of a two-dimensional space

provides a mechanism to speed up the search for the closest code vector to an input vector, which can be quantized by traversing a root-to-leaf path of the quantization tree. This reduces the amount of search time required compared with closest search in a full VQ where no codebook structure is required.

3   Performance of Tree-Structured VQ

A tree-structured VQ can be designed by successive partitioning of an input space into two regions, seeking to minimize the expected distortion at each two-partition (Buzo, Gray Jr., Gray, and Markel [1980], Makhoul, Roucos, and Gish [1985]). Improvement to these design algorithms have been proposed and the TSVQ obtained achieves performance close to that of full VQ (Chou, Lookabaugh, and Gray [1989], Lin and Storer [1991], and Lin [1992]).

To see how we can further improve TSVQ, we first analyze its performance. For a given input space, a tree-structured VQ can be viewed as an approximation to the optimal VQ. If D_{opt} is the expected distortion of the optimal VQ and D_{tree} is that of a tree-structured VQ, it is clear that $D_{opt} \leq D_{tree}$. The approximation ratio, $D_{tree}/D_{opt} \geq 1$, measures the performance of the tree-structured VQ. It is most desired that the approximation ratio can be bounded by a small constant.

If we look at the tree-partition shown in Figure 2 as an approximation to the optimal partition shown in Figure 1, this approximation can be divided into two parts, the approximation of the code vectors and the approximation of the partitioning regions. The first approximation is caused by the approximate design, while the second approximation is due to the approximate tree search. For the same set of

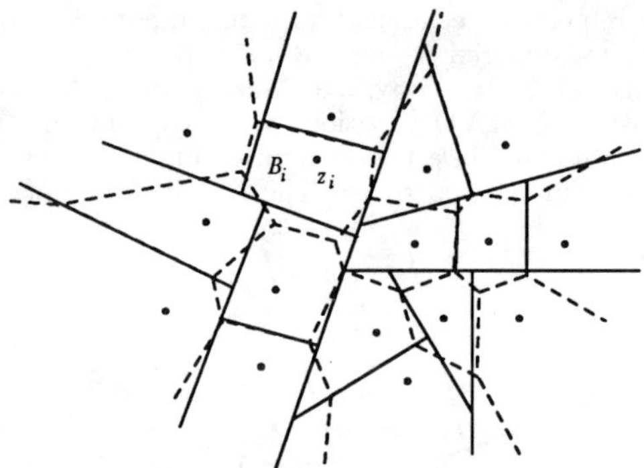

Figure 3: Relationship between code vectors and their partitioning regions

code vectors of the tree-partition in Figure 2, the partitioning regions determined by closest search would be the dash lines shown in Figure 3. If we represent the expected distortion of the dash-line partition by D_{closest}, the following inequality holds,

$$D_{\text{opt}} \leq D_{\text{closest}} \leq D_{\text{tree}}.$$

It is our hope that analyzing the approximation ratio $D_{\text{closest}}/D_{\text{opt}}$ and $D_{\text{tree}}/D_{\text{closest}}$ separately may help us obtain $D_{\text{tree}}/D_{\text{opt}}$.

Most of the effort in the past has been devoted to improving the design of tree-structured VQ. In this paper, we analyze the approximate performance of tree-search and seek to improve its performance. Because the calculation of the expected distortion requires a density function, providing a general bound for the approximation ratio does not seem to be an easy task. Thus, we first look at a simplified problem: the performance bound of tree search compared with the closest search for a single input vector. This may provide some more insight into the expected case.

4   Performance Bound for Scalars

We start with the simplest one-dimensional space. Suppose we have a quantization tree of three leaves shown in Figure 4. The number shown next to the nodes are the code scalars. If we use the mean square error and quantize an input 6, tree search quantizes it to 9 because 6 is closer to 9 than to 2. However, the closest of the three code scalars at the leaves to 6 is 4. Clearly, tree search does not quantize an input to its nearest code scalar. The question is: can a quantization tree such as the one shown in Figure 4 ever be actually constructed? The answer depends on how quantization trees are designed. We show that if the design is based on successive optimal 2-partitioning of a training set, which is most frequently used (Buzo, Gray Jr., Gray, and Markel [1980], Makhoul, Roucos, and Gish [1985], Chou, Lookabaugh, and Gray [1989]), then such a tree can indeed be constructed.

We consider all the code scalars at the leaves of a quantization tree as a training set. In practice, it is not realistic to have only one sample in each subset of the partition. But multiple samples can be obtained by simply replicating each code

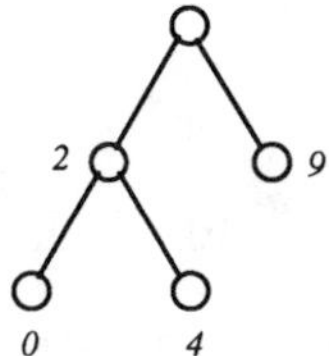

Figure 4: A simple quantization tree

scalar an arbitrary number of times without affecting the validity of the tree. If the replication is bothersome, a more realistic scheme is to choose a sequence of very small values $\delta_1 \geq \delta_2 \geq \cdots \geq \delta_n \geq 0$, and consider

$$y - \delta_1, y - \delta_2, \cdots, y - \delta_n, y, y + \delta_1, y + \delta_2, \cdots, y + \delta_n$$

as the training samples for each code scalar y. In the discussion to follow, we will consider only the code scalars themselves for simplicity.

Suppose we have a simple quantization tree as shown in Figure 5, where m, a,

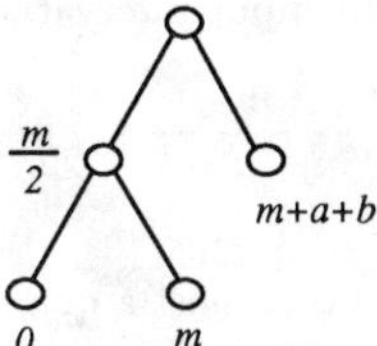

Figure 5: A generic quantization tree

and b are all non-negative numbers. We are to quantize an input $m + a$. If we choose

$$b \leq \frac{m}{2} + a, \tag{1}$$

then $m + a$ will be quantized to $m + a + b$ by tree search. However, if we also choose

$$a \leq b, \tag{2}$$

the closest code scalar to $m + a$ is m. It is clear that both conditions (1) and (2) can be satisfied easily at the same time.

Consider the training set $\{0, m, m + a + b\}$. To insure that the tree shown in Figure 5 is obtained from successive optimal 2-partitioning, we need to have smaller distortion for partition

$$\{\{0, m\}, \{m + a + b\}\}$$

than that for partition

$$\{\{0\}, \{m, m + a + b\}\}.$$

For the mean square error, this can be satisfied by

$$\frac{m^2}{2} \leq \frac{(a + b)^2}{2},$$

which results in the requirement,

$$m \leq a + b. \tag{3}$$

This condition is met simultaneously with conditions (1) and (2) as shown in the quantization tree of Figure 4, where $m = 4$, $a = 2$, and $b = 3$. Thus, the tree of Figure 4 can be actually constructed by successive optimal partitioning of a training set. For input 6, the square error from tree search is 9 while that from closest search is 4.

For the quantization tree shown in Figure 5, the square error from tree search for the input $m + a$ is b^2 while that from closest search is a^2. How do we measure the amount of performance loss caused by tree search? The problem with the ratio b^2/a^2 is that it can not be bounded by any constant. The difference $b-a$, on the other hand, depends on the magnitude of a and b. We thus choose to normalize the difference by the size of the input space, which is the length of the interval in a one-dimensional case. There exist nice upper bounds for such a measure as shown below.

From condition (1), we have

$$b - a \leq \frac{m}{2}.$$

Normalizing this by the length of the input interval, $m + a + b$, we obtain

$$\frac{b-a}{m+a+b} \leq \frac{1}{2}\frac{m}{m+a+b} \leq \frac{1}{2}\frac{m}{m+m} = \frac{1}{4}.$$

The second inequality follows from inequality (3). Thus, for this simple case shown in Figure 5, the difference $b - a$ can be at most a quarter of the length of the interval. This is not the worst general case, however. An upper bound for the difference is given below.

Theorem 1 *For an input interval of length M, if x is quantized by tree search with square error b^2 and the closest code scalar to x has square error of a^2, the following upper bound holds*

$$\frac{b-a}{M} \leq \frac{1}{2}.$$

Proof: Suppose $[0, M]$ is the input interval, and 0, m, and $m + a + b$ are three code scalars in a quantization tree. Also, suppose input $m + a$ is quantized to $m + a + b$ by tree search while m is the closest to $m + a$, as shown in Figure 6. Clearly, to insure

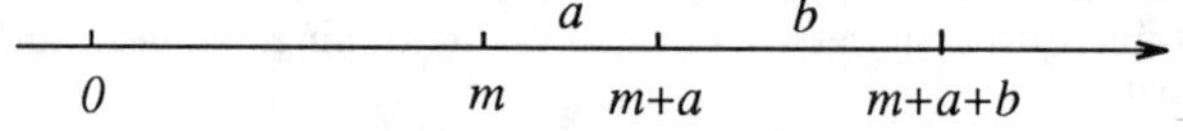

Figure 6: Example points on a real line

that $m + a$ be quantized to $m + a + b$ by tree search, b can be at most $M/2$. Since a has to be non-negative, we immediately have

$$b - a \leq \frac{M}{2} - a \leq \frac{M}{2}. \qquad \text{Q.E.D.}$$

The above upper bound seems rather conservative. It is, however, a tight bound since there exist instances which have a factor arbitrarily close to half. For example, we can replicate both (0) and $(m + a + b)$ n times in the previous example to create the following training set,

$$\{\underbrace{0, 0, \cdots, 0}_{n}, m, \underbrace{m + a + b, m + a + b, \cdots, m + a + b}_{n}\}.$$

We would like the quantization tree constructed from the training set to look like the one shown in Figure 7. The requirements for our construction are now

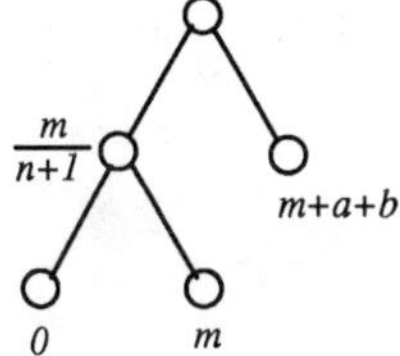

Figure 7: A worst case quantization tree

$$\begin{cases} b \leq \frac{n}{n+1} m + a; \\ a \leq b; \\ m \leq a + b. \end{cases}$$

As a result, we have

$$b - a \leq \frac{n}{n + 1} m,$$

and

$$\frac{b - a}{m + a + b} \leq \frac{n}{n + 1} \frac{m}{m + a + b} \leq \frac{1}{2} \frac{n}{n + 1},$$

which can be made arbitrarily close to a half by choosing n big enough. This demonstrates that the upper bound in Theorem 1 is tight.

5   Performance Bounds for Vector Spaces

Can the bound for one-dimensional space be extended to spaces of higher dimension? Let us next look at the case on the plane and assume that the input space is a bounded square region of size $M \times M$ as shown in Figure 8. Suppose $\vec{u}$ and $\vec{v}$ are two code vectors at the leaves of a quantization tree. For any input point $\vec{x}$, let a^2 be the square distance between $\vec{u}$ and $\vec{x}$, and let b^2 be the square distance between $\vec{v}$ and $\vec{x}$. If $\vec{x}$ is quantized to $\vec{v}$ by tree search and $\vec{u}$ is the closest code vector to $\vec{x}$, then $b \geq a$. Clearly, $b \leq M\sqrt{2}$ since the maximum distance between any two points within the input square shown in Figure 8 is $M\sqrt{2}$. From the fact that $a \geq 0$, we obtain the following bound.

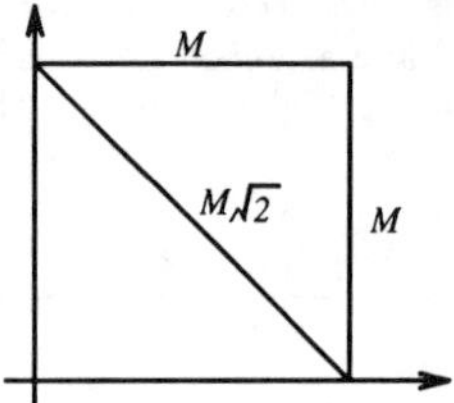

Figure 8: An input space on the plane

Theorem 2 *For an input square of size $M \times M$, if $\vec{x}$ is quantized by tree search with square error b^2 and the closest code vector to $\vec{x}$ has square error of a^2, the following upper bound holds*

$$\frac{b-a}{M} \leq \sqrt{2},$$

and is tight.

The proof of the tightness again involves the construction of an instance which achieves the bound. Similar techniques demonstrated in the proof for the one-dimensional case are used here. However, the construction is much more complex and is omitted in this extended abstract due to the space constraint. Also the result for the plane can be extended to any higher dimensional spaces.

Theorem 3 *For an input h-dimensional cube of size $\underbrace{M \times M \times \cdots \times M}_{h}$, $h \geq 2$, if $\vec{x}$ is quantized by tree search with square error b^2 and the closest code vector to $\vec{x}$ has square error of a^2, the following upper bound holds*

$$\frac{b-a}{M} \leq \sqrt{h},$$

and is tight.

6   Improving the Search Performance

We can see from the above analysis that the output vector from tree search may be quite far away from the closest code vector. The bounds are, however, for the worst possible single input vector. The expected result for multiple input vectors does not seem to be as bad since experimental results have shown that tree-structured VQ can perform quite well compared with full VQ (Chou, Lookabaugh, and Gray [1989], Lin and Storer [1991]). We are still working on the expected case but have not yet obtained any similar bounds.

The above analysis does indicate that the performance of tree search needs to be improved. Most of the work in the past has been devoted to improving the design of tree-structured VQ. In fact, when we separated the two levels of approximation and evaluated the performance of TSVQ obtained by some recently developed algorithms

(Chou, Lookabaugh, and Gray [1989], Lin [1992]), we found that the performance loss of TSVQ is almost entirely due to the search. We thus believe that improvement to TSVQ may be further obtained by improving tree search instead.

From the relationship between the tree partitioning regions and those determined by closest search shown in Figure 3, we can see that when an input vector $\vec{x}$ is quantized to a code vector $\vec{y}$ by tree search, the closest code vector to $\vec{x}$ is one of the neighboring code vectors of $\vec{y}$. Thus, the closest code vector can be obtained by searching through all the neighboring code vectors of the output vector obtained from tree search. Unfortunately, this is no simple matter. Although the average number of neighboring code vectors for a given code vector on the plane is six, the number increases rapidly with the vector dimension and can be as many as $O(k)$ for a codebook of size k (Preparata and Shamos [1985]). Searching through all the neighboring code vectors is thus essentially the same as searching through all the code vectors.

A simple heuristic we propose is to search a limited number of the closest neighboring code vectors following tree search. Depending on the computational resource, the number may vary from a constant to proportional in the codebook size. We prefer a number logarithmic in the codebook size since this overhead does not affect the asymptotic time complexity of tree search. Our experimental results in image compression also show that it provides significant performance improvement to tree search alone.

The experiments we performed were based on original black-and-white images of 512×512 with 8-bit grey levels per pixel. We used the algorithm presented in Lin, Storer, Cohn [1992] or Lin [1992] for the design of tree-structured VQ based on a training sequence of 16 images of various objects, faces, and animals. The algorithm finds an optimal pruned tree which has minimal expected distortion over all pruned tree of a given number of leaves. The constructed tree is then applied to compress a test image, *the woman with a hat*, which is NOT in the training sequence. The distortion measure we used is the mean square error. We performed expertments with various number of closest neighboring code vectors searched following tree search. Figure 9 shows results for a constant number 5, $\log k$, $\sqrt{k}$, and closest search for codebook of size k. Also shown in the figure are the results from basic tree-structured VQ and full VQ designed using the generalized Lloyd algorithm (Lloyd [1957], and Linde, Buzo, and Gray [1980]).

From Figure 9, we can see that if we use the closest code vector in the code tree to quantize the input, the compression result is almost the same as that of a full VQ. The performance loss in such a tree-structured VQ is thus almost entirely due to approximate tree search. The design algorithm provides a very close approximation to the optimal code vectors. Further improvement need to be obtained from improving the search performance. Our experimental results show that searching just a constant 5 closest neighboring code vectors following tree search gives much performance improvement. For large size codebooks, searching a logarithmic number provides significant improvement without increasing the asymptotic search time complexity.

References

A. Buzo, A. H. Gray Jr., R. M. Gray, and J. D. Markel [1980], "Speech coding based upon vector quantization," *IEEE Trans. Acoust., Speech, Signal Processing*, vol. 28, pp. 562-574.

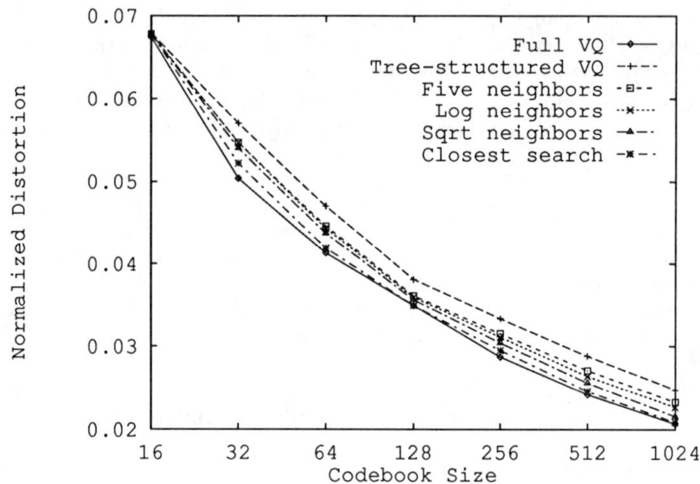

Figure 9: Comparison of improved search performance

D. Cheng and A. Gersho [1986], "A fast codebook search algorithm for nearest neighbor pattern matching," in *Proc. ICASSP*, IEEE Acoustics, Speech, and Signal Processing Society, pp. 265-268.

P. A. Chou, T. Lookabaugh, and R. M. Gray [1989], "Optimal pruning with applications to tree-structured source coding and modeling," *IEEE Trans. Inform. Theory*, vol. IT-35, no. 2, pp. 299-315.

A. Gersho and R. M. Gray [1992], *Vector Quantization and Signal Compression*, Boston, MA: Kluwer Academic Publishers.

J. Lin [1992], *Vector Quantization for Image Compression: Algorithms and Performance*, Ph.D. Dissertation, Brandeis University, MA.

J. Lin and J. A. Storer [1991], "Resolution-constrained tree-structured vector quantization for image compression," *1991 IEEE International Symposium on Information Theory*, Hungary.

J. Lin, J. A. Storer, and M. Cohn [1992], "Optimal pruning for tree-structured vector quantization," *Journal of Information Processing and Management*, in press.

Y. Linde, A. Buzo, and R. M. Gray [1980], "An algorithm for vector quantizer design," *IEEE Trans. Commun.*, vol. 28, pp. 84-95.

S. P. Lloyd [1957], "Least squares quantization in PCM," unpublished Bell Lab. Memorandum, also in *IEEE Trans. Inform. Theory,* vol. IT-28, no. 2, pp. 129-136, Mar. 1982.

J. Makhoul, S. Roucos, and H. Gish [1985], "Vector quantization in speech coding," *Proceedings of the IEEE,* vol. 73, pp. 1551-1588.

N. M. Nasrabadi and R. A. King [1988], "Image coding using vector quantization: a review," *IEEE Trans. Commun.*, vol. 36, no. 8, pp. 957-971.

F. P. Preparata and M. I. Shamos [1985], *Computational Geometry: An Introduction*, New York: Springer-Verlag.

An Adaptive High-Speed Lossy Data Compression

Oscal T.-C. Chen, Student Member, IEEE,   Zhen Zhang, Senior Member, IEEE
Bing J. Sheu, Senior Member, IEEE

Department of Electrical Engineering,
Signal & Image Processing Institute, and Communication Sciences Institute,
University of Southern California, Los Angeles, CA 90089-0271.

Abstract -- An adaptive method for lossy data compression and the associated VLSI architecture have been developed. This scheme does not require a-priori knowledge of the source statistics and codebook training. The codebook is generated on the fly and is constantly updated to capture local textual features of data. The algorithm is proven to reach rate distortion function for memoryless sources. We also propose a computing architecture which consists of a vector quantizer and an encoded-data generator. By using this method, a high-speed VLSI processor with good local adaptivity, less complexity and fair compression ratio can be achieved.

I. Introduction

One of the major goals of data compression is to compress information files in order to consume less storage or transmission resources [1,2]. The source data are to be encoded into a form that can be decoded with a high fidelity. Source data are a sequence of letters drawn from the alphabet, such as English text, numerical data, computer programs, electron mails, digital sampled images, music and speech. A fundamental result of Shannon's rate-distortion theory [3] states that better performance can always be achieved by coding vectors instead of scalars. Vector quantization [4] is a process in which data are divided into small vectors, which are then individually encoded in sequence. The objective is to identify a set of possible vectors which are representative of the information to be encoded. For each source vector, the vector quantization encoder selects the closest matching vector from the codebook. Vector quantization is a very effective technique for speech waveform coding and image data compression [5,6].

Recently, theoretical foundation for a new vector-quantization-based lossy data compression approach was reported [7]. A detailed working algorithm for such an adaptive lossy data compression is presented and proven. This adaptive vector quantization (AVQ) does not need any *a-priori* knowledge of the source statistics. The codebook is generated on the fly as the data flow in. There is no separate codebook training or preprocessing before the actual vector quantization. The codebook is constantly updated in order to capture the local textual features of the data. In the VLSI architecture, the main modules are a vector quantizer (VQ) and an encoded-data generator.

This research was partially supported by NSF under Grant No. NCR-8905052, and by DARPA under Contract No. J-FBI-91-194.

The source data are piped into VQ and then the output index value is applied to the encoded-data generator. If there exists a codevector which can meet the distortion requirement, the output index value and an identification code together form the compressed data. If not, the encoded-data generator uses an interpolation method to estimate a new compact codeword for the source data.

II. The Algorithm

A. Theoretical foundation

Several authorative papers addressed the modified adaptive lossy data compression subject [7,8]. Many of them share a common feature that they used derived methods from lossless move-to-front algorithm [9,10]. If the current source word is used as the new codeword to update the codebook, the rate distortion function can not be reached. Ornstein and Shields [8] used a greedy algorithm to choose the codebook. They demonstrated that their method can reach the rate distortion function in the almost-sure sense. However, a fixed codebook is used. When the statistics of the source data changes from time to time, the performance of their algorithm could be poor. Zhang and Wei [7] developed the basic theory for the "Gold-Washing" technique, and showed that for memoryless sources and Markov sources, the rate distortion function can be achieved.

Since the source statistics is unknown, the optimal codeword distribution is unavailable to the encoder. Therefore the key problem in the design of this type of adaptive lossy data compression algorithms is how to choose the new codewords. The basic idea for the Gold-Washing technique is to use a finite buffer, and to keep on replacing codewords. Notice that there is a survivability associated with each codeword. A good codeword has much better chance to survive than a bad codeword. The Gold-Washing technique uses this property to retain good codewords in the codebook and to discard bad codewords.

B. Gold-Washing method

There are two buffers (buffer-1 and buffer-2) for the codebook shown in Fig. 1. In buffer-2, a frequency table for each codevector is used. For each incoming data x_i, the best matched codevector is searched by calculating distortion measure $\mu(x_i,y_j)$. If the distortion measure is less than a threshold, then the match has been achieved. Here $\mu(x_i,y_i) = \frac{1}{n} \sum_{k=1}^{n} (x_{ik}-y_{ik})^2$. If a best-matched codevector y_j exists, then two possible cases are to be considered:

(1) If codevector y_j is in buffer-1, move it to the top of buffer-1 and push down the first j-1 entries of buffer-1 by one notch; and

(2) If codevector y_j is in buffer-2, then increase the corresponding frequency counter entry by 1.

Otherwise, a new codevector is created by using block-data interpolation. This new codevector is put on the top of buffer-2 and its initial frequency counter is set to be zero. All previous entries of buffer-2 are pushed down by one notch. If the content of the frequency counter for the last codeword entry is below a frequency threshold value S, this entry is deleted. Otherwise, this entry is copied to the top of buffer-1 and the whole entries of buffer-1 are pushed down by one notch. In this case, the previous last entry in buffer-1 is discarded. The flow-chart of the updating rule for the Gold-Washing algorithm is shown in Fig. 2.

In image processing, the buffer-1 functions as a frame adaptive buffer and the buffer-2 functions as a block adaptive buffer. The sizes of buffer-1 and buffer-2 can be adjusted according to different statistical data. For example, if buffer-1 is not used completely after encoding one frame image data, it means that either the size of buffer-1 is too big or the size of buffer-2 is too small, which can be caused by an inadequate frequency threshold value.

C. Gold-Washing theorem [7]

In the theoretical analysis of the algorithm, the new codevectors are not created by an interpolation method. Instead, they are selected randomly according to a predefined probability distribution in the space of codevectors. Let p be the distribution of a memoryless information source $\{x(t)\}_{t=0}^{\infty}$, q be the probability used to select new codewords, $P_e(t, v_0)$ be the probability of a new codeword being introduced, where v_0 is the initial codebook distribution. $d(R)$ is the distortion-rate function of the source and R is the design rate of the algorithm. When the block length n is fixed, we use P_e in place of $P_e^{(n)}$. The average distortion of the algorithm $\bar{d}$ is bounded by

$$\bar{d} \leq d + P_e \, d_{max} \,,$$

and the average rate of the algorithm $\bar{R}$ is bounded by

$$\bar{R} \leq R + \varepsilon + P_e R_{max} + o(n^{-1}),$$

where $d_{max} = \max \mu(x, y)$ and $n \, R_{max}$ is the maximum number of bits needed to code the new codeword y. Since we can make d very close to $d(R)$, the performance of the algorithm mainly depends on P_e. Therefore, the following theorem is the key result needed in the performance analysis of the algorithm.

Theorem 1 : _(Gold–Washing Theorem)_

For all $p, q, d > d(R)$ and $\varepsilon > 0$, there exists a positive integer $S = S(p, q, d, \varepsilon)$ independent of n such that

$$P_e^{(n)} \to 0 \,, \quad as \ n \to \infty \,, \tag{1}$$

where S is a frequency threshold. Gold-Washing theorem guarantees that even though a suboptimal method is used to select new codewords, an optimal codebook can be built up and the average distortion tends to the distortion-rate function. One of the most important issue of Gold-Washing algorithm is its convergence speed defined as follows:

$$t(v_0, \delta) = \min\{t : P_e(t, v_0) \leq \delta\} \,. \tag{2}$$

Define

$$t(\delta) = \max_{v_0} t(v_0, \delta) \,. \tag{3}$$

For $t \leq t(\delta, v_0)$, we have $P_e(t, v_0) > \delta$. If the system started with an arbitrary initial distribution v_0, we have

$$t(v_0, \delta) \leq t(\delta) \leq C_2 L_2 2^{n \, D(d,q,p)} + C_1 L_1 \,, \tag{4}$$

where L_1 and L_2 are the lengths of the two buffers and $D(d, q, p)$ is a function which measures the difference between the two probability distributions p and q. C_1 and C_2 are absolute constants. This is true for sufficiently large n.

352

Although, Gold-Washing Theorem is proved only for memoryless sources, it is not a very difficult matter to generalize the proof to Markov Sources. But, the generalization to an arbitrary ergodic source could be very difficult. We believe even for non-Markov ergodic sources, similar results should hold. This should be the most important research problem in this direction.

D. Block-data interpolation

Selective data from the block source information are quantized. The quantized data are used to find the neighboring data values by the interpolation method. The coefficient codes for the neighboring data are also constructed. The quantized level and jumping step for the coefficient table are selected according to performance requirements. For example, 4 bits are used to quantize image pixel data such that the maximum distortion for each pixel is 8 gray-levels. Based on these quantized data, linear interpolation is used to estimate other pixel results. Here, the jumping step is assumed to be 32. If the difference between the original pixel value and interpolated value is within (-16,16), then "0" is used to encode this pixel and the linearly interpolated value represents this pixel. If the difference is larger than 16, then "10" code is used, and the interpolated value is increased by 32 to represent the pixel. Otherwise, it is encoded by "11" and the interpolated value is decremented by 32 to represent the pixel. Without a large gray-level difference among neighboring pixels, the maximum distortion can be limited in 15 gray-levels for each pixel.

In image processing, if the block size is 16 for a 4x4 window, the 4 corner pixels are quantized and the other are estimated by these 4 quantized values using the interpolation method. The difference between the original and interpolated values can form a coefficient table. Fig. 3 illustrates one such example. If a larger block size is used, more sampled data are required in order to maintain a good quality for reconstruction.

The selection for a new representative codevector is very important. If the source data are used as a new codevector, the rate distortion function cannot be achieved, and the compression ratio is decreased due to transmitting or storing the entire source data. Therefore, the block-data interpolation method tries to introduce a small change to the source data in order that the new codevector can represent a possible group of source data. This process increases the possibility of matching codevectors. The code for source data is also reduced by using the block-data interpolation method.

E. Adaptive vector quantization scheme

Encoding:
1. Create the initial codebook from a random generator or the previous codebook data.
2. Encode the incoming data x_i by using codevector matching. If a best-matched codevector y_j exists such that $\mu(x_i,y_j)$ is smaller than the threshold, then an identification bit (type 1) and a j index are used to encode x_i. The codebook is updated by the Gold-Washing method.
3. If no codevectors can meet the minimum distortion requirement, the block-data interpolation is used to generate a new codevector. This new codevector is added to the codebook according to the Gold-Washing method. An identification bit (type 2), quantized sample data and coefficient table are used to encode this x_i.

Decoding:
Upon receiving data, the decoder checks the identification bit first. If it is type 1, the received index is used to reconstruct data by using table lookup and to update the

codebook according to the Gold-Washing method. Otherwise, the data is produced from quantized sample data and a coefficient table. The codebook also needs to be updated by using the Gold-Washing method.

In the Gold-Washing method, the adequate values for the codebook size (buffer-1 and buffer-2), distortion threshold and frequency threshold are very important. The variance for the distortion threshold can affect the surviving probability of codevectors. In some cases, the compression ratio can be increased by increasing the distortion threshold. Table 1 illustrates the relationship between compression ratio and distortion threshold. If the block-data interpolation occurs frequently, it indicates inefficient encoder operation. In this situation, the codebook size can be increased to reduce such occurrences. If swapping of codevectors between buffer-1 and buffer-2 occurs frequently, the frequency threshold is too small for the size of buffer-2. The frequency threshold should be increased. The quantized level and jumping step for the block-data interpolation can be varied in order to achieve a good estimation for the source data. Therefore, the values of the codebook size, the distortion threshold, the frequency threshold, quantized level and jumping step should be chosen in order to ensure that block-data interpolation occurs infrequently, and an acceptable performance is maintained.

III. Simulation Results

In the computer analysis, the sum of the buffer-1 size and the buffer-2 size is 512. The individual sizes for buffer-1 and buffer-2 are selected according to image statistics. The frequency threshold is set to be 2 for a moderate size of buffer-2. It makes the codevectors in buffer-2 easy to survive and migrate to buffer-1. The initial codebook is created from a random generator. The distortion threshold is chosen such that the performance of reconstruction can be similar to the results from the LBG method [4] for an 8-bit codebook. The original Girl image and its reconstructed images using AVQ and LBG are shown in Fig. 4. Most edges from the AVQ method are estimated by using the block-data interpolation method so that they are clearer than those from the LBG method. Similar simulation results for Pepper image are shown in Fig. 5. The UNIX command "compress" (LZW) [11,12] is used to reduce the size of encoded data. A more reduction is achieved in the AVQ method since a lot of indices are repeated for the type-1 data. The mean-squared errors and compression ratios for the images in Fig. 4 and Fig. 5 are illustrated in Table 2.

The codebook which was trained from the synthetic aperture radar (SAR) image by using the LBG method is applied to encode and decode the Girl image. In this example, the mean-squared error increases to 1063. On the other hand, the AVQ method is not sensitive to the initial codebook selection. Fig. 6 shows the original SAR image and the adaptive characteristics of the AVQ method compared to the LBG method. The computational time for the AVQ method is much less than that for the LBG method. From simulation results, the AVQ method has good local adaptivity, less complexity and fair compression ratio.

IV. VLSI Architecture

The proposed VLSI architecture for the AVQ is shown in Fig. 7. The major functional modules in the vector quantizer are SRAM [13] for codebook data, distortion-computation processing elements (PE), a winner calculation module, a priority calculation module, an index generator, and a priority updating module [14,15]. The source data are piped into a latch and then applied to the input of each PE. In each PE, there is a counter for generation of the codebook memory address. The host machine will reset the counter before the PE starts to calculate the distortion error between source data and codevector. The detailed functional block diagram of the PE is shown in Fig. 8. If the distortion is smaller than the threshold ($Z < T$), the sign bit is set to logic "1". If the distortion is larger than the threshold ($Z > T$), the sign bit remains at logic "0". The sign bit and difference value from each PE are stored in the corresponding latches. The winner calculation module uses the sign bit and difference value to determine the winner. In Fig. 9(a), the AND function is used on the sign bit and the corresponding difference value to filter out the codevectors which are larger than the threshold. The maximum difference value is obtained from the possible winners, as shown in Fig. 9(b). In Fig. 9(c) the winner index is generated by matching the maximum difference value with the stored difference value for each PE. If there exists one winner, then the logic "1" signal for the corresponding codevector is generated. If there are no winners, all output signals are set to logic "0". In the priority calculation module shown in Fig. 10, the signals from the winner calculation module are combined with the corresponding priority values using the AND function. The index generator selects the winner value as the output index. Figure 11 shows the index generator. The priority updating module compares the output index value from the index generator with values from the index table. If the difference is zero and the priority is contained in codevectors of buffer-1, the priority value is set to $2^N - 1$ (high priority). If the difference is negative and the priority is contained in codevectors of buffer-1, the old priority value is decreased by one. In other cases, there is no change in the priority value. The functional block diagram of the priority updating module is shown in Fig. 12.

The index value is also used by the host machine to update the frequency entry or priority value of the corresponding codevector. If further codebook updating is needed, the correct codebook memory address can be obtained using the frequency table and the priority table. The encoded-data generator uses the source data and index value from the VQ to generate the compressed data. If the index value is non-zero, then an identification code and the index value are the output results. If the index value is zero, then a new codevector and a code are generated using the block-data generation method. The new codevector is stored in the extra memory buffer of VQ. In this situation, the host machine will generate the codebook memory address, and simultaneously update a block of data from this extra memory buffer during one clock cycle. A new priority set-up signal is also issued by the host machine in order to maintain the correct priority entry for each codevector.

V. Conclusion

A new adaptive method for lossy data compression has been described. The method has good local adaptivity, low complexity and fair compression ratio. The Gold-Washing algorithm has been proven to reach rate distortion function for memory-less sources. Based on the Gold-Washing method and the block-data interpolation method, an adaptive vector quantizer and its associated VLSI architecture have been developed to achieve high-speed data compression. The block diagrams of various functional modules and simulation results on the image data compression have been presented.

Acknowledgment

Professor Alvin Despain provides useful discussion on advanced computing.

References

[1] A. Netravali, F. Mounts, "Ordering techniques for facsimile coding: a review," *Proc. IEEE,* vol. 68, pp. 796-807, July 1980.

[2] N. Nasrabadi, R. King, "Image coding using vector quantization: a review," *IEEE Trans. on Communications,* vol. 36, no. 8, pp. 957-971, Aug. 1988.

[3] C. Shannon, "A mathematical theory of communication," *Bell Syst. Tech. Journal,* vol. 27, pp. 379-423, and 623-656, 1948.

[4] R. Gray "Vector quantization," *IEEE ASSP Magazine,* pp. 4-29, Apr. 1984.

[5] Y. Linde, A. Buzo, R. Gray, "An algorithm for vector quantizer design," *IEEE Trans. on Communication,* vol. com-28, no. 1, pp. 84-95, Jan. 1980.

[6] A. Buzo, A. Gray, R. Gray, J. Markel, "Speech coding based upon vector quantization ," *IEEE Trans. on Acoustics Speech and Signal Processing,* ASSP-28, pp. 562-574, Oct. 1980.

[7] Z. Zhang, V. Wei, "An adaptive lossy data compression algorithm," *Technical Report, Communication Sciences Inst.,* Dept. of Electrical Engineering, Univ. of Southern California, June 1991.

[8] D. Ornstein, P. Shields, "Universal almost sure data compression," *The Annual of Probability,* vol. 18, no. 2, pp. 441-452, 1990.

[9] J. Bentley, D. Sleator, R. Tarjan, V. Wei, "A locally adaptive data compression scheme," *Communications of the ACM,* vol. 29, pp. 320-330, 1986.

[10] P. Elia, "Interval and recency rank source coding: two on-line adaptive variable length scheme," *IEEE Trans. on Information Theory,* vol. IT-33, pp. 1-15, Jan. 1987.

[11] T. Welch, "A technique for high performance data compression," *IEEE Computer Magazine,* vol. 17, no. 6, pp. 8-19, June 1989.

[12] A. Lempel, J. Ziv, "On the complexity of finite sequence," *IEEE Trans. on Information Theory,* vol. IT-22, pp. 75-81, Jan. 1976.

[13] H. Okuyama, T. Nakano, S. Nishida, E. Aono, H. Satoh, S. Arita "A 7.5-ns 32K x 8 CMOS SRAM," *IEEE Jour. of Solid-State Circuits,* vol. 23, no. 5, pp. 1054-1059, Oct. 1988.

[14] N. Weste, K. Eshraghian, *Principles of CMOS VLSI Design: A Systems Perspective,* Addison Wesley: Reading, MA, 1985.

[15] S. Kung, *VLSI Array Processors,* Prentice Hall: Englewood Cliffs, NJ, 1988.

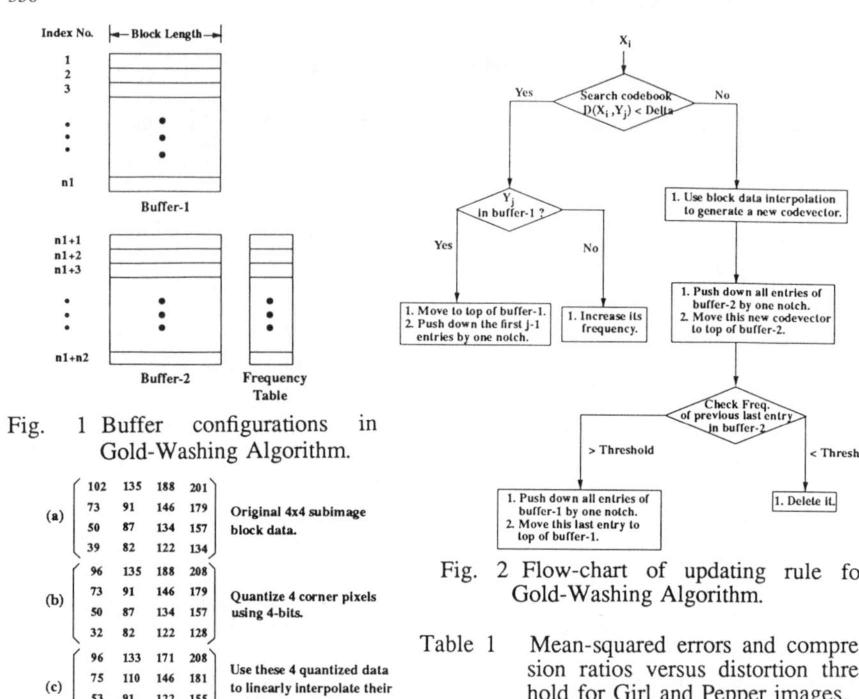

Fig.   1 Buffer   configurations   in Gold-Washing Algorithm.

Fig. 2 Flow-chart of updating rule for Gold-Washing Algorithm.

Table 1   Mean-squared errors and compression ratios versus distortion threshold for Girl and Pepper images.

Images	Girl		Pepper	
Performance Distortion Thrd.	Mean-Squared Error	Compression Ratio	Mean-Squared Error	Compression Ratio
800	50.28	7.20	61.75	7.65
1000	48.79	8.34	62.86	8.05
1200	49.57	9.13	66.50	8.39
1400	52.60	9.69	68.86	8.68
1600	56.36	10.14	70.94	8.91

Fig. 3 One example for block-data interpolation.

(a)   (b)   (c)

Fig. 4 Image compression using the AVQ method and the LBG method on 4x4 subimage block. (a) Original Girl image; 512 x 512 pixels. (b) Reproduced image using the LBG method. (c) Reproduced image using the AVQ method.

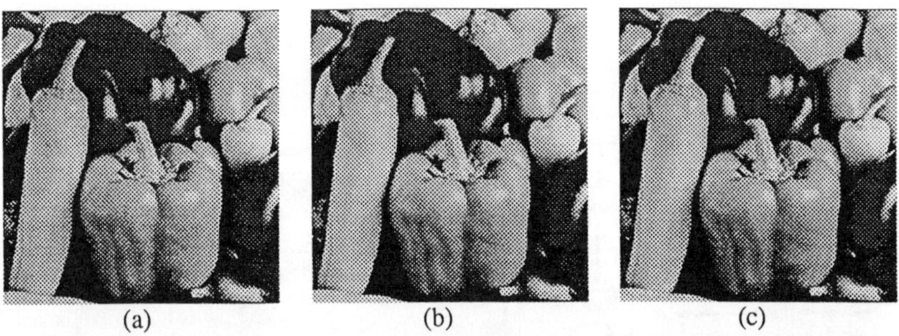

(a)   (b)   (c)

Fig. 5 Image compression using the AVQ method and the LBG method on 4x4 subimage block. (a) Original Pepper image; 512 x 512 pixels. (b) Reproduced image using the LBG method. (c) Reproduced image using the AVQ method.

(a)   (b)   (c)

Fig. 6 Adaptive image compression using the AVQ method. (a) Original SAR image. (b) Reconstructed Girl image by the LBG codebook from the SAR image. (c) Reconstructed Girl image using the AVQ method with initial codebook from the SAR image.

Table 2 Mean-squared errors and compression ratios for Fig. 4 and Fig. 5.

Algorithms\Images	LBG			AVQ			
	MSE	SNR	CR*	MSE	SNR	CR**	CR***
Fig. 4	45.04	26.63	16	49.57	26.21	9.13	12.82
Fig. 5	64.83	24.67	16	62.86	24.80	8.05	10.65

Note: CR* : Compression ratio without codebook data.
CR** : Compression ratio with codebook data.
CR*** : Compression ratio with codebook data and entropy reduction.

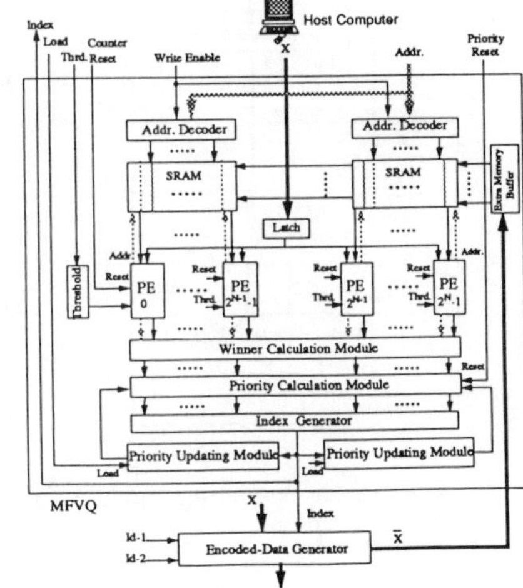

Fig. 7 Block diagram of the VLSI implementation for AVQ method.

358

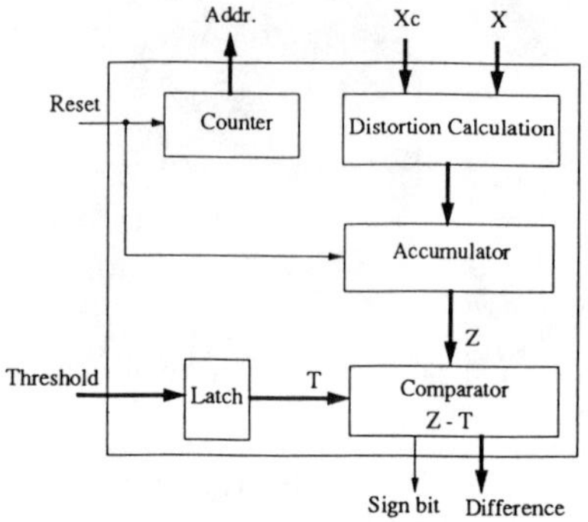

Fig. 8 The functional block diagram of the PE.

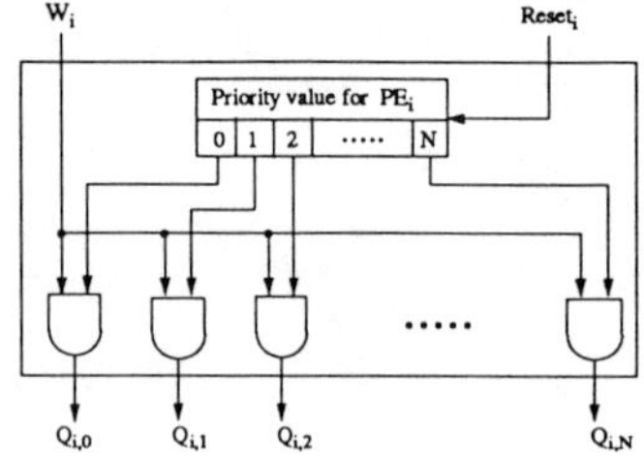

Fig. 10 The priority calculation module for one codevector.

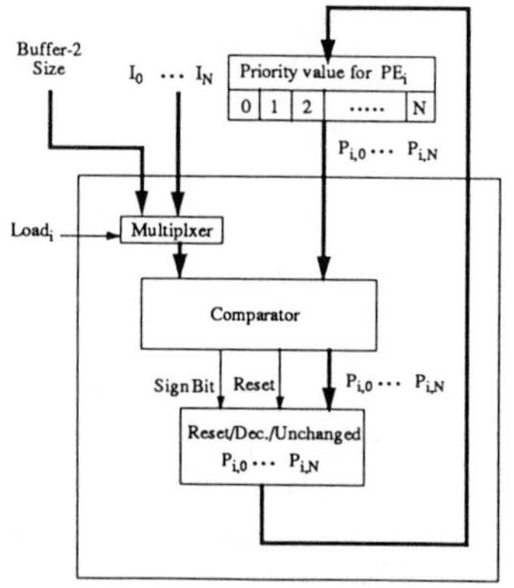

Fig. 12 The priority updating module for one codevector.

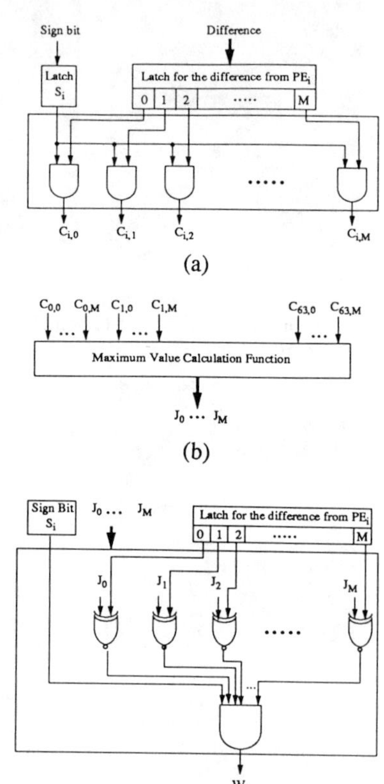

Fig. 9 The functional block diagram of the winner calculation module. (a) The possible winner selector for one codevector. (b) Maximum value calculation. (c) Winner generator for one codevector.

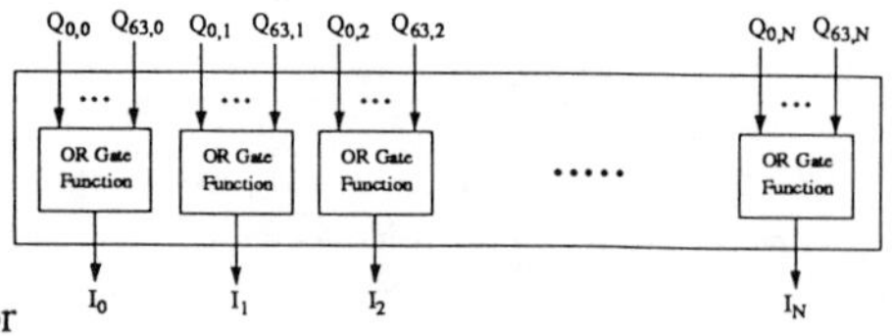

Fig. 11 Index generator.

The hypothetical encoding actually used in Emily is based on that developed by Solomonoff 1964 (but uses the information measure instead of the algorithmic probability measure). Basically, this encoding method is related to Shannon-Fano's non-redundant coding theory where each symbol of the high-level logical language is encoded with a length of

$$-\log_2 (f)$$

where f is the estimated frequency of the symbol in the data.

The actual data length calculations used are too complex to describe properly in this abstract, but in general the length of encoding does come to reflect the length of the data as it is written.

2.3. Searching for a Minimal Encoding

Once an encoding mechanism has been developed so that different possible encodings of the same data can be compared by relative length, Emily then has to search for that particular encoding of the data that gives the minimal length; the concept definitions utilized in that encoding are directly interpretable as the theories which explain the data. The extent to which each of these concept definitions is used in the data reflects precisely the strength of each theory.

In terms of the MDL Principle, the search for the minimal encoding is equivalent to the search for the set of concept definitions which when utilized in the data will minimize the description; thus we can concentrate our search procedure on attempting to generate and test concept definitions.

It has been proved by Solomonoff, 1978, that in general a search for the minimal encoding is an incomputable task, thus any search procedure that is developed will only ever give an approximation to the minimal encoding : we can never guarantee that it will be the minimal. Ultimately, the development of the search procedure will be a heuristic affair; the search used in the Emily system was developed through much experimentation and alterations of the code. The procedure that was finally chosen for the current Emily system does work relatively well but it is believed that further research in this area will yield a better search algorithm.

Complex heuristics need to be used to make the search move through to the most likely extensions of the root definitions, and thus find the correct solution with reasonable efficiency. The A* search, has been an important model in the construction of this search procedure, as has been Levin's search described in Solomonoff, 1986.

2.4. Implementation Details

Emily was implemented on a Sun 4 workstation, and was written in the New Jersey version of Standard ML. This language was chosen as it is a very good development and specification language for a prototype system such as Emily.

Learning problems can be loaded into the Emily system through standard input in the notation described above, with one small exception : the system is able to deal with alternative *extrapolations* which may follow from the raw data given, and this is expressed by placing a colon after the data, then citing each possible extrapolation to the data.

3.0. GEOMETRIC ANALOGY PROBLEMS

In general, an analogy learning task is one where the learner is presented with two background situations which he is told are related; then, given a new reference situation, he must say which of a set of possibilities best relates to that reference; that is, relates in the same way as the two background situations are related.

Geometric analogy problems are a form of the above that are widely used in human intelligence tests (see Winston, 1984) and were chosen to test the capacity of Emily to solve analogy-type problems. Fundamentally, a geometric analogy problem involves pictures of shapes in various relations to one another. Given two such pictures 1 and 2, which we are told are related, the task is to match a third picture 3 to one of several other pictures, X1, X2, etc., according to that relationship. That is, the relationship between picture 3 and some picture X is *analogous* to the relationship between picture 2 and picture 1.

For example, consider the following set of shapes that form such a problem :

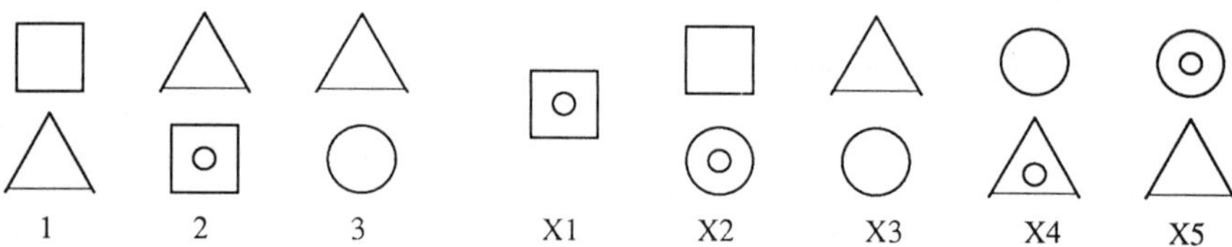

To solve this problem we need to conceive of rules which relate picture 1 to picture 2; then of these rules determine which one allows a mapping between picture 3 and any of the pictures X1 to X5. Perhaps the best rule to be found is the one that says that the two shapes in the first picture, one of which is above the other, swap places in the second picture, and a circle is popped into the shape which is then on the bottom. With this rule it is clear that picture X4 is the best match to picture 3.

3.1. Representing the Problems

In order to get this geometric analogy problem solved by Emily, we need to write the information given in the pictures as a list of logical facts. This can be done by using predicates to indicate shape (ie. `form`), and relations such as `above` and `inside`. Then, the various objects in the pictures, and the pictures themselves can be indicated by variable names. Also, the various shapes, circle, square and so on, can also be represented by variable names. The predicate `in_fig` will be used to indicate that an object is inside a picture (ie. figure), and the predicate `relate` will be used to indicate that two pictures are meant to be related. Thus, with these logical forms we can build the problem in the notation of section 2 as :

```
/   ANALOGY PROBLEM :

/   the following analogy problem has been taken from
/   Winston's 'Artificial Intelligence'. The machine
/   is told that two figures are related, and must
/   then extrapolate which of a set of figures is best
/   related to a third figure.

      graph( square, triangle, circle ) =

/  Figure 1 : contains a square above a triangle

        form( a, square), form( b, triangle),
        above( a, b),
        in_fig( a, 1), in_fig( b, 1),

/  Figure 2 : contains a triangle above a square, and a circle
/  inside the square

        form(c, triangle), form(d, square), form(e, circle),
        above( c, d), inside(e, d),
        in_fig( c, 2), in_fig(d, 2), in_fig(e, 2),

/ Figures 1 and 2 are related :

        relate(1, 2),

/ Figure 3 : contains a triangle above a circle

        form( f, triangle), form( g, circle),
        above( f, g),
        in_fig( f, 3), in_fig( g, 3),

/ Figure 3 is related to some other figure 4 :

        relate(3, 4)


      :


/ Extrapolation X1 : contains a circle inside a square
```

```
            form( h, square),  form( i, circle),
            inside( i, h),
            in_fig( h, 4),  in_fig( i, 4).


/ Extrapolation X2 : contains a square above a circle which
/ has another circle inside

            form(h, square),  form(i, circle),  form(j, circle),
            above( h, i),  inside( j, i),
            in_fig( h, 4),  in_fig( i, 4),  in_fig( j, 4).


/ Extrapolation X3 : contains a triangle above a circle

            form( h, triangle),  form( i, circle),
            above( h, i),
            in_fig( h, 4),  in_fig( i, 4).


/ Extrapolation X4 : contains a circle above a triangle
/ which has a circle inside

            form(h, circle),  form(i, triangle),  form(j, circle),
            above( h, i),  inside( j, i),
            in_fig( h, 4),  in_fig( i, 4),  in_fig( j, 4).


/ Extrapolation X5 : contains a circle, which has another
/ circle inside, above a triangle

            form(h, circle),  form(i, triangle),  form(j, circle),
            above( h, i),  inside( j, h),
            in_fig( h, 4),  in_fig( i, 4),  in_fig( j, 4).
```

This is precisely in the format that was loaded into Emily; note that lines beginning with a '/' are comment lines and are not themselves part of the problem statement.

3.2. Solving the Problems

When the above example is run through Emily, it will return the minimal encoding lengths found for each extrapolation X1 to X5 in conjunction with the given analogy problem data, and will also indicate whatever concept definitions were used to encode the data. The extrapolation which gives the minimal encoding is chosen as the preferable solution. The example of section 3.1 gave the results shown in the table overleaf. Extrapolation X4 was correctly isolated as the solution to the problem, as it gives the least encoding of 134 bits : that is, picture X4 was related to picture 3 as picture 2 was related to picture 1, better than any of the other possible extrapolations were.

Extrapolation	Total length of minimal-length encoding (in bits)
X1	174
X2	180
X3	148
X4	134
X5	194

The concept definitions which were discovered in order to form this solution, are also of interest, and came to encode the data as :

```
R( x, s1, f, s2 ) =   form( x, s2 ),
                      in_fig( x, f ),
                      in_fig( y, f ),
                      form( y, s1),
                      above( y, x).


S( s1, s2, s3 )    =  form( z, s3 ),
                      inside( z, x ),
                      R( x, s1, f2, s2 ),
                      R( y, s2, f1, s1 ),
                      relate( f1, f2 ),
                      in_fig( z, f2 ).
```

```
S(triangle, square, circle),  S(circle, triangle, circle).
```

This is visibly a great reduction in encoding from the original problem specification of section 3.1 : the data of the problem being reduced to the two facts involving the derived concept S. Note also that the concept definitions are nested : that is, the concept R is utilized in the concept definition of S. The output of Emily is exactly as given above except that the variable names are more cryptic : this is because when generating variable names during processing, the system cannot attempt to give them the human mnemonics that we might give (for example, where we might have written `form(object, shape)`, Emily would write something like `form( _x3, _v )`). The variables have been written above in human mnemonics in order to make the concepts better understood to the reader.

The above concept definitions can be interpreted as explaining the relationship that exists between pictures 1 and 2, and pictures 3 and X4. The concept R is an auxiliary concept which expresses simply that within any one picture f that there will be one shape s1 above another s2. The object below, that is x, is a parameter of R so that it can be referred to whenever R is utilized. The concept S is the more important concept which expresses the relationship that there are two pictures `f1` and `f2` such that `R` holds for both of them, and the positions of the shapes in `f2` are the reverse of those in `f1`. It also says that the object at the bottom in picture `f2` will have another object inside (that is, a circle).

Finally, the facts about pictures 1 and 2 can then be compressed into the statement `S( triangle, square, circle )` and those of pictures 3 and X4 can be compressed to `S( circle, triangle, circle)`.

3.3. Conclusions

The Emily system has been used to solve several geometric analogy problems of the above kind, and the results so far have been very impressive and supportive of the MDL Principle. If there were any fault then it would be with the minimal encoding search procedure which occasionally gets trapped in bad sections of the search space and thus is liable to give good but imperfect solutions to the problems.

REFERENCES

Cheeseman, P. (1984), "Learning of Expert Systems from Data", *IEEE Proceedings: Workshop on Principles of Knowledge-Based Systems*, December 1984, Denver, Colorado.

Dawid, A. P. (1991), "Prequential Analysis, Stochastic Complexity and Bayesian Inference", *Bayesian Statistics*, Vol.4.

Gammerman, A. (1991), "The Representation and Manipulation of the Algorithmic Probability Measure for Problem Solving", *Annals of Mathematics and Artificial Intelligence 4*, pp.281-300.

Goodman, N. (1955), "Axiomatic Measurement of Simplicity", *The Journal of Philosophy LII*, pp. 709-722.

Kemeny, J.G. (1953), "The Use of Simplicity in Induction", *Philosophical Review 62*, pp. 391-408.

Li, M. and Vitanyi, P.M.B. (1989), *Inductive Reasoning and Kolmogorov Complexity*, Report CS-R8915 (Centrum voor Wiskunde en Informatica).

Quinlan, J.R. (1986), "Induction of Decision Trees", Machine Learning 11.

Reichenbach, H. (1938), Experience and Prediction.

Solomonoff, R.J. (1964), "A Formal Theory of Inductive Inference", *Information and Control*, Vol.7, pp. 1-22 & 224-254.

Solomonoff, R.J. (1978), "Complexity-Based Induction Systems", *IEEE Transactions on Information Theory*, Vol.IT-24, No. 4.

Wallace, C.S. (1984), "An Improved Program for Classification", Monash University Computer Science Technical Report 47.

Winston, P.H. (1984), Artificial Intelligence (2nd. ed.), Addison-Wesley Publishing Company.

Wolff, J. (1990), "Simplicity and Power: some unifying ideas in computing", *The Computer Journal*, 33(6), pp. 518-534.

Random Access in Huffman-coded Files

Guy Jacobson
AT&T Bell Laboratories
Murray Hill, NJ 07974

Abstract

In this paper, I present a technique for building an index into a Huffman-coded file that permits efficient random access to the encoded data. It gives the ability to find the starting position of the jth symbol of the uncompresed file in an n-bit compressed file in $O(\log n)$ bit-examinations of the compressed file plus its index. Furthermore, the size of the index is $o(n)$ bits. In other words, the ratio of space occupied by the index to the space occupied by the data goes to zero as the length of the data file increases without bound.

1   Introduction

When compressing a file to save space, we often pay a cost in data accessibility. We cannot access a random piece of the data without first uncompressing a potentially large part of the file. We have traded off the ability to perform random access for a savings in space. In this paper, I consider ways to recover the ability to seek to an arbitrary position that was present with the uncompressed file, without paying too high a price in extra space.

There are many practical reasons to desire random access to a large static file that has been compressed. Witten *et al.*[5], for example, describe a full-text retrieval system where a compressed King James Bible is the source. Random access is critical to the efficiency of any indexed database system.

A traditional source-coding data compressor reads input symbols sequentially from the source and writes out a string of bits, and the corresponding decompressor reads the bits and outputs symbols. High-performance data compressors/decompressors typically maintain a great deal of state information during this encoding/decoding computation, and ranges of bits in the output may not correspond exactly to substrings of the input, if, for example, arithmetic coding[6] is used. Adapting a decompressor of this type to allow efficient random access would be difficult, because recovering the state information at some intermediate point in the computation would be costly. For this reason, I limit the investigations in this paper to adding random access to Huffman coding[2], a lower performance encoding technique where each symbol in the input stream maps to a discrete range of bits in the output, and there is no state carried between symbols. Even this limited form of compression often provides a significant savings in space. Also, rather than modify the encoding scheme itself, I am looking for a solution where a small quantity of extra data (an *index*) is added to the Huffman-coded file in order to make random access efficient.

Here, then, is the central problem: we are given a file of Huffman coded symbols. We would like to prepare an index to make random access into the symbols encoded in the file efficient; that is, given an index j, find the jth symbol in the original file quickly. We would like to use a vanishing proportion of extra space for this index. (Note that I am ignoring the space cost of the Huffman tree here.)

An obvious idea is to build an index by storing the bit-addresses of every kth symbol in the encoded file. For a file of N symbols that compress to n bits, this index costs $\lg n \cdot N/k$ bits. To access the jth symbol in the file, we use our index to find where the $k \cdot \lfloor j/k \rfloor$th symbol's encoding starts, and decode $j \bmod k$ symbols from that starting point to reach the proper place in the file. If the space cost for our index is to be $o(n)$ as we desire, we need to choose $k > \Theta((N/n)\log n)$. This means that, to access a random position, we need to examine more than $\Theta(\log n)$ bits from the data *on the average*, since the average symbol takes n/N bits.

This simple scheme may be quite practical, since the value of k may be adjusted to trade space for fast access as desired. Can we do better? This raises two questions:

1. Can the query time be reduced to $O(\log n)$ bit-accesses? (We can't really do better than this, because the size of an address in the data file must be at least $\lceil \lg n \rceil$ bits long.)

2. Can this bound be achieved in the *worst case*? (The simple practical scheme may do badly in regions of the file where the encoded symbols take many more bits than the average.)

In the rest of this paper, I present a scheme, based on the space-efficient ranking and selection directories developed by Jacobson[3], that answers these two theoretical questions in the affirmative. First, I present the problem of efficient ranking and selection in ordered sets, and then I use the tools developed to solve the problem of random access in Huffman-coded files.

2   Ranking and selection

Ordered sets are a most fundamental data type. Given a static subset of $1 \ldots n$, it is trivial to design a data structure that supports membership testing in optimal space; a simple bit-vector will do. If the set is sparse, with m elements chosen from $1 \ldots n$ where $m \ll n$, we desire to store the set in $\lg \binom{n}{m}$ bits, which is roughly $m \lg \frac{n}{m}$. Various hashing techniques allow us to approach this limit.

What if we desire a richer set of set operations? Two very useful operations on a subset S of $1 \ldots n$ are:

rank(m) Returns the number of elements in S less than or equal to m.

`select(m)` Returns the mth smallest element in S.

These are inverses of each other, in the sense that `rank(select(m))` $=$ m, for $1 \leq m \leq ||S||$, and `select(rank(m))` $=$ m, for $m \in S$. These operations can, of course, be performed directly when a bit-map implementation is used, but that would be very inefficient. We generally must perform a linear scan through the bits to rank and select, so the worst-case cost of these operations is $O(n)$.

Ranking and selection are basic operations that can be used to implement a variety of useful functions on ordered sets. For example, let $j, k \leq n$, and $m \in S$:

`rangecount(j,k)` Returns the number of elements in S in the interval $j \ldots k$.
This is `rank(k)` $-$ `rank(`$j-1$`)`.

`next(j)` Returns the smallest element in S greater than j.
This is `select(rank(`j`)+1)`.

`prev(j)` Returns the largest element in S less than j.
This is `select(rank(`$j-1$`))`.

`skip(m,j)` Returns the element in S that comes j positions after m in a sorted list.
This is `select(rank(`m`)+j)`.

One way to add the operations of ranking and selection to a bit-map implementation of a set data type is to augment the bit-map with an auxiliary structure which we shall call a *directory*. This data structure will help make the additional operations efficient.

The term *directory* is taken from Elias[1], where he examines a similar problem: efficient ranking and selection in multisets (which he calls *inventories*). For multisets, there is a pleasing symmetry between ranking and selection, which Elias exploits. However, his scheme is only efficient in the average case. The number of bit-inspections required for any particular operation may be large, but when averaged over all possible inputs he gets logarithmic performance. This average-case efficiency is not good enough for us, since we plan to use ranking and selection as tools. Once they are incorporated into another algorithm, it will be difficult to describe the distribution of inputs to rank and select in a meaningful way. Still, Elias's construction is the inspiration for the two-level directory structure we develop later in section 2.1.2.

Simply storing all the precomputed values of `rank(`m`)` and `select(`m`)` would produce a kind of directory. Since the range values are $1 \ldots n$, we need about $\lg n$ bits per value stored. So the space for this would be $O(n \log n)$, which is unacceptable. The term *directory* implies that the auxiliary data is not too large compared to the bit-map itself. We know that there is a great deal of "fat" in this representation, since the values don't change much from one to the next.

2.1 Ranking directories

To achieve good performance with small directories, we will have to be a little more sophisticated. For now, let's restrict our attention to the problem of creating a directory to make ranking efficient. We will add in extra information to facilitate selection later.

2.1.1 One-level directories

Rather than storing *all* the precomputed values of the rank operation, we will store only a fraction of them. The other values can be reconstructed by interpolation, by counting **1** bits in a small region of the bit-map. If we store some of the n values, with equal spacing k between each stored value, we can compute $\mathtt{rank}(m)$ by computing $\lfloor m/k \rfloor$, doing one table lookup, and then scanning through at most k bits of the bit-map adding up **1**'s to get the desired answer. This requires about $(n/k)\lg n$ bits in the directory (which is organized as an n/k element array of numbers, each of $\lg n$ bits), and does $\lg n + k$ bit accesses in the worst case to compute ranks. The choice of k produces a trade-off of space for time. The bits are chopped up into consecutive blocks of size k, and the information in the directory limits our inspection of the bits from the bit-map to a single block.

Choosing $k = \lg n$ gives a scheme that uses $O(n)$ space (in bits) and takes $O(\log n)$ time (in bit-accesses). The time used is within a constant factor of optimal, as is the space. But we would really like a scheme that uses $1 + o(1)$ times the minimal number of bits; since we are retaining the n bits in the bit-map, we want the space for the directory to be $o(n)$.

If we choose k to grow faster than $\log n$, say $\log^2 n$, we need only $O(n/\log n)$ bits, but the time increases to $O(\log^2 n)$. (We can choose any monotonic unbounded $f(n)$, set $k = f(n)\log n$, and achieve $O(n/f(n))$ space and $O(f(n)\log n)$ time). This gets the space down to where we want it, but now the time grows too quickly.

2.1.2 Two-level directories

The directory schemes proposed above are *one-level* schemes. We know how many bits in positions less than m are **1**'s (except for those in the same block as m) with a single lookup in the directory. Since the maximum number of **1** bits in a block is k (which is small) the values in the directory still don't change too much from one to the next. This suggests using a multi-level directory to recoup some of the space lost to this redundancy. As long as the number of levels is bounded by a constant, we need only inspect $O(\log n)$ bits of the directory. If the final, smallest block size is $\lg n$, this will lead to a total time of $O(\log n)$.

Let's consider two-level directories. The first-level directory is simply a one-level directory, with block size j. Each block is treated as a independent subset of $1 \ldots j$, with its own directory (with block size k) forming the second level directory. This is shown in figure 1. To find $\mathtt{rank}(m)$, we first compute the first-level block number $b_1 = \lfloor m/j \rfloor$. We look up the value of $\mathtt{rank}(j \cdot b_1)$ in the first-level directory, a table

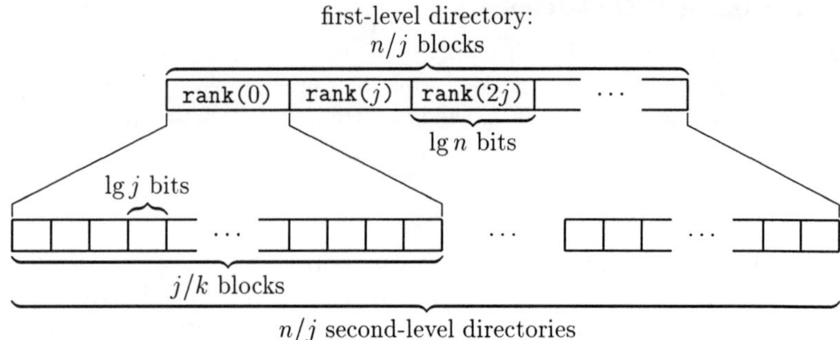

Figure 1: A two-level directory for set ranking.

of n/j numbers each of $\lg n$ bits. Then we proceed to the appropriate second-level directory. We compute the second-level block number $b_2 = \lfloor (m \bmod j)/k \rfloor$. Then we look at element number b_2 in the second level directory; this will be $\mathtt{rank}(k \cdot b_2)$ in the subrange $(b_1 \cdot j) \ldots (b_1 \cdot j + b_2 \cdot k)$. Adding this value to the value from the first-level directory gives the number of **1** bits in the whole set, except for those in the same second-level block as m. These last few bits (at most k) can be scanned directly in the bit-map and added in to get the total value of $\mathtt{rank}(m)$.

The extra space required by this scheme is as follows: $(n/j) \cdot \lg n$ bits for the first-level directory; n/j second-level directories at $(j/k) \cdot \lg j$ bits each for a total of $(n/k) \cdot \lg j$ bits. The number of bits accessed is: $\lg n$ in the first-level directory; $\lg j$ in the second level; and at most k in the bit-map itself. The total time is therefore $O(\log n + k)$. Choosing $k = \lg n$ to make the total time $O(\log n)$, the total space used is $n \cdot [(\lg n)/j + (\lg j)/(\lg n)]$. This space is at a minimum when $j = \lg n \cdot \ln n$. The space needed at this value of j is $2n \ln \ln n / \ln n + O(n \log^{-1} n)$ bits, which is $O(n \log \log n / \log n) = o(n)$. Since the extra space for the directory becomes a vanishing fraction of the space for the bit-map itself, the two-level directory scheme achieves the time and space bounds we seek simultaneously.

Since two levels outdo one, it is tempting to try using the same scheme with more levels to get better results. However, this doesn't lead to improvement over the $1 + O(\log \log n / \log n)$ bit per element ratio that the two-level scheme realizes. Observe that the bulk of the space in any multi-level directory will be found in the bottom level. If the block size at the bottom level is $k(n)$ and the block size at the penultimate level is $j(n)$, the total space used by the bottom level will be $(n/k(n)) \cdot \lg j(n)$. We know that $j(n) > k(n)$, and we require $k(n) = O(\log n)$ to achieve the time bound of $O(\log n)$ bit-accesses. The number of bits in the directories per element must therefore be $\Omega(\log \log n / \log n)$. This is not to say, however, that some fundamentally different scheme could not achieve better performance.

2.2   Selection directories

Now that we know how to construct a succinct directory to make ranking efficient, we would like to do the same thing for selection. First, note that a directory that does ranking in time $t(n)$ can be used to do selection (with no additional space) in time $t(n) \cdot \lg n$, by binary search. If we seek the mth element in the set, we start by doing $\texttt{rank}(\lfloor n/2 \rfloor)$ and compare the returned value with m to determine in which half of $1 \ldots n$ the value of $\texttt{select}(m)$ lies. After $\lg n$ such bisections, we will know the value of $\texttt{select}(m)$ exactly.

While this is better than no directory at all, it doesn't get us down to the bound of $O(\log n)$ bit inspections we are after. The ranking directories we built require $O(\log n)$ time per operation, so this binary search technique will only get us down to $O(\log^2 n)$.

Another line of attack is to do what we did when building the ranking directories: keep a table of precomputed values of $\texttt{select}(m)$ for m a multiple of some suitably chosen j. Then to find $\texttt{select}(m)$, we can look up the value of $\texttt{select}(j \cdot \lfloor m/j \rfloor)$, and begin scanning the bit-map, starting at the returned position until $m \bmod j$ more $\mathbf{1}$ bits are encountered. The problem with this idea is that the number of bits we need to scan through in the bit-map may be very large in the worst case (where the set is sparse).

2.2.1   Putting the ideas together

Neither of the two ideas proposed above is powerful enough to get us the $O(\log n)$ time bound we are after by itself. But if we skillfully combine them, we can make things work.

Assume we have the optimal two-level ranking directory of the previous section available to us. If we knew which second-level block contained $\texttt{select}(m)$, we could compute the rank of the first element in that block, and look through at most $\lg n$ bits in the bit-map to find the value we want. This means that once we locate the second-level block containing $\texttt{select}(m)$, we need only look at $O(\log n)$ more bits to get the exact value.

What if we knew which *first-level* block contained $\texttt{select}(m)$? We could compute the rank of the first element in that block, subtract from m, and do binary search to find the second-level block containing $\texttt{select}(m)$. The binary search would require only $\lg j$ bisections, and each bisection would require us to inspect a number with only $\lg j$ bits, for a total of $\lg^2 j$ bit-inspections. We chose $j = \lg n \cdot \ln n$, so this works out to $O((\log \log n)^2) = O(\log n)$ time. This, together with the result of the previous paragraph, shows that if we could locate the first-level block containing $\texttt{select}(m)$ in $O(\log n)$ time, we could compute the exact value in $O(\log n)$ time.

We are still left with the problem of finding the correct first-level block. A binary search of the whole first-level directory would be too slow. But we can use a table of precomputed values of $\texttt{select}(m)$ to find a subarray of the first-level directory to start the binary search. Furthermore, if we know that the values in that subarray are in the range $a \ldots (a+b)$, we need only inspect the $\lg b$ least significant bits of the numbers in the subarray. The other bits can be deduced from the value of a.

In our precomputed table of `select`(m) we will store all values where m is a multiple of $j = \lfloor \lg n \cdot \ln n \rfloor$. If we want to find `select`(m) for m not a multiple of j, we know that the answer lies between `select`$(j \cdot \lfloor m/j \rfloor)$ and `select`$(j \cdot \lceil m/j \rceil)$, both of which can be obtained via table lookup. Dividing these upper and lower bounds by j, we get a pair of values that bound b_1, the first-level block that contains `select`(m). We can use these indices to define the subarray of the first-level directory on which we start the binary search. We know that in this initial subarray, there are at most $3j$ elements of the set (at most j in the first block, at most j in the last block, and at most j in between).

At this point we run into a small problem. The upper and lower bounds we get out of the table might be quite far apart, if the set is very sparse in this region. Luckily, there is a simple fix for this problem. We will prepare a compressed ranking directory consisting of the values in the first-level ranking directory with duplicates removed. Also, we prepare a two-way index between the compressed and non-compressed ranking directories. The index will store, for each value in the non-compressed ranking directory, the *unique* position in the compressed directory where that value occurs, and for each value in the compressed directory, the *first* position in the non-compressed directory where that value occurs.

With the aid of the compressed ranking directory and the two-way index, we can use the bounds from the table of select values to start the binary search with a small subarray. After finding the upper and lower bounds from this table, we use the non-compressed to compressed index to find a subarray of the compressed ranking directory. Since there are at most $3j$ elements in the subarray, and the subarray is *strictly* increasing, the subarray is at most $3j$ long. We can then perform binary search through this subarray of the compressed directory with only $\lg 3j = O(\log \log n)$ bisections, and use the compressed to non-compressed index to find b_1, the true first-level block number. As we remarked earlier, we do not need to inspect all of the bits of the numbers in the compressed directory to do the binary search either. If we read the first number in its entirety, then we only need to look at the least significant $\lg 3j$ bits of the others, since we know the other values cannot differ from the first value by more than $3j$. Therefore each bisection can be performed using only $O(\log \log n)$ time, and the total time for the binary search is $O((\log \log)^2) = O(\log n)$.

This completes the demonstration that `select` (m) can be carried out in $O(\log n)$ time. But we have been pretty free and easy with the space, adding new structures as needed. How much did we actually use?

2.2.2   Extra space for the selection directory

First we have the table of precomputed values of `select`. There are $n/j = n/(\lg n \cdot \ln n)$ of these at $\lg n$ bits each, for a total of $n/\ln n$ bits here. Then there is the compressed ranking directory, which cannot be bigger than the non-compressed first-level directory, weighing in at $n/\ln n$ bits. Finally, there is the two-way index. Once again, each of these structures is $n/\ln n$ bits. The total additional space used by the selection directory (not counting the ranking directory) is $O(n/\log n)$. Recall that we previously showed that the two-level ranking directory used $O(n\log\log n/\log n)$ bits. Thus the bit-map itself, the ranking directory and the selection directory come to $n \cdot [1 + O(\log\log n/\log n)] = n \cdot [1 + o(1)]$.

2.2.3 A summary of selection

Here is a summary of the steps performed in computing $\texttt{select}(m)$. (Remember that j is defined to be $\lfloor \lg n \cdot \ln n \rfloor$.)

1. If j divides m, then we can find $\texttt{select}(m)$ by table lookup.

2. Otherwise, we do two lookups to obtain a lower bound l of $\texttt{select}(j\lfloor m/j \rfloor)$ and an upper bound u of $\texttt{select}(j\lceil m/j \rceil)$.

3. The subarray of the (non-compressed) ranking directory we want is from locations $\lfloor l/j \rfloor$ to $\lceil u/j \rceil$ inclusive. We use table lookup to find the appropriate range l' to u' in the compressed ranking directory.

4. We read the value s stored in the compressed ranking directory at location l'. We know that between l' and u', all the values are between s and $s + 3j$.

5. Using s, l' and u', we do a binary search through a subarray of the compressed ranking directory. We examine *only* the least significant $\lg 3j$ bits of each number. This yields an index into the compressed ranking directory of the first-level block holding $\texttt{select}(m)$.

6. We map the index into the compressed directory into the true (non-compressed) first-level block number using a table lookup into the two-way index.

7. We do a binary search through the second-level index to find which second-level block contains $\texttt{select}(m)$.

8. Finally, we scan through the bits of the proper second-level block in the bit-map until we find the right **1** bit. The address of this bit is the value of $\texttt{select}(m)$.

3 Random access by selection

With the ranking and selection tools in hand, we can now return to the original problem of random access in Huffman-coded files. This is really a kind of selection problem. Let us begin by preparing a selection directory for the set of positions in the binary Huffman-coded file that begin new symbols in the original file. If our encoded file is of n bits long, we only use $o(n)$ extra bits for the directory. This means that if Huffman-coding achieves some compression factor over a fixed-codeword-length encoding, we can (given long enough files) achieve the same compression factor and enjoy random-access to the symbols.

Of course, there is a big problem with the proposed solution. To do selection, we need to store the original set bit-map as well as the directory. This would double the storage required, which is unsatisfactory. We can get as far as computing the second-level block in which the desired codeword begins without storing the bit-map of start positions. But we cannot scan through the second-level block (the final step in selection) because the blocks are out of synch with the codewords; we do not know how many bits of this block are part of the the last codeword beginning in a previous block.

We do not need to store all $\lg n$ bits of the second-level blocks to recover this synchronizing information. It suffices to store, for each of the $n/\lg n$ blocks, the number of bits in the block that belong to a codeword that begins in a previous block. These numbers are at most $\lg n$, so we only need $\lg \lg n$ bits each, and only $(n/\lg n) \cdot (\lg \lg n) = o(n)$ extra bits for all of them.

With the select directory (minus the set bit-map) and the synchronizing table, we can find the start position of the jth symbol in $O(\log n)$ time, using only $o(n)$ extra bits.

4   Conclusions

A scheme was presented that allows efficient random access to symbols in an n-bit Huffman-coded file, by adding a small index to the file. We can find the start of the jth symbol in only $O(\log n)$ bit-accesses to the index and encoded file, and the size of the encoded file is $o(n)$. Because of the complexity of the scheme, it is more of theoretical than practical interest, although a number of the ideas from the scheme (two-level directories, in particular) could be quite useful in practice.

A question for future research is this: how can we add efficient random access to higher performance compression techniques where there is a great deal of state information needed during the decompression computation? The results shown here do not apply directly, because there is no provision for reconstructing this information.

Also, there are some important ways in which these rank/select structures might be improved:

- The directory schemes presented are complicated, and this makes them unattractive for practical implementation. Is there a simpler data structure that does the same job?

- The number of extra bits per universe element goes as $\log \log n / \log n$. While this quantity does vanish as n grows without bound, it does so quite slowly. Even for very large n, it doesn't even half as n squares! We would rather use less extra space. An asymptotic value of something like $n^{1-\epsilon}$ for some positive ϵ would be better.

- Access time was measured in bit-accesses to the data. A careful examination of the construction of the ranking directory shows that we only examine a constant number of consecutive strings of bits, and each string examined is only $O(\log n)$ bits long. Therefore ranking can be done in constant number of accesses to the data, if accesses can fetch a consecutive string of $\lg n$ bits at unit cost. (The same is not true of the construction of the selection directory; the binary search steps may access a non-constant number of consecutive bit-strings.)

References

[1] ELIAS, P. "Efficient Storage and Retrieval by Content and Address of Static Files." *Journal of the ACM* **21**(2):246–260, 1974.

[2] HUFFMAN, D. A. "A method for the construction of minimum-redundancy codes." *Proceedings of the IRE* **40**:1098–1101, 1952.

[3] JACOBSON, G. *Succinct Static Data Structures*. Ph.D. Thesis, Carnegie Mellon University, 1988.

[4] TARJAN, R. E., AND YAO, A. C. "Storing a Sparse Table." *Communications of the ACM* **22**(11):606–611, 1979.

[5] WITTEN, I. H., BELL, T. C., AND NEVILL, C .G. "Models for Compression in Full-Text Retrieval Systems." in *Proceedings Data Compression Conference* 23–32, IEEE Computer Society Press, 1991.

[6] WITTEN, I. H., NEAL, R., AND CLEARY, J .G. "Arithmetic Coding for Data Compression" *Communications of the ACM* **30**(6):520–540, 1987.

Posters Session

Adjustable Lossless Image Compression
Based on a Natural Splitting of an Image into
Drawing, Shading, and Fine-Grained Components

Dmitry A. Novik
Mail Code 610.3
Universities Space Research Association
Greenbelt, Maryland 20771

James C.Tilton
Mail Code 936
NASA Goddard Space Flight Center
Greenbelt, Maryland 20771

Abstract. The compression, or efficient coding, of single band or multispectral still images is becoming an increasingly important topic. While lossy compression approaches can produce reconstructions that are visually close to the original, many scientific and engineering applications require exact (lossless) reconstructions. However, the most popular and efficient lossless compression techniques do not fully exploit the two-dimensional structural links existing in the image data. We have devised a general approach to lossless data compression that effectively exploits two-dimensional structural links of any length. We briefly describe this general approach and mention two main variants.

Our approach utilizes a natural splitting of an image into drawing, shading and fine-grained components. The drawing component is a kind of contour map of boundaries between connected regions in a digital image. For four nearest neighbor connectivity between pixels, a two bit per pixel region boundary representation is sufficient to select and label separately all connected regions for an image. Eight nearest neighbor connectivity requires three bits per pixel. For an m-band image, the shading component is a list containing m feature values for each region. For an image that is divided into N_{cr} connected regions, there are $m*N_{cr}$ values in the feature list. The fine-grained component (or error term) is the difference between the original image and the image created by placing the value from the feature list at each pixel in each region. An important aspect of our approach is the limiting the fine-grained component to a preset number of bits per pixel. The number of elements in the fine-grained component is the same as the number of pixels in the image (N_0).

Each variation on our general approach uses a different method for dividing (or segmenting) the image into N_{cr} connected regions. One method is based on setting the fine-grained component equal to a preset number of least significant bits. Connected component labeling is then utilized to divide the image created by dropping the specified number of least significant bits into N_{cr} connected regions (regions consist of spatially adjacent pixels with identical values). In a second method, iterative parallel region growing is used to find regions in which each pixel's difference from the region's minimum values can be represented in a preset number of bits. The "drop least significant bits" variation is designed to run quickly, possibly real-time, on currently available computing machines, while the variation based on image segmentation is designed to find and extract the longest possible two-dimensional structural links between image pixels. The image segmentation variation must be implemented on an SIMD massively parallel computer to obtain reasonable execution times.

Preliminary results obtained from 5-spectral band AVHRR (Advanced Very High Resolution Radiometer) data and 7-spectral band Landsat TM (Thematic Mapper) data show compression improvements from 1% to better than 35% over the compression obtained with the UNIX "compress" algorithm.

An Analysis of Frame Interpolation in
Video Compression and Standards Conversion

C. Fenimore and B. F. Field

National Institute of Standards and Technology *

Gaithersburg MD 20899-0001

The interpolation of frames into a video stream is a problem common to the design of video compression techniques [1] and of conversion schemes for the transfer between various video standards and formats, such as frame rate conversion and de-interlacing. For much video material the sampling rate in the spatial domain is sufficiently high that resampling or other processing to change the spatial resolution does not routinely introduce objectionable artifacts. However, the temporal sampling rate, measured in frames per second, is low enough that conversions between framing rates commonly introduce undesirable artifacts.

This study considered metrics for use in assessing the quality of interpolation schemes. Recently, it has been suggested that the L^1 norm is a preferred metric in the comparison of images [2]. We applied both the time-averaged L^1 and L^2 norms ([2]) to video streams, processed according to each of two interpolation schemes. The norms were compared for their ability to detect various levels of interpolation error.

We implemented two interpolation schemes: a frame dropping/repeating scheme, which has roots in telecine conversions, and a linear interpolator. Because the effectiveness of any algorithm is dependent on the motion content in the material to which it is applied, it was necessary to analyze these techniques on 'live video', for which we employed standard material [3]. A simple, yet relatively stringent, test is whether the interpolation algorithm regenerates, with 'small' residual, single frames which have been dropped periodically from the sequence.

The L^2-based norm discriminated between low and high levels of interpolation error more effectively than did the L^1-based norm. Short sequences of interpolated video were generated and viewed in real time to provide a comparison. The study was carried out on a real-time video supercomputer, the Princeton Engine at NIST.

[1] 'Coding of moving pictures and associated audio', Committee Draft of Standard ISO11172: ISO/MPEG 90/176, Dec. 1990.

[2] R. A. DeVore, B. Jawerth, and B. J. Lucier, 'Data Compression using Wavelets: Error, Smoothness, and Quantization', Proceedings DCC 1991, 186-195, Snowbird, Utah USA, 8–11 April 1991.

[3] S. Wolf, M.H. Pinson, S.D. Voran, amd A.A. Webster, 'Objective Quality Assessment of Digitally Transmitted Video', IEEE Pacific Rim Conf. on Comm., Computers, and Signal Proc., Victoria, BC Canada, 9–10, 1991.

---

*Electronics and Electrical Engineering Laboratory, U.S. Department of Commerce, Technology Administration

Bayesian Approach to A Family of Fast Attack Priors for Binary Adaptive Coding

Ahmad Zandi   Glen G. Langdon Jr.

zandi@cse.ucsc.edu   langdon@cse.ucsc.edu

Department of Computer Engineering
University of California at Santa Cruz
Santa Cruz, CA 95064

ABSTRACT

In the compression of black and white (bilevel) images with one-pass adaptive binary arithmetic coding, some conditioning contexts that are all white or all black are highly skewed. When estimating symbol probabilities from counts with the Laplacian estimator (or "cumulative count" in Langdon and Rissanen 1981) the learning phase is too long. In a report of Moffatt (1988), initial counts are 1, but seen events have a count of 10, allowing the ratio to change rapidly thus accelerating the time before the counts are halved. In ISO/CCITT standard work for bilevel images, and a working group document for JBIG (Joint Bilevel Image Group) contributed by members Don Dutweiler and Cristos Chamzas devised an approach called "fast attack" to more rapidly (based on fewer samples) reach a more highly skewed estimate in the initial phases of adaptation. We have devised a single family of Bayesian priors and show it covers all the known methods of initializing the counts and prior statistics employed in binary coding, including the Haldane and Jeffrey priors [1].

Let θ be the probability of the first symbol seen, and let ϵ be different from 0. Also assume that x is the count of the first symbol to be seen and y the count of the other symbol. Therefore at the beginning we have $\theta = \frac{1}{2}$ for every ϵ as it must be. Formula $\hat{\theta} = \frac{x+\epsilon}{x+y+2\epsilon}$ is interpreted as initializing both counts to ϵ and updating by one as they occur. Treating ϵ as $\frac{p}{q}$ then we interpret the formula as initializing the counts to p and updating them by q as they are observed. Letting $p = 1$ initializes each count to one and updates by q, a method already used by Moffat. The avoidance of probabability 1 by using $p_{max} < 1$ is treated.

References

[1] A. Zandi and G. Langdon. Bayesian approach to early probability estimation in binary adaptive coding. Technical Report 91–11, Computer Research Lab, University of Calfornia, Santa Cruz, 1991. Available on ftp site *ftp.cse.ucsc.edu*.

Cascading Modified DPCM with LZW for Lossless Image Compression*

Ratan K. Guha and Ashok I. Roy
Department of Computer Science,
University of Central Florida,
Orlando, Florida 32816-0362
Phone: (407) 823-2341
E-mail: guha@cs.ucf.edu

Extended Abstract

In this paper we consider lossless image compression techniques by combining Differential Pulse Code Modulation (DPCM) [1, 2] and variations of DPCM (called MDPCM) with Lempel-Ziv-Welch (LZW) [3, 4]. There are one and two dimensional predictors for DPCM [1]. Applying any DPCM predictor to an image leads to difference values between -255 and + 255. On cascading DPCM with LZW, the initial LZW code size is increased to 10 bits in place of 9. Two lossless algorithms are implemented using one and two dimensional DPCM predictors cascaded with LZW.

We propose two ways of modifying DPCM (MDPCM) which leads to difference values between 0 and 255, and on cascading with LZW the initial code size remains at 9 bits. Since differences outside the range of -127 to +127 are rare, we give a positive bias of +127 to all the differences within this specified range. The differences outside this range are coded in two different ways resulting in two algorithms, MDPCM1 and MDPCM2. By using one dimensional and two dimensional predictors with these developed algorithms in conjunction with LZW, four different lossless image compression algorithms are developed.

We executed these seven algorithms (LZW, DPCM with LZW and MDPCM with LZW) on approximately 75 different images of various types. We achieved a considerable improvement in compression performance over LZW by cascading DPCM and MDPCM with LZW. The highest improvement in compression performance over LZW of 33.57% was achieved by two dimensional MDPCM2 with LZW and the lowest improvement of 6.4% over LZW was achieved by one dimensional DPCM with LZW. Two dimensional MDPCM2 with LZW performed the best for all the images very closely followed by two dimensional DPCM with LZW. Both the one dimensional MDPCM1 and MDPCM2 cascaded with LZW performed better than one dimensional DPCM with LZW.

References

1. Anil K. Jain, Fundamentals of Digital Image Processing, Prentice Hall, 1989.

2. Rafael C.Gonzalez and Paul Wintz, "Digital Image Processing", Addison-Wesley. 1987.

3. Jacob Ziv and Abraham Lempel, "A Universal Algorithm for Sequential Data Compression", IEEE Transactions on Information Theory, pp. 337 - 343, May 1977.

4. Terry A. Welch, "A Technique for High-Performance Data Compression", IEEE Computer, pp. 8-19, June 1984.

* This work was partially funded by Florida High Technology and Industry Council.

Collision String Repopulation of Hash Tables

Glenn Davis

Arthur D. Little, Inc.
955 L'Enfant Plaza SW, # 4200
Washington, DC 20024-2119

Abstract

Collision string repopulation is an information-lossless structural method for compressing hash data structures that consist of a hash table and a separate collision table containing all collision strings (lists of two or more database record pointers). It successively repopulates individual strings from the collision table into empty hash table locations. The repopulated table is then used in compressed form.

This method is motivated by the need to choose a load factor compromising hash table size with average collision frequency while there are empty locations in the hash table. Collision string repopulation uses these empty locations, and changes how the load factor is chosen, allowing a better compromise.

The compression process is highly structured in order to be almost optimal. During compression, repopulation proceeds string by string, attempting to store each collision string in a single sequence of contiguous empty hash table locations, or space, reversing the direction of string storage if necessary. When no single space is available, it breaks the string into fragments and attempts to repopulate them separately while linking them with pointers called jump references. Repopulation eliminates the collision table and appends an overflow region to the hash table holding any strings and fragments it could not repopulate, and removes pointers to the collision table while generating jump references to other hash table locations. It augments each location in the repopulated table with additional information stored in a 3-bit link field as an opcode describing the location's content and specifying the connection to and direction of the next element of the string.

For hash tables built from random hash addresses, actual compression performance meets theoretical predictions. The compression ratio exhibits a sharp maximum of 1.45:1 at the critical load factor 0.81. At that point, the length of the original collision table equals the amount of empty space in the original hash table, so all strings are repopulated and no overflow region is appended. At higher and lower load factors, an initial imbalance of collision strings or space exists, and an overflow region is present or absent, respectively. For tables built from hash address distributions that are not random, the critical load factor is higher.

Research sponsored by U.S. Postal Service Technology Resource Department.

Color Video Compression Using Motion-Compensated Vector Quantization

Carol W. Wong

Lockheed Engineering & Sciences Company
Houston, Texas

Abstract

Color video compression using a motion-compensated vector quantization (MCVQ) method is being investigated for the National Aeronautics and Space Administration (NASA) Lyndon B. Johnson Space Center (JSC) as part of the Space Station development work. The vector quantization (VQ) coding technique has been used widely in various data compression applications. In VQ coding a finite group of samples, a vector, is compared to a set of predetermined vectors, which is usually referred to as a codebook, to find the closest representative vector. Compression is achieved by replacing the representative vector with an address. Video images, which are usually generated by scanning a scene 30 times a second, contain a significant amount of frame-to-frame redundancy. Motion-compensated coding can achieve significant compression by discriminating stationary areas from moving areas in an image frame and estimating the displacement vectors of the moving areas by comparing the picture elements (pels) in the image frame with those in the previous frame. This coding technique is often combined with transform coding and has been applied extensively to motion picture coding applications.

This paper discusses the implementation and the performance of the MCVQ color video compression system. Color video image sequences, including images collected from a Shuttle mission, are used for testing. By combining VQ with motion-compensated coding, we are able to improve the bit rate of the system significantly without sacrificing the picture quality, when compared with results from using VQ alone. Experiments with real video image sequences show that this method can reproduce good quality color video images at a bit rate of approximately 1 to 1.4 bit per pel (bpp) while the same image sequences coded with VQ alone yields a bit rate of approximately 1.8 bpp.

Compression for Medical Digital Fluoroscopy

John Bloomer jbloomer@crd.ge.com General Electric Corp. R&D, Sch'dy NY 12301

The diagnostic review of digital fluoroscopic X-ray sequences is considered. An economic alternative is the interconnection of the imager, archive server(s) and viewing nodes via a broadcast network. Analysis of clinical procedures show that (1) scheduling of server-to-viewing node transfers and (2) data compression may be used. Access times must be maintained while saturation of the network is avoided. Video compression algorithms and associated VLSI are surveyed. We do not seek to rationalize the need for hospital-wide picture archival systems (PACS), rather discuss one implementation of a specific clinical imaging function: cardiac fluoro review.

We enumerate viewing node needs, thereby generating and analysing design conclusions:
• *Digital Data* - Film viewers no longer make sense with digital imagers.
• *Minimal Cost* - Film and viewer costs establish a $15-$20K baseline for viewing nodes. Networked archive servers are preferred over portable digital media for the communication of data. Compression is needed if low-cost broadcast networks and conventional computer I/O buses and peripherals are to be exploited.
• *Data Availability* - Access times of clinical review procedures might be met if (a) compression and (b) scheduling is used on the broadcast LAN [2].
• *Compression and Data Scheduling* - Observations at one cardiology center suggest a variability in the amount of data recorded per procedure type: 8.6 to 12.9 GB for diagnostic procedure; 9.68 to 32.25 GB for corrective procedures. With no more than one patient per hour in each of four rooms, one hospital center produces data at 11 MB/sec on the average during 8 hours of imaging per day. Amortized over the typical 24 hour review cycle, the 3.67 MB/sec will fit into the (usable) bandwidth of an Ethernet-like LAN with about 15:1 compression. This compression must be performed before storage to use conventional winchester technology. A compression survey involving the author produced no commercially-available hardware that met this constraint without loosing clinical value [3]. It is assumed that the storage server is dual-ported with only server-viewing node transfers appearing on the network.

Note - published hospital PAC system annual volumes are smaller than this cardiac fluoro application by itself. A large hospital generates about 2E12 bytes of digital imagery a year [1]. If the aggregate bandwidth is scheduled over a 260 day year, 12 hour day, transfers may be accommodated by a conventional Ethernet-type network given modest or no compression $(\frac{2E12 \text{ bytes}}{\text{year}} \times \frac{\text{year}}{260 \text{ day}} \times \frac{\text{day}}{12 \text{ hours}} \times \frac{\text{hour}}{3600 \text{ sec}} = \frac{178 \text{ Kbytes}}{\text{sec}})$.

• *Hardware* - Compression at the imager must be capable of functioning at a video rate of $\frac{512 \times 512 \text{ bytes}}{\text{sec}} = \frac{250 \text{ Kbytes}}{\text{sec}}$, given no buffering exists. The viewing node must be equiped with a high-speed frame buffer with adequate storage and memory to loop through images at a 30 frame/sec rate, support back and forth shuttling and freeze frame. Audio and graphic annotation and additional image processing functions are optional. Decompression hardware or software at the viewing node need only consume data at network rates. Compression necessary for authorized individuals to annotate the storage information is not time-constrained. Compression/decompression algorithms with computational asymmetry are therefore acceptable.

References

[1] M. Britt, et.al, *Optical archive organization and strategies for the 1990s,* SPIE Medical Imaging III, PACS System Design and Evaluation, vol. 1093, 1989.
[2] William Stallings, <u>Data and Computer Communications</u>, Macmillan Publishing, 1991.
[3] J.Bloomer, G. Robinson, *Compression VLSI Survey Tutorial*, CICC 1992.

Compression of Object Boundaries in Digital Images by Using Fractional Brownian Motion

James R. Schiess and Kathryn Stacy
NASA Langley Research Center, Hampton, VA 23665-5225
and
Christine G. Matthews, Computer Sciences Corporation, Hampton, VA 23666

ABSTRACT

In many digital images the background and object interiors consist of homogeneous colors and textures. A direct approach to compressing the image is to reduce the image to background and object interior information and object boundary information. For simple geometric boundaries, the boundary information is easy to extract, such as the center location and radius of a circle.

For irregularly or stochastically shaped boundaries, representing the boundary is more difficult if the decompressed boundary is to be a visually reasonable replicate of the original boundary. The present paper addresses this problem by presenting a method which combines existing mathematical techniques. The basic shape of the boundary is represented by a parametric interpolating cubic spline; the stochastic nature of the boundary is represented by a fractional Brownian motion model centered on the cubic spline. Fractional Brownian motion is a fractal-like Gaussian stochastic process that is a generalization of ordinary Brownian motion; it is a form of "one over f" noise.

In the method presented here, the boundary pixels are first sorted so that when listed they progress around the boundary in a clockwise fashion. Spline knots are determined from the sorted pixels by applying an algorithm for locating the endpoints of polygonal segments. The spline knot locations are used to determine a parametric interpolating cubic spline which defines the general shape of the boundary. Deviations of actual boundary pixels from the cubic spline are used to estimate the two fractional Brownian motion (fBm) parameters. As a result, the boundary pixels have then been compressed into the spline knot locations and two fBm parameters.

The method was applied to images of a wind tunnel experiment on helicopter blade turbulence. The method produced 96% to 98% compression of turbulence structure boundaries and regenerated reasonable replicates of the original boundaries.

Compression of Spectral Meteorological Imagery

by

Kristo Miettinen
General Electric, Astro–Space Division
Valley Forge, Pennsylvania

Data compression is essential to current low–earth–orbit spectral sensors with global coverage, *e.g.* meteorological sensors. Such sensors routinely produce in excess of 30 Gb of data per orbit (over 4 Mb/s for about 110 min.) while typically limited to less than 10 Gb of downlink capacity per orbit (15 minutes at 10 Mb/s). Both figures are conservative; actual compression ratios vary from as little as three to as much as twenty–to–one for high–fidelity reconstructions.

Astro–Space division continues to develop and study image compression techniques specifically for application to large–volume spaceborne sensors. Techniques have been both lossless and lossy, spatial and spectral (and stereo). Data quality has been evaluated subjectively as well as with a battery of objective tests (*e.g.* automated weather data calculation based on reconstructed imagery). Algorithms have been evaluated not only for the quality of reconstructed images but also for hardware requirements at the transmitter, vulnerability to communications errors, compatibility with packeting and encryption, and exploitation of error–correcting codes and retransmission.

Current hardware production and development at Astro–Space division focuses on discrete cosine transform (DCT) systems implemented with the GE PFFT chip, a 32x32 2D–DCT engine. Spectral relations in the data are exploited through block mean extraction followed by orthonormal transformation. The transformation produces blocks with spatial correlation (pseudoimages) that are suitable for further compression with any block–oriented spatial compression system, *e.g.* Astro–Space division's laplacian modeler and analytic encoder of DCT coefficients.

The spatial compression system consisting of the DCT, laplacian modeler and analytic encoder is specifically designed for superior performance at bitrates near those achievable by optimized lossless compressors, producing nearly lossless performance (85% of pixels reconstructed exactly) at the lossless bitrate. The DCT–Laplacian system generally outperforms JPEG draft rev. 8 by about 0.5 b/p (or an MSE ratio of about 1:2) when compressing more lossily.

The benefits of the initial spectral transformation vary greatly depending on the design of the sensor, from as little as 0.5 b/p to as much as 4 b/p relative to spatial–only compression with bits assigned among the spectral channels as needed to match the reconstruction quality of the spectral–spatial compressor. For example, for the AVHRR sensor aboard NOAA TIROS spacecraft, the benefit of spectral transformation is about 1.0 bits per channel per pixel (b/cp) for very high fidelity reconstruction (MSE = 0.0833) dropping to a steady 0.8 b/cp for the broad range of lossier reconstructions.

Astro–Space division and its contract team members continue to develop DCT systems, including DCT postprocessors to approach the performance of the Karhunen–Loéve transform and block edge filters to exploit boundary discontinuities, as well as optimal quantizers (vector and scalar), predictors and encoders.

Data Compression using Pattern Matching, Substitution and Morse Coding

G A King, Information Systems Division

Southampton Institute of Higher Education

SOUTHAMPTON, United Kingdom

Overview

The hypothesis is that fast vector signal processors (VSPs) may be used in real time data compression systems. A scheme is suggested involving Matched Filter classifiers in pattern matching and substitution of text entities segmented from bit mapped or scanned documents. The techniques used require very fast correlation/convolution in the frequency domain. An alternative neural net equivalent classifier implemented as an array of matched filters is proposed.

The Pattern Matching Method

A proposed system is described in which a configurable matched filter is implemented as a non-recursive FIR filter using an Altera EPLD. The filter coefficients are a time reversal of the candidate symbol waveform. When a symbol is applied, the output of the matched filter is the cross-correlation function (CCF). The main matching algorithm judges the similarity of the output CCF to the autocorrelation function (ACF) of the candidate entity by means of statistical methods. Both the Matched filter requirements and the Correlation needs can be provided by the VSP.

Before the main matching process proceeds, a rough comparison or screening stage is implemented using majority vote algorithms.

The main statistical estimation technique described calculates the Standard Error of the Difference. The actual difference between the two sample set means is then compared with the Standard Error of the difference, yielding a match figure of merit which is interpreted in accordance with the normal distribution. A short code is allocated to each library symbol.

Secondary Encoding - Further Data Compression

A new approach is proposed which uses an innovative Morse coding principle espousing variable length coding and the stationary statistics of natural language, combined with a dictionary encoding scheme. The 2 pass procedure first performs a word frequency analysis. On the second pass of the source data, words extracted are searched for in the dictionary and substituted for by a single byte code. Uncoded symbols/characters that are non-word sourced are then subjected to the Morse encoding scheme.

Results have produced overall compressions of around 6.5:1 for 10 point characters, comparing favourably with standard benchmarks.

DATA SECURITY IN ARITHMETIC
CODING COMPRESSION ALGORITHMS

Helen A Bergen and James M Hogan*
School of Computing Science
Queensland University of Technology
GPO Box 2434, Brisbane Qld 4001, AUSTRALIA.

KEYWORDS:

Cryptanalysis, Arithmetic Coding, Fixed Model, Adaptive Model, Adaptive Dependent Model, Data Compression, Chosen Plaintext Attack.

ABSTRACT:

The data security provided by fixed and adaptive model arithmetic coding compression algorithms is investigated following recent proposals of their use as encryption systems. For such systems, the model probabilities constitute the key, and knowledge of the model at all times constitutes a successful attack. We examine the case of an open-channel communications line between two users.

Fixed model systems generate non-random output and a chosen plaintext attack allows ready determination of the model. These algorithms are not recommended for encryption purposes. Adaptive systems have a model which changes constantly to reflect the input. This provides protection from the attack used against the fixed model, but allows reduction of the model to a form in which only several thousand states are possible. By implementing a similar system at an interception point on the line, the attacker may scroll through the possible states until a test string is successfully decoded. The models are now synchronised and further messages may be decoded at will. We implement this attack for both a simple adaptive scheme and an adaptive-dependent model. We conclude that adaptive model systems provide significant protection from the casual observer but are vulnerable to a concerted cryptanalytic attack.

* Support from a QUT R & D grant is gratefully acknowledged

Design and Analysis of self-synchronising Codeword Sets using various Models

Eckhard Koch and Manfred Sommer
Department of Mathematics
Philipps University, 3550 Marburg, Germany

Statistical compression algorithms as compared to the dictionary-based compression algorithms have regained importance in the last years. This is partly due to the fact that the important process of modeling the data can easily be separated from the process of coding when using the arithmetic coding scheme.
Although in practice the arithmetic coding is an almost optimal coding scheme, it has the disadvantage of very slow coding. On the other hand, faster coding schemes (such as Huffman coding, e.g.) cannot always be combined with efficient models, which predict the symbols very well that are to be coded next.

In this paper we propose the use of fixed codeword sets for the process of coding. This has the advantage that coding is very fast because of the easy assignment of codewords and symbols. For that purpose a family of codeword sets is presented. Each codeword in a set is characterized by the same prefix and the codewords vary in length. The chosen prefix that all codewords of a set have in common may not occur anywhere else in the codeword except at the beginning. The codeword sets are uniquely decodable and self-synchronising, even though a delay may occur.
Another big advantage of fixed codeword sets is the flexibility in the combination with various models. In arithmetic coding and Huffman coding the frequency distribution of the possible symbols is used for modeling the data (frequency models). Other coding schemes utilize the sequence of occurrence of the symbols (range models). Besides these common models which can be combined with the presented codeword sets a mixed form that uses both principles is proposed here: After a symbol has been processed the new position in the range is determined by the old position and the adapted frequency distribution of the symbol (range&frequency model). Additionally the above models (order-0) are extended to context-based models, in this case order-1 fixed-context models.

The codeword set with '11'-prefix was chosen here. This set, combined with the various models, and some compression algorithms, such as adaptive arithmetic coding, Huffman coding, and Unix-Compress (12-bit table) were applied on a corpus of 'standard' files that has been prepared and released by Bell, Cleary and Witten.
The compression rates of the investigated codeword set in combination with the frequency and the range&frequency model (order-0) are about 0.5 bits per symbol worse (on an average) than the compression rates with adaptive arithmetic coding or Huffman coding.
With order-1 fixed-context models the difference in compression rates between arithmetic coding and the codeword set decreases. When the codeword set is combined with the range&frequency order-1 model the compression rate for some data types (such as object-data or program-data) is even better than the compression rate with arithmetic coding (order-1 model). The compression rates of the codeword set are about the same as those of the Unix-Compress.
With order-0 models the execution time for compression resp. decompression with fixed codeword sets is shorter than with arithmetic coding by a factor 10. With order-1 models this factor increases.

ON DIGITAL DATA COMPRESSION –
THE ASYMPTOTIC LARGE DEVIATIONS APPROACH

Ilan Sadeh

Department of Computer Science
School of Mathematical Sciences
Raymond and Beverly Sackler Faculty of Exact Sciences
Tel Aviv University, Ramat Aviv, Tel Aviv 69978, Israel
Telephone: office (972-3)–5450–849, home (972-53)–59761
E-mail: sade@math.tau.ac.il
7 January, 1992

Abstract

In this work we apply an asymptotic theory of large deviations to the classical compression problem. Following Knessl-Matkowsky-Schuss-Tier (1985) and Covo-Schuss (1990) we obtain the exact asymptotic expansion of the probability distribution of the empirical distribution and the information of blocks of length n. The solution was known only in the limit. The relations between the blocklength $-n$, the distortion D , the rate R and the probability of error P_e. are determined from a set of equations which are solved analytically or by numeric methods. In particular we find the function $R(D, n)$ - "the rate distortion blocklength function". The explicit expression of "the rate distortion function" R(D) is obtained as a limiting case as $n \to \infty$. The error probability $P_e(R, D, n)$, which describes the event of a sourceword of blocklength n occurring that cannot be encoded within block distortion at most nD -as defined in the random coding bound- is also derived. The random- coding theorem concerning the probability of error is presented in its accurate form for large n, rather than bounds in the limit as $n \to \infty$. Thus, we unify together almost all of the classical source compression coding theorems due to Shannon (48, 59), Berger (71) , Blahut (72,74 ,76), Marton (74), Arimoto (73), Sakrison (69), Ziv(72), Dueck and Korner (79) and others.

We use the theory to analyze the performance bounds of limited memory parsing compression schemes. In addition we obtain the asymptotic properties of the parsing method. The analysis of the limited memory cases is carried out under the assumptions that the number of tree nodes in the data base is fixed. The results for compression in various cases are studied. Further results are obtained when some error is allowed in a fixed data base and a fixed compression. Implementations in practical systems are discussed.

A Dynamic Dictionary Compression Method with Genetic Algorithm Optimization

Walter M. Anderson, Anderson Associates
64 Wildwood Drive, Bedford, MA 01730, (617)-275-4060

The use of note-book computers to access remote corporate mainframe data on a timely basis can greatly increase productivity and effectiveness of sales persons and other field organization personnel. Up to date price lists, order status, and other reports can increase service to customers, but at the cost and time of transmitting bulky reports. Fortunately, such reports often contain substantial redundancy that can be exploited to achieve significant reductions in modem transmission costs.

An ad hoc compression scheme was developed that takes advantage of the repetitive nature of mainframe report data. The method developed is an adaptation of the methods described by Ziv and Lempel [1], [2], Welch [3], and Storer [4]. The two principal variations that are employed in the method are: (1) the initial dictionary is seeded with strings that are known to occur often because of the communication framing and (2) the form of the data suggested that parsing should be forced based on character transitions (numeric, alphabetic, blanks, punctuation, etc.). Beyond this, the scheme is similar to that described by Storer; it uses an LRU queue to discard strings after the dictionary is full.

Initial results (compressing by up to 80% or more with a 4K dictionary) were encouraging using dictionary seeding and parsing boundaries that were arbitrarily chosen. It seemed that it ought to be possible to do better if compression parameters were set based on more than an intuitive feel for the data. The seeding of the dictionary was optimized using large quantities of raw data in the following steps: (1) all strings parsed during compression were sorted in an order of decreasing length times number of occurrences and (2) the dictionary was seeded with the most important strings found above for as long as there was room.

Optimizing the selection of parsing boundaries was less straightforward because of the impossible number of variations. This suggested that a Simple Genetic Algorithm (SGA) [5] might be a fruitful approach. An SGA attempts to optimize a function of many variables by examining the performance of independent variable sets and "cross-breeding" those solutions that have the best performance. When the SGA was applied to parsing boundaries, a solution converged within 40-50 generations. The overall results showed a file of 35.6K bytes was reduced to around 6K bytes using the initial, intuitive seeding and parsing boundaries; optimizing dictionary seeding reduced this to about 5.5K bytes; and the SGA optimization of parsing boundaries further compressed this to around 5K bytes. To date too little effort has been spent in exploration of the optimization methods even within the context of the specific communications problem. Further, since optimizing compression encoding often leads to NP-Complete problems, it seems that the use of an SGA optimization algorithm should have applicability to more general compression problems than the specific situation studied here.

[1] J. Ziv and A. Lempel. A Universal Algorithm for Sequential Data Compression, *IEEE Transactions on Information Theory*, Volume IT-23, Number 3, May, 1977, pp. 337-343. [2] J. Ziv and A. Lempel. Compression of Individual Sequences via Variable-Rate Coding, *IEEE Transactions on Information Theory*, Volume IT-24, Number 5, September, 1978, pp. 530-536. [3] T. A. Welch. A Technique for High Performance Data Compression, *IEEE Computer*, June, 1984, pp. 8-19. [4] J. A. Storer. *Data Compression: Methods and Theory*, Computer Science Press, Rockville, MD, 1988. [5] D. E. Goldberg. *Genetic Algorithms in Search, Optimization, and Machine Learning*, Addison-Wesley Publishing Company, Inc., Reading, MA, 1989.

DZ a universal compression algorithm specialized in text.

D REVUZ revuz@litp.ibp.fr   **M ZIPSTEIN** zipstein@litp.ibp.fr

Abstract: «Natural language texts are essentially made of words of this language».
We use this obvious fact, and an extensive lexicon represented with a DAWG (Directed Acyclic Word Graph) to estimate the statistical behaviour of the letters after a given prefix of a word of the language. This estimation used with the arithmetic coding scheme yields an efficient universal data compression method. An average gain of 70% is obtained on French and English test files. The average gain of Ziv & Lempel's algorithm on the same files is 50%. On other kinds of test files results are of the same order as Ziv & Lempel's.

Natural Language: a Distinct Case.

In natural languages the behavior of the letters of the text is highly context dependent. For example, in French after the letter "q" the letter "u" is much more frequent than any other letter. The originality of our method is in the use of a DAWG to produce the probabilities used by the arithmetic coding method. The DAWG represents a 655 000 word French lexicon. The minimized and compacted DAWG takes less than 500K bytes .
The choice of arithmetic coding is motivated by the clear separation that exists between the estimation of the probabilities and the coding itself. The version of arithmetic coding used is the version presented by Witten, Neal et Cleary in 1987. We use an order 1 Markov Chain to estimate the probabilities of the letters of words not recognized by the DAWG.

A DAWG

Both encoder and decoder contains the same DAWG so there is no need to transmit it.
The encoding (resp. decoding) is done simultaneously with the traversal of the DAWG.
Each edge of a state contains the frequency of use of its label (a letter). From these frequencies the probabilities of letters are computed. This corresponds to an estimate of the probability of appearance of a letter after the prefixes that lead to the state.
The frequency of an edge is updated after each use hence the algorithm is adaptative.
Initially all the frequencies are set to 1.

An upper bound for the entropy of French

The average of the compression results for French texts yields an estimate of 2.4 bits per character for an upper bound for the entropy of French. Our corpus size is 3Mbytes

Practical complexity

The present implementation is faster than Abrahamson's implementation of arithmetic coding because of the small out degre of each state, an average number of 1.6 edges per state.The present overall memory usage is 1.6 M bytes.

I.H. Witten, R.M. Neal, J.G. Cleary, Arithmetic coding for data compression, Commun. ACM 30,6 (1987), 520-540 (Arithmetic coding).
D. Abrahamson, An adaptive dependency source model for data compression, Communi. ACM 32,1 (1989), 77-83 (Markov chaine & Arithmetic coding).
D. Revuz, *Dictionnaires et Lexiques Méthodes et Algorithmes*, These de Doctorat Université Paris 7, (1991) (Huge DAWG)
M. Zipstein, *Les méthodes de compression de textes, algorithmes et performances*, Thèse de Doctorat Université PARIS 7, (1990) (Arithmetic Transducer).

The Effects of Video Compression on Acceptability of Images
for Monitoring Life Sciences' Experiments

Richard F. Haines
Foothill-DeAnza College
Los Altos Hills, CA
94022

Sherry L. Chuang
Spacecraft Data Systems Research Branch
Ames Research Center - NASA
Moffett Field, CA 94035

Abstract

Future manned scientific space operations for Space Station Freedom (SSF) will call for a carefully planned variety of multimedia, analog and digital communications including still and full frame rate color video to support remote operations of science experiments. This paper presents results of an investigation to determine if video compression is a viable solution to current transmission bandwidth constraints. Static and dynamic imagery related to three different non-human life sciences scientific disciplines (plant physiology, rodent behavior, and primate behavior) were studied. Thirty three volunteer subjects from NASA Ames viewed three broadly representative scenes (each in their own discipline) that had been compressed to four levels. Still (*plant* growth) imagery was compressed using the JPEG standard at compression ratios (file size in kbytes) of approximately 6:1 (133), 20:1 (47), 40:1 (23), and 80:1 (11). For each scene, viewers had to judge (a) image quality and acceptability of two images presented side by side on a high resolution monitor using a paired comparison experimental technique, (b) which image possessed the best resolution, and (c) the degree of image acceptability to support their own personal research. No information about actual compression levels involved was presented. It was found that the larger the difference in compression the greater was judgment accuracy, however, the two images had to be three levels (of compression) apart before their judgments were reliably correct (above chance). While there was not a statistically significant difference in image acceptability across these four compression levels, a large difference in acceptability was found associated with the three scenes by analysis of variance (F = 8.25; df = 2; p = 0.009). Resolution by itself was the single most important image characteristic, regardless of scene content. In summary, the highest JPEG compression level studied here (i.e., approx. 80:1) appears to provide acceptable image quality for carrying out precise image detail and color discriminations.

In the second series of experiments conducted, different viewers (than above) watched short video segments either of small white rats in SSF cages or a squirrel monkey. Again, three different scenes were used in each situation to sample and evaluate different behavioral aspects, image color, resolution, and contrast. Each scene was then compressed using a CLI Rembrandt codec to 384, 448, 768, and 1540 kb/s and presented in random order. All imagery was presented on a 20" color NTSC monitor 32 inches from the eyes. The *rodent* results showed that these subjects did not rate image quality to be significantly different across these four levels of image compression. The largest difference in mean image quality ratings was between the three scenes (F = 5.01; df = 2; p = 0.0025). In short, scene type plays a very important role in rating images. Resolution, motion, and brightness/contrast were most frequently cited as being the most important image characteristics. The *primate* results indicated that the four bandwidths produced significant differences in image rating for each of the three scenes (typ. F = 4.8; df = 3; p = 0.005) with higher bandwidths yielding higher mean ratings. Type of scene also significantly influenced image ratings (F = 11.1; df = 2; p = 0.0001). Image resolution and color were the most important characteristics. The greatest increase in mean image acceptance occurred between 384 and 576 kb/s, increasing from 45 to 79 percent. In summary, close-up, high resolution imagery and wide-angle "general situation" color video dynamic imagery can be compressed as much as 576 kb/s (using the proprietary CLI algorithm) and still adequately support life science remote coaching operations on SSF for most life science investigators.

Efficient Codebooks for Vector Quantization Image Compression

Vijay S. Sitaram and *Chien M. Huang*
Department of Electrical Engineering, Utah State University
Logan, Utah 84322-4120

This abstract presents some algorithms to be used for the generation of efficient and robust codebooks for vector quantization (VQ). These algorithms are variations to the basic Linde, Buzo and Gray algorithm for VQ codebook generation. Some of the algorithms presented below generate "universal" codebooks that are insensitive to scenery changes in different images.

Mean-residual vector quantization (MRVQ) is a very popular technique of improving the performance of VQ. Similarly, gain normalization has been shown to increase the performance, by reducing the dynamic range of the generated codebook. The combination of mean removal and gain normalization can be expected to yield a significantly better codebook. Our results show that this indeed is the case and saves about 4 bits of codebook size to achieve the same level of performance as MRVQ. In predictive vector quantization (PVQ) the error or residual vector is formed by taking the difference between the actual value of the vector and its predicted value. The residual vector is used for encoding/decoding by VQ. Mean removal and/or gain normalization can also be incorporated into the residual vector. It is found that mean removal and gain normalization of the residual vector performs the best and it saves nearly 8 bits in the required codebook size.

Testing and comparison of each of the algorithms was done by generating tree structured codebooks with a vector dimension of 4x4 image pixels. The codebook is a 4 level codebook with 16 branches in each node. All the testings were done with these codebooks, with three different images which were not present in the training set. Since the codebook was a tree structured codebook, we used the same codebook for evaluating the performance when using 4, 8, 12 and 16 bit. The Fig. shows the performance of MRVQ, mean removed and gain normalized VQ (MGVQ) and PVQ combined with MGVQ. The **SNR** shown is the average for the three images on which testing was done. This improvement in the performance is obtained at the additional cost of slight increase in computational complexity.

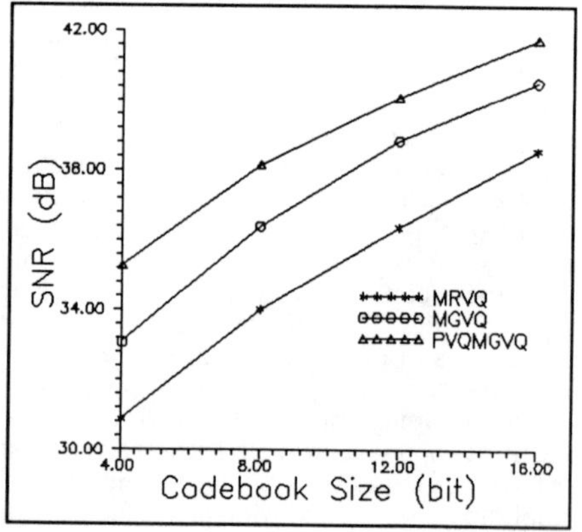

Reducing the codebook size by 8 or even 4 bits helps in greatly reducing the complexity of codebook generation and encoder/decoder. Such codebooks can be used in several applications such as high definition television.

EFFICIENT DATA CODING AND ALGORITHMS
FOR VOLUME COMPRESSION

ZUO MING YIN , KUAN TSAE HUANG
REN BEN SHU and CHEE KONG CHUI

Institute of System Science
National University of Singapore
Heng Mui Keng Terrace, Kent Ridge, Singapore 0511

ABSTRACT

Volume data compression is becoming increasingly important in scientific visualization. We have proposed a new compressed data structure called Linear Level Octree (LLO) and several efficient algorithms. LLO differs from other data structures in its node representation. In linear level octree, each octant is labeled with a unique code key (L_i,x_i,y_i,z_i), where : L_i is the level of the leaf node, x_i, y_i, z_i is x-level coordinate, y-level coordinate , z-level coordinate of the node respectively. Let code key of root node be (0, 0, 0, 0) and the code of an arbitrary node A at level L_i be (L_i, x_i, y_i, z_i) , then A's front-south-west subnode at level $L_i + 1$ is $(L_{i0}, x_{i0}, y_{i0}, z_{i0})$, where $L_{i0} = L_i + 1$, $x_{i0} = x_i * 2$, $y_{i0} = y_i * 2$, $z_{i0} = z_i * 2$. The code keys of A's subnodes at level $L_i + 1$ can be derived by adding the following vectors (0, 0, 0, 0), (0, 0, 0, 1), (0, 0, 1, 0), (0, 0, 1, 1), (0, 1, 0, 0), (0, 1, 0, 1), (0, 1, 1, 0), (0, 1, 1, 1) to $(L_{i0}, x_{i0}, y_{i0}, z_{i0})$.

Escalated representation of octants of linear level octants can be easily implemented. One octant at level L-1 corresponds 8 adjacent octants at level L. 8 adjacent octants Pi (i = 0,1,...,7) in level L can be represented as an octant at level L-1, encoded Q(L, x, y, z, *Children*), $(0 \leq Children \leq 255)$, are not stored separate octants at level L, where *Children* is the byte encoding of the black and white children octants. The compressed format only stores those octant which contain at least one black child octant. It is obvious that this escalated representation format of octants further reduced memory space.

Linear level octree can be also grouped stored. Octants in the same level are first grouped together in a block. The level number and number of octants are stored in the block header. Octants within the block that have the same x values are again grouped together, and similarly for octants with same y values. Experimental results have shown that this compressed storing format can further reduced space required.

Linear level octree has been shown to be very effective in memory saving and processing time reduction. We have shown how to generate linear level octree from voxels. Our octree generation algorithm can grately reduce memory space and has many advantages like generating procedure without search and there is no need for intermediate temporary memory space. The proposed linear level octree based volume display algorithm is optimal in the sense that its time complexity is O(N). The proposed fast neighbor finding algorithm of linear level octree is optimal in the sense that its time complexity is O(logN) and its space complexity is O(N), where N is the number of black nodes. Linear level octree based volume visualization system have being developed successfully.

Entropy Reduction via Simplified Image Contourization.

Martin J. Turner. Research Student, University of Cambridge.
mjt@uk.ac.cam.cl

Contourization

An image can be represented as a contoured landscape with a surjection mapping intensity values to height values. A complete description can be achieved by stating the heights and dimensions of all plateaus in this landscape. As most images have a high two dimensional cross-corrolation the process of contourization gives us a compact image format to aid both storage and manipulation.

A Contour Tree is defined as a contour hierarchical structure describing which plateaus are totally enclosed by other plateaus. This is similar to a Quadtree structure except that the branching is imposed by the image rather than by artificial boundaries.

Contour Merging

For each contour in the Contour Tree we can assign a level of noticeability to the human eye, according to its shape, intensity and surroundings. Repeatedly merging contours, when their noticeability does not exceed a certain specified threshold value, creates a simplified pruned Contour Tree, which can be subsequently coded to give a higher compression ratio.

The current knowledge and theories of the physiological property of the human eye allow us now to some extent quantify this level of noticeability.

Comparisons

This technique offers a complimentary lossy compression system to the popular Quantized Discrete Cosine Transform (QDCT). The artifacts imposed by the two methods are very different; QDCT introduces a general blurring and adds extra highlights in the form of overshoots, whereas Contour Merging (CM) sharpens edges, reduces highlights and introduces a degree of false contouring.

Compression ratios for real images (for example those captured by camera or scanner) at 8bpp giving pleasant acceptable results, depend greatly upon the image contents, but are about 8–10 to 1 for QDCT, and at present about 6 to 1 for CM. For synthetic computer generated images the CM technique often outperforms the QDCT.

Executing Compressed Code: A New Approach

Olaf S. Schoepke, University of Bath

Instruction fetch time is still a major bottleneck in processor performance, particularly with shared memory multiprocessors [R. Duncan, *A Survey of Parallel Computer Architectures*, IEEE Computer, February 1990]. The increasing gap between memory and processor speed therefore requires drastic changes in computer architecture to overcome the communication delays and to allow the execution unit to run more often at peak performance [J.L. Hennessy, *Computer Technology and Architecture: An Evolving Interaction*, IEEE Computer, September 1991]. We show that there is considerable redundancy in instruction stream encoding. Our strategy is therefore to substantially reduce memory–processor bandwidth by a suitable encoding of the instruction stream.

Our measurements show that the entropy of an instruction stream, treated as a higher-order Markov source, is significantly lower than one bit per opcode. We chose arithmetic coding [I.H. Witten, *Arithmetic Coding for Data Compression*, Communications of the ACM, June 1987] as an encoding method for the instruction stream that can approach these levels of compression. Arithmetic coding gives good compression, it clearly separates the model from the channel encoding, and it is amenable to efficient software and hardware implementations. It also is a coding technique which can get as close as desired to the entropy.

We present a technique, in which the object code is compressed prior to execution and then decoded dynamically during execution. We address the problems of encoding the fields of SPARC^{TM} RISC instructions, showing how variable length contexts are useful in dealing with different sized fields within the instruction. We demonstrate the problem posed by branch instructions and present a solution. The coding algorithm must be able to detect branch targets during the encoding process, where a new encoding and decoding phase has to be started. After a branch has been taken, we start the coding phase with little information about the instruction stream seen so far, i.e. a zero–order model. After the first symbol has been coded, we can use a higher order model, i.e. the first–order model. Continuing in this fashion we can get a higher order after each symbol has been coded until an instruction alters the control flow. As we know that on average eight instructions are between branch instruction and branch target we can achieve a limited order only.

In conclusion we give estimates of the improvements in memory–processor bus traffic. With the method presented it is possible to reduce bus traffic considerably. As processors get faster they lose more and more of their performance to the memory system. This research outlines one direction to improve system performance.

Acknowledgement: I would like to thank Siemens AG in Germany which supports this research.

FASVQ: The Filtering And Seeking Vector Quantization

Steve Shih-Yu Huang, Jia-Shung Wang, and Wen-Tsuen Chen
Institute of Computer Science, National Tsing Hua University
Hsinchu, Taiwan 30043, R.O.C.

EXTENDED ABSTRACT

In this decade, vector quantization(VQ) [1, 2] has been proven to be an efficient technique for image/video compression. In the encoding process, full search [1] is a straightforward method to find the quantized codevector of a given input vector. It exhaustively selects the minimum distortion codevector among all given codevectors. The drawback of this approach is that it doesn't adopt any knowledge of correlations between codevectors. Therefore, many redundant works may be done. The computational overhead of it is surely very heavy. Recently, partial distance method [2] was proposed as a technique to reduce the computation time. In this paper, we propose a fast and high-quality method for VQ, called FASVQ (filtering and seeking vector quantization).

The FASVQ procedure consists of two phases. The first one looks like a filter which employees a cost function to prune away those codevectors with small costs. The cost function is defined as follows. From every dimensional point of view, if codevector Y is one of the z (z is a parameter and is set to be 64 in our experiments) closest codevectors of input vector X, cost $C^x(Y)$ is increased by 1. And, the first phase uses the heuristic rule: *"The larger $C^x(Y)$ is, the closer Y is to X,"* to prune away those codevectors with possible large distortions. The second phase chooses the codevector with the minimum distortion among these m candidates (m is a parameter and is set to be 6 in our experimrnts) selected in the first phase.

The experimental results, shown in Table 1, list the comparisons between the full search, the partial distance, and our method. The speedup of FASVQ over the full search algorithm is 6.18, and the fidelity (measured by SNR) is only down 0.24dB on the average. The quality is high enough. The speedup of FASVQ over the partial distance method is 2.11 on the average.

The hardware architecture of the FASVQ method has already been designed [3]. It is a possible way of meeting the real time requirement for the high resolution image.

REFERENCES:

1   R. M. Gray, "Vector Quantization," *IEEE ASSP Mag.*, vol. 1, no. 2, pp. 4-29, Apr. 1984.

2   C. D. Bei and R. M. Gray, "An Improvement of the Minimum Distortion Encoding Algorithm for Vector Qunatization," *IEEE Trans. Commun.*, vol. COM-33, pp. 1132-1133, Oct. 1985.

3   S. S. Huang, H. J. Liu, J. S. Wang, and W. T. Chen, "FASVQ: A Feasible Vector Quantization Architecture", to appear in 1992 *ISCAS*.

		lena	pep.	car	air.	boat	toys	fam.	bar.	bab.	ave.
Full	SNR	32.3	32.3	32.8	33.8	29.2	30.3	29.8	27.2	24.4	30.2
Search	Time	16.7	16.7	16.7	16.7	16.7	16.7	16.7	16.7	16.7	16.7
Partial	SNR	32.3	32.3	32.8	33.8	29.2	30.3	29.8	27.2	24.4	30.2
Distance	Time	4.87	4.6	5.6	6.3	5.3	5.1	5.5	6.1	7.7	5.7
FASVQ	SNR	32.2	32.2	32.7	33.7	29	30.1	29.5	26.8	23.7	30
	Time	2.7	2.7	2.7	2.7	2.7	2.7	2.7	2.7	2.7	2.7

Table 1. The results of the full search, the partial distance, and FASVQ.

This research was sponsored by MOEA and supported by Institute for Information Industry, R.O.C.

FRACTAL IMAGE COMPRESSION

A RESOLUTION INDEPENDENT REPRESENTATION FOR IMAGERY

by

Alan D. Sloan
Iterated Systems, Inc.
5550 Peachtree Parkway, Norcross, Georgia 30092
Phone 404-840-0728   Fax 404-840-0029

Fractal Image Compression, when used in a lossy mode, provides approximations to a large class of images which contain a high frequency of occurrence of large scale correlations under affine transformations. A straight line is encoded in a computer by a formula, not by a bit map image of a representative line. Output and display questions are, for the most part, independent of the formula for the line. When an output device is attached to a computer, a software program which targets the output specific format (resolution, aspect ratio, pixel/depth, number of colors, etc.) of the output device, is used to generate a suitable display from the resolution independent formula which represents the line. Analogously, Fractal Image Compression provides a description of an image which is independent of the output device. No inherent scale is introduced during the Fractal Compression process. Relational information and not resolution specific data is retained. As a consequence, high compression ratios are achievable for high resolution images.

This paper provides some background on Fractal Image Compression, a description of the methodology of Fractal Image Compression, a comparison with discrete cosine based techniques and an evaluation of resolution independence.

Further Study of the DMC Data Compression Scheme

Tong Lai Yu

California State University at San Bernardino

Kin Wah Yu

Chinese University of Hong Kong

The Dynamic Markov Compression (DMC) model described by Cormack and Horspool[1] is an adaptive data compression scheme that uses finite-state modeling and simple arithmetic coding. In contrast with most other text compression methods, DMC works at the bit-level. That is, one bit of the input is processed at a time rather than one symbol at a time; its implementation is particularly simple and might be faster than other models if implemented appropriately. The main advantage of DMC is that it is not tailored to compress any particular language but it achieves English-text-compression comparable to other variable-order Markov models that are tailored to compress English text. Also, DMC achieves better results for non-homogeneous binary files. We find that good compression could be achieved when the model is applied to compress Chinese text which requires a 16-bit word to represent each character. The DMC may have the potential of serving as a universal model for compressing international languages.

In general, it is a rather formidable (if not impossible) task to calculate the entropies of a long string. However, we find that the entropies of some semi-infinite strings generated using some type of deterministic substitution rule can be calculated precisely; a common characteristic of these strings is that the zeroth-order entropy is substantially larger than the first-order entropy which in turn is significantly larger than the second-order entropy and so on. Thus they are appropriate to help analyse the behavior of a compression model. We use these sequences to study the DMC and find that the compression of a Markov binary source varies with use of different n-bit initial models. Also the compression achieved by DMC has not approached the theoretical entropy limit (0) of the sequences implying that there is still room for improvement of the model.

References

[1] G.V. Cormack, and R.N. Horspool, "Data compression using dynamic Markov modeling", Comput. J. 30 (Dec), 541-550 (1987).

High-Performance Compression of Astronomical Images

Richard L. White

Space Telescope Science Institute
3700 San Martin Drive
Baltimore, MD 21218
rlw@stsci.edu

Astronomical images have some rather unusual characteristics that make many existing image compression techniques either ineffective or inapplicable. A typical image consists of a nearly flat background sprinkled with point sources and occasional extended sources. The images are often noisy, so that lossless compression does not work very well; furthermore, the images are usually subjected to stringent quantitative analysis, so any lossy compression method must be proven not to discard useful information, but must instead discard only the noise. Finally, the images can be extremely large. For example, the Space Telescope Science Institute has digitized photographic plates covering the entire sky, generating 1500 images each having 14000×14000 16-bit pixels. Several astronomical groups are now constructing cameras with mosaics of large CCDs (each 2048×2048 or larger); these instruments will be used in projects that generate data at a rate exceeding 100 MBytes every 5 minutes for many years.

An effective technique for image compression may be based on the H-transform (Fritze *et al.* 1977). The method that we have developed can be used for either lossless or lossy compression. The digitized sky survey images can be compressed by at least a factor of 10 with no noticeable losses in the astrometric and photometric properties of the compressed images. The method has been designed to be computationally efficient: compression or decompression of a 512×512 image requires only 4 seconds on a Sun SPARCstation 1.

Fritze, K., Lange, M., Möstl, G., Oleak, H., and Richter, G. M. 1977, *Astron. Nachr.*, **298**, 189.

**A High Performance Data Compression Coprocessor
With Fully Programmable ISA Interface**

Xiaoming Li and Bob Woo
InfoChip Systems Inc.
2840 San Tomas Expressway
Santa Clara, CA 95054
Phone: (408)-727-0514
Fax: (408)-727-4190
email: xiaoming@infochip.com

This report presents a high performance lossless data compression coprocessor IC106 that is designed to be used as a single-chip data compression function for applications where minimum area and power are required such as notebook computers, labtop computers, and X terminals.

IC106 implements high performance adaptive compression and decompression algorithms and supports flowthrough operations for previously compressed or incompressible data. The dictionaries used for compression and decompression are constructed on the fly and stored in a local memory. From 16K to128K local SRAM can be used to support multiple dictionaries (up to 8) and multiple input and output data buffers. IC106 is capable of performing compression at throughput rate of up to 2 megabytes/second and decompression at throughput rate of up to 4 megabytes per second. A lossless compression ratio of 3 to 1 is usually achieved for PC applications.

The complete on-chip ISA (AT) interface results in a single-chip lossless data compression system. The chip can operate either in a master or in a slave mode. In the master mode the onchip DMA function is active, the IC106 controls the system bus through the bus arbitration scheme, and the internal FIFOs are used to buffer the data transfers. In the slave mode the chip behaves like an I/O device controlled directly by the host CPU.

The IC106 is dynamically reconfigurable under program control. Control bytes are first loaded into an internal register file specifying system configurations and data processing options. The register file also holds base and current memory addresses and data byte counts for input and output buffers. The IC106 then performs data compression, decompression, or simple flowthrough on a single command. A fully programmable interrupt mechanism is implemented to communicate to the ISA interrupt controller upon end of the programmed processing.

The chip is packaged in 120-pin PQFP and controlled by two clocks. A High frequency clock up to 40 MH is used for internal data processing and can be either generated onchip from a crystal oscillator or supplied by the system. A low frequency clock of 8-10 MH is used by the interface circuits and should be connected to the BCLK in ISA applications.

Image Compression by Moment-Preserving Edge Detection

Shyi-Chyi Cheng[†] and *Wen-Hsiang Tsai*[‡]
†Institute of Computer Science and Information Engineering
‡Department of Computer and Information Science
National Chiao Tung University, Hsinchu, Taiwan, Republic of China

Abstract

A new image compression algorithm based on a new edge detection technique is proposed. The edge feature in a given window is detected by applying the moment-preserving principle to the image data. The edge directions are approximated by multiples of 45° to speed up the direction process without introducing obvious distortion. For larger block sizes, a more accurate model of a two-step edge is employed in the detection process. The proposed algorithm offers excellent reconstructed image quality agreeing with human perception, high compression ratios, and greatly reduced coding complexity. The solution to the edge detection problem in a given block is also analytic. The algorithm so can be performed very fast for real-time applications with no need of special hardware.

A given image is compressed by dividing the image into nonoverlapping square blocks. Each given block is coded either as a uniform block or an edge block. The edge in each block is detected by the proposed edge detection technique. The image can be reconstructed according to the parameters of these blocks. The window size 4×4 or 5×5 is adopted, which can be assumed to be small for high resolution images. Instead of detecting edges in any directions, it is assumed that the possible directions of an edge in a 4×4 or 5×5 window are limited to be multiples of 45°, or equivalently, $i \times 45°$, i=0, 1, ..., 7.

The proposed approach has been tested on several images. The experiments were conducted on a Sun/4 Spark workstation using the C language. The performance of the proposed method has been compared with the BTC and DCT methods. The BTC method is known to spend less computational expense, and the DCT is a widely used method in image compression. The reconstructed image quality is compared in terms of the SNR. The block size of the BTC method is implemented to be 4×4; however, the block size of the DCT method is implemented to be 16×16. For the DCT method, only the DC term and 11 AC coefficients (11 bits per coefficient) are retained such that the compression ratios are close to those of the proposed method. From the results, it is noticed that the operation speed of the proposed method is faster than that of the BTC method with a comparable image quality. The distortion introduced by the DCT method is large under the range of the compression ratios of the proposed method. Accordingly, the proposed compression scheme is efficient in both operation speed and compression quality.

Image Data Compression Using
Vector Transformation and Vector Quantization

WEIPING LI

EECS DEPARTMENT, LEHIGH UNIVERSITY, BETHLEHEM, PA 18015

Vector transformation has been proposed for image coding. The difference between a vector transform and many well known transforms, such as the discrete Fourier tranform (DFT) and the discrete cosine transform (DCT), is that the vector transform takes a set of vectors as input and generates a set of vectors as output, whereas the DFT or the DCT takes a set of scalars as input and generates a set of scalars as output. In the sense, the DFT and the DCT may be called scalar transforms. In transform coding (or more precisely scalar transform coding), a set of pixels is transformed from the image domain to the transform domain using an orthogonal transform, such as the DCT. The transform domain coefficients have less correlations than the image domain pixels so that they can be coded individually and the energy is packed into a few lower order transform coefficients so that many higher order coefficients can be either coded with very few bits or discarded.

Vector transform coding is a vector generalization of scalar transform coding. In such a vector generalization, a pixel is replaced by a block of pixels (a vector), the scalar transform is replaced by a vector transform, and quantization in the scalar transform domain is replaced by vector quantization (VQ) in the vector transform domain. In other words, an image is divided into blocks, each block is considered to be a vector, and a group of adjacent blocks is considered to be a set of image vectors. Each set of image vectors is transformed into another set of vectors using a vector transform. VQ is performed in the vector transform domain using a set of codebooks. The indexes of the codebooks are transmitted or stored. At the reproduction end, each set of indexes is used to address out a set of code vectors from the same set of codebooks as used in the encoding process. Finally, the inverse vector transform is taken on each set of code vectors to reproduce the image. Similar to scalar transform coding, vector transform coding consists of two parts. One part is to find a vector transform which has the desired properties for image coding. The other part is to find a bit-allocation and coding algorithm in the vector transform domain. Since the vectors in the vector transform domain have different energy concentrations, we should use different codebooks with different sizes to quantize them. The vectors with a higher energy level should be quantized using a larger codebook whereas the vectors with a lower energy level may be quantized using a smaller codebook.

Simulation results of vector transform coding are compared with those using memoryless VQ, scalar transform coding (JPEG), and DCT plus VQ. The comparison shows that, at a compression ratio of 32:1 (0.25 bits/pixel), vector transform coding provides the best image quality. Performance of vector transform coding can be further improved if an adaptive coding algorithm is used in the vector transform domain.

IMAGE DATA COMPRESSION WITH ADAPTIVE DISCRETE COSINE TRANSFORM

Srinivasan.V.S. & Chandrasekhar.L.

CMC Ltd, 115 Sarojini Devi Road, Secunderabad - 500 003 (INDIA)

Extended Abstract

Image data compression using transform techniques have been traditionally block-based necessarily because of the fact that image sizes are large. The image to be compressed is broken into blocks of a fixed size arrived empirically and transform coding is applied over each of the smaller blocks. The transform is basically mapping the image onto another domain to enable processing of the decorrelated components easily. Discrete Cosine Transform (DCT) is one of the most widely used tools in the process of decorrelating image components and retaining only those coefficients which contribute to the major percentage of the energy or activity.

The non-adaptive image data compression technique is based on transforming blocks of image independently and coding each of the blocks by storing a fixed number of coefficients. Performance of such techniques can be drastically improved by making the coding process adaptive in nature by incorporating it with the ability to store only those number of coefficients required for a particular block based on the image data activity within the block and the use of heuristics to decide the number of coefficients based on the entropy within a block.

The fidelity of the decompressed image vis-a-vis the original image is an important parameter in measuring the efficacy of any compression algorithm. The nature of the various DCT coefficients mandates the use of different quantization parameters for DC coefficients and AC coefficients in a block. Quantization is done on each block independently of the other blocks depending on the magnitude distribution of its transform coefficients. The decision and necessity to arm the compression technique with an adaptive dimension is to achieve greater compression over uniform areas of the image. Adaptive compression technique uses a two pronged approach from both the coding and quantizer point of view and delivers greater compression without compromising on the image quality of the decompressed image.

Deciding the number of coefficients to be selected for storing is the primary feature of adaptive coding. Adaptive coder is provided with an activity classifier table. The coder uses spectral entropy of the block as the activity parameter and obtains from the classifier table the number of coefficients to be retained for that particular value of activity parameter. It also invariably retains the DC-coeff of the transformed block as it provides information about the average energy within the block on which the AC-coeffs are modulated.

The adaptive quantizer puts the quantization error low enough not to significantly degrade the image quality. The adaptive quantizer is nonlinear in nature even within the block as the quantizer used for DC-coefficients is different from that used for nonDC-coefficients. In a transformed block DC-coefficients are known to follow a Laplacian distribution and nonDC-coefficients follow a Gaussian distribution. As the number of bits allocated for a quantized coefficient needed to be fixed the number of quantizing levels are fixed. The quantisation levels for the DC-coefficients are fixed over all the blocks whereas for AC-coefficients, the coefficients were normalised with respect to the maximum in the block before quantisation.

The compression performance of the adaptive technique outlined here is highly image dependent. This technique gives a performance, of 0.23 bits/pixel for human faces and 0.33 bits/pixel for finger print images and cartographic map images on an average which compares favourably with the 0.5 bits/pixel of a non-adaptive DCT coding.

Acknowledgements : The authors wish to extend their thanks to Dr.A.Agarwal, University of Hyderabad for many useful suggestions during the course of this work.

IMAGE ENCODING BY POLYNOMIAL APPROXIMATION

Ilan Sadeh and Amir Averbuch

Department of Computer Science
School of Mathematical Sciences
Tel-Aviv University
Tel-Aviv 69978, Israel
E-Mail: sade@MATH.TAU.AC.IL

Abstract

We present a transform method for compressing digital data on a multidimensional lattice. Basically, we generalize the well known polynomial approximation as a method for low-pass filtering of the image. The typical character of high-spatial correlation at the image is used to achieve 2-D "best approximation". One method is to divide the image to subimages (say 8×8 JPEG standard) and approximate each subimage by say 2×2 polynomial coefficients matrix and encode the compressed subimages. The method takes advantage of the limited human eye resolution.

A second approach for exact reconstruction of the image $F(i,j)$ at a given rate, is to calculate the best approximated image $\hat{F}(i,j)$ and the error $E(i,j)$, where $F(i,j) = \hat{F}(i,j) + E(i,j)$.

The argument is: $\hat{F}(i,j)$ is a low pass filtered image and may be encoded at a reduced sample rate and $E(i,j)$ may be represented with fewer bits per pixel than $F(i,j)$. Further data compression is achieved by iterating this process. Using Burt-Adelson's terminology: $g_0(i,j)$ is the original image, $g_1(i,j)$ is the approximated image and $L_0(i,j)$ is the error. The n-step is $L_n(i,j) = g_n(i,j) - g_{n+1}(i,j)$.

By repeating such steps several times we obtain a sequence of two-dimensional arrays $L_0, L_1, \cdots, L_n$. In order to simplify the computation, we choose, a resolution step equal to 2. The details at each resolution 2^j are calculated by best approximation of the difference of previous "filtered" images and by sub-sampling the resulting image by a factor 2^j. So $g_0(i,j)$ with $M \times N$ pixels is approximated to $g_1(i,j)$ by polynomials of $\frac{M}{2}, \frac{N}{2}$ degrees.

The MN equations have a matrix form of dimension $M \times N$ (Eden-Unhr-Leonardi -1985) $\hat{F}(\underline{k},l) = V'_{(M')}(\underline{k})AV'_{(N')}(l)^T$ where $V'_{(M')}(\underline{k})$ and $V'_{(N')}(\ell)$ consist of the first M', N' columns of the $M \times M$ and $N \times N$ Vandermonde matrix, respectively, and A is the optimal compressor- $A \in \tilde{A}(M'N')$.

The main topics are:

1. Solving the problem of determination the set of matrix-compressors $\tilde{A}$ which minimizes the distance $d(A) = \|F - F(A)\|$,and proving that $\tilde{A}$ is a convex set.
2. Calculation of the matrix-transform A,and the minimal error.
3. Proof of the optimal-compression.
4. The reconstructed signal $\hat{F}$ is unique.
5. A necessary and sufficient condition for "distortion-free compression" (i.e. zero-error-compression).

This research is supported by the Ministry of Science of Israel by Eshkol Fellowship no. 0375

IMAGE–SEQUENCE COMPRESSION OF COMPUTATIONAL FLUID DYNAMIC ANIMATIONS

Stephen C. Jones and Robert J. Moorhead II
MSU/NSF Engineering Research Center for Computational Field Simulation
P.O. Box 6176, Mississippi State, MS 39762

The visualization and animation of computational fluid dynamics (CFD) data is vital in understanding the varied parameters that exist in the solution field. Scientists need accurate and efficient visualization techniques. The animation of CFD data is not only computationally expensive but also expensive in the allocation of memory, both RAM and disk. Preserving animations of the CFD data visualizations is useful, since recreation of the animation is expensive when dealing with extremely large data structures. Researchers of CFD data may wish to follow a particle trace over an experimental fuselage design, but are unable to retain the animation for efficient retrieval without rendering or consuming a considerable amount of disk space. The spatial image resolution is reduced from 1280 x 1024 to 512 x 480 in going from the workstation format to a video format, therefore, a desire to save these animations on disk results. Saving on disk allows the animation to maintain the spatial and intensity quality of the rendered image and allows the display of the animation at approximately 30 frames/sec, the standard video rate.

The goal is to develop optimal image compression algorithms that allow visualization animations, captured as independent RGB images, to be recorded to tape or disk. If recorded to disk, the image sequence is compressed in non–realtime with a technique which allows subsequent decompression at approximately 30 frames/sec to simulate the temporal resolution of video. Initial compression is obtained through mapping RGB colors in each frame to a 12–bit colormap image. The colormap is animation sequence dependent and is created by histogramming the colors in the animation sequence and mapping those colors with relation to specific regions of the L*a*b* color coordinate system to take advantage of the uniform nature of the L*a*b* color system. Further compression is obtained by taking interframe differences, specifically comparing respective blocks between consecutive frames. If no change has occurred within a block a zero is recorded otherwise the entire block containing the 12–bit indices of the colormap is retained. The resulting block differences of the sequential frames in each segment will be saved after huffman coding and run length encoding. Playback of an animation will avoid much of the computations involved with rendering the original scene by decoding and loading the video RAM through the pixel bus. The algorithms will be written to take advantage of the systems hardware, specifically the Silicon Graphics VGX graphics adapter.

Incorporation of Imaging System and Visual Parameters into JPEG Quantization Tables

Scott Daly, Electronic Imaging Research Laboratories
Eastman Kodak Company, Rochester, NY 14650–1816

In the JPEG image compression standard for still images, the *quantization tables* describe the quantization used for the 8 x 8 array of DCT coefficients. The standard has left the exact values of these tables up to the user, so that they can be tuned for specific applications or even specific images. Two components that have significant impact in the optimization of these tables are the display and the human observer. The role of the observer is readily acknowledged as the quantization table is often referred to as the *visibility matrix*. Since the basis functions of the DCT coefficients approximately represent two-dimensional spatial frequencies [1], the relevant property of the visual system is its sensitivity to frequency, which is most generally referred to as the contrast sensitivity function (CSF). However, the CSF is adaptive and changes shape as the viewing conditions vary. This adaptivity must be incorporated to accurately model different applications.

Further, for optimal use of the quantization table, the characteristics of the imaging system must also be taken into account. Previous work has addressed the optimization of the normalization array for noise both before and after the compression process [2]. This work extends those results to include other systems parameters such as display frequency response, tone scale, contrast per grey level, and image processing operations. Whether the effects of these parameters occur prior to or after the image compression step will have a significant impact on how the quantization table incorporates their effects. This poster will describe both the incorporation of an adaptive CSF model and imaging system parameters in the design of the JPEG quantization tables. Hardcopy demonstrations of this optimization will be shown for a number of imaging system parameter changes. The results will also be shown on a number of hardcopy display devices, including the Kodak XL 7700 Digital Continuous Tone Printer.

1. R. J. Clarke, "Spectral response of the discrete cosine and Walsh-Hadamard transforms", IEE Proc. V.130 #4, pp 309–313.
2. S. Daly, "Application of a noise-adaptive contrast sensitivity function to image data compression", Optical Engineering V.29 #8, pp 977–988.

Incremental Data Compression
—abstract—

Johan Jeuring

Utrecht University, Department of Computer Science

P.O. Box 80.089, 3508 TB Utrecht, The Netherlands

(jt@cwi.nl)

Consider the case in which an organisation (for example Interpol) maintains a database (containing information about murderers, terrorists, forgers, etc.) that has to be sent to many places (such as the immigration offices of several countries). The organisation edits the database regularly, and sends the updated database to the users. To speed up data transmission, a compressed version of the database is sent. For this purpose the database has to be compressed regularly. Usually, the updated database does not differ much from its original, and for some compression methods, the same holds for their compressed versions. Hence it might pay to use an incremental algorithm for data compression.

Incremental computations can improve the performance of interactive programs such as spreadsheet programs, program development environments, text-editors, etc. Suppose we want to find the value of a function on some input, and that this input is interactively edited. An incremental algorithm prescribes how to recompute the required function-value of the input, after the input has been edited, using the old function-value and possibly some extra information.

Data may be compressed using textual substitution. Textual substitution identifies repeated substrings and replaces some or all substrings by pointers to another copy. We construct an incremental algorithm for a specific textual substitution method: coding a text with respect to a dictionary. With this incremental algorithm it is possible to combine two coded texts in constant time. Furthermore, the time required for deleting or inserting a piece of text and coding the resulting text is linearly dependent on the length of the deleted or inserted piece of text. The algorithm is constructed by means of a theory of incremental algorithms on the data type list[1], based on the Bird-Meertens calculus for program transformation. The algorithm consists of several parts that correspond to the edit actions available on the data type list. The most important part of the algorithm is the part that combines two coded texts, which is essentially a dynamic programming algorithm.

---

[1]J. Jeuring. Incremental algorithms on lists. In J. van Leeuwen, editor, *Proceedings SION Computing Science in the Netherlands*, pages 315–335, 1991.

Interframe Coding Using Quadtree Decomposition and Concentric-Shell Partition Vector Quantization

Hien Nguyen and Jon W. Mark
Dept. of E&CE, University of Waterloo
jwmark@bbcr.waterloo.edu

We consider the problem of interframe coding images using vector quantization so that a constant image quality is always maintained. It is shown in an earlier work (DCC91 pp. 119-128), that a **concentric-shell partition vector quantizer** (CSPVQ) coder yields good image quality using a static codebook. With a relatively low complexity the CSPVQ is able to capture the visual perceptive qualities such as edges and textures in the image representation. It is shown that CSPVQ can also be used effectively in the design of a variable rate coder for moving images. The idea is to suitably identify various homogeneous regions within the *error image* and compactly represent them in a quadtree. Then, the CSPVQ is used to selectively encode various nodes of the tree.

The error image is comprised of several large homogeneous region that make quadtree coding very efficient. Each homogeneous region is classified into one of the four types: **Non-informative, Mean-informative, Variance-informative** and **Mean-Variance-informative.**

When there is no scene change in a video sequence, it is expected that there would be large regions in the current image that need no update information since the previous image. *Non-informative* is the term used to address these regions in the error image. If it is decided that the current image needs resplenishment information, then the resplenishment can be classified into one of *three* types. First, for a *Mean-informative* region, it is only necessary to transmit the mean of the region to the receiver. It is not necessary to transmit the shape of the region to the receiver since it is essentially a constant grey level region. This will result in a bit rate reduction for the coder. Second, for the *Variance-informative* region, it is sufficient that the shape of the region be transmitted to the receiver since the mean of this region can be taken to be zero. This also reduces the bit rate of the coder. The third and last type of resplenishment is the one that requires the most number of coding bits. For *Mean-Variance-informative* region, it is needed to transmit both the *mean* and the *shape* of the region to the receiver. Experiments are conducted to show that error images are largely dominated by homogeneous regions of *non-informative* type and thus are ideal for quadtree representation. That is, for video scenes with an intermediate amount of motion, e.g., horseback riding and conferencing type of video, the percentage of the *non-informative* region in a frame ranges from 70% to over 90%. Experimental results also indicate that the probability of occurrence of *Mean-Variance-informative* region is very small compared to that of *Non-informative* region, *Mean-informative* region, and *Variance-informative* region; therefore, quadtree representation coupled with CSPVQ will result in a low coding bit rate while maintaining high picture quality. A *bottom-up* decomposition technique is described which has better performance characteristic than the conventional top-down decomposition approaches. For the vector quantizer, it only needs a codebook of one size, i.e., the smallest block size (4×4). This will help to reduce the complexity of the coder and enhance the detailed reproduction in the encoded image.

**Large Vector Quantization Codebook Generation
Problems and Solutions**
C.-M. Huang and R. W. Harris
Department of Electrical Engineering
Utah State University

From information theory, it is known that the larger the vector is, the better the performance. That is, with the same quality of decompressed images, a higher compression ratio can be achieved by increasing the vector dimension. However, increasing the vector dimension requires that the codebook size be increased to keep the same quality of the decompressed images. Also, increasing the vector dimension causes the complexity of codebook generation to grow exponentially. This makes large codebook generation very difficult using current computer resources.

A feasible solution is to generate a tree structured codebook instead of a full search codebook. Because of the tree structure, the codebook generation can be easily divided into separate processes of classification and then generating several subtree codebooks. These processes can be done by using several workstations. In this way, the memory for large codebook generation and the required CPU time problems can be solved. Thus, the large codebook can be generated in a reasonable time and cost.

The empty cell problem can be reduced by increasing the number of training images. But when the codebook size increases, this is still a problem to store huge number of training images on disk memory. However, there are several ways that can be used to increase the number of training vectors without increasing the disk space. One such method is overlapping partition method. This method partitions an image into vectors which can have pixels in common. For example, by allowing overlapped 6x6 vectors, an image can be expanded into 36 images. The number of training images can also be increased by performing different linear or non-linear operations on the original set of training images.

To test these ideas, several 16 bit tree structured mean-residual codebooks were generated. Each codebook has 4 levels, and each level of the codebook has 16 branches (that is, each level has a 4 bit representation). The vector sizes used are 5x3, 3x6, 5x4, 6x4, 5x5, 6x5, 4x8, 7x7 and 8x8. About 300 training images were used in each case. Each training image is of dimension 512x512 pixels and each pixel is 8 bits deep. Three Sun 4/110 workstations were used and each of the codebooks were generated in less than 1 week. Three images which are not included in the training set were used for verifying the performance. Since these codebooks are tree structured, they can be used as 4 bit codebooks, 8 bit codebooks, 12 bit codebooks or 16 bit codebooks. The mean rate-distortion curves for these codebooks with different vector sizes demonstrate the result which is consistent with the Shannon theory. That is, the larger the vector size becomes, the better the performance or rate for a given distortion becomes. From the results of our simulation, even larger codebook generation, such as a 20 bit codebook, is feasible and the quality of the decompressed images are even better than 16 bit codebooks.

Lossless Image Compression Using a Codebook of Prediction Trees [1]

Abstract

Nasir D. Memon
Spyros S. Magliveras
Dept. of Computer Science
University of Nebraska
Lincoln, NE 68588-0115

Khalid Sayood
Dept. of Electrical Eng.
University of Nebraska
Lincoln, NE 68588-0511
ksayood@eecomm.unl.edu

Prediction schemes for image compression implicitly assume that the image is scanned in a particular order. Clearly, depending on the picture, a different scanning pattern may give better compression. Earlier [1], we introduced the notion of a *prediction tree* of an image and also its *minimum entropy prediction tree*. A depth-first traversal of a prediction tree can be interpreted as a scan of the image subject to the constraint of visiting neighbors of already scanned pixels. A minimum entropy prediction tree minimizes the entropy of the prediction errors over all such scans.

There is a trade-off involved between minimizing the number of bits needed to encode the shape of a tree and the entropy of the weights on the tree. Depending on the application, there are many ways to strike a favorable trade-off. In this paper we present one such approach, namely, using a codebook of prediction trees.

If we partition an image into fixed size blocks, it would be reasonable to expect to find prediction trees which are near optimal for several blocks. We can construct a codebook of prediction trees and for each block in the image identify the best prediction tree from within the codebook. Although the prediction tree obtained in this way will not be optimal we would have considerably reduced the overhead required to encode the prediction tree.

Like any other dictionary or codebook scheme, there are three ways to proceed. We can have a static codebook which we construct from our general knowledge about image characteristics, or we can have a semiadaptive codebook which is constructed explicitly for each image or class of images. Finally, we could have an adaptive codebook which we construct on the fly as we are encoding the image. We design algorithms for each of these approaches and give implementation results on a test set of images. The bit rates achieved with initial implementations compare favorably with the lossless schemes proposed by the JPEG standard.

References

1. N. D. Memon, S. S. Magliveras and K. Sayood, Prediction trees and lossless image compression - an extended abstract, *Proceedings of the Data Compression Conference*, pages 83–92, IEEE Computer Society Press, 1991.

---

[1]This work was supported in part by the NASA Lewis Research Center and by the Center for Communication and Information Science, University of Nebraska, lincoln.

Low Complexity Subband Encoding For HDTV Images

Naresh Coppisetti and S. C. Kwatra
Department of Elec. Engg.
University of Toledo
Toledo, Ohio 43606

Awad Kh. Al-Asmari
Asst. Professor, Elec. Engg. Dept.
King Saud University, Box 800,
Riyadh, Saudi Arabia 11421

The transmission of high definition television (HDTV) signals on available digital networks and satellites requires the adoption of sophisticated compression techniques to limit the bit rate requirements and to provide high quality and reliable service to customers. For processing and transmission of image signals, a low complexity codec without visible degradation is desired. In this paper, a low complexity intraframe subband image coding algorithm is presented. The low band is DPCM encoded and the high bands are PCM encoded. An efficient entropy coder is designed which reduces the overall bit rate significantly. It is shown that high quality HDTV images can be obtained at as low a bit rate as 45 Mbits/sec or less with a very low complexity encoder. For dividing the image into subbands, a new class of quadrature mirror filters (QMFs) called generalized quadrature mirror filters (GQMFs) are introduced for filtering. Four band and eight band GQMF schemes which have smaller overall delay are developed. Performance is also evaluated by using short kernel filters (SKFs) which are easy to implement and require very few computations.

It is shown that 4 band GQMF scheme gives computational savings of 33.3% due to its tree structure over the conventional QMF schemes. More significant savings are obtained with 8 band GQMF scheme. Due to the fact that there is insignificant information in the eighth band this band is neither processed nor coded. The overall computational savings from this scheme are 70.8% over the conventional QMF schemes. The simulation results of the filtering schemes show that good quality pictures can be obtained at a low bit rate between 0.4 and 0.8 bpp (about 20 to 45 Mbits/sec). Particularly, the GQMF filtering schemes have the ability to achieve very low bit rate such as 0.4 to 0.77 bpp and still give good picture quality images. These filtering schemes, implemented along with the developed simple fixed dead zone algorithm can be a good choice for high data rate applications such as HDTV image processing.

MARVLE: A VLSI Chip of a Memory Based Architecture for Variable Length Encoding and Decoding

Amar Mukherjee

Dept. of Computer Science
Univ. of Central Florida
Orlando, Florida
amar@cs.ucf.edu

Jeff Flieder and N. Ranganathan

Dept. of Computer Science
University of South Florida
Tampa, Florida.

We present the design and implementation of a 2-micron VLSI chip for real time compression and decompression of data. The architecture is based on a novel idea of mapping the decode/encode tree of any tree-based codes on to a memory device that corresponds to simultaneous decoding of multiple bits [Mukherjee et. al.,1991]. The chip has a 512X12 static RAM with an access time of 4 ns and logic circuitry for compression as well as decompression. The chip can be operated as a compression or a decompression chip encoding or decoding two bits on the average per machine cycle by setting the value of a control signal. The chip occupies a silicon area of 6.8x6.9 millimeters and consists of about 50,000 transistors. The chip has an estimated compression rate of 88 Mbits/sec and a decompression rate of 53 Mbits/sec with a clock rate of 50 Mhz. The chip has been fabricated by MOSIS and the test results will be reported in the final presentation. The VLSI chip can be used to implement the JPEG baseline compression scheme using the on-chip static RAM.

Amar Mukherjee, H. Bheda, M.A. Bassiouni and T. Acharya "Multibit Encoding/ Decoding of Binary Codes Using Memory Based Architectures", Proc. Data Compression Conference, Snowbird, Utah, April 8-11,1991.

This work is partically supported by a grant from PM-TRADE Contract No. N61339-89-C-0132 from DOD/NTSC.

Minimization of Expected Distortion
Through Simulated Annealing of Codebook Vectors

Larry K. Barrett and Ronald K. Boyd
CTA Incorporated
Rockville, MD 20852
email: lbarrett@cta.com and boyd@cta.com

Vector Quantization has been shown to be a very effective technique for the compression of video image data, providing acceptable compression factors in the range of 16:1 or 0.5 bits per pixel. Still, vector quantization (VQ) is a lossy compression technique that inherently introduces a level of distortion in the end-to-end transfer of information. Some algorithmic enhancements of the VQ process have been implemented and verified that reduce this distortion. However, these enhancements make no attempt to reduce or minimize the distortion introduced by simple communications or storage device errors. Since the data is in a compressed form, a single bit error results in an incorrect vector being selected during the reconstruction process. Because of the lack of order of vectors within the codebook, this effectively results in a random vector being selected during the reconstruction process, thus increasing the overall image distortion.

In order to quantify the amount of additional distortion introduced by bit errors, we defined a Normalized Distortion Metric (NDM) to measure the level of structure in the codebook. The NDM is a statistical measure of the expected amount of distortion produced by single bit transmission errors and is independent of the data being compressed. This metric can be used to compare two codebooks that contain the same vectors, but have them stored in a different order. Therefore, all we need to do to find an optimal codebook is to determine the NDM value for all possible codevector orderings and then pick the one that produces the least distortion. However, for even a trivially small codebook the number of possible organizations increase factorially, making this process computationally impossible. Instead, we must apply a heuristic search technique that can locate good (if not optimal) codebook organizations.

Simulated annealing is such a search process and is well suited to this specific problem. The NDM value was used as the cost function for the annealing process. Other variables associated with the annealing process itself were determined empirically (i.e. annealing schedule). The annealing process generates a reordered codebook containing the original data vectors. Since this process is non-destructive, it can be applied iteratively until additional (problem specific) acceptability criteria are also met.

The codebook reordering process has been successfully applied to both linear and tree-structured codebooks. Results collected during the annealing process of linear codebooks indicate that the NDM value can be reduced by up to 35 percent with between 20 and 25 percent reductions seen on the average. The results for tree-structured codebooks were similar, with the most significant improvements seen by reordering the upper levels of the tree. A qualitative assessment was performed by introducing the same bit error pattern into pairs of compressed data, that were encodings of the same image with both the original and reordered codebooks. In general, the reconstructed image produced by the annealed codebook appears to show less distortion than that produced by the original codebook.

In summary, the reorganization of VQ codebooks using simulated annealing provides positive results. Follow on work will address adapting the annealing process to handle the introduction of non-white noise by the communication channel.

Modeling Adaptive Multilevel-Dictionary Coding Scheme by Cache Memory Management Policy

Chia-Lun Yu and Ja-Ling Wu
Department of Computer Science and Information Engineering
National Taiwan University, Taipei, Taiwan, R. O. C.
wjl@csman.csie.ntu.edu.tw

Abstract

Data compression is a very important technique to reduce the data transmission time on a network and to save the space in which data should be stored. Many methods have been developed to achieve better compression performance. Dictionary techniques can be applied to data compression. Common substrings or patterns which appear frequently are factorized in a dictionary so that the source data can be encoded using dictionary pointers instead of their original representations. The well-known Lempel-Ziv coding can be classified as one of the adaptive dictionary techniques.

Cache memory has some similar characteristics in comparison with Lempel-Ziv coding. Cache memories are high speed buffers which are inserted between the processors and the main memory to capture those portions of the contents of main memory which are currently in use. The cache is smaller and faster than main memory. Success or failure of a memory access is designated as a hit or a miss: A hit is a memory access found in cache, and a miss means it is not found in that level. Important management policies for cache memory are block placement, block identification, block replacement, and write strategy.

The fast access feature of cache is applicable to data compression. If we collect frequently occurring patterns (substrings) in a small cache-like dictionary and encode these patterns with shorter codewords, and gather other patterns in another large dictionary with long codewords, the overall compression performance should be improved. Policies which maintain the contents of dictionaries can be adopted from those of cache management.

We proposed a model for adaptive multilevel-dictionary coding based on cache memory management policy. It allows multiple dictionaries served as memory hierarchies and provides the capability of adaptive contents exchange to keep the locality during encoding process. Coding operations are characterized by management policies similar to those of cache memory. Parameters under this coding model include: the number of dictionaries, the sizes of dictionaries, the policies to augment the vocabulary of dictionaries, the codeword representation, the placement policies, the replacement policies, the policies to update the vocabulary of dictionaries, and the policies to adjust the codeword representation.

MR-CDF: Managing Multi-Resolution Scientific Data

Kenneth Salem
Computer Science Department, University of Maryland
College Park, MD 20742
and
CESDIS, NASA/GSFC, Code 930.5
Greenbelt, MD 20771

Data management libraries, such as NASA's publicly-distributed Common Data Format (CDF), implement simple data models that are tailored for scientific data. Data managed using these libraries is machine-independent, portable, and self-describing. Access to the data is performed through a set of interface functions that shield the details of storage and retrieval from application programs.

The Multi-Resolution Common Data Format (MR-CDF) is a prototype extension of CDF which permits *variable-resolution* data sets to be stored and manipulated. The goal of MR-CDF is to combine the advantages of CDF (scientifically-oriented abstract data models, common functional interfaces, portability of data) with the advantages of multi-resolution data. Applications requiring full-resolution data should be able to obtain it, while those that can use lower resolutions (e.g., browse-quality images) be able to do so simply and quickly.

Multi-resolution data sets are often produced applying a "compress and subtract" procedure to a data set. The data is compressed using a lossy compression technique. So that the original data can be reconstructed exactly if necessary, both the compressed data and the error introduced by the compression are stored. This procedure results in two resolutions: compressed and full. By repeated application of this procedure to the error data, a multi-resolution data set can be produced. Data at a specified resolution can be reconstructed by applying the inverse "decompress and add" procedure iteratively.

A wide variety of data compression techniques (e.g., various vector quantization and region-growing techniques) can be employed during each iteration of the compression procedure. Building any single technique into MR-CDF would have severely limited its applicability. Instead, MR-CDF incorporates a general decompression framework which is flexible enough to accommodate any "decompress and add" decompression technique. MR-CDF's framework can customized by providing functions which implement the decompression and merging operations performed at each stage of the general iterative procedure. By providing these functions, applications can tailor MR-CDF to accommodate a multi-resolution data sets produced by a wide variety of compression techniques.

The MR-CDF library is being implemented on top of CDF Version 2.0 running on Sun UNIX workstations. It is being tested using multi-resolution images produced by three types of compression techniques: simple, regular block averaging, vector quantization, and an irregular region-growing technique.

A New Compression-based Signature Extraction Method *

Jia-Shing Shiau
email: *7923562@twnctu01.bitnet*
Institute of Computer and
Information Science

Judy C. R. Tseng
email: *7617501@twnctu01.bitnet*
Institute of Computer Science
and Information Engineering

Wei-Pang Yang[†]
email: *wpyang@twnctu01.bitnet*
Institute of Computer and Information Science
National Chiao Tung University
Hsinchu, 300, Taiwan, R.O.C.

Signature file is a promising text retrieval method. A signature is an abstraction of a document in the textual database. The collection of signatures forms a signature file. The objective of a signature file access method is to quickly filter out a large number of non-qualified documents by examining the signature file before actually searching a document. Since the signature file is simply an abstraction of the textual database, *false drop* may occur in the filtering process. Therefore, further searches must be performed on the passed documents to ensure their qualification. The false drop probability depends on the signature extraction method used. In general, a method with lower false drop probability is preferred, since it has less chances to search a document, which is an extremely costly operation.

Various signature extraction methods have been proposed. They include *Word Signature* (WS), *Superimposed Coding* (SC), *Run-Length compression* (RL), and *Bit-block Compression* (BC). The latter two signature extraction methods (RL and BC) are based on *compression*. The basic idea of compression-based approach is to make the signatures formed by traditional superimposed coding as sparse as possible, and then store the results of compression. Comprehensive studies in previous works show: for the same signature size, the compression-based signature extraction methods achieve lower false drop probabilities compared to WS and SC.

In our work, a new compression-based signature extraction method, Huffman Compression (HC), is proposed. HC split the sparse signature into bit-blocks, each contains the same number of bits. Two parts are then generated for each bit-blocks: part 1 is one bit long indicating whether there is a 1 in this bit-block; part 2 is the Huffman code of this bit-block. Finally, the part 1's of all the bit-blocks are stored consecutively, followed by the part 2's. The false drop probability of the new method is also analyzed. The analytical results show that the new approach achieves lower false drop probability than previous compression-based methods, RL and BC. We therefore conclude that the new approach is a preferable one.

---

*This research was supported by the National Science Council, Taiwan, R.O.C. under contract: NSC 76-0408-E009-14 (1987).

†To whom all correspondence should be sent.

A New Locally Adaptive Data Compression Scheme using Multilist Structure

Henry Ker-Chang Chang and Shing-Hong Chen
National Defense Management College, Taipei, Taiwan, R.O.C.

Extended Summary

Data compression technique is important to many applications since the cost of both transmission time and storage space can be reduced. The purpose of this paper is to suggest a new locally adaptive data compression scheme. The proposed scheme is designed based on the application of multilist structure with hashing function. The objective is to improve the previous work of Bentley et al.[1]. The multilist structure helps to shorten the length of a transmitted code word and the hashing function helps in fast encoding and decoding algorithms.

To evaluate the performance of the proposed new scheme, we consider two different types of test data. The first test data consists of five text files of various sizes. Other four PASCAL programs are also tested in the second trial. We have compared three compression techniques including byte-level Huffman coding, Bentley's locally adaptive coding, and the proposed scheme. The comparison results are illustrated in the following Table. From the experimental results, we can assure that the proposed compression scheme has improvement over other methods for text file compression. The improvement is originated from a phenomenon that the average length of the word list is less than 20 for all text files in the experiments. A shorter word list will generate a shorter coded word and will provide faster encoding process. The same result may also be found in the second experiment.

Table Compression results of different techniques

data type	size in bits	byte-level Huffman code	Bentley's method	the proposed scheme
text files	136216	74476	38494	25275
	148960	83015	46155	31780
	155408	87133	49028	34902
	170568	93521	48946	32705
	243408	134273	72243	50535
	258760	142873	77386	54604
PASCAL program	95168	57663	38400	37283
	102880	63192	42166	41085
	114784	69522	46172	45036
	125608	76804	50747	48715

1. Jone L. Bentley, Daniel D. Sleator, Robert E. Tarjan, and Victor K. Wei, A Locally Adaptive Data Compression Scheme, *Communications of the ACM* 29, (4), 320-330, 1986.

A New VLSI Image Codec for Digital Still Video Camera Applications

Abbas Razavi

Zoran Corporation, 1705 Wyatt Drive, Santa Clara, CA 95054

This paper describes a new image compression chip set with bit rate control capability. The chip set is comprised of a Discrete Cosine Transform (DCT) Processor and an Image Compression Coder/Decoder (Codec), which together implement a DCT-based image compression/expansion algorithm, similar to the algorithm specified in the Joint Photographic Expert Group (JPEG) standard. The new chip set is a sophisticated system which is well suited to many applications requiring bit rate control capability, such as Digital Still Video Cameras (DSVCs).

The compression procedure begins by inputting image data into the DCT Processor where 2-D forward DCTs are performed. The input data may be one of the following formats: 8-bit unsigned with or without internal shift of 7, 8-bit 2's complement, and 9-bit 2's complement. The output of the DCT Processor is sent to the Codec where scaling, quantization, and variable-length coding with bit rate control is performed. In addition to the standard variable-length coding, the total number of bits available (Target Code Volume) to compress the entire image can be specified. In this case, the following steps will be performed: 1) the Codec computes the total activity of the image (Accumulated Code Volume) and activity of each 8x8 image block (Block Code Volume) and, 2) the Codec computes a new set of quantization tables based on the global image activity and the required compressed file size, which causes the total code volume to be within 5% of the Target Code Volume. However, if this results in truncation of the code, then up to 5% of the last part of the image will be deleted. To avoid this problem, the Codec allocates a variable number of bits (Allocated Block Code Volume) to each block based on its activity. If the block requires more bits than its Allocated Block Code Volume, then the block code will be truncated and hence, the truncated code will be spread over the entire image rather than just the last part of the image.

The compressed image data can be stored to a memory card or transmitted over a communications channel. The Codec provides four different encoding processes for the user to choose from, depending on speed, memory, and image accuracy requirements.

The compressed data is decoded, dequantized, and rescaled in the expansion mode. The resulting coefficient values are sent to the DCT Processor where 2-D inverse DCTs are performed, producing a close match to the original image.

A Parallel Algorithm for Vector Quantizer Design

Ying Cheng, Paul Fortier
Dept. of Electrical Engineering, Laval University
Quebec, Canada, G1K 7P4

I. Introduction

Efficient algorithms have been applied to vector quantization, such as the conventional LBG algorithm, and some neural networks, using strategies from Kohonen techniques or simulated annealing learning. In this paper, we propose a parallel algorithm for vector quantization which uses a codebook generating machine mainly based on the mechanisms of the ART neural network.

II. Algorithm

A modified neural network mainly based on the ART mechanism is built to generate a codebook. Its architecture is shown in Figure 1. Every node in *F1* is connected to every node in *F2* that represents a category and these bidirectional connections implement bottom-up and top-down adaptive filtering.

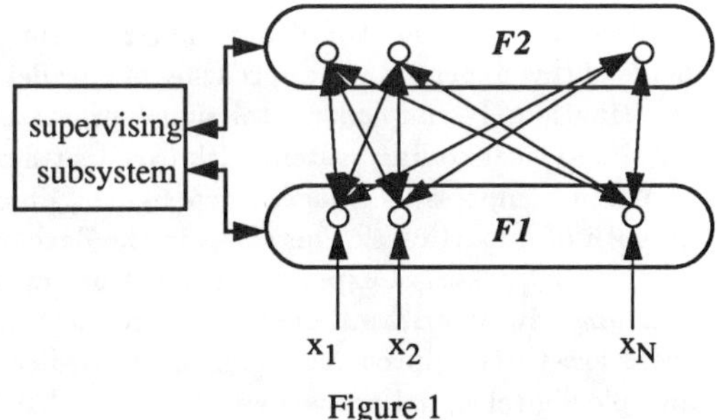

Figure 1

A training vector **x**, presented at *F1* where it is normalized, is mapped to *F2* through a leading pathway in the bottom-up adaptive filter. The nodes in *F2* undergo cooperative and competitive interactions in parallel. The winner is probably the right category to which the input vector belongs. In this framework, however, it is a second, top-down adaptive filter that leads to the crucial property of code self-stabilization. Once the winner is found, it is mapped back to the *F1* field through the top-down adaptive filter, where an expectation value is obtained, evaluating the similarities between the current input vector and the category of the winner. If this value is high enough, the current input vector is considered to be one of the members in that category. If not, the current active output node will be reset and another search will happen among the rest of the output nodes.

According to the expectation value and different situations, a supervising subsystem is designed to manage the actions such as reset, searching, modifying of the weight of the connections, surveying the quality of the categories, etc.

III. Simulation Experiments

In the experiments, the algorithm is applied to speech waveform vector quatization. The vector quantizer for both 4k bits/s and 8k bits/s was implemented with an 8kHz sampling rate and a vector dimension of 8. The results are very promising. Additionnally, a comparison between three-layer perceptron and the algorithm proposed in this paper as a code searching machine is studied. The former performs better because of its powerful learning ability for uncertainty knowledge.

Parallel Image and Video Coding Schemes in Multi-computers

Wei-Jou Duh and Ja-Ling Wu

Department of Computer Science and Information Engineering,
National Taiwan University, Taipei, Taiwan, R.O.C.

Abstract: The use of multi-computer for image/video compression is the main theme of this paper. Many approaches of parallel image/video coding are discussed. By using loosely-coupled digital signal processors, one can construct a powerful real-time visual coding system with excellent flexibility.

When compressing image/video signals, objective and subjective assessments are both of importance. Therefore, in the developing phase of a compression algorithm, many passes of experiments must be carried out. Therefore, in the stage of designing new algorithms, short turn-around time simulation is urgently required. There are three approaches: (1). using dedicated compression chip; (2). using multiple digital signal processors; (3). using distributed computers. The dedicated chips are too expensive for developing, and distributed computing suffers from communication overheads. Therefore, using multiple DSPs seems to be the most cost-effective way.

The coarse grain multi-computer is chosen as the target in this paper. The performance of a parallel system relys upon an appropriate problem decomposition strategy. Here are some commonly-used partition strategies that can be applied to parallel image/video coding: (1). spatial partition; (2). chronological partition; (3). characteristic partition; (4). hybrid partition; (5). control decomposition; (6). object decomposition. Summing up these approaches, the spatial partition is deemed to be the most simple and straightforward. The workloads are approximately equal and the programming is the same as usual in spatial partition approach.

An example system based on distributed transputer array was developed for parallel video coding. In the parallel coding system, 9 transputers coordinate to simulate the encoding/decoding operations of H.261, the CCITT recommendation for visual telephone. 2.14 frames/sec. intra-frame encoding rate was achieved. The distribution and collection of video data take most of the communication time. It is easy to verify that the distribution/collection time is irrelevant to interconnecting topology for such a one pass coding algorithm. When performing multiple-pass coding algorithms, the network topology affects the communication time as nodes interchanging their data. Therefore, using simple network topology and spatial decomposition strategy, most image/video compression algorithms can be accelerated in multi-computer environments.

ON PARALLEL IMPLEMENTATIONS AND EXPERIMENTATIONS OF LOSSLESS DATA COMPRESSION ALGORITHMS [1]

Tassos Markas[2]
Department of Electrical Enginnering,
Duke University,
Durham, NC 27706

John Reif
Department of Computer Science,
Duke University,
Durham, NC 27706

James A. Storer
Department of Computer Science
Brandeis University
Waltham, MA 02254

Extended Abstract

In this paper we present a new systolic-type parallel architecture that is capable of compressing data at very high rates without any loss of information. The proposed architecture implements a hybrid data compression algorithm that belongs in the class of textual substitution methods which can be considered as a generalization of the Lempel-Ziv-Welch (LZW) type algorithms. The innovative aspect of this architecture is that it can achieve high-speed parallel searching by distributing the dictionary among several processing elements, and by utilizing Content Addressable Memories to identify matches between the incoming data and the local vocabulary entries within a single clock cycle. In this paper, we also analyze the compression performance of several variations of the textual substitution methods and we examine their trade-offs when considering their implementation in silicon. Finally, we give a detailed description of the encoding and the decoding operations of the proposed architecture.

---

[1]This work has been supported by the Center of Excellence in Space Data and Information Sciences under NASA/CESDIS NAS USRA subcontract 550-63 of prime contract NAS5-30428. Additional support has been provided by DARPA/ISTO Contracts N00014-88-K-0458, N00014-91-C-0114, N00014-91-J-1985, and NSF Grant 88-00282/2

[2]Also with Center for Systems Engineering, Research Triangle Institute, RTP, NC 27709

PREDICTIVE VECTOR QUANTIZATION OF GRAYSCALE IMAGES

Ajai Narayan & Tenkasi V. Ramabadran
Dept. of Elec. Engg. & Comp. Engg..
Iowa State University
Ames, IA 50011.

In recent years, Vector Quantization (VQ) has received a lot of attention as a viable app-roach to data compression and has been successfully applied to both speech and image coding. There are many possible compression methods that can effectively use of VQ. Pre-dictive vector quantization (PVQ) is one such method that combines linear prediction and vector quantization. In this abstract, an implementation of predictive vector quantization (PVQ) for coding grayscale images is described. The method applies vector quantization (VQ) techniques to quantize innovations values generated by the well known scalar DPCM (Differential Pulse Code Modulation) method. The essential idea is to combine scalar prediction with vector quantization thereby taking advantage of the simplicity of DPCM and the high compressibility of vector quantization.

Implementation of the PVQ method has been accomplished using the was implemented using the 'Analysis by Synthesis approach' wherein the structure of the decoder is duplicated at the encoder in its entirety. The image to be encoded is first partitioned into blocks of dimension 4x4 resulting in vectors of dimension 16. This partitioning however, is for the purpose of quantization alone. Linear prediction is performed on a pixel-by-pixel basis. The encoder and decoder start with the same codebook. The codebook is a collection of vectors consisting of representative innovations values. The encoder builds contestant versions of each input block (to be encoded) using linear prediction, one due to every single vector in the codebook. Each version of the image block so constructed is successively compared with the actual image block being coded. The codevector that const-ructed a block that was closest to the actual image block in some sense is selected as the innovation vector for that image block. The index of that vector is transmitted achieving a reduction in bit rate. During reconstruction, the selected innovations vector is substituted for the original innovations vector. This is the source of error in the reconstruction. The prediction of the successive pixels at the encoder and decoder is based on the reconstructed versions of the previous pixels rather than their actual values.

The method was tested using two types of codebook: 1) Deterministic codebook 2) Ran-dom codebook. The deterministic codebook was generated using the well known LBG algorithm. Innovations vectors from representative images for the particular class of images were used for the training sequences. The random codebook consisted of a set of suitably scaled ran-dom numbers with a distribution similar to that of the innovations sequences obtained from the representative images. The first and second moments of the random number sequence that formed the codebook were made approximately equal to the first and secondmoment values calculated from the innovations sequences of the representative images.

The performance of the PVQ method on several industrial radiographic images was compared with that of standard Discrete Cosine Transform (DCT) coding (with a block size of 8x8) for an identical compression factor of 24. The reconstructions obtained from the PVQ method was found to be better both subjectively and objectively than those obtained from the DCT method.

PROVING THE CORRECTNESS OF
A DATA COMPRESSION PROGRAM

Prof. W. D. Maurer
Department of Electrical Engineering and Computer Science
The George Washington University
Washington, DC 20052

Extended Abstract

Despite the non-mathematical nature of most computer programming, debugging, and testing today, the mathematically based Inductive Assertion Method of Floyd is still around, and there are still people trying to make it useful. An important refocusing of the thrust of this work has been engendered by a famous CACM paper, written by DeMillo, Lipton, and Perlis, which attacks the legitimacy of the entire subject. Most of the points made by these authors were refuted in my reply to this paper, published there a few months later. However, one point bears careful consideration: that of the importance of specification errors.

Most work in the Inductive Assertion Method has focused on huge programs, which are difficult to understand because of their sheer size. However, this method is useful only in proving the absence of software errors (the software does not meet the specifications). It can do nothing about specification errors (the specifications are not what the users really want). Furthermore, the preponderance of specification errors over software errors increases as programs get larger. Both of these points were made by DeMillo, Lipton, and Perlis.

We have therefore refocused our effort on the proof of correctness of small programs. Some small programs are hard to debug because they are unstructured; we have a very fast version of heapsort which is like this. Others are hard to debug because the output does not "look meaningful"; data compression programs are a good example of this.

We have succeeded in using the Inductive Assertion Method to prove the correctness of a data compression program. The main point to prove is that compression followed by expansion yields the original file back. We start by defining compression and expansion in the abstract, and then showing, in the abstract, that one is the inverse of the other. Having done this, the compression program is proved correct if we can show that the old and new files are representations of two abstract sequences, the second of which is the abstract compression of the first. We are currently working on the proof of correctness of the corresponding data expansion program.

QM–AYA Adaptive Arithmetic Coder

Joe-Ming Cheng * Glen Langdon [†]

IBM Corporation
5600 Cottle Road, F86/029
San Jose CA 95193

Department of Computer Engineering
University of California at Santa Cruz
Santa Cruz, CA 95064

ABSTRACT

The QM-AYA arithmetic coder offered balanced improvements to the QM probability estimation used for adaptive arithmetic coding in the JBIG and for JPEG image compression algorithms. Improvement on either JBIG score or JPEG total compression byte could be made relative easier if were not constrained by the other. For the balanced improvements on JBIG and JPEG, the leverage identified is to improve the low-skew probability estimation.

Summary of compression results

	JPEG-FA	QM	QM-AYA
States	46	113	71
JBIG			
score	99.406	99.860	99.871
total_bytes	950633	951793	950142
JPEG			
total_bytes	541683	541386	540430

Our study of CCITT images with 7-pel model shows that less than 5% of the low skew ($p(lps) > 2^{-3}$) pels contributed to more than 63.4% of the final coded length. The renorm-driven Q-Coder, however, is less efficient at low-skews. A conventional solution to this problem is increasing the number of adapter states at low skews, however at an increase in hardware gate complexity and computational delay. The SPIRAL concept is a probability estimation sub-graph of adapter states where the deeper the state the more difficult to achieve a higher skewed estimate, and the inertia to leave the low skews is quite high. The 17 state non-planar SPIRAL behaves as if it were longer than the 56 state low-skew sub-graph of the QM coder.

The 71 state QM-AYA is a composite of QM (final Q-Coder selected for JBIG), and QM-FA (early Q-Coder selected) plus the Spiral idea. The QM-AYA coding inefficiency is less than 2% (3% for QM) for binary sequences of low skew.

---

*Work performed as employee of IBM Almaden Research Center, San Jose CA 95120-6099.

[†]Part-time support, and work performed at, the IBM Almaden Research Center, San Jose CA 95120-6099.

**Real-Time Demonstration Hardware for
Enhanced DPCM Video Compression Algorithm**

Thomas P. Bizon and Wayne A. Whyte, Jr.
NASA Lewis Research Center
Cleveland, Ohio

Vincent R. Marcopoli
Case Western Reserve University
Cleveland, Ohio

The lack of available wideband digital links as well as the complexity of implementation of bandwidth efficient digital video CODECs (encoder/decoder) has worked to keep the cost of digital television transmission too high to compete with analog methods. Terrestrial and satellite video service providers, however, are now recognizing the potential gains that digital video compression offers and are proposing to incorporate compression systems to increase the number of available program channels. NASA is similarly recognizing the benefits of and trend toward digital video compression techniques for transmission of high quality video from space and therefore, has developed a digital television bandwidth compression algorithm to process standard NTSC (National Television Systems Committee) composite color television signals. The algorithm is based on differential pulse code modulation (DPCM), but additionally utilizes a non-adaptive predictor, non-uniform quantizer and multilevel Huffman coder to reduce the data rate substantially below that achievable with straight DPCM. The non-adaptive predictor and multilevel Huffman coder combine to set this technique apart from other DPCM encoding algorithms. All processing is done on an intra-field basis to prevent motion degradation and minimize hardware complexity. Computer simulations have shown the algorithm will produce broadcast quality reconstructed video at an average transmission rate of 1.8 bits/pixel.

Hardware implementation of the DPCM circuit, non-adaptive predictor and non-uniform quantizer has been completed providing real-time demonstration of the image quality at full video rates. Video sampling/reconstruction circuits have also been constructed to accomplish the analog video processing necessary for the real-time demonstration. Performance results for the completed hardware compare favorably with simulation results. Hardware implementation of the multilevel Huffman encoder/decoder is currently under development along with implementation of a buffer control algorithm to accommodate the variable data rate output of the multilevel Huffman encoder. A video CODEC of this type could be used to compress composite NTSC color television signals where high quality reconstruction is desirable (e.g. Space Station video transmission, transmission direct-to-the-home via direct broadcast satellite systems or cable television distribution to system headends and direct-to-the-home).

(The complete technical report is available from the authors.)

REDUCING INFORMATION LOSS DURING SPATIAL COMPRESSION
OF DIGITAL MAP IMAGE DATA

Henry Rosche III

Naval Oceanographic and Atmospheric Research Laboratory
Mapping Sciences Branch
John C. Stennis Space Center, MS 39529-5004

ABSTRACT

The Naval Oceanographic and Atmospheric Research Laboratory's (NOARL) Map Data Formatting Facility (MDFF) is tasked with the production of the Compressed Aeronautical Chart (CAC).   Inherent in this work is the necessity to improve the quality of the final product.   Vector Quantization (VQ) is a stable and well known method of spatially compressing many types of image data. Digital maps, which are a copy of the original paper map, suffer the same defects as the originals with regard to paper folds, roll scallops, smudges and other imperfections. Scanning at the 100 micron level also reveals paper weave and forces light reflections at different angles of incidence to the weave to appear as distinct colors from otherwise homogenous areas.   Therefore it is desirable to locate these areas in the digital form and return them to a state closer to the original form. This leaves fewer color combinations for the classification vectors, thus allowing VQ to produce a compressed image while retaining more of the source information.

The compression method used here is a two step process. The first step is the color compression of the data to a standard color palette. The second step is the spatial compression of this color compressed data.

The technique used to achieve these ends is called color cleanup.   It consists of an a priori analysis of the color digital data to be used and then may be applied without human intervention. The first of the two major components of this analysis is concerned with the location of colors in the standard color palette that are close enough together in color space so as to appear as the same color.   The second component is concerned with studying the use of these color in a representative variety of map segments and determining what features are composed by which colors. This analysis is used to replace color indices.

The cleanup of large areas, such as oceans and deserts, allows codebook vectors to represent more of the image leaving more vectors in the codebook to represent lettering and other detailed features. During the testing of this technique, 11,377 map segments were color and spatially compressed with 1,107 of these segments achieving lossless spatial compression.

This work is sponsored by the Naval Air Systems Command and funded by the AV-8B, F/A-18, V-22, and AX programs under Aircraft Procurement, Navy H1CC, program elements 9410101 (64262N) and 980101 (APN). This paper has been approved for public release, and distribution is unlimited. NOARL contribution number is PR92:010:351.

Robust Measures for Fuzzy Entropy
and Fuzzy Conditioning

Chua-Chin Wang and Hon-Son Don
Department of Electrical Engineering
State University of New York
Stony Brook, NY 11794

Abstract

A robust nonprobabilistic entropy measure is proposed in the context of fuzzy sets. This measure of entropy for a fuzzy message is shown to be the minimum of two ratios, which are the ratios of two distances: the distance from the fuzzy message to its nearest nonfuzzy message, and the distance from the message to its farest nonfuzzy message. Fuzzy conditioning is reconsidered not only by the degree of subsethood, but also by the distance between two fuzzy messages. The theory of subsethood is also shown to solve the major shortcoming of the Bayesian's learning, the problem of requiring that the space must be partitioned into disjoint exhaustive hypotheses.

Many entropy measures were proposed, e.g., the measure suggested by De Luca and Termini, Yager's entropy measure, Kaufmann's measure, and Kosko's measure. In these previously proposed measures, the first two only focus on the intersection of a fuzzy message and its complement fuzzy message, but they are lack of the information where the the message is between its nearest nonfuzzy message and farthest message. Kaufmann, however, only considered the distance from the message to its nearest nonfuzzy message without the acknowledgement of its farthest message. Kosko's measure is proven not to obey De Luca and Termini's entropy axioms, i.e., it is essentially incorrect. We propose an appropriate measure for fuzzy entropy,

$$W_p(A) = \frac{1}{2}\left[\left(\frac{l^p(A,\bar{A})}{l^p(A,\underline{A})} + \frac{l^p(A,\underline{A})}{l^p(A,\bar{A})}\right) - \left|\frac{l^p(A,\bar{A})}{l^p(A,\underline{A})} - \frac{l^p(A,\underline{A})}{l^p(A,\bar{A})}\right|\right]$$

where $\bar{A}$ and $\underline{A}$ are the fuzzy message A's nearest and farthest nonfuzzy messages, respectively, and $l^p(A,B) = (\sum_{i=1}^{n} |m_A(x_i) - m_B(x_i)|^p)^{\frac{1}{p}}$ in which $m(x)$ if the membership function of the fuzzy message.

As far as the subsethood is concerned, Kosko suggested a method to represent the degree of subsethood. However, it is proven that his subsethood measure is not completely to present the degree of violation (subsethood). We propose the following measure to present the degree of subsethood,

$$S(A,B) = 1 - \frac{1}{n}\sum_i^n \frac{\max(0, m_A(x_i) - m_B(x_i))}{m_A(x_i)}$$

where n is the dimension of the fuzzy message. Basing on the measurement of subsethood, a fuzzy Bayesian's theorem can be derived,

$$S(E,H_i) = \frac{1}{n}\sum_{k=1}^n S_k(H_i,E)\frac{m_{H_i}(x_k)}{m_E(x_k)}$$

where E is the evidence, and H_is are the hypotheses of a hypothesis space X.

"

Short Encodings of Planar Graphs and Maps

Kenneth Keeler[1]
National Broadcasting Corporation, New York, NY.

Jeffery Westbrook[2]
Yale University, New Haven, CT.

We discuss space-efficient binary encoding schemes for several classes of unlabeled connected planar graphs and maps. In encoding a graph we must encode the incidences among vertexes and edges. By maps we understand topological equivalence classes of planar embeddings of planar graphs. In encoding a map we are required to encode the topology of the embedding *i.e.*, incidences among faces, edges, and vertexes, as well as the graph. Each map embeds a unique graph, but a given graph may have multiple embeddings. Following Tutte we allow graphs and maps to have multiple edges between two vertexes, and to contain loop edges.

There are a number of recent results on space-efficient encoding. The best to compare our results against is that of Turán, who gives an encoding of unlabeled connected planar graphs and maps which uses asymptotically 4 bits per edge[3]. We show encodings for

- 2-connected maps and graphs in 3 bits per edge,
- arbitrary planar graphs in $\lg 12$ bits per edge,
- arbitrary maps without loop edges in $\lg 12$ bits per edge,
- proper planar triangulations in $(3 + \lg 3)/3$ bits per edge.

The unusual constant $\lg 12 \approx 3.58$ is of particular significance in view of Tutte's enumeration of the connected planar maps with m edges[4] which implies that that in any code for maps with m edges the fraction of maps whose codewords are shorter than $m \lg 12 + O(1)$ bits is asymptotically vanishing.

Our goal is primarily theoretical: to move towards encoding schemes for planar maps that are the shortest possible according to Tutte's results. Our encoding and decoding algorithms, however, are simple, run in linear time, and provide the most compact encoding currently known, so our results may have some practical application in areas such as vision and graphics. In addition, our schemes immediately imply an encoding for labeled planar graphs that improves on the best previous result.

Our basic idea is to construct a particular depth-first search tree of a map, then sequentially to delete the non-tree edges and add labels to the tree edges in such a way that the non-tree edges can be reconstructed from the labels. This converts the map into a labeled version of the search tree. We then encode the tree in any standard way, followed by an encoding of the string of labels.

[1] Parts of this research were performed while this author was with the Division of Applied Sciences, Harvard University (supported by U.S. Army Research Office Contract DAAL03-86-K-0171) and the Performance Analysis Department, AT&T Bell Laboratories.

[2] Research partially supported by National Science Foundation Grant CCR-8610181.

[3] G. Turàn. Succinct representation of graphs. *Discrete Applied Math*, 8:289–294, 1984.

[4] W. T. Tutte. A census of planar maps. *Canadian Journal of Mathematics*, 15(2):249–271, 1963.

A Single-chip Data Compression/Decompression Processor

Duat Tran

Belle W. Y. Wei†

Mehul Desai

Department of Electrical Engineering
College of Engineering
San Jose State University

The gap between huge data requirements of many applications and limited capabilities of transmission and storage systems dictates the need for developing high-performance data compression hardware. This project describes the architecture and design of a single-chip implementation of the Lempel-Ziv data compression scheme. The chip performs compression or decompression on byte-oriented input data. It uses on-chip memory for construction and maintenance of the string dictionary. On-chip memory facilitates string comparison and dictionary update operations and results in a high-performance circuit. In addition, it incorporates a flushing scheme for updating a full string dictionary for adaptive data compression.

Our data compression/decompression chip uses full custom layout that includes on-chip Associative RAM (ARAM) and SRAM. The chip was implemented in 1.2 um CMOS technology with a single 5v power supply. Blocks on the chip are pipelined and interfaced with hand-shaking operations. The critical path is a self-timed signal which emulates the worst-case delay of data comparison within an ARAM module. For maximum performance, this self-timed signal is used as the clock signal by its neighboring ARAM module. The clock speed is 25 ns with the corresponding frequency of 40 MHZ and data rate of 120 Mb/sec.

† This work was supported in part by National Science Foundation grant MIP-9019862.

Singular Value Decomposition for Texture Compression

Chaur–Chin Chen and *Jun–Hsing Hsieh*

Department of Computer Science
National Tsing Hua University
Hsinchu 300, TAIWAN
e-mail: *cchen@cs.nthu.edu.tw*   fax: 011–886–35–723694

The singular value decomposition (SVD) theorem states that $A \in R^{n \times n}$ can be decomposed as $A = U \Lambda V^t$, where U and V are orthogonal matrices and

$$\Lambda = diag\,(\sigma_1, \sigma_2, \ldots, \sigma_k, \ldots, \sigma_n)\ \ with\ \ \sigma_1 \geq \ldots \geq \sigma_k > 0 = \sigma_{k+1}, = \ldots = \sigma_n.$$

The SVD theorem can also be stated as $A = \sum_{i=1}^{k} \sigma_i \mathbf{u}_i \mathbf{v}_i^t$. The $\sigma_i's$ are called singular values and k is the rank of matrix A. The more dependent the column vectors, the smaller the k value. A gray level image can be viewed as a matrix consisting of highly dependent columns and can be represented with few singular values $\sigma_i's$ associated with eigenvectors $\mathbf{u}_i's$ and $\mathbf{v}_i's$. Due to the limitation of computer hardware and its environments, traditional image compression techniques, such as DCT, VQ, KLT, SVD, tend to partition an image into several blocks of small size (e.g. 16×16) and compress each subimage. This may cause blocking effects and increases the difficulty of reconstruction. This paper investigates singular value decomposition for *texture compression*. The performance of encoding a 128×128 gray level image with 0.5bpp by SVD requires 45 seconds on a Sun 4/370 server. The following images are an experimental comparison, (a) is the original 128× image, (b-d) are the reconstructions of using 128×128, 64×64, and 32×32 blocks. The experiment suggests that compression techniques should be carefully adjusted for images of *busy regions* such as *textures*.

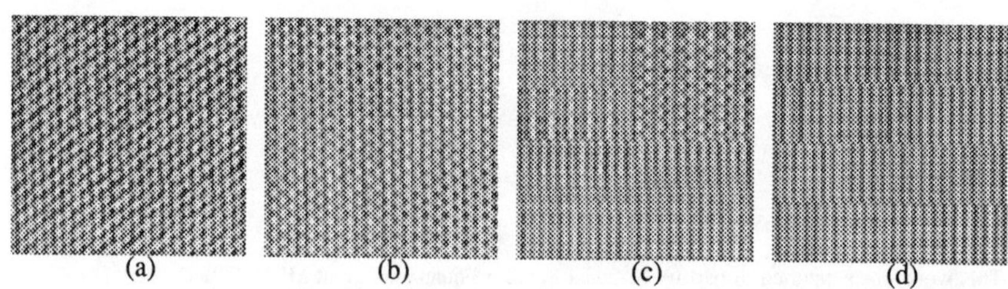

(a)   (b)   (c)   (d)

A Study of Methods for Reducing Blocking Artifacts Caused by Block Transform Coding.

John A. Greszczuk and Mary Deshon
Polaroid Corp. , Cambridge, Mass

Block transform coding is a commonly used image compression technique that involves segmenting the image into blocks which are then transformed into a representation that facilitates coding. One phenomenon that arises out of block transform coding is that as the compression ratio is increased, the edges of the blocks that were used in the compression process become visible. These blocking artifacts are the dominant factor in the degradation of the image quality. Applying the transform on small blocks is normally done to reduce the amount of computation and memory required for a coder, however it is susceptible to discontinuities at the block boundaries since no inter-block information is used. Analysis of the coding error showed that it was higher for boundary pixels, in images that had artifacts. Three methods for reducing these artifacts were considered in this study.

The JPEG draft specification is a popular block transform algorithm which applies the Discrete Cosine Transform (DCT) on non-overlapping 8x8 blocks, followed by selective quantization of the coefficients and entropy coding. It was used as the baseline coding algorithm in the experiments that were conducted.

Reductions in blocking artifacts by edge filtering have been discussed in the literature[Reeve and Lim,84]. It is an effective method which involves low-pass filtering the points on the block boundaries. Enhancements to this technique that were evaluated in the study include a 1-D directional edge filter instead of a general low pass filter and the application of a pre-emphasis filter before compression to compensate for the blurring effect of the low-pass filter.

Another solution to the problem is to introduce inter-block correlation by overlapping the blocks. This technique improved the artifacts, but at the penalty of decreasing the compression rate. Better picture quality was obtained by decreasing the compression rate by the same amount while leaving the blocks non-overlapping.

The draft JPEG specification contains a suggestion for alleviating blocking artifacts in some applications. If any of the five lowest AC coefficients of the DCT have been truncated to zero, then their value can be predicted by using the DC values of the neighboring blocks. For the images used in this study it was found to not be a very effective technique.

SUBBAND CODING FOR IMAGE DATA ARCHIVING
Extended Abstract

Daniel Glover, NASA Lewis Research Center
S. C. Kwatra, The University of Toledo

The fact that a low frequency subband can be a low resolution version of the original image makes subbanding attractive as a browsing tool. The low frequency band is generated as a natural consequence of subbanding and can be tracked separately from the higher frequency subbands in a browsing catalog. The low band can then be retrieved and viewed separately. If a higher resolution version is desired, the higher frequency bands can be retrieved and the image reconstructed. Color images are handled by subbanding each component separately. For browsing, the most significant component can be used (e.g., luminance for color images) or all the components can be retrieved and viewed separately or recombined into a low resolution color image.

A typical approach to generating multiple subbands is to cascade sets of two-channel filters in a tree structure. Although it is possible to design multiple band filter banks, it is usually easier to just cascade a simple two band filter bank to get four, seven, sixteen, or whatever number of bands is appropriate. A corresponding tree structure is used for the synthesis bank and this lends itself to progressive resolution reconstruction. The two most common tree structures are the octave-band split and the uniform-band split. Either structure is equivalent from a browsing standpoint. For progressive resolution, the octave-band split is most efficient in terms of reconstructing a series of increasing resolution images.

Subbanding is a strategy for coding and as such can be used in either a lossless or lossy manner. There are two places where losses can be intentionally introduced: 1) in the coders, and 2) in the way subband values are treated in terms of maintaining accuracy. Lossy coders deliberately throw out "data" that is irrelevant or is predominantly noise. The signal reconstructed from lossy coders does not (in most cases) exactly match the original signal. This "loss" is by design and in some cases can result in a reconstructed signal that is better than the original. The term "lossy" is unfortunate in that it conjures up thoughts of lost data in scientists' minds when most of what is usually lost is noise. The second area where losses can be introduced is in the accuracy of subband values. A typical original signal sample size might be eight bits. When that signal is subbanded, it may take larger sample sizes in the subbands to maintain the accuracy needed for perfect reconstruction. For example, a simple but non-trivial two-channel split will require a minimum of 1/2 bit/sample larger average sample size to maintain accuracy. For a more conventional filter, the sample size requirements are much greater. Although the number of samples doesn't increase over the original signal due to subbanding, the total amount of data increases due to the required accuracy if perfect reconstruction is desired. The full paper (NASA TM 105407) presents some simple algorithms for producing subbands of image data using the Walsh-Hadamard transform and a new non-orthogonal transform.

Subband Image Coding using Watershed and Watercourse Lines

Lawrence H. Croft and John A. Robinson
Department of Systems Design Engineering, University of Waterloo
Waterloo, Ontario, Canada, N2L 3G1

We describe a variable-rate image compression system using thread-like visual primitives. The visual primitives describe 2-dimensional extrema of a multiresolution second derivative operator. Second derivative extrema identify important object-space features, such as occluding contours, within natural images by locating ridges, valleys and the feet and shoulders of edges on the image luminance surface.

The image spectrum is exactly divided into four subband images with a pair of 2-dimensional, non-orthogonal dyadic wavelets. Three high frequency subbands are created by convolutions with a quadratic approximation of a Laplacian of a Gaussian (L-o-G) operator. A dilated set of this wavelet approximates a bank of L-o-G filters with increasing Gaussian Variance. The low pass information not contained in the L-o-G subbands is extracted by a convolution with a Gaussian shaped low pass wavelet.

The coder locates watershed and watercourse lines along surface extrema of the L-o-G subbands with an immersion simulation algorithm. The locations of a thresholded subset of these extrema are compressed with a chain code. Amplitudes values along the watersheds and watercourse lines are transmitted with predictive coding. The low pass subband is regularly subsampled and transmitted with predictive coding. The chain code and amplitude symbols are entropy coded with a set of arithmetic coders.

Figure 1: 0.217 bpp, SNR 14.9 dB.   **Figure 2**: 0.142 bpp, SNR 11.7 dB.

The decoder recovers an image estimate using the iterative method of convex projections from the transmitted primitives and an interpolated low pass image. Each iteration projects the subbands onto the set of valid wavelet transforms, and onto the set of subbands with the transmitted primitives and low pass values. Figures 1 and 2 show results at two compression rates for a 480 × 512 × 8 bit image.

Symmetric-Context Coding Schemes
Martin Cohn and Constantine Kozhukhin
Computer Science, Brandeis University, Waltham MA 02254

We describe the use of recursively contracting, symmetric contexts in the lossless compression of digital data. The approach is motivated by the empirical observation that a context which straddles the symbol being encoded gives significantly lower sample entropy than equal-sized contexts preceding or succeeding the symbol. Here are data for *wsj1*, a one-megabyte file in a corpus of Wall Street Journal articles; these data remain consistent throughout the corpus. $H_{prec} = H(x_t|x_{t-2}, x_{t-1}) = 0.330;$ $H_{strad} = H(x_t|x_{t-1}, x_{t+1}) = 0.259;$ $H_{succ} = H(x_t|x_{t+1}, x_{t+2}) = 0.330.$ While there is no logical necessity, similar discrepancies also appear routinely in text files, images, digitized audio, etc.

It is not possible to take complete advantage of this phenomenon via on-line or off-line lossless compression, but we can gain partially by using a succession of ever-contracting contexts. For initial conditions, the encoder sends to the decoder a sequence (possibly compressed) consisting of every $2^k th$ symbol. Then in round r it sends every $2^{k-r}th$ symbol that is not a $2^{k-r+1}th$ symbol, conditionally encoded in the context of its two distance-2^{k-r} neighbors. The following chart shows the round-by-round sample conditional entropies for the file *wsj1*. The over-all average entropy is 0.364.

Round	0	1	2	3	4
Spread	∞	16	8	4	2
Entropy	1.0	0.448	0.428	0.362	0.259

Below we compare the sample entropy for the 2-byte contracting symmetric contexts with the compression ratios for 1) 2-byte Symmetric Context Arithmetic Coder; 2) 2-byte Conditional Fixed Arithmetic Coder 3) Adaptive Incrementing Arithmetic Coding; 4) UNIX compress; 5) Lempel/Ziv buffer algorithm in tandem with AIA; 5) Adaptive Arithmetic Coding; 6) Q coder with a 2-byte context. The frequencies for fixed arithmetic coding were drawn from files wsj10 through wsj41.

File	H_{CSC}	2SCA	2CFA	AIA	Compress	LZAIA	Q-r16
wsj1	.364	.366	.339	.624	.401	.423	.715

Time-Space Compression Method using Simultaneous Program Execution

Emmanouel Antonidakis and David A. Perreault
Boston University

There are many circumstances in which users at geographically separated sites desire to view the same computer generated information and displays. This is often accomplished by communicating this information over wideband links to provide real time displays. An approach which provides the same services with greatly reduced communications requirements, is presented based on the "Compute rather than Communicate" philosophy.

With the existing methods of computer conferencing, using compression, the transmitting computer takes the screen information, compresses it and transmits it through the communications line. The receiving computer gets the compressed information, it decompresses it and presents it to the screen for display. Compression and decompression have to be done on the fly, to provide real time displays.

A computer conference is based on a supporting program. For example, if the conference is about the design of a building, the conference supporting or application program could be AutoCad^T. The screen data is nothing else but the outputs of the supporting program when specific inputs were presented to the supporting program at specific times. Therefore the inputs are a compressed form of the outputs.The time that the input was presented to the supporting program may affect the outputs. For instance, if a key was pressed at different time during the playing of an electronic game, the game will take a different track. Thus the inputs, and the way that they get entered to the supporting program, is a compressed form of the outputs of that program in time and in space.

An important term needed is "the time that an input was presented to the supporting program." When a computer program is ready to receive an input, it periodically checks for the presence of the input. The number of times, C, that the program checks for the presence of an input, I, until the input was entered to the program, is the time parameter. Inputs can originate from the keyboard, the disk, external ports, the timer, etc. A parameter T will designate the type of the input I. If an application program is deterministic then the set of triplets $S = \{ (I_1,C_1,T_1) , (I_2,C_2,T_2), \ldots ,(I_n,C_n,T_n) \}$ in the order happening, is a unique representation of an execution of the program and therefore and of the outputs of the program. The ordered set of inputs S is a compressed form of the outputs. The decompressor is the supporting program itself. The set S is presented to the decompressor, on an element by element basis. As the inputs get entered on the computer, the supporting program (decompressor) will generate the exact same outputs.

A shell program called COMSAVER was developed to facilitate computer conferencing of two computers with DOS operating system. COMSAVER runs between the application (or supporting) program and the operating system on both computers. When COMSAVER initializes, it sets up the connection through a low speed modem line and the conference can start. COMSAVER becomes transparent to the users and handles the inputs from both computers, defines their order and validity and presents them synchronously to both computers. The application programs get the same inputs, at the same relative point in their execution, they run identically generating the same outputs.

In situations where the outputs are much grater than the inputs (as in most programs) a tremendous bandwidth reduction is achieved.

Variable Rate, Real Time Image Compression for Images Dominated by Point Sources

A. Kris Huber, Scott E. Budge, and Richard W. Harris
Department of Electrical Engineering, Utah State University
Logan, Utah 84322-4120

An image compression system recently developed for real-time compression of images of space which are dominated by point sources, such as stars, is presented. Simulations show that radiometric quality can be preserved exactly for point sources with low signal-to-noise ratios (SNR) and high point source densities while maintaining a reduced output bit rate. Encoding and decoding hardware has been built and tested which can process 552,960 12-bit pixels per second at compression rates of 10:1 and 4:1.

The compression algorithm involves a combination of a traditional lossy algorithm, mean-residual vector quantization (MRVQ), and the lossless algorithms run-length and Huffman encoding. The mean calculation in the MRVQ is the minimum of a collection of sample means so that it approximates the scene background and avoids artifacts that can occur if bright point sources are included in the mean calculation. The VQ codebook is a 16-child/node two-level tree. The MRVQ residual values are subtracted from the original values. If the difference exceeds a time-varying threshold the difference is encoded, otherwise a zero is encoded. Runs of zeroes and non-zero differences are Huffman encoded. The threshold varies with the fullness of a buffer of compressed data waiting to be transmitted, so that the average output bit rate is controlled by the rate at which the buffer is emptied.

The image model assumed in this paper was a simplified model of an infrared telescope being built by the Space Dynamics Laboratory in Logan, Utah. Background photon noise was modeled by zero-mean, unity-variance Gaussian noise, $x(n)$. This field was observed by 1536 detectors, each with response modeled by

$$a_i x^2 + b_i x + c_i$$

where the a_i, b_i, and c_i were uniformly distributed over the intervals $[0, -10^{-6}]$, $[0.8, 1.2]$, and $[10, 20]$, respectively. The detector outputs were uniformly quantized to 12-bit values. The detector nonuniformities effectively increased the root-mean-square (RMS) noise at the input to the data compressor from 1.0 to 5.5 counts. SNR was therefore referenced to the latter noise level. Point sources were positioned randomly and uniformly throughout each image. The point source SNR was defined as the point source amplitude (in counts) minus offset c_i, divided by 5.5. An ideal optical system was assumed; in practice blurring would reduce the SNR of the point source somewhat.

For the 10:1 rate (1.21 bits per pixel), RMS error in background pixels was nearly constant at 4 counts over the entire ensemble of simulation images. No error occurred to point sources for images with point-source SNR greater than 7 and number of point source pixels up to 24,000, which corresponded to a point source density of 3000 per $\deg^2$. For SNR less than 7, error in point source pixels increased until it was comparable to error caused to background pixels.

This work was funded by Space Dynamics Laboratory in Logan, Utah.

VLSI Architectures for Vector Quantization Based on Clustering

Heonchul Park, Viktor K. Prasanna and Cho-Li Wang

Department of Engineering-Systems, EEB-244

University of Southern California

Los Angeles, CA 90089-2562

Abstract

Tree Search Vector Quantization (TSVQ) has become feasible to be used in real-time applications by employing VLSI technology. Known TSVQ architectures have $O(\log N)$ memory modules requiring different memory sizes and require $O(\log N)$ Processing Elements (PEs) having multipliers, which results in $O(\log N)$ I/O bandwidth with $O(kN)$ memory, where $N = 2^{rk}$ is the number of codevectors, $0 < r < 1$, and k is the number of dimensions in input vectors. It leads to a multiple-chip solution.

In this paper, we propose a new search algorithm using box decomposition scheme based on efficient clustering algorithm, which results in a tree each of which node has a simple hyperplane such that $x_i = c$, where i is the index of a dimension and c is a constant. For an input vector, one comparison is performed at a node between an element of the input vector, which corresponds to the dimension i, and constant c. The index corresponding to the input vector is the path from the root of the tree to a leaf. This algorithm has $O(max(k, \log N))$ sequential time complexity for an k-dimensional input vector assuming unit time corresponding to an addition operation. It requires $O(N)$ external memory for storing N hyperplanes. No multiplication operation is employed, since the search method is independent of any L_q metric, $1 \leq q \leq \infty$.

The proposed search algorithm is mapped onto a linear array with a shared memory which corresponds to a heap structure. Each PE consists of a comparator and $O(k)$ registers acting as a shift register. An element of the input vectors is fed into the array every cycle. Each PE makes a comparison during the kth cycle over a window of k cycles. PE_i fetches a node information during the ith cycle over a window through a bus using the comparison result of PE_{i-1} stored in $\log N$ bits wide index register, $1 \leq i \leq \log N$. Output can be obtained from the index register in $PE_{\log N}$. Thus, the array outputs an index corresponding to an input vector every k cycles. Compared with known architectures, it has area efficient PEs and requires less memory by a factor of $O(k)$. In addition, the architecture has fixed I/O bandwidth, which is attractive to implement in a single chip. Details can be found in [1].

Selected References

[1] H. Park, V. K. Prasanna and C-L Wang, "VLSI Architectures for Vector Quantization Based on Clustering," *USC Tech. Report, Dept. of EE-Systems, IRIS #283*, Sep. 1991.

WAVELET COMPRESSION WITH FEATURE PRESERVATION AND DERIVATIVE DEFINITION

Oleg Kiselyov and Paul Fisher

University of North Texas
Department of Computer Science
P.O. Box 13886
Denton, TX 76203-3886
Phone: 817-565-2767
Fax: 817-565-2799
Email: oleg@ponder.csci.unt.edu

In this paper, a technique is presented which modifies the standard wavelet compression technique to permit the preservation of certain features of an image. The features of the image to be preserved are called criteria sets, and are established a priori to the compression technique. In addition, using the wavelet transform, a discrete derivative of an image can be computed. The formulation of this discrete derivative is defined and examples are provided.

The compression achieved in the wavelet transform algorithms is due to the quantization of the wavelet coefficients with following variable-bit encoding. The standard algorithms make use of the uniform quantizing the coefficients within the scale (resolution) band that amounts to the uniform loss of details over the entire picture. In the present paper, the quantization algorithm is modified to include the weight function defined over the image. The function (to be specified a priori) controls the level of detail to be retained in any particular region of the picture. Examples are presented that demonstrate that the significant compression ratio can be achieved with almost lossless encoded areas of special interest turning smoothly into the regions with only large scale features preserved.

The wavelet decompression algorithm has also been modified to obtain the discrete "gradient" of the image. The gradient image emphasizes lines and/or regions with large intensity changes, and is a goal in some applications. The modified algorithm used together with sieving and quantizing the coefficients according to the specified threshold and/or the weight function allows one to control the scale of the non-regularities to emphasize and avoid the noise enhancement in the gradient image.

Word Position as Context

Usha Kondragunta and Debra A. Lelewer
California State Polytechnic University, Pomona CA

Abstract

We suggest that a generalization of the notion of context to include elements
other than previous characters may lead to the development of more powerful models
for data compression. Our current investigation considers the use of word position as
a contextual element. We find that while word position is of little value as a primary
contextual element, it has merit as a secondary element of context information.

Context modeling algorithms such as PPMC[1] and the algorithms of Lelewer
and Hirschberg[2] define context to be previous characters, and the order of a context
model to be the number of previous characters (i.e., number of contextual elements)
used in predicting the current character. The PPMC-type context modeling algorithms do not easily generalize since the data structure at the heart of these algorithms
is a trie. The algorithms of Lelewer and Hirschberg, however, use hashing to map
contexts to a table structure that stores frequency data. This model is more robust in
the sense that with an appropriate hash function any type of context may be represented and exploited to improve compression.

The use of word position for data compression was suggested by Basu[3] who
proposed an ad hoc scheme combining word position and Huffman trees. Our
approach is to generalize the notion of context to include information other than
previous characters and investigate the merits of novel contextual elements such as
word position. Our work indicates that word position is not a powerful primary
contextual element, but has merit as a secondary element. That is, when word
position is combined with previous-character information, the resulting model requires
less memory and provides compression performance that is very close to that of a
previous-character model of the same order.

Empirical results on the Calgary corpus show that an order-2-0 predecessor
model (using 2 previous characters and unconditioned frequencies) requiring 45
Kbytes of memory yields average compression of 3.23 bits per character (bpc). An
order-2-0 position model (using word position and 1 previous character as order-2
context) requires 41 Kbytes and yields 3.42 bpc. On a collection of PC files the
compression results are closer, 3.62 bpc for predecessor and 3.67 bpc for position.

---

[1]Bell, T., Cleary, J.G., and Witten, I.H. *Text Compression*, Prentice-Hall,
Englewood Cliffs, N.J., 1990.

[2]Lelewer, D.A. and Hirschberg, D.S., Streamlining context models for data
compression. *Proc. Data Compression Conf.*, Snowbird, Utah (Apr., 1991), 313-322.

[3]Basu, D. Text compression using several Huffman trees. *Proc. Data Compression Conf.*, Snowbird, Utah (Apr., 1991), 452.

Space and Earth Science Data Compression Workshop
Snowbird, Utah, March 27, 1992

Held in conjunction with the **Data Compression Conference (DCC '92)**
Snowbird, Utah, March 24-26, 1992

The goal of this Workshop is to explore the opportunities for data compression to enhance the collection and analysis of space and Earth science data. Papers were invited on all aspects of data compression research applied to space and Earth science data. Of particular interest to this workshop is research that is integrated into, or has the potential to be integrated into, a particular space and/or Earth science data information system. Preference was given to data compression research that takes into account the scientist's data requirements, and the constraints imposed by the data collection, transmission, distribution and archival system.

Papers were selected from submissions to DCC '92. (Most papers also appeared as poster papers for DCC '92.) Full papers (nominally 8 to 12 pages) will be published in a NASA Conference Publication after the workshop. Copies may be obtained from the Workshop organizers.

WORKSHOP SCHEDULE

Session 1: 8:00-9:45am

8:00   *Subband Coding for Image Data Archiving*
Daniel Glover, NASA Lewis Research Center, and
S. C. Kwatra, The University of Toledo

8:30   *Adjustable Lossless Image Compression Based on a Natural Splitting of an Image into Drawing, Shading, and Fine-Grained Components*
Dmitry A. Novik, Universities Space Research Association, and
James C. Tilton, NASA Goddard Space Flight Center

9:00   *Entropy Reduction via Simplified Image Contourization*
Martin J. Turner, University of Cambridge

9:30   Discussion

9:45   Break

Session 2: 10:15am-NOON

10:15   *Image Compression for Meteorological Remote Sensing*
K. Miettinen, D. B. Hogan and G. M. Binge, General Electric Company,
and D. W. Johnson, G. B. Gustafson, J. M Sparrow and R. G. Isaacs,
Atmospheric and Environmental Research, Inc.

10:45   *Methods of Evaluating the Effects of Encoding on SAR Data*
M. J. Dutkiewicz and I. G. Cumming, MacDonald Dettwiler

11:15   *Fractal Image Compression: A Resolution Independent Representation for Imagery*
Alan D. Sloan, Iterated Systems, Inc.

11:45   Discussion

NOON   Lunch Break

Session 3: 1:30-3:15pm

1:30   *The Implementation of a Lossless Data Compression Module in an Advanced Orbiting System: Analysis and Development*
Pen-Shu Yeh and Warner H. Miller, NASA Goddard Space Flight Center, Jack Venbrux and Norley Liu, Microelectronics Research Center, and Robert Rice, Jet Propulsion Laboratory

2:00   *Lossless Compression for Image Data Products on the FIFE CD-ROM Series*
Jeffrey A. Newcomer, Hughes STX Corporation, and Donald E. Strebel, VERSAR, Inc.

2:30   *The Effects of Video Compression on Acceptability of Images for Monitoring Life Sciences' Experiments*
Richard F. Haines and Sherry L. Chuang, NASA Ames Research Center

3:00   Discussion

3:15   Break

Session 4: 3:45pm-5:00pm

3:45   *High-Performance Compression of Astronomical Images*
Richard L. White, Space Telescope Science Institute

4:15   *Variable Rate, Real Time Image Compression for Images Dominated by Point Sources*
A. Kris Huber, Scott E. Budge and Richard W. Harris, Utah State University

4:45   Discussion

5:00   Close

ACKNOWLEDGMENT

The organization of this workshop was supported by the Office of Aeronautics, Exploration and Technology, NASA Headquarters, Washington, DC.

WORKSHOP ORGANIZERS

James C. Tilton, NASA Goddard Space Flight Center, Mail Code 930.4, Greenbelt, MD 20771; phone: (301) 286-9510; Internet: tilton@chrpisis.gsfc. nasa.gov; GSFCMAIL: JTILTON.

Sam Dolinar, Jet Propulsion Laboratory, Mail Stop 238-420, 4800 Oak Grove Drive, Pasadena, CA 91109; phone: (818) 354-7403; Internet: sam@rtop71.jpl.nasa.gov.

Author Index